P9-CJC-894

 Human Development

DATE DUE

			on at a crossroads
			an unequal world
			PRINTED IN U.S.A.

Published for the
United Nations College

REF HD 72 .H85 2005

Human development report.

Copyright © 2005
by the United Nations Development Programme
1 UN Plaza, New York, New York, 10017, USA

All rights reserved. No part of this publication may be reproduced, stored in a
retrieval system or transmitted, in any form or by any means, electronic, mechanical,
photocopying, recording or otherwise, without prior permission.

ISBN 0-19-530511-6

9 8 7 6 5 4 3 2 1
Printed by Hoechstetter Printing Co. on chlorine-free paper with vegetable inks and
produced by means of environmentally compatible technology.

Cover and layout design: Grundy & Northedge Information Designers, London
Information design: Gerald Quinn, Quinn Information Design, Cabin John, Maryland
Technical editing, layout and production management: Communications Development
Incorporated, Washington, D.C.
Editor: Charlotte Denny, Wellington, New Zealand

For a listing of any errors or omissions in HDR2005 found subsequent to printing, please
visit our website at http://hdr.undp.org

Team for the preparation of Human Development Report 2005

Director and lead author
Kevin Watkins

Research, writing and statistics
Haishan Fu (Chief of Statistics), Ricardo Fuentes, Arunabha Ghosh, Chiara Giamberardini, Claes Johansson, Christopher Kuonqui, Andrés Montes, David Stewart, Cecilia Ugaz (Senior Policy Advisor) and Shahin Yaqub.

Statistical adviser: Tom Griffin
Editor: Charlotte Denny
Production Manager: Marta Jaksona
Technical editing and production:
    Communications Development Incorporated
Cover and layout design: Grundy & Northedge Information Designers
Information design: G. Quinn Information Design

The Human Development Report Office (HDRO)

The *Human Development Report* is the product of a collective effort. Members of the National Human Development Report Unit (NHDRU) provide detailed comments on drafts and advice on content. They also link the Report to a global research network in developing countries. The NHDRU team is led by Sarah Burd-Sharps (Deputy Director) and comprises Sharmila Kurukulasuriya, Juan Pablo Mejia, Mary Ann Mwangi and Timothy Scott. The HDRO administrative team makes the office function and includes Oscar Bernal, Mamaye Gebretsadik and Melissa Hernandez. HDRO operations are managed by Yves Sassenrath with Ana Maria Carvajal. HDRO's outreach and communications programme is managed by Marisol Sanjines and Nena Terrell.

Foreword

This is, sadly, the last *Human Development Report* for which I will write the foreword, as I will step down as United Nations Development Programme (UNDP) Administrator in August. When I arrived at UNDP in 1999, I said that the *Human Development Report* was the jewel in the crown of the organization's global intellectual and advocacy efforts. Six years and six reports later, I can report with some pride that its lustre has only grown.

Building on the powerful foundation laid during the Report's first decade, when successive *Human Development Reports* introduced and fleshed out the concept of human development, the Reports have gone from strength to strength. From examining how best to make new technologies work for rich people and poor people alike to highlighting the critical importance of strengthening human rights and deepening democracy to protect and empower the most vulnerable, the *Human Development Report* has steadily widened the intellectual frontiers of human development in the new millennium. And that shift has been increasingly mirrored in development practice through work by UNDP and its many partners on the ground in all these critical areas.

In short, as a robustly independent and articulate voice that, while sponsored by UNDP, does not necessarily reflect UN or UNDP policy, the *Human Development Reports* over the years have won a well deserved global reputation for excellence. They have played an indispensable catalytic role in helping frame and forge concrete responses to the key development policy debates of our time. Today, as this Report makes clear, the single greatest challenge facing the development community—and arguably the world—is the challenge of meeting the Millennium Development Goals by the target date of 2015.

Human Development Report 2003, drawing on much of the early work of the UNDP-sponsored UN Millennium Project, laid out a detailed plan of action for how each Goal could be achieved. But even as significant progress has been made in many countries and across several Goals, overall progress still falls short of what is needed. Earlier this year the UN Secretary-General's own five-year review of the Millennium Declaration, drawing heavily on the final report of the UN Millennium Project, laid out a broad agenda for how this can be achieved by building on the 2001 Monterrey consensus. The cornerstone of that historic compact is a commitment by developing countries to take primary responsibility for their own development, with developed countries ensuring that transparent, credible and properly costed national development strategies receive the full support they need to meet the Millennium Development Goals.

But, as this Report persuasively argues, that agenda simply will not succeed unless we can decisively resolve bottlenecks currently retarding progress at the pace and scale that are needed over the next decade in three broad areas: aid, trade and conflict. Across each of these critical areas this Report takes a fresh look at the facts and delivers a compelling and comprehensive analysis on how this can be done—and done now. The year 2005 will be remembered as a year of choice, when world leaders had the opportunity at the UN September Summit to turn pledges and promises into concrete actions to help eradicate extreme poverty in our world. It is an opportunity we cannot afford to miss if we are to bequeath a safer, more secure and more just world to our children and future generations.

Finally, while this may be my own last Report as Administrator, it marks the first to be written under the leadership of Kevin Watkins as Director of the Human Development Report Office. The strength and depth of its analysis make clear that the *Human Development Report* and the legacy of human development it represents and symbolizes could not be in safer hands. I wish him, his dedicated team and my own successor, Kemal Dervis, all the very best for the future.

Mark Malloch Brown
Administrator, UNDP

The analysis and policy recommendations of this Report do not necessarily reflect the views of the United Nations Development Programme, its Executive Board or its Member States. The Report is an independent publication commissioned by UNDP. It is the fruit of a collaborative effort by a team of eminent consultants and advisers and the *Human Development Report* team. Kevin Watkins, Director of the Human Development Report Office, led the effort.

Acknowledgements

This Report could not have been prepared without the generous contribution of many individuals and organizations. The authors wish to acknowledge their special debt to Amartya Sen, whose work has shaped the evolution of the *Human Development Report* over the years. Mark Malloch Brown, the outgoing Administrator of the United Nations Development Programme (UNDP), has provided consistent support and encouragement. His personal commitment is deeply appreciated. The Report benefited greatly from detailed and substantive comments from Kemal Dervis, the newly appointed Administrator of UNDP. Errors of commission and omission are the sole responsibility of the authors.

Contributors

Background studies, papers and notes were prepared on a wide range of thematic issues relating to the Report. Contributors were Charlie Arden-Clarke, Catherine Barber, Helen Barnes, Graham K. Brown, Oli Brown, Sarah Burd-Sharps, Simon Chesterman, Bernard Choulai, Giovanni Andrea Cornia, John Crabtree, Carolyn Deere, Nelson Giordano Delgado, Yuri Dikhanov, Kate Dyer, Xibo Fan, Juan Alberto Fuentes, Tony German, Jayati Ghosh, Peter Gibbon, Alissa Goodman, Adele Harmer, Ruth Hill, Catherine Hoffman, Michael Friis Jensen, Alison Johnson, Naila Kabeer, Roman Krznaric, Arnim Langer, Matthew Martin, Ruth Mayne, Kieren McGovern, Calum Miller, Tanni Mukhopadhyay, Ciru Mwaura, Simon Nangiro, Adriano Campolina de Oliveira Soares, Trudy Owens, Franzetska Papadopoulou-Zavalis, Cintia Quiliconi, Judith Randel, Andrew Rogerson, Jorge Oswaldo Romano, Diane Rowland, Emma Samman, Timothy Scott, Abby Stoddard, Diana Tussie and Patrick Watt.

Several organizations generously shared their data and other research materials: Carbon Dioxide Information and Analysis Center, Caribbean Community Secretariat, Center for International Comparisons at the University of Pennsylvania, Development Initiatives, Economic and Social Commission for Asia and the Pacific, Economic and Social Commission for Latin America and the Caribbean, European Commission, Food and Agriculture Organization, Global IDP Project, International Institute for Strategic Studies, International Labour Organization, International Monetary Fund, International Organization for Migration, International Telecommunication Union, Inter-Parliamentary Union, Joint United Nations Programme on HIV/AIDS, Kaiser Family Foundation, Luxembourg Income Study, Organisation for Economic Co-operation and Development, Stockholm International Peace Research Institute, United Nations Children's Fund, United Nations Conference on Trade and Development, United Nations Development Fund for Women, United Nations Educational, Scientific and Cultural Organization Institute for Statistics, United Nations High Commissioner for Refugees, United Nations Office on Drugs and Crime, Treaty Section, United Nations Office of Legal Affairs, United Nations Population Division, United Nations Statistics Division, UN Millennium Project,

World Bank, World Health Organization, World Trade Organization and the World Intellectual Property Organization.

Advisory Panel

The Report benefited greatly from intellectual advice and guidance provided by an external advisory panel of experts. The panel comprised Ekrem Beqiri, Nancy Birdsall, Francesca Cook, Justin Forsyth, Frene Ginwala, Richard Jolly, Donald Kaberuka, Nanak Kakwani, Rashid S. Kaukab, Tony Killick, A.K. Shiva Kumar, Jean-Pierre Landau, Callisto Madavo, Moisés Naím, Deepa Narayan, Benno Ndulu, Dani Rodrik, Mohammad Sahnoun, Ransford Smith, Rehman Sobhan, Frances Stewart, Paul Streeten, Ana Toni, Shriti Vadera, Ngaire Woods and Susan L. Woodward. An advisory panel on statistics made an invaluable contribution. The panel members were Carla Abou-Zahr, Tony Atkinson, Hubert Escaith, Andrew J. Flatt, Rebeca Grynspan, Gareth Jones, Irena Križman, Ian D. Macredie, Anna N. Majelantle, John Male-Mukasa, Marion McEwin, Francesca Perucci, Tim Smeeding, Eric Swanson, Pervez Tahir and Michael Ward. The team is grateful to Brian Hammond, Ian Macredie, Angela Me and David Pearce, the statistical peer reviewers who scrutinized the data in the Report and lent their statistical expertise.

Consultations

Many individuals consulted during the preparation of the Report provided invaluable advice, information and material. The Report team thanks Yuhanna Aboona, Carla Abou-Zahr, Yasmin Ahmad, Serge Allegrezza, Anna Alvazzi del Frate, Jacob Assa, Christina Barrineau, Bob Baulch, Elena Bernaldo, Izzy Birch, Eva Busza, Shaamela Cassiem, Duangkamon Chotikapanich, Giovanni Andrea Cornia, Francesca Coullare, Angus Deaton, Yuri Dikhanov, Adama Diop-Faye, Sherman Dorn, Hubert Escaith, Jens Eschenbaecher, Gonzalo Fanjul Suárez, Sally Fegan-Wyles, Angela Ferriol Muruaga, Marzia Fontana, Marc-André Franche, Enrique Ganuza, Rosario Garcia Calderon, Leonardo Gasparini, Patrick Gerland, Peter Ghys, Erlinda Go, Luc Grégoire, Michèle Griffin, Brian Hammond, Daniel Hanspach, Lotta Harbom, Rubina Haroon, Nick René Hartmann, Rana Hasan, Sukehiro Hasegawa, Alan Heston, Catherine Hoffman, Valeria Izzi, Kareen Jabre, Lisa Jones, Alberic Kacou, Douglas Keh, Reetika Khera, Frederik Kok, Suraj Kumar, Muthuswamy Lakshminarayan, Andrea Lall, Jean Langers, Fiona Legg, Clare Lockhart, Charles Lufumpa, Frances Lund, Nyein Nyein Lwin, Esperanza C. Magpantay, Carlos Maldonado, Lamin Manneh, Kieren McGovern, Marcelo Medeiros, Alvaro Melendez, Jorge Mernies, Johan Mistiaen, Jaime Moll-de-Alba, Bruno Moro, Céline Moyroud, Christine Musisi, Ciru Mwaura, Suppiramaniam Nanthikesan, John Ohiorhenuan, Saeed Ordoubadi, Said Ould A. Voffal, Paola Pagliani, Amy Pate, Paul André de la Porte, Mohammad Pournik, Seeta Prabhu, William Prince, Agnès Puymoyen, Jan Van Ravens, Luca Renda, Yue Renfeng, Rodolfo Roque Fuentes, Diane Rowland, Anuja Singh, Elizabeth Sköns, Jelena Smoljan, Sophia Somogyi, Devi Sridhar, Petter Stalenheim, Mark Stoker, Michel Thieren, Mandy Turner, Fabio Veras, Lotta Viklund, Yan Wang, Michael Ward, Siemon Wezeman, Ian Whitman, Tony Williams and Eduardo Zepeda.

The Report team gratefully acknowledges the stimulating contribution of the Scenario Building workshop participants: Larry Elliot, Alisher Ilkhamov, Bruce Jenks, William Kalema, Nawal Kamel, Melinda Kimble, Claudia Martinez, Pei Minxin, David Morrison, Archbishop Njongonkulu W. H. Ndungane, Shoji Nishimoto, Precious Omuku, Surin Pitsuwan, Jorge Quiroga, Jose Ramos Horta, Mattia Romani, Adnan Shihab Eldin, Roberto Soares, Angela Wilkinson, HRH Prince Willem-Alexander of the Netherlands and Ngaire Woods.

UNDP Readers

A Readers Group, made up of colleagues in UNDP, provided extremely useful comments, suggestions and inputs during the writing of the Report. The Report team is especially grateful to Hakan Bjorkman, Philip Dobie, Ghaith Fariz, Marc-André Franche, Cherie Hart, Gilbert Fossoun Houngbo, Bruce Jenks,

Inge Kaul, Bruno Lemarquis, Kamal Malhotra, Lamin Manneh, Rosemary Nuamah, Eleanor O'Gorman, Hafiz Pasha, Stefano Pettinato, Richard Ponzio, Liliana de Riz, Turhan Saleh, Ben Slay, Ramaswamy Sudarshan, Mark Suzman, Mounir Tabet, Jan Vandemoortele, Antonio Vigilante and Louisa Vinton.

Editing, Production and Translation

The report benefited from the main editor Charlotte Denny. Technical and production editing and layout were provided by Meta de Coquereaumont, Thomas Roncoli, Bruce Ross-Larson, Christopher Trott, Timothy Walker and Elaine Wilson of Communications Development Incorporated. The Report (including cover) was designed by Grundy & Northedge Information Designers. Statistical information appearing in the Report was designed by G. Quinn Information Design.

The production, translation, distribution and promotion of the Report benefited from the help and support of the Communications Office of the Administrator: Maureen Lynch, David Morrison, Bill Orme and Elizabeth Scott Andrews. Translations were reviewed by Jean Fabre, Vladimir Scherbov, Moustapha Soumare, Fayiz Suyyagh and Oscar Yujnovsky.

The Report also benefited from the dedicated work of Noha Aboueldahab, Maria Kristina Dominguez, Laurel Gascho, Tugba Gokalp, Ramzi Mabsout, Aurélie Mazel, Agueda Perez, Gillan Richards, Frederic Rozeira de Mariz and Hanna Schmitt. Özer Babakol and Matthew Bell made valuable contributions to the statistical team.

Daniela Costantino and Michele Jack of the UN Office of Project Services provided critical administrative support and management services.

Kevin Watkins
Director
Human Development Report 2005

Contents

Chapters

Tables

Figures

Special contribution

Map

Human development indicators

Monitoring human development: enlarging people's choices . . .

. . . to lead a long and healthy life . . .

. . . to acquire knowledge . . .

. . . to have access to the resources needed for a decent standard of living . . .

Overview

International cooperation at a crossroads
Aid, trade and security in an unequal world

Every hour more than
1,200 children die
away from the glare
of media attention

The year 2004 ended with an event that demonstrated the destructive power of nature and the regenerative power of human compassion. The tsunami that swept across the Indian Ocean left some 300,000 people dead. Millions more were left homeless. Within days of the tsunami, one of the worst natural disasters in recent history had given rise to the world's greatest international relief effort, showing what can be achieved through global solidarity when the international community commits itself to a great endeavour.

The tsunami was a highly visible, unpredictable and largely unpreventable tragedy. Other tragedies are less visible, monotonously predictable and readily preventable. Every hour more than 1,200 children die away from the glare of media attention. This is equivalent to three tsunamis a month, every month, hitting the world's most vulnerable citizens—its children. The causes of death will vary, but the overwhelming majority can be traced to a single pathology: poverty. Unlike the tsunami, that pathology is preventable. With today's technology, financial resources and accumulated knowledge, the world has the capacity to overcome extreme deprivation. Yet as an international community we allow poverty to destroy lives on a scale that dwarfs the impact of the tsunami.

Five years ago, at the start of the new millennium, the world's governments united to make a remarkable promise to the victims of global poverty. Meeting at the United Nations, they signed the Millennium Declaration—a solemn pledge "to free our fellow men, women and children from the abject and dehumanizing conditions of extreme poverty". The declaration provides a bold vision rooted in a shared commitment to universal human rights and social justice and backed by clear time-bound targets. These targets—the Millennium Development Goals (MDGs)—include halving extreme poverty, cutting child deaths, providing all of the world's children with an education, rolling back infectious disease and forging a new global partnership to deliver results. The deadline for delivery is 2015.

There is more to human development than the MDGs. But the goals provide a crucial benchmark for measuring progress towards the creation of a new, more just, less impoverished and less insecure world order. In September 2005 the world's governments will gather again at the United Nations to review developments since they signed the Millennium Declaration—and to chart a course for the decade to 2015.

There is little cause for celebration. Some important human development advances have been registered since the Millennium Declaration was signed. Poverty has fallen and social indicators have improved. The MDGs have provided a focal point for international concern, putting development and the fight against poverty on the international agenda in a way that seemed unimaginable a decade ago. The year 2005 has been marked by an unprecedented global campaign dedicated to relegating poverty to the past. That campaign has already left its imprint in the form of progress on aid and debt relief during the summit of the Group of Eight (G-8) major industrial economies. The

This is the moment to prove that the Millennium Declaration is not just a paper promise, but a commitment to change

lesson: powerful arguments backed by public mobilization can change the world.

Yet as governments prepare for the 2005 UN summit, the overall report card on progress makes for depressing reading. Most countries are off track for most of the MDGs. Human development is faltering in some key areas, and already deep inequalities are widening. Various diplomatic formulations and polite terminology can be found to describe the divergence between progress on human development and the ambition set out in the Millennium Declaration. None of them should be allowed to obscure a simple truth: the promise to the world's poor is being broken.

This year, 2005, marks a crossroads. The world's governments face a choice. One option is to seize the moment and make 2005 the start of a "decade for development". If the investments and the policies needed to achieve the MDGs are put in place today, there is still time to deliver on the promise of the Millennium Declaration. But time is running out. The UN summit provides a critical opportunity to adopt the bold action plans needed not just to get back on track for the 2015 goals, but to overcome the deep inequalities that divide humanity and to forge a new, more just pattern of globalization.

The other option is to continue on a business as usual basis and make 2005 the year in which the pledge of the Millennium Declaration is broken. This is a choice that will result in the current generation of political leaders going down in history as the leaders that let the MDGs fail on their watch. Instead of delivering action, the UN summit could deliver another round of high-sounding declarations, with rich countries offering more words and no action. Such an outcome will have obvious consequences for the world's poor. But in a world of increasingly interconnected threats and opportunities, it will also jeopardize global security, peace and prosperity.

The 2005 summit provides a critical opportunity for the governments that signed the Millennium Declaration to show that they mean business—and that they are capable of breaking with "business as usual". This is the moment to prove that the Millennium Declaration is not just a paper promise, but a commitment to change. The summit is the moment to mobilize the investment resources and develop the plans needed to build the defences that can stop the tsunami of world poverty. What is needed is the political will to act on the vision that governments set out five years ago.

The 2005 *Human Development Report*

This Report is about the scale of the challenge facing the world at the start of the 10-year countdown to 2015. Its focus is on what governments in rich countries can do to keep their side of the global partnership bargain. This does not imply that governments in developing countries have no responsibility. On the contrary, they have primary responsibility. No amount of international cooperation can compensate for the actions of governments that fail to prioritize human development, to respect human rights, to tackle inequality or to root out corruption. But without a renewed commitment to cooperation backed by practical action, the MDGs will be missed—and the Millennium Declaration will go down in history as just one more empty promise.

We focus on three pillars of cooperation, each in urgent need of renovation. The first pillar is development assistance. International aid is a key investment in human development. Returns to that investment can be measured in the human potential unleashed by averting avoidable sickness and deaths, educating all children, overcoming gender inequalities and creating the conditions for sustained economic growth. Development assistance suffers from two problems: chronic underfinancing and poor quality. There have been improvements on both fronts. But much remains to be done to close the MDG financing gaps and improve value for money.

The second pillar is international trade. Under the right conditions trade can be a powerful catalyst for human development. The Doha "Development Round" of World Trade Organization (WTO) talks, launched in 2001, provided rich country governments with an opportunity to create those conditions.

Four years on, nothing of substance has been achieved. Rich country trade policies continue to deny poor countries and poor people a fair share of global prosperity—and they fly in the face of the Millennium Declaration. More than aid, trade has the potential to increase the share of the world's poorest countries and people in global prosperity. Limiting that potential through unfair trade policies is inconsistent with a commitment to the MDGs. More than that, it is unjust and hypocritical.

The third pillar is security. Violent conflict blights the lives of hundreds of millions of people. It is a source of systematic violations of human rights and a barrier to progress towards the MDGs. The nature of conflict has changed, and new threats to collective security have emerged. In an increasingly interconnected world the threats posed by a failure to prevent conflict, or to seize opportunities for peace, inevitably cross national borders. More effective international cooperation could help to remove the barrier to MDG progress created by violent conflict, creating the conditions for accelerated human development and real security.

The renovation needs to take place simultaneously on each pillar of international cooperation. Failure in any one area will undermine the foundations for future progress. More effective rules in international trade will count for little in countries where violent conflict blocks opportunities to participate in trade. Increased aid without fairer trade rules will deliver suboptimal results. And peace without the prospects for improved human welfare and poverty reduction that can be provided through aid and trade will remain fragile.

The state of human development

Fifteen years ago the first *Human Development Report* looked forward to a decade of rapid progress. "The 1990s", it predicted optimistically, "are shaping up as the decade for human development, for rarely has there been such a consensus on the real objectives of development strategies." Today, as in 1990, there is also a consensus on development. That consensus

has been powerfully expressed in the reports of the UN Millennium Project and the UK-sponsored Commission for Africa. Unfortunately, the consensus has yet to give rise to practical actions—and there are ominous signs for the decade ahead. There is a real danger that the next 10 years, like the last 15 years, will deliver far less for human development than the new consensus promises.

Much has been achieved since the first *Human Development Report*. On average, people in developing countries are healthier, better educated and less impoverished—and they are more likely to live in a multiparty democracy. Since 1990 life expectancy in developing countries has increased by 2 years. There are 3 million fewer child deaths annually and 30 million fewer children out of school. More than 130 million people have escaped extreme poverty. These human development gains should not be underestimated.

Nor should they be exaggerated. In 2003, 18 countries with a combined population of 460 million people registered lower scores on the human development index (HDI) than in 1990—an unprecedented reversal. In the midst of an increasingly prosperous global economy, 10.7 million children every year do not live to see their fifth birthday, and more than 1 billion people survive in abject poverty on less than $1 a day. The HIV/AIDS pandemic has inflicted the single greatest reversal in human development. In 2003 the pandemic claimed 3 million lives and left another 5 million people infected. Millions of children have been orphaned.

Global integration is forging deeper interconnections between countries. In economic terms the space between people and countries is shrinking rapidly, as trade, technology and investment link all countries in a web of interdependence. In human development terms the space between countries is marked by deep and, in some cases, widening inequalities in income and life chances. One-fifth of humanity live in countries where many people think nothing of spending $2 a day on a cappuccino. Another fifth of humanity survive on less than $1 a day and live in countries where children die for want of a simple anti-mosquito bednet.

There is a real danger that the next 10 years, like the last 15 years, will deliver far less for human development than has been promised

At the start of the twenty-first century we live in a divided world. The size of the divide poses a fundamental challenge to the global human community. Part of that challenge is ethical and moral. As Nelson Mandela put it in 2005: "Massive poverty and obscene inequality are such terrible scourges of our times—times in which the world boasts breathtaking advances in science, technology, industry and wealth accumulation—that they have to rank alongside slavery and apartheid as social evils." The twin scourges of poverty and inequality can be defeated—but progress has been faltering and uneven.

Rich countries as well as poor have an interest in changing this picture. Reducing the gulf in wealth and opportunity that divides the human community is not a zero-sum game in which some have to lose so that others gain. Extending opportunities for people in poor countries to lead long and healthy lives, to get their children a decent education and to escape poverty will not diminish the well-being of people in rich countries. On the contrary, it will help build shared prosperity and strengthen our collective security. In our interconnected world a future built on the foundations of mass poverty in the midst of plenty is economically inefficient, politically unsustainable and morally indefensible.

Life expectancy gaps are among the most fundamental of all inequalities. Today, someone living in Zambia has less chance of reaching age 30 than someone born in England in 1840—and the gap is widening. HIV/AIDS is at the heart of the problem. In Europe the greatest demographic shock since the Black Death was suffered by France during the First World War. Life expectancy fell by about 16 years. By comparison, Botswana is facing an HIV/AIDS-inflicted fall in life expectancy of 31 years. Beyond the immediate human costs, HIV/AIDS is destroying the social and economic infrastructure on which recovery depends. The disease is not yet curable. But millions of lives could already have been saved had the international community not waited until a grave threat developed into a fully fledged crisis.

No indicator captures the divergence in human development opportunity more powerfully than child mortality. Death rates among the world's children are falling, but the trend is slowing—and the gap between rich and poor countries is widening. This is an area in which slowing trends cost lives. Had the progress of the 1980s been sustained since 1990, there would be 1.2 million fewer child deaths this year. Sub-Saharan Africa accounts for a rising share of child deaths: the region represents 20% of births worldwide and 44% of child deaths. But the slowdown in progress extends beyond Sub-Saharan Africa. Some of the most highly visible globalization "success stories"—including China and India—are failing to convert wealth creation and rising incomes into more rapid decline in child mortality. Deep-rooted human development inequality is at the heart of the problem.

Debates about trends in global income distribution continue to rage. Less open to debate is the sheer scale of inequality. The world's richest 500 individuals have a combined income greater than that of the poorest 416 million. Beyond these extremes, the 2.5 billion people living on less than $2 a day—40% of the world's population—account for 5% of global income. The richest 10%, almost all of whom live in high-income countries, account for 54%.

An obvious corollary of extreme global inequality is that even modest shifts in distribution from top to bottom could have dramatic effects on poverty. Using a global income distribution database, we estimate a cost of $300 billion for lifting 1 billion people living on less than $1 a day above the extreme poverty line threshold. That amount represents 1.6% of the income of the richest 10% of the world's population. Of course, this figure describes a static transfer. Achieving sustainable poverty reduction requires dynamic processes through which poor countries and poor people can produce their way out of extreme deprivation. But in our highly unequal world greater equity would provide a powerful catalyst for poverty reduction and progress towards the MDGs.

What are the implications of the current global human development trajectory for the MDGs? We address this question by using country data to project where the world will be in relation to some of the main MDGs by

2015. The picture is not encouraging. If current trends continue, there will be large gaps between MDG targets and outcomes. Those gaps can be expressed in statistics, but behind the statistics are the lives and hopes of ordinary people. Human costs can never be captured by numbers alone. But our 2015 projection provides an indication of the scale of the costs. Among the consequences for developing countries of continuing on the current path:

- The MDG target for reducing child mortality will be missed by 4.4 million avoidable child deaths in 2015—a figure equivalent to three times the number of children under age 5 in London, New York and Tokyo. Over the next 10 years the gap between the target and the current trend adds more than 41 million children who will die before their fifth birthday from the most readily curable of all diseases—poverty. This is an outcome that is difficult to square with the Millennium Declaration's pledge to protect the world's children.
- The gap between the MDG target for halving poverty and projected outcomes is equivalent to an additional 380 million people living on less than $1 a day by 2015.
- The MDG target of universal primary education will be missed on current trends, with 47 million children still out of school in 2015.

These are simple forward projections of current trends—and trends are not destiny. As the financial market dictum puts it, past performance is not a guide to future outcomes. For the MDGs that is unambiguously good news. As the UN Secretary-General has put it: "The MDGs can be met by 2015—but only if all involved break with business as usual and dramatically accelerate and scale up action now." Some of the world's poorest countries—including Bangladesh, Uganda and Viet Nam—have shown that rapid progress is possible. But rich countries need to help meet the start-up costs of a global human development take-off.

As governments prepare for the 2005 UN summit, the 2015 projection offers a clear warning. To put it bluntly, the world is heading for a heavily sign-posted human development

disaster, the cost of which will be counted in avoidable deaths, children out of school and lost opportunities for poverty reduction. That disaster is as avoidable as it is predictable. If governments are serious about their commitment to the MDGs, business as usual is not an option. The 2005 UN summit provides an opportunity to chart a new course for the next decade.

Why inequality matters

Human development gaps within countries are as stark as the gaps between countries. These gaps reflect unequal opportunity—people held back because of their gender, group identity, wealth or location. Such inequalities are unjust. They are also economically wasteful and socially destabilizing. Overcoming the structural forces that create and perpetuate extreme inequality is one of the most efficient routes for overcoming extreme poverty, enhancing the welfare of society and accelerating progress towards the MDGs.

The MDGs themselves are a vital statement of international purpose rooted in a commitment to basic human rights. These rights—to education, to gender equality, to survival in childhood and to a decent standard of living—are universal in nature. That is why progress towards the MDGs should be for all people, regardless of their household income, their gender or their location. However, governments measure progress by reference to national averages. These averages can obscure deep inequalities in progress rooted in disparities based on wealth, gender, group identity and other factors.

As shown in this Report, failure to tackle extreme inequalities is acting as a brake on progress towards achieving the MDGs. On many of the MDGs the poor and disadvantaged are falling behind. Cross-country analysis suggests that child mortality rates among the poorest 20% of the population are falling at less than one-half of the world average. Because the poorest 20% account for a disproportionately large share of child mortality, this is slowing the overall rate of progress towards achieving the MDGs. Creating the conditions under which the poor can catch up as part of an

Some 130,000 young Indian lives are lost each year because of the disadvantage associated with being born with two X chromosomes

overall human development advance would give a dynamic new impetus to the MDGs. It would also address a cause of social injustice.

Multiple and interlocking layers of inequality create disadvantages for people throughout their lives. Income inequality is increasing in countries that account for more than 80% of the world's population. Inequality in this dimension matters partly because of the link between distribution patterns and poverty levels. Average income is three times higher in high-inequality and middle-income Brazil than in low-inequality and low-income Viet Nam. Yet the incomes of the poorest 10% in Brazil are lower than those of the poorest 10% in Viet Nam. High levels of income inequality are bad for growth, and they weaken the rate at which growth is converted into poverty reduction: they reduce the size of the economic pie and the size of the slice captured by the poor.

Income inequalities interact with other life chance inequalities. Being born into a poor household diminishes life chances, in some cases in a literal sense. Children born into the poorest 20% of households in Ghana or Senegal are two to three times more likely to die before age 5 than children born into the richest 20% of households. Disadvantage tracks people through their lives. Poor women are less likely to be educated and less likely to receive antenatal care when they are pregnant. Their children are less likely to survive and less likely to complete school, perpetuating a cycle of deprivation that is transmitted across generations. Basic life chance inequalities are not restricted to poor countries. Health outcomes in the United States, the world's richest country, reflect deep inequalities based on wealth and race. Regional disparities are another source of inequality. Human development fault lines separate rural from urban and poor from rich regions of the same country. In Mexico literacy rates in some states are comparable to those in high-income countries. In the predominantly rural indigenous municipalities of southern poverty belt states like Guerrero literacy rates for women approximate those in Mali.

Gender is one of the world's strongest markers for disadvantage. This is especially the case in South Asia. The large number of "missing women" in the region bears testimony to the scale of the problem. Disadvantage starts at birth. In India the death rate for children ages 1–5 is 50% higher for girls than for boys. Expressed differently, 130,000 young lives are lost each year because of the disadvantage associated with being born with two X chromosomes. In Pakistan gender parity in school attendance would give 2 million more girls the chance of an education.

Reducing inequality in the distribution of human development opportunities is a public policy priority in its own right: it matters for intrinsic reasons. It would also be instrumental in accelerating progress towards the MDGs. Closing the gap in child mortality between the richest and poorest 20% would cut child deaths by almost two-thirds, saving more than 6 million lives a year—and putting the world back on track for achieving the MDG target of a two-thirds reduction in child death rates.

More equitable income distribution would act as a strong catalyst for accelerated poverty reduction. We use household income and expenditure surveys to simulate the effect of a growth pattern in which people in poverty capture twice the share of future growth as their current share in national income. For Brazil this version of pro-poor growth shortens the time horizon for halving poverty by 19 years; for Kenya, by 17 years. The conclusion: when it comes to income poverty reduction, distribution matters as well as growth. That conclusion holds as much for low-income countries as for middle-income countries. Without improved income distribution Sub-Saharan Africa would require implausibly high growth rates to halve poverty by 2015. It might be added to this consideration that a demonstrated commitment to reduce inequality as part of a wider poverty reduction strategy would enhance the case for aid among the public in donor countries.

Scaling up national simulation exercises using a global income distribution model highlights the potential benefits of reduced inequality for global poverty reduction. Using such a model, we ask what would happen if people living on less than $1 a day were to double their share of future growth. The result: a decline of one-third—or 258 million people—in the projected number of people living on less than $1 a day by 2015.

Exercises such as these describe what outcomes are possible. Working towards these outcomes will require new directions in public policy. Far more weight should be attached to improving the availability, accessibility and affordability of public services and to increasing poor people's share of the growth. There is no single blueprint for achieving improved outcomes on income distribution. For many countries, especially in Sub-Saharan Africa, measures are needed to unlock the productive potential of smallholder agriculture and rural areas. More universally, education is one of the keys to greater equity. Socially transformative fiscal policies that provide security and equip the poor with the assets needed to escape poverty are also vital.

None of this implies that achieving greater equity in human development is easy. Extreme inequalities are rooted in power structures that deprive poor people of market opportunities, limit their access to services and—crucially—deny them a political voice. These pathologies of power are bad for market-based development and political stability—and a barrier to achieving the MDGs.

International aid—increasing the quantity, improving the quality

International aid is one of the most effective weapons in the war against poverty. Today, that weapon is underused, inefficiently targeted and in need of repair. Reforming the international aid system is a fundamental requirement for getting back on track for the MDGs.

Aid is sometimes thought of in rich countries as a one-way act of charity. That view is misplaced. In a world of interconnected threats and opportunities aid is an investment as well as a moral imperative—an investment in shared prosperity, collective security and a common future. Failure to invest on a sufficient scale today will generate costs tomorrow.

Development assistance is at the heart of the new partnership for development set out in the Millennium Declaration. As in any partnership there are responsibilities and obligations on both sides. Developing countries have a responsibility to create an environment in which aid can yield optimal results. Rich countries, for their part, have an obligation to act on their commitments.

There are three conditions for effective aid. First, it has to be delivered in sufficient quantity to support human development take-off. Aid provides governments with a resource for making the multiple investments in health, education and economic infrastructure needed to break cycles of deprivation and support economic recovery—and the resource needs to be commensurate with the scale of the financing gap. Second, aid has to be delivered on a predictable, low transaction cost, value for money basis. Third, effective aid requires "country ownership". Developing countries have primary responsibility for creating the conditions under which aid can yield optimal results. While there has been progress in increasing the quantity and improving the quality of aid, none of these conditions has yet been met.

When the Millennium Declaration was signed, the development assistance glass was three-quarters empty—and leaking. During the 1990s aid budgets were subject to deep cuts, with per capita assistance to Sub-Saharan Africa falling by one-third. Today, the aid financing glass is approaching half full. The Monterrey Conference on Financing for Development in 2001 marked the beginning of a recovery in aid. Since Monterrey, aid has increased by 4% a year in real terms, or $12 billion (in constant 2003 dollars). Rich countries collectively now spend 0.25% of their gross national income (GNI) on aid—lower than in 1990 but on an upward trend since 1997. The European Union's commitment to reach a 0.51% threshold by 2010 is especially encouraging.

However, even if projected increases are delivered in full, there remains a large aid shortfall for financing the MDGs. That shortfall will increase from $46 billion in 2006 to $52 billion in 2010. The financing gap is especially large for Sub-Saharan Africa, where aid flows need to double over five years to meet the estimated

Tied aid remains one
of the most egregious
abuses of poverty-focused
development assistance

costs of achieving the MDGs. Failure to close the financing gap through a step increase in aid will prevent governments from making the investments in health, education and infrastructure needed to improve welfare and support economic recovery on the scale required to achieve the MDGs.

While rich countries publicly acknowledge the importance of aid, their actions so far have not matched their words. The G-8 includes three countries—Italy, the United States and Japan—with the lowest shares of aid in GNI among the 22 countries on the Organisation for Economic Co-operation and Development's Development Assistance Committee. On a more positive note the United States, the world's largest aid donor, has increased aid by $8 billion since 2000 and is now the world's largest donor to Sub-Saharan Africa. The setting of more ambitious targets is another welcome development. However, donors do not have a good record in acting on aid targets—and some major donors have failed to move from setting targets to making concrete and binding budget commitments. The next 10 years will have to mark a distinct break from the past 15 years if the MDGs are to be achieved. Since 1990 increased prosperity in rich countries has done little to enhance generosity: per capita income has increased by $6,070, while per capita aid has fallen by $1. Such figures suggest that the winners from globalization have not prioritized help for the losers, even though they would gain from doing so.

The chronic underfinancing of aid reflects skewed priorities in public spending. Collective security depends increasingly on tackling the underlying causes of poverty and inequality. Yet for every $1 that rich countries spend on aid they allocate another $10 to military budgets. Just the increase in military spending since 2000, if devoted to aid instead, would be sufficient to reach the long-standing UN target of spending 0.7% of GNI on aid. Failure to look beyond military security to human security is reflected in underinvestments in addressing some of the greatest threats to human life. Current spending on HIV/AIDS, a disease that claims 3 million lives a year, represents three day's worth of military spending.

Questions are sometimes raised about whether the MDGs are affordable. Ultimately, what is affordable is a matter of political priorities. But the investments needed are modest by the scale of wealth in rich countries. The $7 billion needed annually over the next decade to provide 2.6 billion people with access to clean water is less than Europeans spend on perfume and less than Americans spend on elective corrective surgery. This is for an investment that would save an estimated 4,000 lives each day.

Donors have acknowledged the importance of tackling problems in aid quality. In March 2005 the Paris Declaration on Aid Effectiveness set out important principles for donors to improve aid effectiveness, along with targets for monitoring progress on new practices. Coordination is improving, there is less use of tied aid, and more emphasis is being placed on country ownership. But good practice lags far behind declared principle. Aid delivery still falls far short of pledges, undermining financial planning for poverty reduction. At the same time the specific form that conditionality takes often weakens national ownership and contributes to disruptions in aid flows. Donor reluctance to use national systems adds to transaction costs and weakens national capacity.

Tied aid remains one of the most egregious abuses of poverty-focused development assistance. By linking development assistance to the provision of supplies and services provided by the donor country, instead of allowing aid recipients to use the open market, aid tying reduces value for money. Many donors have been reducing tied aid, but the practice remains widely prevalent and underreported. We conservatively estimate the costs of tied aid for low-income countries at $5–$7 billion. Sub-Saharan Africa pays a "tied aid tax" of $1.6 billion.

In some areas the "new partnership" in aid established at the Monterrey conference still looks suspiciously like a repackaged version of the old partnership. There is a continuing imbalance in responsibilities and obligations. Aid recipients are required to set targets for achieving the MDGs, to meet budget targets that are monitored quarterly by the International Monetary Fund (IMF), to comply with a bewildering array of conditions set by donors and to deal with donor practices that raise transaction costs and reduce the value of aid. Donors, for their part, do not set targets for themselves. Instead, they offer broad, non-binding commitments on aid quantity (most of which are subsequently ignored) and even broader and vaguer commitments to improve aid quality. Unlike aid recipients, donors can break commitments with impunity. In practice, the new partnership has been a one-way street. What is needed is a genuine new partnership in which donors as well as recipients act on commitments to deliver on the promise of the Millennium Declaration.

This year provides an opportunity to seal that partnership and forge a new direction in development assistance cooperation. Donor countries need first to honour and then to build on the commitments made at Monterrey. Among the key requirements:

- *Set a schedule for achieving the aid to GNI ratio of 0.7% by 2015 (and keep to it).* Donors should set budget commitments at a minimum level of 0.5% for 2010 to bring the 2015 target within reach.
- *Tackle unsustainable debt.* The G-8 summit in 2005 produced a major breakthrough on debt owed by the heavily indebted poor countries (HIPCs). However, some problems remain, with a large number of low-income countries still facing acute problems in meeting debt service obligations. Final closure of the debt crisis will require action to extend country coverage and to ensure that debt repayments are held to levels consistent with MDG financing.
- *Provide predictable, multiyear financing through government programmes.* Building on the principles set out in the Paris Declaration on Aid Effectiveness, donors should set more ambitious targets for providing stable aid flows, working through national systems and building capacity. By 2010 at least 90% of aid should be disbursed according to agreed schedules through annual or multiyear frameworks.
- *Streamline conditionality.* Aid conditionality should focus on fiduciary responsibility and the transparency of reporting through national systems, with less emphasis on wide-ranging macroeconomic targets and a stronger commitment to building institutions and national capacity.
- *End tied aid.* There is a simple method for tackling the waste of money associated with tied aid: stop it in 2006.

Trade and human development—strengthening the links

Like aid, trade has the potential to be a powerful catalyst for human development. Under the right conditions international trade could generate a powerful impetus for accelerated progress towards the MDGs. The problem is that the human development potential inherent in trade is diminished by a combination of unfair rules and structural inequalities within and between countries.

International trade has been one of the most powerful motors driving globalization. Trade patterns have changed. There has been a sustained increase in the share of developing countries in world manufacturing exports—and some countries are closing the technology gap. However, structural inequalities have persisted and in some cases widened. Sub-Saharan Africa has become increasingly marginalized. Today, the region, with 689 million people, accounts for a smaller share of world exports than Belgium, with 10 million people. If Sub-Saharan Africa enjoyed the same share of world exports as in 1980, the foreign exchange gain would represent about eight times the aid it received in 2003. Much of Latin America is also falling behind. In trade, as in other areas, claims that global integration is driving a convergence of rich and poor countries are overstated.

From a human development perspective trade is a means to development, not an end in itself. Indicators of export growth, ratios of trade to GNI and import liberalization are not proxies for human development. Unfortunately, this is increasingly how they are treated. Participation in trade offers real opportunities for raising living standards. But some of the greatest models of openness and export growth—Mexico and Guatemala, for example—have been less successful in accelerating human development. Export success has not always enhanced human welfare on a broad front. The evidence suggests that more attention needs to be paid to the terms on which countries integrate into world markets.

Fairer trade rules would help, especially when it comes to market access. In most forms of taxation a simple principle of graduation applies: the more you earn, the more you pay. Rich country trade policies flip this principle on its head. The world's highest trade barriers are erected against some of its poorest countries: on average the trade barriers faced by developing countries exporting to rich countries are three to four times higher than those faced by rich countries when they trade with each other. Perverse graduation in trade policy extends to other areas. For example, the European Union sets great store by its commitment to open markets for the world's poorest countries. Yet its rules of origin, which govern eligibility for trade preferences, minimize opportunities for many of these countries.

Agriculture is a special concern. Two-thirds of all people surviving on less than $1 a day live and work in rural areas. The markets in which they operate, their livelihoods and their prospects for escaping poverty are directly affected by the rules governing agricultural trade. The basic problem to be addressed in the WTO negotiations on agriculture can be summarized in three words: rich country subsidies. In the last round of world trade negotiations rich countries promised to cut agricultural subsidies. Since then, they have increased them. They now spend just over $1 billion a year on aid for agriculture in poor countries, and just under $1 billion a day subsidizing agricultural overproduction at home—a less appropriate ordering of priorities is difficult to imagine. To make matters worse, rich countries' subsidies are destroying the markets on which smallholders in poor countries depend, driving down the prices they receive and denying them a fair share in the benefits of world trade. Cotton farmers in Burkina Faso are competing against US cotton producers who receive more than $4 billion a year in subsidies—a sum that

exceeds the total national income of Burkina Faso. Meanwhile, the European Union's extravagant Common Agricultural Policy (CAP) wreaks havoc in global sugar markets, while denying developing countries access to European markets. Rich country consumers and taxpayers are locked into financing policies that are destroying livelihoods in some of the world's poorest countries.

In some areas WTO rules threaten to systematically reinforce the disadvantages faced by developing countries and to further skew the benefits of global integration towards developed countries. An example is the set of rules limiting the scope for poor countries to develop the active industrial and technology policies needed to raise productivity and succeed in world markets. The current WTO regime outlaws many of the policies that helped East Asian countries make rapid advances. WTO rules on intellectual property present a twin threat: they raise the cost of technology transfer and, potentially, increase the prices of medicines, posing risks for the public health of the poor. In the WTO negotiations on services rich countries have sought to create investment opportunities for companies in banking and insurance while limiting opportunities for poor countries to export in an area of obvious advantage: temporary transfers of labour. It is estimated that a small increase in flows of skilled and unskilled labour could generate more than $150 billion annually—a far greater gain than from liberalization in other areas.

The Doha Round of WTO negotiations provides an opportunity to start aligning multilateral trade rules with a commitment to human development and the MDGs. That opportunity has so far been wasted. Four years into the talks and nothing of substance has been achieved. The unbalanced agenda pursued by rich countries and failure to tackle agricultural subsidies are at the core of the problem.

Even the best trade rules will not remove some of the underlying causes of inequality in world trade, however. Persistent problems such as weak infrastructure and limited supply capacity need to be addressed. Rich countries have developed a "capacity-building" aid agenda. Unfortunately, there is an unhealthy concentration on building capacity in areas that rich countries consider strategically useful. Some long-standing problems do not even figure on the international trade agenda. The deep crisis in commodity markets, especially coffee, is an example. In Ethiopia falling prices since 1998 have reduced the average annual income of coffee-producing households by about $200.

The emergence of new trading structures poses new threats to more equitable trade in agriculture. Supermarket chains have become gatekeepers to agricultural markets in rich countries, linking producers in developing countries to consumers in rich countries. But smallholder farmers are excluded by the purchasing practices of some supermarkets, weakening the links between trade and human development. Creating structures to facilitate the entry of small farmers into global marketing chains on more equitable terms would enable the private sector to play a crucial role in the global fight against poverty.

Strengthening the connection between trade and human development is a long-haul exercise. The Doha Round remains an opportunity to start that exercise—and to build the credibility and legitimacy of the rules-based trading system. Viewed in a broader context the round is too important to fail. Building shared prosperity requires multilateral institutions that not only advance the public good, but are seen to operate in a fair and balanced way.

The WTO ministerial meeting planned for December 2005 provides an opportunity to address some of the most pressing challenges. While many of the issues are technical, the practical requirement is for a framework under which WTO rules do more good and less harm for human development. It would be unrealistic to expect the Doha Round to correct all of the imbalances in the rules—but it could set the scene for future rounds aimed at putting human development at the heart of the multilateral system. Among the key benchmarks for assessing the outcome of the Doha Round:

- *Deep cuts in rich country government support for agriculture and a prohibition on export subsidies.* Agricultural support, as measured by the producer support estimates of the OECD, should be cut to no more than 5%–10% of the value of production, with an immediate prohibition on direct and indirect export subsidies.

- *Deep cuts in barriers to developing country exports.* Rich countries should set their maximum tariffs on imports from developing countries at no more than twice the level of their average tariffs, or 5%–6%.

- *Compensation for countries losing preferences.* While rich country preferences for some developing country imports deliver limited benefits in the aggregate, their withdrawal has the potential to cause high levels of unemployment and balance of payments shocks in particular cases. A fund should be created to reduce the adjustment costs facing vulnerable countries.

- *Protection of the policy space for human development.* Multilateral rules should not impose obligations that are inconsistent with national poverty reduction strategies. These strategies should incorporate best international practices adapted for local conditions and shaped though democratic and participative political processes. In particular, the right of developing countries to protect agricultural producers against unfair competition from exports that are subsidized in rich countries should be respected in WTO rules.

- *A commitment to avoid "WTO plus" arrangements in regional trade agreements.* Some regional trade agreements impose obligations that go beyond WTO rules, especially in areas such as investment and intellectual property. It is important that these agreements not override national policies developed in the context of poverty reduction strategies.

- *Refocusing of services negotiations on temporary movements of labour.* In the context of a development round less emphasis should be placed on rapidly liberalizing financial sectors and more on creating rules allowing workers from developing countries improved access to labour markets in rich countries.

OECD agricultural support should be no more than 5%–10% of production value

The interaction between poverty and violent conflict in many developing countries is destroying lives on an enormous scale

Violent conflict as a barrier to progress

In 1945 US Secretary of State Edward R. Stettinius identified the two fundamental components of human security and their connections: "The battle of peace has to be fought on two fronts. The first front is the security front, where victory spells freedom from fear. The second is the economic and social front, where victory means freedom from want. Only victory on both fronts can assure the world of an enduring peace." It was this reasoning that led the United States to play a central role in founding the United Nations.

Sixty years later, and more than a decade after the end of the cold war appeared to mark the start of a new era of peace, security concerns again dominate the international agenda. As the UN Secretary-General's report *In Larger Freedom* argues, we live in an age when the lethal interaction of poverty and violent conflict poses grave threats not just to the immediate victims but also to the collective security of the international community.

For many people in rich countries the concept of global insecurity is linked to threats posed by terrorism and organized crime. The threats are real. Yet the absence of freedom from fear is most marked in developing countries. The interaction between poverty and violent conflict in many developing countries is destroying lives on an enormous scale—and hampering progress towards the MDGs. Failure to build human security by ending this interaction will have global consequences. In an interdependent world the threats posed by violent conflict do not stop at national borders, however heavily defended they may be. Development in poor countries is the front line in the battle for global peace and collective security. The problem with the current battle plan is an overdeveloped military strategy and an underdeveloped strategy for human security.

The nature of conflict has changed. The twentieth century, the bloodiest in human history, was defined first by wars between countries and then by cold war fears of violent confrontation between two superpowers. Now these fears have given way to fears of local and regional wars fought predominantly in poor countries within weak or failed states and with small arms as the weapon of choice. Most of the victims in today's wars are civilians. There are fewer conflicts in the world today than in 1990, but the share of those conflicts occurring in poor countries has increased.

The human development costs of violent conflict are not sufficiently appreciated. In the Democratic Republic of the Congo deaths attributable directly or indirectly to conflict exceed the losses sustained by Britain in the First World War and Second World War combined. In the Darfur region of Sudan nearly 2 million people have been displaced because of conflict. The immediate victims of these and other conflicts periodically make it into the international media spotlight. But the long-run human development impact of violent conflict is more hidden.

Conflict undermines nutrition and public health, destroys education systems, devastates livelihoods and retards prospects for economic growth. Of the 32 countries in the low human development category as measured by the HDI, 22 have experienced conflict at some time since 1990. Countries that have experienced violent conflict are heavily overrepresented among the group of countries that are off track for the MDGs in our projections for 2015. Of the 52 countries that are reversing or stagnating in their attempts to reduce child mortality, 30 have experienced conflict since 1990. The immensity of these costs makes its own case for conflict prevention, conflict resolution and post-conflict reconstruction as three fundamental requirements for building human security and accelerating progress towards the MDGs.

Part of the challenge posed by human insecurity and violent conflict can be traced to weak, fragile and failing states. Compounded failures to protect people against security risks, to provide for basic needs and to develop political institutions perceived as legitimate are standing features of conflict-prone states. In some cases deep horizontal inequalities between regions or groups are a catalyst for violence. External factors also play a role. The "failure" of states such as Afghanistan and Somalia was facilitated by the willingness of external powers to intervene in pursuit of their own strategic goals. Imports of weapons and the capture by narrow interest groups of the flows of finance from the sale of natural resources help to sustain and intensify conflict. Political leadership in conflict-prone states is a necessary condition for change, but not a sufficient one. Rich countries also need to provide leadership.

New approaches to aid are a starting point. Weak and fragile states are not just underaided in relation to their ability to use finance effectively, but they are also subjected to high levels of unpredictability in aid flows. Evidence suggests that aid flows are 40% lower than would be justified by the institutions and policy environment. The nature and sequencing of aid is another problem. Too often donors make large commitments of humanitarian aid in immediate post-conflict periods without following through to support economic recovery in subsequent years.

Mineral and other natural resource exports do not create violent conflict. Neither do small arms. But markets for natural resources and small arms can provide the means to sustain violent conflict. From Cambodia to Afghanistan and countries in West Africa exports of gems and timber have helped finance conflict and weaken state capacity. Certification schemes can close off opportunities for export, as demonstrated by the Kimberley certification process for diamonds. Small arms claim more than 500,000 lives a year, the majority of them in the world's poorest countries. Yet international efforts to control the deadly trade in small arms have had limited impact. Enforcement remains weak, adherence to codes is voluntary, and large legal loopholes enable much of the trade to escape regulation.

One of the most effective ways in which rich countries could address the threats to human development posed by violent conflict is by supporting regional capacity. The crisis in Darfur could have been diminished, if not averted, by the presence of a sufficiently large and well equipped African Union peacekeeping force—especially if that force had a strong mandate to protect civilians. During the peak of the crisis there were fewer than 300 Rwandan and Nigerian troops monitoring what was happening to 1.5 million Darfuris in an area the size of France. Building regional capacity, in areas from the creation of effective early warning systems to intervention, remains a pressing requirement for human security.

If prevention is the most cost-effective route for addressing the threats posed by violent conflict, seizing opportunities for reconstruction runs a close second. Peace settlements are often a prelude to renewed violence: half of all countries coming out of violent conflict revert to war within five years. Breaking this cycle requires a political and financial commitment to provide security, oversee reconstruction and create the conditions for the development of competitive markets and private sector investment over the long haul. That commitment has not always been in evidence.

While the MDGs have provided a focus for progress towards "freedom from want", the world still lacks a coherent agenda for extending "freedom from fear". As the UN Secretary-General's report *In Larger Freedom* has argued, there is an urgent need to develop a collective security framework that goes beyond military responses to the threats posed by terrorism, to a recognition that poverty, social breakdown and civil conflict form core components of the global security threat. Among the key requirements for reducing that threat:

- *A new deal on aid.* Starving conflict-prone or post-conflict states of aid is unjustified. It is bad for human security in the countries concerned—and it is bad for global security. As part of the wider requirement to achieve the aid target of 0.7% of GNI, donors should commit themselves to a greater aid effort, with greater predictability of aid through long-term financing commitments. Donors should be more transparent about the conditions for aid allocations and about their reasons for scaling down investments in conflict-prone countries.
- *Greater transparency in resource management.* As parties to the natural resource markets that help finance conflict and, in some cases, undermine accountable government,

transnational companies involved in mineral exporting should increase transparency. The international legal framework proposed by the UK-sponsored Commission for Africa to allow for the investigation of corrupt practices by transnational companies overseas—as already practised under US law—should be developed as a priority.

- *Cutting the flow of small arms.* The 2006 Small Arms Review Conference provides an opportunity to agree on a comprehensive arms trade treaty to regulate markets and curtail supplies to areas of violent conflict.
- *Building regional capacity.* For Sub-Saharan Africa an immediate priority is the development, through financial, technical and logistical support, of a fully functioning African Union standby peacekeeping force.
- *Building international coherence.* The UN Secretary-General's report calls for the creation of an International Peace-Building Commission to provide a strategic framework for an integrated approach to collective security. As part of that approach a global fund should be created to finance on a long-term and predictable basis immediate post-conflict assistance and the transition to long-term recovery.

* * *

When historians of human development look back at 2005, they will view it as a turning point. The international community has an unprecedented opportunity to put in place the policies and resources that could make the next decade a genuine decade for development. Having set the bar in the Millennium Declaration, the world's governments could set a course that will reshape globalization, give renewed hope to millions of the world's poorest and most vulnerable people and create the conditions for shared prosperity and security. The business as usual alternative will lead towards a world tarnished by mass poverty, divided by deep inequalities and threatened by shared insecurities. In rich and poor countries alike future generations will pay a heavy price for failures of political leadership at this crossroads moment at the start of the twenty-first century.

This Report provides a basis for considering the scale of the challenge. By focusing on three pillars of international cooperation it highlights some of the problems that need to be tackled and some of the critical ingredients for achieving success. What is not in doubt is the simple truth that, as a global community, we have the means to eradicate poverty and to overcome the deep inequalities that divide countries and people. The fundamental question that remains to be answered five years after the Millennium Declaration was signed is whether the world's governments have the resolve to break with past practice and act on their promise to the world's poor. If ever there was a moment for decisive political leadership to advance the shared interests of humanity, that moment is now.

e MDG target for

ng child mortality

 missed, with the

rgin equivalent to

re than 4.4 million

ble deaths in 2015

The MDG target for reducing child mortality will be missed, with the margin equivalent to more than 4.4 million avoidable deaths in 2015. Over the next 10 years the cumulative gap between the target and the current trend adds more than 41 million children who will die before their fifth birthday from the most readily curable of all diseases—poverty. This is an outcome that is difficult to square with the Millennium Declaration's pledge to protect the world's children.

- The gap between the MDG target for halving poverty and projected outcomes is equivalent to an additional 380 million people in developing countries living on less than $1 a day by 2015.

- The MDG target of universal primary education will be missed on current trends, with 47 million children in developing countries still out of school in 2015.

Statistics such as these should be treated with caution. Projections based on past trends provide insights into one set of possible outcomes. They do not define the inevitable. As the financial market dictum puts it, past performance is not a guide to future outcomes. In the case of the MDGs, that is unambiguously good news. There is still time to get back on track—but time is running out. As the UN Secretary-General has said: "The MDGs can

be met by 2015—but only if all involved break with business as usual and dramatically accelerate and scale up action now."[4]

The first section of this chapter is a brief overview of the progress and setbacks in human development over the past decade and a half. It highlights the great reversal in human development inflicted on many countries by HIV/AIDS, and the slowdown in progress on child mortality. Uneven progress across countries and regions has been accompanied by a divergence in human development in some key areas, with inequalities widening. The second section of the chapter turns to the MDGs. The limited—and slowing—advances in human development achieved over the past decade have a direct bearing on prospects for achieving the MDGs. Average incomes in developing countries have been growing far more strongly since 1990. Yet this income growth has not put the world on track for the MDGs—most of which will be missed in most countries. Part of the problem is that growth has been unequally distributed between and within countries. The deeper problem is that increased wealth is not being converted into human development at the rate required to bring the MDGs within reach. Our country-level data projections set out one possible set of outcomes that will follow if the world remains on the business-as-usual trajectory that the UN Secretary-General has warned against.

Progress and setbacks in human development

Human development is about freedom. It is about building human capabilities—the range of things that people can do, and what they can be. Individual freedoms and rights matter a great deal, but people are restricted in what they can do with that freedom if they are poor, ill, illiterate, discriminated against, threatened by violent conflict or denied a political voice. That is why the "larger freedom" proclaimed in the UN Charter is at the heart of human

development. And that is why progress towards the MDGs provides a litmus test for progress in human development. There is more to human development than the MDGs themselves—and many of the MDG targets reflect a modest level of ambition. But failure on the MDGs would represent a grave setback.

The most basic capabilities for human development are leading a long and healthy life, being educated and having adequate resources

1 THE STATE OF HUMAN DEVELOPMENT

"The test of our progress is not whether we add more to the abundance of those who have much; it is whether we provide enough for those who have too little."

US President Franklin D. Roosevelt, second inaugural address, 1937 [1]

"We have a collective responsibility to uphold the principles of human dignity, equality and equity at the global level. As leaders we have a duty therefore to all the world's people, especially the most vulnerable and, in particular, the children of the world, to whom the future belongs."

Millennium Declaration, 2000 [2]

Sixty years ago the UN Charter pledged to free future g⌐
of war, to protect fundamental human rights and "to ⌐
better standards of life in larger freedom". At the start ⌐
world's governments renewed that pledge. The Millenn⌐
in 2000, sets out a bold vision for "larger freedom" in the⌐
vision holds out the promise of a new pattern of globa⌐
foundations of greater equity, social justice and respect f⌐
lennium Development Goals (MDGs), a set of time-bou⌐
for reducing extreme poverty and extending universal ri⌐
benchmarks for measuring progress. More fundamentall⌐
aspirations of the global human community in a period of⌐

This year marks the start of the 10-year count-down to the 2015 target date for achieving the MDGs. Today, the world has the financial, technological and human resources to make a decisive breakthrough in human development. But if current trends continue, the MDGs will be missed by a wide margin. Instead of seizing the moment, the world's governments are stumbling towards a heavily sign-posted and easily avoidable human development failure—a failure with profound implications not just for the world's poor but for global peace, prosperity and security.

Fifteen years after the launch of the first *Human Development Report,* this year's Report starts by looking at the state of human development. Writing in that first report, Mahbub ul Haq looked forward to a decade of rapid advance: "The 1990s", he wrote, "are shaping up as the decade for human development, for rarely has there been such a consensus on the real objectives of development strategies." [3] Since those words were written a great deal has been achieved. Much of the developing world

has experienced ra⌐
living standards. N⌐
globalization. Yet ⌐
vances fall short of ⌐
Development Repo⌐
what was possible. ⌐

Viewed from th⌐
is a growing danger ⌐
the past 10—will g⌐
decade of accelerated⌐
as a decade of lost op⌐
deavour and failed i⌐
This year marks a cro⌐
community can eithe⌐
tinue on its current h⌐
or it can change direc⌐
policies needed to turr⌐
lennium Declaration i⌐

The consequences ⌐
current path should ⌐
Using country-level tre⌐
human cost gaps in 2015⌐
and predicted outcomes⌐
tinue. Among the headli⌐

for a decent standard of living. Other capabilities include social and political participation in society. In this section we look at the record of human development over the past decade—a period of deepening global integration.

The era of globalization has been marked by dramatic advances in technology, trade and investment—and an impressive increase in prosperity. Gains in human development have been less impressive. Large parts of the developing world are being left behind. Human development gaps between rich and poor countries, already large, are widening. Meanwhile, some of the countries most widely cited as examples of globalization "success stories" are finding it harder to convert rising prosperity into human development. Progress in reducing child mortality, one of the most basic of human development indicators, is slowing, and the child death gap between rich and poor countries is widening. For all of the highly visible achievements, the reach of globalization and scientific advance falls far short of ending the unnecessary suffering, debilitating diseases and death from preventable illness that blight the lives of the world's poor people.

Advances in human development— a global snapshot

Looking back over the past decade the long-run trend towards progress in human development has continued. On average, people born in a developing country today can anticipate being wealthier, healthier and better educated than their parents' generation. They are also more likely to live in a multiparty democracy and less likely to be affected by conflict.

In a little more than a decade average life expectancy in developing countries has increased by two years. On this indicator human development is converging: poor countries are catching up with rich ones (figure 1.1). Increased life expectancy is partly a product of falling child death rates (figure 1.2). Today, there are 2 million fewer child deaths than in 1990, and the chance of a child reaching age 5 has increased by about 15%. Improvements in access to water and sanitation have contributed by reducing the

Figure **1.1** **Life expectancy improving in most regions**

Life expectancy (years)

High-income OECD
Latin America & the Caribbean
East Asia & the Pacific
Central & Eastern Europe & the CIS
Arab States
South Asia
Sub-Saharan Africa

1980 1990 2003

Source: UN 2005d.

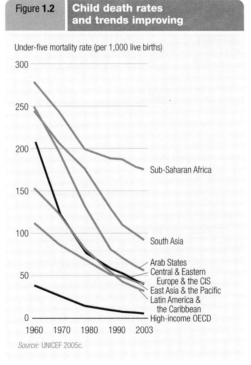

Figure **1.2** **Child death rates and trends improving**

Under-five mortality rate (per 1,000 live births)

Sub-Saharan Africa
South Asia
Arab States
Central & Eastern Europe & the CIS
East Asia & the Pacific
Latin America & the Caribbean
High-income OECD

1960 1970 1980 1990 2003

Source: UNICEF 2005c.

threat of infectious disease. Another 1.2 billion people have gained access to clean water over the past decade. The rapid scale-up in global immunization since 2001 through the Global Alliance for Vaccines and Immunization has also brought down the death toll, saving an estimated half a million lives.

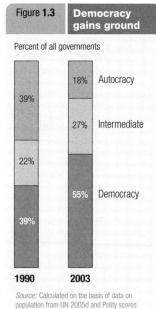

Figure **1.3** **Democracy gains ground**

Percent of all governments

1990: 39%, 22%, 39%
2003: 18% Autocracy, 27% Intermediate, 55% Democracy

Source: Calculated on the basis of data on population from UN 2005d and Polity scores from CIDCM 2005.

Advances in education have been equally impressive. There are still 800 million people in the world lacking basic literacy skills. Women account disproportionately for two-thirds of the total. Even so, literacy levels in developing countries have increased from 70% to 76% over the past decade, and the gender gap is narrowing.[5] Illiteracy today reflects past deficits in access to education. These deficits are shrinking. Compared with the position in 1990, there are 30 million fewer primary school–age children out of school, and the average number of years in school has climbed by half a year. The gender gaps in primary school enrolment, admittedly a limited indicator for gender equity, have narrowed, though girls still account for more than half of children out of school.

Extreme income poverty has been falling. Legitimate concerns have been raised about the use of the $1 a day poverty line to chart cross-country trends—and extreme caution is merited in using this indicator.[6] Measurement problems aside, poverty is a dynamic process that can only be partially captured by static indicators. But the trend points in a positive direction. Extreme poverty fell from 28% in 1990 to 21% today—a reduction in absolute numbers of about 130 million people.[7] Economic growth is one of the obvious requirements for accelerated income poverty reduction and sustained human development. Here, too, the headline news story is encouraging. Average per capita income growth in developing countries in the 1990s was 1.5%, almost three times the rate in the 1980s.[8] Since 2000, average per capita income growth in developing countries has increased to 3.4%—double the average for high-income countries. After two decades of declining average income, Sub-Saharan Africa has posted an increase of 1.2% a year since 2000. It is too early to treat this recovery as a turning point, but there are encouraging signs that growth may be taking root in a growing number of countries in the region.

Conflict is a less obvious good news story. Since 1990 the world has witnessed genocide in Rwanda, violent civil wars in the heart of Europe, wars in Afghanistan and Iraq and setbacks in the Middle East. The conflict in the Democratic Republic of the Congo has claimed almost 4 million lives—the greatest death toll since the Second World War. In Sudan a peace settlement in one of Africa's longest running civil wars served as a prelude to a new humanitarian crisis in Darfur, with more than 1 million people displaced. New threats to collective security have emerged. Yet despite the challenges posed for human development by violent conflict, there is some positive news. The number of conflicts has fallen since 1990. The last 15 years have seen many civil wars ended through negotiation under UN auspices. From Timor-Leste to Afghanistan, El Salvador and Sierra Leone peace has brought new opportunities for human development and democracy. Violent conflict poses one of the greatest barriers to accelerated human development. But the barrier can be lowered.

Progress towards democracy also has been mixed. Democracy is a fundamental aspect of human development. It is both intrinsically valuable, and therefore a human development indicator in its own right, and a means towards wider human development goals. Measuring progress is inherently difficult. Multiparty elections—now the world's preferred form of governance—are one condition. An independent judiciary, constraints on executive power, freedom of the press and respect for human rights give substance to the form of electoral choice. By the Polity indicator of democracy, a composite benchmark, the share of the world's countries with multiparty electoral systems that meet wider criteria for democracy has risen since 1990 from 39% to 55% (figure 1.3). This represents an increase of 1.4 billion people living under multiparty democracy.[9] More than two-thirds of Africans now live in countries with democratic multiparty election systems—and African governments themselves took the lead in opposing an anti-democratic coup in Togo.

However, multiparty elections are not a sufficient condition for democracy—and even on this measure the glass is almost half empty. Multiparty elections are largely absent from the Middle East, though countries such as Egypt and Jordan are increasing the democratic space for electoral politics. Of the world's two most populous countries, India is a thriving democracy, but in China political reforms have lagged behind economic reforms. Many countries with multiparty elections, notably some countries of the former Soviet Union, are democracies in name and electoral autocracies in practice, with political leaders seen by their people as corrupt, tyrannical and predatory. Multiparty elections can provide a smokescreen that obscures overbearing executive power, limitations on press freedom and human rights abuses that strip democracy of its meaning. In some countries public protest has been a powerful antidote to such practices. During 2004 and 2005 long-serving presidents were driven from power in Georgia, Ukraine and Kyrgyzstan by public protest over perceived abuses of democratic process.

The scale of the human development gains registered over the past decade should not be underestimated—nor should it be exaggerated. Part of the problem with global snapshots is that they obscure large variations across and within regions. They also hide differences across dimensions of human development. Progress towards human development has been uneven across and within regions and across different dimensions.

Progress viewed through the human development index

The human development index (HDI) is a composite indicator. It covers three dimensions of human welfare: income, education and health. Its purpose is not to give a complete picture of human development but to provide a measure that goes beyond income. The HDI is a barometer for changes in human well-being and for comparing progress in different regions.

Over the last decade the HDI has been rising across all developing regions, though at variable rates and with the obvious exception of Sub-Saharan Africa (figure 1.4). Amid the overall progress, however, many countries suffered unprecedented reversals. Eighteen countries with a combined population of 460 million people registered lower scores on the HDI in 2003 than in 1990 (table 1.1). (Only six countries suffered such reversals in the 1980s.) The reversals have been heavily concentrated in two

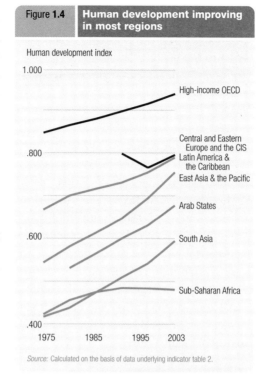

Figure **1.4** Human development improving in most regions

Human development index

Source: Calculated on the basis of data underlying indicator table 2.

Table **1.1** Countries experiencing HDI reversal

1980–90	1990–2003
Congo, Dem. Rep. of the	Botswana
Guyana	Cameroon
Haiti	Central African Republic
Niger	Congo
Rwanda	Congo, Dem. Rep. of the
Zambia	Côte d'Ivoire
	Kazakhstan [a]
	Kenya
	Lesotho
	Moldova, Rep. of [a]
	Russian Federation [a]
	South Africa
	Swaziland
	Tajikistan [a]
	Tanzania, U. Rep. of [a]
	Ukraine [a]
	Zambia
	Zimbabwe

a. Country does not have HDI data for 1980–90, so drop may have begun before 1990.
Source: Indicator table 2.

regions. Twelve of the countries with reversals are in Sub-Saharan Africa. Just over one-third of Sub-Saharan Africa's population—240 million people—live in countries that have suffered an HDI reversal. The former Soviet Union accounts for the other six countries in which the HDI slid backwards.

HDI reversals are reflected in the relative standing of countries. In Sub-Saharan Africa the lethal interaction of economic stagnation, slow progress in education and the spread of HIV/AIDS has produced a free fall in HDI ranking (box 1.1). Southern Africa accounts for some of the steepest declines—a fall of 35 places for South Africa, 23 places for Zimbabwe and 21 places for Botswana. Of the countries of the former Soviet Union the biggest declines were in Tajikistan, which fell 21 places; Ukraine, 17 places; and the Russian Federation, 15 places. The economic disruption that followed the disintegration of the Soviet Union has been one of the two drivers for decline in HDI ranking. The other is a catastrophic drop in life expectancy. Russia fell 48 places in world life expectancy ranking from 1990 to 2003 (box 1.2).

The relationship between wealth ranking and HDI ranking varies across countries. Bangladesh and China are two of the fastest climbers in the HDI ranking. Since 1990 Bangladesh has risen 14 places in the HDI ranking but just 10 places in the global wealth ranking. What this suggests is that social progress in Bangladesh has outstripped economic advance relative to the performance of other countries. Conversely, China has continued its impressive ascent of the HDI ranking, but economic advance has outpaced social advance. The country has climbed 20 places in the HDI ranking and 32 places in the wealth ranking.

Simple decomposition of the HDI provides some insight into the underlying drivers of change. From very different starting points Bangladesh, China and Uganda have all increased their HDI score by about 20% since 1990. In China economic growth has been the biggest component in the change. In Bangladesh income growth was important, though far less so than in China: average income increased at about one-quarter of the rate for China. However, Bangladesh achieved balanced advances across the three dimensions of the HDI, registering stronger gains in life expectancy and education than China did. In Uganda minimal gains were achieved in life expectancy, with the bulk of the HDI gain coming from progress in school enrolment and, to a lesser extent, income. The decomposition exercise is explained in more detail in box 2 of *Note on statistics*.

Decomposition exercises raise important issues for policy-makers. Progress in human development requires advances across a broad front: losses in human welfare linked to life expectancy, for example, cannot be compensated for by gains in other areas such as income or education. Moreover, gains in any one area are difficult to sustain in the absence of overall progress. For example, poor health can constrain economic growth and performance in education, and slow growth reduces the resources available for social investment. The HDI decomposition exercises highlight the challenges facing different groups of countries. For China the challenge is to ensure that surging income growth is converted into sustained progress in non-income

---

Box 1.1	HIV/AIDS generates multiple human development reversals

Falling life expectancy is one indicator capturing the impact of HIV/AIDS. But the epidemic is generating multiple human development reversals, extending beyond health into food security, education and other areas.

HIV-affected households are trapped in a financial pincer as health costs rise and incomes fall. Costs can amount to more than one-third of household income, crowding out spending in other areas. In Namibia and Uganda studies have found households resorting to distress sales of food and livestock to cover medical costs, increasing their vulnerability. Meanwhile, HIV/AIDS erodes their most valuable asset: their labour. In Swaziland maize production falls on average by more than 50% following an adult death from HIV/AIDS.

Beyond the household, HIV/AIDS is eroding the social and economic infrastructure. Health systems are suffering from a lethal interaction of two effects: attrition among workers and rising demand. Already overstretched health infrastructures are being pushed to the brink of collapse. For example, in Côte d'Ivoire and Uganda patients with HIV-related conditions occupy more than half of all hospital beds.

HIV/AIDS is eroding human capacity on a broad front. Zambia now loses two-thirds of its trained teachers to HIV/AIDS, and in 2000 two in three agricultural extension workers in the country reported having lost a co-worker in the past year.

The spread of AIDS is a consequence as well as a cause of vulnerability. HIV/AIDS suppresses the body's immune system and leads to malnutrition. At the same time, nutritional deficiencies hasten the onset of AIDS and its progression. Women with HIV/AIDS suffer a loss of status. At the same time, gender inequality and the subservient status of women are at the heart of power inequalities that increase the risk of contracting the disease. Violence against women, especially forced or coercive sex, is a major cause of vulnerability. Another is women's weak negotiating position on the use of condoms.

Source: Gillespie and Kadiyala 2005; Yamano and Jayne 2004; Carr-Hill 2004; Swaziland, Ministry of Agriculture and Co-operatives and Business 2002.

Box 1.2   **Mortality crisis in the Russian Federation: 7 million "missing" men**

Life expectancy at birth in the Russian Federation is among the lowest for industrial countries: 65 years compared with 79 years in Western Europe. Since the early 1990s there has been a marked increase in male mortality over and above the historical trend. The number of additional deaths during 1992–2001 is estimated at 2.5–3 million. In the absence of war, famines or health epidemics there is no recent historical precedent for the scale of the loss.

Mortality is higher among men than women, especially among single and less educated men. In 2003 life expectancy was 59 years for Russian men and 72 years for women, one of the widest gender gaps in the world. If normal mortality ratios prevailed, 7 million more men would be alive in Russia. Put differently, gender inequality reduces the overall population by about 5%.[1]

Looking at the immediate causes of death provides part of the explanation. Russia suffers from a high incidence of cardiovascular disease, reflecting dietary and lifestyle factors. Alongside this "First World" epidemic, the Russian Federation is increasingly marked by infectious disease problems, with tuberculosis and HIV/AIDS growing threats. Homicide and suicide rates are high by industrial country standards and increased in the 1990s, with both indicators closely associated with overconsumption of alcohol.

Labour market restructuring, the deep and protracted economic recession of the 1990s and the collapse of social provision may have increased the levels of psychosocial stress experienced by the population. This was reflected in an increase in alcohol consumption and alcohol-related illness. At the same time, there was an increase in violent crime linked to a breakdown in state institutions dealing with law, order and security. Informal economic activity and contract enforcement through violence contributed to the decline in life expectancy: male homicide rates doubled in the first half of the 1990s.

Beyond violent crime and psychosocial stress the spread of preventable infectious diseases— tuberculosis, acute intestinal infections and diphtheria, in particular—points to flaws in the healthcare system. Public healthcare expenditure declined from 3.5% of GDP in 1997/98 to an average of 2.9% during 1999–2001. Wealthier households made increasing recourse to new private health services, but for many poorer families widespread demands for bribes and other informal payments put "free" public healthcare out of reach.

Russian mortality trends pose one of the gravest human development challenges of the early twenty-first century. Such an acute upsurge in mortality highlights the need for better research to identify the causes of excess male mortality and proactive public policies to identify and protect vulnerable populations during periods of rapid socio-economic transition. Particularly important is the development of institutions perceived as legitimate by the population and capable of overseeing a complex process of economic reform. Other transition economies—Poland, for instance—have managed to reverse negative mortality trends and to increase life expectancy.

1. "Missing women" is a term more often encountered in the literature. It has been used to illustrate the female mortality differentials in some parts of Sub-Saharan Africa and South Asia (Sen 1999). The number of missing women or men is calculated by comparing the current ratio of women to men to the ratio considered normal in the absence of significant gender bias.

Source: Shkolnikov and Cornia 2000; World Bank 2005e; Men and others 2003; Malyutina and others 2002.

dimensions of human development. Income, after all, is a means to human development, not an end. In Uganda the challenge is to build on the achievements in education while identifying the reasons that advances in this area and in income are not extended to health. Bangladesh demonstrates that it is possible to sustain strong human development progress across a broad front even at relatively modest levels of income growth. Maintaining this progress, while accel-

erating economic growth and income poverty reduction, is critical for future development.

Some countries are far better than others at converting wealth into human development, as measured by the HDI. Saudi Arabia has a far higher average income than Thailand but a similar HDI ranking (figure 1.5). Guatemala has almost double the average income of Viet Nam but a lower HDI ranking. Large gaps between wealth and HDI rankings are usually

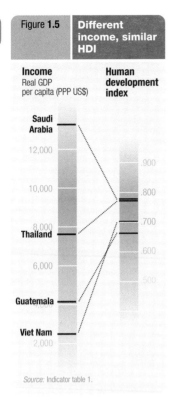

Figure **1.5** **Different income, similar HDI**

Income
Real GDP
per capita (PPP US$)

Human
development
index

Saudi
Arabia

12,000

10,000

.900

.800

8,000
Thailand

.700

.600

6,000

.500

Guatemala

Viet Nam

2,000

Source: Indicator table 1.

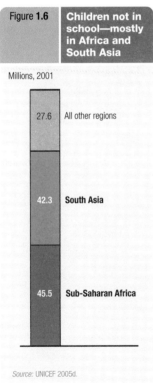

Figure **1.6** **Children not in school—mostly in Africa and South Asia**

Millions, 2001

27.6   All other regions

42.3   South Asia

45.5   Sub-Saharan Africa

Source: UNICEF 2005d.

an indicator of deep structural inequalities that block the transmission from wealth creation to human development. They also point to shortcomings in public policy, with governments failing to put in place strategies for extending opportunities among poor, marginalized or disadvantaged groups. As chapter 2 shows, structural inequalities have a major bearing on the rate of progress towards the MDGs.

Beyond the HDI, very large deficits in human capability remain. Metaphors about the human development glass being half empty or half full distract attention from one overwhelming fact: the extraordinary level of avoidable deprivation that prevails in the midst of an increasingly prosperous world.

The limits to human development

There is no more powerful—or disturbing—indicator of capability deprivation than child mortality. More than 10 million children die each year before their fifth birthday.[10] Sub-Saharan Africa's share of child mortality is growing. The region accounts for 20% of births but 44% of child deaths. Almost all childhood deaths are preventable. Every two minutes four people die from malaria alone, three of them children. Most of these deaths could be prevented by simple, low-cost interventions. Vaccine-preventable illnesses—like measles, diphtheria and tetanus—account for another 2–3 million childhood deaths.[11] For every child who dies, millions more will fall sick or miss school, trapped in a vicious circle that links poor health in childhood to poverty in adulthood. Like the 500,000 women who die each year of pregnancy-related causes, more than 98% of children who die each year live in poor countries. They die because of where they are born.

Progress in reducing poverty has been partial. One in five people in the world—more than 1 billion people—still survive on less than $1 a day, a level of poverty so abject that it threatens survival. Another 1.5 billion people live on $1–$2 a day. More than 40% of the world's population constitute, in effect, a global underclass, faced daily with the reality or the threat of extreme poverty.

Income poverty is closely linked to hunger. In a world of plenty, millions of people go hungry every day. More than 850 million people, including one in three preschool children, are still trapped in a vicious cycle of malnutrition and its effects.[12] Malnutrition weakens the immune system, increasing the risk of ill health, which in turn aggravates malnutrition. Around half of the deaths of preschool children are directly attributable to interactions between malnutrition and infectious disease.[13] Children who are moderately under weight are more than four times more likely to die from infectious disease than are well nourished children.

In turn, vulnerability to infectious disease is exacerbated by inadequate access to clean water and sanitation. More than 1 billion people lack access to safe water and 2.6 billion lack access to improved sanitation. Diseases transmitted through water or human waste are the second leading cause of death among children worldwide, after respiratory tract infection. The overall death toll: an estimated 3,900 children every day.[14]

Gaps in opportunities for education remain large. In an increasingly knowledge-based global economy about 115 million children are denied even the most basic primary education.[15] Most of the children who are not enrolled in school are in Sub-Saharan Africa and South Asia (figure 1.6). On average, a child born in Mozambique today can anticipate four years of formal education. One born in France will receive 15 years at vastly higher levels of provision. Average schooling in South Asia, at eight years, is half the level in high-income countries. Moreover, while the primary school enrolment gap may be closing, the gap between rich and poor countries measured in terms of average years of education is widening (figure 1.7). This is before taking into account differences in education quality: less than one-quarter of Zambian children emerge from primary school able to pass basic literacy tests.[16] Meanwhile, access to higher education remains a privilege available mainly to citizens of high-income countries. These education inequalities of today are the global social and economic inequalities of tomorrow.

Gender inequalities continue to limit girls' education. Even with the narrowing of gender gaps, on average girls can expect to receive one year less of education than boys in African and Arab States and two years less in South Asia. In 14 African countries girls represent less than 45% of the primary school population. In Pakistan they represent just 41%—gender parity would put another 2 million girls in the country in school. In the developing world as a whole primary school completion rates are 75% for girls but rise to 85% for boys. Gender disparities are even wider at the secondary and tertiary levels. These deep gender disparities represent not just a violation of the universal right to education but also a threat to future human development prospects: girls' education is one of the most powerful catalysts for social progress across a wide range of indicators.

The end of convergence?

For most of the past 40 years human capabilities have been gradually converging. From a low base, developing countries as a group have been catching up with rich countries in such areas as life expectancy, child mortality and literacy. A worrying aspect of human development today is that the overall rate of convergence is slowing—and for a large group of countries divergence is becoming the order of the day.

In a world of already extreme inequalities human development gaps between rich and poor countries are in some cases widening and in others narrowing very slowly. The process is uneven, with large variations across regions and countries. We may live in a world where universal rights proclaim that all people are of equal worth—but where you are born in the world dictates your life chances. The following sections look at three areas in which inequalities between countries both reflect and reinforce unequal opportunities for human development: divergences in life expectancy, the slowdown in progress on child mortality and slowing reductions in income poverty and inequality.

Life expectancy—the great reversal
Leading a long and healthy life is a basic indicator for human capabilities. Inequalities in this area have the most fundamental bearing on

well-being and opportunities. Since the early 1990s a long-run trend towards convergence in life expectancy between rich and poor has been slowed by divergence between regions linked to HIV/AIDS and other setbacks.

Viewed at a global level, the life expectancy gap is still closing. Between 1960 and today life expectancy increased by 16 years in developing countries and by 6 years in developed countries.[17] Since 1980 the gap has closed by two years. However, convergence has to be put in context. All but three months of the two years' convergence since 1980 happened before 1990. Since then, convergence has ground to a halt, and the gaps remain very large. The average life expectancy gap between a low-income country and a high-income country is still 19 years. Somebody born in Burkina Faso can expect to live 35 fewer years than somebody born in Japan, and somebody born in India can expect to live 14 fewer years than somebody born in the United States.

Life expectancy is also an indicator of how healthy you can expect to be. One way of measuring risk is to assess the level of avoidable mortality—the excess risk of dying before a specified age in comparison with a population group in another country. With the high-income country average as a point of comparison, over half of mortality in developing countries is avoidable. Adults ages 15–59

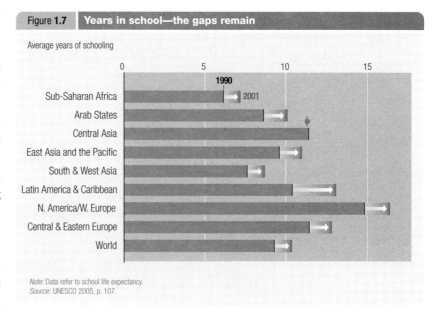

Figure 1.7 Years in school—the gaps remain

Average years of schooling

Note: Data refer to school life expectancy.
Source: UNESCO 2005, p. 107.

On current indicators a child born in Zambia today has less chance of surviving past age 30 than a child born in 1840 in England

account for just under one-third of all deaths in developing countries but only one-fifth in developed countries.[18] The large health inequalities behind these figures draw attention to what has been described as the "law of inverse care"—the availability of medical care is inversely related to need. Health financing inequalities are central to this law. Per capita spending on health ranges from an average of more than $3,000 in high-income OECD countries with the lowest health risks to $78 in low-income countries with the highest risks and to far less in many of the poorest countries.[19]

Gains in life expectancy have been unequally shared. Latin America, the Middle East and Asia have been converging with rich countries. In South Asia life expectancy has increased by a decade in the past 20 years. By contrast, the countries of the former Soviet Union and Sub-Saharan Africa have been falling further behind.

In the countries of the former Soviet Union life expectancy has dropped dramatically, especially for males. In the Russian Federation life expectancy for males has dropped from 70 years in the mid-1980s to 59 years today—lower than in India. Economic collapse, the erosion of welfare provision and high rates of alcoholism and

disease have all contributed (see box 1.2). Noncommunicable ailments—such as cardiovascular disease and injuries—account for the greatest share of the rise in deaths, though infectious diseases are also resurgent. If the death rate remains constant, about 40% of 15-year-old Russian males today will be dead before they reach age 60.[20]

Sub-Saharan Africa is the region that explains the slowdown in progress towards greater global equality in life expectancy. Twenty years ago somebody born in Sub-Saharan Africa could expect to live 24 fewer years than a person born in a rich country, and the gap was shrinking. Today, the gap is 33 years and growing. HIV/AIDS is at the heart of the reversal. In 2004 an estimated 3 million people died from the virus, and another 5 million became infected. Almost all of these deaths were in the developing world, with 70% of them in Africa. Some 38 million people are now infected with HIV—25 million of them in Sub-Saharan Africa (see box 1.1).[21]

Statistics alone cannot capture the full scale of suffering associated with HIV/AIDS. But they can provide an insight into the scale of the demographic shock inflicted on the worst affected countries. On current indicators a child born in Zambia today has less chance of surviving past age 30 than a child born in 1840 in England (figure 1.8). For Sub-Saharan Africa as a whole a child born today has less chance of surviving beyond age 45.

Stark as they are, such statistics understate the human impact of HIV/AIDS. In Europe the greatest single demographic shock since the Black Death was experienced by France between 1913 and 1918, when the combined effects of the First World War and the 1918 influenza outbreak reduced life expectancy by about 16 years. Traumatic as that episode was, it pales against losses in life expectancy of 31 years in countries like Botswana (figure 1.9). In Zambia life expectancy has fallen by 14 years since the mid-1980s. And the projected rate of recovery is far slower than it was in France.

Looking to the future, Africa faces the gravest HIV/AIDS-related risks to human development. But new threats are emerging. Serious epidemics have emerged in several Indian states. In

Figure 1.8 | **Chances of survival in Sub-Saharan Africa are not much better than in 1840s England**

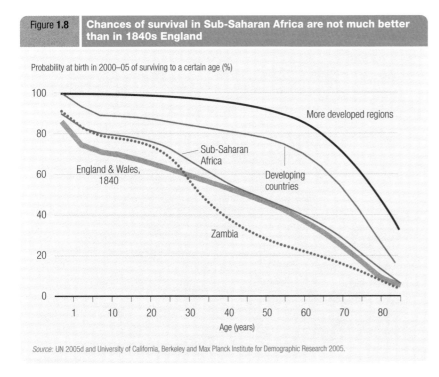

Probability at birth in 2000–05 of surviving to a certain age (%)

Source: UN 2005d and University of California, Berkeley and Max Planck Institute for Demographic Research 2005.

Tamil Nadu HIV prevalence rates higher than 50% have been found among female sex workers, while both Andhra Pradesh and Maharashtra have passed the 1% prevalence mark.[22]

The incidence of HIV/AIDS is also growing in the countries of the former Soviet Union. Ukraine now has one of the fastest growing rates of HIV infection in the world, while the Russian Federation, with the second fastest growth rate (and 1 million infected), is home to the largest epidemic in the region.[23] The vast majority of people living with HIV are young, with intravenous drug use being the main accelerator. As in other parts of Eastern Europe the epidemic is in its early stages—which means that timely intervention can halt and reverse it. If neglected, there is considerable scope for the epidemic to expand as it reaches the general population.

The international response to HIV/AIDS has been profoundly inadequate. In an age of science, technology and economic affluence nothing demonstrates more powerfully the failure of rich countries to tackle the diseases that ravage a large section of humanity. Awareness of the AIDS virus emerged in the early 1980s. When the first *Human Development Report* was published in 1990, only 133,000 cases were reported to the World Health Organization (WHO), more than two-thirds of them in North America. The Report concluded: "AIDS is likely to reverse many of the successes in... raising life expectancy." Yet only now—some 20 million deaths later—is a credible international effort emerging. Just a small fraction of those in need have access to prevention and treatment services. Fewer than 8% of pregnant women have access to treatment for preventing mother-to-child transmission. In Africa fewer than 4% of people in need of antiretroviral treatment are receiving drugs.[24] There are some islands of success. Countries such as Senegal and Uganda have contained and started to reverse the crisis. Brazil and Thailand have saved lives with vigorous public health policies that improve access to medicines. These success stories demonstrate that the goal of treating 3 million people by the end of 2005, a first step towards rolling back the epidemic, is achievable.

The slow and limited international response to the HIV/AIDS crisis has contributed directly to the deepening of global health inequalities. It also demonstrates the costs of delayed action. In 2004 the world spent an estimated $6 billion combating the virus through the Global Fund to Fight AIDS, Tuberculosis and Malaria.[25] Had resources been mobilized on this scale 20 years ago, the epidemic could have been reversed. Today, that amount is insufficient even to contain the crisis, let alone to meet the MDG target to "have halted by 2015 and begun to reverse the spread of HIV/AIDS". The international community's response to a global public health threat has been plainly inadequate. At the same time many governments in the worst affected countries have responded to the unprecedented challenge of HIV/AIDS with denial, stereotyping and neglect, exposing their citizens to grave risks.

Women and children last

Child survival is one of the most sensitive indicators of human welfare, the comparative health of nations and the effectiveness of public policy. Against this backdrop child death trends are fast approaching the point that merits declaration of an international health emergency. Of the 57 million deaths worldwide in 2002 one in five was a child less than five years old— roughly one child died every three seconds. An estimated 4 million of these deaths happened in the first month of life, the neonatal period.[26] Almost all child deaths happen in developing countries, while most of the spending to prevent child deaths happens in rich ones.

The interventions that could prevent or effectively treat the conditions that kill children and women of reproductive age are well known. Most are low cost—and highly cost-effective. Two in every three child deaths could be averted through provision of the most basic health services. Yet a health catastrophe that inflicts a human toll more deadly than the HIV/AIDS pandemic is allowed to continue. Nothing more powerfully underlines the gap between what we are able to do to overcome avoidable suffering and what we choose to do with the wealth and technologies at our disposal.

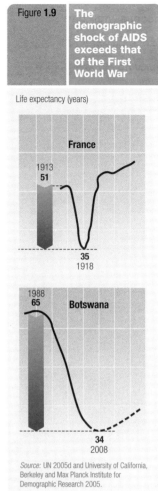

Figure **1.9** The demographic shock of AIDS exceeds that of the First World War

Life expectancy (years)

France
1913
51
35
1918

1988
65
Botswana
34
2008

Source: UN 2005d and University of California, Berkeley and Max Planck Institute for Demographic Research 2005.

While the decline in child mortality has continued over the past decade, the rate of decline appears to be slowing over time. During 1990–2003 child deaths rates in developing countries fell at a pace one-third slower than during the 1980s (figure 1.10).[27] The slowdown has cost lives. Had the progress of the 1980s been sustained during the 1990s and the current decade, more than 1 million fewer children

would have died in 2003.[28] Neonatal mortality has been falling far more slowly than child mortality, with the result that a rising share of child deaths occurs in the first month.[29] Of the 4 million deaths in this period, three-quarters occur in the first week of life.

The child survival story of the past decade is also one of divergence. The gap between rich and poor countries is widening, most spectacularly between rich countries and countries in Africa but also for other regions (figure 1.11). In 1980 child death rates in Sub-Saharan Africa were 13 times higher than in rich countries. They are now 29 times higher. The child mortality challenge extends beyond Sub-Saharan Africa. Even countries that are performing more strongly on economic growth are experiencing slowing progress in reducing child mortality. There is no single cause for the slowdown. Much of the decline in mortality since 1970 can be traced to rising living standards and fewer deaths from diarrhoeal disease and vaccine-preventable conditions. Other major killers linked directly to poverty—such as malnutrition and acute respiratory infection—have been declining more slowly. And deaths from malaria have been increasing.

Child mortality rates underline one of the central lessons of human development: the links between income and social progress are not automatic. On average, mortality rates fall as incomes rise. However, countries at similar levels of income display large variations (figure 1.12). For example, Honduras and Viet Nam have far lower levels of neonatal mortality than India and Pakistan. As such facts suggest, economic growth is not a guaranteed route to faster progress in cutting child deaths.

That conclusion is supported by the record of the past decade. Some of the most visible success stories in economic growth and globalization have been less successful in reducing child mortality. China and, to a more modest degree, India are in the front rank of high-growth, globalizing countries. Yet the annual progress in cutting child deaths has slowed in both countries since 1990, even as economic growth has increased (figure 1.13). The case of China demonstrates that even the most spectacular

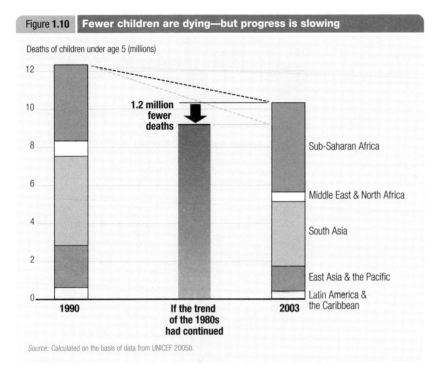

Figure 1.10 | **Fewer children are dying—but progress is slowing**

Deaths of children under age 5 (millions)

1.2 million fewer deaths

Sub-Saharan Africa
Middle East & North Africa
South Asia
East Asia & the Pacific
Latin America & the Caribbean

1990

If the trend of the 1980s had continued

2003

Source: Calculated on the basis of data from UNICEF 2005b.

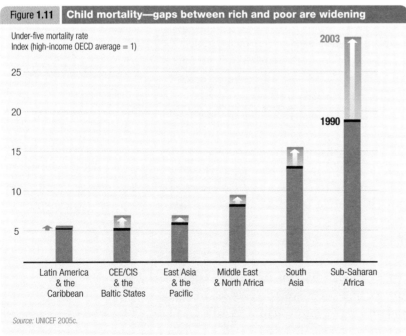

Figure 1.11 | **Child mortality—gaps between rich and poor are widening**

Under-five mortality rate
Index (high-income OECD average = 1)

2003
1990

Latin America & the Caribbean
CEE/CIS & the Baltic States
East Asia & the Pacific
Middle East & North Africa
South Asia
Sub-Saharan Africa

Source: UNICEF 2005c.

economic growth rates and rising living standards do not translate automatically into more rapid declines in the child mortality rate. Per capita income growth increased from 8.1% in the 1980s to 8.5% in 1990–2003, maintaining a spectacular advance in poverty reduction. Indeed, China has already achieved the MDG target of halving income poverty from 1990 levels. However, based on UN data, the annual rate of decline in the incidence of child mortality fell from 2.3% in the 1980s to 1.9% in 1990–2003.[30] There are variations within this trend—and shifting the reference years would produce different outcomes. But the slowdown has prompted questions about whether China, despite a strong track record in a wide range of human development indicators, will meet the MDG target of reducing child mortality by two-thirds by 2015.[31]

At a far higher level of child mortality than China, India seems to be headed in a similar direction. More rapid growth may have put the country on track for the MDG target of halving poverty, but India is widely off track for the child mortality target. The annual rate of decline in child mortality fell from 2.9% in the 1980s to 2.3% since 1990—a slowdown of almost one-fifth. As in China, the slowdown has occurred during a period of accelerating economic growth. Developments in India and China have global implications. India alone accounts for 2.5 million child deaths annually, one in five of the world total. China accounts for another 730,000—more than any other country except India.

Why has the rate of progress slowed? One view is that a slowdown in the rate of decline in child mortality is inevitable. Expanding public health provision through immunization programmes and other services can yield big public health gains, especially in reductions from high levels of mortality. Once these "low hanging fruits" have been collected, so the argument runs, the problem becomes more concentrated in populations that are harder to reach, more vulnerable and less accessible to public policy interventions, driving up the marginal costs of saving lives and dampening progress.

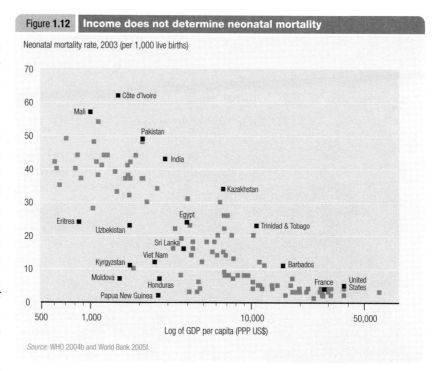

Figure **1.12** Income does not determine neonatal mortality

Neonatal mortality rate, 2003 (per 1,000 live births)

Log of GDP per capita (PPP US$)

Source: WHO 2004b and World Bank 2005f.

Applied in the current context, the low hanging fruit argument lacks credibility. Some countries—Malaysia is an example—have accelerated the rate of reduction in child mortality from already relatively low levels. Others have sustained rapid progress over time, even during periods of low growth. In 1980 Egypt had a higher child mortality rate than Ethiopia does today. At its current rate of progress it will reach Sweden's level by 2010. Egypt has already achieved the MDG target.

Low income is not a barrier to progress. Viet Nam and Bangladesh have both accelerated the pace of child mortality rate reduction. Indeed, at a lower level of income and a comparable rate of economic growth, Viet Nam has now overtaken China on improvement in child mortality. Similarly, at a lower level of income and with far lower growth, Bangladesh has overtaken India (figure 1.14). These differences matter. Had India matched Bangladesh's rate of reduction in child mortality over the past decade, 732,000 fewer children would die this year. Had China matched Viet Nam's, 276,000 lives could be saved. Clearly, there is still a huge scope for rapid reductions in child death in India and China.

For both countries child mortality trends raise wider questions for public health and the distribution within developing countries of the

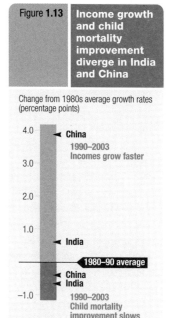

Figure **1.13** Income growth and child mortality improvement diverge in India and China

Change from 1980s average growth rates (percentage points)

Source: Calculated on the basis of data on child mortality from UNICEF 2005e and data on GDP per capita (2000 US$) from World Bank 2005f.

Figure **1.14** China and India fall behind in child mortality

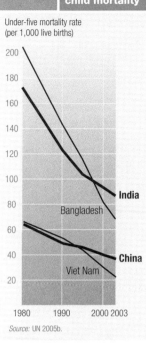

Under-five mortality rate
(per 1,000 live births)

India

Bangladesh

China

Viet Nam

Source: UN 2005b.

benefits from globalization. Integration into global markets has manifestly enhanced wealth creation, generated economic dynamism and raised living standards for many millions of people in India and China. At the same time the human development benefits of economic success have been slow to trickle down to large sections of the population—and the trickle appears to be slowing in some key areas of public health.

Changing this picture will require public policies that address deep-rooted inequalities between rich and poor people, between men and women and between more prosperous and less prosperous regions. These inequalities are rooted in power differences—and they are perpetuated by public policy choices. Were India to show the same level of dynamism and innovation in tackling basic health inequalities as it has displayed in global technology markets, it could rapidly get on track for achieving the

MDG targets. There are encouraging signs that public policy may now be moving in the right direction. During 2005 the announcement of ambitious new programmes aimed at overhauling the health system and extending services in poor areas appeared to mark a new direction in policy. Economic success has expanded the financial resources available for these programmes—and some states have shown that rapid progress can be achieved. The challenge is to ensure that effective reform takes root in the states and areas that account for the bulk of India's human development deficit (box 1.3).

Child mortality is intimately linked to maternal mortality. More than 15 years after the world's governments launched a Safe Motherhood Initiative, an estimated 530,000 women die each year in pregnancy or childbirth. These deaths are the tip of an iceberg. At least 8 million women a year suffer severe complications in pregnancy or childbirth, with grave risks to their

---

Box **1.3**   India—a globalization success story with a mixed record on human development

"The slow improvement in the health status of our people has been a matter of great concern. We have paid inadequate attention to public health."

Dr. Manmohan Singh, Prime Minister of India, April 2005[1]

India has been widely heralded as a success story for globalization. Over the past two decades the country has moved into the premier league of world economic growth; high-technology exports are booming and India's emerging middle-class consumers have become a magnet for foreign investors. As the Indian Prime Minister has candidly acknowledged, the record on human development has been less impressive than the record on global integration.

The incidence of income poverty has fallen from about 36% in the early 1990s to somewhere between 25% and 30% today. Precise figures are widely disputed because of problems with survey data. But overall the evidence suggests that the pick-up in growth

has not translated into a commensurate decline in poverty. More worrying, improvements in child and infant mortality are slowing—and India is now off track for these MDG targets. Some of India's southern cities may be in the midst of a technology boom, but 1 in every 11 Indian children dies in the first five years of life for lack of low-technology, low-cost interventions. Malnutrition, which has barely improved over the past decade, affects half the country's children. About 1 in 4 girls and more than 1 in 10 boys do not attend primary school.

Why has accelerated income growth not moved India onto a faster poverty reduction path? Extreme poverty is concentrated in rural areas of the northern poverty-belt states, including Bihar, Madhya Pradesh, Uttar Pradesh and West Bengal, while income growth has been most dynamic in other states, urban areas and the service sectors. While rural poverty has fallen rapidly in some states, such as Gujarat and Tamil Nadu, less progress has been achieved in the

Differences among states in India

Indicator	India	Kerala	Bihar	Rajasthan	Uttar Pradesh
Female share of population (%)	48	52	49	48	48
Under-five mortality rate (per 1,000 live births)	95	19	105	115	123
Total fertility rate (births per woman)	2.9	2.0	3.5	3.8	4.0
Birth attended by health professional (%)	42	94	23	36	22
Children receiving all vaccinations (%)	42	80	11	17	21

Source: IIPS and ORC Macro 2000.

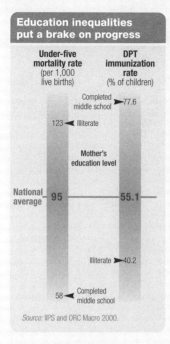

Education inequalities put a brake on progress

Under-five mortality rate (per 1,000 live births) / DPT immunization rate (% of children)

Completed middle school ► 77.6

123 ◄ Illiterate

Mother's education level

National average 95 — 55.1

Illiterate ► 40.2

58 ◄ Completed middle school

Source: IIPS and ORC Macro 2000.

northern states. At a national level, rural unemployment is rising, agricultural output is increasing at less than 2% a year, agricultural wages are stagnating, and growth is virtually "jobless". Every 1% of national income growth generated three times as many jobs in the 1980s as in the 1990s.

The deeper problem facing India is its human development legacy. In particular, pervasive gender inequalities, interacting with rural poverty and inequalities between states, is undermining the potential for converting growth into human development.

Perhaps the starkest gender inequality is revealed by this simple fact: girls ages 1–5 are 50% more likely to die than boys. This fact translates into 130,000 "missing" girls. Female mortality rates remain higher than male mortality rates through age 30, reversing the typical demographic pattern. These gender differences reflect a widespread preference for sons, particularly in northern states. Girls, less valued than their brothers, are often brought to health facilities in more advanced stages of illness, taken to less qualified doctors and have less money spent on their healthcare. The low status and educational disadvantage suffered by women have a direct bearing on their health and their children's. About one-third of India's children are under weight at birth, reflecting poor maternal health.

Inadequate public health provision exacerbates vulnerability. Fifteen years after universal childhood immunization was introduced, national health surveys suggest that only 42% of children are fully immunized. Coverage is lowest in the states with the highest child death rates, and less than 20% in Bihar and Uttar Pradesh. India may be a world leader in computer software services, but when it comes to basic immunization services for children in poor rural areas, the record is less impressive.

Gender inequality is one of the most powerful brakes on human development. Women's education matters in its own right, but it is also closely associated with child mortality. The under-five mortality rate is more than twice as high for children of illiterate mothers as for children whose mothers have completed middle school (see figure). Apart from being less prone to undernutrition, better educated mothers are more likely to use basic health services, have

fewer children at an older age and are more likely to space the births—all factors positively associated with child survival. As well as depriving girls of a basic right, education inequalities in India translate into more child deaths.

State inequalities interact with gender- and income-based inequalities (see table). Four states account for more than half of child deaths: Bihar, Madhya Pradesh, Rajasthan and Uttar Pradesh (see figure). These states also are marked by some of the deepest gender inequalities in India. Contrasts with Kerala are striking. Girls born in Kerala are five times more likely to reach their fifth birthday, are twice as likely to become literate and are likely to live 20 years longer than girls born in Uttar Pradesh. The differences are linked to the chronic underprovision of health services in high-mortality northern states, which is in turn linked to unaccountable state-level governance structures.

Translating economic success into human development advances will require public policies aimed explicitly at broadening the distribution of benefits from growth and global integration, increased public investment in rural areas and services and—above all—political leadership to end poor governance and address the underlying causes of gender inequality.

There are encouraging signs that this leadership may be starting to emerge. In 2005 the government of India launched a $1.5 billion National Rural Health Mission, a programme targeting some 300,000 villages, with an initial focus on the poorest states in the north and north-east. Commitments have been made to raise public health spending from 0.9% of national income to 2.3%. Spending on education has also been increased. In an effort to create the conditions for accelerated rural growth and poverty reduction, ambitious public investment programmes have been put in place to expand rural infrastructure, including the provision of drinking water and roads.

Translating increased financial commitment into improved outcomes will require a stronger focus on effective delivery and measures to improve the quality of public services. There is no shortage of innovative models to draw upon. States such Himachal Pradesh and Tamil Nadu have sustained rapid progress in education, not just by increasing budget provision but by increasing the accountability of service providers and creating incentives—such as free school meals, scholarships and free textbooks—aimed at increasing the participation of poor households.

Overcoming the legacy of decades of underinvestment in human development and deep-rooted gender inequalities poses immense challenges. Political leadership of a high order will be needed to address these challenges. Failure to provide it and to extend health and education opportunities for all, regardless of wealth and gender, will ultimately act as a constraint on India's future prospects in the global economy.

1. BBC News 2005a.

Source: BBC News 2005a; Cassen, Visaria and Dyson 2004; Kijima and Lanjouw 2003; Joshi 2004; Dev 2002; Drèze and Murthi 2001.

health. As with child mortality, the vast majority of these deaths occur in developing countries, with South Asia (where the maternal mortality ratio is 540 deaths per 100,000 live births) and Sub-Saharan Africa (where the ratio is 920 per 100,000 live births) accounting for 75% of the total. The risk of dying from pregnancy-related causes ranges from 1 in 18 in Nigeria to 1 in 8,700 in Canada. And as with child mortality, most deaths are avoidable: around three-quarters could be prevented through low-cost interventions. Despite this, overall levels of maternal mortality appear to have changed little over the past decade, especially in the majority of countries that account for the bulk of deaths. Underreporting and misreporting of maternal death make cross-country comparisons and precise trend analysis difficult (see box 5 of *Note on statistics*). However, proxy indicators—such as fertility rates and attendance by skilled health workers—indicate that the annual decline in mortality is slowing.[32]

Child health and maternal health are barometers for other areas of human development: the state of public health, the state of nutrition and the empowerment of women, among others. Failures in public health provision are reflected in the fact that the lives of about 6 million children's lives a year could be saved through simple, low-cost interventions (box 1.4). Measles causes more than half a million deaths a year. Diphtheria, pertussis (whooping cough) and tetanus (DPT) claim another half a million lives. Almost all of these deaths could be averted through immunization.[33] Yet 37 million children worldwide are not immunized with the DPT vaccine, and progress in immunization coverage has stalled across much of the developing world, notably among the poor. Immunization coverage is less than 50% for children living in households with incomes below the $1 a day international poverty line.[34] Three children die every two minutes as a result of malaria in Africa alone.[35] Many of these deaths happen for want of a simple insecticide-treated bednet. Fewer than 2% of children living in malaria-infected zones sleep under bednets that protect them from mosquitoes.[36] At an average cost of $3 per bednet this would appear to be a small investment in the prevention of a disease

that claims more than 1 million lives a year and accounts for one in four of all child deaths in Africa. Yet it is an investment that the international community and national governments have been loath to make. Spending on malaria by the Global Fund to Fight AIDS, Tuberculosis and Malaria is just $450 million a year.[37]

Factors beyond the health sector are equally important. Louis Pasteur wrote that "the microbe is nothing, the terrain everything."[38] Poverty and inequalities in power, and a failure to reduce them, define the terrain for child and maternal death. Malnourishment among mothers is a major contributor to neonatal deaths. And malnutrition is implicated in half of all deaths in children under age 5. Poor and malnourished children are more likely to become sick and less able to resist childhood diseases. It is estimated that about 3,900 children die each day because of diseases transmitted through dirty water or poor hygiene.[39] These poverty-related impediments to progress are intimately linked to gender inequality and the low status of women. In much of the developing world—especially South Asia—women lack the power to claim entitlements to nutrition and health resources, exposing them and their children to increased risk of mortality.[40]

While child death is the most extreme indicator for inequality in life chances, the disparities between rich and poor draw attention to a wider problem. The vast majority of people who live in rich countries have access to the financial resources, technologies and services that prevent or, for diseases like AIDS, at least postpone death. Conversely, the vast majority of people in poor countries—especially if they happen to be poor—do not. It is this continued inequality in health outcomes that raises fundamental questions about the failure of governments in wealthy countries to develop a pattern of globalization that incorporates redistributive mechanisms to correct fundamental imbalances in life chances.[41]

Income poverty—slowing progress in an unequal world

"The tide of poverty and inequality that has previously engulfed the world is starting to turn", declares one influential report on globalization.[42] The sentiment reflects a widespread belief that,

Box 1.4	**Saving 6 million lives—achievable and affordable**

Most child deaths are avoidable. While faster economic growth would reduce mortality rates, mortality rates are higher than they need to be because of the indefensible underuse of effective, low-cost, low-technology interventions—and because of a failure to address the structural causes of poverty and inequality.

Cross-country research published in *The Lancet* in 2003 identified 23 interventions having the strongest impact on child mortality. These interventions—15 of them preventive and 8 curative—ranged from the provision of oral rehydration therapy to drugs and insecticide-treated bednets for preventing malaria and antenatal and obstetric care. Most of the interventions can be provided on a low-cost basis through trained health workers and local communities. Using 2000 data and assuming 100% coverage for these interventions, the authors of the study concluded that around two in every three child deaths—6 million in total—could have been avoided.

The findings highlight the huge potential for tackling one of the gravest human development problems facing the international community. Communicable diseases and systemic infections, such as pneumonia, septicaemia, diarrhoea and tetanus, cause two in every three child deaths—nearly all of them preventable. The 2.5 million deaths from diarrhoea and pneumonia could be dramatically reduced through community-level interventions supported by government agencies. The precise intervention priorities vary by country, and there is no single solution. But the common problem is one of low coverage of services, high levels of inequality linked to poverty and neglect of neonatal mortality in public health policy.

Several myths reinforce the idea that the MDG target of reducing child mortality by two-thirds may be unattainable. The following are among the most common:

- *Myth 1. Achieving rapid decline is unaffordable.* Not true. Some countries do face major financial constraints—hence the need for increased aid. But child mortality is an area in which small investments yield high returns. Recent cross-country research on neonatal mortality identifies a set of interventions that, with 90% coverage in 75 high-mortality countries, could reduce death rates by 59%, saving 2.3 million lives. The $4 billion cost represents two days' worth of military spending in developed countries.
- *Myth 2. High-technology interventions such as intensive care units hold the key to success.* Not true. Sweden at the end of the nineteenth century and the United Kingdom after 1945 achieved rapid declines in neonatal mortality with the introduction of free antenatal care, skilled attendance at childbirth and increased availability of antibiotics. Developing countries such as Malaysia and Sri Lanka have similarly achieved steep

declines in neonatal deaths through simple, home-based, district-level interventions supported through training for health workers and midwives and publicly financed provision.

- *Myth 3. Poor countries lack the institutional capacity to scale up.* Not true. Institutions matter, but many poor countries have achieved rapid advances by using institutional structures creatively. Egypt has sustained one of the fastest declines in child mortality rates in the world since 1980. Bangladesh, Honduras, Nicaragua and Viet Nam have also achieved rapid progress. In each case decentralized district-level programmes have integrated child health and maternal health programmes—including immunization, diarrhoea treatment and antenatal care—into health service delivery. They also invested in training health workers and midwives and in targeting vulnerable populations. Even poor-performing countries do not lack evidence of the potential for scaling up. In the Indian state of Maharashtra a three-year pilot project covering 39 villages extended basic antenatal care programmes through home-based care provision and simple clinical interventions costing $5 per person covered. The infant mortality rate fell from 75 deaths per 1,000 live births in the baseline period (1993–95) to 39 three years later. The mortality rate in an adjacent district declined only from 77 deaths per 1,000 live births to 75 over the same period.

The potential for rapid progress reflects the large deficit in current provision. In Sub-Saharan Africa less than 40% of women deliver with skilled care and in South Asia less than 30% do. More than 60 million women each year deliver without skilled care. Inequality in service use—a theme taken up in chapter 2—adds to vulnerability. The poorest women are more likely to be malnourished and less likely to take advantage of services because they are unavailable, unaffordable or of inadequate quality. Beyond service provision, deeper gender inequalities exacerbate the problem. Estimates suggest that birth spacing could reduce death rates by 20% in India and 10% in Nigeria, the countries with the highest neonatal mortality rates. Lack of control over fertility, which is linked to imbalance in power within the household and beyond, is central to the problem.

The real barriers to progress in reducing child deaths are not institutional or financial, though there are constraints in both areas. Poor quality service provision and chronic financing shortfalls have to be addressed. At the same time, poverty reduction strategies need to focus more on the structural causes of high mortality linked to the low status of women, inequalities in access to healthcare and a failure to prioritize child and maternal health.

Source: Cousens, Lawn and Zupan 2005; Mills and Shilcutt 2004; Wagstaff and Claeson 2004.

when it comes to income, global integration has ushered in a new era of convergence. At best, the sentiment is weakly supported by the evidence. Poverty is falling, but slowly since the mid-1990s.

Meanwhile, global inequality remains at extraordinarily high levels.

In the aggregate the past two decades have witnessed one of the most rapid reductions in

At the other end of the spectrum, Sub-Saharan Africa had almost 100 million more people living in poverty in 2001 than in 1990

poverty in world history. However, any assessment of trends in income poverty has to take into account large variations across regions. Global poverty reduction has been driven largely by the extraordinary success of East Asia, particularly China. At the other end of the spectrum, Sub-Saharan Africa had almost 100 million more people living on less than $1 a day in 2001 than in 1990. South Asia reduced the incidence of poverty, though not the absolute number of poor people. Latin America and the Middle East registered no progress, while Central and Eastern Europe and the CIS experienced a dramatic increase in poverty. The number of people living on less than $2 a day in Central and Eastern Europe and the CIS rose from 23 million in 1990 to 93 million in 2001, or from 5% to 20%.

In a military metaphor, the war against poverty has witnessed advances on the eastern front, massive reversals in Sub-Saharan Africa and stagnation across a broad front between these poles. The worrying trend for the future is that overall progress is slowing. Much of the success in pushing back poverty over the past two decades was achieved in the 1980s and the first half of the 1990s (table 1.2). Since the mid-1990s $1 a day poverty has been falling at one-fifth the 1980–96 rate. This is despite the fact that average growth for developing countries picked up in the 1990s, increasing at more than double the per capita rate of the previous decade. In China the rate at which growth is converted into poverty reduction has fallen sharply. Between 1990 and 2001 the incidence of $1 a day

poverty declined by 50%, with 130 million fewer people living below the international poverty line. However, more than 90% of the decline took place between 1990 and 1996.

The rate of progress in income poverty reduction is a function of two factors: economic growth and the share of any increment in growth captured by the poor. No country has successfully sustained progress in reducing income poverty with a stagnating economy. In East Asia high growth has been central to the reduction of income poverty. More recently, economic take-off in India has created the potential for accelerated poverty reduction. At the 4% annual per capita growth rate achieved since 1980, incomes double every 17 years. With the 1% per capita growth rate India experienced in the two decades before 1980 it took 66 years for incomes to double.

In other regions the growth picture has been less encouraging. Average incomes in Sub-Saharan Africa are lower today than in 1990. Recent years have witnessed signs of recovery in several countries, including Burkina Faso, Ethiopia, Ghana, Mozambique and Tanzania. However, recovery has to be put in context. It will take Sub-Saharan Africa until 2012 just to restore average incomes to their 1980 levels at the 1.2% per capita annual growth experienced since 2000. In the countries of the former Soviet Union transition brought with it one of the deepest recessions since the Great Depression of the 1930s—and in many cases despite positive growth over the last few years, incomes are still lower than they were 15 years ago. Since

Table **1.2**	Decline in income poverty, 1981–2001							

Share of people living on less than $1 (PPP US$) a day (%)

Region	1981	1984	1987	1990	1993	1996	1999	2001
East Asia & Pacific	56.7	38.8	28.0	29.5	24.9	15.9	15.3	14.3
Europe & Central Asia	0.8	0.6	0.4	0.5	3.7	4.4	6.3	3.5
Latin America & Caribbean	10.1	12.2	11.3	11.6	11.8	9.4	10.5	9.9
Middle East & North Africa	5.1	3.8	3.2	2.3	1.6	2.0	2.7	2.4
South Asia	51.5	46.8	45.0	41.3	40.1	36.7	32.8	31.9
Sub-Saharan Africa	41.6	46.3	46.9	44.5	44.1	46.1	45.7	46.4
World	40.4	33.0	28.5	27.9	26.3	22.3	21.5	20.7

Source: World Bank 2005d.

1990 real per capita incomes have fallen by more than 10% in Kyrgyzstan, Russia and Ukraine and by 40% or more in Georgia, Moldova and Tajikistan. In Russia 10% of the population live on less than $2 a day, and 25% live below the national subsistence poverty line. Most countries of the Middle East and Latin America have seen only a marginal increase in average income.

These figures underscore the mixed experience of countries with regard to economic growth. While global integration has been associated with accelerated growth for some countries, current growth patterns remain incompatible with achieving the MDGs. On average, countries have to grow at 1%–2% per capita a year to halve poverty over a 25-year period, as envisaged under the MDGs. In 1990–2003 more than 1 billion people were living in countries growing at less than this rate—about half of them in Sub-Saharan Africa (table 1.3). Fifteen countries in Central and Eastern Europe also

posted growth rates of less than 1% per capita during this period. However, recent years have been more encouraging, with a robust economic recovery driving a reduction in poverty. Russia and Ukraine have averaged growth rates of 6%–9% since 2000, rising to 9%–13% for Armenia, Azerbaijan and Tajikistan. In Russia poverty levels were halved between 1999 and 2002, with about 30 million people escaping poverty.

Economic stagnation has been a widespread feature of the globalization era: during the 1990s, 25 countries in Sub-Saharan Africa and 10 in Latin America experienced a sustained period of economic stagnation.[43] Volatility linked to crises in capital markets has been another recurrent problem under globalization—and one with a major bearing on poverty. In the two years after Russia was engulfed by a financial crisis in 1998, 30 million people were forced below the poverty line.[44] In Argentina the population living below the extreme poverty line

| Table 1.3 | Income growth bands | | | |

Annual GDP per capita growth rate, 1990–2003 (%)

Region	Negative	0%–1%	1%–2%	More than 2%
Arab States				
Countries	5	4	2	5
Population (millions)	34	70	19	139
East Asia & Pacific				
Countries	4	1	3	13
Population (millions)	3	6	81	1,814
Latin America & Caribbean				
Countries	4	8	9	12
Population (millions)	43	74	345	79
South Asia				
Countries	0	0	1	7
Population (millions)	0	0	152	1,324
Sub-Saharan Africa				
Countries	18	8	8	11
Population (millions)	319	108	171	76
Central & Eastern Europe & the CIS				
Countries	10	5	1	11
Population (millions)	253	58	10	85
High-income OECD [a]				
Countries	0	2	6	15
Population (millions)	0	135	224	510
World				
Countries	41	28	32	76
Population (millions)	653	450	1,081	4,030

a. Excludes the Republic of Korea, which is included in East Asia and Pacific.
Source: Indicator tables 5 and 14.

Box 1.5 | **The champagne glass effect—the global distribution of income**

Building a global income distribution model from national household expenditure surveys reveals just how unequal the world is. It also helps to identify the global underclass living on less than $2 a day and to compare their position with that of people at the top end of the global income distribution.

If the world were a country, it would have had an average purchasing power parity income of $5,533 and a median income of $1,700 in 2000. The gap between median and average income points to a concentration of income at the top end of the distribution: 80% of the world's population had an income less than the average. Meanwhile, the average income of the top 20% of the world's population is about 50 times the average income of the bottom 20%.

Global income distribution resembles a champagne glass (see figure 1.16 in text). At the top, where the glass is widest, the richest 20% of the population hold three-quarters of world income. At the bottom of the stem, where the glass is narrowest, the poorest 40% hold 5% of world income and the poorest 20% hold just 1.5%. The poorest 40% roughly corresponds to the 2 billion people living on less than $2 a day.

How has the regional composition of the poorest 20% changed over time? The share of South Asia has fallen sharply, from one half in 1980 to one third today. Reflecting two decades of declining average incomes, Sub-Saharan Africa accounts for a rising share of the poorest 20%. Since 1980 that share has more than doubled from 15% to 36%, and it is still rising. One in every two people in Sub-Saharan Africa is now located in the poorest 20% of world income distribution, compared with one in every five people in East Asia and one in every four people in South Asia.

Unsurprisingly, rich countries dominate the top 20%. Nine of every 10 of their citizens are among the richest 20%. And Organisation for Economic Co-operation and Development countries account for 85% of income in the richest decile.

The global income distribution also highlights the extraordinarily high degree of inequality in Latin America. One-quarter of the region's population enjoys an income that puts it in the richest 20%, while more than 8% are in the poorest 20% of the global distribution.

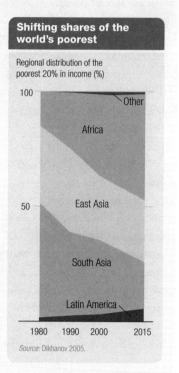

Shifting shares of the world's poorest

Regional distribution of the poorest 20% in income (%)

Other
Africa
East Asia
South Asia
Latin America

1980 1990 2000   2015

Source: Dikhanov 2005.

Source: Dikhanov 2005.

---

more than tripled from 2000 to 2003, underlining yet again a lesson delivered by the 1997 East Asian financial crisis: integration into global capital markets comes with high human development risks attached.[45]

Inequality and poor countries' share of increased global wealth

Globalization has given rise to a protracted and sometimes heated debate over trends in global income distribution, their links with poverty and whether integration into global markets is leading to a convergence or a divergence of income between rich and poor countries. The trends matter because the share of increases in global wealth captured by poor countries has a bearing on average income and so on prospects for poverty reduction.

The answer to the question of whether poor countries are capturing a larger or smaller share of global increases in wealth depends partly on how it is asked.[46] For most of the world's poorest countries the past decade has continued a disheartening trend: not only have they failed to reduce poverty, but they are falling further behind rich countries. Measured at the extremes, the gap between the average citizen in the richest and in the poorest countries is wide and getting wider. In 1990 the average American was 38 times richer than the average Tanzanian. Today the average American is 61 times richer. Purchasing power parity income in low-income countries as a group is one-thirteenth that in high-income countries.

Weighting for population changes the picture. Because incomes have been growing more rapidly in China and (less spectacularly) in India than in high-income countries over the past two decades, the average gap has been closing in relative terms. This reverses a trend towards increased global inequality that started in the 1820s and continued until 1992.[47] Even here, though, the idea of convergence has to be put in context. High growth in India has been one of the most powerful forces for convergence. But on 2000–05 growth trends it will still take India until 2106 to catch up with high-income countries. For other countries and regions convergence prospects are even more limited. Were high-income countries to stop growing today and Latin America and Sub-Saharan Africa to continue on their current growth trajectories, it would take Latin America until 2177 and Africa until 2236 to catch up.

Most developing regions are falling behind, not catching up with, rich countries. Moreover, convergence is a relative concept. Absolute income inequalities between rich and poor

countries are increasing even when developing countries have higher growth rates—precisely because the initial income gaps are so large (figure 1.15). If average incomes grow by 3% in Sub-Saharan Africa and in high-income Europe, for example, the absolute change will be an extra $51 per person in Africa and an extra $854 per person in Europe.

Part of the problem with the debate over global inequality is that it misses an important point. Income inequality is exceptionally high however it is measured and regardless of whether it is rising or falling. On the (conservative) assumption that the world's 500 richest people listed by *Forbes* magazine have an income equivalent to no more than 5% of their assets, their income exceeds that of the poorest 416 million people.[48]

The scale of global inequality is best captured by global income distribution models. These models use national household survey data to create a unified global income distribution, placing everybody in the world in a unified ranking regardless of where they live (box 1.5). Presented in graphic form, global income distribution resembles a champagne glass, with a large concentration of income at the top and a thin stem at the bottom (figure 1.16).[49] The gap between top and bottom is very large—far greater than that found in even the most unequal countries. In Brazil the ratio of the income

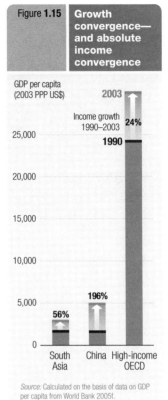

Figure **1.15** Growth convergence—and absolute income convergence

GDP per capita (2003 PPP US$)

Source: Calculated on the basis of data on GDP per capita from World Bank 2005f.

Figure **1.16** | Where the money is

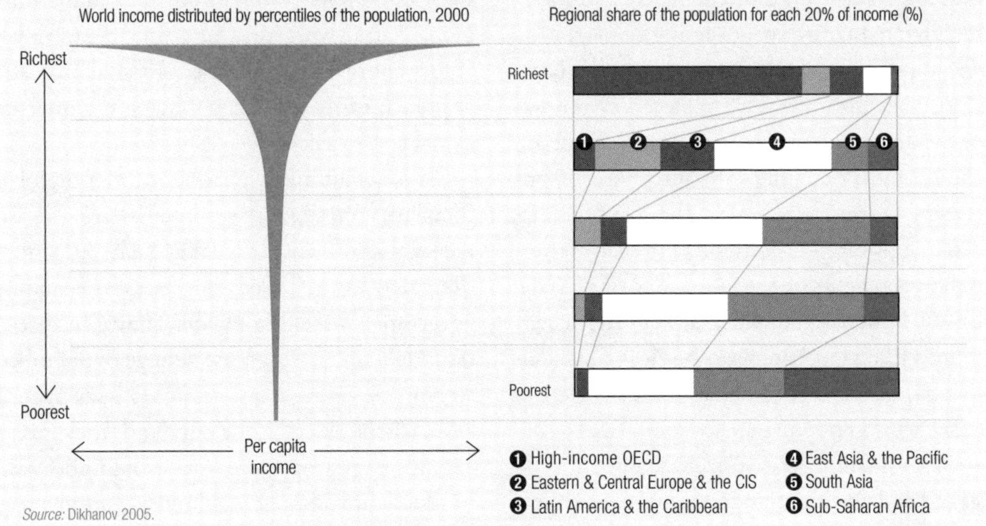

World income distributed by percentiles of the population, 2000

Regional share of the population for each 20% of income (%)

Richest

Poorest

Per capita income

Source: Dikhanov 2005.

❶ High-income OECD
❷ Eastern & Central Europe & the CIS
❸ Latin America & the Caribbean
❹ East Asia & the Pacific
❺ South Asia
❻ Sub-Saharan Africa

of the poorest 10% of the population to the richest 10% is 1 to 94. For the world as a whole it is 1 to 103. Measured more systematically by the Gini coefficient, the most widely used yardstick for inequality, the overall pattern of distribution for the world is more unequal than for any country except Namibia. On a scale where 0 is perfect equality and 100 is total inequality, the Gini coefficient for the world is 67.

Income inequalities between countries account for the bulk of global income inequality. About two-thirds of overall inequality can be traced to this source. Inequality within countries accounts for the balance. Reproduced at a national level, the gap between rich and poor countries would be regarded as socially indefensible, politically unsustainable and economically inefficient even in high-inequality regions such as Latin America. Global inequalities are less visible, but no less damaging to public interest, than inequalities within countries (explained in more detail in chapter 2). A world economy in which 40% of the population live on incomes so low as to preclude fully participating in wealth creation is hardly good for shared prosperity and growth.

Beyond the dysfunctional outcomes the extreme concentration of wealth at the top end of the global income distribution has one important consequence. Even small transfers relative to the income of the wealthy could generate very large increases in the incomes of the poor. Using the global income distribution model, we have estimated the overall financing that would be required to take everybody living below the $1 a day poverty line above the line. The calculation thus takes into account the depth of poverty, or the distance between household income and the income poverty line. Measured in 2000 purchasing power parity terms, the cost of ending extreme poverty—the amount needed to lift 1 billion people above the $1 a day poverty line— is $300 billion. Expressed in absolute terms, this sounds like a large amount. But it is equivalent to less than 2% of the income of the richest 10% of the world's population.

This is an illustrative exercise only. It is designed to draw attention to the modest financial resources, measured in global terms, needed to overcome extreme poverty. Achieving lasting redistributive outcomes, rather than describing their potential benefits, raises more complex challenges. Shares of global income reflect past and present growth trends. More fundamentally, as in any national economy global inequalities reflect disparities in technology, human capital and investment resources, as well as in factors linked to geography, history and—crucially—political and economic power. Redressing unequal outcomes requires measures to reduce these deeper structural inequalities that they reflect.

Some people claim that policy-makers have no need to consider inequalities beyond national boundaries. The distribution of income and opportunity between countries, so the argument runs, is not an issue for public policy. Writing in this vein, one commentator claims that "cross-country comparisons, no matter what measure is deployed, are just so much irrelevant data-mongering".[50] In an increasingly interconnected and interdependent world such views are at variance with both public perceptions and political realities. If we are part of a global human community, moral concern over unacceptable inequalities cannot be confined to national borders. This is especially the case when the policies adopted in one country have repercussions in another. As the growth of global social justice coalitions on issues such as aid, trade and debt amply demonstrates, international distribution does matter to a large constituency in rich and poor countries alike. Championing globalization while turning a blind eye to global equity concerns is an increasingly anachronistic approach to the challenges facing the international community.

It is sometimes argued that, even if global inequality matters, governments lack the capacity to influence distributional outcomes. That view too is flawed. In a national economy governments seeking greater equity in distributional outcomes can use a range of policy instruments. Fiscal transfers, public spending to enhance the assets of the poor and measures to extend market opportunities would all figure in. Public investment would play a critical role not just in overcoming immediate disadvantage but also in equipping people with the capacities they need to work their way out of poverty and increase their self-reliance. There are analogies at a global level. International aid is the equivalent of a redistributive fiscal transfer mechanism with a potential to effect dynamic change, for instance, through investments in health, education and infrastructure. Similarly, international trade practices can open—or close—opportunities for poor countries and their citizens to capture a bigger share of the economic pie. The problem, as we show in chapters 3 and 4, is that these redistributive mechanisms are heavily underdeveloped.

Scenario 2015—prospects for the Millennium Development Goals

Forty-two years ago, on the steps of the Lincoln Memorial in Washington, DC, Martin Luther King, Jr. delivered the speech that defined the civil rights movement. Describing the US constitution as a "promissory note" guaranteeing freedom and social justice for all, he charged successive governments with giving African Americans "a bad check which has come back marked 'insufficient funds'". He went on: "But we refuse to believe that the bank of justice is bankrupt. We refuse to believe that there are insufficient funds in the great vaults of opportunity of this nation."[51]

The MDGs can also be thought of as a promissory note. Written by 189 governments to the world's poor people, that note falls due in 10 years time. Without an investment of political will and financial capital today, it too will come back marked "insufficient funds". Beyond the immediate human costs, a default on the scale in prospect will have implications for the credibility of the governments that made the pledge and on the future of international cooperation to resolve global problems.

There is more to human development than the MDGs. But progress towards the MDGs reflects progress towards human development. The MDGs represent the most comprehensive and most detailed set of human development goals ever adopted (box 1.6). They embody basic indicators for human development in its many dimensions, including income poverty, education, gender equity, progress in combating infectious disease and access to clean water and sanitation. The MDGs are also basic human rights. While measures such as global gross national income (GNI), the value of trade and the scale of foreign

Box 1.6	The Millennium Development Goals

In September 2005 the UN General Assembly will review achievements since the Millennium Declaration of 2000, including progress towards the eight Millennium Development Goals. These goals provide tangible benchmarks for measuring progress in eight areas, with a target date for most of them of 2015:

Goal 1 Eradicate extreme hunger and poverty. Halving the proportion of people living on less than $1 a day and halving malnutrition.

Goal 2 Achieve universal primary education. Ensuring that all children are able to complete primary education.

Goal 3 Promote gender equality and empower women. Eliminating gender disparity in primary and secondary schooling, preferably by 2005 and no later than 2015.

Goal 4 Reduce child mortality. Cutting the under-five death rate by two-thirds.

Goal 5 Improve maternal health. Reducing the maternal mortality rate by three-quarters.

Goal 6 Combat HIV/AIDS, malaria and other diseases. Halting and beginning to reverse HIV/AIDS and other diseases.

Goal 7 Ensure environmental stability. Cutting by half the proportion of people without sustainable access to safe drinking water and sanitation.

Goal 8 Develop a global partnership for development. Reforming aid and trade with special treatment for the poorest countries.

If solemn promises, ambitious pledges, earnest commitments and high-level conferences lifted people out of poverty, the MDGs would have been achieved long ago

investment say something about the world's success in creating wealth, the MDGs provide a marker for something more fundamental: the moral and ethical underpinnings of our interactions as a global community. That is why, as the report of the UN Millennium Project puts it, "The MDGs are too important to fail."[52]

But fail they will unless there is a change of gear in human development. Continuation of the trends described earlier in this chapter will have fatal consequences for the MDGs. Almost all of the goals will be missed by most countries, some of them by epic margins. In this section we use country by country projections to estimate the size of these margins. These projections highlight the potential costs of continuing on a business-as-usual basis between now and 2015.

This is not the first time that the international community has embraced ambitious goals. If solemn promises, ambitious pledges, earnest commitments and high-level conferences lifted people out of poverty, put children in school and cut child deaths, the MDGs would have been achieved long ago. The currency of pledges from the international community is by now so severely debased by non-delivery that it is widely perceived as worthless. Restoring that currency is vital not just to the success of the MDGs but also to the creation of confidence in multilateralism and international cooperation—the twin foundations for strengthened international peace and security.

Scenario 2015—projections not predictions

"Stocks have reached what looks like a permanently high plateau", declared Irving Fischer, a professor of economics at Yale University, on the eve of the Great Depression in October 1929. As events a few days later were to demonstrate, predicting the future is a hazardous affair. Future outcomes are seldom a continuation of past trends.

Our projections for 2015 are not predictions. Using trend analysis for 1990–2003, we look at where the world would be in 2015 on key MDGs if current trends continue. The trend projections are based on national data rather than regional

averages, giving a more precise picture of the direction of current trends.[53] However, trends do not lead to inevitable outcomes. Trends can be improved—or worsened—through public policy choices, as well as by external factors over which governments have limited influence. But projecting the past into the future can help to focus public attention by providing one possible version of the future.

Several caveats have to be attached to our trends analysis. Good quality data are not available for many countries and several goals. Time-series data on education are lacking for 46 countries, for example. There are also problems with reviewing trends on a goal-by-goal basis. Progress in any one area is heavily conditioned by progress in other areas, with strong multiplier effects operating across the goals—for example, from health to education. Finally, some of the forces that might affect MDG progress are difficult to anticipate, including what might be thought of as systemic threats. As the International Monetary Fund (IMF) has warned, current imbalances in the global economy have the potential to result in slower growth—an outcome that would hurt poverty reduction efforts in developing countries. Beyond the global economy there are potentially grave threats to public health. For example, if the widely predicted outbreak of avian flu were to materialize, it would have devastating implications for the MDGs as well as for public health across all countries. Similarly, the full consequences of global warming and other ecological pressures on food systems could dramatically change the scenario for reducing malnutrition.

We make no attempt to factor in systemic risk, and so our results may err on the side of optimism. Even so, the results point unambiguously to a large gap between MDG targets and outcomes on current trends. The overall country by country progress report for child mortality and school enrolment is summarized in figure 1.17. This shows how many countries would achieve each MDG target by 2015 if current trends continue. It also shows how many countries will not meet the target until 2035 or later. As illustrated in map 1.1, Sub-Saharan Africa is not the only region off track for the MDG target of reducing child mortality by two-thirds.

Looking more broadly at progress towards five of the MDGs—child mortality, school enrolment, gender parity in education and access to water and sanitation—produces a similarly bleak prognosis. Among the summary findings to emerge from our trend analysis:

- Fifty countries with a combined population of almost 900 million people are going backwards on at least one MDG. Twenty-four of these countries are in Sub-Saharan Africa.
- Another 65 countries with a combined population of 1.2 billion will fail to meet at least one MDG until after 2040. In other words, they will miss the target by an entire generation.

Below, we briefly outline the 2015 projections behind these trends.

Child health and maternal health—millions more children will die

No indicator more powerfully demonstrates the scale of the challenge facing the international community than child mortality. The slowdown in progress since 1990 has set the world on course for comprehensive failure in meeting the MDG.

On current trends the world will achieve the two-thirds reduction in child deaths targeted by the MDGs in 2045—31 years late. Achieving the MDG target implies an average annual reduction of about 2.7% in the incidence of child mortality. This is more than double the observed rate for 1990–2002. Less than one-fifth of the developing world's population live in countries that are on track to meet the target. Not one Sub-Saharan African country with a significant population is on track to meet the target. Neither are China and India.

The projected gap between the 2015 target and the outcome that would take place if current trends continued represents a huge loss of life. It translates into an additional 4.4 million child deaths in 2015 above those that would occur if the MDG target were achieved (figure 1.18). Charting a linear trend from the cumulative cost of additional child deaths for 2003–15 provides an indicator for the annualized gap between target and outcome. The cumulative cost of that gap represents more than 41 million additional child deaths between now and 2015—almost all of them in developing countries (figure 1.19). These are lives that would be saved if the targets were met.

The following are among the main findings from the trend projection:

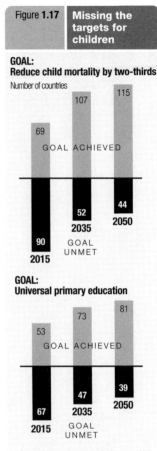

Figure **1.17** | **Missing the targets for children**

GOAL: Reduce child mortality by two-thirds

Number of countries

Source: Calculated on the basis of data on child mortality and primary enrolment from UN 2005b; for details see *Technical note 3*.

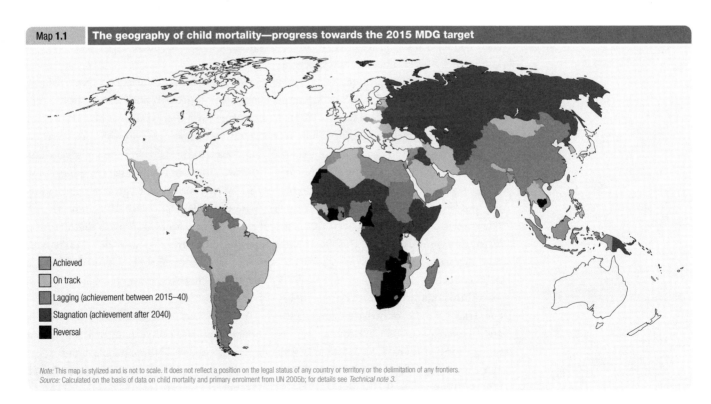

Map **1.1** | **The geography of child mortality—progress towards the 2015 MDG target**

Achieved
On track
Lagging (achievement between 2015–40)
Stagnation (achievement after 2040)
Reversal

Note: This map is stylized and is not to scale. It does not reflect a position on the legal status of any country or territory or the delimitation of any frontiers.
Source: Calculated on the basis of data on child mortality and primary enrolment from UN 2005b; for details see *Technical note 3*.

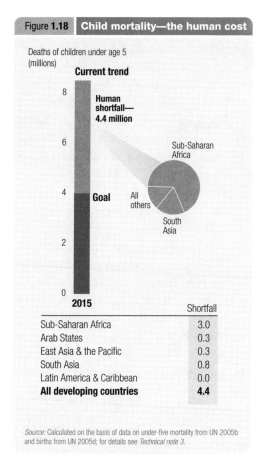

Figure 1.18 Child mortality—the human cost

Deaths of children under age 5 (millions)

Current trend

Human shortfall— 4.4 million

Sub-Saharan Africa

Goal   All others

South Asia

2015

	Shortfall
Sub-Saharan Africa	3.0
Arab States	0.3
East Asia & the Pacific	0.3
South Asia	0.8
Latin America & Caribbean	0.0
All developing countries	**4.4**

Source: Calculated on the basis of data on under-five mortality from UN 2005b and births from UN 2005d; for details see *Technical note 3*.

- More than 45% of child deaths—4.9 million in all—occur in 52 countries that are going backwards or making little progress in reducing the death toll. Children born in these countries today who survive to adulthood will see barely improved prospects of survival for their own children.

- On current trends it will take Sub-Saharan Africa until 2115 to achieve the MDG target, putting it off track by a century. The two largest centres of child deaths in Sub-Saharan Africa are the Democratic Republic of the Congo, where conditions are deteriorating, and Nigeria. The child mortality rate in Nigeria has fallen from 235 per 1,000 live births to 198 since 1990. At this rate it will take Nigeria another 40 years to achieve the MDG target.

- Two-thirds of all child deaths occur in 13 countries. Of these, only two—Bangladesh and Indonesia—are on track for the MDG target. Another four—China, India, Niger and Pakistan—will achieve the goal between 2015 and 2040. The remainder—a

group that includes Afghanistan, Angola, the Democratic Republic of the Congo, Ethiopia, Nigeria, Tanzania and Uganda — are either more than a generation off track or going backwards.

Data limitations make it impossible to track trends in maternal mortality with any accuracy. Best estimates for trends are derived from models that use proxy indicators, such as fertility rate and attendance at delivery by skilled medical personnel. The most widely used of these models suggests that the world is off track and that the rate of progress is slowing. For the developing world as a whole, the population-weighted rate of decline needed to achieve the MDG target is just over 3%. Sub-Saharan Africa is reducing maternal mortality at less than half that rate.[54]

Water and sanitation—more than a billion unserved

Progress in access to water and sanitation will have an important bearing on child death rates. Our trend analysis suggests that the target of halving the number of people without sustainable access to improved water sources will be missed by about 210 million people (figure 1.20). Another 2 billion people will also lack access to an improved sanitation source in 2015. Sub-Saharan Africa will account for the bulk of the deficit.

Halving extreme poverty and malnutrition depends on growth and distribution

Prospects for halving extreme poverty will be shaped by two factors: growth and distribution. Poverty will fall faster the higher the rate of growth for poor countries and the bigger the share of any increment to growth captured by poor people. Projections to 2015 indicate that if the current pattern of growth and distribution continues, the aggregate global target will be met, largely because of high growth in China and India. However, most countries will miss the target.

Our estimates indicate that there will be about 800 million people living on less than $1 a day and another 1.7 billion people living on less than $2 a day in 2015. The incidence of global $1 a day poverty will fall from 21% today to 14% in

2015. The regional composition of poverty will also change. Sub-Saharan Africa's share of $1 a day poverty will rise sharply, from 24% today to 41% in 2015. How does this picture compare with one in which each country meets the target of halving poverty? On our estimates there would be around 380 million fewer people living in $1 a day poverty if all countries achieved the target (figure 1.21). More than half of these people would be in Sub-Saharan Africa.

Sub-Saharan Africa's rising share of global poverty to 2015 reflects its weak growth record since 1990, exacerbated by highly unequal income distribution. The region would need to attain an implausibly high annual per capita growth rate of around 5% over the next decade to achieve the 2015 target. A mix of accelerated growth and improved distribution offers a better hope of getting on track.

Prospects for reaching the MDG target on malnutrition are even less promising. The incidence of malnutrition has fallen since 1990, from 20% to 17%. However, population growth has left the number of malnourished people unchanged. The pace of progress will have to double to reach the 2015 target. On the current trajectory there will still be around 670 million people suffering from malnutrition in 2015, 230 million more people than if the target were achieved. Sub-Saharan Africa accounts for almost 60% of the deficit.

Regional projections show a different pattern for malnutrition than for $1 a day poverty. While South Asia is projected to make strong progress on income poverty, it will still account for 40% of malnutrition in 2015. This is consistent with the current pattern in which South Asian countries record levels of malnutrition comparable to those in Sub-Saharan Africa, despite higher average incomes—an outcome that highlights the central role of gender inequalities in blocking advances in nutrition.

Education—missing the universal enrolment target

Education is a crucial human development goal in its own right and a key to progress in other areas. The promise to get every child into school and to close gender gaps in education powerfully

symbolizes the hope that the transmission of poverty across generations can be broken.

That hope will remain unfulfilled if current trends continue. While the world is moving in the right direction, progress is too slow to achieve the 2015 target (figure 1.22). If current trends continue:

- The target of achieving universal primary education by 2015 will be missed by at least a decade. There will be 47 million children out of school in 2015, 19 million of them in Sub-Saharan Africa.
- Forty-six countries are going backwards or will not meet the target until after 2040. These countries account for 23 million of the 110 million children currently out of school in developing countries.

Gender parity and empowerment— one target already missed

One set of targets has already been missed. The MDG targets for gender parity in primary and secondary enrolment were supposed to be met

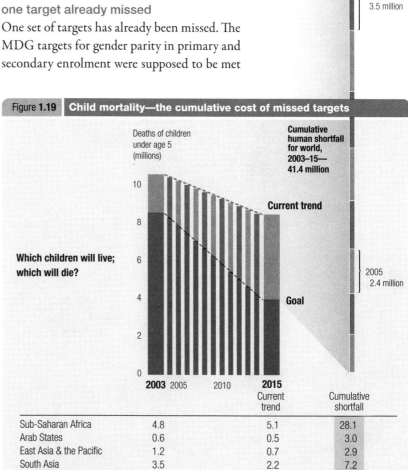

Figure 1.19 Child mortality—the cumulative cost of missed targets

Deaths of children under age 5 (millions)

Cumulative human shortfall for world, 2003–15— 41.4 million

Current trend

Which children will live; which will die?

Goal

2003 2005 2010 2015 Current trend

Cumulative shortfall

	Current trend	Cumulative shortfall
Sub-Saharan Africa	4.8	5.1	28.1
Arab States	0.6	0.5	3.0
East Asia & the Pacific	1.2	0.7	2.9
South Asia	3.5	2.2	7.2
Latin America & Caribbean	0.4	0.1	0.2
All developing countries	**10.5**	**8.6**	**41.4**

Source: Calculated on the basis of data on under-five mortality from UN 2005b and births from UN 2005d. For details see *Technical note 3.*

40 million — 2015 4.4 million

30 million —

20 million — 2010 3.5 million

2005 2.4 million

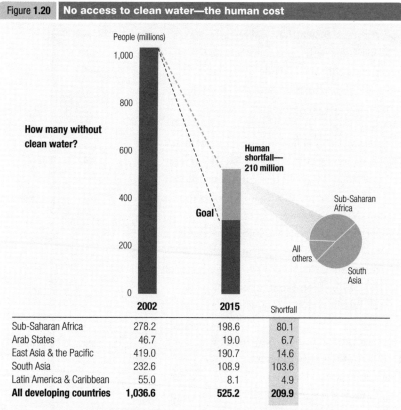

Figure 1.20 No access to clean water—the human cost

People (millions)

How many without clean water?

Human shortfall— 210 million

Goal

Sub-Saharan Africa

All others

South Asia

	2002	2015	Shortfall
Sub-Saharan Africa	278.2	198.6	80.1
Arab States	46.7	19.0	6.7
East Asia & the Pacific	419.0	190.7	14.6
South Asia	232.6	108.9	103.6
Latin America & Caribbean	55.0	8.1	4.9
All developing countries	**1,036.6**	**525.2**	**209.9**

Source: Calculated on the basis of data on people with access to improved water sources from UN 2005b and data on population from UN 2005d; for details see *Technical note 3.*

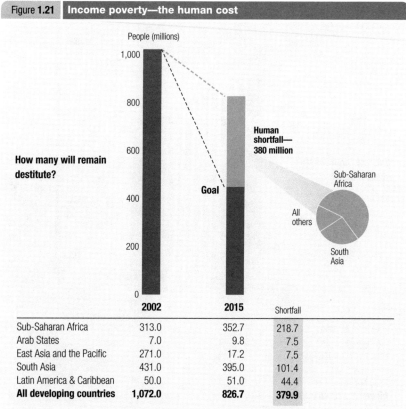

Figure 1.21 Income poverty—the human cost

People (millions)

How many will remain destitute?

Human shortfall— 380 million

Goal

Sub-Saharan Africa

All others

South Asia

	2002	2015	Shortfall
Sub-Saharan Africa	313.0	352.7	218.7
Arab States	7.0	9.8	7.5
East Asia and the Pacific	271.0	17.2	7.5
South Asia	431.0	395.0	101.4
Latin America & Caribbean	50.0	51.0	44.4
All developing countries	**1,072.0**	**826.7**	**379.9**

Source: Calculated on the basis of data on people living on less than $1 a day (PPP US$) from World Bank 2005d and data on population from UN 2005d; for details see *Technical note 3.*

by 2005. Had that target been achieved, there would be 14 million more girls in primary school today, 6 million of them in India and Pakistan and another 4 million in Sub-Saharan Africa. Trend projections are not encouraging. By 2015 the shortfall from the gender parity target will be equivalent to 6 million girls out of school, the majority of them in Sub-Saharan Africa (figure 1.23). In 41 countries accounting for 20 million of the girls currently out of school the gender gap is either widening or closing so slowly that parity will not be achieved until after 2040. Of course, there is more to gender parity than attendance in school. Research from many countries highlights wider aspects of gender disadvantage rooted in attitudes and cultural practices that diminish the value of girls' education. Progress in these areas is inherently more difficult to track on a comparative basis, though it is equally fundamental.

Beyond parity in education the MDGs include female representation in parliaments as an indicator of progress towards the empowerment of women. The gender empowerment measure (GEM) developed by the *Human Development Report* includes this indicator in a broader composite indicator that tracks female representation in legislative bodies, governments and the private sector, along with a range of income indicators.

Decomposing the GEM to provide a snapshot of women's current position highlights the limited progress towards gender empowerment. Globally, women hold only about 15% of legislative assembly seats. In only 43 countries is the ratio of female to male parliamentarians more than 1 to 5, and in only two—Rwanda and Sweden—is the ratio even close to parity. In most countries politics remains an overwhelmingly male domain.

Nigeria is one of 57 countries in which women account for less than 10% of legislative presence. Women account for 6% of Nigeria's House of Representatives, less than 4% of the Senate and no state governors. In Saudi Arabia and the United Arab Emirates there is no female representation, in some cases reflecting the use of laws to exclude women from voting or holding office. In countries where gender inequality is a major barrier to progress in health, education and income poverty, such underrepresentation of women points to a worrying continuation of gender inequality and obstacles to social and income progress.

The GEM demolishes two widely held myths about gender empowerment. First, there is no evidence that Islam necessarily represents an obstacle to female empowerment, as measured by political representation. Malaysia, a Muslim country, has a GEM far higher than Saudi Arabia's and comparable to that of Greece. Second, there is no clear evidence that gender inequalities automatically diminish at higher levels of income (figure 1.24). Two members of the Group of Seven (G-7) industrial countries are poor performers on the GEM. Both Italy (ranked 36) and Japan (ranked 42) occupy a lower position than Costa Rica and Argentina. Similarly, both Japan and Sweden are democracies at comparable levels of human development as measured by the HDI, but Sweden's GEM score is almost double that of Japan. The conclusion: social norms, political culture and public attitudes matter as much as economic wealth and overall human development in defining opportunities for women.

Changing course and getting on track

Trend projections identify one set of possible outcomes for the MDGs. Actual outcomes will reflect policy choices made by governments and the international community over the next decade. What emerges from the projections set out here is a clear warning. The gap between trend projections and MDG targets represents a huge loss of human life and human potential. The good news is that the gap can be closed.

Some countries have registered an extraordinary rate of advance towards the MDGs, often from very low levels of income. Viet Nam is one.[55] Income poverty has already been cut in half, falling from 60% in 1990 to 32% in 2000. Child mortality rates have fallen from 58 per 1,000 live births (a far lower rate than income would predict) to 42 over the same period. Rapid, broad-based economic growth has

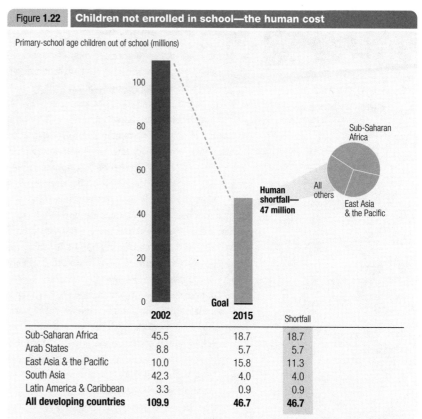

Figure 1.22 Children not enrolled in school—the human cost

Primary-school age children out of school (millions)

	2002	2015	Shortfall
Sub-Saharan Africa	45.5	18.7	18.7
Arab States	8.8	5.7	5.7
East Asia & the Pacific	10.0	15.8	11.3
South Asia	42.3	4.0	4.0
Latin America & Caribbean	3.3	0.9	0.9
All developing countries	**109.9**	**46.7**	**46.7**

Source: Calculated on the basis of data on children attending school from UNESCO 2005, data on children out of school from UNICEF 2005d and data on population from UN 2005d; for details see *Technical note 3.*

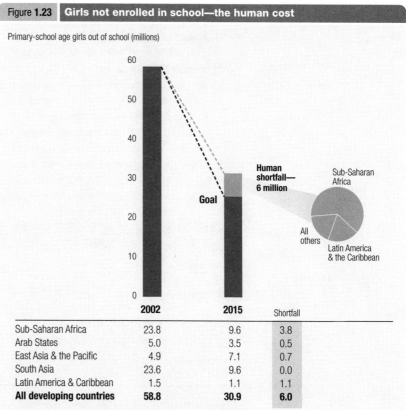

Figure 1.23 Girls not enrolled in school—the human cost

Primary-school age girls out of school (millions)

	2002	2015	Shortfall
Sub-Saharan Africa	23.8	9.6	3.8
Arab States	5.0	3.5	0.5
East Asia & the Pacific	4.9	7.1	0.7
South Asia	23.6	9.6	0.0
Latin America & Caribbean	1.5	1.1	1.1
All developing countries	**58.8**	**30.9**	**6.0**

Source: Caclulated on the basis of data on girls attending school from UNESCO 2005 and population growth rates from UN 2005d. For details see *Technical note 3.*

Figure 1.24 Income does not predict gender empowerment

Ranking among the 78 countries with a gender empowerment measure

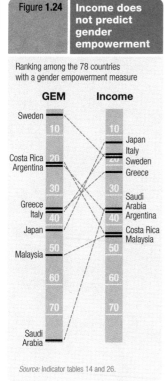

Source: Indicator tables 14 and 26.

Box 1.7 Bangladesh—moderate growth, rapid human development

At the start of the 1990s pessimism about development prospects for Bangladesh was as deeply ingrained as pessimism is about Sub-Saharan Africa today. Slow economic growth, rapid population growth, limited progress on social indicators and acute vulnerability to natural disasters provoked descriptions of Bangladesh as "a landscape of disaster". That landscape has changed dramatically.

Since 1990 Bangladesh has recorded some of the developing world's most rapid advances in basic human development indicators. Child and infant mortality rates have been falling at more than 5% a year, the fertility rate has fallen sharply, and malnutrition among mothers has fallen from 52% in 1996 to 42% in 2002. Primary school enrolment rates have reached more than 90%, up from 72% in 1990, with close to gender parity, and enrolment in secondary education has been rising.

How did Bangladesh achieve this transformation of the human development landscape? Not by economic growth alone. True, the 1990s saw more rapid growth, with average incomes rising at just under 3% a year. However, Bangladesh is still a desperately poor country—average income is $1,770—and income poverty has been falling relatively slowly, by 10% between 1990 and 2002.

Four strategies have contributed to Bangladesh's human development take-off:

- *Active partnerships with civil society.* Non-governmental organizations (NGOs) have played a critical role in improving access to basic services through innovative programmes. For example, the Bangladesh Rural Advancement Committee (BRAC) has pioneered programmes to recruit and train local female teachers, develop relevant curriculum material and support parental involvement in school management. More than 2 million children go to school outside the formal government system. But NGO schools act as feeders for government middle schools.

- *Targeted transfers.* Wide-ranging social programmes have targeted improved nutrition while also creating wider incentives for human development. The Food for Schooling programme offers free rations to poor households if their children attend primary school. About 7% of government spending on education is allocated through this programme, reaching 2.1 million children and providing a stipend of $3 a month. Participating schools have achieved higher rates of girls' participation and lower drop-out rates, demonstrating how incentives can counteract the economic pressures and cultural prejudices that keep girls out of school.

- *Extended health programmes.* Immunization coverage against six major childhood diseases increased from 2% in the mid-1980s to 52% in 2001. Immunization programmes have been implemented through partnerships with international agencies and national NGOs.

- *Virtuous cycles and female agency.* Improved access to health and education for women, allied with expanded opportunities for employment and access to microcredit, has expanded choice and empowered women. While gender disparities still exist, women have become increasingly powerful catalysts for development, demanding greater control over fertility and birth spacing, education for their daughters and access to services.

Bangladesh achieved this remarkable progress at low levels of income and starting from a position of low literacy, high malnutrition and weak institutions. Its successes demonstrate what can be achieved through stronger state action and civic activism.

Rapid progress in a low-income country

Indicator	1990	2000
Income poverty (%)	59	50
Gini coefficient	25	30
Children under age 5 under weight for age (%)	72	51
Under-five mortality rate (per 1,000 live births)	144	69 [a]
Ratio of girls to boys in primary school (girls per 100 boys)	87	104 [b]

a. Data refer to 2003.
b. Data refer to 2002.

Source: Ahluwalia and Hussain 2004; Drèze 2004; Yunus 2004; Ahmed and del Ninno 2001; Sen, Mujeri and Quazi 2005.

contributed to Viet Nam's success. So have investments in human development during the 1980s. The challenge for Viet Nam is to sustain the rate of advance by reaching some of the country's most marginalized regions and groups.[56]

Viet Nam is an example—Chile is another—of a country that has converted high growth into rapid human development. Other countries have shown that rapid advance towards the MDGs is possible even at lower levels of growth. In Bangladesh public policies and interventions by civil society have expanded access to basic services and opportunities, propelling Bangladesh into a higher human development trajectory (box 1.7). As a region Sub-Saharan Africa has been slipping down in the human development rankings. However, some countries have registered marked advances. Ghana reduced income poverty from 51% in 1991 to 40% at the end of the 1990s.[57] Uganda has combined economic reform with an improved record in income poverty and education, though progress has been uneven (box 1.8).

Conflict remains a potent barrier to human development. Peace creates opportunities to

---

Box 1.8 **Uganda—impressive progress, but uneven**

Over the past decade Uganda has experienced sustained economic growth and made important advances in human development. Poverty reduction has been a national priority reflected in planning and budgeting. However, progress has been uneven—and the gains remain fragile:

- *Income poverty.* In the first half of the 1990s government policies focused on stabilization and growth. Average incomes grew 5% a year from 1990 to 2000. Income poverty fell rapidly in the 1990s, from 56% to 34%, putting the country on track for the 2015 MDG target. However, since 2000 income growth has slowed and the incidence of poverty has risen. Poverty is concentrated in rural areas, especially in the north and east, and is far higher among producers growing only food staples.

- *Education.* In the second half of the 1990s poverty reduction priorities shifted to education. Free primary education was introduced and public spending increased. Primary school enrolment rose from 5.3 million to 7.6 million between 1997 and 2003. Enrolment rates are the same for the poorest 20% of the population as for the richest 20%, and the gender parity gap has been closed at the primary level. Universal enrolment is now within reach, but drop-out rates make achieving universal completion by 2015 unlikely.

- *Health.* Outcome indicators for health, including infant, child and maternal mortality have either stagnated or deteriorated, with under-five mortality rising since 1995. One of the strongest MDG performers in Africa, Uganda is now off track for all of the major health goals. Recognizing that failure to reduce child and maternal mortality threatens to undermine social and economic progress, the government has convened a cross-ministry task force under the auspices of the Ministry of Finance to identify solutions.

These diverse trends draw attention to the challenges facing Uganda. Some challenges are driven by external forces, notably the price of coffee. Until 1997 producers of coffee, the main cash crop for smallholders, benefited from rising domestic prices and favourable terms of trade. The collapse in coffee prices since then has reversed these gains, partly accounting for the reversal in income poverty.

Another problem is that falling growth has coincided with rising inequality. The Gini coefficient has increased from 34 to 42 since 1997, suggesting that Uganda may be in transition from a low-inequality to a high-inequality country. Correcting this trend will require action to broaden the base of economic growth around smallholder farmers in rural areas, alongside a focus on more capital-intensive export agriculture.

Progress in the health sector has been hampered by deep structural problems. Malnutrition is implicated in two-thirds of childhood deaths, less than one-third of women give birth under the supervision of trained staff, and there has been no decrease in major childhood killers, such as malaria and measles. High fertility rates and inadequate birth spacing are another problem. Uganda has the third highest fertility rate in the world.

The contrast between progress in education and stagnation in health partly reflects public spending priorities. Not until the late 1990s was health identified as a major public spending priority, though the health sector budget has tripled in the past four years. Poor quality service provision is another barrier.

Mixed performance on human development

Indicator	1992	2002
Income poverty (%)	56	38
Gini coefficient	36	42
Children under age 5 under weight for age (%)	62	86
Under-five mortality rate (per 1,000 live births)	167 [a]	152
Maternal mortality ratio (per 100,000 live births)	523	505

a. Data are for 1990.

Source: Uganda, Ministry of Finance, Planning and Economic Development 2003; Ssewanyana and others 2004.

Changing course and getting the world on track for the MDGs will require new partnerships in development

remove that barrier. In Afghanistan there are encouraging early signs that improved human security is leading to opportunities for a rapid recovery from the human development free fall it experienced during two decades of conflict. Under a "back to education" plan adopted in 2001 the government aimed to increase school enrolments by 1.5 million. More than twice this number of children enrolled in primary school, with the figure rising to 4 million in 2003. An ambitious basic health programme has been adopted that aims at extending services across the country. Meanwhile, economic recovery is taking root. Seizing these opportunities depends critically on aid donors signing up for the long haul. The danger: the international community will lose interest as the strategic focus shifts elsewhere.

Attempts have been made to isolate the costs and benefits of investments in specific MDGs. Such exercises are unhelpful. Progress in any one area is heavily conditioned by progress across the MDGs—and beyond. Getting children into well equipped schools staffed by motivated teachers is a vital requirement for achieving the MDG target of education for all. But the full value of investments in education will not be realized if children are sick because their families lack access to clean water and affordable medicine. The multiplier effects that operate across the MDGs are especially strong for women's education. The education and empowerment of women are a human development goal in their own right: they are ends in themselves. Gender empowerment is also an accelerator towards the

MDGs and wider human development goals. Educated women are better able to control their fertility and demand basic health services, less likely to contract HIV/AIDS and more likely to educate their daughters (see box 1.3).

Changing course and getting the world on track for the MDGs will require new partnerships in development. Many of the countries that are falling far short of achieving the MDGs, especially in Africa but also in other low-income regions, lack the financial resources for the public investments needed to create a virtuous circle of increased investment in human development and faster growth. The UN Millennium Project report of 2005 sets out an ambitious but practical framework for a new partnership based on two building blocks. First, each developing country needs to set out clear national strategies for reaching the MDGs, including the financing gaps that have to be covered. Second, rich countries, as part of their MDG commitment, need to mobilize the development assistance resources to cover these gaps—an issue that we look in more detail in chapter 3.

Beyond the question of financing is another fundamental requirement for getting the world back on track: a renewed focus on inequality and distributional equity. As we show in the next chapter, deep structural inequalities in human capabilities, opportunities and income act as a powerful brake on the MDGs. Releasing that brake by putting strategies for greater equality at the centre of national strategies for achieving the MDGs would dramatically enhance chances of success.

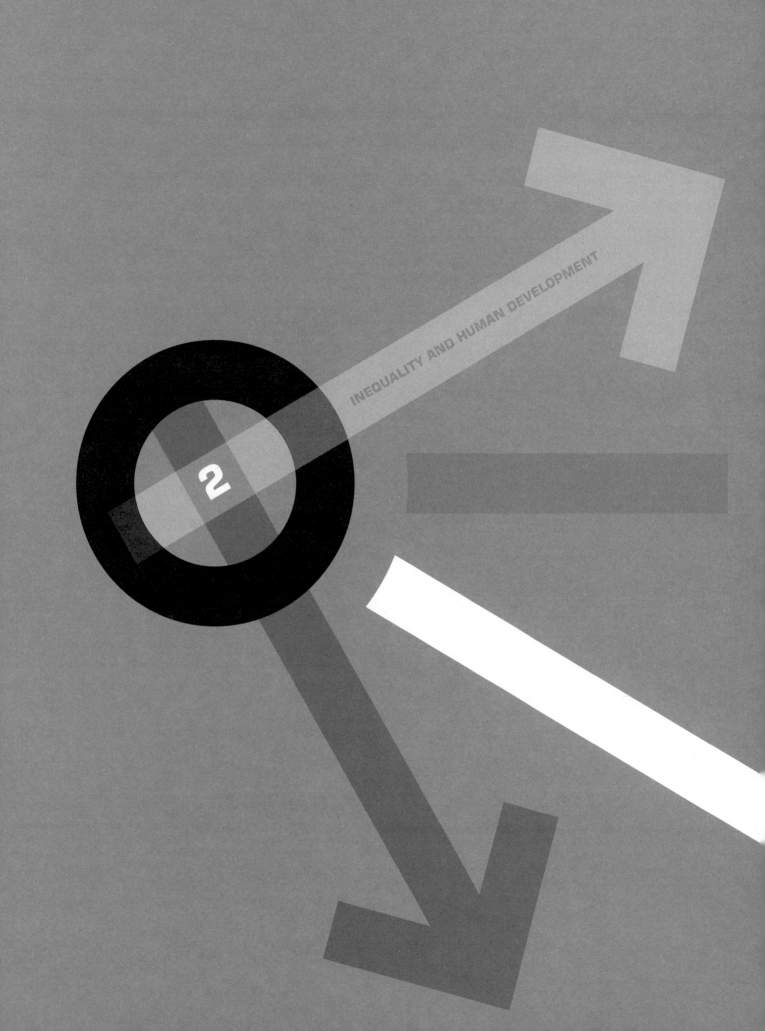

2

INEQUALITY AND HUMAN DEVELOPMENT

"There are only two families in the world, as my grandmother used to say: the haves and the have-nots."

Sancho Panza in *Don Quixote de la Mancha*, Miguel de Cervantes

Inequality and human development

Across many of the
MDGs poor people are
being left behind

"What is it that impels the powerful and vocal lobby to press for greater equality?" asked Margaret Thatcher, then UK prime minister, in 1975. She offered her own answer: "Often the reason boils down to an undistinguished combination of envy and bourgeois guilt."[1] Plato took a different view. Writing in the fifth century BC he warned Athenian lawmakers of the threat posed by extreme inequality. "There should exist among the citizens neither extreme poverty nor again excessive wealth", he wrote, "for both are productive of great evil."[2]

Two contrasting views on a question that retains a powerful relevance today: does inequality matter? If so, why? In this chapter we argue that inequality matters because it is a fundamental issue for human development. Extreme inequalities in opportunity and life chance have a direct bearing on what people can be and what they can do—that is, on human capabilities. Children facing a higher risk of death because they are born into a low-income or indigenous household or because they are female, for example, clearly have less opportunity to realize their potential. Inherited disadvantage in opportunity is wrong for intrinsic reasons: it violates basic precepts of social justice. There are also strong instrumental reasons for a concern with inequality. Deep disparities based on wealth, region, gender and ethnicity are bad for growth, bad for democracy and bad for social cohesion.

They are also bad for the Millennium Development Goals (MDGs). The MDGs do not directly address inequality. In this sense they are distribution neutral. Progress is measured by aggregating and averaging change at a national level. In theory, the MDGs could be met even if, say, households with low incomes were falling behind on the income poverty and health targets, or if the rate of reduction in child deaths among boys was sufficient to compensate for a slower rate of reduction among girls.

The distributional blind spot of the MDGs is a weakness on two counts. First, the MDGs themselves are rooted in ideas about global justice and human rights. They are universal entitlements, not optional or discretionary allowances. It follows that progress should be for all, regardless of economic status, gender, parents' wealth or location in a country. Yet the MDGs do not remind governments that success in advancing towards the MDGs should be measured for all of society, and not just in the aggregate. The opportunities that shape the distribution of income, education, health and wider life chances in any society are not randomly distributed. As we show in this chapter, the disparities hampering progress towards the MDGs are systemic. They reflect complex hierarchies of advantage and disadvantage that are transmitted across generations—and they reflect public policy choices.

The second reason for a focus on inequality relates to progress within the MDG framework. Across many of the MDGs poor people are being left behind. As we show in this chapter, a recurring theme in data from a large group of countries is that progress among the poorest 20% of the population is far below the national average. Apart from being unjust, this is suboptimal from the perspective of MDG attainment. People who are poor account for a far

The idea that people should be consigned to an early death, illiteracy or second-class citizenship because of inherited attributes beyond their control violates most people's sense of what is fair

larger share of deprivation than people who are not. It follows that accelerated progress among poor people is one of the most effective routes to faster national progress. Put differently, current patterns of progress are slowing the overall advance because the smallest gains are being registered among the households that account for the biggest part of the problem.

These considerations have important implications for the design of MDG strategies. For many of the MDGs the jury is now in, with the evidence that a "trickle down" approach to reducing disparities and maintaining overall progress will not work. The MDGs set quantifiable targets that lend themselves to policy responses rooted in technical and financial terms. Ultimately, however, the real barriers to progress are social and political. They are rooted in unequal access to resources and distribution of power within and

among countries. Unless these inequalities are corrected, the first principles of the Millennium Declaration—commitment to social justice, equity and human rights—from which the MDGs are derived will not be translated into progress in human development at the required rate. The appropriate response is to ensure that inequality and the measures to overcome disparities in life chances figure more prominently in the design of poverty reduction strategies.

This chapter sets out the reasons why inequality matters. It then looks at different dimensions of inequality and shows how interlocking inequalities in income, health and education disadvantage the poor. It concludes by showing how even modest moves towards greater distributional equity could advance human development and accelerate progress towards the MDGs.

Why inequality matters

Ideas about inequality, like ideas about fairness and social justice, are rooted in values. As Amartya Sen has argued, virtually everybody today believes in equality of something: equal rights before the law, equal civil liberties, equality of opportunity and so on.[3] Similarly, most people would accept that not all inequalities are unjust. Inequality in income is an inevitable product of any functioning market economy, though there are questions about the justifiable extent of income inequality. At the same time, few people would accept in principle that inequalities in opportunity are tolerable when based on gender, inherited wealth, ethnicity or other accidents of birth over which individuals have no control. The idea that people should be consigned to an early death, illiteracy or second-class citizenship because of inherited attributes beyond their control violates most people's sense of what is fair.[4]

From a human development perspective there are a range of mutually reinforcing

intrinsic and instrumental reasons why inequality matters. These can be broadly summarized under five headings.

Social justice and morality

The view that there are limits to tolerable deprivation is fundamental to most societies and value systems. Adam Smith powerfully expressed the basic concept: "No society can be flourishing and happy", he wrote, "of which the far greater part of members are poor and miserable."[5] It was Smith who went on to elaborate the idea of relative poverty, arguing that all members of society should have an income sufficient to enable them to appear in public "without shame". All major religions express concerns with equity and place obligations on their adherents to address extreme deprivation as a moral duty. Public ideas reflect wider normative concerns. Opinion surveys show that more than 80% of the public in (very unequal)

Latin America believe that the gap between rich and poor is too large, with only a slightly smaller share echoing this concern in the (less unequal) United Kingdom.[6] While few of the respondents to these surveys might be able to indicate what an acceptable level of inequality would be, the surveys point clearly to an underlying perception of social justice.

Putting the poor first

Pareto efficiency or optimality—one of the core ideas of modern economics—declares that only a change that leaves nobody worse off can be declared "welfare enhancing". Redistribution from rich to poor is not a "Pareto improvement", because by definition it makes someone worse off. But, as Amartya Sen has said: "A society can be Pareto optimal and still be perfectly disgusting."[7] That sentiment powerfully captures the idea that there are limits to the acceptable level of inequality.

In fact, economics itself provides strong arguments for redistribution. Most people, and most democratically elected governments, accept in principle that more weight should be given to improvements in the well-being of the poor and disadvantaged than to the rich and highly privileged.[8] An economy's income is not a sufficient statistic for evaluating welfare, precisely because it ignores the distribution of income generated by growth. The idea of diminishing returns to increased wealth provides a framework for understanding a simple idea: an extra dollar in the hands of a landless agricultural labourer in South Asia or an urban slum dweller in Latin America generates greater welfare than an equivalent amount in the hands of a millionaire. In fact, a policy that increases the income of the poor by $1 can be worthwhile, even if it costs the rest of society more than $1. From this perspective it might make sense for governments choosing between alternative growth paths to choose the option that generates the biggest return to the poor, even where overall growth effects are less certain.

Beyond income, many of the same arguments apply. For example, most people would accept in principle that an additional unit of public spending directed towards reducing child deaths or extending access to primary school would be preferable on social grounds to a similar amount spent on transfers to services for high-income groups.

Growth and efficiency

If there were a trade-off between growth and distribution, governments would face tough choices: the welfare-enhancing gains of greater equity could be eliminated by the losses associated with lower growth. In fact, the evidence suggests that the trade-offs work in the other direction. Extreme inequality is not just bad for poverty reduction—it is also bad for growth. Long-run efficiency and greater equity can be complementary. Poor people remain poor partly because they cannot borrow against future earnings to invest in production, the education of their children and assets to reduce their vulnerability. Insecure land rights and limited access to justice can create further barriers to investment.

Deprived of public goods—such as information and legal rights—poor people are denied opportunities to contribute to growth. They enter markets on unequal terms and leave them with unequal rewards. Where extreme inequalities based on wealth, gender or region leave a large section of society with insufficient assets and endowments, society as a whole suffers from the resulting inefficiency. Denying half the population access to education opportunities is not just a violation of human rights. It is also bad for growth. Gender-based education inequalities have held back Pakistan's economic development, for example. Allowing unequal asset distribution to perpetuate mass poverty is clearly bad for poor people, but it also restricts the development of investment opportunities and markets for the rest of society.

Political legitimacy

Extreme inequalities also weaken political legitimacy and corrode institutions. Inequalities in income and human capabilities often reflect inequalities in political power. Disadvantaged

Extreme inequality is not just bad for poverty reduction—it is also bad for growth

Absolute poverty and
inequality may be
different, but they are
intimately related

groups—poor people, women, rural populations, indigenous communities—are disadvantaged partly because they have a weak political voice, and they have a weak political voice because they are disadvantaged.

Where political institutions are seen as vehicles for perpetuating unjust inequalities or advancing the interests of elites, that undermines the development of democracy and creates conditions for state breakdown. In countries such as Bolivia and Ecuador conflicts over natural resources management have, at a more fundamental level, become a focal point for disadvantaged indigenous groups denied a political voice by institutions that are seen as unresponsive.

Public policy goals

Most societies see reducing poverty and removing unjust inequalities as important goals for public policy. Extreme disparities undermine the pursuit of these goals. As we show in this chapter, extreme inequalities in income limit the rate at which growth can be converted into lower levels of poverty. Similarly, extreme disparities in health and education reduce the scope of disadvantaged groups to take advantage of opportunities for improving welfare.

Counter-arguments—countered

There are counter-arguments to the claim that inequality matters. Some libertarians deny the existence of "social justice". The free market theorist F.A. Hayek famously argued that it was nonsense to talk about resources being fairly or unfairly distributed. On his account it was up to free markets, not human agency, to determine the appropriate allocation of wealth and assets. This perspective overlooks the role of human agency and unequal power relationships in structuring markets.

Another widely held view is that some inequalities matter more than others and that equality before the law matters first and foremost.[9] However, rights and freedoms cannot stand alone. People are likely to be restricted in what they can do with their freedom and their

rights if they are poor, ill, denied an education or lack the capacity to influence what happens to them. To be meaningful, formal equalities have to be backed by what Amartya Sen has called the "substantive freedoms"—the capabilities—to choose a way of life and do the things that one values. Deep inequalities in life chances limit these substantive freedoms, rendering hollow the idea of equality before the law.

Others have argued that the proper focus for social justice is absolute deprivation, not distribution. Where poor people stand in relation to others, so the argument runs, is less important than their command over income or access to health and education services. "We are against poverty," runs the common refrain, "but inequality is a different matter, and nothing to do with social justice or the MDGs." This argument too is flawed. Absolute poverty and inequality may be different concepts, but they are intimately related. Disparities in life chances define prospects for escaping poverty. For example, inequality in access to healthcare, education or political rights can diminish an individual's prospects for escaping poverty. In this chapter we examine some of the basic disparities that interact with poverty. What links these diverse disparities is that they are rooted in inequalities in power that perpetuate deprivation and destitution. The "pathologies of power", as one author has described them, are at the very core of the processes that are driving countries off track for the MDGs.[10]

As we show later, progress towards the reduction of absolute poverty is heavily conditioned by inequality. This is true not just for income, but also for wider inequalities in areas such as health, education and politics. Moreover, the idea that poverty and human welfare can be defined solely in absolute terms to the exclusion of relative considerations flies in the face not just of attitude survey evidence, but of basic ideas elaborated in 1776 by Adam Smith. Smith forcefully argued that relative distribution is integral to any assessment of human welfare: "By necessities I understand not only the commodities necessary for the support of life, but whatever the custom of the country renders it necessary for creditable people, even of the lowest order, to be without. A linen shirt, for example, is strictly speaking not a necessity of life....But in present times, throughout the greater part of Europe, a creditable day labourer would be ashamed to appear in public without a linen shirt."[11]

Chains of disadvantage—inequality within countries

Chapter 1 looked at inequalities between rich and poor countries. These inequalities are mirrored within countries. Deep human development disparities persist between rich people and poor people, men and women, rural and urban areas and different regions and groups. These inequalities seldom exist in isolation. They create mutually reinforcing structures of disadvantage that follow people through life cycles and are transmitted across generations.

Income inequality varies markedly across regions. In broad terms Latin America and Sub-Saharan Africa register very high levels of inequality, while South Asia and Organisation for Economic Co-operation and Development (OECD) countries register much lower levels. Although there are no clear threshold points, countries with Gini coefficients above 50 can be said to be in the high inequality category (figure 2.1).

Cross-country evidence is often cited in support of the proposition that, on average, inequality changes very little over time. That proposition is misleading in important respects. While it is difficult to compare different surveys across countries and time, there has been a clear trend over the past two decades towards rising inequality within countries. Of the 73 countries for which data are available, 53 (with more than 80% of the world's population) have seen inequality rise, while only 9 (with 4% of the population) have seen it narrow.[12] This holds true in both high- and low-growth situations (such as China in the first case and Bolivia in the second) and across all regions.

Differences in the Gini coefficient relate to differences in the share of national wealth captured by the poorest people. In broad terms the higher the Gini coefficient, the lower is the share of national income captured by the poorest

sections of society. The poorest 20% of the population in low-inequality countries such as Indonesia and Viet Nam capture three to four times

Figure 2.1 **Inequality in income—selected countries and regions**

Gini coefficient, income distribution
(GDP per capita, PPP US$)

GINI

Sub-Saharan Africa 72.2 ➤ 70

World 67.0 ➤

Latin America & the Caribbean 57.1 ➤ 60

East Asia & the Pacific 52.0 ➤ 50

Central & Eastern Europe & CIS 42.8 ➤ 40

High-income OECD 36.8 ➤

South Asia 33.4 ➤ 30

Inequality within countries

Namibia	70.7
Brazil	59.3
South Africa	57.8
Chile	57.1
Zimbabwe	56.8
Mexico	54.6
Zambia	52.6
Argentina	52.2
Malaysia	49.2
Philippines	46.1
China	44.7
Thailand	43.2
Kenya	42.5
United States	40.8
Viet Nam	37.0
United Kingdom	36.0
Egypt	34.4
Poland	34.1
Sri Lanka	33.2
France	32.7
Russian Federation	31.0
Ethiopia	30.0
Albania	28.2
Hungary	26.9
Sweden	25.0

Source: Regional data, Dihkanov 2005; country data, indicator table 15.

more national income than their counterparts in high-inequality countries such as Guatemala and Peru (figure 2.2). While income gaps between countries account for the lion's share of global inequality, income disparities within many countries rival in scale the inequalities in global income distribution. In Brazil the poorest 10% of the population account for 0.7% of national income, and the richest 10% for 47%. Inequalities within Sub-Saharan Africa are also very large. In Zambia, for example, the ratio of the income of the richest to the poorest 10% is 42:1.

Distribution patterns have an important bearing on the relationship between average incomes and poverty levels. A more nearly equal distribution can mean that poor people in countries with low levels of inequality have higher incomes than poor people in countries at higher average income levels. This provides a clear example of how distribution affects absolute poverty. For example, average income in Brazil is three times higher than average income in Viet Nam. But the poorest 20% of Brazilians have an income well below the average income in Viet Nam and comparable to the income of the poorest 20% of that country (figure 2.3). The poorest 20% of the population in the United Kingdom have an income comparable to that of the poorest 20% in the Czech Republic, a far less wealthy country.

As these comparisons suggest, average incomes obscure the effects of distribution patterns on real welfare. The human development index (HDI) is also an average indicator. In this sense it too provides a picture of what is happening to the hypothetical average person in a country, not to the average poor person. This can be demonstrated through a simple exercise. Adjusting the income component of the HDI from average income to average income of the poorest 20%, holding everything else constant—including the health and education scores—drops Brazil 52 places in the HDI ranking (to 115) and Mexico 55 places (to 108).

Comparisons between low-income countries and high-inequality countries are revealing in another way. They highlight how, at any given

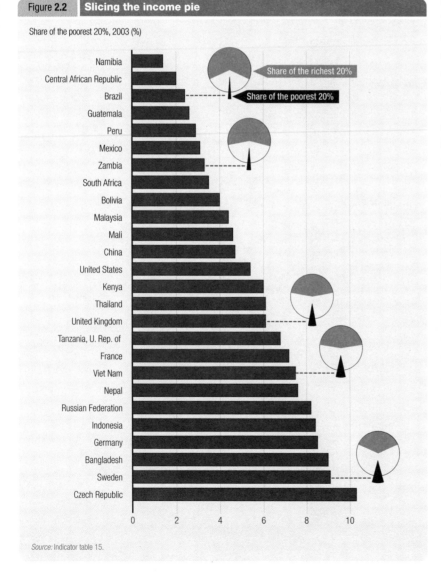

Figure 2.2   Slicing the income pie

Share of the poorest 20%, 2003 (%)

Share of the richest 20%
Share of the poorest 20%

Namibia
Central African Republic
Brazil
Guatemala
Peru
Mexico
Zambia
South Africa
Bolivia
Malaysia
Mali
China
United States
Kenya
Thailand
United Kingdom
Tanzania, U. Rep. of
France
Viet Nam
Nepal
Russian Federation
Indonesia
Germany
Bangladesh
Sweden
Czech Republic

0   2   4   6   8   10

Source: Indicator table 15.

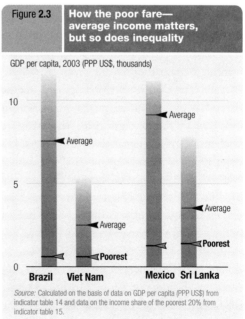

Figure 2.3   How the poor fare— average income matters, but so does inequality

GDP per capita, 2003 (PPP US$, thousands)

10

5

0

Brazil   Viet Nam   Mexico   Sri Lanka

Average
Average
Average
Average
Poorest
Poorest
Poorest
Poorest

Source: Calculated on the basis of data on GDP per capita (PPP US$) from indicator table 14 and data on the income share of the poorest 20% from indicator table 15.

level of average income, more equitable distribution can be associated with lower poverty levels. One way to illustrate this is to consider how the incomes of different parts of the overall distribution in a country might change if the distribution patterns of a more equal country were imposed. Currently, the poorest 20% of the population in Guatemala have an average income of $550 a year, or 46% below the $2 a day international poverty line. Were this group to capture the same share of national income as the poorest 20% in Viet Nam, their average incomes would rise to $1,560, or 66% above the $2 a day line.[13] Of course, it could be argued that this example ignores the potentially negative effects on growth and hence on the overall size of the economy of a transition to greater equity in Guatemala. But the example of Viet Nam, a dynamic, high-growth economy with lower inequality, suggests that there may be positive benefits for Guatemala, which has experienced two decades of low growth.

Income inequalities both reflect and affect wider life chance inequalities, starting with the chance of staying alive.[14] In Bolivia and Peru infant death rates are four to five times higher for the children of the poorest 20% of the population than the children of the richest 20%. With more births, the poor are heavily overrepresented in the distribution of child deaths (figure 2.4). This is a stark demonstration of how inequality deprives people of substantive freedoms and choices, regardless of their formal legal rights and freedoms.

Wealth-based differences are the first link in a cycle of inequality that tracks people through their lives. Women in poor households are less likely to receive antenatal care and less likely to have their births attended by a trained medical assistant (figure 2.5). Their children are less likely to survive or to complete school. Children who do not complete school are more likely to have lower incomes. Thus the cycle of deprivation is transmitted across generations.

In rich countries, too, basic life chances are unequally distributed. Chapter 1 highlighted the chasm in life chances separating the average person in a rich country from the average person in a poor country. Beyond this chasm, some deprived groups in the "First World" have life chances comparable to the average in

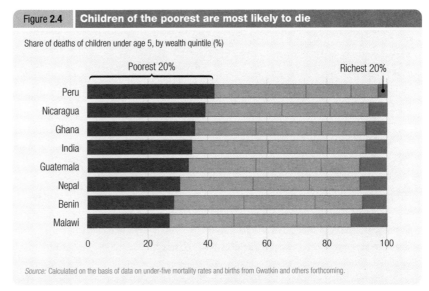

Figure 2.4   **Children of the poorest are most likely to die**

Share of deaths of children under age 5, by wealth quintile (%)

Source: Calculated on the basis of data on under-five mortality rates and births from Gwatkin and others forthcoming.

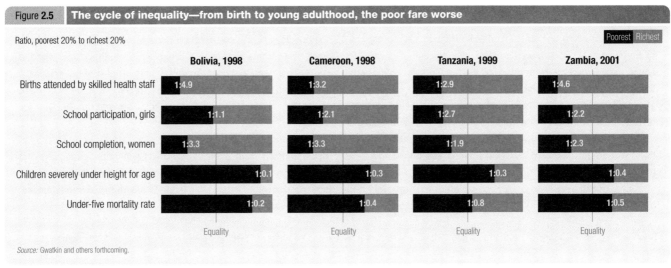

Figure 2.5   **The cycle of inequality—from birth to young adulthood, the poor fare worse**

Ratio, poorest 20% to richest 20%

	Bolivia, 1998	Cameroon, 1998	Tanzania, 1999	Zambia, 2001
Births attended by skilled health staff	1:4.9	1:3.2	1:2.9	1:4.6
School participation, girls	1:1.1	1:2.1	1:2.7	1:2.2
School completion, women	1:3.3	1:3.3	1:1.9	1:2.3
Children severely under height for age	1:0.1	1:0.3	1:0.3	1:0.4
Under-five mortality rate	1:0.2	1:0.4	1:0.8	1:0.5

Source: Gwatkin and others forthcoming.

Box **2.1**   **Inequality and health in the United States**

The United States leads the world in healthcare spending. On a per capita basis the United States spends twice the Organisation for Economic Co-operation and Development average on healthcare, or 13% of national income. Yet some countries that spend substantially less than the United States have healthier populations. US public health indicators are marred by deep inequalities linked to income, health insurance coverage, race, ethnicity, geography and—critically—access to care.

Key US health indicators are far below those that might be anticipated on the basis of national wealth. Infant mortality trends are especially troublesome. Since 2000 a half century of sustained decline in infant death rates first slowed and then reversed. The infant mortality rate is now higher for the United States than for many other industrial countries. Malaysia—a country with an average income one-quarter that of the United States—has achieved the same infant mortality rate as the United States (figure 1). And the Indian state of Kerala has an urban infant death rate lower than that for African Americans in Washington, DC.

Wide differences in health across socio-economic groups partly explain the poorer health outcomes in the United States than in other industrial countries. From the cradle to the grave the health of US citizens shows extreme divergence. For example, racial and ethnic health disparities are persistent—a result of differences in insurance coverage, income, language and education, among other factors (figure 2). African American mothers are twice as likely as white mothers to give birth to a low birthweight baby. Their children are twice as likely to die before their first birthday. Income differences are closely correlated with health differences. A baby boy from a family in the top 5% of the US income distribution will enjoy a life span 25% longer than a boy born in the bottom 5%.

Many factors contribute to health inequalities. One important driver is the coverage of healthcare provision. The United States is the only wealthy country with no universal health insurance system. Its mix of employer-based private insurance and public coverage has never reached all Americans. While more than half the population have health insurance coverage through their employers and almost all the elderly are covered through Medicare, more than one

in six non-elderly Americans (45 million) lacked health insurance in 2003. Over a third (36%) of families living below the poverty line are uninsured. Hispanic Americans (34%) are more than twice as likely to be uninsured as white Americans (13%), and 21% of African Americans have no health insurance. Health insurance coverage also varies widely across the 50 states, depending on the share of families with low incomes, the nature of employment and the breadth of each state's Medicaid programme for low-income people.

More than in any other major industrial country the cost of treatment is a major barrier to access in the United States. Over 40% of the uninsured do not have a regular place to receive medical treatment when they are sick, and more than a third say that they or someone in their family went without needed medical care, including recommended treatments or prescription drugs, in the last year because of cost.

Unequal access to healthcare has clear links to health outcomes. The uninsured are less likely to have regular outpatient care, so they are more likely to be hospitalized for avoidable health problems. Once in a hospital, they receive fewer services and are more likely to die than are insured patients. They also receive less preventive care. The Institute of Medicine estimates that at least 18,000 Americans die prematurely each year solely because they lack health insurance. Being born into an uninsured household increases the probability of death before age 1 by about 50%.

Unequal access to healthcare has a powerful effect on health inequalities linked to race, which are only partly explained by insurance and income inequalities. One study finds that eliminating the gap in healthcare between African Americans and white Americans would save nearly 85,000 lives a year. To put this figure in context, technological improvements in medicine save about 20,000 lives a year.

The comparison highlights a paradox at the heart of the US health system. High levels of personal healthcare spending reflect the country's cutting-edge medical technology and treatment. Yet social inequalities, interacting with inequalities in health financing, limit the reach of medical advance.

Figure 1   Infant mortality comparison

Infant mortality rate, 2003
(deaths per 1,000 live births)

15 — ◄ Urban Kerala, India
       ◄ US African Americans
       ◄ Uruguay

10
       ◄ Malaysia, United States
       ◄ US White

5
       ◄ Japan

0

Source: India data, IIPS and ORC Macro 2000; US data, The Henry Kaiser Family Foundation 2005; national data, indicator table 10.

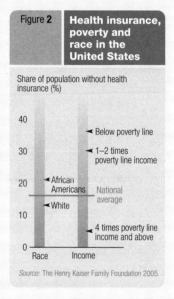

Figure 2   Health insurance, poverty and race in the United States

Share of population without health insurance (%)

40   ◄ Below poverty line

30   ◄ 1–2 times poverty line income

20 ◄ African Americans   National average

       ◄ White

10   ◄ 4 times poverty line income and above

0
    Race   Income

Source: The Henry Kaiser Family Foundation 2005.

Source: Rowland and Hoffman 2005; Proctor and Dalaker 2003; Munnell, Hatch and Lee 2004; The Henry Kaiser Family Foundation 2005; Deaton 2002.

Inequality and human development

countries at far lower levels of income. Poorer people die younger and are sick more often. Men in the top 5% of the income distribution in the United States live about 25% longer than men in the bottom 5%.[15] Meanwhile, high levels of health spending have failed to eradicate large disparities in infant death rates based on race, wealth and state of residence. These disparities have limited progress in reducing infant mortality. The infant mortality rate in the United States compares with that in Malaysia—a country with a quarter the income. Infant death rates are higher for African American children in Washington, DC, than for children in Kerala, India. While other socio-economic factors are involved, financial barriers to adequate healthcare are an important contributor (box 2.1).

Layers of inequality constrain life choices

Life chances in any country are constrained by complex layers of inequality. Disparities in opportunities for health, education, income and political influence are to be found in every country, in varying magnitudes. Inequalities linked to wealth, gender, location, race and ethnicity, along with other markers for disadvantage, do not operate in isolation. They interact to create dynamic and mutually reinforcing cycles of disadvantage that are transmitted across generations. Breaking these cycles is one of the keys to accelerated progress towards the MDGs.

Regional inequalities

In many countries regional disparities are a major source of inequality. In Brazil the infant mortality rate is 52 deaths per 1,000 live births in the north-east but drops to 20 deaths in the south-east. The 10 municipalities with the lowest infant mortality rates have an average of 8 deaths per 1,000 live births—a level comparable to that in some high-income countries. The 10 worst municipalities have a death rate of 117 deaths per 1,000 live births, which is higher than in Bihar, India. Per capita spending on health is inversely related to the infant mortality rate: it is twice as high in the south-east as in the north-east.[16]

Breaking down national HDIs graphically reveals the scale of regional inequality within countries. The HDI in China ranges from 0.64 in Guizhou to 0.80 in Guangdong and 0.89 in Shanghai (figure 2.6). If they were countries, Guizhou would rank just above Namibia and Shanghai alongside Portugal. The HDI in Mexico ranges from 0.71 in Chiapas and 0.72 in Oaxaca to 0.89 in Mexico City, a range that extends from El Salvador to the Republic of Korea. Education differences are one explanation. Illiteracy rates range from 3% in Mexico City to more than 20% in Chiapas and Guerrero. Figure 2.7 uses an inequality tree to investigate inequalities below the state

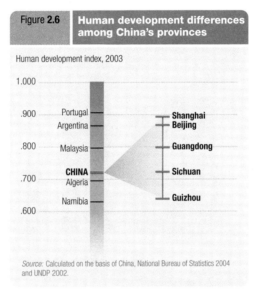

Figure 2.6 Human development differences among China's provinces

Human development index, 2003

Source: Calculated on the basis of China, National Bureau of Statistics 2004 and UNDP 2002.

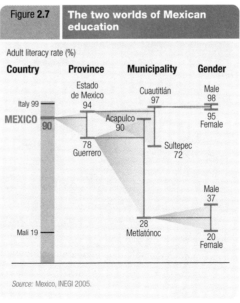

Figure 2.7 The two worlds of Mexican education

Adult literacy rate (%)

Source: Mexico, INEGI 2005.

level in Mexico. The richest municipalities in Guerrero, such as the resort of Acapulco, have literacy levels comparable to those in high-income countries, and with limited gender gaps. Meanwhile, in the predominantly rural, indigenous and mountainous municipalities literacy levels fall to 28%—half the level in Sudan—and to 20% for women. Inequality trees provide a way of tracking the complex patterns of inequality that operate beneath the national average.

Urban-rural disparities

Living in a rural area is, in many countries, a marker for disadvantage. Poverty rates are higher, and access to services is lower. In Ghana the incidence of poverty is 2% in the capital city of Accra but 70% in the rural savannah. The rural savannah accounts for one-fifth of Ghana's population, but two-fifths of the population living in poverty. While poverty has been declining in Accra, it has remained unchanged in the savannah.[17]

Ghana's rural-urban divide is equally marked in access to basic services. One in five rural residents has access to piped water compared with four in five urban residents. Death rates for children under age 5 are far higher in rural areas, reflecting a higher incidence of poverty and more limited coverage of basic services. In Bolivia death rates are nearly 1.9 times higher among rural children than among urban children (figure 2.8). The rural-urban divide magnifies gender inequalities, dramatically so in many countries. In Pakistan the rural-urban gap in school attendance is 27 percentage points, but the gap between rural girls and urban boys is 47 percentage points (figure 2.9). In many countries the rural-urban divide also exacerbates inequalities within and between groups. Indigenous people in Guatemala are far more likely to live in poverty, but rural indigenous people have an incidence of poverty almost five times the average for urban non-indigenous people (figure 2.10).

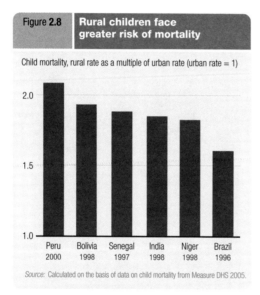

Figure **2.8** **Rural children face greater risk of mortality**

Child mortality, rural rate as a multiple of urban rate (urban rate = 1)

| | Peru 2000 | Bolivia 1998 | Senegal 1997 | India 1998 | Niger 1998 | Brazil 1996 |

Source: Calculated on the basis of data on child mortality from Measure DHS 2005.

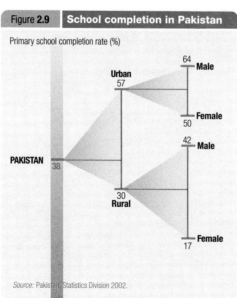

Figure **2.9** **School completion in Pakistan**

Primary school completion rate (%)

PAKISTAN 38
Urban 57 — Male 64, Female 50
Rural 30 — Male 42, Female 17

Source: Pakistan, Statistics Division 2002.

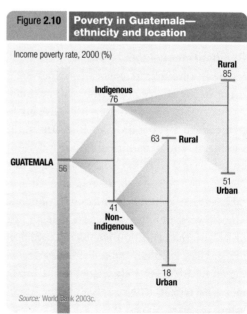

Figure **2.10** **Poverty in Guatemala— ethnicity and location**

Income poverty rate, 2000 (%)

GUATEMALA 56
Indigenous 76 — Rural 85, Urban 51
Non-indigenous 41 — Rural 63, Urban 18

Source: World Bank 2003c.

Gender inequality

Gender disparities are among the deepest and most pervasive of inequalities. They are revealed most brutally in parts of South Asia. In India the mortality rate among children ages 1–5 is 50% higher for girls than for boys. These girls, deprived of life because they were born with two X chromosomes, are among the 100 million "missing women" in South Asia. The higher mortality rates among girls and women from birth to about age 30 inverts the normal demographic gender balance, pointing to structural inequalities in nutrition, healthcare and status.

Income inequality reinforces unequal health outcomes for women. In Indonesia maternal mortality ratios are four times higher among women in the poorest 20% of the population than among women in the richest 20%. Women who die during pregnancy are twice as likely to be unschooled and 50% less likely to have access to clean water.[18] Across the developing world poor women are less likely than women in higher income groups to have their births attended by a trained assistant—a key indicator for maternal mortality. In Peru and Yemen women in the richest 20% of the population are six to seven times more likely to have births attended by trained assistants than are women in the poorest 20%. Gender-based inequalities, including infant mortality, link back to wider life chance inequalities. In Burkina Faso infant mortality rates are three times higher for children of uneducated mothers than for children of educated mothers.

The very visible disparities in human development described here are the product of deeper structural inequalities, including less visible inequalities in power. Empowerment of the poor is both an instrument to reduce poverty and, because participation in society is a dimension of human development, an aspect of poverty reduction. Poor people and disadvantaged groups often lack the capacity to influence institutions controlled by elite groups. More broadly, the disadvantage is perpetuated by inequalities in what can be thought of as the factors shaping the political capabilities of the poor: self-confidence, capacity to influence political processes and recognition by the rest of society.

Nowhere are power inequalities and their consequences more clearly displayed than for women. Women experience inequality in power relative to men from the household level to the national level, where they are universally underrepresented in legislative bodies, organs of government and local political structures. Women, especially those with low incomes, tend to have less control over household resources, less access to information and health services and less control over their time. These factors are closely linked to their nutritional status, the quality of care they receive and the nutritional status of their children (see box 1.3).

Unequal chances—health inequalities and the MDGs

Life chance inequalities on the scale described above are not just inherently unjust. They are also bad for the MDGs. Deep inequalities are holding back progress in many areas. To demonstrate how strategies to reduce inequality could accelerate progress, this section considers child mortality.

Income

As chapter 1 shows, the MDG target of reducing child deaths by two-thirds will be missed by a wide margin on current trends. Two interrelated factors explain much of the deficit. First, in most countries the poor account for a far larger share of child deaths than is commensurate with their share of the population. Put differently, the children of the poor are overrepresented among the victims of child death—heavily so in many countries. In Ghana 36% of child deaths occur among the poorest 20% of the population, while 7% occur among the richest 20% (see figure 2.4). Second, the rate of child mortality is falling much more slowly among the poor than the average rate of decline in most countries. Cross-country data suggest that the child mortality rate among the poorest 20% is falling at half the average rate of decline, so that the mortality gap between rich and poor children is widening. In Zambia child mortality among the richest 20% fell by 6% a year in the second half of the 1990s—three times as fast as for the poorest 20% (figure 2.11).

2

Inequality and human development

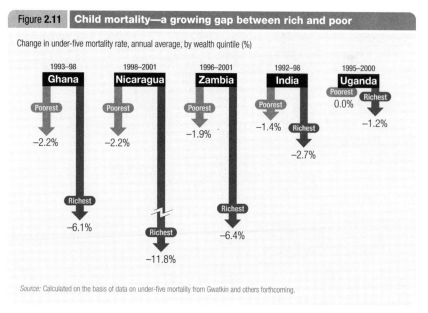

Figure 2.11 Child mortality—a growing gap between rich and poor

Change in under-five mortality rate, annual average, by wealth quintile (%)

1993–98	1998–2001	1996–2001	1992–98	1995–2000
Ghana	**Nicaragua**	**Zambia**	**India**	**Uganda**

Ghana: Poorest −2.2%, Richest −6.1%

Nicaragua: Poorest −2.2%, Richest −11.8%

Zambia: Poorest −1.9%, Richest −6.4%

India: Poorest −1.4%, Richest −2.7%

Uganda: Poorest 0.0%, Richest −1.2%

Source: Calculated on the basis of data on under-five mortality from Gwatkin and others forthcoming.

No avoidable child death should be tolerated. But this current pattern of progress is also suboptimal from the perspective of achieving the MDG target of a two-thirds reduction. The slowest decline is happening in precisely the population group in which accelerated progress could lead to the biggest reductions in child mortality. On one estimate, closing the gap in child mortality rates between the poorest 20% and the national average would cut child deaths by 60%, saving about 6.3 million lives a year. This would also put the world on track for achieving the MDG target.[19] This suggests that the failure of national governments and the international community to overcome inequalities based on wealth costs the lives of more than 6 million children a year.

It could even be argued that this comparison yields an unduly conservative assessment. Using Demographic and Health Survey data, we estimate what would happen if the average child mortality rate fell to the rate of the richest 20%. For many countries this would translate into very large declines in child deaths, reducing the overall total by more than one-half in India and in Nicaragua. For India the reduction in child mortality would reduce overall deaths by about 1.4 million. In just three countries—Bangladesh, India and Nepal—half a million of the lives saved would be of children in the first month of life.

Gender

Reducing gender inequality would have a catalytic effect on cutting child deaths. That effect would be especially pronounced in South Asia, where gender inequality is most deeply entrenched. If India closed the gender gap in mortality between girls and boys ages 1–5, that would save an estimated 130,000 lives, reducing its overall child mortality rate by 5%.[20]

Overcoming wider gender inequalities would have even more pronounced effects because of the negative links between maternal nutritional deprivation and child mortality. The percentage of underweight women is four times higher in South Asia than in Sub-Saharan Africa, and deficiencies in nutrients and vitamins linked to child death are far greater. South Asia has lower levels of poverty and higher average incomes than Sub-Saharan Africa but South Asia's child malnutrition rate is 20% higher than Sub-Saharan Africa's. Half of the world's underweight children live in South Asia. These human development deficits are strongly associated with gender inequalities.

Greater gender equity would act as a powerful force for reducing child mortality. Using cross-country data, the International Food Policy Research Institute has estimated that equalizing the access of men and women to education, nutrition, income and property rights could reduce the underweight rate among children less than three years old by 13 percentage points in South Asia, meaning 13.4 million fewer malnourished children vulnerable to early mortality. For Sub-Saharan Africa child malnutrition would fall by 3 percentage points, with 1.7 million fewer malnourished children.[21] The pathways through which the empowerment of women influences child well-being include wider spacing of births through enhanced control over fertility, greater use of health facilities and better knowledge of health interventions.

Public policy

Reducing the deeply rooted inequalities based on gender, income and region that generate unequal child mortality rates requires wide-ranging reforms. Public policy has a critical role to play in addressing the three "As" for reducing inequality:

- *Access.* The poor often live in areas that are sparsely covered by basic health services or covered by facilities that lack drugs and trained staff. Chronic underfinancing is part of the problem. Providing basic healthcare coverage in a low-income country costs an estimated $30–$40 per capita. Across much of Africa spending is less than $6 per capita. Under these conditions, even where facilities exist, they are likely to lack essential medicines.

- *Affordability.* Charging for basic healthcare increases inequality. Payments for healthcare can represent a large share of the income of poor people, leading to reduced demand, uncompleted treatments or increased debt. In Viet Nam a single hospital visit costs 40% of the monthly income of people in the poorest 20% of the population. High levels of household health spending not only deter use of services, but by one estimate have pushed 3 million people in Viet Nam into poverty.[22] In China the erosion of the public health system after the economic reforms of the late 1970s has exacerbated inequalities in health (box 2.2). Removing fees can improve equity. When Uganda did that in 2001, visits to public

---

Box 2.2   China—rising inequalities in health

Over the past four decades China has registered some of the most rapid advances in human development in history. During the 1990s the country climbed 14 places in the HDI ranking (to 85). China has been the world's fastest growing economy over the past two decades, with per capita incomes rising threefold in constant purchasing power terms. However, there are worrying indications that social progress is starting to lag behind economic growth performance, with the slowdown in the rate of reduction in child deaths a special concern.

Health inequalities appear to be contributing to the problem. Children living in the poorest provinces and in rural China face the highest death risks. Child mortality levels in urban areas average about one-third of those in rural areas. Under-five mortality rates range from 8 per 1,000 live births in Shanghai and Beijing (comparable to the United States) to 60 in the poorest province of Guizhou (comparable to Namibia). The gap between rich and poor provinces appears to be widening. So does the survival gap between girls and boys. Recent research indicates that child mortality rates are rising at 0.5% a year for girls while falling at 2.3% a year for boys.

Public policies have contributed to these inequalities. Until 1980 most of China's poor people living in rural areas were covered by the Cooperative Medical System. That system was dismantled with market reforms. One effect was to shift the burden of financing healthcare costs from public providers to household transfers. Most people now have to buy health insurance, meet costs as they arise or go without healthcare. Today, China spends 5% of GDP on health, which is relatively high for countries at comparable levels of income, but public spending on health amounts to less than 2% of GDP. In effect, health financing has been privatized.

Fiscal decentralization has reinforced the transition to a market-based system. Poorer counties and districts have been unable to raise sufficient revenue through taxation, intensifying the pressure on health service providers to demand payment for services. This includes basic immunization and other preventive health services. Charging for services that are public goods is economically inefficient and inequitable.

The erosion of public provision has resulted in a mismatch between need and provision: average per capita spending on health in urban areas is now 3.5 times the level in rural areas. Between 70% and 80% of the rural population have no health insurance coverage. This means that treatment for sickness episodes has to be paid for out of pocket. High healthcare costs are a cause of household poverty and a deterrent to using health services. One study commissioned by the Chinese Ministry of Health covering three provinces (Guangdong, Shanxi and Sichuan) found that half of respondents reported not seeking healthcare despite needing it in the past year. The main reason cited was cost.

Price barriers may be partly responsible for a downturn in immunization coverage. During the 1980s immunization for diphtheria, pertussis and tetanus (DPT3) increased from 58% to 97%—one of the highest rates of coverage in the developing world. Since then coverage has slipped back to 90%, according to data from the World Health Organization and the United Nations Children's Fund.

There is now a danger that China will miss the Millennium Development Goal target for child mortality and that deepening inequalities will slow progress towards other health goals. These inequalities are rooted in a privatized health financing system that seems inappropriate in a country with high levels of poverty. While economic reform has clearly generated important gains, market principles have been extended too far into the health system. The Chinese government itself is now reviewing healthcare financing with a view to strengthening service provision for poor households.

Source: Lim and others 2004; Liu, Liu and Meng 1994; Sen 2004.

health facilities rose by 80%, with half of the increase among the poorest 20% of the population. The share of households that reported not having used a health service because of high costs decreased from about 50% in 1999 to 35% in 2002—a reduction that was particularly pronounced in the country's poorest region.[23]

- *Accountability.* Even where public health services are available, they are often not used by poor people. For example, in India a large share of demand is directed towards poorly qualified private providers. A survey in one of the poorest districts of Rajasthan found that poor households used private health providers even when nominally free public services were available. One reason: over half of health centres were closed during periods when they were supposed to be open. When facilities are open they often lack a trained staff member on site. For India as a whole survey evidence based on unannounced visits to health clinics found that 40% of clinics lack a trained person on site at the time of the visit.[24] Developing more accountable health systems can dramatically improve access and health indicators. For example, in 1987 the Brazilian state of Cereá, one of the poorest in the country, set up a decentralized, community-based healthcare system that now employs more than 170,000 health workers. The programme has been accompanied by strategies to support community monitoring of health providers. In less than 15 years the infant death rate fell to one-third of its 1987 level.

The human development potential of pro-poor growth

Trends in income inequality have an important bearing on wider dimensions of human development as well as on income poverty. Moves towards greater distributional equity could sharply reduce the rate of income poverty, with attendant benefits for the MDGs and wider human development goals.

Improved distribution can enhance development through two pathways: one static and the other dynamic. At any given growth rate the larger the share of any increment in economic wealth that is captured by the poor, the higher the ratio of poverty reduction to growth— referred to as the poverty elasticity of growth. This is a static effect. Dynamic effects emerge when changes in distribution affect the growth rate. Extreme inequality can act as a brake on growth. This effect is especially strong for asset inequality. Limited access to productive assets, or limited capacity to enforce legal claims, can restrict poor people's ability to borrow and invest, holding back growth.[25] Cross-country evidence suggests that greater distributional equity can accelerate growth and that there are no inherent trade-offs between growth and equity. Thus improved distributional equity can generate a double benefit: it increases growth and the size of the economic pie and it enables the poor to capture a bigger slice of that pie.[26]

Improving the distribution of growth

In countries where inequality and poverty levels are high even small shifts in distribution can significantly reduce poverty.

Accelerating poverty reduction in individual countries

Using national household income and expenditure data for several countries, we estimated the potential impact on income poverty of doubling the national income share of the poorest 20% of the population through a transfer from the top 20% (see *Technical note 2*). For high-inequality countries with large populations in poverty, shifting even a small share of the income of the top 20% could lift large numbers of people above the poverty line. For Brazil and Mexico the transfer of 5% of the income of the richest 20% would have the following effects:

- In Brazil about 26 million people would be lifted above the $2 a day poverty line, cutting the poverty rate from 22% to 7%.
- In Mexico about 12 million people would be taken out of poverty, as nationally defined, reducing the poverty rate from 16% to 4%.

Of course, this is a static exercise. It illustrates the poverty impact of a hypothetical transfer from rich to poor. In a society that attaches greater weight to welfare gains for the poor than the rich the transfer might be considered welfare enhancing for the whole of society even if some lose.

Another route to improved distribution is progressive growth—a growth pattern in which average incomes are growing, but the incomes of poor people are growing even faster. This is a positive-sum process in which nobody loses and

the poor gain proportionately more. Progressive growth can be thought of as a dynamic process in which poor people produce their way out of poverty, while increasing their contribution to national wealth (box 2.3).

Even modestly progressive growth can have a powerful impact on poverty. Once again, we use growth simulation models based on national household income survey data to demonstrate the effects for Brazil and Mexico. We build two scenarios. The first, a distribution-neutral scenario, assumes a continuation of current growth trends with no change in distribution. Increases to income are distributed in line with existing income shares: if the poorest 20% account for 1% of current income, they would receive 1 cent of every $1 generated by growth. The second, a progressive growth scenario, assumes that people living below the poverty line double their share of future growth. In the case mentioned above, if the poorest 20% represented the population living in poverty, their

---

Box 2.3	Pro-poor growth and progressive growth

Like motherhood and apple pie, everybody is in favour of "pro-poor growth". The concept, like its increasingly popular and more recent variant "shared growth", captures the idea that the quality of growth, as well as the quantity, matters for poverty reduction. But the concept means very different things to different people. The World Bank and international development agencies favour an absolute definition of pro-poor growth. What matters in this definition is not whether the incomes of poor people are rising in relation to average income, but how fast their incomes are rising. Pro-poor growth on this definition can be consistent with rising inequality, even in countries already marked by extreme inequalities.

The progressive definition of pro-poor growth adopted in this Report focuses on the relative position of poor people. It highlights the potential for small distributional shifts to produce major gains for poverty reduction.

Are these just semantic differences? Or do they have a direct relevance for human development? The differences can be overplayed: all parties in the debate favour rapid poverty reduction. By extension, nobody argues that low levels of inequality are inherently good for poverty reduction. If they were, low-growth, low-inequality (a Gini coefficient of about 36 throughout the 1990s) Benin would be outperforming China. However, two important issues are at stake, both connected to the balance between economic growth and distribution.

The first issue is one of social justice. In the absolute definition distribution-neutral growth is pro-poor: any growth that increases the income of the poor can be deemed pro-poor. It is difficult to square this with basic ideas of social justice. If everybody in Brazil shared in increments to growth on the current distribution pattern, the richest 20% would receive 85 cents of every $1. The poorest 20% would receive 3 cents. Everybody—including the poor—is better off, so growth might be deemed pro-poor. But if more weight is attached to the well-being of poor people, that distribution pattern is not consistent with basic principles of fairness and social justice.

The second, related concern is about the conversion of growth into poverty reduction. If maximizing the impact of growth on poverty reduction is a central policy goal, then distribution matters. Other things being equal, the bigger the share of any increment to growth captured by poor people, the faster the rate of poverty reduction. Increasing their share of additional growth can accelerate the rate at which rising prosperity reduces poverty, while at the same time raising the overall growth rate.

The progressive growth approach focuses attention on the structural inequalities that deny poor people and marginalized groups an opportunity to contribute to and participate in growth on more equitable terms. It puts redistribution, alongside growth, at the centre of the policy agenda for reducing extreme poverty.

Source: Kakwani, Khandker and Son 2004; Ravallion 2005; DFID 2004b.

The smaller the poor's share of any increment to income the less efficient growth is as a mechanism for poverty reduction

share of future growth would rise from 1 cent to 2 cents of every $1. Considering the high degree of inequality in both Brazil and Mexico, this is a modest scenario for pro-poor growth. Even so, the results are striking. For Brazil it shortens the time it takes the median household to cross the poverty line by 19 years. For Mexico it shortens the time by 15 years (see *Technical note 2*).

It is sometimes argued that distribution has more relevance for high-inequality middle-income countries than for the low-growth low-income countries that are farthest off track for meeting the MDGs. This is correct in the sense that, as the Brazil and Mexico simulations demonstrate, even modest redistribution can produce big results for poverty reduction in high-inequality middle-income countries. But the distribution of growth also matters a great deal for low-income countries.

Sub-Saharan Africa demonstrates the point. One consequence of economic stagnation for the region has been a rise in the growth rate required to achieve the MDG target of halving poverty. Some countries—Ethiopia, Senegal, South Africa and Tanzania among them—need to grow at about 3% per capita a year to reach the target. However, analysis based on household surveys (in countries accounting for 78% of the region's population) suggests that the weighted average annual growth rate required to achieve the MDG for the region is 5% per capita for 10 years.[27] This is in a region where the average annual growth per capita for 2000–06 is 1.6%. Even if the current recovery in some countries is sustained, for a large group of countries the MDG growth requirements are implausible.

Does this mean that Sub-Saharan Africa is destined to fail on the MDGs? Not if the region combines a more modest increase in growth with an improved pattern of income distribution.

The point can be demonstrated by reference to Kenya—a country that is unequivocally off track for halving extreme poverty by 2015. If Kenya were to achieve a 1% per capita growth rate on current distribution patterns, it would not halve poverty until 2030. Doubling the share of the poor in future growth even at the 1% per capita growth rate would enable Kenya to halve poverty by 2013, meeting the MDG target. In

other words pro-poor growth would reduce the time horizon for halving poverty by 17 years. The broader point here is that extreme inequality can constrain poverty reduction in low- and middle-income countries for the same reason: the smaller the poor's share of any increment to income the less efficient growth is as a mechanism for poverty reduction. In Viet Nam the ratio of average income growth to poverty reduction is approximately 1:1. For high inequality countries such as Bolivia and Zambia the ratio is about 1:0.5.[28] In other words, it takes twice as much growth to achieve the same level of poverty reduction.

These cases demonstrate that the quality and composition of growth matter as much as the quantity. As Sub-Saharan African governments seek to consolidate economic recovery, prioritizing the quality of growth has become increasingly urgent. There is a danger that on current growth patterns economic recovery will leave the poor behind. For example, Tanzania's success in raising overall growth has had a negligible impact on poverty rates. Average per capita incomes have risen 1.8% a year since 1995, but poverty has been falling far too slowly to achieve the MDG. Between 1991 and 2001 the poverty rate fell from 39% to 36%, with large underlying variations. Poverty levels have fallen sharply in Dar es Salaam, but only marginally in rural areas (figure 2.12). The problem: rural areas account for 82% of poverty.

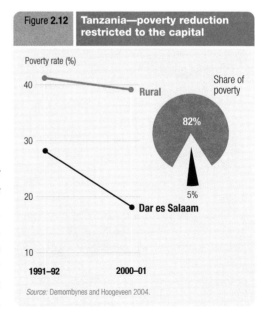

Figure **2.12** Tanzania—poverty reduction restricted to the capital

Source: Demombynes and Hoogeveen 2004.

Across much of Africa the challenge then is not just to accelerate growth, but to ensure that poor people contribute to the growth process, through increased output and rising productivity, and capture a bigger share of increments to growth than they do now. For public policy this means far more attention to smallholder farmers; to marginal, rain-fed agricultural areas; and to public investments to build the assets of the poor and the infrastructure serving them.

The role of the private sector is also critical for pro-poor growth. Small and medium-size enterprises in particular play a pivotal role—as employers, as suppliers of inputs and as a link to markets. Private firms can contribute to poverty reduction by empowering people, extending choice and providing a broad range of goods and services. In Bangladesh, GrameenPhone, the country's largest cellular phone service provider, operates a rural programme that serves more than 50 million people, enabling microenterprises to operate more efficiently by improving access to market information. Elsewhere, the absence of microenterprises can reduce competition, driving up costs of inputs and driving down prices for goods sold by communities in poor or remote areas. The high costs of government regulation and limited access to credit are among the major constraints on small-scale private enterprises' ability to operate as a more dynamic force for poverty reduction. On average, the cost of starting a company in Sub-Saharan Africa is 224% of average national income, compared with 45% in South Asia and 7% in high-income countries.

Accelerating poverty reduction globally

So far, we have looked only at the potential benefits of pro-poor growth in accelerating poverty reduction in individual countries. Using the global income distribution model outlined in chapter 1, we scale up this exercise. The model provides an approximation of the global distribution of income adjusted for purchasing power parity to take into account price differences across countries. We use the model to simulate what would happen to the global poverty trends set out in our projection to 2015 if people living below the poverty line captured a share of future growth that is double their current share—in effect, extending the national propoor growth model to the global stage. As in the national exercises, for countries with positive growth trends, we assume that the trend will continue. For countries with negative growth trends we use a positive growth projection based on regional averages for 2000–06.

The results of the simulation are striking (figure 2.13). Redistribution in favour of the poor has a marginal effect on overall world income distribution, but it has a marked effect on poverty. Under the pro-poor growth scenario in 2015:

- The number of people living in extreme poverty drops from 704 million to 446 million—a decline of one-third.
- The worldwide incidence of poverty falls from 10% to 6%.
- The pro-poor growth track reduces poverty sharply in all regions, though it also increases the share of poverty accounted for by Sub-Saharan Africa—an outcome that demonstrates the importance of boosting economic growth as well as improving distribution.

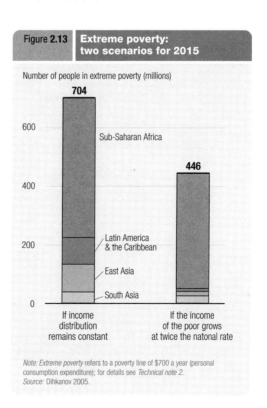

Figure 2.13 Extreme poverty: two scenarios for 2015

Number of people in extreme poverty (millions)

704

Sub-Saharan Africa

446

Latin America & the Caribbean

East Asia

South Asia

If income distribution remains constant

If the income of the poor grows at twice the natonal rate

Note: *Extreme poverty* refers to a poverty line of $700 a year (personal consumption expenditure); for details see *Technical note 2*.
Source: Dihkanov 2005.

Box 2.4   Targeting child poverty reduction in the United Kingdom

In most developed countries poverty is measured in relative terms rather than absolute terms. This means that the benchmark for measuring poverty—and poverty reduction—is usually defined in relation to average or median income. It follows that when governments set targets for reducing poverty, they are targeting changes in distribution that involve narrowing the gap between the poorest end of the income distribution and the benchmark.

Experience in the United Kingdom highlights some of the problems associated with reducing relative poverty. At the end of the 1990s the UK government set ambitious targets for reducing the incidence of child poverty, thus putting the issue of distribution at the centre of government policy. Child poverty in this context is defined as living in a household with income below 60% of the median after housing costs. Fiscal policy and targeting transfers to the poor have been central planks in measures aimed at achieving the target. However, labour market developments, including rising incomes at the top of the distribution, have pulled in the opposite direction.

At the end of the 1990s the United Kingdom had one of the highest rates of child poverty in Europe. In 1998 some 4.6 million children—around one in three—were living below the poverty line. These high poverty levels, double those at the end of the 1970s, were a legacy of the 1980s—a decade characterized by a distinctly pro-rich growth pattern that left poor people behind. At the end of the 1970s the richest 10% of the population received 21% of total disposable income. Twenty years later it received 28%, nearly as much as for the entire bottom half of the population. Average annual incomes for the richest 20% increased at about 10 times the rate for the poorest 20% (3.8% compared with 0.4%). The United Kingdom's Gini coefficient climbed from 25 to 35 by the mid-1990s—one of the biggest increases in inequality in the world.

Two main forces drove the rise in inequality: changes in the underlying distribution of earnings, and the impact of government policies that cut taxes for higher earners and lowered benefits for the poor.

While the rise in inequality stabilized at high levels by the early 1990s, child poverty remained exceptionally high by historic standards. More than one in four children still lived below the poverty line during the economic boom of the late 1990s, reflecting a further rise in the Gini coefficient.

In 1999 ambitious targets were announced for eradicating child poverty within a generation. The first stage was to reduce child poverty by a quarter from the 1998 level by 2004–05 and then to halve it by 2010.

Fiscal redistribution has played a central role in strategies for meeting the target. Large increases in financial support for families with children have been introduced. Most of the extra spending was directed to in-work benefits and tax credits that boosted the incomes of low-income working families with children. Out of work income benefits were also increased for families with children.

The gains for the poorest families have been considerable. The Institute for Fiscal Studies estimates that the incomes of the poorest fifth have risen by over 20% as a result of the reforms between 1997 and 2004. While government has played down the redistributive effect, that effect has been pronounced. Labour market effects have also had a bearing on progress towards the targets. As the United Kingdom's jobless rate fell to historic lows from the end of the 1990s, wage gains at the lower end of the spectrum contributed to substantial falls in relative child poverty. By 2003–04, 600,000 fewer children were living in poverty than in 1998.

Impressive as the decline has been, prospects for meeting the target remain uncertain. Another 400,000 children will have to be lifted out of poverty over the next year to achieve the 2004–05 target. The next target—halving child poverty by 2010—will prove even more challenging. Why has it been so difficult to achieve the target even with strong fiscal redistribution?

The answer is because fiscal policy has its limits. While fiscal transfers have reduced inequality since 1997, labour markets and other changes appear to be pulling in the other direction. Income levels are rising at below the median rate among roughly the poorest 15%. Meanwhile, the overall level of inequality now remains effectively unchanged from its 1997 level.

Beyond the labour market, analysis by the Institute for Fiscal Studies shows that much of the rise in the United Kingdom's child poverty rate is accounted for by the changing relative position of families in the income distribution. For example, the number of single-parent families and families where both parents are jobless has risen sharply. Both factors are strongly associated with poverty. This suggests that meeting the 2010 target will require more redistribution, a change in working and employment patterns among parents and more fundamental changes to the underlying distribution of earnings and incomes.

The importance of changing the distribution of earnings can be demonstrated by reference to a variant of the pro-poor growth model used elsewhere in this chapter. As noted earlier, the 1980s was a pro-rich decade, with incomes at the top end of the spectrum rising far more rapidly than those at the bottom end. In an exercise carried out for the *Human Development Report* the Institute for Fiscal Studies simulated what would happen to child poverty over the next 10 years if the distribution pattern of the 1980s were reversed. So, for example, the income of the poorest 10% was estimated to grow at 3.7% a year, the average rate of growth experienced by the richest 10% between 1979 and 1990, while the richest 10% was estimated to grow at 0.4%, the average growth of the poorest 10% between 1979 and 1990.

The distributional shift would have cut the incidence of child poverty from 23% to 17% by 2010 (see figure). While this is still above the 2010 target, the simulation does not take into account the potential for fiscal policy to close the gap. In other words, if the next 10 years did for the poor what the 1980s did for the rich, that

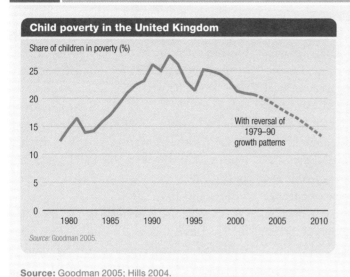

Child poverty in the United Kingdom

Share of children in poverty (%)

With reversal of 1979–90 growth patterns

Source: Goodman 2005.

would bring the United Kingdom within touching distance of the child poverty goals.

Developments in the United Kingdom raise poverty issues that are different in character than those associated with the MDGs, though with some striking similarities. Perhaps most obviously, the setting of targets has brought a crucial human development problem to the centre of public policy debate. The target itself signals an important message about government priorities. Fiscal policies have been geared towards that priority. At the same time, the wider social and economic forces shaping income distribution patterns during a period of high growth and low unemployment are slowing progress towards the target. Ironically, economic success, combined with the limits to fiscal redistribution, can raise the absolute income of the poor without accelerating progress towards child poverty reduction.

Source: Goodman 2005; Hills 2004.

Relative poverty in rich countries

These simulation exercises look at absolute poverty. The effects of growth on distribution depend on the definition of poverty used. Distribution effects are stronger for a relative definition of poverty for the obvious reason that the poverty indicator becomes a function of distribution. Ultimately, the decision about the appropriate measure is a value judgement.

Most rich countries define poverty in relative terms. Child poverty is a particularly sensitive indicator for income poverty in rich countries. It provides an insight into the scale of deprivation, and it is also an indicator for inherited disadvantage and the transmission of poverty across generations. For 17 of 24 OECD countries in the 1990s research by the United Nations Children's Fund shows a rise in child poverty, defined as living in a family with an income below 50% of the national median.[29] This means that 40–50 million children are growing up in poverty in the world's richest countries. Two OECD members—Mexico and the United States—have the dubious distinction of having child poverty rates of more than 20%. The United Kingdom has had some recent success in reversing a rapid rise in child poverty. Redistribution through fiscal transfer has played a central role, suggesting that pro-poor spending can be a potent force for reducing child poverty.

But it also demonstrates that wider forces shaping income distribution, notably labour market inequalities, are difficult obstacles to overcome (box 2.4).

Achieving pro-poor growth

What emerges from the simulation exercises presented in the previous section is that policies and growth patterns that improve distribution can be powerful weapons in the fight against poverty. Of course, not all policies to improve distribution are inherently good for growth— and low levels of inequality are not a substitute for accelerated growth. But policy-makers are not always forced to make trade-offs—many strategies for narrowing inequality will have positive effects on growth. This suggests that increasing poor people's share of growth should be a central part of strategies for achieving the MDGs and wider human development goals (see box 2.3).

There is no single path for achieving this objective. Closing gaps in educational opportunity is a critical starting point. In almost all countries inequalities in education are among the most powerful drivers of inequalities in income, health and opportunity, including opportunities to participate in society and influence political processes. Education has the potential to act as an equalizer of opportunity, as well as a force for economic growth and efficiency. But that potential can only be unlocked through public policies that systematically remove the social, economic and cultural barriers facing disadvantaged groups. Similarly, deep inequalities in health and the increased vulnerabilities associated with unequal access to healthcare are associated with deep differences in opportunities. Repeat episodes of ill-health undermine productivity, diminish the ability of children to benefit from education and lock households into cycles of poverty. As in the education sector, overcoming these inequalities in health requires public investment to increase the supply of good quality education, and measures to reduce obstacles to demand.

Inequalities in income reflect the distribution of assets and opportunity and the operation of markets. But they are influenced by government taxation and spending. In many countries fiscal transfers are already narrowing extreme inequalities. In Chile, for example, they narrow the gap between the income ratios of the richest and the poorest 20% of the population from 20:1 to 10:1. From a human development perspective the fiscal transfers with the highest returns are investments that build capabilities and provide protection during periods of acute vulnerability (box 2.5).

An obvious requirement for meaningful fiscal transfers to alleviate poverty is the willingness—and capacity—of the state to

---

Box 2.5   Public investment in social transformation

At the end of the eighteenth century the great thinkers of the European Enlightenment advocated ambitious social programmes to reduce inequality and poor people's vulnerability and dependence on welfare—with a central role for public policy in financing the needed socially transformative investments. The ideas remain profoundly relevant.

In France Antione-Nicola de Condorcet set out a bold plan for eradicating all inequality "entailing either poverty, humiliation or dependence". The plan saw publicly financed education, protection against sickness and old-age pensions as the key to social progress. The practical application of this approach in England was set out in Thomas Paine's *Rights of Man,* which advocated a system of universal insurance financed through taxation. Underpinning these approaches was the idea that public policy needed to create a sustainable exit from poverty by equipping people with the assets, security and opportunities needed to break out of the cycle of poverty.

Well designed fiscal transfers provide more than temporary relief. They provide a redistributive mechanism through which investments in poverty reduction can yield human development and economic returns far greater than the initial investment. Among the strategies:

- *Income transfers to vulnerable groups.* Income transfers enable policy-makers to raise the income of vulnerable groups. Take South Africa's old-age pension system, for example. Originally intended to provide benefits for white people, it has been extended to elderly black people and to vulnerable families with children. In 2001 the payment was over 80% of the welfare budget. Transfers have been instrumental in lowering income inequality (South Africa's Gini coefficient fell from 67 in 1991 to 59 in 2000). The payments have enabled households to secure credit and invest in productive activities (hire equipment,

buy improved agricultural inputs), refuting the idea that social transfers crowd out private initiative. The transfers have also resulted in tangible health gains. Among black children under age 5 these transfers have led to an estimated 8 centimetre increase in height—equivalent to six months' growth.
- *Employment-based transfers.* Transfers linked to employment can provide vulnerable households with security during periods of extreme stress—in the aftermath of drought, for example. The Maharashtra Employment Guarantee Scheme is one of the best known examples. Since the mid-1970s it has provided agricultural labourers and small farmers with up to 100 days in paid employment on rural works programmes. Women account for just under half the beneficiaries. Extending the programme to the whole of India would cost an estimated 0.5%–1% of national income in transfers to 40 million rural labourers and smallholders. If effectively targeted, this would lift most of the recipients above the poverty line.
- *Incentive-based transfers.* Governments can use fiscal transfers to promote wider human development goals. In Mexico the Oportunidades programme targets income transfers to households in vulnerable municipalities, with eligibility being conditional on children attending school and visiting health clinics. More than 5 million families are covered, and there is strong evidence of improvements in school attendance, nutrition and income status: recent evaluations suggest that more than 60% of the transfers reach households in the poorest 20% of the population. The programme currently costs 0.2% of GDP. Low income is not a barrier to incentive-based transfer. Several very poor countries have used such systems, for example to increase girls' participation in school (see box 1.7 on Bangladesh).

Source: Jones 2004; Lund 2002, 2004; ODI 2004; Case and Deaton 1998; Indiatogether.org 2004; Coady, Grosh and Hoddinott 2004; Coady and Parker 2005; Mexico, Secretaría de Desarrollo Social 2005.

mobilize revenue. In much of Latin America aversion to taxation restricts this condition. Mexico raises only 13% of GDP in revenue—less than Senegal does. India's capacity to redistribute the benefits of higher growth through the fiscal system is similarly constrained by a tax to revenue ratio of only 10%. After two decades of growth that ratio has not increased.

Fiscal transfer is one mechanism for raising the income of the poor above the level dictated by current growth and distribution patterns. More broadly, pro-poor growth requires a public investment focus on the markets in which poor people operate. In many countries the challenge is to shift the policy focus to the smallholder producers and to the more marginal areas that account for the bulk of poverty. The problem is that the production of food staples and cash crops in poor areas is constrained by limited access to markets, high transport costs and restricted access to credit. Compounding this problem, poor people—especially poor women—lack the assets, legal entitlements and political power needed to raise productivity and income.

Control over assets is critical. It is sometimes argued that there is a potential trade-off in agriculture between greater equity through land reform and greater growth. Here too the trade-offs are more apparent than real. Redistributive reforms in agriculture have proven results in reducing poverty, leading to major advances in countries such as China, the Republic of Korea and Viet Nam. In West Bengal, India, agricultural output and incomes rose following tenancy reform and recognition of the land rights of the poor. The contrast with Pakistan is striking. The *Pakistan National Human Development Report* found that the poorest tenant farmers pay 28% of the value of their production to landlords, while other tenant farmers pay 8%.[30] Cash and crop transfers from poor tenant farmers to landlords are a major source of income poverty. Many of the payments are disputed. Yet the poor do not use the legal system to pursue claims. The main reason: the median cost of a dispute is 20% higher than the annual average household income of the poorest tenant farmers.

*   *   *

The central message of this chapter is that distribution should be put at the centre of strategies for human development. At a national level this implies that plans for achieving the MDGs, including the Poverty Reduction Strategy Papers that set out a framework for cooperation between developing countries and aid donors, should include measures for redressing extreme inequalities. The MDG agenda needs to go beyond national averages to address the structural inequalities linked to wealth, gender, location and assets that are hampering progress in human development. Governments should expressly commit themselves to targets for reducing inequality and gaps in opportunity, in addition to aggregate MDG targets.

At a global level the international community needs to act on the commitments made in the Millennium Declaration to overcome extreme international inequalities. International action cannot compensate for poor governance and bad national policies. But it can create an enabling environment in which governments committed to human development can succeed. The rest of this Report focuses on three pillars of international cooperation that need reconstruction for human development: international aid, trade and the prevention of violent conflict.

3

AID FOR THE 21ST CENTURY

"Hunger is actually the worst of all weapons of mass destruction, claiming millions of victims every year. Fighting hunger and poverty and promoting development are the truly sustainable way to achieve world peace....There will be no peace without development, and there will be neither peace nor development without social justice."

Brazilian President Luiz Inácio Lula da Silva [1]

CHAPTER 3

Aid for the 21st century

> "This growing divide between wealth and poverty, between opportunity and misery, is both a challenge to our compassion and a source of instability."
>
> **US President George W. Bush** [2]

International aid is one of the most powerful weapons in the war against poverty. Today, that weapon is underused and badly targeted. There is too little aid and too much of what is provided is weakly linked to human development. Fixing the international aid system is one of the most urgent priorities facing governments at the start of the 10-year countdown to 2015.

This chapter sets out an agenda for rethinking international aid that is relevant to rich countries and poor countries alike. Many people equate aid with charity—a one-way act of generosity directed from high-income countries to their low-income counterparts. That belief is wrong. Aid should be thought of as a hand up, not a hand-out—and as an investment in shared security and shared prosperity. By enabling poor people and poor countries to overcome the health, education and economic resource barriers that keep them in poverty, aid can spread the benefits of global integration, expanding shared prosperity in the process. It can also reduce the mass poverty and inequality that increasingly threaten the collective security of the international community.

Aid has not always played a positive role in supporting human development, partly because of failures on the side of aid recipients and partly because donor countries have allowed strategic considerations to override development concerns. But whatever the failings of the past, today there are new opportunities for reshaping development assistance. For the first time in history there is an international consensus that human development should be the primary objective of aid. That consensus was reinforced in March 2002 when world leaders, gathered at the International Conference on Financing for Development in Monterrey, Mexico, agreed to make aid one of the building blocks of a new "global partnership" for poverty reduction.

Three years later, the scorecard on delivery is, at best, mixed. It would be wrong to understate what has been achieved. When the Millennium Declaration was signed in 2000, international aid budgets were at an all-time low as a share of national income. Aid to Sub-Saharan Africa, the world's poorest region, was lower at the end of the 1990s than at the start. Allied to these problems in aid quantity, serious problems in aid quality were not being addressed, undermining aid effectiveness and imposing huge transaction costs on recipient governments. Today, aid budgets are rising despite the severe fiscal and public debt problems facing some donor countries, and an intensive dialogue is under way aimed at improving aid quality.

The rise in aid has been particularly marked. Official development assistance increased by $12 billion from 2002 to 2004. The United States, the world's largest aid donor, has announced the biggest increases in its national aid programmes since the 1960s. It accounts for $8 billion of the increase in development assistance, although admittedly the increase has been from a low base measured in terms of aid as a share of national income, and it includes large aid transfers for Afghanistan and Iraq. Meanwhile, countries in the European Union have also set targets for a step increase in development assistance.

In terms of targets set, the aid quality debate has also delivered some impressive results. In March 2005 donors agreed on a wide-ranging

As rich countries ratchet
up aid flows, they need
to ratchet down the
transaction costs

framework for enhancing aid effectiveness through greater emphasis on harmonization, coordination and country ownership. The Paris Declaration on Aid Effectiveness incorporates some 50 commitments to improve aid quality, with progress to be monitored against 12 indicators.

These are encouraging developments. At the time of the Millennium Declaration the aid glass was three-quarters empty. It is now half full and rising. The Group of Eight (G-8) summit in 2005 provided a further boost to development assistance in the form of additional debt relief and new commitments on aid. Monitoring delivery against these commitments is a priority. But even a three-quarters full aid glass will not bring the Millennium Development Goals (MDGs) within reach, especially if resources do not come on-stream for several years. Having signed up for the Millennium Declaration, from which the MDGs emerged, donor governments have failed to align their development assistance programmes with the requirements for achieving the targets. The most immediate indicator of misalignment is a large—and growing—financing gap. Without an increase in aid, by 2010 the shortfall between aid needed to achieve the MDGs and actual delivery will reach more than $30 billion. Failure to close this gap will compromise progress towards achieving the MDGs. Yet several major donors have not put in place the necessary spending plans, calling into question their commitment to the MDGs.

The record on aid quality is also mixed. Poor countries need aid that is delivered in a predictable fashion, without too many strings attached and in ways that minimize transaction costs and maximize value for money. All too often they get aid that is unpredictable, hedged with conditions, uncoordinated and tied to purchases in donor countries. We estimate the costs of tied aid at $2.6 billion a year for low-income countries—a tied-aid "tax" of about 8%. That tax costs Africa alone $1.6 billion a year—a huge diversion of resources from investments in poverty reduction.

Not all of the problems in aid can be traced to the donor side of the equation. Many developing countries have put planning for poverty

reduction and the MDGs at the heart of public policy. Too often, however, a failure to translate MDG commitments into effective action undermines aid effectiveness. Weak governance, corruption and a failure to adopt policies that sustain economic growth reduce the human development returns to aid investments. This chapter focuses on donors, but it recognizes that effective aid requires a partnership of shared responsibilities and obligations.

Two simple messages emerge from the analysis in this chapter, one on aid financing and one on aid structures. First, without a sustained increase in aid, the MDGs will not be achieved. The time for incremental change is past. If donor countries are serious about tackling global poverty, reducing inequality and securing a safer and more prosperous future for their own citizens, they need to set their sights firmly on the target of delivering 0.5% of their national income in aid by 2010 and 0.7% by 2015. More aid is no guarantee of development—and concerns about the capacity of poor countries to absorb and deploy aid effectively have to be taken seriously. But increased aid is a necessary condition for accelerated progress towards the MDGs—and there is clear evidence that many countries can absorb far more aid than they are now receiving.

The second message is that more aid delivered through current aid structures will yield suboptimal results. As rich countries ratchet up aid flows, they need to ratchet down the transaction costs that reduce aid effectiveness. That does not mean compromising on fiduciary responsibility to taxpayers. But it does mean ending tied aid, reducing the volatility and unpredictability of aid flows and rethinking the scope of conditionality. More aid will produce better results only if it is delivered though streamlined management structures that are more accountable to developing country governments and their citizens.

The case for increasing and improving aid is reinforced by the huge—and growing—potential benefits. In the past various factors have diminished the impact of aid on human development—cold war politics, the use of aid to promote commercial objectives in donor countries, the absence of effective national poverty reduction strategies, corruption and economic mismanagement all contributed. It would be naïve to claim that all of these problems have disappeared. Yet the policy environment has improved dramatically, as have the human development returns to aid. This is a moment when a step increase in aid could transform prospects for the MDGs.

The balance of responsibility and obligation between aid recipients and aid donors also needs attention. Developing countries wanting aid must set targets linked to the MDGs, undergo budget monitoring by the International Monetary Fund (IMF) and comply with extensive conditions. Yet donors, the other party to the "new partnership", can with impunity fail to meet targets for increasing aid quantity (including those that they have stipulated) and ignore the vague principles that they have set for improving aid quality.

New approaches to aid are affordable and achievable. The starting point is for donors and aid recipients to agree on a financial needs assessment that identifies the aid requirements for achieving the MDGs. Donors then need to provide predictable, multiyear funding to cover these requirements, and developing countries need to implement the reforms that will optimize returns to aid. Overcoming capacity constraints in recipient countries is vital.

At one level aid is a simple transfer of finance from rich to poor countries. At another it is an indicator of something more fundamental. The aid policies of rich countries reflect how they think about globalization, about their own security and prosperity and about their responsibilities and obligations to the world's most vulnerable people. Ultimately, aid policies are a barometer for measuring the rich world's tolerance for mass poverty in the midst of plenty.

Mahatma Gandhi, when asked how policymakers should judge the merits of any action, replied: "Recall the face of the poorest person you have seen, and ask yourself if the step you contemplate is going to be any use to them."[3] With 10 years to go to the MDG target date, that advice should resonate in current debates on aid. Declarations of commitment to the MDGs are of little use to the world's poor people unless backed by real financial commitments and real improvements in aid quality. Having specified the ends in the Millennium Declaration, rich countries must now play their part in delivering the means.

The first section of this chapter briefly sets out the case for aid in an increasingly interdependent world. It highlights the pivotal role that aid can play as an investment in human development. The chapter then looks at the record on aid quantity and reviews trends since the Monterrey conference. The third section turns to aid quality, as measured by indicators of predictability, transaction costs and tied aid. The chapter concludes with a review of important governance issues raised by reform of international aid.

Rethinking the case for aid

The current aid architecture, like the global security architecture discussed in chapter 5, was established more than half a century ago. Like the security architecture, it also suffered through the distortions of the cold war. Fifty years later, it is time to ask fundamental questions about the role of aid in meeting the challenges of the twenty-first century.

Aid as moral imperative and enlightened self-interest

Part of the answer can be provided by a report written 175 years ago. During the 1830s, Britain's overcrowded industrial centres were swept by a wave of epidemics, prompting a government inquiry led by the great social reformer,

Edwin Chadwick. His report spelled out the human cost of neglect: "The annual loss of life from filth and bad ventilation are greater than the loss from death or wounds in any wars in which the country has been engaged in modern times."[4] Beyond these human costs the report drew attention to the efficiency savings of preventive measures: the expense of treating sickness and the losses associated with reduced labour productivity dwarfed the costs of providing public drainage. In an era of government aversion to raising taxes for public goods, it took another 20 years and a series of epidemics that threatened rich people as well as poor people to galvanize action. But Chadwick's report established the principle that social investment in a public good was imperative on grounds of morality and common sense economics.

The same logic underpins international aid today. Infectious diseases, security threats, illicit weapons and drugs, and environmental problems cross the borders separating rich countries from poor countries as readily as diseases crossed between rich and poor areas of Britain's major industrial centres in the 1830s. International aid in this context is an investment in public goods, such as reduced health and security risks.

Shared prosperity and reduced vulnerability provide other powerful rationales for aid. Episodes of crisis have acted as strong catalysts for the development of social insurance systems in industrial countries. US President Franklin D. Roosevelt responded to the Great Depression of the 1930s by establishing government employment programmes and income transfers, a "New Deal" providing millions of vulnerable people with employment and a source of security. The New Deal created the conditions for economic recovery, restored social cohesion and established a principle that remains central to human development: economic security has to underpin markets and individual freedom.[5] Thirty years later, in the mid-1960s, President Lyndon B. Johnson's "Great Society" programme declared an "unconditional war" on poverty, initiating a raft of legislation aimed at empowering people to work their way out of extreme deprivation (box 3.1). In both cases social protection went hand in hand with programmes to get people back to work.

Today, rich countries spend about a quarter of their wealth on social transfers.[6] These transfers are an investment in avoiding or reducing the waste and social dislocation associated with extreme deprivation. Global poverty also represents a massive waste of human potential and a barrier to shared prosperity. In a world tightly linked by trade and investment flows, poverty in one country diminishes the potential for prosperity elsewhere. Yet the international community lacks a credible global social insurance mechanism—a gap that development assistance could fill.

International aid is the point at which moral values and enlightened self-interest intersect. The moral imperative behind aid is reflected in many value-based systems of thought. Most major religions call on their followers to aid the poor. In Islam *zakat,* an obligation to give to those in need, is one of the five pillars of the

---

Box 3.1	The Great Society

US President Lyndon B. Johnson's Great Society speech in 1964 marked a new era in social legislation. It also set out principles that continue to resonate in debates on aid.

Underpinning the Great Society reforms was a simple idea: public action was needed to equip people with the skills and assets to escape cycles of poverty. Growth alone was not enough. Transfers to the poor were not just welfare payments but an investment in skills and in security against risk. Government programmes would empower people, providing a hand up, not a hand-out. As President Johnson put it: "It is not enough to open the gates of opportunity. All our citizens must have the ability to walk through those gates."

What followed was a raft of legislation—Medicare, Medicaid, the Economic Opportunity Act, education programmes for low-income groups and vocational training—aimed at supporting an exit from poverty and preventing entry into poverty. Between 1963 and 1967 the federal grant programmes behind the legislation doubled to $15 billion. The results were reflected in a period of falling inequality and rising mobility for previously excluded groups.

Good international aid has a similar rationale. It can equip poor countries and poor people with the education, skills and health assets needed to contribute to growth and to produce their way out of poverty and dependence. Assistance to economies such as Botswana, the Republic of Korea and Taiwan Province of China in the early stages of their development helped them escape dependence on aid and make the transition to higher economic growth and reduced poverty.

Source: Burnham 1989; Brown-Collier 1998; Johnson 1964; Advisory Commission on Intergovernmental Relations 1984 (table 75).

religion. The Christian tradition of the jubilee calls on creditors to write off debt. Other values systems also emphasize protecting vulnerable people and limiting inequality within communities. For the global community aid represents a mechanism for expressing human solidarity and for extending opportunity. Whether motivated by human rights, religious values or wider ethical systems, aid's role in eliminating mass poverty, hunger and avoidable child deaths is a moral imperative.

Enlightened self-interest underlies the security rationale for aid. Poverty does not automatically feed terrorism. Neither does inequality. Yet political leaders in rich countries increasingly recognize that failure to address the perceived injustices that perpetuate mass poverty in an increasingly prosperous global economy does pose a security threat. President Roosevelt in his last inaugural address in 1945 summarized what he saw as a central lesson of the Second World War: "We have learned that we cannot live alone, at peace; that our well-being is dependent on the well-being of other nations far away." That observation retains a powerful resonance. The threats posed by fragile and conflict-prone states are partly rooted in poverty but also in a perceived sense of injustice in a world order that allows wide divisions between haves and have-nots. As the current US National Security Strategy puts it: "A world where some live in comfort and plenty, while half of the human race lives on less than $2 a day, is neither just nor stable."[7]

Aid and human development

Controversies about the effectiveness of aid stretch back over several decades. Critics argue that the case for more development assistance is undermined by the limited benefits produced by the large amounts of aid disbursed during the past four or more decades. That claim demonstrates how a partial understanding of evidence can lead to flawed conclusions.

Assertions about aid's ineffectiveness based on the historical record are on shaky ground. Until the end of the cold war much of what passed as aid was, at best, tenuously connected to

human development objectives. Brutal, corrupt and inefficient regimes were shown a benign tolerance by donors less interested in development than in geopolitical goals. President Mobutu Sésé Seko of Zaire and President Ferdinand Marcos of the Philippines got wealthy, while their citizens were left with large debts. From Afghanistan to Central America and the Horn of Africa aid was part of the rivalry between East and West.

The motivations for the aid distortions of the cold war collapsed with the Berlin Wall. All aid did not suddenly shift towards well defined human development goals, however. Large amounts of aid are still spent on non-development objectives, such as disposing of agricultural surpluses or creating markets for companies in rich countries. Moreover, the "war on terror" risks bringing a new set of distortions to aid allocation decisions: some countries with dubious human development records, at best, are receiving windfall aid. Even so, for the first time in history donor countries have an opportunity to direct their aid towards the central goal of improving the human condition.

Reducing financing constraints

The MDGs provide benchmarks for measuring progress. However, as chapter 1 shows, on current trends most of the world's poorest countries will miss most of the targets. Financing constraints, rooted in low average incomes and pervasive poverty, limit the capacity of these countries to alter these trends. Aid can ease those constraints by providing governments with new investment resources.

To get a sense of the severity of the financing problem, consider the health sector. Average spending on health in low-income countries is about $11 per capita. In much of Sub-Saharan Africa the average ranges from $3 to $10. Meanwhile, the cost of providing basic healthcare is estimated at $30 a person. For a country like Mali, where more than half the population lives on less than $1 a day, it would cost an additional $26 per person—or about 10% of GDP—to finance this one goal.

Costing studies consistently point to a large financing gap for the MDGs, even if

Under the right conditions
aid can advance human
development

governments scale up spending and improve its efficiency. One study of financing requirements for universal primary education considered the financing implications if developing countries were to direct 4% of GDP to education, allocating half to primary education. For developing countries as a group the financing gap was about $5–$7 billion, with low-income countries accounting for $4 billion.[8]

Economic growth in developing countries can help to increase the domestic resources available for financing development. For many countries, however, capacity constraints impede economic growth. Inadequate access to basic infrastructure such as water, roads, electricity and communications limits opportunities for households, restricts private investment and constrains government revenue. The financing shortfall is greatest in the poorest countries. World Bank estimates suggest that Sub-Saharan Africa needs to double infrastructure spending as a share of GDP, from less than 5% to more than 9%. The UK-sponsored Commission for Africa puts the additional aid required at $10 billion a year for 10 years.[9] Failure to make this investment will perpetuate a vicious circle. Underinvestment in roads, ports, electricity and communication systems reduces growth, diminishes opportunities to participate in trade and lowers the revenue available to governments for future investment in infrastructure.

Factoring in financing requirements for the MDGs as a package demonstrates even more starkly the critical importance of external financing. Estimates by the UN Millennium Project, based on work in five low-income countries, put the financing requirements for achieving the MDGs at $40–$50 billion in 2006, rising to $70–$100 billion by 2015.[10] Tanzania, even with reasonable growth performance and increased government revenue collection, is facing a $35 per capita financing shortfall today—equivalent to more than 14% of average income. By 2015 the shortfall will be $85 per capita. In a country where the average annual per capita income is $100, this is a very large gap. Increased revenue collection from domestic resources could—and should—bridge part of this gap. But in countries with low average incomes and high levels of poverty there are limits to what can be achieved. If Ethiopia doubled the share of GDP it collects as revenue it would gain an extra $15 per capita—less than one-quarter of the estimated financing requirement for achieving the MDGs.[11] Ethiopia already raises 15% of gross national income (GNI) as revenue—far higher than the average for a country at its income level.

None of this diminishes the importance of national financing. Even with a severely constrained resource base, performance in developing countries varies. For example, Mozambique has mobilized 4% of GDP for public investment in health, which is more than double the level in countries such as Burkina Faso, Côte d'Ivoire, Mali and (at a far higher average income) Pakistan. In education Chad spends less than half as much of GDP as Ethiopia. However, in most regions—notably in Sub-Saharan Africa—there has been a clear upward trend in spending on health and education, partly supported by aid and debt relief.

The obvious question is whether aid is an effective complement to domestic revenues in countries unable to meet the costs of MDG financing. The answer is yes. Increased aid is not a panacea for low growth or for poverty. Not all aid works—and some aid is wasted. But under the right conditions (an important caveat) aid can advance human development through various channels. These range from macroeconomic effects—including increased growth and productivity—to the provision of goods and services vital for building the capabilities of the poor.

Increasing economic growth

Aid allows recipients to increase consumption and investment. It creates opportunities to raise living standards progressively through higher growth over time. Past cross-country research has tended to find a positive relationship between aid and growth.[12] That finding is strengthened when spending on emergency aid—by definition associated with countries in crisis—and spending on long-term assistance not linked to growth are removed. The Center for Global Development estimates that for the roughly one-half of aid flows that can be expected to generate "short impact" growth, every $1 in aid generates $1.64 in increased income.[13]

Country evidence confirms the potential for strong growth effects. High-growth economies in Africa such as Mozambique, Tanzania and Uganda depend heavily on aid to sustain investments in social and economic infrastructure. Mozambique has been growing at 8% a year since the mid-1990s, one of the fastest rates in the developing world. That growth could not have been sustained without net aid transfers per capita of $54—providing vital support for infrastructure and balance of payments.[14]

Improving the provision of basic services
Underfinancing of basic services such as health and education leads to weak coverage and poor-quality provision. Aid plays a critical role in financing the investments in health and education needed to build human capital.

Aid financing is a lifeline for basic service provision in many countries. In Tanzania external assistance constitutes more than one-third of social sector budgets. In Zambia health sector spending would fall from $8 per capita to $3 without aid, with devastating implications for the fight against HIV/AIDS and other public health problems. In Uganda foreign aid increased by 5% of GDP between 1997 and 2001, and per capita spending on health has tripled since 2000, with about half the health budget financed by donors. Several aid programmes have demonstrably reduced child deaths. In Egypt a national diarrhoea control programme supported by the US Agency for International Development (USAID) and the World Health Organization (WHO) helped reduce infant deaths by 82% in five years, preventing 300,000 child deaths.[15] Aid plays a central role in filling service delivery gaps. To achieve the 2015 MDG health and education targets, Sub-Saharan Africa alone will need an additional 1 million health workers, and eight countries in the region will need to increase the number of teachers by one-third or more.[16] Without increased aid, expansion on this scale is not feasible.

Cost barriers often prevent people from using basic services even when services are available. Aid can lower those barriers. In Tanzania an additional 1.6 million children enrolled in school after user fees were dropped in 2003 (box 3.2). In Uganda attendance at health clinics rose 80% when cost sharing in health was ended in 2002, with poor people capturing a large share of the benefits. Neither of these policy interventions would have been possible in the absence of aid financing. In Bangladesh aid has played a central role in financing school-based meals programmes designed to create incentives for parents to send their children—especially girls—to school. These programmes now reach more than 2 million children and have led to dramatic increases in school enrolments and progress towards gender parity.[17] Aid can also build demand by improving the quality of education. A recent review of World Bank support for education during 1988–2003 found that primary and middle school enrolments had risen by 10% and that test scores had improved by more than 60%,[18] gains in outcomes that were linked to improved classroom quality, access to textbooks and teacher training.

Box 3.2	Reducing cost barriers

The inability of poor people to afford basic services is a powerful driver of inequality—and a cause of poverty. Aid can increase demand for basic services by lowering costs.

In Tanzania an additional 1.6 million children enrolled in school between 1999 and 2003 because of aid-financed budget support to education. The government doubled per capita education spending and financed the transition to a system of free primary schooling.

Building on Tanzania's example, one of the first acts of the new Kenyan government in 2003 was to institute free primary education. Within a year an additional 1.5 million children were in school. Kenya has also created programmes to help poor households overcome cost constraints, such as the textbook fund and the school feeding programme. None of these investments would have been possible without increased aid.

In health, as in education, aid can reduce barriers by providing governments with the resources to reduce the cost of access. In 2001, as part of the national poverty reduction strategy, Uganda removed user fees for most lower level health facilities. In 2002/03 outpatient attendance rose by more than 6 million—an 80% increase over attendance in 2000. Attendance increased more sharply among poor people than among the better-off.

Source: Inyega and Mbugua 2005; Tanzania, Government of, 2004; World Bank and Republic of Kenya 2004; World Bank 2001.

Extending social insurance

The world's poorest countries have the greatest need for social insurance and the least capacity to finance it. Most low-income countries have exceptionally weak welfare provision. One consequence is that the poorest households are trapped in cycles of poverty, with low income, poor nutrition and vulnerability to shocks blocking exit from poverty.

Aid can help to break the cycle of poverty. Yet social insurance provision suffers from chronic underfinancing in aid. Programmes in this area have the potential to put resources directly in the hands of the poorest, most vulnerable households. Such programmes provide an international extension of the social welfare principle applied in rich countries, including the principle of enhanced equity. With donor assistance a pilot cash transfer scheme in Zambia targets the poorest 10% of the population, who cannot meet even the most basic nutritional standards. The

transfer—$6 a month—enables beneficiaries to have two meals a day, rather than one, with large spillover benefits for child nutrition and household livelihoods (box 3.3).[19] In Viet Nam health inequalities are widening despite the government's strong record on human development. In response the government has created Health Care Funds for the Poor (HCFP) to provide social insurance to households unable to meet health costs. Working closely with donors, the government has developed strategies to target the poorest social groups and the poorest regions, such as the Central Highlands. Aid accounts for less than 4% of GNI in Viet Nam, but more than one-quarter of the HCFP budget.[20] Without donor support the investment in health equity would be heavily underfinanced.

Supporting reconstruction

In poor countries emerging from civil conflict, aid financing can help create the conditions for peace and human development. Mozambique shows what is possible. More recently, aid has been central to the rapid social progress achieved in Timor-Leste, with development assistance now representing more than one-half of GNI. In Afghanistan more than 4 million children enrolled in school as a result of the government's "Back to School" campaign, and the government has ambitious plans to restore the public health system. Donor financing has been a critical ingredient for success, financing more than 90% of social sector budgets in Afghanistan.[21] In Liberia and Sierra Leone long-term aid investment holds the key to moving forward after settlements that brought to an end two of the world's most brutal civil wars.

Meeting global health challenges

Some of the great achievements in global public health were made possible by multilateral aid initiatives. In the 1970s targeted aid of some $100 million, largely from the United States, led to the eradication of smallpox. The continuing savings on vaccinations and treatment heavily outweigh the initial investment. Polio has been eliminated as a threat in the Western Hemisphere. In West Africa a programme

Box 3.3	Aid for social insurance in Zambia

About half of Zambia's population of more than 10 million people live on less than the minimum energy standard set by the food poverty line. Malnutrition threatens lives, reduces opportunities for earning income, undermines the education of children and increases vulnerability to ill health.

Working with the Zambian Ministry of Community Development and Social Services, the German Agency for Technical Cooperation (GTZ) developed a pilot cash transfer programme in the southern Kalomo district. Covering 143 villages and 5 townships, the programme targets the 10% of households identified as most destitute on the basis of criteria agreed and administered through community-based welfare committees. Two-thirds of beneficiary households are headed by women, most of them elderly. Two-thirds of household members are children, 71% of them orphaned by HIV/AIDS.

Transfers under the programme amount to $6 a month. The pilot programme covers 1,000 households. Initial evaluations of the programme, which started in 2004, point to some successes. School attendance has increased and targeted households have been receiving regular monthly incomes.

Scaling up the transfer scheme to cover 200,000 destitute households would imply an annual cost of $16 million, or about 4% of total aid flows to Zambia. What this scheme demonstrates is the potential for such programmes to provide a conduit for poverty-focussed redistribution programmes. Very small transfers from rich countries can generate significant gains for poor households in countries like Zambia. However, the success of such social insurance schemes depends critically on donors and governments working together over a long time horizon.

Source: Goldberg 2005; Development Initiatives 2005a.

supported by 14 donors has halted the spread of river blindness at a treatment cost of about $1 per person. So far 60,000 cases of blindness have been prevented, and 18 million vulnerable children have been protected.[22] Donors have committed $1 billion through the Global Alliance for Vaccination and Immunization since 2000, averting more than 600,000 deaths from vaccine-preventable diseases.[23]

From a different perspective these multilateral success stories highlight the extent of failure in other areas. More than 27 million children miss out on immunizations in the first year of life, and 1.4 million children still die each year from vaccine-preventable diseases. Malaria results in another 1 million deaths annually, and yet the global initiative to reduce this death toll—the Roll Back Malaria Campaign—suffers from chronic underfunding and has achieved little as a result. As the UN Millennium Project argues, this is an area in which aid can deliver "quick wins". For example, a global initiative to ensure that every child in a malaria-endemic region in Africa receives a free anti-malarial bednet by 2007 would be a low-cost route to saving up to 60% of the lives claimed by malaria. USAID has been developing public-private partnerships to address this challenge. In Ghana, Nigeria, Senegal and Zambia a public-private partnership supported through USAID's NetMark programme sold more than 600,000 insecticide-treated bednets.

However, these initiatives have yet to be scaled up to a level commensurate with the challenge.

Prevention through aid is a good investment as well as a humanitarian imperative. Apart from the human toll in lost lives and sickness, malaria reduces economic growth per capita by an estimated 1.3 percentage points a year in affected countries. This represents a severe handicap for achieving the MDG target of halving poverty. But the average figure understates the size of the handicap. Malaria cases are heavily concentrated among poor people: one study estimates that the poorest 20% of the world's population account for two-thirds of malaria cases.[24] In rural communities the malaria transmission season often coincides with planting and harvesting, leading to losses of output and income. Subsistence farmers suffer the heaviest burden because their margin for survival is so thin and their dependence on labour so critical. Even brief periods of illness can produce catastrophic consequences for households. Releasing households from the burden of malaria would generate high returns for poverty reduction as well as economic growth. Cutting malaria incidence by one-half in Africa would cost about $3 billion a year while generating an economic benefit of $47 billion a year.[25] That benefit is more than double total aid to Sub-Saharan Africa—and much of it would be concentrated in the hands of the poorest households.

Financing aid—the record, the problems, the challenge

The people of this country are distant from the troubled areas of the earth and it is hard for them to comprehend the plight and consequent reactions of the long-suffering peoples, and the effect of those reactions on their governments in connection with our efforts to promote peace in the world. The truth of the matter is that Europe's requirements are so much greater than her present ability to pay that she must have substantial additional help or face economic, social and political deterioration of a very grave character.
—George C. Marshall[26]

With these words at a Harvard University commencement ceremony in 1947 US Secretary of State George C. Marshall outlined his plan for European reconstruction. Over the next three years the United States transferred $13 billion in aid to Europe—equivalent to more than 1% of US GDP.[27] The transfers were driven partly by moral conviction, but also by the recognition that US prosperity and security ultimately depended on European recovery. The Marshall Plan provided a vision backed by a practical strategy for action.

At the end of the 1960s the Commission on International Development, convened by the World Bank under the auspices of former Canadian Prime Minister Lester Pearson, revived the spirit of the Marshall Plan.[28] It argued for donors to provide 0.7% of GNI in development assistance by 1975, asserting that "The fullest possible utilization of the world's resources, human and physical, which can be brought about only by international cooperation, helps not only those countries now economically weak, but also those strong and wealthy."[29] Thus, the case for the target was partly moral and partly enlightened self-interest.

Aid quantity

That argument retains relevance for current debates on aid. So, too, does the central principle of setting a target with a date for achievement. Without a schedule, targets risk remaining aspirations. In the 36 years since the Pearson report there has been no shortage of commitments to the 0.7% target, but rich countries have habitually failed to back promises with actions.

Aid targets and trends

Measured against the 0.7% target argued for in the Pearson report, let alone the standards set by the Marshall Plan, international aid in 2005 reflects a legacy of sustained underperformance. Aid is increasing, but from a low base—and financing still falls far short of what is needed to achieve the MDGs and wider human development goals.

At the 1992 United Nations Conference on Environment and Development (Earth Summit) in Rio de Janeiro, most donors revived their pledge to achieve the 0.7% target. They then spent the next five years cutting aid budgets as a share of national income to an all-time low of 0.22% in 1997. Aid flows stagnated until 2001, when a gradual recovery began. A key motivating event was the 2002 UN Conference on Financing for Development, where donors committed themselves to providing more—and better—aid.

Delivery on aid quantity commitments since then has been encouraging, but partial. In 2002 aid levels finally surpassed the 1990 benchmark. Provisional estimates for 2004 put aid at $78 billion, or some $12 billion higher than in 2000 in real terms. The recovery in aid volume looks less encouraging assessed against other benchmarks for generosity. In 1990 donors gave 0.33% of their GNI in aid. Since 2000 that share has climbed from 0.22% to 0.25% of GNI, highlighting the limits to aid recovery. From a longer term perspective those limits are even more starkly defined. As a share of GNI the weighted average for aid from Organisation for Economic Co-operation and Development (OECD) countries is one-third lower than at the start of the 1980s and one-half the level in the 1960s (figure 3.1). Translated into per capita aid receipts, much of the post-2000 recovery can be viewed as a process of restoring cuts. For Sub-Saharan Africa per capita aid fell from $24 in 1990 to $12 in 1999. In 2003 it was still just below the 1990 level.

Development assistance comes through a variety of channels. Aid today is roughly divided at a ratio of 2:1 between bilateral aid allocated directly by individual countries and multilateral aid allocated to concessional finance facilities

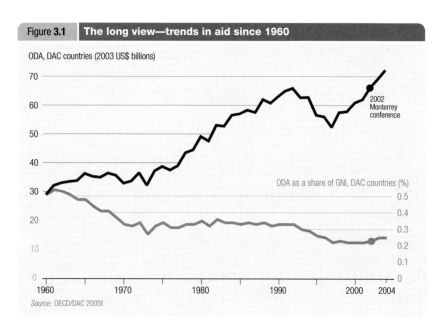

Figure 3.1 The long view—trends in aid since 1960

ODA, DAC countries (2003 US$ billions)

2002 Monterrey conference

ODA as a share of GNI, DAC countries (%)

Source: OECD/DAC 2005f.

such as the World Bank's International Development Association (IDA), regional development banks and global mechanisms like the Global Fund to Fight AIDS, Tuberculosis and Malaria. The Group of Seven (G-7) leading industrial countries dominates international aid flows, accounting for three-quarters of development assistance. That gives them tremendous influence on prospects for closing the MDG financing gap. Measured by the standards of their wealth, some of the world's largest economies are among the least generous donors. Only one member of the G-7 is among the top 10 donors when aid is measured as a share of GNI. The bottom three places in the donor generosity league as measured by this indicator are held by G-7 countries (figure 3.2).

In financial terms the United States is the world's largest donor. Since 2000 its ratio of aid to GNI has increased from an exceptionally low base of 0.10% to 0.16% in 2004. The United States has climbed above Italy, but it remains second to last in the share of aid to GNI. The steady decline in Japanese aid, which fell by another 4% in 2004, has pushed Japan into the third slot from the bottom. At the other end of the list five small countries—Norway, Luxembourg, Denmark, Sweden and the Netherlands—have consistently met or surpassed the UN target.

A new category of donors is emerging: the transition economies of Eastern Europe, which have graduated from being aid recipients to being donors. Their contributions are still relatively small—the Czech Republic, which gives 0.1% of GNI, is the most generous. Since acceding to the G-7, the Russian Federation has also emerged as a donor and contributor to debt relief in low-income countries. The Russian government is working with the United Nations Development Programme (UNDP) to create an aid agency (called, for now, RUSAID), and it too is set to become a more important player in international aid. With oil revenues rising, Arab states are also making a greater contribution to aid flows, with transfers reaching about $2.6 billion in 2003. However, the G-7 countries still account for 70% of official development assistance, an obvious corollary of which

is their influence on future aid levels and prospects for MDG financing.

Over the longer term rich-world prosperity has been inversely related to aid generosity. Since 1990 income per capita in rich countries has increased by $6,070 in constant prices,

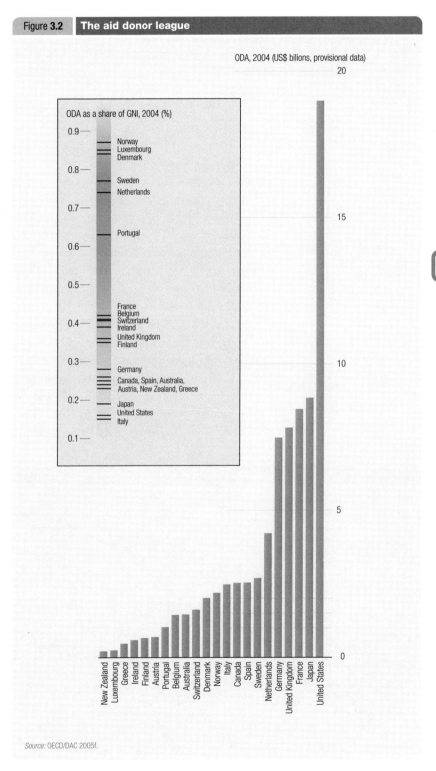

Figure 3.2   The aid donor league

Source: OECD/DAC 2005f.

while aid fell by $1 per capita (figure 3.3). The winners from globalization have not prioritized compensating the losers or spreading prosperity. Investment in aid per capita ranges widely in donor countries, from more than $200 in Sweden and the Netherlands to $51 in the United States and $37 (and falling) in Italy (figure 3.4). At constant prices four of the G-7 countries—Germany, France, Italy and Canada—are still giving less today than they were in 1992. Italy's 2004 aid spending was roughly one-half of its 1992 level.

At the 2002 Conference on Financing for Development in Monterrey donors agreed to collectively undertake "efforts to reach" the 0.7% target—words that stop some way short of a commitment (and with different meaning to different donors). However, as the Pearson report correctly identified, broad pledges without target dates are of limited use. Because effective planning for poverty reduction requires that resources be predictable, donors need to translate broad targets for increased aid into tangible budget commitments. Some donors have incorporated the 0.7% target into budget planning. Apart from the five donors that have achieved the target, another six have now set timetables, with varying degrees of ambition, for joining this group: including Belgium by 2010 and the United Kingdom and France by 2012–13.[30] Others—notably Japan and the United States—

have set no timetables. The United States has clearly stipulated that it does not see the 0.7% target as an operational budget commitment.

The galvanizing effect of the Monterrey conference is reflected in the fact that all donors have pledged to increase their aid budgets, though it took New Zealand until 2005 to make that pledge. The US Millennium Challenge Account was the centrepiece of a commitment to raise aid spending by 50%, or $4–$5 billion annually, by 2006. The European Union's 15 richest member states, building on a commitment made before Monterrey to achieve an aid to GNI target of 0.33% by 2006, agreed in 2005 to a supplementary minimum target of aid to GNI of 0.51% by 2010 as an interim step to meeting the 0.7% commitment by 2015. The 10 poorest members agreed to a 0.17% target for 2010 and 0.34% by 2015. The EU decision marks a bold step in the right direction. If honoured, the commitments could mobilize an additional $30–$40 billion in aid by 2010. Other commitments are more open ended. For example, Canada has set a target of doubling its 2001 aid level by 2010 and doubling aid to Africa by 2008. Even with these commitments, Canada's aid will reach only about 0.33% of GNI by 2010. While Japan has pledged to double aid to Africa, it has made no meaningful commitment on overall aid to GNI levels.

The impact of these pledges is already apparent in the increases in aid in real terms in every

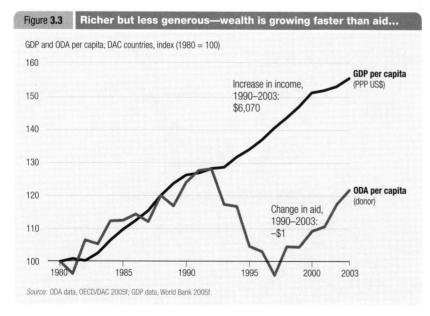

Figure **3.3** Richer but less generous—wealth is growing faster than aid...

GDP and ODA per capita, DAC countries, index (1980 = 100)

Increase in income, 1990–2003: $6,070

GDP per capita (PPP US$)

ODA per capita (donor)

Change in aid, 1990–2003: –$1

Source: ODA data, OECD/DAC 2005f; GDP data, World Bank 2005f.

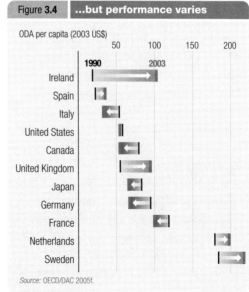

Figure **3.4** ...but performance varies

ODA per capita (2003 US$)

Source: OECD/DAC 2005f.

Aid for the 21st century

3

year since 2002, an increase of $6 billion (in 2003 prices and exchange rates). Aid has clearly emerged as a more important public spending priority. But while the trend of rising aid budgets appears firmly established, it cannot be taken for granted that donors will deliver completely on their Monterrey commitments. Italy's aid has fallen back to its 2001 level, a 30% drop since Monterrey. It will have to more than double current spending next year to meet the European Union's 2006 commitment. Germany froze spending in real terms in 2004 and faces a considerable challenge in raising aid from its current level of 0.28% of GNI to 0.33% by next year. Japan has also cut aid spending and will have to find an extra $1 billion by 2006 if its limited goal of keeping aid at the 2001–03 average level is to be achieved.

While the United States has sharply increased its aid budget, allocations under the Millennium Challenge Account have fallen short of administration requests. In 2005 Congress authorized $1.5 billion against a request of $2.5 billion. While all countries with per capita incomes below $1,435 are eligible, as of mid-2005 only two grants had been allocated. These were a $110 million programme for Madagascar to be disbursed over four years and a $215 million programme for Honduras to be disbursed over five years.[31]

Given the short time since the Monterrey conference, it would be premature to draw strong conclusions from trend analysis. Much will depend on whether governments translate current aspirations into hard budget choices. If achieving the 0.7% goal by 2015 were used as a benchmark, current performance would appear in a less positive light. Figure 3.5 shows where aid levels would be today in a hypothetical world where all donors set an aid to GNI target of 0.7% by 2015, assuming that their aid budgets increased by equal annual increments of aid to GNI ratios from 2000. The size of the gaps between current levels and the stylized target are self-explanatory. Admittedly, the exercise is an artificial one because not all donors accept the 0.7% target. Even so, it provides a useful point of reference. Even for donors that have committed to the 0.7% target, the gap

between performance and progress needed is large. However, the recent summit meeting of the G-8 leaders at Gleneagle in Perthshire, Scotland, proved that progress on bridging these gaps is possible (box 3.4).

Aid flows cannot be considered in isolation. This is especially the case for low-income countries facing debt service difficulties. In 2003 the 27 countries receiving debt relief under the Heavily Indebted Poor Countries (HIPC) Initiative transferred $2.6 billion to creditors, or 13% of government revenue.[32] These transfers have been diverting resources from investment in human development and economic recovery. In 2005, almost a decade after the creation of the HIPC Initiative, creditors finally agreed to a plan for writing off 100% of multilateral debt. This represents a huge step in the right direction. However, the new deal on debt does not adequately cover several countries—including

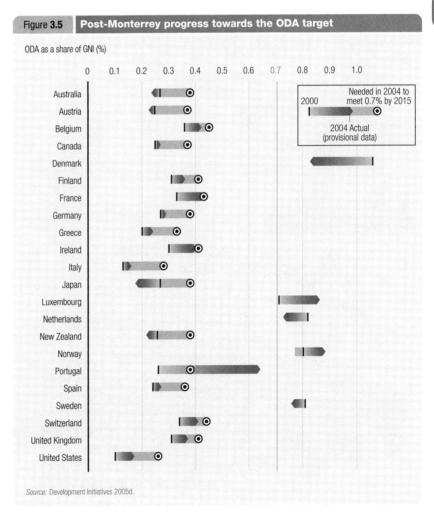

Figure **3.5** **Post-Monterrey progress towards the ODA target**

ODA as a share of GNI (%)

Source: Development Initiatives 2005d.

3

Aid for the 21st century

Box 3.4 **From the G-8 summit to the General Assembly—following up words with action**

Group of Eight (G-8) summits have a long track record in delivering lofty promises, that are swiftly broken, especially to the world's poorest countries. Will it be different after the July 2005 summit in Gleneagle, Scotland?

The G-8 communiqué makes some important commitments. The pledge to increase aid by $50 billion over 2004 levels, with half the increase going to Sub-Saharan Africa, could close a substantial part of the MDG financing gap. Moreover, for the first time the G-8 leaders have signed a communiqué specifying concrete targets, which may reduce the risk of backsliding.

Looking ahead, there are three challenges on aid. First, G-8 leaders must be held to their word. There is a real danger that at least two EU members—Germany and Italy—will not translate G-8 summit commitments into public expenditure plans. Second, some countries need to go much further. Even with aid increases Japan and the United States will still be spending only 0.18% of GNI on aid in 2010 (putting them at the bottom of the OECD aid table)—and Canada is also an aid underperformer. Third, it is important that a sizeable share of the increased aid commitment be delivered up-front, not in five years time.

Beyond aid, the G-8 communiqué receives mixed marks. The commitment to free and compulsory primary education, free basic health care and "as close as possible to universal access" to treatment for HIV/AIDS could accelerate progress towards the MDGs. So, too, could the pledge to train and equip some 75,000 troops for African Union peace-keeping operations by 2010 (see chapter 5). On trade, by contrast, the G-8 communiqué makes for unimpressive reading. The general commitment to phase out a limited range of agricultural export subsidies within an unspecified time-frame will come as cold comfort to Africa's farmers.

Two critical ingredients combined to make the G-8 summit in Gleneagle different: political leadership and the political momentum generated by global campaigning and public opinion. The same ingredients will be needed if the UN summit in September 2005 is to consolidate and build on what has been achieved.

Source: G-8 2005.

Figure 3.6 **The MDG financing gap**

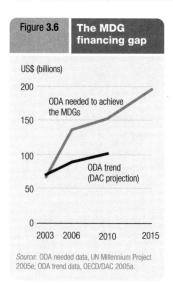

US$ (billions)

Source: ODA needed data, UN Millennium Project 2005e; ODA trend data, OECD/DAC 2005a.

Nigeria—for which unsustainable debt remains a barrier to achieving the MDGs (box 3.5).

The adequacy of current aid and debt relief efforts must be considered in the proper context. From an MDG perspective what matters is how current aid commitments square with the financing requirements for reaching the targets. Estimating MDG financing gaps is an inexact science. Cost structures vary widely from country to country, and there is a dynamic interaction among the MDGs: progress on, say, girls' education can reduce the costs of achieving progress on child mortality, for example. The UN Millennium Project estimates that overall aid will need to roughly double by 2006 and then rise by another 50% (to $195 billion) by 2015 to meet the MDG targets. Proposals set

out in a report by the UK-sponsored Commission for Africa are broadly consistent with this assessment.[33] They recommend a doubling over the next three to five years of the $25 billion in aid currently provided to the region, with a further $25 billion increase to 2015. Current aid projections fall far short of these levels.

Financing gaps. One of the problems with estimating the MDG financing gap is that the budget targets set by donors may not be achieved. If acted on—and this remains a big if—the pledges made during and after the Monterrey conference would result in aid budgets rising to 0.30% of donor countries' national income by 2006, an increase to $88 billion (at 2003 prices and exchange rates). That figure falls $47 billion short of the $135 billion that the UN Millennium Project estimates rich countries should be spending next year to keep the world on track for the MDGs (figure 3.6). The financing gap increases to $52 billion by 2010. By that point, if rich countries fail to follow through on their commitments, developing countries will be unable to make the investments in health, education and infrastructure needed to improve welfare and support economic recovery on the scale required to achieve the MDGs. Admittedly, these figures do not factor in the European Union's 2010 target of 0.51%, but this target is not yet enshrined in concrete budget commitments. It is also important to bear in mind that not all of the additional aid mobilized since Monterrey will be directed specifically towards MDG financing gaps.

Real aid and headline figures
If anything, the financing gap figures may understate the problem. Closing financing gaps requires real money, but not all of the money counted as aid translates into a transfer of resources. This is especially the case for the three categories of assistance that accounted for more than 90% of the $11.3 billion increase in bilateral aid between 2000 and 2004: debt relief ($3.7 billion), technical cooperation ($5.2 billion) and emergency assistance ($1.7 billion; figure 3.7). Increases in these areas generate headline figures that are larger than real aid transfers.

Box 3.5   Debt relief—going the extra mile

Twenty years ago, Julius Nyerere, then President of Tanzania, asked the governments of rich countries a pointed question: "Should we really starve our children to pay our debts?" Almost a decade after the launch of the Heavily Indebted Poor Countries (HIPC) Initiative was supposed to consign Africa's debt crisis to the history books, creditors have at last started to answer that question in the negative. While details of the debt relief deal agreed by the G-8 finance ministers in June 2005 remain sketchy, real progress has been made, though some important questions still have to be addressed.

Headline numbers on debt relief provided under the HIPC Initiative before the 2005 G-8 meeting were impressive. In total, 27 countries eligible for loans from the World Bank's concessional facility, the International Development Association (IDA)—all but 4 in Africa—were benefiting from debt stock reduction commitments valued at $32 billion (in net present value terms). The debt relief premium has helped advance progress towards the MDGs. According to the World Bank, public spending on health, education and other poverty reduction investments has risen by 2% of GDP in countries receiving debt relief. Savings generated through the HIPC Initiative have helped finance free primary education in Uganda and Tanzania, anti-HIV/AIDS programmes in Senegal, health programmes in Mozambique and rural development in Ethiopia.

The bad news was that the headline numbers on debt stock reduction obscured other parts of the balance sheet—notably the columns dealing with debt service and government revenue. In 2003 the 27 countries receiving debt relief still spent $2.8 billion in repayments to creditors. On average, that figure represented 15% of government revenues, rising to more than 20% in countries like Bolivia, Zambia and Senegal (figure 1). For a group of the world's poorest countries these were very large transfers, averaging some 3% of national income.

The upshot is that debt repayments have been diverting resources from social priority areas critical to progress towards the MDGs. For example, Zambia, with one of the highest levels of HIV/AIDS infection in the world, has been spending more than $2 on debt repayments for every $1 it allocates to health sector

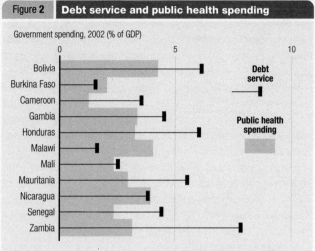

Figure 2   Debt service and public health spending

Government spending, 2002 (% of GDP)

Source: Calculated on the basis of data on debt service and public health expenditures from indicator table 20, data on population from indicator table 5 and data on GDP from indicator table 14.

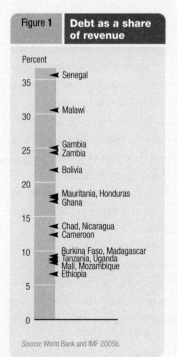

Figure 1   Debt as a share of revenue

Percent

Source: World Bank and IMF 2005b.

spending (figure 2). While aid flows continue to exceed debt payments (an important difference from the Latin American debt crisis of the 1980s), high levels of debt service have deprived HIPC governments of revenue and made them more dependent on aid—and their budgets more susceptible to the vagaries of donor priorities.

Delivery fell short of expectation under the HIPC Initiative for several reasons. First, the primary criterion adopted for debt sustainability—a debt stock threshold of 150% of exports in net present value terms—attached too much weight to export indicators and insufficient weight to the impact of debt on national budgets and capacity to finance progress towards the MDGs. Second, whereas most major bilateral creditors have been providing 100% debt relief, multilateral donors such as the World Bank, the IMF and the regional development banks have not, with the result that their share in debt service payments has been rising. Third, eligibility for full debt relief has been contingent on complying with IMF programmes and loan conditions. Interruptions to these programmes have delayed debt relief for a large group of HIPCs, including Honduras, Rwanda and Zambia.

Will the June 2005 agreement resolve these problems? The agreement provides for 100% debt relief for 18 countries that have passed through the full HIPC process to reach the "completion point". Crucially, it also stipulates that the costs for reducing multilateral debt owed to IDA and the Africa Development Fund will be met through additional finance from creditors, thereby avoiding the diversion of development assistance into debt relief. In the case of the IMF debt relief financing will be generated through internal resources, possibly including the sale or revaluation of part of the IMF's gold stock. Another eight countries will become eligible for 100% debt reduction in the next one to two years as they reach the HIPC completion point. This group includes countries embarking

(continued on next page)

Box **3.5** **Debt relief—going the extra mile** (continued)

on reconstruction—such as the Democratic Republic of the Congo and Sierra Leone—and countries like Cameroon and Chad that have had interrupted IMF programmes. For all of these countries the new debt relief deal has the potential to release new resources for development—and it is crucial for MDG financing that the resources be deployed efficiently to support social sector services and broad-based growth.

Implementation of the new agreement will need to be closely monitored to ensure that debt relief finance is genuinely additional. Particular concerns have been raised about the failure of the financing arrangements to cover the costs of debt reduction for the Inter-American Development Bank, which will need to meet part of the bill for financing debt relief in Bolivia, Honduras and Nicaragua. Nonetheless, for the 27 HIPCs now receiving debt relief the agreement is unambiguously good news.

More problematic is the question of how to deal with countries beyond this group. HIPC membership has now been closed on the basis of countries covered in 2004. Ironically, this means that some countries eligible for IDA loans have debt indicators that are worse than those of the HIPCs following HIPC debt relief and yet these countries do not qualify for debt relief on the grounds that they were not on the 2004 list. For example, Haiti, Kenya and Kyrgyzstan all have debt stock to export ratios that exceed 150%, yet they are not

eligible for debt relief. So far, individual creditors have responded unilaterally to the anomalies in the HIPC framework. For instance, the United Kingdom has developed proposals for cancelling its share of debt service payments owed by countries such as Armenia, Mongolia, Nepal, Sri Lanka and Viet Nam. Looking ahead, what is needed is a more coherent strategy for reducing debt obligations to a level consistent with MDG financing requirements.

Nigeria's experience highlights other limitations in the current debt relief framework. In contrast to the HIPCs, Nigeria owes the bulk of its debt—some 80% of the total—to bilateral creditors rather than to the World Bank or the IMF. Creditors have cited Nigeria's oil wealth as grounds for refusing debt relief. Yet although Nigeria is the world's eighth largest oil exporter, it ranks 158 on the HDI, has one of the poorest populations in Sub-Saharan Africa and receives less than $2 per capita in aid—one of the lowest levels for the region. Nigeria's annual debt service bill is more than $3 billion a year—exceeding public spending on health. Moreover, because less than half the external debt is being serviced, arrears are accumulating. True, Nigeria's debt problems could have been avoided had previous governments not indulged in economic mismanagement and transferred oil revenues to Swiss bank accounts. But this hardly provides a rationale for penalizing poor Nigerians today or for undermining a government committed to reform.

Source: World Bank and IMF 2004c; Martin and others 2004.

Consider debt relief. A highly effective form of development assistance, it gives governments greater control over domestic revenues and reduces their dependence on aid. Forgiveness of debts that are actually being serviced releases budget resources for other purposes. However, OECD reporting arrangements allow governments to report the entire stock of debt reduction as aid given in the year it is written off. This inflates the actual value of debt relief since the real financial savings to the recipient country come in the form of reduced debt servicing.

In cases where the debts were not being fully serviced, debt relief is in part an accounting operation. Much of the $4 billion increase in aid to the Democratic Republic of the Congo in 2003 fits into this category. Ethiopia received debt stock reduction under the HIPC Initiative of $1.3 billion in 2003, for a reduction in debt servicing of $20–$40 million a year. This is not an argument against debt relief but against current accounting practices that give a misleading

impression of how much aid donors are giving. Over the next few years large debt reduction operations are in prospect for Iraq and for countries under the HIPC Initiative. It is important that the high face value of these operations not divert attention either from the relatively modest budget savings that result or from the need to see debt relief as one part of a wider financing package for achieving the MDGs.

Many of the same arguments apply to technical assistance and emergency aid. Technical assistance accounted for $1 in every $4 in aid provided in 2003. Often, this assistance plays an important role in supporting development and building capacity, but much of it represents expenditure in donor countries—a problem compounded by tied aid (discussed later in this chapter). Aid to education demonstrates the problem. The greatest financing gaps are in training, remuneration and retention of teachers; construction of classrooms; and the provision of textbooks. Yet three-quarters of

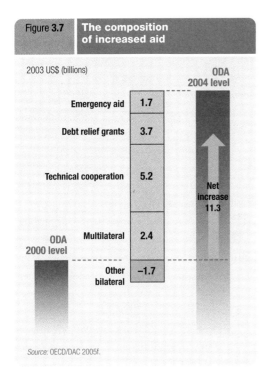

Figure 3.7 The composition of increased aid

2003 US$ (billions)

Emergency aid	1.7
Debt relief grants	3.7
Technical cooperation	5.2
Multilateral	2.4
Other bilateral	–1.7

ODA 2004 level

Net increase 11.3

ODA 2000 level

Source: OECD/DAC 2005f.

donor support to education comes as technical assistance. Much of this is swallowed up in payments for scholarships, external technical advice and consultancy fees. The quality of technical assistance varies widely, but as with debt relief the important point for MDG financing is that resources do not flow automatically into priority areas. Emergency aid, and assistance to fragile states, are a priority, but they are also a response to financing requirements over and above those estimated for the MDGs. Afghanistan and Iraq together accounted for $3.2 billion of the increase in official development assistance between 2001 and 2003—and for a large slice of the increase in aid from the United States. In fact, more than 40% of the $3.8 billion increase in U.S. development assistance in 2003 was earmarked for Iraq. To date, most of the increase in aid for emergencies has been through the mobilization of additional funds, though in practice additionality is hard to confirm. For example, Japan has combined increased aid for Afghanistan and Iraq with deep cuts in overall development assistance. Whatever the current position, the diversion of aid from MDG financing into post-conflict reconstruction or wider strategic objectives remains a real threat.[34]

Aid selectivity

Another reason that headline figures may understate the scale of the MDG financing problem is that donors vary in their aid allocation patterns. Low-income countries and Sub-Saharan Africa, which face the biggest financing gaps, figure more prominently in some aid programmes than in others (figure 3.8). Aid delivered through multilateral mechanisms such as IDA and the Global Fund to Fight AIDS, Tuberculosis and Malaria are probably the most strongly targeted at MDG financing gaps—in IDA's case because eligibility is largely restricted to low-income countries (box 3.6). This does not imply that aid to middle-income countries is not justified on human development grounds. But it remains the case that donors vary in the share of aid allocated to the poorest countries facing the most serious financing constraints for the MDGs.

Donor selection of preferred aid recipients affects the distribution of aid. A highly influential 1997 study argued on the basis of cross-country evidence that aid was effective only in "good" policy environments (fiscal stability, low inflation, open markets and other criteria).[35] That study led to the new orthodoxy that aid should be used selectively to reward strong reformers.

Figure 3.8 Donors vary in aid to the poorest countries

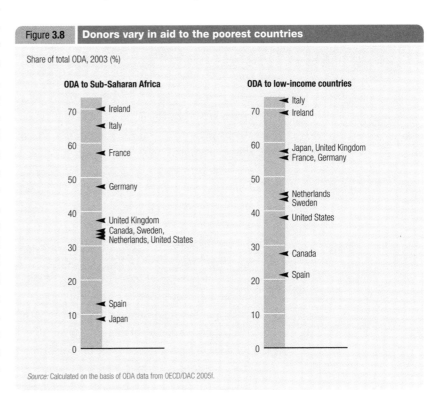

Share of total ODA, 2003 (%)

ODA to Sub-Saharan Africa

- 70 — Ireland
- — Italy
- 60 — France
- 50 — Germany
- 40 — United Kingdom / Canada, Sweden, Netherlands, United States
- 30
- 20
- 10 — Spain / Japan
- 0

ODA to low-income countries

- 70 — Italy / Ireland
- 60 — Japan, United Kingdom / France, Germany
- 50 — Netherlands / Sweden
- 40 — United States
- 30 — Canada
- 20 — Spain
- 10
- 0

Source: Calculated on the basis of ODA data from OECD/DAC 2005f.

Box **3.6** | **The future of the International Development Association**

As the international mechanism most effectively targeted to the poorest countries, the International Development Association (IDA) occupies a pivotal position in MDG financing: $1 given through IDA is more likely to reduce an MDG financing gap than $1 delivered through any other channel. Moreover, because IDA operates on a three-year budget cycle, it is less prone to the unpredictability associated with bilateral aid provided through annual budgets.

In 2005 donors allocated $34 billion to IDA through 2008—a 25% increase in real terms. This is the largest expansion in two decades, though far below the 40%–50% that most European governments wanted. Had the European proposals been adopted, that would have increased the multilateral share in aid and the share of aid earmarked for the poorest countries. IDA is the third largest source of aid to Sub-Saharan Africa (after France and the United States) and the main source of aid for education and health.

Important questions remain about IDA's future role in financing for development. About one-fifth of IDA loans are provided on grant terms to countries vulnerable to debt problems. The remainder is allocated as concessional loans: repayments over 40 years with a 10-year grace period. Some donors want to retain this balance. Others favour transforming IDA into a predominantly grant-based agency.

These are dangers in going down the grants-only route. Donors currently provide about one-half of IDA's income. Another 40% comes from repayments of past loans by countries like China, which have risen from low- to middle-income status. Moving to a grant system could choke off this flow of payments, reducing the resource base. Moreover, some countries—Bangladesh and India, for example—are in a position to use soft loans while others could use IDA to make a transition from reliance solely on grants.

There is another reason for caution. Donors could neutralize the financial effects by agreeing to compensate any loss of IDA repayments through binding commitments of increased grants. But no donors have done so. Without such guarantees of increased long-term financing, IDA flows would become dependent on unpredictable donor support.

Source: Rogerson 2005.

However, subsequent studies found that aid can also be effective in countries with a less favourable institutional environment and weaker economic reform record. This conclusion does not mean that the policy environment is unimportant: on the contrary, effective macroeconomic management is vital. But the evidence does caution strongly against using uniform "good policy" checklists as a basis for aid allocation.

Best evidence suggests that aid can be effective in a diverse range of environments—and that policy precondition blueprints are not helpful.[36] There is a danger of these blueprints dividing aid recipients into donor darlings and donor orphans based on flimsy evidence about their capacity to make good use of aid. This is already happening to some degree, with an overconcentration of donor darlings in Anglophone Sub-Saharan Africa (and Mozambique and Ethiopia) and an overrepresentation of donor orphans in Francophone Africa and Latin America.

Recent research using the World Bank's policy selectivity index, a measure of the correlation between aid and the quality of institutions in aid recipient countries, suggests that development assistance flows are increasingly sensitive to the quality of institutions (as defined in the index).[37] At the same time the donor focus on institutional performance is far more stringent in low-income countries than in middle-income countries. More worrying, some low-income countries receive aid at levels some 40% lower than their institutional capacity would indicate.[38]

None of this is to deny the obvious importance of the national policy environment in determining the effectiveness of aid. Countries as diverse as Bangladesh, Mozambique and Viet Nam are able to generate high human development returns for aid because they have effective strategies for poverty reduction. Conversely, endemic corruption, weak governance and economic mismanagement diminish the potential benefits of aid. Corruption undermines aid efforts in two respects. First, poor households suffer disproportionately from corrupt practices. A survey in Cambodia found that corruption cost low-income households three times as much of their income as it did high-income households, partly because low-income households depend more on public services.[39] Second, financial outflows associated with corruption can dwarf aid inflows: on one estimate public financial assets exceeding the value of Africa's external debt have been illegally transferred to foreign banks accounts.

Aid donors can most effectively address these problems through partnerships with governments committed to financial transparency and accountability rather than through the imposition of blueprints.

Aid and the MDGs: can rich countries afford them?

Can rich countries afford to deliver on their long-standing commitment to spend 0.7% of

GNI on aid? That question has a critical bearing on prospects for achieving the MDGs and wider human development goals.

In any democracy what governments regard as affordable will reflect an assessment of the costs and benefits of public spending. That assessment will be guided by judgements about political priorities mediated through political processes that lead to choices about the merits of competing claims. Aid budgets reflect how governments and the public view world poverty and their obligations and interests in combating it.

Affordable costs

Assessed against the wealth and resources of rich countries, the cost of achieving the MDGs is modest. More than 1 billion people in the world lack access to clean water and 2.6 billion to sanitation. Overcoming these deficits would cost just under $7 billion a year over the next decade. This investment could save some 4,000 lives each day as a result of reduced exposure to infectious diseases. It would address a problem that robs poor people of their health, undermines economic development and imposes huge demands on the time and labour of young girls and women. The investment required seems like a lot of money—and for low-income developing countries it is. But it is no more than the $7 billion a year that Europeans spend on perfume or the $8 billion a year that Americans spend on elective corrective surgery.

Such comparisons are not to deny the effort that will be required to increase aid on a scale commensurate with achieving the MDGs. In all of the G-7 countries—except Canada—fiscal deficits remain high—indeed, their fiscal position as a group has deteriorated (figure 3.9). The US fiscal deficit (as a percentage of GDP) is now the largest of any major industrial country except Japan. Current budget proposals envisage the halving of this deficit by 2009, with a reduction in non-military spending to its lowest share of GDP in over 40 years. Clearly, this is not a propitious environment for expanding aid budgets. The same is true for Japan, where the structural fiscal deficit is projected to decline only slightly, to just over 6% of GDP by 2006. Over the medium term Japan's budget plans

envisage converting the deficit into a surplus by 2010—a target that will translate into intense pressure for cuts in public investment.

The position in the European Union is scarcely more encouraging. Although fiscal deficits are smaller in the euro area than in Japan or the United States, both France and Germany have fiscal deficits exceeding 3% of GDP, while Italy's projected deficit will reach more than 4% by 2006. The smaller scale of fiscal deficits in the European Union than in the United States or Japan conceals three other underlying pressures. Public debt levels are high in the euro zone. The fiscal pressures associated with an aging population are mounting. And rates of joblessness have forced unemployment to the top of the political agenda of some countries. Since 2003 unemployment rates have been locked at more than 9% in France, Germany and Italy. While reforms to the European Union's Stability and Growth Pact have increased flexibility, EU governments are facing intense fiscal pressures in the context of low growth, high unemployment and mounting pressure on public spending. Against this backdrop the European Union's decision to set an aid target of 0.51% of GNI was an important political statement of intent. However, an exceptional effort will be required to ensure that the target is translated into hard budgetary commitments.

While the fiscal pressures facing G-7 and other industrial country donors are real, it is important to recognize that aid budgets, even at expanded levels, represent a modest source of that pressure. For two of the G-7 countries—Italy and the United States—development assistance accounts for 1% or less of public spending, far below the OECD average. In 2004 total aid budgets were equivalent to only 3% of the overall fiscal deficit for both Japan and the United States and 5% for Germany. Even if all the G-7 countries were to increase their aid to the EU target level, any detrimental impact on their fiscal position would be limited. Conversely, constraining aid spending will have a similarly marginal effect on improving that position.

In practice, how governments prioritize public spending, just as how they respond to fiscal pressures, will reflect their ordering of political priorities, as well as policy judgements

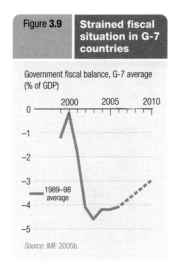

Figure 3.9 Strained fiscal situation in G-7 countries

Government fiscal balance, G-7 average (% of GDP)

1989–98 average

Source: IMF 2005b.

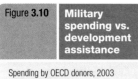

Figure 3.10 Military spending vs. development assistance

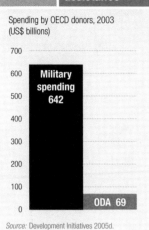

Spending by OECD donors, 2003 (US$ billions)

Military spending 642

ODA 69

Source: Development Initiatives 2005d.

Table 3.1 Military expenditure dwarfs official development assistance in rich countries

Share of government spending, 2003 (%)

Country	ODA	Military expenditure
Australia	1.4	10.7
Austria	1.1	4.3
Belgium	2.7	5.7
Canada	1.2	6.3
Denmark	3.1	5.7
Finland	1.6	5.4
France	1.7	10.7
Germany	1.4	7.3
Greece	1.4	26.5
Ireland	2.1	4.6
Italy	0.9	9.8
Japan	1.2	5.7
Luxembourg	3.9	4.8
Netherlands	3.2	6.5
New Zealand	1.2	6.3
Norway	4.1	8.9
Portugal	1.0	10.0
Spain	1.3	6.7
Sweden	2.8	6.4
Switzerland	3.5	8.5
United Kingdom	1.6	13.3
United States	1.0	25.0

Source: Calculated on the basis of data on ODA from OECD/DAC 2005f, data on military expenditure from indicator table 20 and data on government spending from World Bank 2005f.

on taxation, the scope of public investment and economic reform. If, as we argue in this chapter, increased aid is an imperative not just on moral and ethical grounds, but also in terms of the enlightened self-interest of rich countries, as reflected in the future prosperity and security of their citizens, then it is important to accord aid a far higher budget priority.

Military spending and aid levels

Comparisons with military spending are instructive. For every $1 invested in development assistance another $10 is spent on military budgets (figure 3.10). No G-7 country has a ratio of military expenditure to aid of less than 4:1. That ratio rises to 13:1 for the United Kingdom and to 25:1 for the United States (table 3.1). In a world where rich countries increasingly recognize that security threats are linked to global poverty, inequality and insufficient hope for large segments of the world's population, this 10:1 ratio of military spending to aid spending makes no sense. On any assessment of threats to

human life there is an extraordinary mismatch between military budgets and human need. The amount that rich countries currently spend on HIV/AIDS, a human security threat that claims 3 million lives a year, represents three days' spending on military hardware.

Budget priorities in many rich countries reflect neither an adequate commitment to the MDGs nor a coherent response to the security challenges posed by mass poverty and deep global inequalities. The discrepancy between military budgets and development budgets puts the affordability of the MDGs in a different light. Had the $118 billion increase in military spending between 2000 and 2003 been allocated to aid, development assistance would now represent about 0.7% of rich country GNI. Just $4 billion—about 3% of the increase in military spending—is needed to finance basic health interventions that could prevent the deaths of 3 million infants a year. If the war against poverty is a priority, it is simply not credible for governments to attach so little weight to aid budgets aimed at saving lives.

None of this detracts from the very real security threats that developed country governments have to address. These threats range from the proliferation of nuclear weapons to international terrorism. However, legitimate questions can be asked about whether military upgrading is the most effective response. For example, a comprehensive test ban treaty and a sharp reduction in operationally deployed nuclear warheads would eliminate the need for some of the extensive—and expensive—programmes now under way for modernizing nuclear forces and developing new launch vehicles. Investment of more political capital in negotiated disarmament and less financial capital in military hardware would enhance security and release resources for development.

Innovative financing

Various innovative proposals have been developed to bridge the MDG financing gap. These involve looking beyond public spending to private capital markets and new forms of financing.

The International Financing Facility (IFF) proposed by the UK government is one example. Underpinning the IFF is a simple idea:

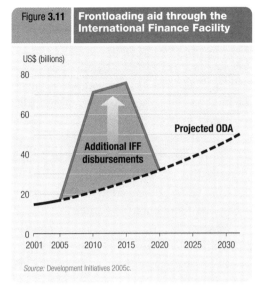

Figure 3.11 Frontloading aid through the International Finance Facility

US$ (billions)

Additional IFF disbursements

Projected ODA

Source: Development Initiatives 2005c.

Box 3.7 The International Finance Facility

To have a lasting effect on poverty, aid should meet three conditions. It should be sustained and predictable, large enough to facilitate simultaneous investment across sectors that reinforce each other's impact and rooted in viable development plans. In the absence of these conditions aid is less an investment in permanent poverty reduction and more an occasional compensation for being poor.

The importance of sustained and predictable aid is self-evident. No responsible private company would embark on a project to increase future returns until it had a fully financed multiyear plan. The same applies to governments in poor countries. If, like Senegal, a country depends on aid for 30% of public spending and 74% of public investment, a secure and predictable flow of aid is a condition for long-run investment. Countries cannot achieve universal primary education by abolishing user fees, constructing schools and training teachers unless funding is ensured to maintain schools and pay teachers beyond the first couple of years. And countries cannot be expected to sustain their investments in education unless they also have a financed health plan that prevents teachers from dying of HIV/AIDS faster than they are being trained or without a financed plan for water and sanitation without which girls drop out of school at puberty—hence the importance of simultaneous investments across sectors.

But the lesson donors have been the least eager to learn is that the need for increased aid is immediate and urgent. The longer they procrastinate, the more intractable the problem and expensive the solution. Frontloading aid can mean savings in the future. Malaria costs $12 billion a year in lost output. Paying to fully treat malaria would cost a fraction of that. Rates of return for infrastructure investment can be as high as 80%, dwarfing standard returns in private capital markets.

The International Finance Facility (IFF) is designed to meet the three conditions for effective aid. Through the sale of government bonds in rich countries, it would mobilize lump sum resources to finance a secure and predictable stream of aid. Because the financing would be frontloaded, it could provide the critical mass of investment needed across a range of sectors.

Could the IFF work in practice? Implementation details are being worked out through the International Finance Facility for Immunization (IFFIm), a pilot programme developed by the Global Alliance for Vaccines and Immunization (GAVI). In the past, GAVI's effectiveness has been compromised by fluctuating and uncertain financial flows. The IFFIm is a financing mechanism designed to provide secure frontloaded funding for vaccines and immunization services in the poorest countries. GAVI has estimated that an increased investment of $4 billion frontloaded over 10 years would save the lives of more than 5 million children ahead of the 2015 target date and would prevent a further 5 million adult deaths (mainly from hepatitis B) after 2015.

Source: Development Initiatives 2005b; GAVI and the Vaccine Fund 2005a, b; UK, HM Treasury 2003.

governments should use their ability to leverage resources in capital markets to provide additional aid. The IFF would use government pledges of increased aid to back the issuance of government bonds. Income from the sale of these bonds would be channelled through aid programmes, with the IFF drawing down future aid flows to pay off the bonds as they fall due.[40]

One of the strengths of the IFF is that it would frontload finance for investment in this critical period (figure 3.11). Even if all donors committed themselves to reaching an aid to GNI target of 0.5% by 2010 and 0.7% by 2015, there would be an MDG financing gap in the short term until the new resources came on-stream. Under the IFF, aid transfers could be expanded with immediate effect, while the budgetary costs to governments would be deferred. This frontloading would enable developing country governments to make key investments in health, education and infrastructure, while high-income countries could act on their MDG commitments without compromising fiscal stability (box 3.7).

Other proposals envisage raising additional revenue through international taxation mechanisms.[41] In practice, any international taxes would have to be implemented by national governments, as they are the only sovereign bodies with revenue raising powers—and the United States, in particular, is opposed to the approach. Support is strongest in the European Union. Several governments are assessing the implications of an international tax on aviation fuel. Even set at a low level, such a tax could raise $9–$10 billion a year.[42] Another proposal calls for a flat-rate tax on airline passenger tickets, with the revenue earmarked for prevention and treatment of HIV/AIDS. This proposal has been advocated by one G-7 country (France) and supported by two others (Germany and the United Kingdom), with several developing countries (including Brazil) backing the idea. These countries and others have reached an agreement in principle to introduce a national air ticketing tax to finance development spending. Other countries have advocated a tax on currency transactions. Indeed, Belgium has already passed legislation on the adoption of a currency tax. Several other countries—including Finland and Norway—have explored using carbon taxes as a new financing mechanism.

Advocates for the use of international levies to mobilize financing for development claim that the approach would produce important benefits for the MDGs and beyond. These levies, so the argument runs, have the potential to bring together the financing of public goods and the financing of poverty reduction. The French government's Working Group on New International Financial Contributions, which reported in 2004, argues that the flow of resources from levies would provide a stream of predictable finance while complementing private capital market approaches, such as the IFF, by taking up the slack left as IFF flows start to diminish as bonds are repaid.

Can more aid be absorbed?

A major expansion of aid will produce results only if poor countries can use the increased flows effectively. Opponents of rapid aid scale-up argue that poor countries lack absorptive capacity—that large increases in transfers will overwhelm their ability to use aid effectively, creating economic distortions and undermining growth prospects. In fact, most of the problems are readily solvable through a combination of domestic policy prudence and improved donor practices. None of the objections raised weakens the case for a step increase in aid to accelerate progress towards the MDGs.

Several recurrent themes dominate the concerns of aid pessimists. One is that countries lacking social and economic infrastructure—roads, nurses, teachers—are not in a position to reap the benefits of higher aid flows and that diminishing returns for growth and human development will rapidly set in. Another is that aid brings its own distortions. Dependence on aid, so the argument runs, can undermine incentives for governments

to develop national revenue systems, weakening the development of accountable institutions. Also cited are macroeconomic issues. Large inflows of foreign exchange can push up exchange rates, making exports uncompetitive, encouraging imports and creating balance of payments problems. The problem is known as Dutch disease, after the experience of the Netherlands in the 1960s when the sudden inflow of wealth from the discovery of North Sea gas pushed up the value of the guilder, crippling manufacturing exporters and stoking inflation.[43]

While each of these concerns raises important questions, the limits to absorptive capacity can be exaggerated. So, too, can the degree of aid dependence. Sub-Saharan Africa is the world's most aid-dependent region. Bilateral aid represents more than 10% of GNI for 23 countries in Africa, reaching more than 60% in Mozambique. But the regional average, at 6.2%, is below the level of the early 1990s.

There is little hard evidence to support the claim that poor countries will be unable to use more aid effectively. Precise circumstances vary, but aid dependence levels are a weak indicator of the ability of countries to harness development assistance to poverty reduction. Where absorptive capacity is a problem, the appropriate response is investment in capacity-building in combination with measures aimed at reducing transaction costs.

Diminishing returns?

Theoretically, diminishing returns to aid have to set in at some point, so that even with good management, marginal benefits will decline as aid increases. Cross-country research by the Centre for Global Development for 1993–2001 indicates that on average aid generates positive returns to growth up to the point where it reaches 16%–18% of GNI. Other studies put the figure at 20%–25%. But cross-country evidence on past performance is a weak guide to future outcomes. As aid quality, governance and economic policy improve over time, the benefits of aid can be expected to increase. Moreover, whatever the average threshold for diminishing returns, some countries are able to effectively absorb aid beyond this point. For example,

Mozambique is both one of Africa's strongest growth performers and one of the world's most aid-dependent countries.

In any case many countries with aid to GNI ratios of 10%–15%—including Bangladesh, Cambodia, Tanzania and Uganda—are facing a financing gap for the MDGs. Detailed country-level research from the World Bank suggests that $30 billion in additional aid could be used productively in low-income countries, a conservative figure that does not take into account the scope for infrastructure investment.[45] It is also the case that aid to GNI ratios in developing countries are a limited way of looking at dependence. For example, Ethiopia has a relatively high ratio, at 19%, but receives $19 in aid per capita compared with an average of $28 for Sub-Saharan Africa and $35 for Tanzania.

Revenue effects

Rapid increases in aid will raise the share of national budgets financed through development assistance. An obvious danger is that this will institutionalize aid dependence, making budgets more vulnerable to volatile aid flows and shifting donor priorities.[46] Some critics argue that large inflows of aid weaken incentives for governments to mobilize domestic taxes, undermining the development of a sustainable revenue base. Evidence from some countries lends weight to this concern. For example, Uganda has not been able to raise its relatively low tax to GDP ratio despite high growth. However, counter-examples suggest that such outcomes are not inevitable. Ethiopia has increased its national tax to GDP ratio from 11% to 15% since 1998 even as aid receipts rose by a factor of three.

Dutch disease—and how to cure it

Dutch disease is a threat that has to be taken seriously. Rapid exchange rate appreciation would have devastating consequences for Africa, making it more difficult for small farmers and manufacturers to expand and diversify their exports, raising the spectre of further marginalization in world trade. In practice, the problems can be avoided.

The most serious problems arise when aid flows finance a consumer boom. If output stays constant and demand rises, inflation, with higher prices for non-traded goods, is inevitable. However, if aid is directed towards areas such as infrastructure, agricultural production and investments in human capital, the supply response can provide an antidote to Dutch disease.[47] Rising productivity can counteract inflationary pressures and maintain the competitiveness of exports. This helps to explain why countries like Ethiopia, Mozambique and Tanzania have been able to absorb increased aid without large-scale inflationary effects.

Governments can also influence the exchange rate effects of aid—for example, by deciding whether to use aid inflows to increase consumption, finance imports or build foreign exchange reserves.[48] Evidence from individual countries confirms that large inflows of aid do not inevitably cause Dutch disease. In Ghana net aid increased from 3% of GDP in the mid-1990s to more than 7% in 2001–03, yet the real exchange rate changed by less than 1% in the second period.[49] In Ethiopia aid has doubled to 22% of national income since 1998. There, too, the real exchange rate has remained stable.[50] In both cases export competitiveness has been maintained through prudent management of reserves. Ghana managed a surge of aid in 2001 not by increasing domestic money supply but by selling into foreign exchange markets to stabilize the currency following a terms of trade shock.

Using aid effectively

While rapid surges in aid are likely to produce suboptimal outcomes, it is important to understand that absorptive capacity is a dynamic process, not a fixed entity. Shortages of teachers and health workers, dilapidated transport infrastructure and weak institutions can constrain the effective use of aid. But government institutions can be developed through capacity building; teachers, health workers and engineers can be trained; and infrastructure can be developed. The critical challenge is to sequence these investments through coordinated national strategies. That is why MDG planning needs to be put at the centre of public expenditure frameworks— and why donors need to commit themselves to predictable, multiyear support.

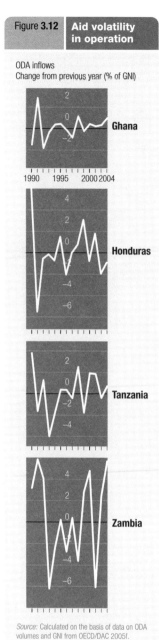

Figure **3.12** | Aid volatility in operation

ODA inflows
Change from previous year (% of GNI)

Ghana

1990   1995   2000 2004

Honduras

Tanzania

Zambia

Source: Calculated on the basis of data on ODA volumes and GNI from OECD/DAC 2005f.

Weakness in the quality and effectiveness of aid

Increased aid is a necessary condition for accelerated progress towards the MDGs. Without it the 2015 targets will be missed by a wide margin. But simply increasing budgets without reforming the unproductive habits of donors will deliver diminishing returns. Creating the conditions for more effective aid means making aid more predictable, reducing excessive conditionality, increasing donor harmonization, ending tied aid and providing more aid as programme support through government budgets.

The volatility and unpredictability of aid

Effective poverty reduction planning in low-income countries requires aid flows that are stable and predictable. The introduction of Poverty Reduction Strategy Papers in 1999 was intended to provide a framework for support based on national plans that would make aid flows more stable and predictable. Unfortunately, those hopes have not been realized.

Predictable aid flows are especially critical in low-income countries where aid flows are large relative to government revenues and budgets. In Burkina Faso more than 40% of budget spending is financed through development assistance. Unanticipated shifts in aid flows can undermine budget management and threaten effective delivery of basic services by interrupting the investments needed to supply schools and health clinics and pay teachers and health workers and by creating balance of payments problems.

Cross-country research shows that aid is more volatile than GNI or government revenue—40 times more volatile on average than revenue.[51] IMF research comparing aid during 1985–88 and 2000–03 shows that the difference in the volatility of aid and government revenue has increased, suggesting that Poverty Reduction Strategy Papers have done little to change practice in this area.[52] Measured by variance from trend, aid volatility has doubled since 2000, and for some countries the

annual variation is very large (figure 3.12). Particularly worrying, aid-dependent countries are most vulnerable to aid volatility, and aid volatility is especially high for these countries. Aid volatility in fragile states is twice the average for low-income countries.

Volatility might be less of a problem if aid recipients knew that donor commitments would translate into real financial flows. In fact, donor pledges are only a partial guide to aid delivery. Commitments may be disbursed over several years, with gaps between pledges and delivery smoothed out across several budget cycles. But such unpredictability can still impede fiscal planning. Decisions to undertake investments in, say, health or education create fiscal commitments for future years. Under the worst conditions unpredictability can give rise to stop-go financing as governments adjust to the delivery or non-delivery of aid pledges.

The gap between aid commitments and disbursements can be thought of as an "aid shock" to which public finances have to adjust. Measuring the scale of this shock is made difficult by sometimes less than comprehensive donor reporting on actual expenditure. Using the OECD Development Assistance Committee's reporting system for bilateral and multilateral flows for 2001–03, we looked at gaps between aid commitments and disbursements for 129 countries. The results are striking. For 47 countries disbursements fell short of commitments by more than 1% of GNI during one of the three years. For 35 countries the shortfall represented more than 2% of GNI. In 2001 both Burkina Faso and Ghana experienced aid shocks of 4% of GNI. Rich countries would struggle to adjust their budgets to fluctuations on this scale. In the case of Ghana and Burkina Faso the shortfall represented about one-fifth of all government revenue.

Shortfalls in aid flows can have a particularly damaging impact in key social sectors in heavily aid-dependent countries. Zambia finances more than 40% of its education budget through aid.

Consistently during 2000–02 donor disbursements amounted to less than one-half of commitments made at the start of the budget year. For Senegal, which relied on aid for one-third of public spending on health, annual disbursements for 1998–2002 fell short of commitments by an average of 45%. Slow and partial disbursements appear to have compromised funding for national immunization campaigns.[53]

Aid volatility and unpredictability might be partially explained if they reflected donor responses to economic shocks in recipient countries. Defining a shock as a decline in prices of at least 10% from one year to the next, the IMF calculates that low-income countries suffer such a shock on average once every three years. These shocks fall disproportionately on poor countries, reducing economic growth and government revenues, and disproportionately harm poor people, for example, by destroying the livelihoods of small farmers. However, there is no evidence that aid compensates for such economic shocks. During 1975–2003 only one in five countries hit by negative GDP shocks of 5% or more received increased aid.[54]

Countries can respond to shortfalls and uncertainty in aid in several ways, all of them with adverse implications for MDG financing. They can cut government spending, with adverse implications for reduced economic growth and social investment. They can maintain spending by borrowing and increasing the fiscal deficit, options with adverse implications for inflation and IMF conditionality. And they can use aid to build up cash reserves in anticipation of future income shocks, an avenue that implies lower levels of public spending.[55] None of these responses is helpful for long-term financial planning for poverty reduction.

The unreliability of aid flows is one reason that aid has not realized its potential. It is difficult for governments to develop stable revenue and financial management systems or to make long-run investments in infrastructure and basic services when they have little control over a large component of national financing. One of the most effective ways to enhance absorptive capacity would be to tackle the problem of unpredictable aid flows head on.

Conditionality and country ownership

All donors stress the virtues of "country ownership", of giving recipients more control over how aid is spent. Yet most link aid to stringent conditions. Country ownership is seen as a requirement for efficient use of aid, while conditionality is seen as a mechanism for leveraging policy change. In many cases the two objectives pull in opposite directions, with conditionality undermining country ownership and adding to the unpredictability and volatility of aid. One reason that donors' commitment to country ownership has failed to improve aid predictability is that it has yet to be put into practice.

Since the late 1990s there have been important changes in the administration of conditionality. Poverty Reduction Strategy Papers, drawn up by national governments, have created a new framework for cooperation. With that has come a streamlining of donor conditions. For example, conditions on IDA loans fell from an average of 30 per loan in the mid-1990s to 15 in 2003.[56] IMF loan conditions under the Poverty Reduction and Growth Facility have fallen to an average of 13. However, there are large variations across countries, and recent analysis of IMF programmes suggests that the number of structural conditions may be on the rise again.

Some of the changes have produced substantive results. But much of what passes for "streamlining" is simply a repackaging of conditionality or the transfer of responsibility for enforcing conditionality to other donors.[57] Aid still comes with a bewildering array of strings attached. Loan conditions linked to Poverty Reduction and Growth Facility programmes still set detailed budget targets—and sweeping targets for broader economic management. Doing business with the World Bank requires compliance with targets set in its country assistance strategies, Poverty Reduction Support Credits and other loan agreements. Bilateral donors and the World Bank have even picked up some of the structural loan conditions dropped by the IMF.[58] Meanwhile, countries seeking HIPC Initiative debt relief have to comply with a further set of spending and economic management targets.

The unreliability of aid flows is one reason that aid has not realized its potential

Loan conditionality
continues to reinforce
unequal power relationships

From the perspective of aid recipients, even slimmed-down conditionality resembles a very long shopping list. Consider Benin. Under its Poverty Reduction and Growth Facility Benin must provide the IMF with quarterly reports on spending in health and education, details of government wage bills and a timetable for privatizing the state bank. The (non-exhaustive) list of triggers for the World Bank's Poverty Reduction Support Credit includes accelerated progress in privatizing cotton; tangible progress in privatizing other public enterprises, including the creation of "sound regulatory frameworks in liberalized sectors"; preparation of a "coherent strategy" for private sector development; and a detailed list of quantitative outcomes in health, education and water. In all, the policy matrix includes more than 90 actions to be monitored. Meanwhile, to qualify for debt relief, Benin was required to meet targets for privatizing a cotton sector marketing agency.[59]

The merits of such specific policy prescriptions aside, individual loan conditions, by their sheer scale, scope and interlocking nature, inevitably diminish national ownership and increase the risk of aid cut-offs for non-compliance. Only one-quarter of IMF programmes are completed without interruption—a fact that helps to explain both the volatility and the unpredictability of aid.[60]

Some conditionality is inevitable and desirable. Aid recipients should report, above all to their own citizens, on public spending and budget priorities. National development strategies setting out clear poverty reduction goals and linked to medium-term financing plans are one vehicle for transparency. Effective auditing and legislative scrutiny of budgets are also vital. The problem with current approaches is the mix of macro-conditionality and micro-management. Loan conditionality continues to reinforce unequal power relationships that limit real progress towards country ownership.

Too many donors—too little coordination

The capacity problems created by excessive conditionality are exacerbated by the donor community's disjointed working habits. All too often, severely constrained government departments in aid recipient countries have to deal with large numbers of weakly coordinated donors, many of them operating overlapping programmes and unwilling to work through government structures. The high transaction costs that result diminish the effectiveness of aid and erode capacity.

When the Marshall Plan was implemented in Europe, a single donor interacted with countries with strong financial, judicial and public administration capacity and a large pool of skilled labour, entrepreneurs and managers. Aid success stories in the Republic of Korea and Taiwan Province of China followed a similar model of one dominant donor interacting with strong governance structures. Times have changed in the aid relationship. Of the 23 members of the OECD's Development Assistance Committee, only five give aid to fewer than 100 countries.

The flip side is that aid recipients are dealing with multiple donors. In 2002 the mean number of official donors operating in recipient countries was 23, though the typical country in Sub-Saharan Africa deals with more than 30 donors (and several dozen international non-governmental organizations).[61] The Ethiopian government received aid from 37 donors in 2003. Each donor may be operating dozens of projects supporting a variety of sector strategies. Tanzania has about 650 donor projects operating through either national ministries or local government.[62]

Meeting donor requirements for reporting, consultation and evaluation imposes a heavy burden on the scarcest of resources in developing country ministries: skilled people. Aid programmes in a typical Sub-Saharan African country will generate demands for thousands of reports to multiple oversight agencies, with hundreds of missions visiting to monitor, evaluate and audit performance. Line ministries may be required to generate not only departmental reports, but dozens of reports on individual projects as well.

Duplication adds to the problem. To meet legal obligations to their shareholders, the IMF and the World Bank conduct extensive annual reviews of budget management, public finance systems and public expenditure. Governments are required to submit accounts audited to international standards. Even so, donors such as the European Union, Italy, Japan and the United States require separate reporting to meet their own requirements—an arrangement that inflicts large and unnecessary transaction costs. Analytical work generates another layer of duplication. Donors conduct overlapping poverty assessments, public expenditure reviews, fiscal policy reviews, assessments of economic policies and fiduciary analysis and are often unaware of similar studies conducted by others or are unwilling to use them. In a case cited by the World Bank, five donors in Bolivia sponsoring a single poverty survey each required separate financial and technical reporting, so that the government official managing the project had to spend more time on reporting than on the survey.[63]

The burden of donor demands goes to the top of government systems. Demands created by weakly coordinated donor actions generate huge opportunity costs. Consider this lament by Ashraf Ghani, Finance Minister of Afghanistan from 2002 to 2004:

As Finance Minister more than 60% of my time was spent on managing donors, in terms of meeting visiting missions and representatives to reiterate government policy, raise funds...to enable the recurrent costs of government to be met, advocate for support to government-led programmes channelled through government financing, procurement, and accounting systems, and discuss and negotiate projects....This time could instead have been devoted to raising domestic revenue and managing internal reform.

Zambia highlights some of the wider problems associated with donor coordination behind nationally owned programmes. Support for the education sector, formerly under a four-year investment programme, is now being channelled through a sectorwide approach, with $87 million in aid committed for 2004. With at least 20 donors supporting education, there is a premium on effective coordination.

The record is mixed. The Zambian government has been arguing for support to be channelled through pooled funds in the overall education budget, and that now accounts for around one-half of support. However, another one-third of support is allocated through funds designated for purposes specified by donors, with the balance allocated for specific projects. In all, there are 20 donor funding lines for amounts of $12 million to $400 million, each requiring separate reporting. There has been little discussion about how to reduce the number of donors without reducing funding. Several key donors that have pooled resources have yet to participate in a joint mission. Senior ministry officials continue to cite the length and frequency of reporting as a problem. While the new joint missions are reducing transaction costs for donors, for developing countries the missions still occupy senior staff for two to three weeks at a time, diverting energy from effective management.[64]

Zambia offers a window on broader problems associated with harmonization in countries perceived as lacking a strong system of public administration. Some donors have been unwilling to move to pooled funding arrangements, partly because of concerns over fiduciary responsibilities. Others have agreed to pool some funds, but with extensive reporting strings attached. Donor reluctance to harmonize is especially marked in countries where there is a perception that governments have failed to design effective harmonization strategies. Thus, while Senegal is one of 13 countries in a pilot OECD scheme to accelerate harmonization, there is little effective coordination even in sectors where sectorwide approaches are in place, such as in health.

Efforts are being made to reduce transaction costs. In March 2005 members of the OECD's Development Assistance Committee signed the Paris Declaration on Aid Effectiveness, much of it dealing with measures to reduce transaction costs. Pilot programmes to strengthen harmonization and coordination are being implemented in Ethiopia, Ghana, Tanzania and Uganda. Some transaction costs have declined, but progress has been uneven. Ugandan officials still cite transaction costs as a major problem. With an average of three missions (some with as many as 35 people) for Uganda's World Bank Poverty

3

Aid for the 21st century

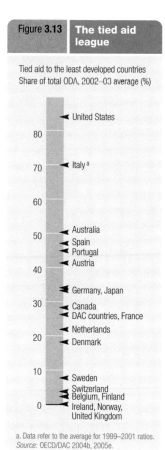

Figure **3.13** The tied aid league

Tied aid to the least developed countries
Share of total ODA, 2002–03 average (%)

- United States
- 80
- 70 Italy a
- 60
- 50 Australia
      Spain
      Portugal
- 40 Austria
      Germany, Japan
- 30 Canada
      DAC countries, France
      Netherlands
- 20 Denmark
- 10
      Sweden
      Switzerland
      Belgium, Finland
- 0   Ireland, Norway,
      United Kingdom

a. Data refer to the average for 1999–2001 ratios.
Source: OECD/DAC 2004b, 2005e.

Reduction Support Credit programme alone, it is not difficult to see why. Elsewhere, harmonization has also promised more than it has delivered. Reportedly, Senegal hosted more than 50 World Bank missions in 2002—roughly one a week. In 2003 Zambia hosted 120 donor missions, excluding those of the World Bank and the IMF. Of these, just 12—and none involving the European Union or the United Nations—were joint missions.[65]

Donors are also attempting to reduce some transaction costs through multilateral initiatives involving greater specialization and cooperation. Mechanisms such as the Global Fund to Fight AIDS, Tuberculosis and Malaria and the Education for All Fast Track Initiative enable donors to pool resources, deliver aid and delegate reporting to a single body. In recent years several donors—including Denmark, the Netherlands, Norway, Sweden and the United Kingdom—have announced intentions to streamline aid programmes around a smaller group of recipients. In theory, this opens the door to greater specialization and cooperation. In practice, the high-priority lists for each donor tend to concentrate on the same set of recipients, raising the risk of widening the gap between donor darlings and donor orphans. In one example of harmonization through greater specialization, Norway and Sweden are implementing a plan in Ethiopia under which Sweden will channel health funding through Norway, and Norway will channel education funding through Sweden. Such arrangements are the exception rather than the rule, however.

Implementing the agenda for improved coordination will be difficult if experience to date is a guide. The efficiency argument for greater specialization and harmonization is clear. But moving in that direction will require donors to share control of resources and to accept reporting systems managed by others—a move that implies major changes in the administration of aid programmes.

Inefficient resource transfers: tied aid

Not every aid dollar has the same value in financing poverty reduction. Much of what is reported as aid ends up back in rich countries, some of it as subsidies that benefit large companies. Perhaps the most egregious undermining of efficient aid is the practice of tying financial transfers to the purchase of services and goods from the donating countries.

Recipient countries lose out from tied aid on several counts. The absence of open market tendering means that they are denied an opportunity to get the same services and goods at a lower price elsewhere. Tied aid can result in the transfer of inappropriate skills and technologies. Price comparisons have found that tied aid reduces the value of assistance by 11%–30% and that tied food aid is on average 40% more costly than open market transactions.[66]

The full extent of tied aid is unknown because of unclear or incomplete reporting by donors. Procurement policies are often untransparent and biased towards contractors in the donor country. Two G-7 donors—Italy and the United States—do not fully report to the OECD on tied aid. Others also report on an incomplete basis. Reporting on the tying of technical assistance, most of it linked to suppliers in donor countries, is not required by the OECD. The upshot: the tying status of between one-third and one-half of aid to low-income countries is unknown. Tying is an area in which donors could usefully apply the principles of openness and accountability that they demand of recipient governments. Taxpayers in donor countries have a right to know how much of the aid that they finance is being used for non-development purposes, while citizens in recipient countries have an interest in knowing how much they lose as a result of aid tying.

While the precise amount of tied aid is unknown, donors clearly vary in the degree to which they tie their aid (figure 3.13). According to OECD reports on tied aid to least developed countries, the United States tops the tied aid list, with Italy close behind.[67] However, aid provided under the Millennium Challenge Account is untied, so the US tied aid ratio will fall as spending from this source increases. Germany and Japan also tie a relatively large share of aid.

The implied financial costs of tying are high. Estimating these costs is difficult because of the restricted nature of donor reporting and the exclusion of technical cooperation. For this Report we attempted to approximate the costs of tied aid. The tied aid ratio used is the average of tied aid reported for 2002 and 2003 by the OECD's Development Assistance Committee for transfers to least developed countries.[68] Gross bilateral aid disbursements for 2003 are used to establish aid levels to specific regions. Tied aid is then discounted at the rate of 20%–30% of face value, reflecting estimates for the costs of such aid against open market arrangements.

For developing countries as a group we estimate overall current losses at $5–$7 billion—enough to finance universal primary education. Low-income countries as a group lose $2.6–$4.0 billion, Sub-Saharan Africa loses $1.6–$2.3 billion, and the least developed countries lose $1.5–$2.3 billion (figure 3.14).

These figures understate the real costs by a considerable margin since they cover only bilateral aid and exclude technical assistance. Losses for individual countries vary according to the structure of their donors. In some cases value for money is severely compromised: 14 cents in every $1 of Italian aid to Ethiopia is spent in Italy. Currently, two-thirds of Australian aid to Papua New Guinea, its biggest aid recipient, is delivered through just six Australian companies.[69] Some forms of tied aid fly in the face of a serious commitment to the MDGs. In 2002–03 some $1 billion in bilateral aid was in the form of grants for university study in donor countries, heavily outweighing donor support for basic education in some cases.

Tied aid often raises transaction costs for recipients. Some donors apply restrictive procurement rules to meet their own requirements, creating multiple procurement structures and weakening coordination. Tying tends to skew aid towards capital-intensive imports or donor-based technical expertise, rather than towards activities with low input and capital costs, such as rural development programmes that draw on local expertise. The bias of some donors towards large-scale trunk roads rather than small-scale rural feeder roads is symptomatic of the problem.

Aid tying raises concerns at several levels. Most obviously, it diminishes the value of a resource in desperately short supply in the war against poverty. More than that, tied aid is incompatible with other stated donor objectives, including the development of national ownership. Many of the procurement policies operated through tied aid programmes suffer the same lack of transparency that donors criticize in countries receiving their aid. Aid tying represents a form of support to industry that most donors frown on in aid recipient countries. And tied aid is an inefficient use of taxpayers' money. While most industrial country taxpayers favour contributing to the fight against global poverty, there is less evidence that they endorse the use of public finance to create markets for large companies.

Project support rather than national budget support

Aid is most effective when it is channelled through budgets and expenditure frameworks that reflect priorities set out in poverty reduction strategies. As countries develop more transparent and efficient public financial management systems, the scope for building national ownership by supporting national budgets is increasing. However, many recipient governments complain that donors acknowledge national priorities in principle but undermine government processes in practice by directing aid towards individual projects—an approach that reduces efficiency, increases transaction costs and erodes capacity.

Project-based aid often reflects donor concerns about government capacity, budget management and financial reporting systems. The belief is that working through projects can circumvent failures in national governance systems. Ironically, project aid has a track record of intensifying problems in all these areas. In many countries donors operate hundreds of projects, many of them financed and managed outside of government systems.

The upshot is that a large share of public spending happens off-budget, weakening public finance management. Meanwhile, project

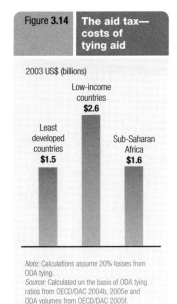

Figure 3.14   The aid tax—costs of tying aid

2003 US$ (billions)

Least developed countries
$1.5

Low-income countries
$2.6

Sub-Saharan Africa
$1.6

Note: Calculations assume 20% losses from ODA tying.
Source: Calculated on the basis of ODA tying ratios from OECD/DAC 2004b, 2005e and ODA volumes from OECD/DAC 2005f.

implementation units set up by donors operate as a parallel system, often attracting government staff to donor agencies and establishing a separate system of rules for procurement, financial management and auditing. Afghanistan's experience since the reconstruction process started shows how this approach erodes government capacity (box 3.8).

The creation of strong public finance systems linked to poverty reduction goals provides opportunities for donors to shift support from projects to the national budget. Over the past decade the Ugandan government has worked with donors to develop one of the strongest budget systems in Africa. Since 1997 priorities set out in the national Poverty Eradication Action Plan have been reflected in a medium-term expenditure framework and in annual budget allocations (see chapter 1). Some donors have responded by transferring aid from projects to the national budget. The share of aid provided through budget support has increased from 35% to 53%. This has made budgets more predictable: between 1998 and 2003 the ratio of disbursements to commitments rose from less than 40% to more than 85%.[70] However, some major donors—including Japan and the United States—are reluctant to shift aid programmes from projects to budgets, even in countries like Uganda.

And even when donors operate in support of national strategies through programme aid, the aid often arrives in forms that limit its effectiveness. Donors have encouraged aid recipients to develop medium-term financing frameworks to create stability and predictability in poverty reduction financing. To be fully effective, these frameworks need to be backed by multiyear donor commitments. Yet fewer than one-half of donors supporting the budget in Bangladesh make such multiyear commitments. A major strength of the Millennium Challenge Account is its framework for multiyear commitments. For example, under Millennium Challenge Account agreements, grants are provided to Honduras under

---

| Box 3.8 | Undermining capacity through project aid—the case of Afghanistan |

After more than two decades of human development free fall, Afghanistan has embarked on a process of reconstruction and recovery. The challenges are immense. It has one of the highest child death rates in the world (257 deaths per 1,000 live births), and three-quarters of the rural population live below the poverty line. Recovery prospects depend heavily on aid, which accounts for more than 90% of spending. But some donor practices have obstructed the development of national capacity.

Two models for financing and implementing reconstruction were developed in Afghanistan. Under a state-supporting model donors channelled their financing into the Afghanistan Reconstruction Trust Fund, jointly managed by the United Nations Development Programme, World Bank and Asian Development Bank. From there it was channelled to the government under strict accountability rules.

Under a state-avoiding model donors implemented projects directly or through UN agencies or non-governmental organizations. Projects operated through parallel organizations and parallel rules for procurement, financial management and audit. There have been at least 2,000 such projects, though many more were unrecorded. More than 80% of donor funding went into this model during the first two years of reconstruction.

Aid through state avoidance posed several problems. Transaction costs were high. Government officials devoted considerable time trying to extract information from donors on what projects were under way and what resources were flowing into the country. Government staff also had to learn new rules and practices, which differ by donor, including multiple reporting systems.

This project-aid economy also introduced distortions in the labour market. Public sector staff were drawn away from core functions as teachers, doctors, engineers and managers to support positions in the aid system. Government managers or engineers could earn many times their standard salaries as drivers or translators in the aid system. National human capital reserves in public governance systems, nearly depleted after 23 years of civil war, were further eroded.

The new Afghan government has developed innovative responses for dealing with the donor community. Faced with the prospect of coordinating 30 donors, each operating across 30 sectors, the government has limited donors to involvement in a maximum of three sectors each. Attempts have been made to align reporting processes with the Afghan budget cycle rather than with individual donor cycles.

Source: Lockhart 2004.

---

a five-year budget framework and to Madagascar under a four-year framework to enable them to develop medium-term financing strategies with greater predictability. Some donors that provide budget support link support to specific projects or earmark funds for individual programmes—a practice that can give rise to onerous reporting requirements. The pooling of donor resources through sectoral programmes is often viewed as a first step towards budget support. However, pooling arrangements sometimes entail enormous transaction costs as donors seek to retain control over specific programme elements. Senegal currently has 23 sectoral groups, with associated reporting requirements.[71]

Rethinking aid governance

Over the coming decade aid has the potential to play a central role in realizing the ambition set out in the Millennium Declaration. But realizing the potential of aid will depend on donors combining increased support with fundamental reforms in aid governance.

An immediate requirement for increasing the effectiveness of aid is basic budgeting. Developing countries have been pressed to adopt nationally owned poverty reduction strategies setting out clear goals linked to the MDGs. Donors, however, have made no commensurate effort to ensure that sufficient aid is available to meet gaps in public investment or to ensure consistency between MDG targets and IMF and other conditionalities. The outcome, as the UN Millennium Project puts it, is that "the public strategy has no direct link to actual public investment programmes". When it comes to the MDGs, donor governments desire the ends but shun the means.

The solution is for donor governments to adopt an aid financing strategy for the period expressly mapped to achievement of the MDGs by 2015. The financing strategy will be more effective if it is backed by a new relationship between aid donors and recipients. The rhetoric of country ownership needs to be translated into actions to empower recipient governments, coordinate donor activities and improve the quality of aid. The Paris Declaration on Aid Effectiveness takes a step in the right direction, with some 50 specific commitments for 2010.

Progress will require fundamental changes in current practices.

Bilateral aid—some lessons from Africa

The aid relationship is still not a partnership of equal responsibility. Developing countries have set targets based on the MDGs and are complying with detailed aid conditions stipulated by donors. The donor community has set no binding targets on the quantity of aid financing and has adopted only broad—and vague—principles on aid quality. If the Millennium Declaration is to be a genuine partnership, new structures are needed to enable both sets of countries to monitor each other's performance.

Developing countries are already showing leadership by example. Aid recipients are developing innovative strategies for improving donor practices. They are creating institutional structures for improved coordination and harmonization and reduced transaction costs. This section draws on a UNDP research programme on capacity building and evidence from a detailed analysis of work by more than 150 officials in 16 aid-recipient countries working daily with donors.[72] The analysis provides insights into the perspectives and solutions in Sub-Saharan Africa and elsewhere.[73]

Concessionality

Aid recipients place a premium on concessional finance, which lowers their risk of future debt

Donors need to ensure a
more stable and reliable
flow of long-term support

problems. Under the Tanzania Assistance Strategy, a homegrown strategy for development assistance, Tanzania has set a minimum grant element of 50% for new government borrowing. Other countries, Rwanda, Senegal and Uganda among them, are reducing their exposure to Poverty Reduction and Growth Facility loans, which are less concessional than IDA loans, for example. There is a clear need for more concessional finance to support poverty reduction strategies.

Coordination

The presence of large numbers of donors can inflate transaction costs, as each donor imposes its own reporting requirements and aid conditions. Some aid recipients have been successful in pushing donors towards improved coordination.

Lessons from Botswana are instructive. Donor interventions are framed under the auspices of a National Development Plan. The plan integrates development assistance and domestic resources. To prevent a proliferation of projects and reporting demands, line ministries are not permitted to negotiate individually with donors. All technical assistance programmes are designed to ensure that local staff are trained, resulting in greater skill transfer than in more traditional arrangements. Botswana has severely restricted the scope for donors to create autonomous project units and parallel structures for reporting and procurement, helping avoid distortions in government pay structures and the loss of trained civil servants.

Other countries are developing similar models of active coordination. Notable examples are the Tanzania Assistance Strategy and the Uganda Poverty Eradication Action Plan. The Cambodian government is developing a Harmonization and Simplification Programme linked to the national poverty reduction strategy. In each case, donors have been supportive.

Programme aid and budget support

Most governments see aid directed through the budget as more efficient and more effective in tackling poverty and as less of a drain on capacity than aid channelled to projects through special units in line ministries or other organizations such as non-governmental organizations. Burkina Faso and Tanzania have improved coordination between government departments by passing a law requiring that all line ministries submit requests for loans and grants to the Ministry of Finance. Donors can reinforce national budgeting and management by reporting all aid to the appropriate ministry and channelling it to programmes that form part of the national strategy for poverty reduction.

Countries have developed other strategies to reduce transaction costs. In Sub-Saharan Africa governments have attempted to lower transaction costs by persuading donors to pool their resources. Eleven HIPCs have established multidonor budget support programmes that release pooled funds on a predictable basis to support poverty reduction expenditures.

These pooled financing approaches are not without risks, however. Conditions for disbursement can reflect the highest common multiple among donors, reducing flexibility and increasing the possibility of aid interruption—especially when disbursements require unanimous agreement that performance targets have been met. One risk is that all donors will suspend disbursements if the country goes off track in its programme with the IMF. Another is the time it takes to negotiate pooled arrangements. It took Mozambique a year and 19 drafts to arrive at a 21-page memorandum of understanding on pooling arrangements with 15 donors. Clearly, donors can do more to avoid such protracted negotiations.

Predictability

Developing countries see the predictability of multiyear aid pledges as essential to effective implementation of the medium-term expenditure plans that underpin their poverty reduction strategies. Mozambique and Rwanda report improvements in their access to multiyear funds. Tanzania has also had some success in pressing donors to provide resources up-front and to improve the predictability of budget support. But too many countries are still forced to adjust budgets to fluctuations in donor transfers. Donors need to ensure a more stable and reliable flow of long-term support.

Multilateral initiatives

Recent years have witnessed a renewed interest in global multilateral aid initiatives. The revival of multilateralism offers great opportunities for human development—and some risks.

There are three good reasons for building on multilateral approaches to aid. First, and most obviously, in some areas the international community faces problems and threats that are global in nature: HIV/AIDS is a case in point. Multilateral initiatives can help finance a range of public goods that would otherwise remain undelivered. One example is the use of pooled multilateral funds to create incentives for research, development and production of vaccines for HIV/AIDS, malaria and other diseases for which market demand is too constrained by poverty to attract large-scale private investment. Advance purchase commitments by governments can provide pharmaceutical companies with a market rationale for developing new medicines—this arrangement has already helped finance a breakthrough in malaria drug trials. Second, multilateral frameworks provide donors with opportunities to pool their resources and reduce transaction costs; not every donor needs to establish high levels of expertise in every sector it wishes to support. Third, international resource pools provide a mechanism for matching finance with needs, thereby overcoming some of the skewed patterns of bilateral aid distribution.

The Global Fund to Fight AIDS, Tuberculosis and Malaria is an example of a multilateral initiative that is starting to produce real results in the fight against HIV/AIDS. Commitments reached $1.5 billion in 2004. For the Roll Back Malaria Initiative, a partnership with more than 200 members—including the World Health Organization, World Bank, United Nations Children's Fund and UNDP—financial constraints and weak coordination have hampered effective action. The situation has improved somewhat. The fight against malaria has gained new momentum since the creation of the Global Fund. In 2003 about $450 million was allocated to fight malaria through the Global Fund. This still falls far short of the $2–$3 billion in additional finance needed to scale up interventions sufficiently to reduce deaths by 75% by 2015, however.

The Fast Track Initiative in education demonstrates some of the strengths of multilateralism—and some of the weaknesses. The Fast Track Initiative grew out of a commitment made at the 2000 World Education Forum in Dakar to ensure that "no countries seriously committed to education for all will be thwarted in their achievement of this goal by lack of resources". Governments were encouraged to draw up plans identifying education financing gaps, and donors committed to bridging these gaps by leveraging resources through bilateral and multilateral channels. By the end of 2004, 13 countries had drawn up national plans endorsed through the Fast Track Initiative process.[74] The external financing needed to cover the plans is estimated at about $600 million, but only a little more than half of this amount has been mobilized.[75] Commitments are also far short of the additional $6–$7 billion a year needed to achieve the MDG education target. Some countries that are farthest off track for the MDG targets of universal completion and gender equity do not receive adequate funds. Francophone West Africa receives far less aid per capita than Anglophone East Africa, for example.

Some very modest investments in multilateral initiatives have generated high returns. The Global Alliance for Vaccines and Immunization (GAVI), launched in 2000 to improve access to underused vaccines, has committed just over $1 billion in five years, averting an estimated 670,000 deaths worldwide. Yet financing has been highly variable and volatile, making long-term planning difficult. Until 2005 revenue levels fell far short of the $400 million annual target. Some 27 million children miss out on immunization in the first year of life, and low or falling coverage rates and the unaffordable cost of some vaccines still represent a threat to MDG progress.

Multilateralism offers advantages for aid governance. Contributions to the Global Fund and GAVI cannot be earmarked, reducing the risks of donor bias. While both funds have rigorous performance standards, neither is linked to the host of conditions demanded by donors through other programmes, thereby reducing the risk of vital

3

Aid for the 21st century

Aid targets without binding
schedules are not a solid
foundation for poverty
reduction planning

public goods being cut off because of failure to achieve targets. Both funds also provide multiyear funding, allowing for greater predictability. But there are dangers that global initiatives might create distortions of their own. Large financial flows could be directed towards a single disease, such as HIV/AIDS, while other diseases are neglected, distorting health budgets in the process. Another danger is that dealing with global initiative secretariats will lock recipients into another set of reporting requirements and high transaction costs.

Changing aid

We live in a globalized world. Security and prosperity cannot be contained within national boundaries. Yet we have no global social policy, no mechanism for social welfare or protection of the poorest. Social security and intracountry transfers in the interests of human security are a standard part of the domestic economies of most high-income countries. Now these principles and practices need to be applied globally.

Aid is a unique resource. It is the only international mechanism that can be directed to the poorest—to secure their rights to basic services, to promote equity, to address the enormous gulf in global living standards and to build human capacity, the foundation of wealth and opportunity.

To make aid more effective and efficient all donors need to recast their approach to aid:

- To make the most of its value as a keystone in the permanent architecture for achieving social justice.
- To recognize that half measures and incremental change will not overcome the scale and depth of global poverty.
- To shed dysfunctional orthodoxies and procedures.

As a starting point the donor community must stop devaluing the currency of aid pledges. For more than 35 years donors have been stating their commitments to quantitative and qualitative targets for aid. With a few exceptions, these have not been met. Donors urgently need to rebuild trust in the reliability of their commitments on international aid, following the lead of the proposed International Finance Facility in making pledges legally binding.

Years of aid cuts have resulted in a culture that rationalizes small and declining aid budgets behind a false logic. Claims about the limited capacity of developing countries, concerns over the economic effects of scaling up aid and publicly expressed fears about governance are often smokescreens behind which donors seek to justify the unjustifiable: a legacy of indifference, neglect and failure to deliver on past pledges. This is not to suggest that the issues raised are unimportant. On the contrary, they are too important to be used by donors as a pretext for weak aid policies.

With 10 years to go to the MDG target date the international aid system is at a crossroads. There is a window of opportunity to put in place the reforms needed to fulfil the potential of aid as a mechanism for achieving the MDGs. Among the key reforms needed:

Set a schedule—and keep to it

The target of 0.7% of GNI in aid was set in 1970. Only five donors currently achieve it. Another seven have committed to a timetable. Targets without binding schedules are not a solid foundation for poverty reduction planning. All OECD donors should take the next step and set a schedule for reaching 0.5% by 2010 and the 0.7% target by 2015 at the latest.

Back MDG and wider human development plans with real money

Each developing country has been urged to adopt national development strategies bold enough to meet the MDG targets. The MDGs reflect the shared aspirations of the international community. It follows that donors should ensure that no national plan fails for want of finance. Increased aid flows should be linked explicitly to achievement of the MDGs. Donor financing should be linked to national financing plans, including medium-term expenditure frameworks. This implies abandoning annualized aid budgeting and moving towards three- to five-year financing strategies that are part of longer term plans for financing the MDGs.

Focus on additionality

Any financing strategy needs to consider the large sums currently included as aid that never leave donor government accounts or donor countries, in particular debt stock cancellation and technical assistance. Realistic accounting is necessary to ensure that donors are meeting their commitments to provide resources for the achievement of the MDGs. Aid reporting should be adjusted to ensure that public statements are not simply an OECD accounting exercise but reflect real resource transfers.

End tied aid

Tied aid includes a hidden taxpayer return to companies in donor countries. That return should be deducted from reported aid, along with the tied component of technical assistance. All tied aid should be phased out between 2006 and 2008.

Link aid to need

There are good reasons for providing aid to countries that are on track for achieving the MDGs and that are not facing a financing gap. However, increments to aid must be targeted effectively to the countries facing the greatest difficulty, especially in Sub-Saharan Africa.

Resolve the debt problem

Unsustainable debt remains a barrier to MDG financing in a large group of countries. An immediate priority is to identify low-income countries that will not qualify for debt relief under the 2005 G-8 agreement but nonetheless face problems in debt servicing.

Tackle inequality

Aid policies should reflect a commitment to reduce inequalities in human capabilities and income. These policies should form an explicit part of poverty reduction strategies and donor strategies. The commitment to reduce inequality should include a strong focus on basic services. It has been 10 years since the World Summit for Social Development set the target of devoting 20% of aid to basic social services. Donors need to ensure that the statistical reporting is in place to make them accountable for spending on basic services—currently estimated at 17%—and to make a quantum leap in the resources going to education, health, water and sanitation, and nutrition, by further increasing this share of the growing total aid.

Improve aid quality

Donors have been calling for better coordination and harmonization of aid since the 1980s. In 2005, for the first time, they set quantitative targets on reforms to enhance aid quality.[76] This is a positive first step. However, the targets lack ambition. Ensuring the effectiveness of aid requires more:

- *Aid flows aligned on national priorities.* The suggested target is to ensure that 85% of aid flows to the government sector be reported through the national budgets of recipient countries. This should be increased to 100% to ensure that public finance reporting reflects expenditures and that financing reflects national MDG priorities.
- *Budget support.* Donors have suggested a 25% target for the share of aid provided as budget support. This is massively under-ambitious. Conditions vary by country, but the aim should be to maximize the share of aid delivered as budget support, with a benchmark target of 70% by 2010.
- *Fewer missions.* Donors should adhere to best practice models. They should also report on a country by country basis on the number of missions and on the separate reports they require.
- *Use of national procurement and public financial management systems.* Failure to use national systems adds to transaction costs and undermines national capacity. No target has yet been set. But the aim should be to use national systems as a first resort and to ensure that 100% of aid goes through national systems by 2010.
- *Predictability and stability.* Donors need to make reliable, multiyear commitments that can be used to underwrite the recurrent costs involved in meeting the MDGs. At a minimum they should cover 90% of disbursements in agreed schedules, and funds should be released on time.
- *Transparency.* All donors should take steps to make their aid transactions fully transparent. Donors should provide timely, transparent and comprehensive information on aid flows to enable proper accountability to the public and parliaments in donor and recipient countries.

All tied aid should be phased out between 2006 and 2008

3

Aid for the 21st century

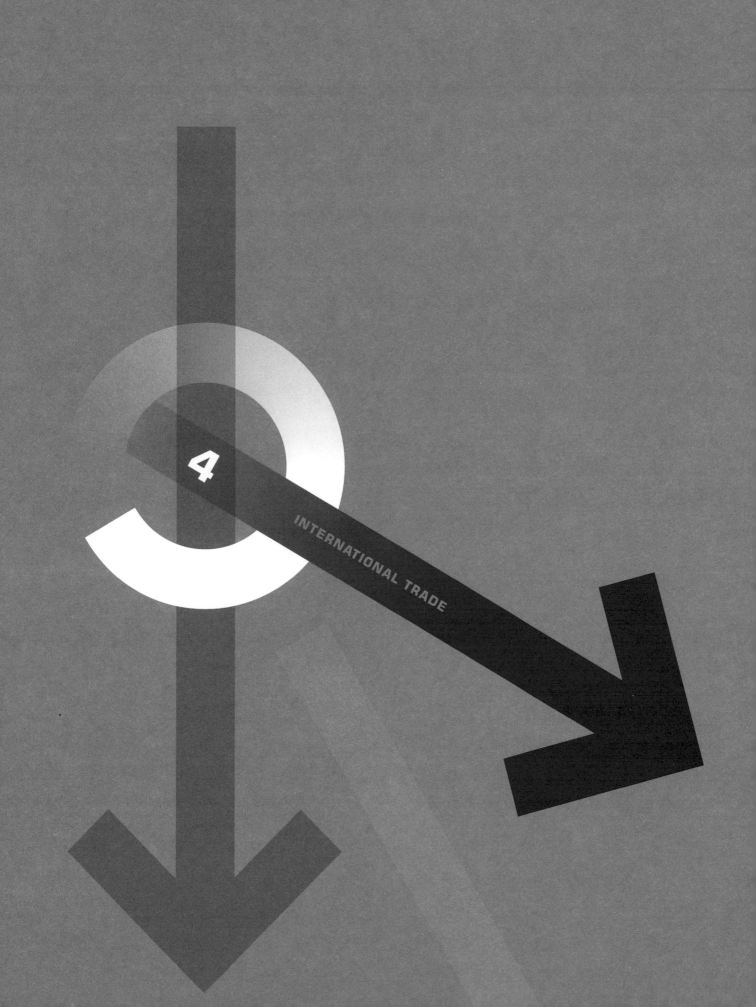

4

INTERNATIONAL TRADE

"The division of labour among nations is that some specialize in winning and others in losing."

Eduardo Galeano [1]

4 International trade—unlocking the potential for human development

Hypocrisy and double standards are not strong foundations for a rules-based multilateral system

"Until the lions have their historians", declares an African proverb, "tales of hunting will always glorify the hunter." The same is true of tales about international trade. For globalization enthusiasts the rapid expansion of world trade over the past two decades has been an unmitigated blessing, notably for the world's poor. Reality is more prosaic. Greater trade does offer enormous opportunities for human development. Under the right conditions it has potential for reducing poverty, narrowing inequality and overcoming economic injustice. For many of the world's poorest countries, and for millions of poor people, these conditions have yet to be created.

Improved multilateral cooperation on trade is vital if the international community is to achieve the Millennium Development Goals (MDGs) and wider development objectives. International trade rules and national trade policies need to be aligned with a commitment to poverty reduction. The starting point should be a recognition that greater openness to trade, like economic growth, is not an end in itself: it is a means to expanding human capabilities. Indicators for increased openness—such as export growth and rising trade to GDP ratios—are important, but they are not proxies for human development.

Trade is at the heart of the interdependence that binds countries together. That interdependence has contributed to some highly visible human development advances, enabling millions of people to escape poverty and share in the prosperity generated by globalization. Yet many millions more have been left behind. The costs and benefits of trade have been unevenly distributed across and within countries, perpetuating a pattern of globalization that builds prosperity for some amid mass poverty and deepening inequality for others.

The rules of the game are at the heart of the problem. Developed country governments

seldom waste an opportunity to emphasize the virtues of open markets, level playing fields and free trade, especially in their prescriptions for poor countries. Yet the same governments maintain a formidable array of protectionist barriers against developing countries. They also spend billions of dollars on agricultural subsidies. Such policies skew the benefits of globalization in favour of rich countries, while denying millions of people in developing countries a chance to share in the benefits of trade. Hypocrisy and double standards are not strong foundations for a rules-based multilateral system geared towards human development.

The Doha Round of World Trade Organization (WTO) negotiations provides an opportunity to change the rules of the game. That opportunity has so far been wasted. Launched in 2001, Doha was billed as a "development round". Rich countries promised practical measures to achieve a fairer distribution of benefits from globalization. Four years later, nothing of substance has been achieved. Trade barriers remain intact, agricultural subsidies have been increased, and rich countries have aggressively pursued rules on investment, services and intellectual property that threaten to reinforce

Living standards in rich and
poor countries alike depend
increasingly on trade

global inequalities. Meanwhile, issues of vital interest to many of the poorest developing countries—notably the protracted decline in commodity prices—scarcely figure on the international trade agenda.

Delivering on the promise of a development round will not address all of the human development problems raised by international trade. Even the best rules will not overcome the systemic disadvantages linked to low income, poverty and inequalities in education and health. Nor will such rules address the structural inequalities within countries that prevent the poor from capturing a fair share of the prosperity generated by trade. However, failure to align multilateral trade rules with a commitment to human development will have grave consequences. Most immediately, it will undermine prospects for accelerated progress towards the MDGs. Failure at the Doha Round would damage the credibility and legitimacy of the rules-based trading system itself, with grave consequences for

the future of multilateralism. At a time when shared security and shared prosperity depend increasingly on rules-based multilateralism, the costs of failure will extend far beyond the trading system.

The first section of this chapter provides an overview of developments in the international trading system under globalization. It challenges the argument that economic integration through trade is leading to convergence and identifies some of the conditions under which trade can help—or hinder—human development. The second section looks at how the current trading system is rigged in favour of rich countries. The third section addresses issues beyond the multilateral rules that lock poor countries out of world trade, including the protracted crisis in commodity markets and the increasingly important role of supermarkets as gatekeepers to western markets. The final section sets out an agenda for turning the current round of trade negotiations into a true development round.

An interdependent world

4

International trade

Deep global integration through trade is not unprecedented. At the end of the nineteenth century cross-border flows of goods, capital and information created a powerful dynamic for global integration. Far more than today, people as well as goods and investment flowed across borders: in the four decades up to the First World War 36 million people left Europe, helping alleviate poverty and narrowing global income inequalities.[2] The globalized world of the early twentieth century was shattered by the First World War and the Great Depression. The revival of global integration began in earnest about 25 years ago, with international trade and finance creating the impetus. Since then there have been major shifts in trade patterns, though continuity has been as important as change.

Trade and global living standards

Trade has been one of the most powerful motors driving global integration. Over the past decade the value of world exports has almost doubled, to $9 trillion in 2003.[3] Global production has grown more slowly, so that the share of exports in global GDP and in the income of most countries and regions has been growing (figure 4.1). Exports now account for more than one-quarter of world income and more than one-third of income in Sub-Saharan Africa.

Interdependence is the corollary of rising exports. Living standards in rich and poor countries alike depend increasingly on trade. Behind the complicated economics, globalization produces one outcome that is very straightforward: the prosperity of any one country in the global

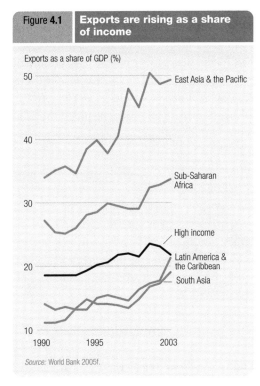

Figure 4.1 Exports are rising as a share of income

Exports as a share of GDP (%)

East Asia & the Pacific
Sub-Saharan Africa
High income
Latin America & the Caribbean
South Asia

1990   1995   2003

Source: World Bank 2005f.

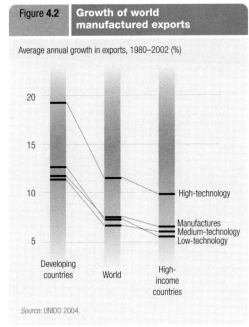

Figure 4.2 Growth of world manufactured exports

Average annual growth in exports, 1980–2002 (%)

High-technology
Manufactures
Medium-technology
Low-technology

Developing countries   World   High-income countries

Source: UNIDO 2004.

trading system is increasingly dependent on the prosperity of others. It is true that the interdependence is asymmetric: developing countries remain more dependent on industrial countries as export markets than industrial countries are on developing countries. But in the globalized world of the early twenty-first century all countries' fortunes are becoming inextricably linked.

Deepening interdependence has gone together with a change in the structure of world trade. Manufacturing exports have been the catalyst for integration, led by trade in high-technology products (such as electronics and computer equipment) and medium-technology products (such as automobile parts; figure 4.2). Trade in commercial services has also been increasing and now represents one-quarter of world trade. Meanwhile, the share of agriculture and primary commodities in the value of world trade has been in steady decline, falling from 15% to 10% since 1980.[4] Patterns of trade have also been changing. One of the most important developments has been the rapid growth of trade between developing countries.[5] More than 40% of developing country exports are now destined for other developing countries.

Developing countries have been expanding their share of world markets. Collectively,

they accounted for about one-quarter of global manufactured exports in 2003, double the share in 1980. In value terms manufactured goods account for 80% of developing country exports. Export growth in developing countries has outstripped growth in industrial countries across all technology sectors—but most spectacularly in high technology. Only in agriculture, an area in which developing countries have an obvious comparative advantage, have industrial countries avoided losing market share—a testimony to the power of protectionism and agricultural subsidies.

Policy change and new technologies have combined to create the conditions for increased trade. Import barriers and restrictions on foreign investment have fallen across the world, especially in developing countries. Tariffs have been cut, tariff schedules simplified and nontariff barriers rolled back. The average tariff in developing countries has fallen from 25% in the late 1980s to 11% today, with most of the liberalization having been carried out on a unilateral basis (figure 4.3).[6] At the same time falling transport costs, cheaper communications and new information technologies have opened up new frontiers.

One of the defining features of contemporary globalization has been the development of worldwide production systems. When the

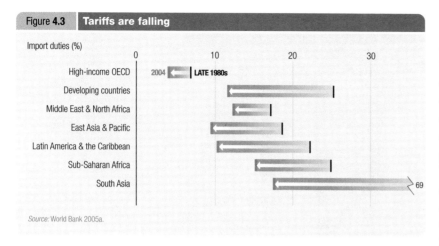

Figure 4.3   Tariffs are falling

Import duties (%)

High-income OECD	2004 ← LATE 1980s
Developing countries	
Middle East & North Africa	
East Asia & Pacific	
Latin America & the Caribbean	
Sub-Saharan Africa	
South Asia	69

Source: World Bank 2005a.

first Model T rolled off the Ford assembly line in Detroit in 1908, it was a genuinely national car assembled under one roof. One hundred years later the United States accounts for only about one-third of value added in domestically produced cars. As in other sectors of manufacturing the production of goods that previously took place in one location has been broken down into discrete parts, with components and products assembled in networks that span many countries.[7]

Consider the Microsoft Xbox—a high-technology game console containing cutting-edge technology. Manufacturing is outsourced to a Taiwanese company. The Intel processors are sourced from any of 11 production sites, including China, Costa Rica, Malaysia and the Philippines. Graphics processors are manufactured by a US company at a plant in Taiwan Province of China. The hard drive is assembled in China from components produced in Ireland. The DVD-ROM is manufactured in Indonesia. Final assembly has recently been moved from Mexico to China.[8]

The Xbox is a microcosm of what is happening under globalization. In computer electronics regional hubs based in East Asia dominate global networks. It has been estimated that two-thirds of computer components marketed in the United States have passed through the Chinese city of Dongguan, in some cases more than once.[9] "National" cars are a thing of the past. General Motors sources gearboxes assembled in Mexico, radiator caps from plants in Chennai, India, and upholstery from suppliers in Indonesia, using materials imported from China.

The fragmentation of production has been accompanied by wider changes. Some services that previously could be provided only domestically can now be traded internationally. Western companies now outsource not just software services but also data management, information services and insurance claims. The vertiginous growth of India's information technology and business outsourcing sectors is one result. Research, as well as data management and technical service provision, is also being outsourced. General Electric now operates one of the world's largest aerospace research laboratories in Bangalore, India, having followed companies like Intel and Texas Instruments in relocating research facilities.

The limits to convergence

One of the prevailing myths of globalization is that increased trade has been the catalyst for a new era of convergence. Expanded trade, so the argument runs, is narrowing the income gap between rich and poor countries, with the developing world gaining from access to new technologies and new markets. Like most myths, this one combines some elements of truth with a hefty dose of exaggeration. Some countries are catching up, albeit from a low base. But successful integration is the exception rather than the rule—and trade is a driver of global inequality as well as prosperity. For the majority of countries the globalization story is one of divergence and marginalization.

Success in world trade depends increasingly on entry into higher value-added markets for manufactured goods. Most of the increase in developing world market share in manufactured goods can be traced to one region—East Asia—and to a small cluster of countries (figure 4.4). Since 1980 East Asia has more than doubled its share of world manufactured exports, to 18% of the total. China has been doubling its share of world trade roughly every five years. China now supplies one-fifth of the world's clothing exports and one-third of the world's mobile phones, and it is the world's largest exporter of domestic appliances, toys and computer electronics. Mexico has also been increasing its world market share. However, the very visible

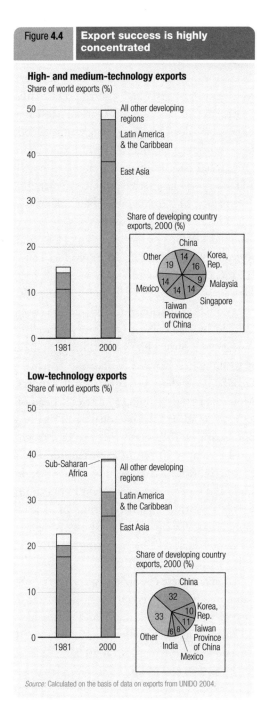

Figure 4.4 — Export success is highly concentrated

High- and medium-technology exports
Share of world exports (%)

All other developing regions
Latin America & the Caribbean
East Asia

Share of developing country exports, 2000 (%)

China 14
Korea, Rep. 16
Malaysia 9
Singapore 14
Taiwan Province of China 14
Mexico 14
Other 19

Low-technology exports
Share of world exports (%)

Sub-Saharan Africa
All other developing regions
Latin America & the Caribbean
East Asia

Share of developing country exports, 2000 (%)

China 32
Korea, Rep. 10
Taiwan Province of China 11
Mexico 8
India 6
Other 33

Source: Calculated on the basis of data on exports from UNIDO 2004.

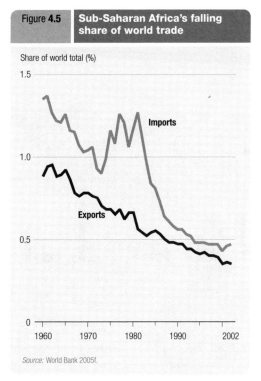

Figure 4.5 — Sub-Saharan Africa's falling share of world trade

Share of world total (%)

Imports

Exports

Source: World Bank 2005f.

base. Mexico now accounts for more than one-half of the region's manufactured exports. South Asia's share of world exports is rising from a low base, led by India's export growth. Meanwhile, the growth of international trade has done little to slow the marginalization of Sub-Saharan Africa. While trade has risen as a share of GDP—from 40% to 55% since 1990—the region's share (excluding South Africa) of world exports has fallen to 0.3% (figure 4.5). Today, the share of world exports of Sub-Saharan Africa, with 689 million people, is less than one-half that of Belgium, with 10 million people.

Sub-Saharan Africa graphically demonstrates how losses from trade can outweigh the benefits associated with aid and debt relief. If Africa enjoyed the same share of world exports today as it did in 1980, its exports today would be some $119 billion higher (in constant 2000 dollars). That is equivalent to about five times aid flows and budget savings from debt service relief provided by high-income countries in 2002.

These limits to convergence through global integration are striking. After more than two decades of rapid trade growth, high-income countries representing 15% of the world's population still account for two-thirds of world exports—a modest decline from the position

presence of a group of dynamic developing country exporters can create a misleading impression. Just seven developing countries account for more than 70% of low-technology exports and 80% of high-technology exports.[10]

As these figures suggest, there are limits to convergence. Much of the developing world has little more than a toehold in manufacturing export markets. Excluding Mexico, Latin America's presence in world manufacturing export markets is limited and shrinking from a low

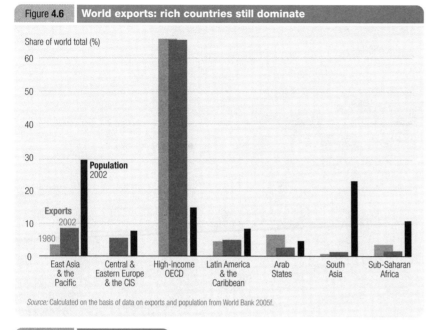

Figure 4.6 World exports: rich countries still dominate

Share of world total (%)

- Population 2002
- Exports 2002
- 1980

East Asia & the Pacific | Central & Eastern Europe & the CIS | High-income OECD | Latin America & the Caribbean | Arab States | South Asia | Sub-Saharan Africa

Source: Calculated on the basis of data on exports and population from World Bank 2005f.

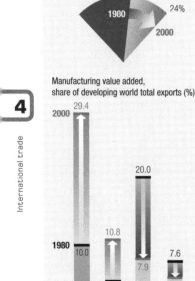

Figure 4.7 Manufacturing value added: shifting shares in the developing world

Developing countries' global share

14%
1900
24%
2000

Manufacturing value added, share of developing world total exports (%)

	2000	1980
China	29.4	10.0
Korea, Rep.	10.8	4.7
Brazil	20.0	7.9
Mexico	7.6	5.2

Source: UNIDO 2004.

in 1980 (figure 4.6). Evidence of convergence is even less impressive based on current market shares. India may be one of the world's fastest growing export economies, with exports rising at more than 10% a year since 1990, but it still accounts for just 0.7% of world exports.

World export market shares give only a partial picture of the extent of divergence in world trade. The ability of countries to convert export success into rising incomes—and so into improved living standards and poverty reduction—depends not just on the volume of production and export, but also on value added—a measure of wealth created. It is value added through manufacturing production that has the biggest bearing on the distribution of global income and the benefits of trade. The bad news from a global distribution perspective is that the balance of power in world manufacturing has barely changed after 25 years of global integration.

Over 1980–2000 manufacturing value added in developing countries increased at more than 5% a year—twice the rate in industrial countries.[11] But almost the entire increase was recorded in East Asia, and industrial countries still account for more than 70% of manufacturing value added worldwide.

Contrasts between East Asia and Latin America demonstrate that export growth and export success are very different concepts. In manufacturing value added Latin America has

been losing market share relative to East Asia (figure 4.7). Even Mexico, Latin America's most dynamic exporter, has been losing market share relative to East Asia and, more spectacularly, relative to China.[12] The explanation: Mexico is a low value-added producer of high value-added, high-technology products. Much of the export growth has been built on the simple assembly and re-export of imported products in maquiladora plants, with limited technological upgrading.[13] At a lower level of technology the Mexican model of high export growth and low value added is characteristic of a larger group of countries. Garment exporters such as Bangladesh, Honduras and Nicaragua fit into this category.

Global integration through trade has been marked by elements of continuity as well as change. Agriculture may be shrinking as a share of world trade, but many poor countries remain heavily dependent on agricultural exports. More than 50 developing countries depend on agriculture for at least one-quarter of their export earnings. These countries are on the downward escalator. They are exporting products that account for a diminishing share of world trade and income, with attendant implications for their position in global distribution. The regional share for agricultural exports is highest for Latin America (29%, excluding Mexico) and Sub-Saharan Africa (16%).

Many of these countries, especially in Sub-Saharan Africa, depend on a very narrow range of commodities for which world prices have been declining steeply. Between 1997 and 2001 the combined price index for all commodities fell by 53% in real terms.[14] This means that African exporters had to double export volumes to maintain incomes at constant levels (see later in this chapter). It is not only commodity-dependent exporters that have faced declining terms of trade. The purchasing power of manufactured exports from developing countries has fallen by 10% since the mid-1990s, with labour-intensive exports facing the biggest decline.[15]

Why do these trends towards convergence and divergence matter for human development? One reason is that international trade has an increasingly important bearing on the distribution of global income. As the share of trade in world

GDP rises, the share of countries in world trade will strongly affect their standing in the global distribution of income. Another reason that distribution trends matter is that success—and failure—in trade is cumulative. Exports are important not just—or even mainly—as a source of income but also as a means of financing imports of the new technologies needed to generate growth, productivity and employment and to improve living standards and maintain competitiveness in world markets. Thus trade marginalization can translate into technological marginalization, with impacts on global income distribution and poverty. Avoiding marginalization implies entry into more dynamic, higher value-added markets. And that demands the development of diversified manufacturing systems capable of adapting new technologies and adding value locally.[16]

Trade and human development

The idea that participation in trade enhances human welfare is as old as modern economics. From different perspectives, Adam Smith, David Ricardo, John Stuart Mill and Karl Marx all argued that specialization through trade would increase productivity, economic growth and living standards. Many of their insights remain valid. But the pathways between trade and human development are complex—and there are no simple blueprints for successful integration into global markets.

Trade policy represents one of the last frontiers of old-style development thinking. In other areas most policy-makers accept in principle that economic growth and consumption are not ends in themselves but means to advance human development. In trade the logic of development is inverted. Success is typically measured in terms of export growth, changes in trade to GDP ratios and the speed at which import barriers are falling. As Dani Rodrik has written: "Trade has become the lens through which development is perceived, rather than the other way round."[17]

The idea that openness to trade is inherently good for both growth and human development now enjoys almost universal support. Translated into policy terms, this belief has led to an emphasis on the merits of rapid import liberalization as the key to successful integration into global markets. When countries such as Cambodia and Viet Nam join the WTO, they are required as a condition of entry to implement deep cuts in tariffs on agriculture and manufacturing, as though this were a test of their trade policy credentials.

Such approaches are unjustified. The evidence to support the proposition that import liberalization is automatically good for growth is weak—almost as weak as the opposite proposition that protectionism is good for growth (figure 4.8 and box 4.1). While properly sequenced and gradual import liberalization can foster gains in productivity, successful trade liberalization and deepening integration are often outcomes of sustained high growth, with countries lowering tariffs as they grow richer. This was true both for rich economies during their industrial development and for successful integrators in the developing world: China, India, the Republic of Korea and Taiwan Province of China started lowering tariffs progressively after the reforms that generated economic take-off.

None of this detracts from the obvious benefits of participation in trade. At a household

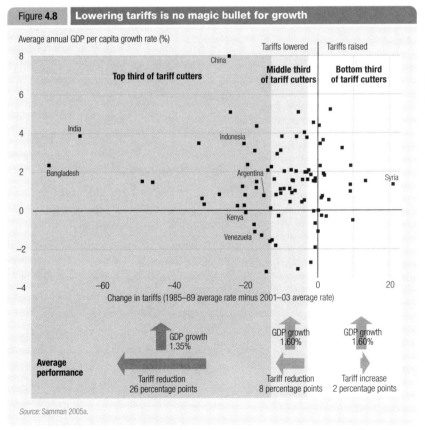

Figure 4.8   Lowering tariffs is no magic bullet for growth

Source: Samman 2005a.

Box **4.1** **How good is openness for growth?**

The idea that openness is good for growth and human development is deeply ingrained. Developing country governments are frequently pressed to liberalize imports, in some cases as conditions for aid or loans and in almost all cases as a requirement for joining the WTO. Does the evidence support the prescription?

One widely cited research exercise proceeds by dividing countries into globalizers and non-globalizers on the basis of the rate of growth in their trade to GDP ratio.[1] It then asks which group grows fastest. The answer that emerges is globalizers, by a ratio of 3:1—a huge margin. Because these countries have also cut their tariffs more deeply, the implication drawn is that import liberalization is good for growth. The same exercise argues that growth is distribution neutral on average, in that the poor share in growth in direct proportion to their current income levels. Openness is thus found to be good for growth and good for the poor.

Running the same exercise to look at the relationship between import liberalization and growth reveals a very different picture, however. Cross-country comparisons show that economic growth is positively associated with export growth, though the effects work in both directions: export growth is as much a consequence as a cause of higher income growth. The relationship between import liberalization and growth is less well defined. Unlike the trade to GDP ratio, which is an indicator of economic outcomes, import liberalization is a policy indi-

cator. Figure 4.8 in the main text summarizes data on the relationship between that indicator, as measured by the percentage change in (unweighted) tariffs, and growth for 92 countries over the period 1985–89 to 2001–03. Clustering countries into three groups on the basis of the depth of their tariff cuts reveals no significant growth differential.

What emerges instead is a diversity of outcomes, highlighting the importance of the interaction between trade policy measures and other variables. Brazil and Peru are more impressive tariff cutters than China and other countries in East Asia, but they perform considerably less impressively on growth. India has combined deep tariff cuts with an improved growth performance in the 1990s. However, the higher growth path predates import liberalization by a decade, and tariffs remain relatively high. In other cases—such as Kenya and Nicaragua—rapid market opening has been associated with stagnation or economic decline.

None of this makes a case for protectionism. There is no evidence that higher tariffs are good for growth. However, the diversity of outcomes associated with import liberalization suggests that the links to growth are more complex than is sometimes argued. In practice, the relationship between trade and growth is determined by a complex array of domestic and external factors. Cross-country evidence provides little foundation for the use of loan conditions or world trade rules to promote rapid liberalization.

1. Dollar and Kraay 2001a, b.
Source: Samman 2005b; Dollar and Kraay 2001a, b.

level exports can provide an important source of income and employment to poor people. In Bangladesh the growth of garment exports since 1990 has created about 1.8 million jobs, more than 90% of them for women.[18] Increased incomes in the garment sector have lowered poverty and contributed to improvements in health and education indicators. When Viet Nam liberalized rice marketing, it gave domestic producers access to global markets, with important gains for living standards and human development indicators.[19] In both cases the broad-based income and employment effects generated by exports provided an impetus for human development.

Beyond the household some of the most important benefits of trade derive from imports of capital goods that are cheaper than those available domestically. Exports of labour-intensive manufactured products in the 1960s and 1970s enabled the Republic of Korea and Taiwan Province of China to import and adapt the technologies needed to diversify their manufacturing

sectors, raise productivity and enter higher value-added areas of world trade.[20] Similarly, export growth, allied to foreign investment, has financed the import of technologies that have enabled Chinese firms to compete successfully in local and international markets.

Like any technological change, restructuring or reform affecting national markets, greater openness to trade can give rise to dislocation and adjustment costs. Participation in trade can produce losers as well as winners. From a human development perspective the challenge is to take advantage of new opportunities presented by trade while ensuring that the benefits are widely distributed and that vulnerable populations are protected from the costs. The six elements discussed below are among the key requirements.

Developing an active industrial and technology policy
Success in global markets depends increasingly on the development of industrial capabilities. In

a knowledge-based global economy cheap labour and exports of primary commodities or simple assembled goods are insufficient to support rising living standards. Climbing the value chain depends on managing the processes of adapting and improving new technologies. This is an area in which market failure is widespread. Free markets may not give the right signals for investment in new technologies when there are high and unpredictable learning costs. Moreover, firms in developing countries face such structural disadvantages as lack of information, weak capital markets and poor support institutions.

Most successful examples of integration into global markets have involved government action to overcome market failure.[21] The governments of the Republic of Korea and Taiwan Province of China, among the first generation of East Asian "tigers", created incentive for the development of local technological capacity by restricting imports, encouraging reverse engineering of imported technologies and regulating foreign investment. China followed a broadly similar path. Foreign investors in the automobile and electronics sectors have been required to transfer new technologies, train domestic workers and use local inputs. Government procurement has been used to create incentives. To qualify for government contracts, foreign software manufacturers have to transfer core technologies to China, invest a minimum proportion of their revenues in the country and meet 50% of development costs for eligible software products.

Managing openness

If openness, as measured by the ratio of trade to GDP, were an indicator of human development progress, Latin America would be an unmitigated success story. The region has led the world in trade liberalization. However, outcomes have been disappointing. After a decade of falling incomes in the 1980s economic growth per capita in the 1990s was just over 1%.[22] Greater openness in Mexico has been associated with negligible reductions in poverty and high levels of inequality. Rapid import liberalization in agriculture has further marginalized the rural poor in particular, in part due to high levels of initial inequality. The contrast with Viet Nam is striking. From far lower levels of average income, openness in Viet Nam has contributed to accelerated human development (box 4.2). Viet Nam has succeeded partly because its export success has been built on domestic reforms that have generated economic growth with equity and partly because it has not pursued greater openness through rapid import liberalization. More important, Viet Nam built integration into global markets on strong human development foundations.

These contrasting cases underline the importance of viewing trade policy, especially import liberalization, as an integral part of

---

Box 4.2	Viet Nam and Mexico—a tale of two globalizers

Both Viet Nam and Mexico are in the premier division of new globalizing countries, as measured by standard economic indicators. Measured on human development indicators, they are in different leagues. Deeper participation in trade has sustained rapid advances in Viet Nam. In Mexico export "success" has gone hand in hand with limited progress in human development (see table).

Viet Nam. Since introducing market reforms at the end of the 1980s, Viet Nam has sustained growth rates in excess of 5% a year—one of the highest in the world. Participation in trade has been critical, providing producers with access to new markets and new technologies. Imports and exports have been rising at more than 20% a year since the early 1990s, with the share of exports in GDP doubling.

Human development advances have accompanied this trade success. During the 1990s income poverty levels fell from 58% to 28%, life expectancy increased by six years, and child mortality was cut in half. Inequality has risen, but from a low base. The Gini coefficient increased from 35.7 at the start of the 1990s to 37 at the end of the decade—still one of the lowest in the world. The country's HDI ranking today is 16 places above its wealth ranking. The factors behind Viet Nam's success include:

• *Prior investments in human development.* Before economic take-off Viet Nam had high levels of income poverty, but other indicators (school enrolment, literacy, life expectancy) were far higher than the average for countries at a similar income level.

(continued on next page)

Box **4.2** | **Viet Nam and Mexico—a tale of two globalizers** (continued)

Global integration and human development: some do it better than others

Country	Exports of goods and services (% of GDP)			GDP per capita (2002 PPP US$)			Extreme poverty rate (%)				Income share of the poorest 20% of population (%)		Gini coefficient	
			Average annual growth 1990–2003			Average annual growth 1990–2003	National extreme poverty line[a] (%)		International extreme poverty line (%)					
	1990	2003	(%)	1990	2003	(%)	1990	2002	1990	2002	1990	2002	1990	2002
Viet Nam	36.0	59.7	20.2	1,282	2,490	5.9	30.0	15.0	60.0	37.0	..	7.5	35.7[b]	37.0
Mexico	18.6	28.4	11.4	7,973	9,168	1.4	22.5[c]	20.3[d]	15.8	9.9	..	3.1	50.3[c]	54.6[d]

.. Not available.
a. Comparisons should not be made across countries because national poverty lines vary considerably.
b. Data are for 1993.
c. Data are for 1992.
d. Data are for 2000.
Source: Exports data, indicator table 16; GDP per capita data, indicator table 14; national extreme poverty data, Mexico, Secretaría de Desarrollo Social 2005 and UN Viet Nam 2002; international extreme poverty data for Mexico, World Bank 2005d, for Viet Nam, UN Viet Nam 2002; poorest 20% of population's income and Gini coefficient data, indicator table 15.

- *Broad-based, inclusive growth.* Export growth was driven by millions of smallholder producers. Economic reform started with liberalization of agricultural markets. Restrictions on rice exports were relaxed, constraints on imports of fertilizer were lifted, and land tenure rights were extended. Rising prices and falling input costs led to rapidly rising income for smallholders. Agricultural wages, domestic trade and local demand all rose.
- *A commitment to equity.* Viet Nam collects about 16% of GDP in revenue—a high share for a low-income country. As a result, the government was able to distribute the benefits of trade more widely through spending on social and economic infrastructure.
- *Gradual liberalization.* Higher growth and export promotion pre-dated import liberalization. Quantitative restrictions were reduced beginning in the mid-1990s, but mean tariffs remained at about 15%. Capital markets remained closed, insulating Viet Nam from the impact of the East Asian financial crisis.
- *Market diversification.* At the end of the 1980s Viet Nam relied almost exclusively on exports of oil to Japan and Singapore. During the 1990s policies promoted diversification of exports (manufactured goods now account for about one-third of the total) and export markets.

Mexico. Over the past decade Mexico has sustained export growth rates for manufactured goods of about 26%. The country now accounts for about half of all manufactured exports from Latin America. Moreover, export growth has been concentrated in high-growth, high value-added technology sectors, such as automobiles and electronics.

In stark contrast to this export success story, economic growth per capita between 1990 and 2003 averaged just over 1%. Real wages are stagnant, and unemployment is higher than at the start of the 1990s. Extreme poverty has fallen only marginally, while inequality has increased. The reasons for Mexico's human development failures are a mirror image of the factors behind Viet Nam's success.

- *A high degree of initial inequality.* Mexico has one of the highest Gini coefficients in the world—and it has risen slightly over the past decade. The poorest 10% of the population account for one-quarter of the share of national income of their counterparts in Viet Nam. The role of the government in developing the social and economic infrastructure for broad-based growth has been constrained by weak revenue collection. Mexico has an average income five times the level of Viet Nam but a lower tax revenue to GDP ratio of 13%, which is comparable to Uganda.
- *Rapid liberalization.* Under the North American Free Trade Agreement Mexico has been one of the developing world's most rapidly liberalizing economies. In some sectors import liberalization has compounded poverty. Imports of subsidized maize from the United States have increased sixfold since liberalization started in 1994, contributing to a 70% decline in real proceeds for Mexico's millions of maize farmers. Agricultural export growth has been concentrated in large irrigated commercial farms, while small farmers have had to adjust to increased import competition.
- *Weak industrial policy.* Export data pointing to a high-technology boom are misleading. Half of Mexico's exports originate in the maquiladora zone, where production is dominated by simple assembly and re-export of imported components. Export activity is associated with limited local value added and minimal skills and technology transfer. Dependence on a low-wage, low-skill export sector has left Mexico highly exposed to competition from lower wage economies such as China. Employment has fallen by 180,000 since 2001 alone.
- *Power imbalances in labour markets.* Despite sustained productivity increases real wages have not risen with rapid export growth, partly because of the concentration of export activity in low value-added sectors. Weak collective bargaining rights and unemployment pressures are contributing factors. Another is wage inequality linked to the feminization of the work force: on average, women's wages are 11% lower than men's.

Source: Viet Nam 2004; IMF 2003b; Audley and others 2003; Oxfam International 2003b.

4

International trade

national poverty reduction strategies rather than as a standalone enterprise. That said, import liberalization can have positive benefits for economic growth and human development. Since 1990 India has reduced its average tariff from more than 80% to 20%, enabling firms to obtain the imports needed to sustain an increasingly dynamic growth process. One of the problems in India may be that import liberalization has not gone far enough in some areas. Tariffs on inputs for manufacturing are far higher than the world average, hindering the competitiveness of products that rely on imported inputs.[23]

Tackling inequality

Participation in trade can exacerbate inequality as poor people absorb the adjustment costs of increased competition from imports, while people with assets and market power take advantage of opportunities provided by exports.

Rapid export growth is not a panacea for poverty. The surge in textile and apparel exports from Madagascar since the late 1990s has created a large number of jobs, but predominantly for skilled workers. The result: rising inequality and a modest impact on poverty. Increased exports of high value-added fruit and vegetables from countries like Kenya and Zambia have been concentrated in large, capital-intensive farms with weak links to the rest of the economy. Similarly, in Brazil, the world's fourth largest agricultural exporter, large commercial farms and agribusiness firms dominate the $20 billion export market: just four or fewer firms account for more than 40% of exports of soy, orange juice, poultry and beef. The other face of Brazilian agriculture is scarred by mass poverty. More than 10 million people in rural areas live below the poverty line, most of them smallholder farmers or landless labourers.[24] Guatemala, another export "success story", is a human development laggard (box 4.3).

Box 4.3   Guatemala—the limits to export-led success

Increased agricultural exports are widely seen as a route to higher rural incomes and reduced poverty. In some cases they are. But the pattern of growth and distribution also matters.

Over the past decade Guatemala has sustained export growth rates of more than 8%, with minimal progress in human development. The country's HDI ranking is 11 places below its economic wealth ranking. While income poverty fell during the 1990s from 62% to 56%, it fell far less than would be predicted on the basis of growth levels. Since 2000 extreme poverty levels have risen. Already extreme income disparities are also rising: from 1989 to 2002 the income share of the poorest 20% of the population fell from 2.7% to 1.7%.

Why the weak link between export growth and human development? One reason is that high initial inequalities exclude poor people from market opportunities and limit human development. Despite being a middle-income country, Guatemala has malnutrition rates that are among the highest in the world, and one-third of its population is illiterate. Extreme inequality extends to land ownership. An estimated 2% of the population owns 72% of agricultural land, including the most fertile land.

Traditional exports—such as sugar, beef and rubber—are dominated by some 20–50 families. At the other extreme, smallholders constitute 87% of farmers, but hold just 15% of land and have limited access to credit and marketing infrastructure. Over half of rural households are landless or own less than 1 hectare. Poverty rates in this group are over 80%.

Smallholders have effectively been excluded from export growth in traditional sectors such as sugar. While jobs have been created, employment conditions are poor. Three-quarters of agricultural labourers receive less than the minimum wage—a share that rises to 82% for indigenous people.

Developments in the non-traditional sector have been more encouraging. Exports of vegetables such as snow peas have increased rapidly over the past decade. Production is dominated by 18,000–20,000 Mayan farmers in highland areas, most of them working on plots of less than 2 hectares.

Non-traditional exports have generated high economic returns, created employment and provided opportunities for diversifying away from coffee. However, only 3% of farmers are involved in the sector. Moreover, there is evidence that small farmers are being pushed out by large exporters linked to the US market. The failure of successive Guatemalan governments to extend credit provision, insurance coverage and marketing support has limited the potential for non-traditional exports to act as a force for poverty reduction.

No export growth strategy in Guatemala is likely to produce substantive benefits for human development without deep structural reforms to reduce inequalities and extend opportunity through the redistribution of land and other productive assets, increased public spending for the poor and targeted programmes aimed at breaking down the barriers facing indigenous people. Such measures will ultimately require a change in the distribution of political power in Guatemala.

Source: Krznaric 2005.

4

Greater openness to trade can exacerbate inequalities linked to education. In Latin America deep inequalities in primary and secondary school completion rates and the resulting shortage of skilled workers have increased the premium on higher education. Wage differentials between people with a college education and people with lower levels of schooling increased during the 1990s: on average a college education in Latin America now generates higher economic returns than in the United States, pointing to an extraordinarily high level of inequality. While trade can play a positive role, policies to overcome structural inequalities are of pivotal importance for converting export success into human development.[25]

Reducing vulnerability

Integration into world markets creates opportunities, but it also creates risk. Participation in trade creates losers as well as winners, and it brings with it adjustment costs. Poorly managed adjustment can inflict high human development costs.

Many poor countries and small island states that depend heavily on trade—especially commodity trade—face high market risks. These risks are linked to price vulnerability and the potential for policy change in importing countries to create external economic shocks—a problem suffered in recent years by exporters of bananas and sugar to the European Union. Exporters of some manufactured goods also face acute vulnerability. Garment exports have created millions of jobs in Bangladesh and Nepal. Today, competition from China threatens to destroy many of these jobs (box 4.4). Vulnerability is not limited to poor countries. The effects of imports from developing countries on wages and employment in rich countries are often exaggerated. Even so, evidence from the United States shows that 75% of people re-entering the labour market following a trade-related job loss received lower wages than before. Unlike poor countries, rich countries have a capacity to reduce adjustment costs for workers, but most fail to do so. The US Trade Adjustment Act, one of the few pieces of legislation designed explicitly to address this task, covers barely 10% of affected workers.[26]

Weak labour rights, allied to the absence of support for labour market adjustments, exacerbate problems of vulnerability. In Latin America only 40% of employed workers are protected by labour laws and have access to social security benefits.[27] Women suffer disproportionately from weak labour rights. Less than one-quarter of women in Chile's fruit industry have a contract, exposing them to excessive levels of risk and insecurity. Workers in export processing zones often have weaker rights than those outside: in 2003 at least 16 countries—including Bangladesh and Malaysia—fell into this category.[28] Weak labour rights and discrimination against female workers, especially in core areas such as freedom of association and collective bargaining, limit the capacity of workers to negotiate reasonable wages and conditions. What is needed is a combination of strengthened labour rights with institutions and policies that can facilitate adjustment and adaptation to change. Basic economics teaches that trade can raise aggregate income, even though part of the population may lose as a result of adjustments. In order to maximize the welfare gains from trade, and to strengthen the political case for participation in trade, it is important that the winners compensate the losers. That compensation can take various forms, including transfers between countries and public policies within countries to create the conditions under which losers are protected and provided with opportunities.

Confronting the "resource curse"

When it comes to human development, some export activities have a better record than others. Oil and mineral wealth generated through exports can be bad for growth, bad for democracy and bad for development.

In the 34 developing countries with oil and gas resources that make up at least 30% of their export earnings, half of their combined populations live on less than $1 a day. Two-thirds of these countries are not democratic.[29] Oil exports have made Equatorial Guinea one of the world's fastest growing economies, but it also holds the record for the largest gap between its national wealth and its human development

Box 4.4   Phasing out the Multifibre Arrangement

The elimination of textile and garment quotas maintained under the Multifibre Arrangement (MFA) starkly illustrates the human development threats posed by the loss of preferences. Handled badly, as it has been so far, the transition to a more liberalized market could jeopardize the welfare of millions of people.

Under the WTO Agreement on Textiles and Clothing, drawn up in 1994, all textile and clothing quotas maintained by industrial countries under the MFA have been phased out. As the last quotas are withdrawn, the shake-up in the $350 billion textile and clothing market will produce winners and losers. Impoverished female workers, who make up two-thirds of the global labour force in this sector, are likely to be the biggest losers.

The MFA provided a powerful stimulus to the development of industries across a large group of countries. In Bangladesh, Cambodia, Nepal and Sri Lanka textile and clothing sectors grew as a result of quota constraints on lower cost producers, such as China and India. Foreign investors from China, the Republic of Korea, Taiwan Province of China and elsewhere arrived to take advantage of the protected market.

Today, the ready-made garment sector in Bangladesh accounts for more than three-quarters of the country's exports and about 40% of manufacturing employment. Apart from the 1.8 million mainly female workers directly employed by the industry, another 10–15 million people are indirectly supported through workers' remittances to the countryside and employment generated in other sectors. Wages earned in producing garment exports help keep children in school and help relatives in the countryside meet health costs and maintain nutrition. In Nepal the industry employs 100,000 people and accounts for 40% of export earnings; in Cambodia 250,000 jobs are directly at stake.

Abolition of the preferences under the Agreement on Textiles and Clothing in 2005 heralds the onset of what could be a brutal process of restructuring. WTO projections show that the share of China and India in the US market could rise to more than 60% in the medium term, or three times current levels. Prospects for Bangladesh are less encouraging. IMF forecasts point to a 25% reduction in exports, with losses of $750 million. Countries such as Lao PDR, the Maldives and Nepal are considerably less competitive than Bangladesh.

Adjustment will inevitably be transmitted from global markets to enterprises as price pressures, affecting wages and employment.

In Bangladesh the scale of the adjustments could roll back some of the human development gains documented in chapter 1, with lower wages translating into reduced income for education and health as well as increased pressure on women to work longer hours.

Industrial countries have directly contributed to the scale of the adjustment costs. For example, instead of removing quotas in a balanced manner over the 10-year phase-out period, the European Union and the United States backloaded quota removal, magnifying the impending 2005 shock.

Strategies that could have been put in place to reduce adjustment costs were ignored. Take the case of Bangladesh. Almost the entire output of its textile and garment sector is exported to protected EU and US markets. Bangladesh continues to face high tariffs for its other exports in the US market, reaching 30% for some products. These tariffs could have been progressively lowered as part of the phase-out to provide a protected breathing space.

The European Union has been equally remiss. Nominally, Bangladesh enjoys duty-free access to the EU market under the Everything but Arms initiative, but the rules of origin present a barrier. Bangladesh's knit garments can generally meet the eligibility requirements because they have a high domestic value-added content. However, woven garments, which rely heavily on imported inputs, face problems in meeting domestic value-added requirements. Well over half of Bangladesh's exports to the European Union are in this category, so less than half of Bangladesh's exports actually receive duty-free treatment.

Having created industries through MFA protectionism, the European Union and the United States are jeopardizing these same industries through the rapid phase-out of quotas. Ironically, the policy response has been to authorize a new wave of antidumping protection against China at the behest of the garment industries of Europe and the United States. Faced with the prospect of further sanctions, the Chinese government has also introduced export taxes. In practice, the protectionist measures directed at China can be traced to vested interests and political pressures. In stark contrast to the sensitivity shown towards protectionist lobbies at home, developed countries have failed to put in place even the most rudimentary forms of protection and adjustment assistance for the losers from the MFA phase-out.

Source: Page 2005; UN Millennium Project 2005g; Alexandraki and Lankes 2004; Mlachila and Yang 2004.

index (HDI), at 93 places. By some estimates less than 10% of Equatorial Guinea's $700 million in oil revenue finds its way into government accounts. And despite Angola's wealth of natural resources it ranks 160 out of 177 countries on the HDI. The rush to exploit oil reserves in the Caspian Sea has led to a surge of foreign investment in Azerbaijan, Kazakhstan and Turkmenistan. Meanwhile, human development indicators have been worsening, and institutions for public accountability suffer from systemic corruption.

The "resource curse" operates by weakening institutions, creating perverse economic incentives and creating conditions for conflict—but it can be broken by sensible policies and democratic governance (see chapter 5).

Counting social and environmental costs

Inappropriately regulated export growth can undermine human development through its impact on the environment. In the 1990s Bangladesh strongly promoted export-led growth in shrimp aquaculture. Today, shrimp exports amount to 1.1% of GDP. Research by the United Nations Environment Programme estimates that water salinization, loss of grazing land and wider environmental impacts have cost 20%–30% of the value of exports. Poor farmers have lost grazing land and suffered lower yields.[30] In Tajikistan the government has promoted intensive cotton production through state companies. Cotton is now the country's third largest export. However, the incidence of water-borne illness is three to nine times higher in cotton growing areas. The reason: weakly regulated use of toxic chemicals that filter into irrigation ditches used for water supply.[31] As these cases demonstrate, export growth figures do not take into account human costs and environmental externalities that weaken the links between trade and human development. Factoring in these costs and externalities is one of the primary conditions for making trade work for human development.

Unfair rules: how the trading system favours developed countries

The Doha Round of multilateral trade negotiations provides developed countries with an opportunity to bring international trade rules and domestic policies in line with their development pledges. It would be unrealistic to expect the Doha Round to fully resolve this long-standing mismatch—but it would be disastrous for the multilateral trading system if it failed to deliver tangible progress.

There are three benchmarks for assessing the outcome of the Doha Round. First, it needs to produce rules that tackle long-standing unfair and unbalanced trade practices by improving market access for poor countries. Second, it needs to focus in particular on agricultural trade and a reduction in agricultural subsidies. Third, it needs to revisit agreements and negotiations that limit the policy space available to developing countries, directly threaten human development or skew the benefits of integration towards rich countries. The issues raised by WTO rules on investment and intellectual property and by current negotiations on services demonstrate the problem in different ways.

Access to markets

To benefit from trade and achieve human development gains developing countries and poor people need access to rich country markets. This was recognized in the declaration that launched the Doha Round, which included a promise by rich countries "to reduce or as appropriate eliminate tariffs as well as non-tariff barriers on products of export interest to developing countries". For a group of self-declared free traders, rich country governments have found it difficult to turn words into action.

System of perverse graduation
Most systems of taxation start from a simple principle: the more you earn, the more you pay. The international trading system flips this principle on its head: when it comes to access to industrial markets, the lower a country's average income, the higher the tax. Although industrial countries apply very low average tariffs in their trade with each other, they reserve some of their highest import barriers for the world's poorest countries.

On average, low-income developing countries exporting to high-income countries face tariffs three to four times higher than the barriers applied in trade between high-income countries (figure 4.9).[32] The average conceals very large differences between countries and the very high tariffs on labour-intensive products of great importance for employment in developing countries. For example, while the average tariff on imports from developing countries to high-income countries is 3.4%, Japan imposes a tariff of 26% on Kenyan footwear. The European Union taxes Indian garment imports at 10%. Canada levies a 17% tariff on garments from Malaysia.[33]

Trading partners' ability to pay has little bearing on developed country tariffs. Developing countries account for less than one-third of developed country imports but for two-thirds of tariff revenues collected. They also account for two-thirds of developed country imports subjected to tariffs higher than 15%.[34] In concrete terms this means that Viet Nam pays $470 million in taxes on exports to the United States worth $4.7 billion, while the United Kingdom pays roughly the same amount on exports worth $50 billion.[35] Customs revenue collection as a share of imports graphically illustrates perverse taxation in operation (figure 4.10). The effective US import duty for countries like Viet Nam and Bangladesh is some 10 times higher than for most countries in the European Union.

Tariff escalation is one of the more pernicious forms of perverse graduation. Developed countries typically apply low tariffs to raw commodities but rapidly rising rates to intermediate or final products.[36] In Japan tariffs on processed food products are 7 times higher than on first-stage products; in Canada they are 12 times higher. In the European Union tariffs rise from 0 to 9% on cocoa paste and to 30% on the final product.

This tariff structure prevents developing countries from adding value to their exports. Tariff escalation is designed to transfer value from producers in poor countries to agricultural processors and retailers in rich ones—and it works. It helps explain why 90% of the world's cocoa beans are grown in developing countries,

while only 44% of cocoa liquor and 29% of cocoa powder exports originate in those countries. Escalating tariffs help to confine countries like Côte d'Ivoire and Ghana to the export of unprocessed cocoa beans, locking them into a volatile, low value-added raw cocoa market. Meanwhile, Germany is the world's largest exporter of processed cocoa, and European companies capture the bulk of the final value of Africa's cocoa production.

In addition to facing high barriers in developed countries, developing countries impose high trade barriers on trade with each other. Indeed, they impose even higher tariffs on each other's imports than those imposed by industrial countries. Average tariffs on low- and middle-income countries exporting to South Asia are more than 20%, for example. Tariff peaks (import duties higher than 15%) are also common in developing countries, rising to more than 100% in Bangladesh and India, for example. Exports from least developed countries to other developing countries face among the highest average tariff barriers in world trade. On a regional basis the highest average tariffs are Sub-Saharan Africa's 18% import duties and South Asia's 15% tariff. High tariffs help explain why intraregional trade accounts for less than 1% of GDP in South Asia and 5% in Sub-Saharan Africa, compared with more than 25% in East Asia. Liberalization of regional trade under the Common Market for Eastern and Southern Africa since 2000 has led to a marked increase in trade value, with imports

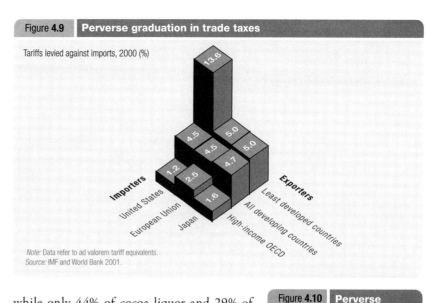

Figure **4.9** **Perverse graduation in trade taxes**

Tariffs levied against imports, 2000 (%)

Note: Data refer to ad valorem tariff equivalents.
Source: IMF and World Bank 2001.

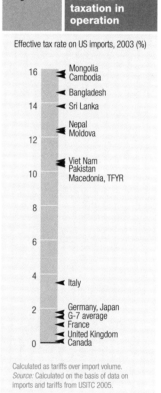

Figure **4.10** **Perverse taxation in operation**

Effective tax rate on US imports, 2003 (%)

- 16 — Mongolia, Cambodia
- Bangladesh
- 14 — Sri Lanka
- Nepal, Moldova
- 12
- Viet Nam, Pakistan, Macedonia, TFYR
- 10
- 8
- 6
- 4 — Italy
- 2 — Germany, Japan; G-7 average; France; United Kingdom
- 0 — Canada

Calculated as tariffs over import volume.
Source: Calculated on the basis of data on imports and tariffs from USITC 2005.

4

International trade

In practice, the European
Union's rules of origin have
protectionist consequences

and exports rising from $4.5 billion in 2002 to $5.3 billion in 2003 alone.

Preferential trade schemes and preference erosion

Preferential trade schemes provide some countries with protection from some discriminatory import duties. The European Union grants preferences for least developed countries through its Everything but Arms initiative—a duty-free and quota-free market access provision introduced in 2001. The US African Growth and Opportunity Act, which gives preferential access to US markets for several products, including textiles and clothing, has spurred garment exports from some countries in Africa. More broadly, however, preference schemes often suffer from limited product coverage, uncertain duration and complex eligibility requirements.

Among the most onerous requirements are rules of origin, which specify how much value must be added to any inputs used to produce exports that are entitled to preferences. Rules of origin are often deployed as protectionist trade barriers. For entry to the European Union, exporting countries must add "the majority" of the value to export products. Canada has set the bar at the lowest level: exporting countries have to add just 25% to the value of imported inputs.

Why do these apparently arcane differences matter? Consider the position of a vegetable exporter in Uganda who uses imported packaging from Kenya. The exporter would not be eligible for duty-free access under the EU Everything but Arms scheme because of the value of the imported items. Similarly, an African garment exporter wanting to import fabric from India to stitch into garments would fall foul of the European Union's rules of origin.[37] The sheer complexity of the rules, allied to unrealistic value-added requirements, undermines the capacity of poor countries to make use of preferences.

In practice, the European Union's rules of origin have protectionist consequences. Only a small proportion of eligible goods are imported to the European Union on a duty-free basis. As a least developed country, Bangladesh is eligible for duty-free status, but less than half of its

exports enter duty free.[38] Similarly, only about one-third of eligible exports from Cambodia enter the European Union duty free.[39] Senegal is nominally eligible for duty-free access, but it pays an effective tariff of about 10%.[40]

Changing Europe's rules of origin could open up new opportunities for some of the world's poorest countries. When Canada lowered its eligibility requirements for local value added in 2003, imports from Bangladesh doubled within a year. Similarly, when the United States waived its rules of origin under the African Growth and Opportunity Act in 2001, eligible imports from Sub-Saharan Africa rose sharply. By 2003 imports had increased in value from $54 million to $668 million. More than 10,000 jobs were created in Lesotho alone.[41] European imports from Sub-Saharan Africa fell over the same period.

Whatever the benefits and limitations of existing trade preferences, developing countries that use them stand to suffer from their erosion. When trade is liberalized, preference margins fall or disappear altogether. Under the Multifibre Arrangement (MFA), some developing countries—such as Bangladesh, Nepal and Sri Lanka—enjoyed protected access to industrial country markets under a quota system. The removal of the quotas through a WTO trade liberalization agreement exposes these countries to competition from more competitive suppliers, such as China and India. China has already been expanding market share, prompting a surge of appeals for protection from the EU and US textile and garment industries, ostensibly on grounds of unfair competition. The appeals are misplaced. There is no substantiated evidence of unfair competition. Moreover, while Chinese imports have surged since the ending of MFA quotas, it is developing country exporters, not industrial country producers, that have borne the adjustment costs (see box 4.4).

Some of the biggest losses from liberalization could happen in agriculture. For example, EU trade preferences mean that countries such as Fiji and Mauritius have quotas for sugar exports for which they receive three times the current world market price. The International Monetary Fund (IMF) estimates the potential losses at 2% of GDP for Fiji and 4% for Mauritius.[42] For Mauritius this translates into a one-quarter reduction in government revenue, threatening vital social sector budgets.

What these cases underline is that trade liberalization creates winners and losers within the developing world. Developed countries are belatedly responding to the challenges posed by preference erosion, but had human development been front and centre in trade policies, assistance schemes would already be in place. Financial support and other measures urgently need to be implemented to protect vulnerable countries and people. More broadly, the failure of developed countries to align their import policies with a commitment to the MDGs has limited the capacity of poor countries to benefit from trade.

Agricultural trade

Agriculture has become the flashpoint for tensions in the Doha Round. At stake is an issue that is central to human development and the MDGs—the rules governing world agricultural trade. More than two-thirds of all people surviving on less than $1 a day live and work in rural areas either as smallholder farmers or as agricultural labourers. Unfair trade practices systematically undermine the livelihoods of these people, hampering progress towards the MDGs in the process.

The problem at the heart of the Doha Round negotiations can be summarized in three words: rich country subsidies. Having promised to cut agricultural support in the last round of world trade negotiations—the Uruguay Round—the world's richest countries have increased the overall level of producer subsidies. Led by the world's farm subsidy superpowers, the European Union and the United States, developed country support to agricultural production amounts to $350 billion a year. Direct support to producers can be calculated on different measures. The Organisation for Economic Co-operation and Development's (OECD) producer support estimate measures the cost of all policies and transfers that maintain domestic prices above world levels at about $279 billion, or one-third of the

value of production—and rising to more than one-half for Japan (figure 4.11).[43] This support comes in different forms, most of which have the effect of raising prices, increasing output and boosting exports. Import tariffs, rising to more than 100% for several products—including rice, sugar, and fruit and nuts[44]—keep domestic prices above world market levels, while budget transfers inflate incomes. Most developed country governments would take a dim view of any developing country contemplating tariffs and subsidies on this scale, but when it comes to agriculture, developed countries are able to set their own standards.

Some political leaders in developed countries seek to justify agricultural support by reference to rural development objectives and the interests of vulnerable communities. There is little evidence to support this justification. In the real world the winners in the annual cycle of multibillion dollar subsidies are large-scale farmers, corporate agribusiness interests and landowners. Research carried out for this Report estimates that subsidy distribution in rich countries is more unequal than income distribution in Brazil (box 4.5). It would be hard to design a more regressive—or less efficient—system of financial transfer than currently provided through agricultural subsidies.

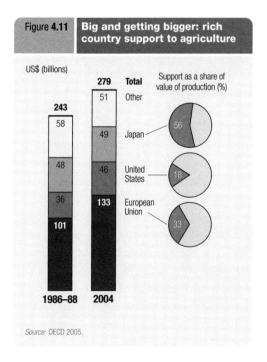

Figure 4.11 **Big and getting bigger: rich country support to agriculture**

US$ (billions)

1986–88: 243 (58, 48, 36, 101)

2004: 279 Total (51 Other, 49 Japan, 46 United States, 133 European Union)

Support as a share of value of production (%)

Japan 56
United States 18
European Union 33

Source: OECD 2005.

Box **4.5**   **Where do the subsidies go?**

One former European agriculture minister has described the EU Common Agriculture Policy (CAP) as an integral part of the EU "social model". In the United States the controversial 2002 Farm Act was presented as an investment in family farming. The facts tell a different story.

Subsidies in Europe and the United States are directly linked to output and the size of land holding, with one overwhelming consequence: the bigger you are, the more you get. In the European Union more than three-quarters of CAP support goes to the biggest 10% of subsidy recipients. In 2003 six sugar processors shared a payment of €831 million. The United States has an even more skewed pattern of distribution. Only 40% of farmers receive any subsidy. Within this group, the richest 5% get over half, or about $470,000 each.

One way of assessing distributional equity for agricultural subsidies is to construct a Gini coefficient for government support. Measured in this way, EU and US subsidy distribution is more unequal than income distribution in the world's most unequal countries, calling into question the idea that subsidies play an important social welfare role (see figure). The subsidy Gini coefficient for the European Union is 77; the income Gini coefficient for Brazil, one of the world's most unequal countries, is 60. These figures understate how regressive agricultural subsidies are. Much of the final value of subsidies is capitalized into rising land values and rents or converted into profits for input suppliers. US farmers retain only about 40% of the value of government payments.

Source: Burfisher and Hopkins 2003; Oxfam International 2004a; Environmental Working Group 2005.

Subsidies are heavily skewed towards the biggest farms

Gini coefficient of farm subsidies, 2001

- 80
- ◄ EU-15
- ◄ United Kingdom
- 75
- ◄ Germany
- 70
- ◄ United States
- 65
- Brazil income
- 60 ◄ France
- 55
- 50

Source: Samman 2005b; data on Brazil from indicator table 15.

The financial commitment to a small group of largely high-income beneficiaries in developed countries puts the financing requirements for the MDGs in perspective. Rich countries spend just over $1 billion a year on aid to developing country agriculture and just under $1 billion a day supporting their own agricultural systems. For a fraction of what rich countries spend subsidizing the overproduction of crops like rice and sugar, it would be possible to meet the financing requirements for achieving the MDGs in areas such as education, health and water. Adding insult to injury, the subsidies in rich countries not only divert resources but also reinforce rural poverty in poor countries. Industrial countries are locked into a system that

wastes money at home and destroys livelihoods abroad. When it comes to world agricultural trade, market success is determined not by comparative advantage, but by comparative access to subsidies—an area in which producers in poor countries are unable to compete.

High levels of agricultural support translate into higher output, fewer imports and more exports than would otherwise be the case. That support helps to explain why industrial countries continue to dominate world agricultural trade. At the end of the 1990s developed countries accounted for two-thirds of world agricultural exports—the same share as in 1980.[45] Rural communities in developing countries are hurt through several channels. Subsidized exports undercut them in global and local markets, driving down the proceeds received by farmers and the wages received by agricultural labourers. Meanwhile, producers seeking access to industrial country markets have to scale some of the highest tariff peaks in world trade.

Recent estimates suggest that developing countries lose about $24 billion a year in agricultural income from protectionism and subsidies in developed countries, not counting the dynamic and spillover effects.[46] Every $1 lost through unfair agricultural trade policies costs more than $1 in rural communities because lost purchasing power means less income for investment and employment. The spillover effects are very large: research in Africa suggests that for every $1 increase in income the rural economy generates another $3 through local markets. This would suggest that the real costs for developing countries of rich country agricultural support may be as high as $72 billion a year—an amount equivalent to all official aid flows in 2003.

The EU Common Agricultural Policy

Nothing better demonstrates the perverse logic of agricultural subsidies than the European Union's Common Agricultural Policy (CAP)—an arrangement that lavishes $51 billion (€43 billion) in support on producers. The CAP supports a sector that accounts for less than 2% of employment but absorbs more than 40% of the total EU budget. Sugar is first among equals as a case study in irrational public policy behaviour (figure 4.12). Farmers and processors are paid four times the world market price for sugar, generating a 4 million tonne surplus. That surplus is then dumped on world markets with the help of more than $1 billion in export subsidies paid to a small group of sugar processors. The result: Europe is the world's second largest exporter of a product in which it has no comparative advantage.

Developing country producers foot the bill. Subsidized EU sugar exports lower world prices by about one-third. As a result, far more efficient sugar exporters in developing countries suffer foreign exchange losses estimated at $494 million for Brazil, $151 million for South Africa and $60 million for Thailand—countries with more than 60 million people living on less than $2 a day.[47] Meanwhile, Mozambique, a country that is building a competitive sugar industry that employs a large number of agricultural labourers, is kept out of EU markets by an import quota allowing it to supply an amount equivalent to less than four hours' worth of EU consumption. When it comes to agriculture, there are distinct limits to EU openness.

US cotton and rice policies

Cotton policy in the United States provides another example of subsidized market distortions that harm human development. As with EU sugar policies, the scale of the subsidies stretches credulity. The US Department of Agriculture estimates that the country's 20,000 cotton farmers will receive government payments of $4.7 billion in 2005—an amount equivalent to the market value of the crop and more than US aid to Sub-Saharan Africa.[48] Subsidies of this order are reminiscent of the state planning systems that characterized the former Soviet Union. Of more direct relevance is the effect of the subsidies on cotton producers in poor countries.

Price distortions caused by US subsidies have a direct impact on these smallholder producers. These subsidies lower world prices by 9%–13% and enable US producers to dominate world markets, accounting for about one-third of total world exports. These exports would

not be possible without subsidies. High levels of government support effectively insulate US producers from world price signals, enabling them to expand production regardless of market conditions. Perversely, the increased subsidy payments triggered when world prices fall create incentives to expand production during periods of low prices, while other countries bear the adjustment costs (figure 4.13). These adjustment costs are very high. When world cotton prices fell to a 50-year low in 2001, losses attributable to US subsidies were estimated at 1%–3% of GDP for countries such as Burkina Faso and Mali in West Africa—a region in which some 2 million smallholders depend on cotton as their main, and in some cases only, source of income. These losses hurt poor households, with lower incomes compromising nutritional status and resources available for health, education and investment in agriculture. In Benin alone the fall in cotton prices in 2001–02 was linked to an increase in poverty from 37% to 59%.[49]

Whole economies are being destabilized by world cotton market distortions, with poor countries bearing the brunt. Cotton exports are of marginal relevance for the United States. For Burkina Faso, by contrast, cotton represents

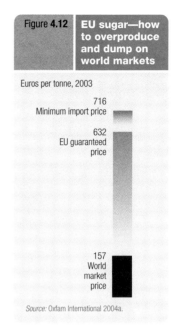

Figure **4.12** EU sugar—how to overproduce and dump on world markets

Euros per tonne, 2003

716 Minimum import price

632 EU guaranteed price

157 World market price

Source: Oxfam International 2004a.

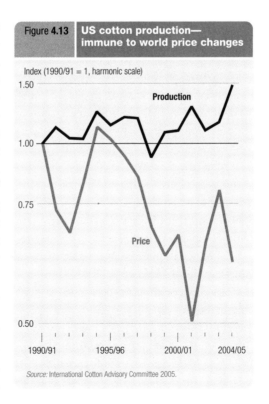

Figure **4.13** US cotton production—immune to world price changes

Index (1990/91 = 1, harmonic scale)

Production

Price

Source: International Cotton Advisory Committee 2005.

The 20,000 cotton farmers in the United States will receive government payments in 2005 equivalent to the market value of the crop and more than US aid to Sub-Saharan Africa

50% of the value of exports and is a mainstay of the national economy. With the world cotton market heading for another deep price slump in 2005, the IMF estimates that worsening terms of trade will reduce economic growth in Burkina Faso by 2.5% of GDP, halving the projected growth rate.[50] This outcome has grave implications for efforts to achieve the MDG target of halving income poverty. It also threatens to destabilize the balance of payments, with aid inflows insufficient to cover a widening deficit. Human development will suffer as a result of both the impact on rural poverty and the diminished capacity to import.

Not all of the problems in international cotton markets can be traced to US agricultural policy. Rising production elsewhere, especially in China, and heavy subsidies in the European Union, also contribute.[51] However, because the United States is the world's largest exporter, its policies have particularly strong global market effects.

It is not only smallholders involved in export crop production that suffer income losses. US rice policies harm domestic producers in many countries. Between 2002 and 2003 rice grown in the United States at a cost of $415 a tonne was exported at $274 a tonne.[52] Rival rice exporters such as Thailand and Viet Nam have to adjust to this unfair competition. So do millions of rice farmers growing for their domestic markets. In countries such as Ghana and Haiti rice farmers have been pushed out of national markets by US imports, undermining prospects for the development of a dynamic rural economy. In Ghana rice farmers in the poorest northern part of the country have seen markets squeezed by cheap US imports. The IMF has opposed the use of tariffs to restrict these imports on the grounds that there is no evidence of unfair competition. That judgement is hard to square with the fact that US budget payments for rice in 2003 amounted to $1.3 billion, or almost three-quarters of the value of output.

Rewriting the rules for agriculture

The Doha Round provides an opportunity to remove one of the most egregious examples of unfair trade. Developed country agricultural subsidies may have a long and ignoble history. But reducing them is now more urgent than ever because doing so would remove a barrier to the realization of the MDGs. Unfortunately, there has been little progress in this direction. Since the Doha Round started, the United States has passed legislation that increases agricultural support by about $7 billion a year.[53] The new legislation also strengthens the links between subsidies and production that had been weakened in previous legislation.

The latest twist in the long-running saga of CAP reform similarly gives little cause for optimism. Under measures agreed in 2003 the European Union has created a framework that will restructure, but not reduce, overall support: the CAP budget is set to increase over the next decade. The European Union argues that the reformed CAP payments will be "WTO-friendly" and therefore exempt from any cuts agreed as a result of the Doha Round. However, national provisions also allow governments the scope to maintain a link between subsidies and output. How will CAP reform affect the overall level of support under the policy? An OECD evaluation based on projections that capture the effect of the new payments structure concludes that producer support will still amount to more than one-third of the value of production (with the producer support estimate falling by just over 1%) as a result of the reform.[54] Because payments are still linked to past production and size of land holding, support will continue to benefit larger and richer farmers. And while the structure of payments will change, market price support will continue to account for 52% of the total under the reformed CAP.

At the WTO itself new threats are emerging. Instead of addressing head on the fundamental challenge of removing market distortions, developed countries have embarked on an elaborate subsidy repackaging exercise (box 4.6). The danger now is that an agreement at the WTO will leave intact the very distortions that the Doha Round was intended to remove, in the process undermining prospects for achieving the MDGs.

Box **4.6** | **When is a subsidy not a subsidy?**

The answer to the question posed in the title is simple: when developed countries say so. One problem now facing developing countries is that industrial countries have transferred support into subsidy areas that are weakly covered by WTO rules—rules crafted under heavy EU and US influence.

The Uruguay Round Agreement on Agriculture, negotiated largely between the European Union and the United States, introduced three categories of subsidy. Amber Box subsidies are subject to any cut in support agreed at the WTO. Green Box subsidies, deemed to be "non-distorting", are permitted. In between are Blue Box subsidies, which are exempt from cuts if the subsidies are linked to taking some land out of cultivation. These were introduced at EU insistence to accommodate CAP reforms, under which eligibility for direct payments was made conditional on producers removing a certain proportion of their holdings from cultivation.

Why do these distinctions matter? Because the WTO framework exercises weak or non-existent disciplines over precisely the forms of support into which developed country governments are now directing agricultural subsidies. In 2001 (the last year for which notifications to the WTO are available) the United States spent $50 billion on Green Box payments—three times what it spent on Amber Box payments (see table). Not to be outdone the European Union spent $50 billion on Green Box and Blue Box payments—more than it spent on Amber Box payments. In both cases the subsidy superpowers have been able to remain below the WTO subsidy

Large subsidies escape World Trade Organization regulation

US$, 2001/02 (billions)

	European Union	United States
Amber Box	44.3	14.4
Maximum Amber Box allowed under WTO rules	75.7	19.1
Blue Box	26.7	0.0
Green Box	23.3	50.7

Source: WTO 2005.

ceiling by restructuring, rather than cutting, overall support. The upshot is that for WTO purposes many of the subsidies that allow Europe to export cereals and the United States to sell rice, cotton, maize and other crops at below cost on world markets are not currently categorized either as export subsidies or trade distorting and are therefore potentially exempt from any agreement to cut such subsidies.

Some developing countries have already used WTO dispute panels to challenge specific subsidies. Brazil successfully challenged the US Green Box categorization of direct payments to cotton. Brazil, India and Thailand have successfully challenged the legality of EU sugar subsidies, with a WTO panel ruling that these subsidies are not in compliance with WTO rules. However, there is a growing danger that a WTO agreement could provide sufficient space to enable overall agricultural support, as defined by the OECD's producer support estimate, to remain around current levels, albeit in repackaged form.

Such an outcome would severely diminish the credibility of any Doha Round agreement on agriculture. Not all subsidies are equally distorting in their effects. However, the annual transfer of billions of dollars to large agricultural producers clearly has market-distorting effects, even if the payments are nominally categorized as non-distorting. This is especially the case in sectors where large surpluses are produced for world markets. At the very least these payments provide a guarantee against risk, capital resources for investment and a source of collateral for loans.

From the perspective of cotton farmers in Burkina Faso or rice farmers in Ghana, the precise legal categorization of subsidies in the WTO is of less immediate relevance than whether subsidies in rich countries undermine their livelihoods. The problem with the current framework of rules in agriculture is that it institutionalizes unfair trade practices behind a veneer of WTO legality, weakening the legitimacy of the rules-based multilateral system in the process. The development of WTO rules that prohibit unfair competition between developed and developing countries should be one of the benchmarks for judging the outcome of the entire Doha Round.

Source: US Department of Agriculture, Economic Research Service 2005b; Watkins 2003b.

Closing down the space for development policies

The last round of world trade negotiations extended the remit of WTO rules into new areas. It also strengthened enforcement mechanisms. Under the new regime WTO members now have to comply with all agreements taken as a package—an arrangement known as the Single Undertaking. Compliance is enforced through a dispute resolution procedure. In parallel to the strengthening of multilateral rules, there has been a proliferation of regional agreements. There are now some 230 regional trade agreements covering about 40% of world trade. In four areas in particular stronger multilateral rules or regional agreements will have a major bearing on human development and the future distribution of benefits from world trade: industrial policy, intellectual property, services, and tariffs and revenue.

4

International trade

Industrial policy

One of the most pressing challenges for developing countries is to develop the capacity to enter higher value-added areas of world trade. For reasons explained earlier, an active industrial and technology policy is a critical requirement. Current rules severely restrict the scope for government action in this area.

Several WTO agreements expressly limit the policy space available to governments. The Agreement on Subsidies makes a wide range of fiscal and credit incentives for export illegal. Similarly, the Trade-Related Investment Measures (TRIMs) agreement prohibits tools that successful economies in East Asia and elsewhere once used to maximize the benefit of foreign investment, including local content requirements, technology transfer, local employment, and research and development provisions.

This is unjustified. Not all industrial policy has worked. There is no shortage of examples of such policies being captured by special interest groups or of leading to industrial white elephants. At the same time, it is difficult to find examples of sectors competing successfully in world markets without active state involvement. Many of the policy measures that underpinned East Asian industrial development are now prohibited by WTO rules.[55] China made extensive use of local content and technology transfer provisions, leading to the emergence of globally competitive firms that rapidly climbed into higher value-added areas of world trade. Brazil's aircraft industry, the country's third largest source of export earnings, was supported through subsidized credit. India's fast-growing automobile components sector has been supported through regulation of foreign investors, including local content rules (box 4.7). In Latin America, where the automobile components industry conforms closely to the proposed WTO rules, domestic firms have been almost entirely displaced by foreign transnational companies.[56]

The aim of industrial policy should be to create the conditions under which countries can acquire the technological capabilities needed to raise productivity, maximize the advantages of trade and develop a dynamic comparative advantage.[57] Blanket protection and disincentives for foreign investment are not helpful. To be successful, industrial policy needs to focus on dynamic new sectors, offer time-bound import protection and promote activities that generate investments and technological dispersion. Transparent interaction between public and private sector bodies is vital.

Broad WTO rules could foster the transparency and predictability needed to ensure that industrial policies do not spark trade disputes,

---

> **Box 4.7   The Indian automobile components sector**
>
> A key driver of industrial development is the integration of local firms into global supply chains. Success depends critically on industrial policy.
>
> The most highly developed supply chain is that of the automobile industry. Over the past decade companies in India have emerged as a powerful force, especially in the components sector. Indian firms—such as Bharat Forge, Brakes India and Sundaram—have moved into high value-added areas of production, often in partnership with multinational companies. The contrast with Latin America is striking. There, a fairly well developed industry has been pushed out of domestic and regional markets by foreign car companies using their own suppliers.
>
> From the early 1990s a wave of multinational investors entered the Indian market. These entrants were required to achieve a high level of domestic content within a specified period (typically 70% within three years). To do that, multinational companies had to switch from importing components to sourcing from local companies. That created incentives for automobile makers to work closely with suppliers to raise quality standards. In addition, the Indian government imposed training requirements on multinational investors.
>
> Export success followed a lengthy period of market protection. High import barriers created an incentive for foreign investors to locate in India and build alliances with local firms. These barriers were reduced slowly, in stark contrast to Latin America. Tariffs on imported automobiles and parts averaged more than 30% in India in the mid-1990s, whereas they were less than 3% in Latin America.
>
> The component supply chain has developed rapidly. The value of output increased from $2.4 billion in 1997 to $4.2 billion in 2001. India has also emerged as a significant exporter. Exports now account for about 15% of the sector's output, reaching $800 million in value terms in 2002–03. International comparisons show that the top Indian companies are globally competitive across a wide range of automobile component products. Local firms have dramatically reduced defect rates and are using skilled labour to master new technologies.
>
> Evidence from firm-level research in India suggests that changes in WTO rules are unlikely to erode the position of local firms. Most foreign investors report that Indian suppliers are as efficient as imported alternatives.
>
> Domestic content restrictions were used to stimulate development of the components industry. Policies of this kind are not always appropriate or successful. But in this case the infant industry was successfully nurtured, with the participation of international automobile companies. The key question in other cases is whether multinational firms will source locally since WTO rules preclude local content rules.
>
> **Source:** Sutton 2004; Tewari 2003.

as is increasingly the case between the European Union and the United States. But the current regime is entirely out of step with what is required to strengthen the links between trade and human development. The starting point for reform should be a recognition that the purpose of multilateralism is not to impose common rules or a free market blueprint on countries with different approaches and different levels of development, but to accept the case for diverse public policies. The rules-based system could then focus on the key challenge of strengthening predictability and avoiding conflict.

Intellectual property

Intellectual property rules have an important bearing on human development. They influence the terms on which poor countries can acquire and adapt the new technologies needed to raise living standards and succeed in world trade. They also influence access to medicines. Any intellectual property rules have to strike a balance between two objectives: creating incentives for innovation through patents and other measures and spreading the benefits of innovation as widely as possible. The WTO's Trade-Related Intellectual Property Rights (TRIPS) agreement, along with "TRIPS plus" variants in regional and bilateral agreements, strikes the wrong balance between the interests of technology holders and the wider public interest.

The TRIPS agreement establishes a global regime for intellectual property rights based on the level of protection provided in the world's most developed countries, including a 20-year patent protection period. Reduced to its essentials, the new regime will increase the price of patented technologies, creating gains for patent holders and raising the cost of technology transfer. Firms in developed countries currently account for 96% of royalties from patents, or $71 billion a year.[58]

The TRIPS agreement threatens to widen the technological divide between technology-rich and technology-poor countries. The ability to copy technologies developed in economically advanced countries has historically been an important element enabling other countries to catch up. In the nineteenth century the United States copied British patents. In East Asia, Japan, the Republic of Korea, Taiwan Province of China and China have all upgraded technologies through reverse engineering and copying. The space for such strategies has now been closed by the countries at the top of the technology ladder. With technology increasingly important to international trade competitiveness, the rising cost of technology imports could further marginalize many developing countries.

The human development threats posed by the TRIPS agreement are especially pronounced in public health.[59] Prices for medicines are heavily influenced by the terms on which generic products, produced through reverse engineering, can enter markets and compete with brand name, or patented, products. For example, when the generic version of fluconazole, a medicine used in the treatment of HIV/AIDS, entered the market in Thailand, prices fell to 3% of the original level. Strengthened intellectual property rules will delay the entry of generic drugs, driving up prices. Demand for medicines is highly sensitive to price in poor countries, where households pay three-quarters of the costs of medicines. One estimate for India suggests that costs to households associated with higher prices for medicine will increase by some $670 million, almost double current spending on all antibacterial medicines.[60] Public health providers will also have to adjust to higher costs. Estimates by the government of Costa Rica suggest that its pharmaceutical budget would have to rise fivefold to maintain universal coverage without access to generic drugs.

Concerns that stronger patent protection would lead to higher drug prices motivated governments in 2003 to adopt the Doha Declaration on Public Health. In principle, the declaration strengthens the right of countries with insufficient manufacturing capacity to use compulsory licensing to import low-cost copies of patented medicines—to promote public health. It stipulates that the TRIPS agreement "should not prevent members from taking measures to protect public health".[61]

It remains to be seen whether the declaration is interpreted in a spirit that reflects this commitment. Following international pressure,

International trade

Easing restrictions on
temporary movements
of labour would offer
developing countries
huge gains

pharmaceutical companies have lowered prices towards cost level for drugs used in treating HIV/AIDS. This is an encouraging development. What is unclear is whether this action will weaken intellectual property protection on patented products for treating less high-profile health problems, such as diabetes (which affects 115 million people in developing countries) and cervical cancer (which affects 400,000 women in developing countries), or for preventing such illnesses as pneumonia (which causes one-quarter of child deaths worldwide).[62]

Even if the declaration is interpreted as intended, developed countries are demanding "TRIPS plus" provisions in many regional trade agreements. These provisions explicitly strengthen the protection afforded to pharmaceutical companies beyond WTO provisions and circumscribe the policy space for governments. Indeed, some developing countries appear to have adopted trade negotiating strategies that accept more stringent patent protection in return for improved market access.[63] The bargains struck have been unequal, reflecting inequalities in negotiating power (box 4.8).

Trade in services

Liberalization of trade in services offers potential benefits to developing countries. The problem is that industrial countries have focussed on areas that threaten to undermine human development prospects, while failing to liberalize areas that could generate gains for poor countries.

The General Agreement on Trade in Services (GATS) sets the framework for legally binding rules in the WTO. It covers four "modes of supply": cross-border (e-commerce and telecommunications are examples); consumption overseas (tourism or health provision, for instance); commercial presence (for example, through the establishment of banks, insurance companies or financial institutions); and temporary movements of people.

Developed countries have concentrated their efforts almost exclusively on commercial presence. Their priority has been to establish WTO rules that enforce the right of multinational banks, insurance companies and other service providers to operate in developing countries on terms equivalent to those applied to domestic providers. This negotiating strategy reflects a sustained lobbying campaign by bodies representing corporate financial service providers, for which such rules would offer expanded global markets. Developing countries have prioritized other areas, notably reducing barriers to the temporary movement of labour.

Efforts to promote across-the-board liberalization of services in developing countries through the WTO are entirely misplaced. In some cases services liberalization does offer benefits. Poor quality services are a major constraint on human development, growth and trade in developing countries. The presence of foreign companies providing services can improve transport infrastructure, reduce the costs of telecommunications and improve access to credit. However, liberalization is best managed through national strategies rooted in planning for the MDGs and wider human development goals, not through multilateral trade rules. This is especially the case in areas such as water, health and education. The starting point for any WTO regime should be a full assessment of the human development implications of the rules on a sector by sector basis—a provision that was included in the GATS but has so far been a dead letter.

Developed countries have been unwilling to enter substantive negotiations on the temporary movement of labour even though this is where developing countries stand to make the greatest gains. Easing restrictions on temporary movements of labour would offer developing countries the opportunity to exploit one of their areas of strongest comparative advantage: low wages linked, in many cases, to high skills. Consider the software sector in India, which accounts for 16% of exports and provides jobs to half a million people. Two-thirds of exports go to the United States and another quarter to Europe. Almost half of these exports—valued at more than $3 billion in 2002—are delivered on site by professional staff.[64] Delivery depends on market access.

Access barriers include some immigration-related issues, along with onerous visa eligibility

| Box 4.8 | **Going beyond the World Trade Organization** |

Recent years have seen a marked shift in US trade policy. While the WTO remains an important focus, regional and bilateral free trade agreements are being used to strengthen and extend multilateral provisions. Intellectual property rules figure prominently. Many of the bargains being struck raise concerns for human development.

Bilateral agreements with Jordan (2000), Viet Nam (2001), Chile (2003), Morocco (2004) and Australia (2004) and the regional agreement with six countries in the Central America Free Trade Agreement (CAFTA, 2004) have all resulted in "TRIPS-plus" provisions. Although the detailed provisions vary, three themes recur:

- *Extension and expansion of patent protection.* All free trade agreements provide patent protection for 20 years, as in the WTO. Under certain conditions, they require an extension of the period of patent protection. Under CAFTA, for example, patent holders can demand extensions to compensate for any delay by national regulatory bodies in granting the patent. All free trade agreements go beyond TRIPS in strengthening patent protection for plants and animals.
- *Restrictions on use of clinical data.* Before drug patents are granted, pharmaceutical companies have to register clinical trial data with national drug registration bodies. Access to that data is important for generics-producing companies, to enable them to produce copies of patented medicines without having to repeat costly trials. The TRIPS agreement states only that governments must prevent "unfair commercial use" of data. By contrast, most free trade agreements establish a five-year "market exclusivity" period in line with US law. During this period access to trial data is prohibited, potentially delaying the market entry of generic drugs and limiting the scope for compulsory licences. In addition, exclusivity applies across borders. The restrictions applied in one country (say, the United States) must be enforced in another (say, Nicaragua) and across all free trade agreement jurisdictions.
- *Restrictions on compulsory licensing and parallel importing.* Under TRIPS governments can authorize compulsory licences to allow generics companies to produce low-cost copies of patented medicines to promote public health. They can also

import patented products being sold more cheaply overseas than in domestic markets, an arrangement known as parallel importing. The free trade agreements weaken both provisions. For example, some agreements restrict the use of compulsory licensing to emergencies and cases of proven anti-competitive behaviour. The onus on poor developing countries to "prove" an emergency or anti-competitive behaviour is likely to limit recourse to compulsory licences. Similarly, while TRIPS allows WTO members flexibility in deciding whether to authorize parallel imports, most free trade agreements allow patent holders to prevent this.

The overall effect of these provisions will be to limit the capacity of governments to put downward pressure on pharmaceutical prices. The danger is that enhanced profit margins for the pharmaceutical industry will compromise the capacity of governments to address public health concerns.

Some developing countries have been willing to commit to stronger intellectual property rules while seeking concessions in other areas. Preferential access to the US market is the main negotiating carrot, especially for agricultural goods. However, the negotiating process has produced some unbalanced outcomes.

CAFTA grants limited market openings for the six developing countries involved (Costa Rica, the Dominican Republic, El Salvador, Guatemala, Honduras and Nicaragua). For sugar, a crop in which these countries have a considerable advantage, tariffs will remain at more than 100% and imports will be restricted to a 1.7% market share. Meanwhile, the United States has secured extensive market openings for rice, gaining immediate duty-free quotas for rice that rise 5% annually. More than one-third of US rice exports will now enter duty free, having previously been subjected to tariffs of 15%–60%.

So in return for, at best, limited market advantages for export crops grown mainly by large commercial farmers, CAFTA developing countries have agreed to accept intellectual property rules that could compromise public health and technological innovation and to expose domestic rice producers to heavily subsidized competition from the US rice sector.

Source: Tussie 2005; Mayne 2005; US Department of Agriculture, Foreign Agricultural Service 2005.

requirements.[65] Would-be importers of Indian professional services are required to conduct prior searches in domestic labour markets to prove that no alternative labour supply is available. They also have to meet wage parity requirements. This means that employers have to pay the wage prevailing in the host country (negating cost advantages), while foreign workers have to contribute to social security schemes (to whose benefits they are not entitled). Software

engineers are also required to meet minimum experience requirements (five years in the United Kingdom and three years in the United States) and to pass through cumbersome procedures for work permits. In addition, there are quota restrictions on how many workers can enter, and complex "economic needs" tests to be passed.

Immigration controls constitute an even more formidable entry barrier for unskilled

4

International trade

labour. The wage differentials between, say, a Zambian mechanic or a Honduran agricultural labourer and their counterparts in Europe or North America are huge. The average wage differential between developed and developing countries is 10:1—five times the differential for the price of goods. It follows that temporary access to the higher wage labour market offers big advantages. Those advantages are closed down by migration policies.

The temporary movement of labour could generate very large welfare gains. One exercise has estimated the potential impact of a transfer of skilled and unskilled workers from the developing world at $157 billion, equivalent to 3% of the work force in industrial countries. While developing countries would be the main beneficiaries, industrial countries would also gain through higher growth and increased revenue collection. Just as in trade in goods, however, there would also be losers in developed countries: unskilled workers competing in the same sector of the labour market as the new entrants could see wages capped or even cut. These estimates should not be taken as indicative of precise outcomes: they merely point to orders of magnitude. But to put the estimated welfare gain in context, a Doha Round agreement that liberalized trade in agriculture and manufacturing by 40% would generate a welfare gain estimated at only $70 billion.[66]

Tariffs and revenue—Economic Partnership Agreements

Multilateral and regional trade rules have a direct bearing on tariffs and other import policies—and on the revenues associated with them. While regional agreements involving the United States have been a focus in international debates, EU policies are also important.

In 2000 the European Union agreed to revise its system of trade preferences with the countries in the African, Caribbean and Pacific (ACP) group by replacing the Cotonou Agreement with a new set of Economic Partnership Agreements with six ACP regions covering 76 countries. The agreement, to be in place by 2008, will define the terms of Europe's trading relationship with some of the world's poorest

countries. It remains to be seen whether these terms will be consistent with a commitment to human development and the MDGs.

Under WTO rules regional trade agreements are required to extend liberalization to "substantially all trade". The European Union has put this commitment at the centre of its negotiating mandate. In addition to tariff reductions the European Union also plans to cover in the negotiations a range of non-tariff charges on imports, trade in services and the so-called Singapore issues of competition policy, investment trade facilitation and government procurement. There are no plans for any special provisions for ACP countries to limit surges of imports. Taken as a package, the negotiations mandate has the potential to produce an unbalanced outcome that is bad for human development.

Consider first the implications of liberalizing "substantially all trade". For rich countries this has limited relevance for government revenue. In Sub-Saharan Africa, by contrast, tariffs account for about one-third of government revenue, rising to about one-half for Lesotho and Uganda. Lower tariffs do not automatically lead to lower revenue—if imports rise enough they can outweigh the effects of lower import tax rates—but the potential for a sharp decline in revenue is marked. One detailed study concludes that three-quarters of the ACP countries could lose 40% or more of tax revenue, with more than one-third of them losing 60%.[67] Such an outcome would have profound implications for government financing of basic services and economic infrastructure.

Other aspects of the mandate are also problematic. During the Doha Round the European Union's attempt to secure a WTO agreement on the Singapore issues contributed to the breakdown of negotiations, with many developing countries—especially in Sub-Saharan Africa—opposing the strengthening of WTO rules in these areas. For practical purposes multilateral negotiations on the Singapore issues have been suspended. Critics now argue that the European Union is using its negotiating leverage over the ACP countries to bypass opposition at the WTO and develop stronger rules through the back door of regional trade negotiations.

Similarly, the European Union's failure to allow for rules that enhance the ability of ACP countries to protect their economies against import surges is problematic—not least in the case of products subsidized under the CAP.

The terms on which the European Union will apply its negotiating mandate remain uncertain. In practice, it has choices. While some EU countries have emphasized the binding nature of the WTO requirement to substantially liberalize all trade, that rule is open to interpretation, and a challenge at the WTO is unlikely. While many countries in Sub-Saharan Africa could benefit from lower tariffs, especially to promote intraregional trade, it would be wrong to use regional trade negotiations to pressure governments into rapid liberalization. Given the potentially damaging impact on ACP countries of opening up to subsidized agricultural trade, the European Union could also allow far more flexibility to provide protection on imports linked to CAP subsidies.

Beyond the rules: commodities, the new gatekeepers and capacity building

It is not just the rigged rules of the world trading system that tilt the balance of power against developing countries. Deep structural changes in the world economy are narrowing the opportunities for vulnerable economies to secure the benefits from trade that they need to help kickstart human development. Two trends, one long standing and one more recent, are proving particularly challenging. The first is the long-run decline in commodity prices. The second is the increasing power of such market gatekeepers as supermarkets. And in addition to these secular changes in the structure of world trade, poor countries, as always, are challenged by capacity constraints in their own economies. What currently passes for capacity building falls far short of what is needed.

The commodity crisis

"Proper economic prices should be fixed not at the lowest possible level, but at a level sufficient to provide producers with proper nutritional and other standards in the conditions in which they live...and it is in the interest of all producers that the price of a commodity should not be depressed below this level, and consumers are not entitled to expect that it should."[68] Half a century has passed since British economist John Maynard Keynes made these comments. His view was moulded by the memory of the Great Depression, when the collapse of commodity prices contributed to the breakdown of the world trading system, caused mass social dislocation and exacerbated international tensions.

Fifty years later millions of primary commodity producers are locked in a depression more severe than that of the 1930s. While surging growth in China has underpinned a recovery in the prices of some commodities, low and unstable prices are undermining progress towards the MDGs across a large group of countries. Yet the crisis in commodity markets is conspicuously absent from the international trade agenda. If the international community is serious about halving extreme poverty and meeting the other MDGs, this picture will need to change.

The protracted crisis in coffee markets demonstrates the devastating consequences of the wider crisis in commodity markets. From the designer coffee bars in high-income countries, where the price of coffee and the profits of retail outlets are soaring, the crisis in coffee is scarcely visible. Yet it is destroying the livelihoods of more than 20 million households in which smallholder production of coffee provides a critical source of income.

For more than a decade coffee producers have been trapped on a downward price escalator, growing more and more coffee in a desperate—and counterproductive—bid to protect their incomes. At the end of the 1980s coffee exporters received about $12 billion for their exports. In 2003 they exported more coffee, but received less than half as much income— $5.5 billion. Meanwhile, the coffee economy in high-income countries has been moving in the opposite direction. Since 1990 retail sales have increased from about $30 billion to $80 billion.[69] Low world prices have reduced costs and boosted profit margins for the six coffee roasters that account for 50% of world trade—and for retailers. Exporting countries, meanwhile, have seen their share of final consumer expenditure fall from one-third to one-thirteenth.[70] Viewed from the farms of coffee smallholders, the change has been even more dramatic. For every $1 worth of high quality Arabica coffee from Tanzania sold in a coffeehouse in the United States, a farmer now receives less than 1 cent (box 4.9).

Developing country exporters have absorbed huge economic shocks as a result of falling prices. Nine countries in Sub-Saharan Africa and Central America depend on coffee for one-quarter or more of export earnings. For each of them the price slump has undermined the growth and revenue generation vital to accelerated progress towards the MDGs. Because most producers are smallholders, falling prices directly affect household income and access to basic services such as health and education.[71]

Ethiopia is one of the most affected countries.[72] Coffee is its single largest cash crop, providing more than 60% of foreign exchange earnings and 10% of government revenue. About one-quarter of the population is involved directly or indirectly in producing and marketing coffee. What happens in international coffee markets has a profound bearing on Ethiopia's prospects for achieving the MDGs. In contrast to agricultural producers in the European Union and the United States, farmers in Ethiopia have no protection from falling prices.

The price shocks absorbed by coffee producers in Ethiopia have been enormous. Exports have increased by two thirds since the mid-1990s, but export earnings have fallen dramatically (figure 4.14). Beyond the adverse implications for the balance of payments and economic growth, lower export earnings translate into diminished opportunities for human development. Coffee, grown alongside food staples, is the primary source of cash for vulnerable households. Sales of coffee finance spending on education, health and other vital household needs.

Estimating the financial losses suffered by households is difficult. Information about production at the household level is incomplete. Moreover, in a market with wildly fluctuating prices the choice of reference years will have a major bearing on estimated losses. Taking as a reference point the 1998 price of $1 per kilo (a level that approximates the average for the past 15 years), we used household-level data to estimate how much the lower price of $0.30 per kilo in 2003 reduced incomes in coffee-producing households. Household-level data indicate that

---

| Box 4.9 | The crisis in coffee |

"Coffee income is very important to this household. I use it for paying school fees, meeting medical bills and running family affairs. But now I am losing hope in coffee. It has disappointed me so much." These are the words of one coffee farmer in the Masaka District near Lake Victoria in Central Uganda. They capture the desperation felt by millions of producers.

As in other countries, coffee in Uganda is predominantly a smallholder crop. It is grown alongside food crops—such as potato, maize and bananas—to provide a source of household income. Surveys of coffee farmers in 1999 and 2002 covering four regions that account for half the country's production capture the impact of falling prices. During the first half of the 1990s rising household incomes among coffee farmers—a result of currency devaluation, reduced taxation on producers and stable world prices—were one of the main forces driving poverty reduction in Uganda. Since 1997, as world prices plummeted, forced adjustments by farmers have begun to reverse this progress:

- *Increased debt.* More than one-third of coffee farmers reported being unable to pay back a loan because of falling prices.
- *Reduced consumption.* Families reported having to cut meat and fish from their diets and to reduce the number of meals eaten. On the day the farmer quoted at the top of this box was interviewed, his 10- and 12-year-old sons had not eaten breakfast.
- *Reduced investment.* Families reported cutting spending on home maintenance and the purchase of goats, an important source of protein.
- *Sale of food crops.* Families reported having to sell food staples to pay for health costs and school fees.

Source: Vargas Hill 2005.

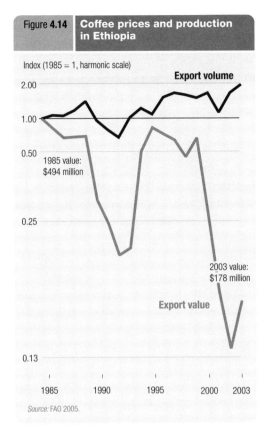

Figure 4.14 Coffee prices and production in Ethiopia

Index (1985 = 1, harmonic scale)

Export volume

2.00

1.00

0.50

1985 value:
$494 million

0.25

2003 value:
$178 million

Export value

0.13

1985   1990   1995   2000   2003

Source: FAO 2005.

the median coffee-producing household sold about 300 kilos of coffee in 2003. The loss in income as a result of the price decline amounts to about $200 per household—a huge loss in a country where more than one-third of the rural population survive on less than $1 a day. At a national level the loss translates into $400 million.[73] This means that for every $2 in aid received by Ethiopia in 2003, $1 was lost through lower coffee prices—a loss that widens the financing gap for achieving the MDGs.

Ethiopia is but one example of a far wider problem. In Central America falling prices produced economic effects amounting to a drop of 1.2% of GDP, without taking into account multiplier effects. The impact on poverty can be traced through household expenditure data. In Nicaragua the incidence of extreme poverty rose by 5% among coffee farmers while declining by 16% for households not growing coffee (table 4.1). Falling household income has affected other areas of human development, including education, illustrating again how problems in commodity markets can undermine progress towards the MDGs across a broad front.

As in other commodity sectors the problems facing coffee producers are easier to describe than to resolve. Oversupply has been driven by intense competition for market share, rising production and a widening gap between output and demand, reflected in rising stocks. Commercial practices have also contributed. For example, coffee roasters have developed clean-steaming techniques that enable them to substitute low-value, low-price coffee for higher value coffees, adding to a global price depression that has inflated their profit margins while consigning millions of producers to poverty.[74]

In the rush to liberalize agricultural marketing systems, donors and governments have sometimes compounded the problems of commodity producers. While state agencies were inefficient and sometimes corrupt, they also provided producers with inputs such as credit. Loss of these services has often made it more difficult for smallholders to enter global markets, especially for higher value-added products. In Tanzania rapid liberalization of coffee marketing led to the collapse of cooperatives that had maintained quality through price differentiation. The coffee price premium subsequently fell much more sharply for Tanzania than for Kenya, where the domestic market was only marginally liberalized.[75] The same process was repeated in cotton. Rapid liberalization of marketing in Tanzania led to the collapse of input,

Table 4.1 Welfare changes in Nicaragua—the cost of falling coffee prices 1998–2001

Percentage change

Household	Poverty rate	Extreme poverty rate	School enrolment	Per capita consumption
Non-coffee producing	−15.0	−16.0	9.0	9.6
Coffee producing	2.4	5.0	−7.0	−7.0

Source: Based on Vakis, Kruger and Mason 2004.

4

International trade

Supermarkets are now the
main gatekeepers of the
fastest growing market
in agricultural trade

credit and market information functions previously performed by state agencies, with adverse consequences for production and producer prices. In West Africa, by contrast, more active state involvement has facilitated increased productivity and maintained a high price premium for quality.[76]

There are no simple or universal solutions to the rolling crisis in global commodity markets. In some cases supply management is needed to restore market balance, though the problems with old-style commodity agreements have been well rehearsed. Market-based risk management tools could provide some protection against price volatility, but not price decline—and extending such tools to the poorest producers is difficult, though not impossible. Compensation is another option, using aid and debt relief to cushion balance of payments shocks. The IMF has a Compensatory Finance Facility, but it provides finance on terms that are unaffordable to most low-income countries in Africa. The EU Flex facility, launched in 2000, is more promising. It provides budget support in the form of grants, but eligibility requirements are so restrictive that few countries qualify: countries have to suffer a 10% loss in overall export earnings and a comparable worsening of the budget deficit. As a result, only $12 million a year on average was disbursed in 2000–03 and to just 6 of the 51 countries that applied.[77]

The role of market gatekeepers

International trade debates tend to focus on governments. Far less attention has been paid to distortions associated with the concentration of economic power in the hands of gatekeepers to developed country markets. Global retail and trading companies are increasingly important in the international trading system, linking millions of producers to consumers worldwide. These companies contribute to the wealth generated through international trade. But their increasing market power poses a threat to efforts aimed at strengthening the links between trade and human development.

Supermarkets are now the main gatekeeper to developed country markets for agricultural produce. Their growth is transforming markets. To sell in world markets, especially markets for higher value-added crops, is increasingly to sell to a handful of large supermarket chains. This has important implications for the distribution of benefits from trade.[78]

The top 30 supermarket chains and food companies account for about one-third of global grocery sales.[79] Within developed countries the market share of the largest operators is increasing rapidly. Wal-Mart, now the world's largest company, accounts for more than one-third of US food industry sales. In the United Kingdom the top five supermarkets account for 70% or more of grocery sales—double the share at the end of the 1980s. Parallel developments are under way in developing countries. In the late 1980s supermarkets accounted for less than 20% of food sales in Latin America. That share has now climbed to 60%. The pace of change has been astonishing: in one decade Latin America experienced a scale of supermarket expansion that took five decades in Europe.[80]

Concentration of power has gone together with the development of global sourcing and supply systems. Wal-Mart buys its supplies from more than 65,000 sources. Carrefour sources its melons in northeast Brazil to supply its retail outlets in that country and its distribution centres in another 21 countries. Royal Ahold sources apples in Chile for distribution through a centre in Peru. Companies such as Tesco in the United Kingdom source fruit and vegetables from more than 200 suppliers, many of them in developing countries.[81]

These trends matter for the distribution of benefits from international trade for three related reasons. First, supermarkets are the gatekeepers to the fastest growing markets in world agricultural trade and to markets with higher levels of value added. Successful participation in these markets has the potential to generate large income gains for small farmers, especially for those able to diversify out of primary commodity markets. Second, the concentration of buying power information gives supermarkets an enormous capacity to influence prices and the wider terms and conditions under which small farmers in developing countries trade with rich

4

International trade

countries. Third, the emergence of global supply networks spanning large numbers of countries gives supermarkets the capacity to shift their demand across large numbers of suppliers, further strengthening their power in the market.

The dominant business model in the supermarket sector places a premium on rapid delivery, high quality and—above all—intense price pressure. As an Oxfam report puts it: "Buyers work in a business culture of performance targets and incentives which encourages them to squeeze suppliers on prices and delivery times, with scant attention to the ethical repercussions down the supply chain."[82] Supermarket purchasing power ensures that adjustments to lower prices are passed back to producers. For example, in 2002 UK supermarket chains engaged in a price war in bananas, the country's most popular fruit. Between 2001 and 2003 prices to producers were cut by one-third, with devastating impacts on smallholder farmers in the Caribbean and plantation workers.[83]

Such trends point to a danger that exporters of higher value-added products in developing countries will be locked into the type of adverse terms of trade trends faced by primary commodity exporters. Supermarkets are also creating barriers to market entry that are far more formidable than tariffs for small producers. While prices are being squeezed, suppliers are required to meet improved product standards, along with stringent criteria for just-in-time delivery. Compliance requires a financial and institutional capacity beyond the means of many smallholders. This is especially the case when supermarkets delay payments; the standard commercial practice is to pay 45–60 days after delivery.[84]

With western consumers increasingly worried about food safety, supermarkets are under pressure to guarantee the standards and provenance of the goods they sell. But the cost of monitoring compliance with standards rises with the number and geographical dispersion of producers. This creates an incentive to contract with large production and distribution centres. The upshot is that the obstacles to market entry are highest in precisely the areas in which trade has the greatest potential to reduce poverty.

The experience of Kenya highlights the problem. Over the past 15 years Kenya has emerged as a dynamic exporter of fresh vegetables to the European Union, a rare example of successful entry by an African country into higher value-added markets. However, smallholders are being left behind. In 1997 almost three-quarters of Kenya's high value-added horticulture exports were supplied by small farmers. By 2000 this share had fallen to 18%.[85] The biggest change to the industry has been the increased importance of farms owned or leased by major export companies. One of the motivating factors behind this change has been the need to comply with UK supermarket standards, especially on traceability. Another has been the requirement to provide guaranteed quantities, which supermarkets can change at short notice. Looking to the future, demands imposed by supermarkets could further marginalize smallholders unable to afford the electricity, greenhouses and artificial lighting needed to provide uniform produce.

Kenya is not an isolated example. Worldwide, there is growing evidence of smallholder exclusion. In Brazil the inability to meet rising technical standards required by supermarkets resulted in 60,000 small-scale dairy farmers being pushed out of the local market in the second half of the 1990s.[86] As supermarkets extend their reach, the danger is that price pressures will intensify and market barriers through product-standard requirements will increase.

Lack of capacity

Export markets can offer huge opportunities for human development. Exploiting those opportunities requires more than open markets. Above all, it requires a capacity to respond to market openings—and to deal with adjustments. Many poor countries and poor producers lack that capacity.

Access to markets is a necessary but not sufficient condition for successful integration into international trade, as Sub-Saharan Africa has found. The region faces the lowest tariff barriers in developed countries, but this has not halted its marginalization. One reason is high

Access to markets is a necessary but not sufficient condition for successful integration into international trade

4

International trade

marketing costs—a problem linked to weak institutions and lack of infrastructure capacity. Transport costs add 15%–20% to the price of Sub-Saharan Africa's exports. At more than three times the world average this is a barrier that dwarfs the tariffs faced by African exporters.[87] The report of the UK-sponsored Commission for Africa has proposed a $10–$15 billion fund to overcome Africa's infrastructure deficit, underlining both the scale of the problems and the critical role of aid in addressing trade concerns.

Invariably, poor producers face the highest marketing costs. Many do not have access to the roads, technologies, market information or productive assets—land, capital and water—required to succeed. In Lao PDR almost 40% of villages are more than 6 kilometres from a main road, and half the roads are inaccessible during the rainy season. This makes it difficult to get output to markets and raises the costs of inputs. In Sub-Saharan Africa the density of the rural road network is only 55 kilometres per square kilometre, compared with more than 800 in India.[88] The inadequacy of rural roads raises transaction costs, reduces farm-gate prices and returns to labour and weakens market incentives. It helps explain why it is not uncommon for small farmers in Sub-Saharan Africa to receive 10%–20% of the export price of their produce, with the remainder being lost to transport and market costs.[89]

At one level the prerequisites for human development through trade are no different from those for human development more broadly. Without measures to overcome the deep deficits and inequalities in access to health, education and productive assets, integration into global markets will bring few gains. That is why trade policy needs to be developed as part of an integrated strategy for poverty reduction and human development. Leaving it to the market is not an adequate approach.

Some of the success stories in agricultural trade teach important lessons. In Senegal exports of fruit and nuts have grown by more than 40% since 1998, with smallholders the driving force. More than 10,000 rural jobs have been created. The key to success: a partnership of smallholders,

government and the autonomous Agricultural Export Promotion project.[90] The project is developing refrigeration centres, providing market information and rehabilitating freight facilities. In Ghana five smallholder cooperatives have created a company that has been at the forefront of an increase in pineapple exports to the European Union and regional markets. Initially supported by the World Bank, the company works with public bodies and private providers to contract for technical services that assist farmers in meeting product standards, procuring credit and exporting.[91] In India the Spices Board provides a regulatory structure and marketing systems linking 2.5 million producers to world markets, providing support for marketing and pest management systems and maintaining quality standards. In each case, public-private partnerships have been critical to success.[92]

Since the start of the Doha Round developed countries have committed to increased efforts in capacity building to overcome the capacity constraints hindering developing country exports.[93] An extensive set of aid measures has emerged under the banner of Trade-Related Technical Assistance and Capacity Building (TACB). On a conservative estimate, about $2.1 billion is now directed towards TACB, 70% of it for relieving supply-side constraints and the remainder allocated for institutional capacity building in trade policy.

While some important benefits have been delivered, TACB suffers from the problems in aid outlined in chapter 3, writ large. There is a multiplicity of technical assistance initiatives, with weak coordination, limited funding and, in many cases, limited ownership on the part of recipient governments. Technical assistance is frequently delivered randomly, indiscriminately and on a stand-alone basis. Equally damaging has been a narrow focus on implementation of WTO agreements, many of dubious benefit to developing countries (box 4.10).

Coherence is important for capacity building. All too often, trade policies undermine the very objectives pursued under TACB programmes. While EU and US aid programmes invest in capacity development for smallholder farmers, their trade policies undermine the

Capacity building is critical to successfully integrating developing countries in world trade. Developed countries have made this a growing priority in their aid programmes. But technical assistance for capacity building suffers from shortcomings that undermine its effectiveness. This is particularly the case under the Trade-Related Technical Assistance for Capacity Building (TACB) measures.

Donor-driven priorities. All too often TACB is biased towards donor priorities. At the start of the Doha Round the EU negotiating agenda prioritized competition policy, trade facilitation and investment—the Singapore issues. The overwhelming majority of developing countries, especially in Africa and among the least developed countries, rejected this agenda. Even so, in 2001 the Singapore issues accounted for one-half of total technical assistance in trade policy recorded by the WTO. By contrast, 1% of policy support was directed towards negotiations on agriculture—an area of vital concern for developing countries. In bilateral programmes bias occurs through negative discrimination (donors refuse to fund activities inimical to their immediate interests) and positive discrimination (support is offered in areas prioritized by donors).

Biased and restricted advice. Too much TACB advice is about how to implement WTO agreements dictated by developed countries, including much of the WTO activity conducted under the Global Trust Fund established in 2001. Too little advice is about

areas that might redress power imbalances and enhance public policy objectives.

Underfunding. Some of the most effective TACB programmes are chronically underfunded. One example is the Joint Integrated Technical Assistance Programme of the WTO, the United Nations Conference on Trade and Development and the International Trade Centre. This programme is highly regarded by African governments in particular. However, the programme is currently financed through a Common Trust Fund amounting to $10 million for 20 countries—hardly commensurate with the scale of disadvantage facing African governments at the WTO. Current funding for the Integrated Framework for Trade-Related Technical Assistance to least developed countries amounts to less than $6 million.

Weak links to development strategies. Donor efforts to make TACB integral in development cooperation and national poverty reduction planning have fallen far short of expectations. The Integrated Framework, a case in point, has carried out several high-quality diagnostic assessments of supply-side constraints, especially as they relate to the poor. Yet there is no evidence that the recommendations have been integrated into Poverty Reduction Strategy Papers, most of which say little about trade policy. Weak coordination, conflicting and overlapping mandates of the agencies involved and bias towards technical assistance over financing for infrastructure have further weakened the Integrated Framework's effectiveness.

Source: Deere 2005.

Box 4.11   Fishing for coherence

Sometimes capacity building suffers from outright policy incoherence. A stark example is EU fisheries policy in Senegal. While one part of EU aid and trade policy aims to support sustainable resource management and to balance export growth with local market needs, another part is undermining these objectives.

The fisheries sector currently accounts for more than one-third of Senegal's export earnings, an estimated 75% of national protein consumption and direct and indirect employment of about 600,000 people, including a large number of small-scale fishers.

Development of a fisheries export industry has been supported by the French Development Agency, which has financed about one-third of the costs associated with meeting EU food safety standards. EU trade preferences have protected Senegal from low-cost competition from Thailand. Other EU donors, along with the World Bank, are supporting projects to improve Senegal's capacity to manage fish stocks on a sustainable basis. The European Union is spending $12 million to support inspection and monitoring. Diagnostic work under the Integrated Framework for Trade-Related Technical Assistance has highlighted the critical importance of developing a national capacity to monitor stocks and control access.

While one part of EU aid and trade policy aims to support sustainable resource management and to balance export growth with

local market needs, another part is undermining these very objectives. Since 1979 the European Union has financed a series of agreements that give European vessels access to Senegal's fish stocks. The latest "cash for access" deal, a $64 million transfer covering the period up to 2006, is part of a wider network of agreements through which the European Union has subsidized access to the fish stocks of other countries to compensate for overfishing in EU waters.

After 15 years of "cooperation" with the European Union, Senegal's fisheries sector is in deep crisis. Stocks have been severely depleted, disrupting the artisan sector, pushing up fish prices in local markets and jeopardizing supplies to canning factories producing for export. Like earlier agreements, the current arrangement puts no limit on harvesting. And since there are no tonnage records, Senegalese authorities are unable to monitor stocks. This is in stark contrast with the European Union's domestic fisheries management, where limits are set on total catches.

The upshot is that the European Union is systematically undermining the development of a fish resource management system. All of this rests uneasily with policy coherence objectives set out in the Treaty of Rome.

Source: Brown 2005b; Kaczynski and Fluharty 2002; UNEP 2002; Picciotto 2004; CTA 2004; Jensen 2005.

4

International trade

markets on which the livelihoods of rural producers depend. One particularly stark illustration of incoherence in operation is the EU's fisheries policy, which actively undermines an industry in Senegal supported through the aid programmes of EU member states (box 4.11).

Turning Doha into a development round

As argued throughout this chapter, strengthening the links between trade and human development will require action across a broad front. The immediate priority is to consider trade policy as a central part of national planning for poverty reduction—and then to ensure that multilateral and regional trade rules support human development priorities.

The Doha Round—and the WTO itself—are an important part of this broader process. Good trade rules will not resolve many of the most pressing problems facing developing countries, but good rules can help. And bad rules can inflict serious damage. The next ministerial meeting of the WTO in December 2005 provides a critical opportunity to adopt a negotiating framework that delivers on the commitment to a development round. It can also set the scene for future negotiations that put human development—alongside progressive and balanced liberalization—at the centre of the WTO's remit. Failure to seize this opportunity will weaken—perhaps fatally—the already strained legitimacy and credibility of the WTO.

Rethinking WTO governance

Rule changes do not take place in a vacuum. They are shaped by institutions and, in the case of the WTO and world trade, by power relationships. The critical challenge for a multilateral system is to provide a framework in which the voices of weaker members carry weight.

In principle, the WTO is a supremely "democratic" body. Unlike the World Bank or the IMF, its decision-making structures do not reflect the financial power of members. The prevailing rule is one country, one vote, with each member having the right to veto decisions taken on what purports to be a consensus basis. In a formal sense, Benin has the same vote as the United States, and Bangladesh as the EU.

In practice, the one-country one-vote facade obscures the unequal power relations that shape the outcome of WTO negotiations. Some countries are more able than others to influence the WTO agenda. In the Uruguay Round developing countries, despite being in the majority, were unsuccessful in opposing the extension of the WTO's rules into areas such as intellectual property, investment and services. The agreement on agriculture left most EU and US farm subsidy programmes intact for the simple reason that it was in all but name a bilateral agreement between the two parties that was forced onto the multilateral rules system. In effect, the world's economic superpowers were able to tailor the rules to suit their national policies.

Institutional factors exacerbate inequalities between countries. The ability to shape agreements depends on the capacity of countries to follow complex, wide-ranging negotiations, an area in which some countries are distinctly more equal than others. In 2004, 33 developing countries, 10 of them in Africa, that were WTO members or in the process of accession had no permanent representative. The average size of a least developed country WTO mission is two professional staff. At the other extreme the European Union has 140 staff to make its case in WTO negotiations. That is without taking into account trade officials in national capitals, which would multiply that number several times over.[94] While some developing countries—such as Brazil, China and

India—field large negotiating teams and are effective participants in negotiations, most developing countries are marginalized.

This deficit in representation matters. In day to day negotiations sheer weight of numbers and easy access to expertise count a great deal. Capacity to use the system is also reflected in the dispute procedure: not a single country in Africa has taken out a WTO case. Correcting these institutional imbalances is a requirement for creating a meaningful democracy at the WTO.

How trade could deliver for the MDGs

Fairer international trade rules could give a powerful impetus to the MDGs. Generating that impetus will require greater coherence between the trade policies of developed country governments and their development polices and commitments. Unfair and unbalanced trade rules are hampering international efforts to achieve the MDGs. The Doha Round provides an opportunity to address this problem, but there has been little progress so far. What is needed is a two-step approach to refocus the round on its development objectives and to set a development framework for future negotiations.

A down payment on the development round
The ministerial meeting in Hong Kong, China (SAR), in December 2005 provides a last chance to restore confidence in the Doha Round. That meeting needs to deliver tangible and practical results. These results should include a down payment on the development round in three specific areas: market access, agricultural support and special and differential treatment for developing countries.

The 2005 ministerial meeting provides an opportunity to remove some of the more egregious market access restrictions that limit the ability of poor countries to benefit from trade. Binding schedules should be agreed upon to:
- Eliminate tariff peaks and reduce tariff escalation by lowering maximum tariffs to no more than twice the average tariff by 2010.
- Implement the proposal of the UK-sponsored Commission for Africa to apply duty-free and quota-free access to all exports from low-income Sub-Saharan Africa and to extend this access to all least developed countries in other regions.
- Relax rules of origin by adopting before 2007 legislation based on international best practice to reduce the value-added requirement for eligible products to 25% of export value and allow countries receiving preferences to source inputs from anywhere in the world.
- Establish in 2006 a trade adjustment compensation fund providing $500 million a year for the next decade to compensate countries for preference erosion.

Progress in agriculture is critical. Developed country policies destabilize and depress world markets, undermine the position of competitive agricultural exporters and increase rural poverty by flooding food markets in poor countries with subsidized exports. After four years of negotiations, nothing has been achieved. No timetable has been set for eliminating export subsidies, and developed countries are restructuring subsidies to evade WTO disciplines. Immediate priorities for a schedule of commitments by developed countries should provide for the following:
- A binding prohibition on all direct export subsidies by 2007.
- A reduction in overall subsidies by 2010 to a level no higher than 10% of the value of production.
- Compensation for developing country producers most affected by developed country agricultural policies in key commodities such as sugar and cotton.
- Phased reduction in import tariffs through the so-called Swiss formula, which makes the deepest cuts on the highest tariffs, with a ceiling of 10% by 2010.
- An end to Blue Box provisions that allow countries to provide unlimited market-based support.

WTO rules recognize in principle that developing countries should not have to make commitments incompatible with their economic status and development needs. In practice, the special and differential treatment

International trade

provision has failed to provide a framework for aligning WTO obligations with a commitment to human development. This was recognized in the Doha Declaration, which called for "more precise, effective and operational" rules. However, developing countries have come under pressure to liberalize imports at a rate inconsistent with their development needs. While import liberalization can offer advantages for human development, it should be applied in a sequenced fashion consistent with national poverty reduction strategies and the MDGs, with which WTO rules should be aligned. The 2005 ministerial meeting provides a chance to elaborate these rules for market access and agriculture. To this end, developed countries should agree to:

- Limit reciprocal demands for market access in non-agricultural goods, allowing developing countries to reduce average tariffs through a formula that allows a high degree of flexibility.
- Exempt "special products" in agriculture from any requirement to liberalize, and permit developing countries to apply safeguard mechanisms to restrict market access when import levels threaten food security. These products should include basic food staples as well as crops that are important for rural livelihoods and the income of poor households.
- Revise WTO accession rules to ensure that new developing country members do not have to comply with liberalization demands inconsistent with their development status.

Looking to the future

It would be unrealistic to expect the Doha Round, let alone the 2005 ministerial meeting, to resolve all of the tensions between WTO rules and developed country trade policies on the one side, and the MDGs and wider human development goals on the other. However, ministerial meetings are important partly because they can signal intent. In the current context industrial countries need to signal their intent to revise agreements and rebalance negotiations in the following areas:

- *Industrial and technology policy.* There should be a commitment to relax the constraints imposed on the development of active industrial and technology policies through Trade-Related Investment Measures and other agreements.
- *Intellectual property.* The TRIPS agreement arguably should not have been brought on to the WTO agenda. While intellectual property protection is important, the current framework suffers from a one size fits all model that fails to take into account the needs and interests of developing countries. The challenge now is to strengthen the public health provisions in the agreement, increase the scope for technological innovation and, for developed countries, to act on the TRIPS commitment to help finance technology transfer.
- *Services.* Liberalization of rules on temporary movements of people under the General Agreement on Trade in Services would do a great deal to achieve a more equitable distribution of the benefits from trade. Developed countries should put the liberalization of service markets in developing countries on the WTO back-burner and prioritize instead a phased liberalization of their domestic labour markets.
- *Commodities.* The crisis facing commodity producers has to be placed squarely at the centre of the international trade agenda. An integrated approach that encompasses increased debt relief, compensation, risk insurance and, in some cases, supply management should be developed.

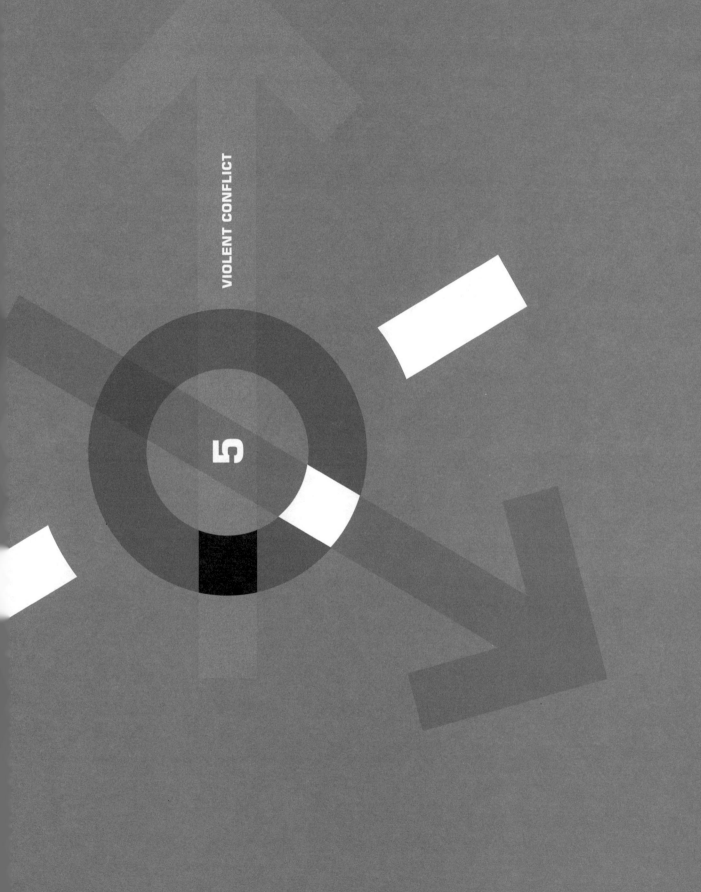

VIOLENT CONFLICT

5

"What begins with the failure to uphold the dignity of one life all too often ends with a calamity for entire nations."

UN Secretary-General Kofi Annan [1]

CHAPTER 5

Violent conflict—bringing the real threat into focus

Every civilian death linked to conflict is a violation of human rights. But the risk is heavily weighted against people living in the poorest countries

If human development is about expanding choice and advancing rights, then violent conflict is the most brutal suppression of human development. The right to life and to security are among the most basic human rights. They are also among the most widely and systematically violated. Insecurity linked to armed conflict remains one of the greatest obstacles to human development. It is both a cause and a consequence of mass poverty. As the UN Secretary-General has put it, "humanity cannot enjoy security without development or development without security, and neither without respect for human rights."[2]

Almost 15 years after the end of the cold war there is a perception that our world is becoming less safe. In industrial countries public opinion polls suggest that this perception is linked to fears of terrorist threats. These threats are real. Yet they also create a distorted perception of the distribution of human insecurity. Since 1998 terrorism has been responsible for nearly 20,000 fatalities globally.[3] Meanwhile, conflict in the Democratic Republic of the Congo is estimated to have caused nearly 4 million deaths, the vast majority not from bullets but from malnutrition and disease. In Sudan the ongoing humanitarian tragedy in the Darfur region flickers intermittently into world news reports, yet it is claiming victims on a scale that dwarfs the threats facing people in rich countries. Every civilian death linked to conflict is a violation of human rights. But the risk of violation is heavily weighted against people living in the world's poorest countries.

Since 1990 more than 3 million people have died in armed conflict.[4] Almost all of the deaths directly attributable to conflict have happened in developing countries. Apart from the immediate human costs, violent conflict disrupts whole societies and can roll back human development gains built up over generations. Conflict disrupts food systems, contributes to hunger and malnutrition and undermines progress in health and education. About 25 million people are currently internally displaced because of conflict or human rights violations.[5] Nine of the 10 countries ranked at the bottom in the human development index (HDI) have experienced violent conflict at some point since 1990.

Violent conflict in developing countries demands the attention of rich countries. Moral responsibility to address suffering and a shared interest in collective security provide the two most compelling reasons for rich countries to participate in the development of a collective security strategy for all. The rights violated by conflict are universal human rights that the entire international community has a moral and legal duty to uphold. The Millennium Development Goals (MDGs) provide another rationale for putting human security in developing countries at the centre of the international agenda. Few things in the future are certain. But one certainty is that preventing and resolving conflict and seizing opportunities for post-conflict reconstruction would demonstrably accelerate progress towards the MDGs. Conversely, failure in these areas will make it difficult for the world to achieve the targets it has set.

5

Violent conflict

Rich countries have another reason to prioritize measures to address the challenges posed by violent conflict in poor countries. That reason can be summarized in two words: enlightened self-interest. One hundred years ago states may have had the option of building security at home by investing in military hardware, strengthening borders and treating their countries as islands that could be insulated from the world beyond. That option has gone. In our globalized world no country is an island. Violent conflict creates problems that travel without passports and do not respect national borders, even when those borders are elaborately defended. As the UN Secretary-General's High-level Panel on Threats, Challenges and Change warned in 2004, in an interdependent world collective security cannot be developed on a purely national basis.[6]

Collective security links people in rich countries directly to communities in poor countries where lives are being devastated by conflict. International drug trafficking and illicit arms transfers provide the financing and the weapons that fuel violent conflicts in countries such as Afghanistan and Haiti—and they create profound threats to public welfare in rich countries. When health systems collapse because of violent conflict, rich countries as well as poor face an increased threat of infectious disease. The breakdown of immunization systems in Central Africa and parts of West Africa is a recent example. When violence uproots people from their homes, the flows of refugees and displaced people, and the export of conflict to neighbours, create challenges for the entire international community. When weak states tip over into violent conflict, they provide a natural habitat for terrorist groups that pose a security risk to people in rich countries while perpetuating violence in poor ones. Above all, when rich countries, through their indifference, display a tolerance for poverty and violent conflict, it challenges the hope that an interconnected world can improve the lot of everyone, including the poor, the vulnerable and the insecure.

Violent conflict in poor countries is one aspect of global insecurity. But threats to security extend not just to war, civil violence, terrorism and organized crime, but also to poverty. Infectious disease, hunger and environmental degradation are still far bigger killers than armed conflict—and each of these killers is both a cause and an effect of violent conflict. While there is no automatic link between poverty and civil conflict, violent outcomes are more likely in societies marked by deep polarization, weak institutions and chronic poverty. The threats posed by terrorism demand a global response. So do the threats posed by human insecurity in the broader sense. Indeed, the "war against terror" will never be won unless human security is extended and strengthened. Today's security strategies suffer from an overdeveloped military response to collective security threats and an underdeveloped human security response.

This chapter looks at the human development challenge posed by violent conflict. The first section outlines the changing nature of conflict and examines the human development costs. It shows how the nature of conflict has changed, along with the geography of conflict: wars between states have given way to conflicts within borders, with poor countries figuring more prominently. The second section looks at some of the structural weaknesses affecting states that are prone to conflict. These range from weak capacity to provide basic services to contested legitimacy and deep horizontal inequalities. The third section turns to questions of what rich countries can do to enhance human security. The fourth section explores the transitions from war to peace to security and the facilitating roles of aid and the private sector. The final section highlights what the international community can do to build collective security. While this is a large agenda, it focuses on four areas: aid for conflict-prone countries, market interventions to deprive conflict areas of finance and arms, the development of regional capacity, and reconstruction.

Violent conflict at the start of the twenty-first century

The international security institutions of today were formed as a response to the two world wars and the threats posed by the cold war

Eleven years ago *Human Development Report 1994* set out a framework for security beyond narrowly defined military concerns. Human security, the report argued, has two aspects: safety from chronic threats, like hunger, disease and repression, and protection from sudden disruptions in the patterns of daily life. Violent conflict undermines human security in both dimensions. It reinforces poverty and devastates ordinary lives.

The international security institutions of today were formed as a response to the two great wars of the first half of the twentieth century and the threats posed by the cold war. Today's world faces new challenges. The nature and geography of conflict have changed. Sixty years ago a visionary generation of post-war leaders sought to address the threats posed by conflicts between states. The United Nations was a product of their efforts. At the start of the twenty-first century most conflicts are within states, and most victims are civilians. The challenges are no less profound than those faced 60 years ago. Yet as UN Secretary-General Kofi Annan pointed out in his proposals for reforming the United Nations, the response has been limited: "On the security side, despite a heightened sense of threat among many, we lack even a basic consensus, and implementation, where it occurs, is all too often contested."[7] The human development costs of failure to provide a vision backed by a practical strategy are immense, but insufficiently appreciated.

Security risks have shifted towards poor countries

Viewed over the long term, we live in an increasingly violent world. The century that just ended was the most violent humanity has experienced. Nearly three times as many people were killed in conflict in the twentieth century as in the previous four centuries combined (table 5.1).

Conflict trends can be interpreted in both a positive and a negative light. The last decade of the twentieth century witnessed a marked reduction in the number of conflicts. From a high of 51 conflicts in 1991 there were only 29 ongoing conflicts in 2003 (figure 5.1). But although the number of conflicts has declined, the wars of the last 15 years have exacted an extremely large toll in human lives. The Rwandan genocide in 1994 killed almost 1 million people. The civil war in the Democratic Republic of the Congo has killed some 7% of the population. In Sudan a two-decade long civil war between the north and the south claimed more than 2 million lives and displaced 6 million people. As that conflict

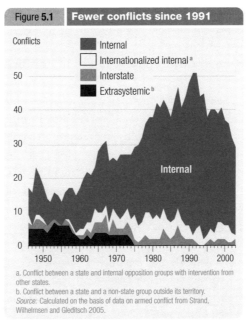

Figure 5.1 **Fewer conflicts since 1991**

Conflicts

- Internal
- Internationalized internal [a]
- Interstate
- Extrasystemic [b]

Internal

a. Conflict between a state and internal opposition groups with intervention from other states.
b. Conflict between a state and a non-state group outside its territory.
Source: Calculated on the basis of data on armed conflict from Strand, Wilhelmsen and Gleditsch 2005.

Table 5.1 **Conflicts steadily cost more in human lives**

Period	Conflict-related deaths (millions)	World population, mid-century (millions)	Conflict-related deaths as share of world population (%)
Sixteenth century	1.6	493.3	0.32
Seventeenth century	6.1	579.1	1.05
Eighteenth century	7.0	757.4	0.92
Nineteenth century	19.4	1,172.9	1.65
Twentieth century	109.7	2,519.5	4.35

Source: Conflict deaths data, Sivard 1991, 1996; twentieth century population data, UN 2005d; other population data, Human Development Report Office interpolation based on Sykes 2004 (table B-10).

5

Violent conflict

Figure **5.2**

Security risks are shifting to Africa

Share of global conflicts

30% 38% Africa[a]

1946–1989 1990–2003

a. The entire continent, not just Sub-Saharan Africa.
Source: Calculated on the basis of data on armed conflict from Strand, Wilhelmsen and Gleditsch 2005.

ended, a new state-sponsored humanitarian crisis erupted in the western region of Darfur. Today, an estimated 2.3 million people are displaced and another 200,000 or more have fled into neighbouring Chad. The 1990s also saw ethnic cleansing in the heart of Europe, as violent civil conflicts swept the Balkans.

The geographical pattern of conflict has changed over time, with a clear shift in security risks towards the poorest countries. During 1946–89 low-income developing countries accounted for just over one-third of all conflicts. Over 1990–2003 low-income countries accounted for more than half of the countries and territories that experienced violent conflict.[8] Nearly 40% of the world's conflicts are in Africa (figure 5.2), including several of the bloodiest of the last decade and a half. Meanwhile, even though the number of conflicts is falling, today's wars last longer. As a consequence, their impact on human development is severe.[9]

Human development costs of conflict

Violent conflict imposes some obvious and immediate human development costs. Loss of life, wounding, disability and rape are all corollaries of conflict. Other costs are less immediately visible and less easy to capture in figures. Collapsing food systems, disintegration of health and education services and lost income are all aspects of conflict that have negative implications for human development. So do psychological stress and trauma. Statistics alone cannot reflect the full costs—and data are often at their weakest in countries undergoing violent conflict. But what is clear is that the immediate human costs, though enormous, represent a small fraction of the price countries pay for conflict.

The HDI provides a tool for looking at the longer term costs of conflict. HDI ranking is affected by many factors, so caution has to be exercised in interpreting the relationship between any given HDI score and the country's conflict status. Even with these caveats there is a strong association between low human development and violent conflict. Indeed, violent conflict is one of the surest and fastest routes to

the bottom of the HDI table—and one of the strongest indicators for a protracted stay there. Of the 32 countries in the low human development section of the HDI table, 22 have experienced conflict at some point since 1990 and 5 of these experienced human development reversals over the decade. The lethal impact of violent conflict on human development is readily apparent from the following:

- Nine of the 10 lowest HDI countries have experienced conflict at some point since 1990. Only two of them were democracies.[10]
- Seven of the 10 countries in the bottom ranking in GDP per capita have undergone conflict in recent years.
- Five of the 10 countries with the lowest life expectancy suffered conflict in the last 15 years.
- Nine of the 10 countries with the highest infant mortality and child mortality rates have suffered conflict in recent years.
- Eight of the 10 countries with the lowest primary enrolment ratio have experienced conflict at some point since 1990.
- Nine of the 18 countries whose HDI declined in the 1990s experienced conflict in the same period. Per capita incomes and life expectancy fell in virtually all of these countries.

As a result of these human development reversals, countries suffering violent conflict are among the group furthest off track for achieving the MDGs. Despite data gaps in conflict countries that make it difficult to link conflict incidence with MDG performance, evidence on child mortality is available for almost all countries. Thirty of the 52 countries with child mortality rates that have stagnated or worsened have experienced conflict since 1990. As in other areas of human development, indicators of child welfare provide a sensitive barometer for measuring the impact of conflict on human well-being.

Striking as they are, HDI indicators for countries in conflict provide a static snapshot of a dynamic picture. The losses in welfare that they reflect are cumulative and extend across different dimensions of welfare. In Sudan violent conflict has not only claimed lives but has created conditions under which human development

5

Violent conflict

reversals are transmitted across generations. In southern Sudan only about one in five children attend school, less than one-third of the population has adequate sanitation, and the maternal mortality ratio (763 deaths per 100,000 live births) is one of the highest in the world. The peace settlement that brought the long-running North-South conflict to a close has created at least the possibility of recovery. Meanwhile, in the Darfur region government-backed militia have engineered another human development crisis. Malnutrition rates are estimated at 40%, and 60% of people have no access to clean water. While the child mortality rate in Sudan is half the Sub-Saharan African average, the latest estimates suggest that the mortality rate in northern Darfur is three times the average and in West Darfur six times the average. Meanwhile, the conflict is creating the conditions for long-term food insecurity. The displacement is so widespread and persistent that few households are expected to return home for the 2005 planting season, with the result that access to food and income will become more precarious.

As the case of Darfur demonstrates in extreme form, violent conflict claims lives not just through bullets but through the erosion of human security more broadly. The disruption of food systems, the collapse of livelihoods and the disintegration of already limited basic services create powerful multiplier effects, with children in the front rank of victims. Of the 3 million deaths worldwide related to violent conflict since 1990, children account for about 2 million. Many of these deaths occurred in the Democratic Republic of the Congo (box 5.1). Since 2002 a tentative ceasefire has reduced the number of deaths resulting directly from violent conflict. But the "excess death rate"—the number of people dying above the expected rate in a normal year—suggests that the violent conflict multiplier effect is still claiming 31,000 lives each month. Most of these deaths are attributable to infectious diseases among children.

Even limited outbreaks of violent conflict can create a downward spiral. Insecurity, losses of physical infrastructure, reduced economic activity, the opportunity costs of military expenditure, loss of assets and related vulnerabilities are

a toxic combination for development. Conflict increases poverty, reduces growth, undermines investment and destroys the infrastructure on which progress in human welfare depends. It encourages high levels of military spending, diverting resources from productive investment. Violent conflict also spreads malnutrition and infectious disease through the breakdown of services and increased numbers of refugees and displaced people. The following sections look at some of the main elements contributing to the human development costs.

Slowed economic growth, lost assets and incomes

Violent conflict creates losses that are transmitted across whole economies, undermining the potential for growth. With fewer assets and less capacity to respond to losses in income and assets, poor people are especially vulnerable to the economic impact of conflict.

The World Bank estimates that a civil war lasts seven years on average, with the growth rate of the economy reduced by 2.2% each year.[11] Few countries losing ground on this scale have a credible prospect of halving poverty by 2015. One study puts the average cost of a conflict as high as $54 billion for a low-income country, taking into account the increased risk of future conflict, although attempts to quantify the impact are open to challenge on methodological grounds.[12] What is clear is that the absolute amounts are very large—and that they dwarf the potential benefits of aid flows. Cumulative losses increase as civil conflict drags on. Long-running conflicts in Latin America have had severe impacts on economic growth.[13] In Colombia armed conflict between government forces and rebel guerrillas since 1992 is estimated to have shaved 2 percentage points annually from the economic growth rate.

Violent conflict gives rise to chain reactions that perpetuate and extend economic losses. A slowing economy and an uncertain security environment represent powerful disincentives for investment, domestic and foreign, and a powerful incentive for capital flight: transfers of almost 20% of private wealth have been recorded in some countries as conflict looms.[14] Alongside

5

Violent conflict

| Box 5.1 | Democratic Republic of the Congo—violent conflict leaves fragile states even worse off |

The conflict in the eastern part of the Democratic Republic of the Congo receives little media attention. Nor does it register any longer as a major international security concern on the radar screens of developed country policy-makers. Yet it is the site of the deadliest conflict since the Second World War.

The conflict illustrates graphically how the number of direct casualties can understate the human costs. Comparing death rates during 1998–2004 with what would have occurred in the absence of violent conflict shows an estimated 3.8 million "excess deaths". The conflict demonstrates another feature of the relationship between violent conflict and human development: peace settlements bring no automatic recovery of losses in human welfare. Despite improvements in the security situation since a tentative ceasefire in 2002 came into effect, the crude mortality rate in the country remained 67% higher than before the conflict and double the average for Sub-Saharan Africa. Nearly 31,000 people still die each month in excess of the average levels for Sub-Saharan Africa as a result of disease, malnutrition and violence.

In addition, whole communities have been dislocated. As of March 2004 the UN's Office for the Coordination of Humanitarian Affairs had recorded 3.4 million Congolese as internally displaced out of a population of 51.2 million. Dislocation and vulnerability at such a massive scale make this the world's worst post-1945 humanitarian disaster.

Poor households have been especially vulnerable. With dislocation has come loss of assets, especially in rural areas, which are more vulnerable to looting by armed factions. Many farmers have been forced to abandon their land in search of short-term cash incomes, often joining work forces in illegal mining operations. Disruption of agriculture has undermined food systems and exacerbated the threat of malnutrition. Agricultural production in eastern provinces is now a tenth of its pre-war levels. Even where crops are produced or goods are available for exchange, the breakdown of river transport links further limits access to markets. In the country as a whole almost three-quarters of the population—some 35 million people—are undernourished.

Children have been in the front line of casualties resulting from the conflict (see figure). Diseases like measles, whooping cough and even bubonic plague have re-emerged as major threats. In 2002 the infant mortality rate in the eastern provinces was 210 deaths per 1,000 live births—nearly double the average for Sub-Saharan Africa and more than 70% higher than the national average for the country. The infant mortality rate in the eastern provinces fell in 2003/04, demonstrating a "peace premium" in terms of lives saved and providing an indication of the costs of conflict. Conflict has also taken a toll on education. School enrolment rates in the country fell from 94% in 1978 to 60% in 2001.

Daily insecurities persist. Despite the All-Inclusive Peace Agreement signed in 2003, hundreds of thousands of people have still not been able to resume normal lives. In fact, since November 2004 nearly 200,000 people have fled their homes in North and South Kivu provinces, seeking safety in the forests.

The ongoing costs of conflict point to weaknesses in the peace agreement. Armed forces from other countries still operate widely in the Democratic Republic of the Congo, along with rebel groups. The eastern region has become a military base for the Democratic Forces for the Liberation of Rwanda (FDLR)—Hutu rebels linked to the 1994 genocide. It is also a magnet for forces from neighbouring states seeking to exploit the region's vast mineral wealth. Disarming the FDLR, expelling the armed forces of foreign states and bringing mineral exploitation under effective state control are immediate requirements for extending real security.

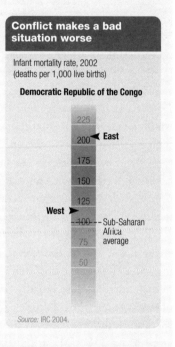

Conflict makes a bad situation worse

Infant mortality rate, 2002
(deaths per 1,000 live births)

Democratic Republic of the Congo

225

200 ◀ East

175

150

125

West ▶

100 --- Sub-Saharan Africa average

75

50

Source: IRC 2004.

Source: FAO 2004b; IRC 2004; Global IDP Project 2005b; Oxfam GB, Save the Children and Christian Aid 2001; UNICEF 2000, 2001b; UN OCHA 2002, 2004a, b; Oxfam International and others 2002; UNHCR 2004; WHO 2004a; Human Rights Watch 2004a.

falling investment is the loss of years of development through the destruction of physical capital. Destroyed roads, bridges and power systems represent a loss of past investment as well as a threat to future recovery. El Salvador lost an estimated $1.6 billion worth of infrastructure during its conflict years, with devastating consequences for the country's growth performance.[15]

The links between growth and violent conflict appear to run in both directions. Poor countries are more prone to conflict. Cross-country econometric research finds that countries with a per capita income of $600 are half as likely to experience civil war as countries with a per capita income of $250.[16] This suggests that poverty and low income are associated with conflict, which in turn reinforces the conditions for poverty and low growth. For many countries, the conflict trap is part of the poverty trap.

The economic costs associated with conflict are not neatly contained within national borders. The most immediate spillover effect of a civil war on a neighbouring country is the influx of refugees, such as Afghans in Pakistan and Iran, Congolese and Burundians in Tanzania and Sudanese in Chad. But the wider impact is the increased risk of being drawn into the conflict, consequent rises in military spending, declining investment in the region as a whole and disruption of trade routes. A country bordering a conflict zone can expect about half a percentage point decline in its own growth rate.[17]

In addition to the direct loss of incomes and investments, there are costs with a bearing on human development. Military spending increases during civil wars, with associated opportunity costs. On average a civil war results in extra military spending of 1.8% of GDP.[18]

These are resources that could be more productively deployed to provide social services and economic infrastructure.

Beyond the macro level, the cost of conflicts falls disproportionately on poor and marginalized people. Fears of violent conflict can disrupt local trading systems and cut people off from the markets on which their livelihoods—and sometimes their survival—depend. In northern Uganda violent conflict has led to the repeated disruption of cattle markets, with devastating consequences for pastoral farmers—one of the poorest groups in the country. The Karamoja region of northeastern Uganda bordering Kenya and Sudan does not appear on the standard media map of conflict hotspots. The scale of suffering caused by violent conflict suggests that it should. Partly generated by intense competition for resources, the conflict has increased the vulnerability of the Karamojong pastoralists to poverty (box 5.2).

A country bordering a conflict zone can expect about half a percentage point decline in its own growth rate

| Box 5.2 | **Impact of insecurity on livelihoods—an example from Karamoja, Uganda** |

Violent conflict destroys livelihoods as well as claiming lives. When peace breaks down, the movement of goods is often disrupted as traders abandon affected areas, lowering the prices of traded products and shrinking the incomes of the poor. Pastoral communities in eastern Africa have been among the most affected.

The Karamoja region in northeastern Uganda, comprising the districts of Kotido, Moroto and Nakapiripirit, shows what can happen when violent conflict and market disruption reinforce each other. Economic insecurities have become chronic. Bordering Sudan and Kenya, Karamoja poses a unique development challenge. It is one of the poorest regions in Uganda, with some of the worst human development indicators. It is semi-arid and vulnerable to drought and has limited access to markets and poor delivery of social services.

Conflict in Karamoja has complex roots. Most of the population are pastoralists. Colonial and, until recently, post-colonial governments viewed the Karamojong pastoral way of life as outdated, economically unproductive and environmentally destructive. Efforts were made to enforce settlement by de-stocking, imposing boundaries, restricting movements to dry season grazing areas and forcing intensification of cropping.

The consequences have included increased competition for scarce resources and destitution of pastoralist households. As livelihoods became more vulnerable, livestock raiding became a survival strategy. Large influxes of small arms following conflicts in Somalia and Ethiopia and, more recently, in the wider Great Lakes

region meant that these raids took increasingly bloody forms, as did the reprisals.

Today, conflicts over livestock and grazing maintain a spiral of violence between different pastoral clans. That violence crosses borders. In March 2004 the Dodoth raided the Kenyan Turkana people when the Turkana crossed over into Dodoth territory to graze their livestock. The Turkana had entered with 58,800 cattle. In a single incident of raiding the Turkana lost 2,915 cattle to the raiders.

Highway banditry has become a standard feature of the conflict. During 2003 and 2004 at least 10 lorries ferrying livestock were ambushed along the Kotido–Mbale highway. Traders are now reluctant to source livestock from pastoral markets in the area. In March 2003 purchases were less than one-tenth the level of a year earlier.

Armed raids have led to the destruction of health and education infrastructure. Many health workers and teachers have deserted their work for fear of being killed in local skirmishes. In 2003–04 two health workers and five teachers were killed at their posts. As a consequence, access to social services has declined.

Failure to address pastoral destitution has encouraged the institutionalization of violent conflict and raiding as part of pastoralism in Karamoja. Conflict is part of daily life. The heavy militarization of the region has created a situation in which lawlessness, deprivation of life and property and gun wielding are now the ordinary way of life.

Source: Gray 2000; Nangiro 2005; Odhiambo 2004.

5

Violent conflict

It is not just low-income countries that manifest a strong link between violent conflict and economic dislocation. Conflict also disrupts labour markets in middle-income economies, reducing the returns on the most important asset of poor people: their labour. In the Occupied Palestinian Territories labour market disruption has contributed to a sharp increase in poverty. Rising unemployment, increased poverty and falling incomes have gone together with a wider deterioration in human development indicators (box 5.3).

Asset loss can have devastating effects, depriving poor households of collateral and the savings that provide security against future risks. Problems are especially pronounced in rural areas when people lose access to arable land, livestock, implements and seeds or when agricultural infrastructure, like irrigation systems, is destroyed. In the Bahr-el-Ghazal region of Southern Sudan 40% of households lost all their cattle in the 20-year conflict.[19] Losses of male labour have intensified the pressures on women seeking to rebuild lost assets and maintain incomes. The female-male ratio in the region has risen to 2:1.[20] Women as heads of households have to not only tend to their children but also find employment and income in highly insecure environments.

Direct losses to agricultural production and infrastructure can have devastating consequences for poverty reduction efforts. Net

---

Box 5.3 **Occupied Palestinian Territories—how human development is being reversed**

The Occupied Palestinian Territories registered some improvements in human development through the 1990s. But the second intifada (uprising) since September 2000, and the associated military incursions in the West Bank and Gaza, have resulted in a sharp deterioration in living standards and life chances.

One effect of the conflict has been a major downturn in the Palestinian economy. Border closures have cut workers off from labour markets in Israel. Meanwhile, small enterprises have suffered disruptions to supplies of inputs and exclusion from markets. The effect has been to drive down wages and drive up unemployment. Unemployment rates rose from 10% before September 2000 to 30% in 2003. In 2004 the figure climbed to 40%.

An educated and, until 2000, increasingly affluent work force has experienced a dramatic increase in poverty. The poverty rate more than doubled from 20% in 1999 to 55% in 2003 (see table).

Conflict has disrupted all economic activities. Consider the relatively prosperous West Bank district of Nablus. Prior to September 2000 the town was a commercial hub. As a result of the conflict there has been a growing military presence, long curfews (a 24-hour curfew during much of the second half of 2002), more checkpoints and blocked access roads. The result: shops closing, workers selling their tools and farmers selling their land.

Restrictions on movement have affected healthcare and education as well. Nearly half the Palestinian population is unable to access health services. Maternal care fell sharply by 2002, and chronic malnutrition in children increased by 50% in both the West Bank and Gaza. In the past four years 282 schools have been damaged, and another 275 are considered in the direct line of confrontation.

Increased insecurity is affecting work opportunities and the provision of basic services, with negative consequences and reversals of human development for the Palestinian population.

Human development reversal on a grand scale

Percent

Indicator	Before September 2000	2001	2002	2003
Poverty rate	20.1	45.7	58.6	55.1
Unemployment rate	10.0	26.9	28.9[a]	30.5
Women receiving antenatal care	95.6	..	82.4	..
Women giving birth at home in the West Bank	8.2	7.9	14.0	..
Chronic malnutrition in children in the West Bank	6.7	..	7.9	9.2
Chronic malnutrition in children in Gaza	8.7	..	17.5	12.7

.. Not available.
a. Data are as of the first quarter of 2002.
Source: UN OCHA 2004b.

Source: World Bank and Palestinian Central Bureau of Statistics 2004; UN OCHA 2004b.

losses to agricultural production from armed violence in Africa are estimated at $25 billion for 1970–97, or three-quarters of all aid in the same period.[21] In Sierra Leone, where some 500,000 farm families were displaced,[22] production of rice (the main staple crop) during the 1991–2000 civil war fell to 20% of pre-war levels.[23]

Lost opportunities in education

Education is one of the building blocks of human development. It is not just a basic right, but a foundation for progress in other areas, including health, nutrition and the development of institutions and democracy. Conflict undermines this foundation and also contributes to the conditions that perpetuate violence.

Violent conflict destroys education infrastructure, reduces spending on schools and teachers and prevents children from attending classes. Schools are often a target for groups hostile to the government because of the association with state authority. During Mozambique's civil war (1976–92) almost half of all primary schools had been closed or destroyed by 1989.[24] Education infrastructure has also been badly damaged in the Occupied Palestinian Territories: 282 schools were damaged during 2000–04 (see box 5.3). The capacity of governments to maintain education systems is further eroded by budget constraints as military spending crowds out social spending. For low-income countries with data, spending on education was 4.2% of GDP for countries not in conflict and 3.4% for countries in conflict since 1990—almost one-fifth lower.[25]

Violent conflict also creates barriers to education. Parents are reluctant to send their children to school when there are security risks. In Colombia children abandon schooling at higher rates in municipalities where paramilitaries and insurgents are active than in other areas.[26] Insecurity linked to violent conflict is strongly associated with gender disparity in education. Even where schooling is available (in relief camps, for instance), fears of personal insecurity are a key factor preventing girls from attending school. The ratio of girls to boys enrolled in primary schools was 0.83 for 18 low-income countries

that were in conflict at some point since 2000 and for which data were available. The ratio for low-income countries not in conflict was 0.90.[27]

Education provides another example of how violent conflict creates a cycle that is hard to break. One survey of ex-combatants in Sierra Leone found that an overwhelming majority of those who joined the brutal rebellions were youths who had been living in difficult conditions prior to the onset of the war. Based on interviews with 1,000 ex-combatants, the survey found that half had left school because they could not afford the fees or because the school had shut down.

Adverse consequences for public health

Like education, health is a primary determinant of human development. Violent conflict generates obvious health risks in the short run. Over the longer term the health impact of violent conflict claims more lives than bullets.

Most of the 2 million child deaths attributable to conflict fall into this category. Similarly, increased vulnerability to disease and injury poses major threats for vulnerable groups, especially for refugees and internally displaced people. Acute malnutrition, diarrhoeal diseases, measles, respiratory infections and malaria are often cited as reasons why mortality rates among refugees have been more than 80 times the baseline rates in parts of Africa.[28] But even the non-displaced suffer because diseases that develop in refugee camps tend to spread easily to local areas. In Chechnya the rate for tuberculosis was found to be 160 cases per 10,000 compared with 90 for the rest of the Russian Federation.[29]

Violent conflict has a proven track record in disrupting the supply of basic health services, especially to poor communities. Like schools, health facilities are often viewed by rebel groups as a legitimate military target. Nearly half of all primary health centres in Mozambique were looted and the surrounding areas mined during the civil war.[30] Medical personnel often flee conflict areas as well. Even areas with good health indicators prior to the onset of violence can experience sharp deterioration. In Bosnia and

Like schools, health facilities are often viewed by rebel groups as a legitimate military target

Violent conflict

While entire communities
suffer from the
consequences of violent
conflict, women and children
are especially vulnerable

Herzegovina 95% of children were immunized before hostilities broke out in the early 1990s. By 1994, at the peak of the fighting, the immunization rate had plunged to less than 35%.[31] Conflict can disrupt the provision of important public goods needed to improve health across society and combat debilitating and deadly diseases. Despite worldwide attempts to eradicate Guinea worm, river blindness and polio, these diseases have taken hold in areas of the most intense conflict in Africa.[32]

Armed conflict has had a role in the spread of the HIV/AIDS pandemic. In 2003 of the 17 countries that had more than 100,000 children orphaned by AIDS, 13 were in conflict or on the brink of an emergency.[33] Several factors can contribute to the spread of HIV during conflict situations, and many of those factors leave women particularly vulnerable: population displacement; breakdown of relationships; use of rape as a weapon; increased sexual coercion in exchange for money, food or protection; collapse of health systems, with a resulting breakdown in access to information and supplies that can help control exposure to HIV; and declining safety of blood transfusions.[34]

Again as with education, armed conflict often results in fewer resources available for healthcare (figure 5.3). In 2002 countries with

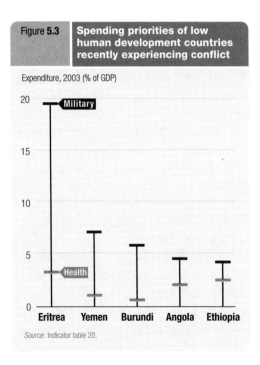

| Figure **5.3** | **Spending priorities of low human development countries recently experiencing conflict** |

Expenditure, 2003 (% of GDP)

Source: Indicator table 20.

a low HDI spent an average of 3.7% of GDP on military expenditures and 2.4% on health.[35] In some cases—for example, Burundi and Eritrea—countries allocate a much higher share to military expenditure than to education and health combined.

Displacement, insecurity and crime

Displacement is an almost inevitable corollary of violent conflict. The consequences are often long term. Following the loss of homes and assets, people are left with no means of sustainable livelihoods. Even once well-to-do families cannot support themselves or poorer relatives. For poor households asset loss translates into increased risk of malnutrition and sickness.

Worldwide, an estimated 25 million people are displaced by conflict. Driven out by armed groups or fleeing to escape violence, these people are acutely vulnerable. The camps housing an estimated 1.8 million people in the region of Darfur have become a symbol of the displaced. Driven from their homes by state-backed militia, people face far higher risks of malnutrition and infectious disease than they did before. In Colombia a protracted civil war has led to one of the largest displacements since those caused by the Second World War in Europe. By 2002, 2 million people of a population of 43.5 million were refugees or displaced.[36] Measured relative to the size of the population, some countries have suffered even worse levels of displacement. Three-quarters of a million people were displaced within Guatemala or had fled to Mexico by the mid-1980s, accounting for nearly a tenth of the population.[37] Over 600,000 Chechens—half of the population—are internally displaced after nearly a decade of conflict.[38]

While entire communities suffer from the consequences of violent conflict, women are especially vulnerable. Many of them suffer the brutality of rape, sexual exploitation and abuse, both during and after conflict. In recent years mass rape during war has been documented in Bosnia and Herzegovina, Cambodia, Liberia, Peru, Somalia and Uganda. During the conflict in Sierra Leone more than half the women experienced some type of sexual violence.[39] Many

5

Violent conflict

of these women continue to suffer from serious long-term physical and mental health problems, and some of them face rejection by their families and communities. Violence and acts of terror perpetrated against women are now institutionalized strategies adopted by warring factions—including government forces—in many countries.

Children too are especially vulnerable to the impact of violent conflict. Not only do they bear the brunt of the human cost, but they are also at risk from a special horror: the risk of forced recruitment as soldiers. The Lord's Resistance Army, which operates across a broad swathe of territory in northern Uganda, is accused of having abducted 30,000 children. Worldwide there are about 250,000 child soldiers.[40] Abduction is a central conscription strategy, though factors operating on the supply side also contribute to recruitment. In particular, poverty drives the children of poor households into the ranks of armed groups. In countries such as Sri Lanka rebel groups have recruited youths from the poorest backgrounds by offering them or their families cash or food.

Less visible than the refugees or child soldiers but no less important for human development is the breakdown of trust and traditional forms of mediation that can happen as a result of violent conflict. When these institutions are weakened, crime and insecurity invariably increase. This is especially the case in situations marked by high unemployment or where the state is too weak to preserve civil law and order. Civilians are often victims of looting and persecution by both state forces and insurgents. During 1998–2001 there were more than 100,000 homicides in Colombia—an average of 61 victims per 100,000 people each year. By comparison, there were about 5.7 homicides per 100,000 people per year in the United States in the same period.[41] This high homicide rate in Colombia reduced life expectancy during the 1990s by an estimated 1.5–2 years.[42]

Poor households often bear the brunt of financing the very conflicts that jeopardize their security. Both rebels and state actors fund themselves by looting assets from ordinary people or exploiting natural resources, creating a war economy that feeds the conflict. Those who benefit have a vested interest in opposing peace agreements. Illegal taxation and extortion are often preferred means of raising revenue. In eastern Democratic Republic of the Congo the Democratic Forces for the Liberation of Rwanda (FDLR) impose illegal taxes and systematically pillage local markets. The weekly "war tax" exceeds the income of most local residents. Civilians are also sometimes forced to pay the FDLR a large part of their profit from mining coltan, one of the few income-generating activities in the area.[43] Banditry, livestock looting and the state's inability to provide protection make insecurity a daily reality in conflict-affected regions.

The emergence of black markets and parallel economies that often accompanies violent conflict creates new opportunities for combatants—and new sources of economic dislocation for society. Limited state capacity to regulate natural resources, for instance, along with widespread corruption makes it easier for informal and illicit networks to develop. In Sierra Leone the informal diamond industry was a rich source of revenue for the rebel Revolutionary United Front and their sponsor, former Liberian President Charles Taylor. Thus, crime and insecurity become the manifestations of conflicts that might originally have had political underpinnings.

Interlocking insecurity

The human development costs associated with violent conflict make a powerful case for prevention. Once under way, violent conflict can lead to problems that are difficult to resolve—and to human development costs that are cumulative and irreversible. When poor people lose assets, their ability to cover health costs, keep children in school and maintain nutrition is diminished, sometimes with fatal consequences. Lost opportunities for education are transmitted across generations in the form of illiteracy and reduced prospects for escaping poverty.

It is not just human development costs that make prevention an imperative. The institutional costs of violent conflict can have

The emergence of black markets and parallel economies creates new opportunities for combatants—and new sources of economic dislocation

5

Violent conflict

The collapse of effective
authority in many countries
has undermined capacity to
prevent and resolve conflict

devastating consequences for long-run development. When conflicts end, roads and bridges can be swiftly rebuilt with external support. But the breakdown of institutions, loss of trust and the trauma inflicted on vulnerable people can make renewed conflict more likely. By weakening states, violent conflict can lock entire populations, and the populations of neighbouring states, into cycles of violence. Breaking these cycles is one of the greatest human development challenges facing the international community.

The challenge of conflict-prone states

For much of the twentieth century violent conflict was the product of a breakdown in relations between states. Today, violent conflict is a product primarily of the failure of states to prevent, contain and resolve conflicts between groups. No two conflicts are the same. Yet states that are prone to conflict share some common features.

Violent conflict can break out for many reasons. Attempts have been made to model individual risk factors. In reality, though, what appears to matter are clusters of risks and catalytic events. Some risk factors are rooted in poverty and inequality, though the linkages are not automatic. Others can be traced to institutional failure and undemocratic political structures, occupation or rival claims over territory. External events such as economic shocks, regional conflicts and changes in society that create tensions between political elites can tip societies over into violent conflict.

The collapse of effective authority in some countries has undermined capacity to prevent and resolve conflict. Governments lacking either the means or the will to fulfil their core functions, including territorial control, provision of basic services, management of public resources and protection of the livelihoods of the poorest people, are both a cause and a consequence of violent conflict.[44] As the International Commission on Intervention and State Sovereignty notes: "In security terms, a cohesive and peaceful international system is far more likely to be achieved through the cooperation of effective states...than in an environment of fragile, collapsed, fragmenting or generally chaotic state entities."[45] While ineffective states vary in form, three common characteristics that increase the risk of political tensions and economic pressures spilling over into violent conflict have been well summarized by the Commission on Weak States and US National Security: the security gap, the capacity gap and the legitimacy gap.[46]

- *The security gap.* Security, including human security in its broadest sense, is a basic foundation for sustainable development and effective government. Providing security is one of the state's most basic functions. This implies protection from systematic human rights abuses, physical threats, violence and extreme economic, social and environmental risks. Many conflict-prone states are unwilling or unable to provide security, creating opportunities for non-state actors to fill the security space. During the conflicts in Liberia and Sierra Leone government capacity to provide security was barely evident beyond a few urban centres. In Sudan the government has actively undermined the security of black Africans through its support for Arab militias and direct military acts against the civilian population.

- *The capacity gap.* State authority depends critically on the ability to provide basic services and infrastructure. When governments are unable or unwilling to do this, the resulting deprivation, suffering and exposure to threats of epidemics can build resentment and add to the loss of public confidence. In Liberia, for instance, the health sector has been essentially organized and paid for by international non-governmental organizations since 1990, not the nominally responsible Ministry of Health. In Sierra Leone only about a quarter of all rural births are registered, betraying the inadequate reach of welfare services. More than 90% of pharmaceuticals distributed by the central state pharmacy do not reach their intended beneficiaries.

- *The legitimacy gap.* Political, social and economic rivalry is part of the development process. Whether these rivalries take violent form depends on the capacity of state institutions to articulate the interests and aspirations of different groups, to arbitrate between them and to mediate conflict. All of this depends on having institutions that are seen as legitimate and accountable, rather than as channels for pursuing private interests. Conflict-prone states tend to have institutions that are dysfunctional, liable to breakdowns in political authority and tending towards violence to advance claims for control over resources, state revenues and state power.

Poverty, insecurity and violent conflict systematically reinforce each other. Not all impoverished countries are conflict prone—and prosperity does not remove the threat of conflict. But interacting with other factors, poverty can exacerbate the tensions created by the security, capacity and legitimacy gaps. The UK Department for International Development (DFID) lists 46 fragile states, which it describes as having governments that are unable or unwilling to perform core functions such as controlling territory, providing security, managing public resources and delivering basic services; 35 of these countries were in conflict in the 1990s.[47] On DFID's estimate these states account for one-third of people living on less than $1 a day. Attempting to establish whether these countries are poor because they are in conflict or in conflict because they are poor is a futile and largely meaningless exercise. What is clear is that poverty is part of the cycle that creates and perpetuates violent conflict—and that violent conflict feeds back to reinforce poverty.

Horizontal inequalities

Just as mass poverty does not lead automatically to violent conflict, so the links between inequality and conflict are complex and varied. High inequality is not an automatic marker for violent conflict. If it were, Latin America would be one of the world's most violent regions. High levels of vertical inequality based on income are associated with social dislocation, including high levels of crime and personal insecurity. Horizontal inequality between regions and groups poses threats of a different order, not least because these inequalities can lead to a perception—justified or unjustified—that state power is being abused to advantage one group over another. In practice, horizontal and vertical inequalities often interact, and the decisive factor may not be the scale of inequality in isolation, but complex political and economic tensions that have been played out over several generations.

The conflict in Nepal illustrates how inequalities across different dimensions can create the conditions for violent conflict.[48] In 1996, the year the current insurgency began, the poverty rate was 72% in the Mid- and Far-Western regions and 4% in the Kathmandu valley. Overlaying these regional disparities are disparities in human development status, with the HDI of upper-caste Nepalese about 50% higher than that of hill ethnic, Tarai ethnic and occupational caste groups. And while indigenous people constituted 36% of the population and *dalits* 15% in 1999, indigenous people held only 8.42% of posts in government agencies and *dalits* held only 0.17%. The insurgency in Nepal has its deepest roots in precisely the western regions where development has lagged behind the rest of the country—and where marginalized groups harbour a deep sense of injustice over the failure of state institutions. More than 8,000 people have died since 1996.

Nepal demonstrates how responses to violent conflict can exacerbate the underlying causes. Faced with a widespread insurgency, the government has responded with a battlefield strategy to counteract the activities of Maoist guerrillas. That strategy has been supported by military aid from some rich countries. The rhetoric of the

5

Violent conflict

Failure to address
challenges posed by
horizontal inequalities can
lead to violent conflict
even in stable states

"war on terror" has been used to justify the strong military response. Serious human rights abuses have been reported on all sides, but in some parts of the country there is a perception that state actors are now part of the security problem.

Political strategies for addressing the deep inequalities that have fuelled the insurgency have been less in evidence. Indeed, the political response to conflict appears likely to exacerbate its underlying causes. Citing overarching security imperatives, the royal government has instituted an absolute monarchy, undermining democratic institutions and outlawing mainstream politicians and human rights groups—prompting India and the United Kingdom to suspend aid. Weakening democracy in this context can only undermine the institutions needed to resolve conflict and restore peace. More viable would be a strategy to unite democratic forces to deal with the very real security threats posed by the insurgency and to develop a peace settlement that includes measures to reduce the deep inequalities driving the conflict.

Failure to address challenges posed by horizontal inequality can lead to violent conflict in more stable states as well as fragile ones. Until the late 1990s Côte d'Ivoire was one of the most stable states in West Africa. Government legitimacy suffered when political changes and rising regional inequalities were perceived as disadvantageous to one part of the political elite. The result was an eruption of political violence at the end of the 1990s followed by a tenuous peace in 2003. The lesson: political legitimacy and stability are fragile commodities that are easier to lose than to restore (box 5.4).

Horizontal inequalities do not exist in isolation. They interact with wider political processes that can generate violent conflict. In Bolivia recent outbreaks of political instability and violence have been linked to disputes over policies for managing the wealth generated by mineral exports. These conflicts have been touchstones for deep grievances among indigenous people over the unequal sharing of benefits from development.

In Indonesia the violent conflict in Aceh can be traced partly to the same source. Indigenous groups have mobilized around a programme that claims for them an entitlement to a greater share of the wealth generated by mineral exports, along with resentment at the perceived advantages in employment and education conferred on migrants from Java.[49] In 2000 Aceh was among the richest regions in Indonesia measured in terms of wealth but among the poorest as measured by the level of income poverty. Over the two decades to 2002, a period marked by rising oil wealth, poverty levels more than doubled in Aceh while falling by half in Indonesia as a whole. Rising mineral wealth has created a demand for skilled labour in the oil and gas industry and in government departments, which has been disproportionately met by migrants from Java. By 1990 (around the time the current conflict began) urban unemployment among Acehnese was double the level for migrant Javanese. At the same time, migration policies encouraged the settlement in Aceh of farmers from Java, most of whom had larger plots than the Acehnese farmers. The perceived injustice of these horizontal inequalities manifested itself in anti-Javanese sentiment, to which the separatist movement continues to appeal.

Conflicts linked to high levels of horizontal inequality or political rifts between groups and regions can be addressed. One approach is to restore political confidence through a process of multistakeholder dialogue. This approach starts from the simple principle that conflict can be resolved peacefully—and lastingly—only through trust and dialogue. The multistakeholder model has been widely used in Latin America, with varying success. In Guatemala the Civil Society Assembly played a crucial role in formulating consensus positions during Guatemala's peace process in 1994, with many proposals becoming part of the final peace accords. The assembly built bridges between government and wider society, although the government's failure to honour some of its pledges on land reform has weakened the outcome. Whatever the form, multistakeholder dialogue is unlikely to produce results if government actors fail to respond effectively to the social and economic inequalities that drive conflict. In Bolivia several rounds of dialogue between civil society and successive governments have failed to deliver tangible results—hence the periodic descent into political violence and chaos (box 5.5).

5

Violent conflict

Ten years ago few people would have considered Côte d'Ivoire a candidate for fragile state status. The country appeared to have institutions and political structures capable of accommodating the interests of different groups and regions. Today, after several bouts of violent conflict, Côte d'Ivoire's political stability remains uncertain. What went wrong?

Côte d'Ivoire has five main ethnolinguistic communities. The Akan (42.1% of the population) and Krou (11%), concentrated in the south and west, are Christian. The Northern Mandé (16.5%) and Voltaic (17.6%) groups live largely in the north and are predominantly Muslim. The fifth group is the Southern Mandé (10%). The country also has a large population of foreign origin who came during the 1940s from the current Burkina Faso to work on coffee and cocoa plantations. Many of these migrants settled permanently in Côte d'Ivoire. In 1998 one-quarter of the population was of foreign origin, though they were born in Côte d'Ivoire.

After independence in 1958 President Felix Houphouet-Boigny instituted a one-party state. But he carefully nurtured a balance among regions and ethnic groups through a system of quotas for government positions. He also enfranchised immigrants and eventually introduced a multiparty system. During the first 20 years after independence Côte d'Ivoire experienced political stability and sustained high growth—a rare achievement in West Africa.

This relative success started to unravel in the 1980s. Falling coffee and cocoa prices increased economic vulnerability, inequalities between the north and the south widened and tensions between locals and economic migrants in the southern regions increased. The 1990s witnessed the rise of Ivorian nationalism. "Foreigners" were no longer allowed to vote, a move that excluded political leaders from the north from contesting elections. The ethnic group of whichever regime was in power came to be increasingly overrepresented in state institutions, including the military.

Social and economic inequalities widened, partly through economic pressures and partly as a result of the use of state power to support favoured groups and regions. By the end of the 1990s five of the six regions with the lowest primary school enrolment rates were in northern areas. As measured by the Socio-Economic Prosperity Index,[1] the period 1994–98 saw the southern groups (Akan and Krou) improve their positions relative to the national average, especially the Baoulé tribe, while the Northern Mandé and Voltaic remained far below the national average (see figure). The Northern

Mandé's position worsened from 1.19 times the national average in 1994 to 0.93 times the national average in 1998.

The rising inequalities interacted with simmering grievances linked to political exclusion and the perceived use of state power to favour certain groups and regions. A coup in December 1999 led to the establishment of a military-dominated government. While this government agreed to hold new elections, it also introduced constitutional changes that barred those whose nationality was "in doubt" from holding political office. Disagreements over election results in October 2000 led to widespread protests and another change of government. The new government continued to favour southern groups, prompting an uprising in 2001 led by the northern-based Patriotic Movement of Côte d'Ivoire, which extended its control over half the country's territory.

Under strong encouragement from France and the Economic Community of West African States, the rival groups signed a peace agreement in January 2003. But implementation lagged, with deadlock over disarmament of rebels, eligibility criteria for presidential candidates and nationality laws. Political fighting has started up again in recent months, together with growing resentment against French peacekeeping troops. The current president recently announced that the opposition leader could contest elections later in the year, but core issues remain unresolved.

Côte d'Ivoire's descent into state fragility is a product of complex social, economic and political forces. However, the failure of the state to redress rising inequalities based on region and on group membership has been an important contributory factor. So has the failure of the state to ensure that it was perceived as reflecting a fair balance among different groups. The conclusion: horizontal economic and political inequalities can destabilize states.

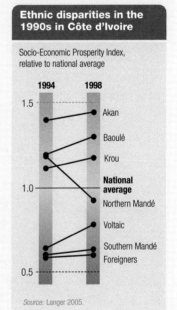

Ethnic disparities in the 1990s in Côte d'Ivoire

Socio-Economic Prosperity Index, relative to national average

1994   1998

- 1.5
  - Akan
  - Baoulé
  - Krou
- 1.0 — **National average**
  - Northern Mandé
  - Voltaic
  - Southern Mandé
  - Foreigners
- 0.5

Source: Langer 2005.

1. The Socio-Economic Prosperity Index is based on five indicators (ownership of a refrigerator, ownership of a car, access to piped water, flooring material in the home and access to flush toilets). It shows the position of a group relative to the national average.

Source: Langer 2005.

Natural resource management

In addition to intensifying inequality, natural resource abundance can magnify the capacity gaps that make some states more prone to conflict. Conflict-prone states are often desperately poor, but enormously rich in resources. Susceptibility to violent conflict appears to be a feature of what has been called the "resource curse". Once again, the links between resources

5

Violent conflict

> **Box 5.5**   **The benefits and limits of participatory dialogue for preventing conflict**

National multistakeholder dialogues are inclusive, participatory exercises intended to build trust among interest groups. With the help of neutral facilitators, national dialogues enable governments to respond to crises or to formulate long-term strategic policies. They are particularly useful when trust in political institutions has eroded or where democratic processes are fragile.

But dialogue cannot resolve conflicts or reduce social tensions where states fail to address deep structural inequalities that cause political breakdown. Bolivia provides living proof of the problem.

In recent years the country experimented with dialogues to frame development strategies. In 1997 a dialogue led to the General Economic and Social Development Plan for 1997–2000, aiming at poverty reduction centred on equity, opportunity, institutionalism and dignity. In 2000 another national dialogue was convened as part of the poverty reduction strategy process. It was run by an independent secretariat, which included many civil society participants. But frustrations increased as the policies emerging from the dialogues were not effectively put into practice. There has been growing disagreement over issues of economic policy: the exploitation of natural gas reserves; the eradication of coca crops in 1998–2001, which cost 59,000 jobs; and opposition to the privatization of public services.

Meanwhile, widespread inequalities persist. The income of the richest 10% of the population is 90 times that of the poorest 10%. Land is unequally distributed—2 million families, mostly indigenous, work 5 million hectares of land, while fewer than 100 families own 25 million hectares. On average Bolivians spend five and a half years in school, but there is a difference of seven years in mean schooling between the richest and poorest 20% of the population. Poverty rates, which had declined to 48.7% in 1999, rose to 61.2% in 2002. Moreover, 88% of indigenous people are poor.

Inequalities and discontent over policy responses resulted in violent demonstrations in 2003 involving peasant unions, worker federations and even middle-class intellectuals, forcing a presidential resignation. With growing protests, and the breakdown in trust they reflect, it becomes harder for governments to respond to demands in a sustained manner.

Source: Barnes 2005; ICG 2004a; Justino, Litchfield and Whitehead 2003; Petras 2004.

and violent conflict are neither automatic nor inevitable. Botswana has converted diamond wealth into high growth and rapid human development, while avoiding group-based conflict over revenue sharing. However, this is the exception rather than the rule across much of the developing world. The combination of weak governance structures and resources that offer the promise of windfall gains to those who control their production and export is a major cause of violent conflict.

In the post–cold war era revenues from natural resources have replaced superpower funding as the fuel of war. Between 1990 and 2002 the world saw at least 17 such conflicts in which natural resource wealth was a primary factor. Diamonds in Angola and Sierra Leone, timber and diamonds in Liberia, gems in Afghanistan, and copper, gold, cobalt and timber in the Democratic Republic of the Congo have all been at the centre of civil conflict, or—in the case of the Democratic Republic of the Congo—incursions supported by neighbouring states (table 5.2). In Cambodia the Khmer Rouge insurgency was financed in large measure by exports of timber.

As discussed in chapter 4, for many countries natural resources have become a curse not a blessing. In the conflict sphere the "resource curse" pathology works through various channels, impeding the development of political institutions and market economies capable of converting natural wealth into human development. Part of the pathology is in the diversion of national wealth. Financial flows that could have been used to support human development have frequently been diverted into funding civil wars, with governments, rebels and assorted warlords seeking control over oil, metals, minerals and timber. Angola is a stark example. The wealth from the second largest oil reserves in Africa and the fourth largest diamond reserves

Table 5.2	Natural resources have helped fuel conflicts in many countries	
Country	**Duration of conflict**	**Resources**
Afghanistan	1978–2001	Gems, opium
Angola	1975–2002	Oil, diamonds
Angola, Cabinda	1975–	Oil
Cambodia	1978–97	Timber, gems
Colombia	1984–	Oil, gold, coca
Congo	1997	Oil
Congo, Dem. Rep. of the	1996–97, 1998–2002	Copper, coltan, diamonds, gold, cobalt
Indonesia, Aceh	1975–	Natural gas
Indonesia, West Papua	1969–	Copper, gold
Liberia	1989–96	Timber, diamonds, iron, palm oil, cocoa, coffee, marijuana, rubber, gold
Morocco	1975–	Phosphates, oil
Myanmar	1949–	Timber, tin, gems, opium
Papua New Guinea	1988–98	Copper, gold
Peru	1980–95	Coca
Sierra Leone	1991–2000	Diamonds
Sudan	1983–2005	Oil

Source: Adapted from Bannon and Collier 2003.

in the world was used to fuel a civil war that killed or maimed 1 million people between 1975 and 2002 and left another 4 million internally displaced. Today, Angola ranks 160 of 177 countries on the HDI, with a life expectancy of about 40 years.

Windfalls of natural resources revenue can weaken the state at various levels. Two perverse incentives exacerbating bad governance stand out. First, the availability of large revenue streams can weaken the incentive for governments to develop stable revenue systems through national tax structures. A state that becomes less dependent on tax revenues will become less accountable to its citizens.[50] Second, natural resource rents offer immensely high returns to corruption for the state—and the individuals and groups that control it. Weak governance structures provide extensive opportunity for "off-budget" activity, and large revenue flows give individuals with power an interest in ensuring that these opportunities remain intact. There is no official figure for oil revenue in Equatorial Guinea, but the World Bank estimate of $710 million points to a large mismatch between reported and actual income. Such practices weaken the conditions of accountability and transparency central to the development of legitimate state authority.

Beyond borders

Not all conflict is the product of state failure. External factors are equally important in many cases. External problems are imported through porous human security borders, and they are re-exported as new security problems for other states.

These external factors take various forms. The unravelling of the Afghan state was actively supported through a Soviet invasion and the recruitment by external powers of mujahideen fighters to end the Soviet occupation. The subsequent civil war among resistance groups devastated the country and enabled the most ruthless elements to emerge victorious. The Taliban government, which was to take Afghanistan into a human development free fall, took advantage of the internal chaos abetted by external influence. In Somalia a process of militarization sponsored first by the Soviet Union and then by the United States led to a war with Ethiopia and to a brutal civil war between rival warlords controlling an estimated 500,000 weapons.

Whatever the balance between internal and external factors in causing conflict, the consequences are invariably regionalized and internationalized. Ethnic cleansing in the Balkans created flows of refugees into Western Europe,

5

Violent conflict

For violent conflict, as in
public health, the first rule
of success: prevention
is better than cure

and violence in Darfur creates refugees in Chad. Once started, conflicts can spill over into neighbouring states, undermining security and creating cross-border cycles of violence. The West African regional war that began in Liberia in 1989, migrated to Sierra Leone, returned to Liberia (where it undermined a disarmament process in 1997) and then moved into Guinea. In September 2002 combatants from Liberia and Sierra Leone were involved in the fighting that erupted in Côte d'Ivoire.

One feature of globalization is the narrowing of the economic space between countries. When states collapse, security threats can cross this narrow space with impunity. The creation of terrorist networks out of the very groups that had been supported by the West to oust Soviet forces provides a striking example of the boomerang effect of the Afghan proxy war.

Conflict-prone states pose an immense threat not just to their own citizens, but to the international community. They are a natural locus for warlords, criminal networks and extremist groups seeking to exploit a vacuum of governance. From Afghanistan to West Africa and beyond, state breakdown opens the door to the creation of havens for groups posing security threats to local people and to the incubation of cross-border threats linked to flows of refugees, arms trafficking, drug economies and disease. Fragile states matter beyond their borders partly because they lack the capacity to effectively control their territories, which can become safe havens for terrorists and criminal organizations.

The international response

In 1945 US Secretary of State Edward R. Stettinius reported to his government on the San Francisco conference that established the United Nations. He identified the two fundamental components of human security and their connections: "The battle of peace has to be fought on two fronts. The first front is the security front, where victory spells freedom from fear. The second is the economic and social front, where victory means freedom from want. Only victory on both fronts can assure the world of an enduring peace."[51]

Sixty years on, those words retain a powerful resonance for the collective security challenges of the early twenty-first century. Victory on both human security fronts remains a condition for success, yet the rate of advance is uneven. Progress on the economic and social front has been limited, obstructing progress on the security front. Improving living standards, extending opportunities for health and education and building the institutions needed to deliver real democracy should be seen as the first line of defence. Overcoming poverty will not only save millions of lives, but it will also make the social and economic tensions that create conflict more amenable to resolution. For violent conflict, as in public health, the first rule of success is this: prevention is better than cure. And development is the most effective strategy for prevention.

The international environment for developing an effective collective security response is marked by threats and opportunities. New peace settlements, fragile as some may be, demonstrate the potential human development benefits of resolving violent conflict: five years ago few people would have predicted that Afghanistan, Liberia or Sierra Leone would be in a position to launch a human development recovery. Industrial country governments are increasingly aware of the importance of building conflict prevention measures into their development assistance programmes. At the same time the military response to security threats is overdeveloped in relation to the broader human security response. The MDGs have given a renewed focus to global poverty reduction efforts. But as earlier chapters

5

Violent conflict

in this Report have argued, agreement on the MDGs has yet to induce the sustained financial and political commitment needed to translate targets into practical outcomes.

How developed countries perceive security will have an important bearing on the effectiveness of the two-fronts strategy. Security in the developed world has increasingly come to mean military security against the threat posed by "terror". Wider objectives have been subordinated to this goal. The threat posed by terrorism is real enough, for poor countries as well as rich. There is, however, a danger that the war on terrorism will distort priorities and give rise to strategies that are either ineffective or counterproductive. For example, the war on terrorism cannot justify brutal violation of human rights and civil liberties and militarized responses to development problems. Yet a number of governments have cited the overwhelming imperatives of that war to strike out against groups conveniently labelled "terrorist". These transgressions threaten to weaken the norms and institutions needed to secure peace. From the perspective of a broader conception of human security, there is a danger that the war on terrorism could sideline the struggle against poverty, health epidemics and other challenges, drawing scarce financial resources away from the causes of insecurity. There remains a very real threat that already limited development assistance budgets could be re-allocated to reflect the perceived imperative of military and foreign policy goals.

Human security can be fully developed only with leadership in developing countries themselves—it is not a commodity that can be imported. Yet human security is one of the key elements of the new partnership for development between rich and poor countries. Developed countries have a central role to play in removing the barrier to human development created by violent conflict—and they have a strong rationale for action rooted in moral imperative and self-interest.

Improving aid

As shown in chapter 3 international aid is one of the main resources available to accelerate the advance on the second front identified by Secretary of State Stettinius: the war against want. But well designed aid can also help address some of the challenges faced by conflict-prone states.

Recognizing that development processes intended to improve human well-being can unintentionally generate conflict is the first step towards conflict prevention. When aid is delivered into conflict-prone environments it can exacerbate tensions between groups—as happened in Rwanda. Development assistance benefiting a small part of the population to the exclusion of the majority contributed to inequality, fuelling resentment and contributing to structural violence.[52] Had donors been more aware of the consequences of their actions and more willing to engage in conflict prevention, it is possible that they could have pre-empted the resulting genocide.

New approaches to aid under the rubric "conflict-sensitive development" now engage donors directly in evaluating the potential impact of development assistance on different groups. Between 1998 and 2000 violence erupted in the Solomon Islands when indigenous groups in Guadalcanal launched violent attacks on communities from a neighbouring island who had settled in the capital city, Honiara. The conflict was defined largely in ethnic terms. A peace settlement was concluded in 2000, but militant groups refused to disarm. In 2003 the United Nations Development Programme (UNDP) and other donors worked with the National Peace Council and the government's Department of National Unity, Reconciliation and Peace to explore, through a wide ranging, multistakeholder consultation process, the grievances and frustrations that led to the violence. The consultation process itself challenged the prevailing idea that the conflict was fundamentally about ethnic identification. Participants identified several major flashpoints, especially tensions over land rights, the roles of traditional and non-traditional authority structures, access to government services, lack of economic opportunities and a breakdown of law enforcement mechanisms. The consultation process thus challenged the widely held and potentially dangerous belief that the conflict was

5

Violent conflict

If the threat of reversion
to conflict in fragile states
is to be averted, then
aid is an investment in
creating the conditions
for sustained peace

fundamentally about ethnic identity. It also exposed the fact that, in some cases, donor actions to support government services taken without prior consultations had inadvertently exacerbated tensions.[53]

External financing can fill some of the capability gaps that make states prone to conflict. To the extent that this financing prevents conflict, it can be expected to generate very high returns for growth and human development. Yet aid to fragile states appears to be disproportionately low, especially when discounting flows to Afghanistan and Iraq. With a few notable exceptions fragile states do not attract large aid flows. The issue is not purely one of poor governance. Cross-country research by the World Bank using a poverty- and performance-based allocation model suggests that aid to fragile states could be increased by as much as 40% based on the quality of their institutions. An additional problem, highlighted in chapter 3, is that aid to fragile states is twice as volatile as aid to other countries. For governments with a weak revenue base, this is likely to be highly destabilizing and to erode already weak capacity. Of course, there are immense challenges facing donors wanting to disburse aid in post-conflict environments. But it is important that allocation decisions be made on the basis of carefully considered and transparent judgements.

International aid is critically important in the reconstruction period. The objective of post-conflict reconstruction is to avoid returning to pre-crisis conditions and to build the foundations for lasting peace. If the threat of reversion to conflict in fragile states is to be averted, then aid is an investment in creating the conditions for sustained peace. Using allocation as a basis for assessment, there is little evidence that aid flows reflect a coherent response to reconstruction financing needs. Per capita spending in the two-year period after conclusion of a peace settlement ranges from $245 in Bosnia and Herzegovina to $40 in Afghanistan and $31 in Liberia (figure 5.4).

Differences in policy performance and absorptive capacity doubtless explain some of the discrepancy—and there is no set formula for squaring need with financing. Even so, there appears to be little internal consistency in a resource allocation pattern that leaves countries such as Burundi, the Democratic Republic of the Congo and Liberia near the bottom. The World Bank has acknowledged this problem in the use of International Development Association (IDA) funds—one of the major international sources for post-conflict reconstruction. Post-conflict reconstruction financing through IDA amounted to $45 per capita in Bosnia and Herzegovina between 1996 and 1999 but to less than $5 per capita in Rwanda in the three-year period after the genocide.[54] These discrepancies point to the need for far greater transparency in donor decisions on post-conflict reconstruction financing.

Aid sequencing presents another problem. In the typical post-conflict aid cycle aid peaks in the early years after conflict and then falls sharply. This is the opposite of what is needed. Capacity to absorb aid is most limited in the immediate post-conflict period, as new institutions are put in place, leading to large gaps between donor commitments and disbursements. Research suggests that the optimal period for absorbing increased aid is about six years after a peace settlement, by which time donor interest has moved on. The cycle just described helps to explain the findings of World Bank research indicating that in post-conflict states

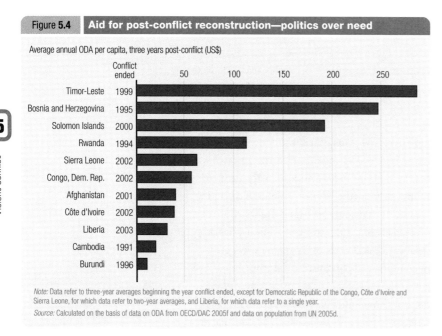

Figure 5.4 **Aid for post-conflict reconstruction—politics over need**

Average annual ODA per capita, three years post-conflict (US$)

Note: Data refer to three-year averages beginning the year conflict ended, except for Democratic Republic of the Congo, Côte d'Ivoire and Sierra Leone, for which data refer to two-year averages, and Liberia, for which data refer to a single year.
Source: Calculated on the basis of data on ODA from OECD/DAC 2005f and data on population from UN 2005d.

5

Violent conflict

aid absorptive capacity is nearly double that in other countries at similar levels of poverty.[55]

After conflict, states are especially susceptible to some of the general problems of aid described in chapter 3. An immediate priority in any post-conflict state is to develop institutional capacity and accountability to local populations. When donors choose to work "off-budget", through projects, and to create parallel structures for reporting, auditing and procuring goods, they undermine development of the institutional structures on which future peace and security depend. The danger is that poor judgement by donors will compound the very problem that donors want to address: the weakening of state structures and local capacity. The failure of coordination and coherence is particularly striking in Bosnia and Herzegovina. The country has received more aid per capita than Europe did under the Marshall Plan. Yet more than six years after the peace agreements were signed it was still in financial crisis.[56] At a far more limited level of institutional development, Afghanistan has also faced serious problems.

Managing natural resources and tackling small arms

Developed countries could be far more active in addressing two problems that generate and sustain violent conflict: the mismanagement of natural resource exports and inadequate management of small arms imports.

Breaking the resource curse

National governments must shoulder the main responsibility for effective governance of natural resources. But the international community can help to sever the links between natural resources and violent conflict. Cutting off markets can stem the flow of finances into areas in conflict and reduce the incentives to control natural

---

Special contribution | **Challenges for post-conflict reconstruction: lessons from Afghanistan**

The form and function of the state have usually been at the centre of conflict. The critical challenge in the wake of the political processes ending overt conflict is to adopt policies, procedures and interventions that would make peace sustainable, lead to an environment of mutual trust and solidarity and build the state as the organized power of society.

More specifically, several issues must receive critical attention:

- *Build consensus on a strategy.* In the immediate post-conflict environment a range of domestic and international actors enters the scene. Each has different perceptions, different capabilities and a different set of priorities, reflecting different mandates, resources and interests. If each of these actors pursues an autonomous strategy, the result will be a waste of resources, growing distrust and possible renewal of conflict. It is therefore imperative for the government and donors to reach agreement on priorities within the framework of a coherent strategy, agree on a division of labour and strive to create modalities of coordination and cooperation.
- *Restore and expand trust in the state.* For trust in the state to be restored, the focus must be on revitalization and reform of processes of governance, with particular attention to security, administration, rule of law and basic services. Creation of parallel institutions to the state, whether through UN or bilateral agencies, can undermine this necessary focus on the state.
- *Ensure adequate public finances.* Restoration of the functions of the state requires that the state have resources at its disposal. Aid flows are a significant part of these resources in the initial phase, but domestic revenue mobilization through activities that can yield major resources should be at the forefront of attention. Trust in the state requires making the budget the central instrument of policy and the arena for determining priorities and building consensus on the use of resources to meet national priorities. The aid system must try to help the government rapidly acquire the capacity for a medium-term expenditure framework and create mechanisms of accountability, including in procurement, financial management and auditing, that would result in donor and citizen confidence.
- *Use the regulatory function of the state to protect residents and build trust.* In addition to the other obvious tasks, stakeholders must pay attention to the regulatory functions of the state. Award of licences and regulation of the activities of the private sector (to protect citizens against such harms as leaded fuel or expired medicine) can be critical to trust. National programs directed in particular towards the urban and rural poor are an instrument for creating a sense of citizenship and using resources effectively.

Dr. Ashraf Ghani
Former Minister of Finance
The Islamic State of Afghanistan

5

Violent conflict

resources. Certification can be used to restrict consumer access to illegal products by informing potential buyers and customs authorities of the legal standing of commodities. In early 2000 southern African governments led efforts to prevent the export of "conflict" diamonds from Angola, Liberia and Sierra Leone. The outcome was the Kimberley process—a scheme under which importing and transit countries agree not to take rough diamonds whose legal status is not confirmed by an official certificate.

It is still too early to draw conclusions about the effectiveness of the process, but indications are that it has had some success: it now covers 42 countries and almost all global production of rough diamonds.[57] The European Union has begun to develop an analogous process to exclude imports of illegal timber products under its Forest Law Enforcement Governance and Trade programme. However, widespread illegal export of timber continues to cause large losses of government revenue, to generate extensive environmental damage and to undermine efforts to control corruption. It is estimated that illegal trade in timber amounts to 10% of the $150 billion annual trade in timber.

Improved transparency is another priority. The Group of Eight (G-8) countries has attached a high priority to improved disclosure and accountability in the minerals sector. An example is the multistakeholder Extractive Industries Transparency Initiative, which calls on oil and gas companies to disclose all payments and calls on governments to disclose all receipts. The initiative is voluntary, however, and lacks clear implementation guidelines. Moreover, progress has been limited by perverse market incentives: any company offering greater transparency runs the risk of losing out to rivals that do not encumber governments with public accountability obligations.

Corporate practices can add to the problems of natural resource management. Inadequate transparency can reinforce corruption and weak governance. The counterpart to off-budget activity by governments is off-the-book payments by companies to key individuals who are seen as gatekeepers to natural resource rights. In Angola more than 30 multinational oil companies

have paid the government for rights to exploit oil, without disclosing either to Angolans or to their shareholders how much they paid or to whom. In the Caspian region oil exploitation rights are governed by multinational partnership agreements between governments and foreign investors. Negotiated in secret, these agreements have given rise to some of the largest foreign corruption investigations in US legal history. Lack of transparency weakens government accountability and can exacerbate the underlying distrust that fuels conflict.

The UK-sponsored Commission for Africa has proposed building on the Extractive Industries Transparency Initiative approach and adding some legal teeth. Under most current legal frameworks it is difficult to prosecute a transnational company headquartered in one country for corrupt practices in another country. The framework proposed by the commission would close this loophole. It would allow governments in the countries in which transnational companies are located to take legal action against corrupt practices overseas. And it would allow developing countries easier access to legal processes for recovering stolen assets. Greater transparency could be encouraged if other industrial economies followed the US lead and strengthened laws to make corruption by transnational companies overseas a crime at home. The argument that such measures run contrary to the principle of open markets for investment is misplaced: such measures would be no different from financial data disclosure requirements imposed on all publicly listed companies in western economies. Moreover, they would be consistent with the UN Convention against Corruption and Organisation for Economic Co-operation and Development Guidelines on Multinational Enterprises.

Controlling small arms

More effective action by the international community to control the spread of weapons is a key requirement for human security. The availability of weapons may not cause conflict. But it makes conflict more likely—and it increases the likelihood that conflicts will take more violent forms.

The weapons of choice in today's conflicts are small arms. They kill 500,000 people a year on average, or one person per minute.[58] Anti-personnel mines kill another 25,000 people a year.[59] In conflict-prone areas small arms are used by warring factions to terrorize, kill and displace vulnerable populations. The dispersal of guns to private armies and militias feeds a cycle of violence. Meanwhile, societies emerging from years of conflict face the threat of continuing violence as the availability of small arms facilitates political and criminal violence.

There are no fully reliable estimates for the number of small arms in circulation. One authoritative source puts the figure at 639 million.[60] Global production of small arms runs at 7–8 million pieces a year, some 1 million of them military-style weapons. The United States, Russia and China dominate production, but there are at least 27 other significant sources of supply. Worldwide, at least 1,249 companies in 92 countries are involved. The small arms economy is an integral part of the collective security threat posed by fragile states. In Afghanistan anti-Soviet mujahideen groups paid for guns with revenue from opium. In Cambodia, Liberia and Sierra Leone revenues from diamonds and timber financed the small arms trade.

In the past decade some governments have moved towards greater transparency in monitoring the small arms trade. Governments in importing countries in Sub-Saharan Africa have been prominently involved. The Moratorium on the Import, Export and Manufacture of Small Arms and Light Weapons in West Africa of 1998, established by the Economic Community of West African States (ECOWAS), was the world's first regional moratorium on small arms. It banned imports of new weapons without approval from other member states. In 2004, 11 African governments in the Great Lakes and Horn of Africa regions—two of the highest conflict areas—signed the Protocol for the Prevention, Control and Reduction of Small Arms and Light Weapons.

Exporting countries have also stepped up cooperation. The European Union's Code of Conduct on Arms Exports prohibits the sale of weapons that could be used for internal repression or external aggression. European countries have also expanded their data sharing activities through the Organization for Security and Co-operation in Europe (OSCE). In 2001 UN Member States negotiated a binding protocol prohibiting the illegal manufacture of and trafficking in firearms to supplement the UN Convention against Transnational Organized Crime. The Wassenaar Arrangement Best Practice Guidelines for Exports of Small Arms and Light Weapons (2002), accepted by 33 states—the majority of global arms manufacturers and exporters—requires that arms transfers be conducted in a manner that minimizes the diversion of human and economic resources.

These are important initiatives. They reflect a growing awareness of the scale of the problem. But current arrangements suffer from a number of shortcomings. They are not legally binding, and they focus solely on illicit arms rather than on state-authorized transfers. Because of multiple suppliers, states have access to weapons from sources with less than scrupulous reporting requirements—a large loophole. Another problem is that regional agreements are not always mutually consistent or effectively coordinated. Major exporters have tightened export practices: it is now more difficult for governments to authorize arms transfers to regimes that do not respect basic human rights. Even here, though, a recipient government's willingness to sign up for the "war on terror" can often override scrutiny of its human rights record.

Since most small arms enter the market legally, supply-side regulations can be very effective. Two powerful barriers have obstructed efforts to stem the flow of small arms at source: diversity of supply, as mentioned, and lack of political will. Considering the threat posed by terrorism, it might be thought that industrial countries would be leading efforts to regulate trade in small arms. Yet this lethal trade remains weakly regulated at best, with devastating consequences for human development. Needed is a comprehensive international arms trade treaty that establishes legally binding agreements on territorial and extraterritorial arms brokering and common standards on enforcement. The 2006

A comprehensive international arms trade treaty should regulate arms brokering and establish common standards of enforcement

Regional bodies in Africa
lack the resources, logistics
and human capacity to act
on ambitious mandates

Small Arms Review Conference at the United Nations provides a critical opportunity to agree on an arms trade treaty to regulate transfers to states and to stop illicit transfers of weapons.

Building regional capacity

Civil wars affect neighbouring countries whether by spilling over directly or by blocking access to trade routes and creating unfavourable conditions for foreign and domestic investment. That gives neighbouring countries an immediate interest in minimizing this impact. The problem is that the poorest countries facing the gravest regional security challenges lack the financial and institutional capacity to mount an effective response. Building that capacity is a vital part of building a more secure world.

Regional organizations can play an important role in addressing security challenges. This is as true for Europe as for Sub-Saharan Africa. The European Union, the OSCE and the North Atlantic Treaty Organization have all made security interventions in recent years. Regional bodies are well placed to monitor peace agreements and produce early warnings of a crisis. Early warning mechanisms developed in Africa, such as the Conflict Early Warning and Response Mechanism of the Intergovernmental Authority on Development, have enabled regional organizations to monitor developments at close quarters. Regional institutions can also mediate among parties to a conflict: the African-led mediation in the Great Lakes in 2004 and in Sudan in 2005 are examples.

When conflicts break out, regional bodies have the strongest vested interest in responding decisively to contain them. In Darfur the African Union sought a strong mandate to send in forces to protect civilians and to monitor a widely ignored ceasefire. This would have been the most effective international response. Yet by August 2004, when the killings were still at a very high level, there were fewer than 300 soldiers in place to guard an estimated 1.5 million Darfuris driven from their homes by government-backed militias. By mid-2005 the African Union forces had increased to 3,000 troops—this to monitor a region the size of France. While donors have increased

their pledges to the African Union's peacekeeping force, pledges still fall far short of requests.[61] Despite these constraints the African Union is considering sending in troops to disarm hardline Rwandan rebel groups in eastern Democratic Republic of the Congo. It is also considering sending forces to Somalia. Success in such operations will require a far higher level of coordinated support from the international community.

The Darfur case points to a wider problem. African governments are recognizing their responsibility to address regional peace and security concerns. Humanitarian intervention has increased. In West Africa ECOWAS has intervened in Liberia (1990), Sierra Leone (1991–99) and Guinea-Bissau (1998–99), albeit with varying success. African governments have recognized that the creation of effective regional security forces is essential for maintaining the territorial integrity of their states and for helping fragile neighbouring states prevent conflict. In 2000 the Constitutive Act of the African Union gave it the right to intervene under circumstances of "war crimes, genocide and crimes against humanity".[62] Subsequently, a Peace and Security Council was established and called for the creation of an African standby force.

The problem is that regional bodies in Africa lack the resources, logistics and human capacity to act on such ambitious mandates. In the early 1990s the Organization for African Unity identified anticipating and preventing conflict as well as peacemaking and peace-building as important objectives. A Peace Fund set up for this purpose was able to mobilize only $1 million a year during 1996–2001, with many member states failing to meet their financial obligations.[63] In the ECOWAS intervention in Liberia, Nigeria ended up covering 90% of the costs of operations, which ran to more than $1.2 billion. Canada, the European Union, Japan, the United Kingdom and the United States also contributed, but not enough.[64] In the absence of adequate financial and logistical support, Tanzania and Uganda withdrew from the Liberia mission in 1995.

Efforts have been made to improve intervention capacities. In 1996 the United States launched the African Crisis Response Initiative

5

Violent conflict

to train African soldiers. By 2004 more than 10,000 troops had been trained. In February 2004 the European Union pledged $300 million for creating five regional, multinational standby brigades.[65] These are a start, but still far short of an effective intervention force for responding rapidly to the region's conflicts.

Establishing the African standby force proposed by the African Union will require continuing support for planning and logistics if the proposed capacity of 15,000 troops is to be in place by the target date of 2010. Investment in the development of the African standby force would be a powerful contribution to human development and collective security. Were such a body in place today, the human toll of the conflict in Sudan might be far less. In April 2004 the African Union, along with the European Union and the United States, mediated a ceasefire agreement between the Sudanese government and rebels in Darfur. But its mission to oversee the ceasefire is constrained by a lack of financial support from developed countries.[66]

While prospects are promising, relying on regional responses has drawbacks. One obvious risk is that regional interventions may be compromised by states with a strategic interest in a particular outcome. Rivalries in the Great Lakes region limit the scope for involving forces from states in the region, for example. Regional peacekeeping bodies also face some of the same constraints that reduce the effectiveness of UN peacekeeping missions. In the case of Darfur the government of Sudan was willing to accept an African Union peacekeeping force in part because it had a mandate to observe rather than to protect civilians.

Challenges for reconstruction

Peace settlements are moments of great opportunity—and great vulnerability. Most fragile states are trapped in cycles of temporary peace and resumed conflict: half of all countries emerging from conflict relapse into violence within five years. Breaking the cycle requires decisive action to seize the opportunities that peace creates by providing security, rebuilding institutions and supporting social and economic recovery.

Security is an immediate priority. In Sierra Leone the United Kingdom has committed to providing a 15- to 25-year "over the horizon" security guarantee, helping to create the conditions for the development of national institutions. Support from donors is financing a programme to integrate former combatants into a national security force and to provide retraining. By contrast, the peace settlement in neighbouring Liberia remains tenuous. Disarmament has been less complete. And parts of the country remain insecure. The challenge for Sierra Leone is to move beyond security to the next phase of reconstruction through a long-term national strategy for economic recovery and the development of accountable institutions. The challenge for Liberia is to create the security conditions for reconstruction.

Creating an effective umbrella for the development of human security is the first step on the road to reconstruction. That step requires a financial commitment—but it is a commitment with a high return in lives saved and economic gains. One estimate puts the cost of UK military intervention in Sierra Leone at $397 million a year for 10 years, with an estimated return of $33 billion, or more than 8 times the investment. Beyond immediate security, restoring or rebuilding institutions capable of overseeing long-term peace and development poses great challenges.

The United Nations has taken on an increasingly important role in building or strengthening institutions of the state—taking charge of organizing elections and providing police personnel (table 5.3). While transitional administrations led by the United Nations—as in Bosnia and Herzegovina—are still the exception rather than the rule, the reconstruction challenge is the same: building effective states that provide basic services and creating secure conditions for development.

Much has been learned since 1990 about the conditions under which reconstruction fails to provide a framework for recovery. Post-conflict peace-building is a complex task, requiring sustained engagement. To be successful it must both address the underlying causes of conflict and develop institutions perceived as legitimate

Post-conflict peace-building is a complex task, requiring sustained engagement

Table 5.3 **Post-conflict peace-building operations exercising governmental powers**

Territory	Mission	Date	Primary responsibility for police?	Primary responsibility for referendum?	Primary responsibility for elections?	Executive power?	Legislative power?	Judicial power?	Treaty power?
Congo	United Nations Operation in the Congo	1960–64	De facto in limited areas			De facto in limited areas			
West Papua	United Nations Temporary Executive Authority	1962–63	Yes		Regional elections only	Yes	Limited		
Namibia	United Nations Transition Assistance Group	1989–90			Yes				De facto (Council for Namibia)
Western Sahara	United Nations Mission for the Referendum in Western Sahara	1991–		Yes					
Cambodia	United Nations Transitional Authority in Cambodia	1992–93	Yes		Yes	As necessary			
Somalia	United Nations Operation in Somalia II	1993–95					Disputed		
Bosnia and Herzegovina	Office of the High Representative (before Bonn powers)[a]	1995–97			Yes (Organization for Security and Co-operation in Europe)				
Bosnia and Herzegovina	Office of the High Representative (after Bonn powers)[a]	1997–			Yes (Organization for Security and Co-operation in Europe)	De facto			
Bosnia and Herzegovina	United Nations Mission in Bosnia Herzegovina	1995–2002	De facto						
Eastern Slavonia (Croatia)	United Nations Transitional Authority in Eastern Slavonia, Baranja and Western Sirmium	1996–98	Yes		Yes	Yes			
East Timor	United Nations Mission in East Timor	1999		Yes					
Sierra Leone	United Nations Mission in Sierra Leone	1999–	De facto					Limited (Special Court)	
Kosovo (Federal Republic of Yugoslavia/Serbia and Montenegro)	United Nations Mission in Kosovo	1999–	Yes		Yes (Organization for Security and Co-operation in Europe)	Yes	Yes	Yes	
East Timor	United Nations Transitional Administration in East Timor	1999–2002	Yes		Yes	Yes	Yes	Yes	De facto
Afghanistan	United Nations Assistance Mission in Afghanistan	2002–							
Iraq	Coalition Provisional Authority[a]	2003–04	As occupying power		Unclear	As occupying power	Limited	Limited	

a. Not a UN operation.
Source: Chesterman 2005.

by all sides. There are no blueprints. However, experience highlights an underlying cause of failure: a lack of strategic and institutional clarity allied to the inability or unwillingness of the international community to make long-term commitments to state-building.[67]

International interventions require strategic clarity of objectives. In East Timor the recognized objective was independence. By contrast, Kosovo's final status remains harder to determine. The mandate never specified whether Kosovo would become independent or remain an autonomous province within Serbia and Montenegro. The result: confusion over the roles of each party in the reconstruction: Kosovars, Serbian and Montenegrins and international institutions. The 2000 Report of the Panel on UN Peace Operations stated bluntly that missions with uncertain mandates and inadequate resources should not be created at all.[68]

Problems of institutional coordination and policy coherence are magnified in post-conflict situations. Coordination problems arise when different agencies pursue similar goals. Coherence problems arise when different agencies pursue different goals, from security to humanitarian assistance to development. At an operational level policy ambiguity undermines chains of authority and command. For international actors coordination problems arise between the civilian administration (run by the United Nations or the national government) and military personnel with independent command (for example, the Kosovo Force and the International Security Assistance Force in Afghanistan). Since

the United Nations cannot wage war, the way to achieve a single chain of command is to bring the political process in line with development assistance. In the 1990s this was called "peacebuilding", but no additional institutional capacity was created for designing policy or providing operational oversight.

The challenge for post-conflict reconstruction can be addressed by focusing on two core objectives: ensuring physical security for civilians and providing adequate finance for both rapid response and long-term commitments.

Any international or regional intervention must ensure the safety and security of civilians. This requires providing peacekeepers with the political and material support needed to protect threatened populations. An Independent Inquiry on Rwanda concluded that whether a peacekeeping operation has a mandate to protect civilians or not, its very presence creates the expectation that it will do so. Protecting civilians also demands that funding to maintain law and order and improve the democratic governance of security forces be a priority.[69]

Financial commitments are critical for meeting the challenges of violent conflict, both before violence becomes generalized and after peace agreements have been signed. Timely financial support can help the authorities provide services that people value, diminishing incentives for conflict. The problem is that financing for reconstruction is fragmented. Peace settlements are typically followed by surges of humanitarian aid, which soon dry up, leaving large gaps in state capacity to meet basic needs.

Transitions from war to peace and from peace to security

High levels of foreign aid are no guarantee of a smooth transition to reconstruction, economic recovery and greater self-reliance. While some post-conflict countries receive exceptionally high levels of per capita aid, many are unable to convert

the peace dividend into an exit from aid dependence. One recurrent theme appears to be the weakness of the private sector response to peace.

Bosnia and Herzegovina is an extreme case of protracted aid dependence and limited

5

Violent conflict

Slow aid disbursement
can retard private
sector recovery

progress towards economic recovery. In the two years after the 1995 Dayton Accord aid per capita reached $245, and today it is $138, still among the highest in the world. The huge surge in aid has generated growth, but private sector investment has not taken off. This matters not just because of the high levels of unemployment, but also because of the critical role of the private sector in taking over functions financed by aid.

The case of Nicaragua provides another illustration of the problem. During the 1980s civil war led to the large-scale destruction of economic and social infrastructure. When the peace accord was signed in 1990, inflation was above 13,000%, the fiscal deficit was at 20% of GDP and military expenditure represented 40% of the national budget. Within a year inflation was under control and military expenditure was cut by half. Yet the 1990s saw a limited economic recovery, with per capita incomes rising at less than 1% a year. Like Bosnia and Herzegovina, Nicaragua remains critically dependent on development assistance, with per capita aid currently running at $152.

Economic stagnation amid high per capita aid is a reflection of the weak response of the private sector. But why is it that, in stark contrast to post-war Europe, large inflows of aid sometimes fail to stimulate the recovery of commercial markets?

Part of the problem appears to be that violence leaves a legacy of disarticulated commercial networks, loss of trust and weakened market institutions. The chronic uncertainty that prevails during conflict situations can spill over into the peace period, leading to suboptimal patterns of investment. For example, fears of future insecurity can generate a preference for short-term investments with high returns, rather than for the longer term investments on which sustained recovery and employment generation depend. Prospects for broad-based recovery suffer as a result. So too does the recovery of the tax base—an essential requirement for reducing aid dependence and financing basic service provision.[70]

Other barriers to private sector recovery can also emerge. In Nicaragua the poor performance of the private sector can be traced in part to uncertainty about the stability of the government—and hence about the future direction of policies on interest rates, public spending and inflation. Moreover, in a post-conflict environment bad policies and weak institutions can magnify the effects of low trust. In Bosnia and Herzegovina the poor business environment is reflected in a range of indicators. For example, the cost of registering a business amounts to 52% of average income, compared with 38% for low- and middle-income countries. Similarly, it takes on average 630 days to enforce a contract—twice the average for Sub-Saharan Africa. The formal banking sector also accounts for a proportionately far lower share of domestic credit than the average for low-income countries. Each of these facts reflects a combination of low trust, weak institutions, flawed policies and fears of future insecurity.

Slow aid disbursement can also retard private sector recovery. Countries moving from conflict to recovery face a daunting array of challenges. The reconstruction agenda includes building peace, securing political stability, recreating basic functions of state administration, resettling refugees and rebuilding social and economic infrastructure. Large aid inflows bring with them a wide range of actors, including multilateral donors, bilateral donors and non-governmental organizations. Meanwhile, weak state structures and a lack of coordination represent an obstacle to effective recovery.

Different components of an "integrated" peace-building programme will have different sources of funding. Donors make assessed contributions (as a percentage of GNP) for peace-keeping operations and voluntary contributions for other specialized UN agencies like UNDP and the UN High Commissioner for Refugees. But multiple criteria for reporting and lack of harmonization can slow the release of funds during the sensitive post-conflict period, hampering reconstruction of the infrastructure needed to support private investment.

Efforts are being made to address problems of reconstruction through a unified framework. The UNDP, the UN Development Group and the World Bank have already developed guidelines for post-conflict needs assessments, feeding into the creation of transitional results matrices. Equivalent to poverty reduction strategies, for fragile and post-conflict states, where capacity development remains the foremost priority, such transitional results matrices are now being used in five fragile states: Central African Republic, Haiti, Liberia, Sudan and Timor-Leste. In Iraq a new cluster approach for reconstruction assigns to each UN agency responsibility for a single sector. Not only does this locate agencies in their areas of expertise, but it also avoids duplication of tasks.

The Report of the UN Secretary-General's High-level Panel on Threats, Challenges and Change has proposed going a step further. It argues for the creation of an intergovernmental peace-building commission—a proposal endorsed in the Secretary-General's Report *In Larger Freedom*. If established, the commission would report in sequence to the Security Council and the Economic and Social Council. It is a bold proposal. Its major benefit would be to straddle three important dimensions of reconstruction activities—mandate, agencies and operations—coordinating all activities from fund raising to fund disbursement and regularly reviewing targets.

A central challenge facing the commission will be to identify the conditions under which private sector recovery can help to reduce dependence on aid. Blueprints are unlikely to help because each conflict arises from a different context and leaves a different set of problems. New approaches need to be explored, including the use of public finance or public credit guarantees to reduce risk and create incentives for private investment. Using aid to promote public-private partnerships in service provision is also important. Perhaps most important is the development of strategies for rebuilding the institutions and trust on which private sector investment depends.

All this requires sophisticated and integrated post-conflict recovery strategies. Different phases of recovery need to be supported by aid and by appropriate incentive policies. The progression would be from a humanitarian focus in the immediate post-war period to an approach based on encouraging private investment and risk pooling in the later recovery stages.

Collective security captures the fundamental realities of the threats facing governments as they seek to build human security

Redefining security and building collective security

While the MDGs provide a focus for progress towards freedom from want, the world still lacks a coherent agenda for extending freedom from fear. As the UN Secretary-General's report on reform of the United Nations argues, there is an urgent need to redefine security. Defining security narrowly as the threat of terrorism encourages military responses that fail to achieve collective security. What is needed is a security framework that recognizes that poverty, social breakdown and civil conflict are the core components of the global security threat—and the world must respond accordingly.

Collective security is not an abstract concept. It captures the fundamental realities of the threats facing governments as they seek to build human security. As the Report of the UN Secretary-General's High-level Panel on Threats, Challenges and Change forcefully argued, today's threats are not confined within national borders. When states fail and violent conflict follows in any one country, the conditions for insecurity are created in other countries. Thus no state can achieve security on its own. Building collective security requires actions on a broad front, from conventions for tackling head-on the threats posed by global terrorism and nuclear weapons to progress in reducing poverty. Investments in equitable development—in economic growth, job creation and human security in the broader sense—remain the key to preventing conflict.

Prevention of violent
conflict should be put at
the centre of planning
for poverty reduction

The following are among the main measures needed to reverse the downward spiral of conflict and underdevelopment:

- *Putting prevention of violent conflict at the centre of planning for poverty reduction.* All governments, donors, financial institutions and the United Nations should undertake comprehensive risk assessments to evaluate how specific policies affect conflict. The assessments should focus on the risks related to recent or ongoing conflicts and on potential risks associated with inequality in the distribution of benefits from development.

- *Establishing a new deal on aid.* Starving conflict-prone or post-conflict states of aid is unjustified. It is bad for human security in the countries concerned—and it is bad for global security. As part of the wider requirement to achieve the aid target of 0.7% of GNI, donors should commit to an increased aid effort and to greater predictability of aid through long-term financing commitments. Donors should be more transparent about the conditions for aid allocations and about their reasons for scaling down investments in conflict-prone countries.

- *Restricting "conflict resource" markets.* Urgent action is needed to weaken the links between violent conflict and natural resources. Creating a Permanent Expert Panel within the UN Security Council to monitor these links is a first step. The second step is creating legal instruments and certification schemes to obstruct trade in conflict resources, building on current initiatives in diamonds and timber. The absence of clear criteria for defining "conflict resources" and restricting their sale remains a major problem. Resolving these problems requires the third step of effective sanctions. The Report of the UN Secretary-General's High-level Panel on Threats, Challenges and Change has identified a number of measures to strengthen sanction arrangements.[71] These include the creation of a senior UN post and effective machinery to monitor trade in conflict resources and to enable the UN Secretary-General to make concrete recommendations on sanctions and compliance to the Security Council. The Security Council, for its part, needs to show greater resolve in imposing secondary sanctions against countries involved in sanctions busting.

- *Encouraging corporate transparency.* The lack of transparency in accounting for the natural resource wealth and the distribution of benefits that it generates is itself a major source of violent conflict. It is also both a symptom and a cause of weak governance. The international community could do far more to increase the transparency of payments by requiring higher reporting standards and by giving current initiatives—such as the Extractive Industries Transparency Initiative—legal teeth. Of course, developing country governments need to report to their own citizens on revenue flows through transparent national channels—and many systematically fail to do so. But more effective international action could also create the right incentives—and disincentives—for the companies that interact with governments. As proposed by the UK-sponsored Commission for Africa, an international legal framework to facilitate the investigation of corrupt practices in developing countries by companies headquartered in industrial countries could raise the legal risks associated with off-budget and off-the-book activities.

- *Cutting the flow of small arms.* The control agreements mentioned in this chapter are not sufficient. Arms have continued to flow into Sudan during the crisis in Darfur. Elsewhere, there is a steady flow of small arms into areas marked by violent conflict and state repression. Some of the largest exporters of the arms that eventually claim innocent lives in the world's poorest countries are to be found in the G-8 and the European Union. Many of these states have weak controls on arms brokering, transit trade and the extraterritorial activities of arms traders and weak enforcement of current rules. The 2006 Small Arms Review Conference provides an opportunity to agree on a comprehensive arms trade treaty to regulate markets and curtail supplies to areas of violent conflict. The treaty would provide a comprehensive international mechanism to restrain arms transfers to areas marked by violent conflict, human rights abuse or terrorism and would create an international legal mechanism for preventing the brokering of deals for supplying such areas.

- *Building regional capacity.* An immediate priority is the development, through financial, technical and logistical support, of a fully functioning African Union standby force. Donors should agree to fund 70%–80% of the African Union's Peace Fund from 2005, with African Union members increasing their own resource mobilization over time. In addition to building this capacity, there is a need for far greater use of early warning systems, linking monitoring activities with action. Though the actors will vary from region to region, this will require a global partnership among bodies such as the OSCE, which has developed extensive early warning systems, other regional bodies and non-governmental organizations.

- *Financing post-conflict recovery.* The UN Secretary-General's High-level Panel on Threats, Challenges and Change has called for an international peace-building commission to provide a strategic framework for an integrated approach to collective security. As part of that approach a global fund should be created to finance immediate post-conflict assistance and the transition to long-term reconstruction on a predictable basis. The panel has recommended creation of a $250 million peace-building fund. The fund would allow for short-term financing to enable governments to discharge their immediate functions by paying civil servants and delivering basic services. It would also finance longer term reconstruction. In parallel, there is a case for expanding the World Bank's Post-Conflict Fund. The UK-sponsored Commission for Africa has called for a phased three-year increase from the current $30 million to $60 million a year. Debt relief also has a critical role to play. One shared characteristic of many post-conflict countries—including the Democratic Republic of the Congo, Liberia and Sierra Leone—is a high level of arrears to multilateral agencies. High debt servicing burdens and the disruption in relations with donors caused by arrears suggest a case for accelerated debt reduction. Allied to increased funding, donors need to create a strategic environment for recovery by committing themselves for the long haul of reconstruction.

There are no blueprints for preventing or resolving violent conflict. However, without much more—and much more effective—international cooperation to tackle the threats posed by violent conflict, the international community cannot hope to protect basic human rights, advance collective security and achieve the MDGs. Putting the threat posed by violent conflict at the heart of the development agenda is an imperative, not just to save lives today but to save the future costs of humanitarian aid, peacekeeping and reconstruction—and to reduce the global threats posed by a failure to advance human security.

Without much more effective international cooperation, the international community cannot protect human rights, advance collective security and achieve the MDGs

Notes

Chapter 1

1 Roosevelt 1937.
2 UN 2000a.
3 UNDP 1990, p. 61.
4 Annan 2005.
5 UNESCO 2005.
6 See UNDP 2003c for a more detailed discussion. Reddy and Pogge 2003.
7 Wolfensohn and Bourguignon 2004.
8 World Bank 2004c, table 1.3.
9 HDRO calculation using data on democracy from CIDCM 2005 and data on population from UN 2003. Countries with a Polity score of 6 or higher were considered democracies.
10 UNICEF 2005e, table 1.
11 GAVI and The Vaccine Fund 2005b.
12 UN Millennium Project 2005a.
13 Pelletier and others 1995.
14 UNICEF 2005e.
15 UNESCO 2005, table 3.3.
16 UNESCO 2005.
17 Mills and Shilcutt 2004.
18 Jha and Mills 2002, p.175.
19 Calculated on the basis of data on health expenditure from indicator table 6.
20 World Bank 2005e.
21 UNAIDS 2004b.
22 UNAIDS 2005a.
23 UNAIDS 2005b.
24 UN Millennium Project 2005a.
25 UN Millennium Project 2005a.
26 Cousens, Lawn and Zupan 2005.
27 At 1.3% a year compared with 1.9%.
28 HDRO calculations based on data on under-five mortality from UN 2005b.
29 Cousens, Lawn and Zupan 2005.
30 The data are derived from UNICEF (2005c) reporting systems available at www.childinfo.org.
31 World Bank 2005b.
32 Wagstaff and Claeson 2004.
33 GAVI and The Vaccine Fund 2005b.
34 World Bank 2003e. This figure is based on estimated numbers receiving the third dose of the diphtheria, pertussis and tetanus (DPT) vaccine—the proxy commonly used for coverage.
35 van der Gaag 2004.
36 WHO and UNICEF 2003.
37 UN Millennium Project 2005a.
38 Quoted in Gillespie and Kadiyala 2005.
39 UNICEF 2005e.
40 IFPRI 2005.
41 Deaton 2004.
42 Collier and Dollar 2002b.
43 Reddy and Minoiu 2005. The onset of a stagnation period is defined as a year in which a country's per capita income is lower than of any time in the past two years and higher than at any time in the subsequent four years.
44 World Bank 2005e.
45 Miller 2005; IMF 2004a, p.21.
46 For a clear overview of the different ways of looking at global inequalities see Birdsall 2002a.
47 Bourguignon and Morrisson 1999.
48 HDRO calculation based on Kroll and Goldman 2005, Chen and Ravallion 2004 and World Bank 2004e.
49 Dikhanov 2005.
50 Bhagwati 2004, p. 66.
51 King 1963.
52 UN Millennium Project 2005e, p. 2.
53 Description of methodology.
54 Wagstaff and Claeson 2004.
55 UN Viet Nam 2002.
56 Klump and Bonschab 2004.
57 UNDP 2003b.

Chapter 2

1 Walker and Walker 1987.
2 Plato 2000.
3 Sen 1992.
4 Bourguignon, Ferreira and Menéndez 2003.
5 Smith [1776] 1976.
6 de Ferranti and others 2003.
7 Quoted in Kanbur 2005.
8 Kanbur 2005.
9 *The Economist* 2004b.
10 Farmer 2004.
11 Smith [1776] 1976.
12 Cornia 2004.
13 The $2 a day poverty line is $978 in 1995 purchasing power parity terms.
14 Based on Gwatkin and others forthcoming.
15 Deaton 2002.
16 World Bank 2003b.
17 McKay and Aryeetey 2004.
18 Graham 2004.
19 UN Millennium Project 2005h.
20 HDRO calculation based on IIPS and ORC Macro 2000.
21 IFPRI 2005.
22 Wagtaff and van Doorslaer 2003.
23 Deininger and Mpuga 2004.
24 Banerjee, Deaton and Duflo 2004.
25 Birdsall and Londono 1997.
26 Killick 2002a.
27 World Bank and IMF 2005a.
28 Thurlow and Wobst 2004.
29 UNICEF 2005a.
30 UNDP 2003d.

Chapter 3

1 Lula da Silva 2004.
2 Bush 2002.
3 Mahatma Gandhi, as quoted in Sethi 1958.
4 Cited in Woodward 1963. Chadwick's report led to the creation of a Royal Commission and, eventually, to the Public Health Act of 1848.
5 Edsforth 2000.
6 Lindert 2005.
7 The White House 2002.
8 Bruns, Mingat and Rakatomalala 2003.
9 Commission for Africa 2005.
10 UN Millennium Project 2005e.
11 Sundberg, Lofgren and Bourguignon 2005.
12 Hansen and Tarp 2000; Foster and Keith 2003a, b.
13 Clemens, Bhavnani and Radelet 2004.
14 Foster and Keith 2003a, b.
15 Levine and the What Works Working Group 2004.
16 Joint Learning Initiative 2004.
17 Akhter and del Ninno 2001.
18 World Bank 2004b.
19 Goldberg 2005.
20 Nguyen and Akal 2003; ADB 2004.
21 UNDP 2005a.
22 Levine and the What Works Working Group 2004.
23 GAVI and The Vaccine Fund 2005a.
24 UN Millennium Project 2005b.
25 Mills and Shilcutt 2004.
26 Quoted in DeLong and Eichengreen 1991.
27 DeLong and Eichengreen 1991.
28 Commission on International Development 1969.
29 Commission on International Development 1969.
30 The other three are Ireland, Portugal and Spain.

31 Millennium Challenge Corporation 2005b.
32 World Bank and IMF 2005b.
33 Commission for Africa 2005.
34 Woods 2005.
35 Dollar and Burnside 2000.
36 Birdsall, Claessens and Diwan 2003.
37 World Bank and IMF 2005a. The World Bank index uses a Country Policy and Institutional Assessment (CPIA) exercise to rank countries.
38 Dollar and Levin 2004. Empirical evidence collected by the World Bank suggests that low-income countries with weak institutions receive around 40% less aid than predicted on the basis of their Country Policy and Institutional Assessment scores.
39 World Bank 2002.
40 UK, HM Treasury 2003.
41 See, for example, Working Group on New International Financial Contributions 2004. Various alternative financing proposals are discussed in Reisen 2004.
42 World Bank and IMF 2004a.
43 Adam and Bevan 2003.
44 Clemens, Bhavnani and Radelet 2004.
45 World Bank and IMF 2003.
46 IMF 2002.
47 Bevan 2005.
48 Bevan 2005.
49 Berg 2005.
50 Sundberg, Lofgren and Bourguignon 2005.
51 Vargas Hill 2005.
52 Bulír and Hamann 2003.
53 Watt 2005.
54 Watt 2005.
55 Adam 2005.
56 World Bank 2005c.
57 Martin and Bargawi 2004.
58 Killick 2004.
59 World Bank 2003a.
60 Killick 2004.
61 Knack and Rahman 2004.
62 World Bank and IMF 2005a.
63 Knack and Rahman 2004.
64 Knack and Rahman 2004.
65 Watt 2005.
66 Jepma 1991; Aryeetey, Osei and Quartey 2003. There are a range of estimates of the costs of tied aid. One study of project-based aid in Ghana found that input costs could have been lowered by 11%–25% by untying aid (McKay and Aryeetey 2004). Earlier studies covering larger groups of countries estimated costs in a higher range, at 15%–30%. The OECD puts the additional cost of tied food aid at 50% (OECD/DAC 2004b).
67 OECD/DAC 2004b, 2005e.
68 For Italy the average for 2001 and 2002 is used since the 2003 figure is not reported.
69 Aid/Watch 2005.
70 Miovic 2004.
71 Watt 2005. On the wider transaction costs associated with pooling arrangements, see OECD/DAC 2003b.
72 UNDP 2004b.

73 Johnson and Martin 2005.
74 UN Millennium Project 2005f. These were: Mauritania, Guyana, The Gambia, Honduras, Burkina Faso, Ghana, Nicaragua, Niger, Guinea, Viet Nam, Mozambique, and Yemen. Ethiopia's plan has also now been endorsed.
75 Global Campaign for Education 2005.
76 OECD/DAC 2005d.

Chapter 4
1 Galeano 1973.
2 James 2001.
3 WTO 2004b.
4 WTO 2004b.
5 IMF and World Bank 2001.
6 World Bank and IMF 2005a.
7 Arndt 1998. "Intra-product" trade is estimated to account for around one-third of the value in world trade.
8 Carey 2002; Intel 2005; Seagate 2003.
9 CAFOD 2005.
10 UNIDO 2004.
11 UNIDO 2002.
12 Lall 2004.
13 When Malaysia exports colour televisions, more than one-quarter of the value added to imported components stays in Malaysia. When Mexico exports high-technology automobile products, the equivalent share is 3%.
14 UNCTAD 2003. The combined price index deflates the unit value of commodities exported by developing countries by the unit value of manufactured exports from developed countries.
15 UNCTAD 2004b.
16 Lall and Pietrobelli 2002.
17 Rodrik 2001b.
18 Bhattacharya 2003.
19 Dollar 2004.
20 Evans 2005.
21 See, for example, Lall 2001.
22 Morley 2002.
23 Jha 2005.
24 Jank and others 2001; World Bank 2004f.
25 Carlson 2001.
26 Rosen 2002.
27 IADB 2004.
28 Oxfam International 2004e.
29 Birdsall and Subramaniam 2004.
30 UNEP 1999.
31 UNDP 2003f.
32 Laird 2002; Stevens and Kennan 2002; Ng, Hoekman and Olarreaga 2001.
33 Figures are trade weighted. UNCTAD and World Bank 2005.
34 Laird 2002.
35 USITC 2005.
36 Data on tariff escalation is derived from UNCTAD TRAINS data (UNCTAD and World Bank 2005). See also Cernat, Laird and Turrini 2003.
37 The European Union's rules of origin are explained in Oxfam International 2004d.
38 Mlachila and Yang 2004.

39 Oxfam International 2004d.
40 Integrated Framework for Trade-Related Technical Assistance to Least Developed Countries 2003.
41 Stevens and Kennan 2004a.
42 Alexandraki and Lankes 2004.
43 Derived from OECD 2004a.
44 Aksoy and Beghin 2004.
45 OECD 2000.
46 Diao, Diaz-Bonilla and Robinson 2003.
47 Oxfam International 2004a.
48 US Department of Agriculture, Economic Research Service 2002, tables 29 and 35.
49 Minot and Daniels 2002.
50 IMF 2005.
51 FAO 2004a.
52 Oxfam International 2005a.
53 US Department of Agriculture, Economic Research Service 2005a.
54 OECD 2004c.
55 Lall 2001.
56 Oxfam International 2002b.
57 Rodrik 2004.
58 Maskus 2004.
59 Mayne 2005.
60 Chauduri, Goldberg and Jia 2003.
61 Cited in Mayne 2005.
62 Mayne 2005.
63 Tussie 2005.
64 Parikh 2002.
65 Parikh 2002.
66 Winters 2002.
67 Stevens and Kennan 2005b. See also Stevens and Kennan 2005a.
68 Keynes 1980.
69 Osorio 2004.
70 Ponte 2001.
71 Gibbon 2005.
72 The following is based on Vargas Hill 2005.
73 Vargas Hill 2005.
74 Gibbon 2005.
75 Ponte 2001.
76 Larsen 2003; Teal and Vigneri 2004.
77 Gibbon 2005.
78 Lang 2003; ACIAR 2004.
79 This section draws on Brown 2005a.
80 Reardon and others 2003.
81 Reardon, Timmer and Berdegue 2003.
82 Oxfam International 2004e.
83 Vorley 2003.
84 Reardon, Timmer and Berdegue 2003.
85 Jaffee 2003, 2005
86 Reardon, Timmer and Berdegue 2003.
87 Aschenaki 2004.
88 Collier and Gunning 1999
89 Diao and Hazell 2003.
90 Diao and Hazell 2003.
91 Jensen 2005.
92 Jaffee 2005.
93 This section draws on Deere 2005; Jensen 2005.
94 This section draws on Deere 2005.

Chapter 5
1 Annan 2002.
2 Annan 2005.

3   MIPT 2005. For the purposes of this database terrorism is defined by the nature of the act, not by the identity of the perpetrators or the nature of the cause. Terrorism is violence or threat of violence, generally targeted at civilians, with the express political purpose of coercing others into actions they would not otherwise undertake, or refrain from actions they desired to take.

4   Data on casualties are from Marshall 2005. *Armed conflict* is defined in this Report as the use of armed force between two parties, at least one of which is the government of a state, that results in at least 25 battle-related deaths (Strand, Wilhelmsen and Gleditsch 2005).

5   Global IDP Project 2005a, p. 10.

6   UN 2004b.

7   Annan 2005, p. 24.

8   Calculations based on Strand, Wilhelmsen and Gleditsch 2005 and World Bank 2005f.

9   Fearon and Laitin 2003.

10   Polity IV data (CIDCM 2005).

11   Collier and others 2003.

12   Collier and Hoeffler 2004a.

13   Fuentes 2005a.

14   Collier and others 2003, p. 21.

15   Lopez 2003 as quoted in Fuentes 2005a.

16   Humphreys 2003.

17   Collier and others 2003, p. 35.

18   Collier and Hoeffler 2004a.

19   Mackenzie and Buchanan-Smith 2005, p. 20.

20   Centre for International Cooperation and Security, Department of Peace Studies 2005.

21   Centre for International Cooperation and Security, Department of Peace Studies 2005, p. 21.

22   Ginifer 2005, p. 17.

23   Centre for International Cooperation and Security, Department of Peace Studies 2005, p. 22.

24   Boyden and Ryder 1996.

25   HDRO calculations based on World Bank 2004e.

26   UNDP 2003a, p.106.

27   HDRO calculations.

28   Toole and Waldman 1997.

29   Global IDP Project 2003.

30   Pedersen 2002.

31   Mann and others 1994; Horton 1993.

32   Ghobarah, Huth and Russett 2004.

33   UNAIDS 2003.

34   UNAIDS 2004b, pp.175-78.

35   SIPRI 2004. Data on health expenditures refer to 2001.

36   Fuentes 2005a and indicator table 5.

37   Fuentes 2005a and indicator table 5.

38   Peimani 2005, p. 19.

39   Physicians for Human Rights 2002.

40   Otunnu 2005.

41   Calculated from FBI various years.

42   UNDP 2003a, p.105.

43   Human Rights Watch 2004b.

44   DFID 2005.

45   ICISS 2001, para 1.34.

46   Commission on Weak States and US National Security 2004.

47   DFID 2005.

48   UNDP 2001.

49   Brown 2005.

50   Fearon and Laitin 2003.

51   Quoted in King 1998.

52   Uvin 1998.

53   McGovern and Choulai 2005.

54   World Bank 2005a.

55   Collier and Hoeffler 2002.

56   See, for example, ICG 2001a.

57   The Kimberley Process 2004.

58   Muggah 2001.

59   Muggah and Batchelor 2002.

60   Small Arms Survey 2002.

61   In May 2005 a donor pledging conference agreed to increase support by $200 million against an African Union request for $350 million (BBC News 2005b).

62   African Union 2000, Article 4(h). See discussion in Cilliers and Sturman 2002.

63   Juma and Mengistu 2002, p. 24.

64   Juma and Mengistu 2002, p. 30.

65   O'Hanlon and Rice 2004.

66   Kagwanja 2004.

67   This analytical framework draws on Chesterman 2005.

68   UN 2000b.

69   OECD DAC 2003a, 2004d.

70   Addison 2003.

71   UN 2004b, pp. 55–56.

Bibliographic note

Chapter 1 draws on Ahluwalia and Hussain 2004; Ahmed and del Ninno 2001; Banister and Zhang 2005; Bardhan 2000; BBC News 2005a; Bhagwati 2004; Birdsall 2002a, 2002b; Bourguignon 2000; Bourguignon and Morrison 1999; Carr-Hill 2004; Cassen, Visaria and Dyson 2004; Castro-Leal, Dayton and Mehra 2004; Chen and Ravallion 2004; Chen and Wang 2001; CIDCM 2005; Claeson and others 2000; Collier and Dollar 2002a; Commission on Macroeconomics and Health 2001; Commission on Social Justice 1993; Corbacho and Schwartz 2002; Cousens, Lawn and Zupan 2005; Das 2001; Datt and Ravallion 2002; Deaton 2003, 2004; Deaton and Drèze 2002; Deaton and Kozel 2004; Demombynes and Hoogeveen 2004; Dev 2002; Devarajan and Reinikka 2003; Dikhanov 2005; Drèze 2004; Drèze and Murthi 2001; Dunning 2003; Egerter and others 2004; Firebaugh 2003; GAVI and The Vaccine Fund 2005b; Gelb 2004; Gillespie and Kadiyala 2005; Gordillo and others 2001; Gupta, Whelan and Allendorf 2003; Hausmann, Pritchett and Rodrik 2004; The Henry Kaiser Family Foundation 2005; IMF 2004a; India, Ministry of Statistics and Programme Implementation 2002a, 2002b; Jha and Mills 2002; Johnson and others 2004; Jones 2004; Joshi 2004; Justino, Litchfield and Niimi 2004; Kabeer 2005; Kakwani 2004; Kasterine 2004; Kijima and Lanjouw 2003; King 1963; Kingdon and others 2004; Klump and Bonschab 2004; Lim and others 2004; Lomborg 2004; Luther 1998; Maison, Bailes and Mason 2003; Malyutina and others 2002; McKay 2002; Men and others 2003; Milanovic 2001, 2003; Mills and Shilcutt 2004; Morley 2001; ODI 2004; Oxfam International 2004e; Pelletier and others 1995; Reddy and Minoiu 2005; Reddy and Pogge 2003; Rodrik and Subramanian 2004; Sachs and Brundtland 2001; Sen 1999; Sen and Drèze 1997; Sen, Mujeri and Quazi 2004; Shkolnikov and Cornia 2000; Ssewanyana and others 2004; Swaziland, Ministry of Agriculture and Co-operatives and Business 2002; Uganda, Ministry of Finance, Planning and Economic Development 2003; UN 2000a, 2003, 2005b, 2005d; UNAIDS 2004a, 2005a; UNDP 1990, 2003b, 2003c; UNESCO 2005; UNESCO Institute of Statistics 2005; UNICEF 2005b, 2005c, 2005d, 2005e; University of California, Berkeley, and Max Planck Institute for Demographic Research 2005; UN Millennium Project 2005a, 2005b, 2005c, 2005d; UN Viet Nam 2002; Visaria 2004a, 2004b; Wade 2005; Wagstaff 2000; Wagstaff and Claeson 2004; Watkins 2000, 2003b; WHO 2004b; WHO and UNICEF 2003; Wolf 2005; Wolfensohn and Bourguignon 2004; World Bank 2003b, 2003d, 2003e, 2005b, 2005e; Yamano and Jayne 2004; Yunus 2004.

Chapter 2 draws on Banerjee, Deaton and Duflo 2004; Birdsall and Londono 1997; Bourguignon, Ferreira and Menéndez 2003; Case and Deaton 1998; China, National Bureau of Statistics 2004; Coady and Parker 2005; Coady, Grosh and Hoddinott 2004; Cornia 2004; Deaton 2002; de Ferranti and others 2003; Deininger and Mpuga 2004; DFID 2004b; Dikhanov 2005; The Economist 2004b; Farmer 2004; Fuentes 2005; Goodman 2005; Graham 2004; Gwatkin and others forthcoming; Hills 2004; IFPRI 2005; IIPS and ORC Macro 2000; Indiatogether.org 2004; Kanbur 2005; Killick 2002a; Lim and others 2004; Lindert and Williamson 2001a; Liu 1996; Liu, Liu and Meng 1994; Lund 2002, 2004; McKay and Aryeetey 2004; Measure DHS 2005; Mexico, INEGI 2005; Mexico, Secretaría de Desarrollo Social 2005; Munnell, Hatch

and Lee 2004; Naschold 2002; ODI 2004; Pakistan, Statistics Division 2002; Plato [360 BC] 2000; Proctor and Dalaker 2003; Ravallion 2005; Ravallion and Chen 2004; Rowland and Hoffman 2005; Sen 1992, 2004; Smith [1776] 1976; Thurlow and Wobst 2004; UN 2004a, 2005b; UNDP 2002, 2003d; UNESCO Institute of Statistics 2005; UNICEF 2005a; UN Millennium Project 2005h; Wagstaff and van Doorslaer 2003, Walker and Walker 1987; World Bank 2003b, 2003d.

Chapter 3 draws on ActionAid International and Oxfam International 2005; ActionAid International, Eurodad and Oxfam International 2005; Adam 2005; Adam and Bevan 2003; ADB 2004; Adenauer and Vagassky 1998; Advisory Commission on Intergovernmental Relations 1984; Aid/Watch 2005, Aryeetey, Osei and Quartey 2003; Atkinson 2004, 2005; Atkinson 2003; AVERT 2005; Baulch 2004; Benn 2004; Bevan 2005; Beynon 2003; Bird 2002; Bird and Milne 2003; Birdsall 2004; Birdsall and Clemens 2003; Birdsall and Deese 2005; Böhning and Schloeter-Paredes 1994; Brown-Collier 1998; Bruns, Mingat and Rakotomalala 2003; Bulír and Hamann 2001, 2003; Burnham 1989; Bush 2002; Center for Global Development 2004; Clemens, Bhavnani and Radelet 2004; Clemens, Kenny and Moss 2005; Collier 1999; Collier and Dehn 2001; Collier and Dollar 2002a, 2004; Commission for Africa 2005; Commission on International Development 1969; Cordella and Dell'Ariccia 2003; Dalgaard, Hansen and Tarp 2004; de Renzio 2005; de Renzio and others 2004; DeLong and Eichengreen 1991; Devarajan, Miller and Swanson 2002; Development Initiatives 2005a, 2005b, 2005c, 2005d; DFID, Foreign and Commonwealth Office and UK, HM Treasury 2005; Dollar and Burnside 2000; Dollar and Levin 2004; Dyer 2005; Edsforth 2000; Elbadawi 1999; EORG 2003; Fedelino and Kudina 2003; Foster and Fozzard 2000; Foster and Keith 2003a, 2003b; Working Group on New International Financial Contributions 2004; GAVI and The Vaccine Fund 2005a; Gemmell and McGillivray 1998; Global Campaign for Education 2005; Goldberg 2005; Gupta and others 2003; Hansen and Tarp 2000; IMF 2001, 2002, 2005b; Inyega and Mbugua 2005; ISMEA 2003; Jepma 1991; Johnson and Martin 2005; Johnson, Martin and Bargawi 2004; Johnson 1964; Joint Learning Initiative 2004; Kattan and Burnett 2004; Kenya, Ministry of Planning and National Development 2003, 2004; Killick 2002b, 2004; Knack and Rahman 2004; Lensink and Morrisey 2000; Levine and the what Works Working Group 2004; Lindert 2005; Lockhart 2004; Lula da Silva 2004; Macrae and others 2004; Martin and Bargawi 2004; Martin and others 2004; Millennium Challenge Corporation 2005b; Miller 2005; Miovic 2004; Mosley, Hudson and Verschoor 2004; Nguyen and Akal 2003; Nkusu 2004; Nyoni 1998; O'Brien 2004; OECD/DAC 2001c, 2002, 2003b, 2004a, 2004b, 2004c, 2004e, 2005a, 2005b, 2005c, 2005d, 2005e, 2005f, 2005g; Oxfam GB 2004; Oxfam International 2005b; Pallage and Robe 2001; PIPA 2001, 2004; Prati, Sahai and Tressel 2003; Radelet 2003a, 2003b; Ramcharan 2002; Reisen 2004; Rogerson 2005; Rogerson, Hewitt and Waldenburg 2004; Roodman 2004; Sagasti, Bezanson and Prada 2005; Sandler and Arce 2005; Sanford 2004; Sethi 1958; Shah 2005; Sundberg, Lofgren and Bourguignon 2005; Tanzania 2004; Torvik 2001; UK, HM Treasury 2003; UN 2004b, 2005b; UNDP 2000, 2004b, 2005a; UNICEF 2001a; UN Millennium Project 2005e, 2005f;

Vargas Hill 2005; Victora and others 2003; Watkins 2000; Watt 2005; White and Dijkstra 2003; The White House 2002; Woods 2005; Woods and research team 2004; Woodward 1963; World Bank 1998, 2001, 2002, 2003a, 2004a, 2004b, 2004c, 2005c; World Bank and IMF 2003, 2004a, 2004b, 2004c, 2005a, 2005b, 2005c; World Bank and the Republic of Kenya 2004, Yunker 2004.

Chapter 4 draws on ACIAR 2004; Aksoy and Beghin 2004; Alexandraki and Lankes 2004; Amsden 2000; Anderson 2003, 2004; Arndt 1998; Aschenaki 2004; Audley and others 2003; Baffes and de Gorter 2003; Baldwin 2003; Bannister and Thugge 2001; Barber 2005; Barrientos, McClenaghan and Orton 2001; Barrientos and others 1999; Beghin and Aksoy 2003; Bhagwati 2002; Bhagwati and Panagariya 1996; Bhattacharya 2003; Binswanger and Lutz 2000; Birdsall and Subramaniam 2004; Birdsall, Claessens and Diwan 2003; Brenton 2003; Brenton and Ikezuki 2004; Brown 2005a, 2005b, 2005c; Burfisher and Hopkins 2003; CAFOD 2005; Carey 2002; Carlson 2001; Cernat, Laird and Turrini 2003; Chanda 1999; Chauduri, Goldberg and Jia 2003; Collier and Dollar 2002b; Collier and Gunning 1999; Cornejo 2002; de Córdoba and Vanzetti 2005; Deere 2005; DFID 2003; Diao and Hazell 2003; Diao, Diaz-Bonilla and Robinson 2003; Diao and others 2005; Dollar 2004; Dollar and Kraay 2001a, 2001b; Dorosh 2002; Drahos 2001; Drahos and Braithwaite 2002; Duncan 2004; Elliott 2000; Environmental Working Group 2005; Evans 2005; FAO 2004a, 2005; Galeano 1973; Ghosh 2005; Gibbon 2005; Gibbon 2003; Gilbert 1996; Gunter 2004; Hausmann and Rodrik 2002; Hocking and McGuire 1999; Hoekman 2002, 2005; Hoekman and Martin 2001; Hoekman, Kostecki and Kostecki 1995; Hoekman, Mattoo and English 2002; Horn, Rodrik and McMillan 2003; IADB 2004; IMF 2003a, 2003b, 2004b, 2005a; IMF and World Bank 2001; Integrated Framework for Trade-Related Technical Assistance to Least Developed Countries 2003; Intel 2005; International Cotton Advisory Committee 2005; Jaffee 2003, 2005; James 2001; Jank and others 2001; Jensen 2005; Jha 2005; Kaczynski and Fluharty 2002; Kelch and Normile 2004; Keynes 1980; Khor 2001; Kibria 2001; Killick 2001; Krznaric 2005; Laird 2002; Laird, de Córdoba and Vanzetti 2004; Laird, Peters and Vanzetti 2004; Lall 2000, 2001, 2004; Lall and Pietrobelli 2002; Landes 1998; Lang 2003; Lanjouw 2001; Larsen 2003; Lindert and Williamson 2001b; Lustig and Szekely 1998; Maddison 2001; Mainuddin 2000; Maizels 2000; Martin 2004; Maskus 2000, 2004; Mayne 2005; McCulloch, Winters and Cirera 2002; Minot and Daniels 2002; Mlachila and Yang 2004; Morley 2002; Ng 2001; Ng, Hoekman and Olarreaga 2001; Nogues 2003; OECD 2000, 2001b, 2003a, 2003b, 2004a, 2004b, 2004d, 2005; Okediji 2004; Olarreaga and Ng 2002; Orden 2003; Osorio 2004; Oxfam International 2002a, 2002b, 2003b, 2004a, 2004b, 2004c, 2004d, 2005a; Page 2005; Page and Kleen 2004; Parikh 2002; Picciotto 2004; Ponte 2001; Potbury 2000; Reardon and Berdegue 2002; Reardon, Timmer and Berdegue 2003; Reardon and others 2003; Rodriguez and Rodrik 2000; Rodrik 2000, 2001a, 2001b, 2001c, 2003, 2004; Rogerson and de Renzio 2005; Rosen 2002; Roy 2000, 2001; Samman 2005a, 2005b; Seagate 2003; Sen 1999; Stevens and Kennan 2002, 2004a, 2004b, 2005a, 2005b; Story 2004; Sutton 2004; Tangermann 2003; Teal and Vigneri 2004; Tewari 2003; Tussie 2005; Tussie and Lengyel 2002; Tussie and Quiliconi 2005; UN 2005c; UNCTAD 2000, 2003, 2004a, 2004b; UNCTAD and World Bank 2005; UNDP 2003f; UNEP 1999, 2002; UNIDO 2002, 2004; UN Millennium Project 2005g; US Department of Agriculture 2002, 2005a, 2005b; US Department of Agriculture, Foreign Agricultural Service 2005; USITC 2005; Vakis, Kruger and Mason 2004; Viet Nam 2004; Vorley 2003;

Watal 2002; Watkins 2003a; Winters 2002; Winters, McCulloch and McKay 2004; World Bank 2003c, 2004c, 2004d, 2004f; WTO 2004a, 2004b, 2004c, 2005.

Chapter 5 draws on Addison 2003; Afghanistan, Ministry of Finance 2005; African Union 2000; Amnesty International, Iansa and Oxfam International 2004; Anderson 1999; Annan 2002, 2005; Ballentine and Nitzschke 2004; Bannon and Collier 2003; Barnes 2005; BBC News 2005b; Berdal and Malone 2000; Boyce 2003; Boyden and Ryder 1996; Brown 2005; Brück, Fitzgerald and Gringsby 2000; Bush 2002; Caplan 2002; CEH 1999; Centre for International Cooperation and Security, Department of Peace Studies 2005; Chesterman 2001, 2005; CIDCM 2005; Cilliers and Sturman 2002; Clark 2003; Collier and Hoeffler 2001, 2002, 2004a, 2004b; Collier and others 2003; Commission for Africa 2005; Commission on Human Security 2003; Commission on Weak States and US National Security 2004; Conflictsensitivity.org 2004; Cousens 2002; Cragin and Chalk 2003; Daalder and Lindsay 2003; Dallaire 2003; de Waal 1997; DFID 2004a, 2005; Dodge 1990; Doyle 2001; Duffield 1994, 1998; *The Economist* 2004a; FAO 2004b; FBI various years; Fearon and Laitin 2003; Feinstein and Slaughter 2004; Fiszbein, Giovagnoli and Adúriz 2002; Freedman 1993; Frum and Perle 2003; Fuentes 2005a, 2005b; Ghobarah, Huth and Russett 2004; Ginifer 2005; Global IDP Project 2003, 2005a, 2005b; Global Witness 2004; Goldstone 2005; Goodhand and Atkinson 2001; Gray 2000; Hegarty 2003; Hegre and others 2001; High-Level Forum on the Health MDGs 2004; Holsti 2000; Horton 1993; Human Rights Watch 2004a, 2004b; Humphreys 2003; ICG 2001a, 2001b, 2002, 2003, 2004a, 2004b; ICISS 2001; IRC 2004; Juma and Mengistu 2002; Justino, Litchfield and Whitehead 2003; Kagan 2002; Kagwanja 2004; Kaldor 2001; Kalipeni and Oppong 1998; Keen 1998; The Kimberley Process 2004; King 1998; King and Martin 2001; Klare 2001, 2005; Krug and others 2002; Langer 2005; Le Billon 2001; Levin and Dollar 2005; Lopez 2003; Mackenzie and Buchanan-Smith 2005; Malan and others 2003; Mann and others 1994; Marshall 2005; McGovern and Choulai 2005; Millennium Challenge Corporation 2005a; MIPT 2005; Muggah 2001; Muggah and Batchelor 2002; Mwaura 2005; Mwaura and Schmeidl 2001; Nangiro 2005; Nicaragua 2001; Odhiambo 2004; OECD 2001a; OECD/DAC 1997a, 1997b, 2003a, 2004d; O'Hanlon and Rice 2004; Omitoogun 2003; Østby 2003; Oxfam GB, Save the Children and Christian Aid 2001; Oxfam GB 2003; Oxfam International 2003a; Oxfam International and others 2002; Partnership Africa Canada 2005; Pedersen 2002; Peimani 2005; Petras 2004; Physicians for Human Rights 2002; Pillay 2002; Ponzio 2005a, 2005b; Prime Minister's Strategy Unit 2005; Reilly 2002; Riascos and Vargas 2004; Rotberg 2004; Rubin and others 2005; Schenkenberg van Mierop 2004; SIPRI 2004; Sivard 1991, 1996; Small Arms Survey 2002; Sommers 2002; Stewart 2000, 2002, 2005; Stewart and Fitzgerald 2001; Stewart, Brown and Mancini 2005; Stoddard and Harmer 2005; Strand, Wilhelmsen and Gleditsch 2004, 2005; Sykes 2004; Thakur and Schnabel 2001; Toole and Waldman 1997; UK, HM Treasury 2003; ul Haq 1995; UN 1992, 2000b, 2000c, 2004b, 2005a, 2005d; UN News Centre 2004; UNAIDS 2003, 2004b; UNDP 1994, 2001, 2003a, 2003e, 2004a, 2005b, 2005c; UNHCR 2004; UNICEF 2000, 2001b; UN OCHA 2002, 2004a, 2004b; US Department of State 1999, 2004; USITC 2005; Uvin 1998; Waldman 2005; Welsh 2002; White 2005; WHO 2004a; Woods and research team 2004; Woodward 2002; World Bank 2004e, 2005a, 2005f; World Bank and Palestinian Central Bureau of Statistics 2004.

Bibliography

Commissioned research

Background papers

Chesterman, Simon. 2005. "State-Building and Human Development."
Development Initiatives. 2005a. "New Thinking on Aid and Social Insurance." Somerset, United Kingdom.

Thematic papers

Barnes, Helen. 2005. "Innovative Measures for Conflict Prevention and Resolution in Latin America: A Comparative Study of Bolivia, Venezuela, and Argentina."
Brown, Oli. 2005a. "Supermarket in Agricultural Trade and Impact of Extractive Industries."
Deere, Carolyn. 2005. "International Trade Technical Assistance and Capacity Building."
Development Initiatives. 2005b. "Aid Data Report." Somerset, United Kingdom.
————. 2005c. "Fund Profiles: Global Fund, GAVI, Fast Track Initiative, and Roll Back Malaria." Somerset, United Kingdom.
Dikhanov, Yuri. 2005. "Trends in Global Income Distribution 1970–2015."
Dyer, Kate. 2005. "'The Cost of Poverty': Transaction Costs and the Struggle to Make Aid Work in the Education Sector in Tanzania."
Fuentes, Juan Alberto. 2005a. "Violent Conflict and Human Development in Latin America: The Cases of Colombia, El Salvador and Guatemala."
Fuentes, Ricardo. 2005. "Poverty, Pro-Poor Growth and Simulated Inequality Reduction."
Ghosh, Jayati. 2005. "Trade Liberalization in Agriculture: An Examination of Impact and Policy Strategies with Special Reference to India."
Gibbon, Peter. 2005. "The Commodity Question: New Thinking on Old Problems."
Goodman, Alissa. 2005. "The Links between Income Distribution and Poverty Reduction in Britain."
Jensen, Michael Friis. 2005. "Capacity Building for Pro-Poor Trade: Learning from the Limitations in Current Models."
Johnson, Alison, and Matthew Martin. 2005. "Empowering Developing Countries to Lead the Aid Partnership."
Krznaric, Roman. 2005. "The Limits on Pro-poor Agricultural Trade in Guatemala: Land, Labour and Political Power."
Mayne, Ruth. 2005. "Regionalism, Bilateralism, and 'TRIPS Plus' Agreements: The Threat to Developing Countries."
Miller, Calum. 2005. "The Human Development Impact of Economic Crises."
Mwaura, Ciru. 2005. "Kenya and Uganda Pastoral Conflict Case Study."
Nangiro, Simon. 2005. "The Impact of Insecurity on Livelihood and Social Service Provision in Kotido District."
Samman, Emma. 2005a. "Openness and Growth: An Empirical Investigation."
Stoddard, Abby, and Adele Harmer. 2005. "Room to Manoeuvre: Challenges of Linking Humanitarian Action and Post-Conflict Recovery in the New Global Security Environment."

Tussie, Diana. 2005. "More of the Same, or a New Threat? Regionalism versus Multilateralism in World Trade Negotiations."
Tussie, Diana, and Cintia Quiliconi. 2005. "The Current Trade Context."
Vargas Hill, Ruth. 2005. "Assessing Rhetoric and Reality in the Predictability and Volatility of Aid."
Watt, Patrick. 2005. "Transaction Costs in Aid: Case Studies of Sector Wide Approaches in Zambia and Senegal."

Issue notes

Barber, Catherine. 2005. "Potential Benefits of Labour Mobility and Mode 4 Negotiations: Rule of Origin and Trade Preferences."
Brown, Graham. 2005. "Horizontal Inequalities, Ethnic Separatism, and Violent Conflict: The Case of Aceh, Indonesia."
Brown, Oli. 2005b. "Policy Incoherence: EU Fisheries Policy in Senegal."
————. 2005c. "Wealth for the Few, Poverty for the Many: The Resource Curse—Examples of Poor Governance/Corporate Mismanagement Wasting Natural Resource Wealth."
Kabeer, Naila. 2005. "Gender Equality and Human Development: the Instrumental Rationale."
Langer, Arnim. 2005. "Horizontal Inequalities and Violent Conflict. Cote d'Ivoire Country Paper."
McGovern, Kieren, and Bernard Choulai. 2005. "Case Study of Solomon Islands Peace and Conflict-related Development Analysis."
Rowland, Diane, and Catherine Hoffman. 2005. "The Impact of Health Insurance Coverage on Health Disparities in the United States."
Samman, Emma. 2005b. "Gini Coefficients for Subsidy Distribution in Agriculture."

References

ACIAR (Australian Centre for International Agricultural Research). 2004. "The Rise of Supermarkets: How Will Smallholder Farmers Fare?" *Linking Farmers with Markets*. [http://www.linkingfarmerswithmarkets.net/index.php?p=3&id=9]. June 2005.
ActionAid International and Oxfam International. 2005. "Millstone or Milestone: What Rich Countries Must Do in Paris to Make and Work for Poor People." Oxford. [http://www.oxfam.org.uk/what_we_do/issues/debt_aid/downloads/aid_millstone.pdf]. May 2005.
ActionAid International, Eurodad, and Oxfam International. 2005. "EU Heroes and Villains: Which Countries Are Living up to Their Promises on Aid, Trade, and Debt?" Joint NGO Briefing Paper. [http://www.oxfam.org.uk/what_we_do/issues/debt_aid/downloads/eu_heroes_villains.pdf]. March 2005.
Adam, Christopher. 2005. "Exogenous Inflows and Real Exchange Rates: Theoretical Quirk or Empirical Reality?" Paper presented at the IMF Seminar on Foreign Aid and Macroeconomic Management, 14–15 March, Maputo.
Adam, Christopher, and David Bevan. 2003. "Aid, Public Expenditure, and the Dutch Disease." CSAE Working Paper. University of Oxford, Department of Economics, Oxford.
ADB (Asian Development Bank). 2004. "Socialist Republic of Viet Nam, Loan VIE 37115-01: Health Care in the Central Highlands." Manila. [http://www.adb.org/Documents/Profiles/LOAN/37115013.ASP]. May 2005.

Adenauer, I., and L. Vagassky. 1998. "Aid and the Real Exchange Rate: Dutch Disease Effects in African Countries." *Intereconomics* 33(4): 177–85.

Addison, T., ed. 2003. *From Conflict to Recovery in Africa.* Oxford: Oxford University Press.

Advisory Commission on Intergovernmental Relations. 1984. "Significant Features of Fiscal Federalism, 1982-83 Edition." In Marshall Kaplan and Peggy L. Cucitit, eds., *The Great Society and Its Legacy: Twenty Years of U.S. Social Policy.* Durham, N.C.: Duke University Press.

Afghanistan, Ministry of Finance. 2005. "National Budget." Development Budget and External Relations Unit, Kabul. [http://www.af/mof/budget/index.html]. April 2005.

African Union. 2000. "Constitutive Act of the African Union." 11 July, Lomé.

Ahluwalia, Isher, and Zahid Hussain. 2004. "Development Achievements and Challenges." *Economic and Political Weekly* 39(36): 4013–22.

Ahmed, Akhter U., and Carlo del Ninno. 2001. "Food for Education Program in Bangladesh: An Evaluation of Its Impact on Educational Attainment and Food Security." FCND BRIEFS. Discussion Paper 138. International Food Policy Research Institute, Food Consumption and Nutrition Division, Washington, DC. [http://www.ifpri.org/divs/fcnd/dp/papers/fcnbr138.pdf]. May 2005.

Aid/Watch. 2005. "Australian Aid: The Boomerang Effect." Erskineville, Australia. [http://www.aidwatch.org.au/assets/aw00669/feb%2016%20boom%20aid%20final.doc]. May 2005.

Aksoy, Ataman M., and John C. Beghin, eds. 2004. "Global Agricultural Trade and Developing Countries." Washington, DC: World Bank. [http://siteresources.worldbank.org/INTGAT/Resources/GATfulltext.pdf]. May 2005.

Alexandraki, Katerina, and Hans Peter Lankes. 2004. "The Impact of Preference Erosion on Middle-Income Developing Countries." IMF Working Paper WP/04/169. Washington, DC.

Amnesty International, Iansa, and Oxfam International. 2004. "The Arms Trade Treaty: Draft Framework Convention on International Arms Transfers." Working draft. [http://www.controlarms.org/the_issues/ATT_0504.pdf]. April 2005.

Amsden, Alice. 2000. "Industrialisation under New WTO Law." Paper prepared for the UNCTAD X High Level Round Table on Trade and Development: Directions for the Twenty-First Century, 12–19 February, Bangkok.

Anderson, Kym. 2003. "How Can Agricultural Trade Reform Reduce Poverty?" University of Adelaide, CEPR and School of Economics and Centre for International Economic Studies, Adelaide, Australia. [http://www.tcd.ie/iiis/pdf/YaleSeminar0403rev.pdf]. May 2005.

———. 2004. "Agriculture, Trade Reform, and Poverty Reduction: Implications for Sub-Saharan Africa." Policy Issues in International Trade and Commodities Study Series 22. United Nations Conference on Trade and Development, Geneva. [http://www.unctad.org/en/docs/itcdtab24_en.pdf]. May 2005.

Anderson, Mary B. 1999. *Do Not Harm: How Aid Can Support Peace—Or War.* Boulder, Colo.: Lynne Rienner.

Annan, Kofi. 2002. "Strategies for World Peace: The View of the UN Secretary-General." *The Futurist* 36(3): 18–21.

———. 2005. "In Larger Freedom: Towards Development, Security, and Human Rights for All." Report of the Secretary-General to the General Assembly. Document A/59/2005. New York. [http://www.un.org/largerfreedom/report-largerfreedom.pdf]. May 2005.

Arndt, S. 1998. "Super-Specialization and the Gains from Trade." *Contemporary Economic Policy* 16(4): 480–85.

Aryeetey, Ernest, Barfour Osei, and Peter Quartey. 2003. "Does Tying Aid Make It More Costly? A Ghanaian Case Study." Center for Global Development and the Global Development Network. Paper presented at the Workshop on Quantifying the Impact of Rich Countries' Policies on Poor Countries, 23–24 October, Washington, DC.

Aschenaki, Bemnet. 2004. "Transport Costs in Ethiopia: An Impediment to Exports." Background Study for the World Bank's FY04 Country Economic Memorandum for Ethiopia. Washington, DC. [http://siteresources.worldbank.org/INTETHIOPIA/Resources/PREM/Ethiopia-Transport_Cost-Final.pdf]. May 2005.

Atkinson, A. B. 2004. "New Sources of Development Finance: Funding the Millennium Development Goals." Policy Brief 10. United Nations University, World Institute for Development Economics Research, Helsinki.

———, ed. 2005. *New Sources of Development Finance.* New York: Oxford University Press.

Atkinson, Tony. 2003. "Innovative Sources for Development Finance—Global Public Economics." Paper presented at the Annual World Bank Conference on Development Economics-Europe, 15–16 May, Paris. [http://wbln0018.worldbank.org/eurvp/web.nsf/Pages/Paper+by+Atkinson/$File/ATKINSON.PDF]. October 2005.

Audley, John J., Demetrios G. Papademetriou, Sandra Polaski, and Scott Vaunghan. 2003. "NAFTA's Promise and Reality: Lessons from Mexico for the Hemisphere." Carnegie Endowment for International Peace, Washington, DC. [http://www.ceip.org/files/pdf/NAFTA_Report._Intro.pdf]. May 2005.

AVERT. 2005. "The Origins of AIDS and HIV and the First Cases of AIDS." West Sussex, United Kingdom. [http://www.avert.org/origins.htm]. March 2005.

Baffes, John, and Harry De Gorter. 2003. "Decoupling Support to Agriculture: An Economic Analysis of Recent Experience." Paper presented at the Annual World Bank Conference on Development Economics-Europe, 15–16 May, Paris. [http://wbln0018.worldbank.org/eurvp/web.nsf/Pages/Paper+by+De+Gorter/$File/DE+GORTER.PDF]. May 2005.

Baldwin, Robert E. 2003. *Openness and Growth: What's the Empirical Relationship?* NBER Working Paper 9578. Cambridge, Mass.: National Bureau of Economic Research.

Ballentine, Karen, and Heiko Nitzschke. 2004. "The Political Economy of Civil War and Conflict Transformation." Berghof Research Center for Constructive Conflict Management, Berlin. [http://www.berghof-handbook.net/articles/BHDS3_BallentineNitzschke230305.pdf]. April 2005.

Banerjee, Abhijit, Angus Deaton, and Esther Duflo. 2004. "Health Care Delivery in Rural Rajasthan." *Economic and Political Weekly* 39(9): 944–49. [http://www.wws.princeton.edu/~rpds/downloads/banerjee_deaton_healthcare.pdf]. May 2005.

Banister, Judith, and Xiabo Zhang. 2005. "China, Economic Development, and Mortality Decline." *World Development* 33(1): 21–41.

Bannister, Geoffrey J., and Kamau Thugge. 2001. "International Trade and Poverty Alleviation." *Finance & Development* 38(4): 48–51. [http://www.imf.org/external/pubs/ft/fandd/2001/12/banniste.htm]. May 2005.

Bannon, Ian, and Paul Collier, eds. 2003. *Natural Resources and Violent Conflict: Options and Actions.* Washington, DC: World Bank.

Bardhan, Pranab. 2000. "Social Justice in the Global Economy." International Labour Organization Social Policy Lecture, 1–6 September, Cape Town, South Africa. [http://www.ilo.org/public/english/bureau/inst/papers/sopolecs/bardhan/]. May 2005.

Barrientos, S., A. Bee, A. Matear, and I. Vogel. 1999. *Women and Agribusiness: Working Miracles in the Chilean Fruit Export Sector.* Basingstoke, United Kingdom: Macmillan.

Barrientos, S., S. McClenaghan, and L. Orton. 2001. "Ethical Trade and South African Deciduous Fruit Exports—Addressing Gender Sensitivity." *European Journal of Development Research* 12(1): 140–58.

Baulch, Bob. 2004. "Aid Distribution and the MDGs." CPRC Working Paper 48. Chronic Poverty Research Centre, Manchester. [http://www.chronicpoverty.org/pdfs/48%20Bob%20Baulch.pdf]. May 2005.

BBC News. 2005a. "India Launches Rural Health Plan." 12 April.
[http://news.bbc.co.uk/1/hi/world/south_asia/4436603.stm].
————. 2005b. "Pledges Mount Up for Darfur Force." 26 May. [http://
news.bbc.co.uk/1/hi/world/africa/4581463.stm]. June 2005.

Beghin, John C., and Ataman Aksoy. 2003. "Agricultural Trade and
the Doha Round: Preliminary Lessons from Commodity Studies."
Briefing Paper 03-BP 42. Iowa State University, Center for
Agricultural and Rural Development, Ames, Iowa. [http://www.
card.iastate.edu/publications/DBS/PDFFiles/03bp42.pdf]. May
2005.

Benn, Hilary. 2004. "The Development Challenge in Crisis States: How
Development Can Help Deal with State Failure." London School of
Economics Public Lecture, 4 March, London. [http://www.lse.ac.uk/
collections/LSEPublicLecturesAndEvents/pdf/20040304Benn.pdf].
March 2005.

Berdal, Mats, and David Malone, eds. 2000. Greed and Grievance:
Economic Agendas in Civil Wars. Boulder, Colo.: Lynne Rienner.

Berg, Andy. 2005. "High Aid Inflows Case Study: Ghana." Paper
presented at the International Monetary Fund Seminar on Foreign
Aid and Macroeconomic Management, 14–15 March, Maputo.

Bevan, David. 2005. "An Analytical Overview of Aid Absorption:
Recognising and Avoiding Macroeconomic Hazards." Paper
presented at the International Monetary Fund Seminar on Foreign
Aid and Macroeconomic Management, 14–15 March, Maputo.

Beynon, Jonathan. 2003. "Poverty Efficient Aid Allocation—Collier/
Dollar Revisited." ESAU Working Paper 2. Overseas Development
Institute, Economic and Statistics Analysis Unit, London. [http://
www.odi.org.uk/esau/publications/working_papers/esau_wp2.
pdf]. March 2005.

Bhagwati, Jagdish. 2002. Free Trade Today. Princeton, N.J.: Princeton
University Press.
————. 2004. In Defense of Globalization. Oxford: Oxford University
Press.

Bhagwati, Jagdish, and Arvind Panagariya, eds. 1996. The
Economics of Preferential Trade Agreements. Washington, DC:
American Enterprise Institute Press.

Bhattacharya, Debapriya. 2003. "Final Countdown of the MFA: Fallout
for the LDCs." Center for Policy Dialogue, Dhaka.

Binswanger, Hans, and Ernst Lutz. 2000. "Agricultural Trade Barriers,
Trade Negotiations, and the Interests of Developing Countries."
Paper presented at the International Association of Agricultural
Economists Meeting, 13–19 August, Berlin.

Bird, Graham. 2002. "The Completion Rate of IMF Programmes: What
We Know, Don't Know, and Need to Know." The World Economy
25(6): 833–47.

Bird, Graham, and Alistair Milne. 2003. "Debt Relief for Low Income
Countries: Is It Effective and Efficient?" The World Economy 26(1):
43–59.

Birdsall, Nancy. 2002a. "Asymmetric Globalization: Global Markets
Require Good Global Politics." Working Paper 12. Center for Global
Development, Washington, DC. [http://www.cgdev.org/docs/cgd_
wp012.pdf]. May 2005.
————. 2002b. "From Social Policy to an Open-Economy Social
Contract in Latin America." Working Paper 21. Center for Global
Development, Washington, DC. [http://cgdev.axion-it.net/docs/
cgd%20wp021.pdf]. May 2005.
————. 2004. "Seven Deadly Sins: Reflections on Donor Failings."
Working Paper 50. Center for Global Development, Washington, DC.

Birdsall, Nancy, and Michael Clemens. 2003. "From Promise to
Performance: How Rich Countries Can Help Poor Countries Help
Themselves." CGD Brief 2(1). Center for Global Development,
Washington, DC. [http://www.cgdev.org/docs/cgdbrief5.pdf].
March 2005.

Birdsall, Nancy, and Brian Deese. 2005. "Delivering on Debt Relief."
CGD Brief 1(1). Center for Global Development, Washington, DC.
[http://www.cgdev.org/docs/cgdbrief1.pdf]. May 2005.

Birdsall, Nancy, and J. Londono. 1997. "Asset Inequality Matters: An
Assessment of the World Bank's Approach to Poverty Reduction."
American Economic Review 87(2): 32–37.

Birdsall, Nancy, and Arvind Subramaniam. 2004. "Saving Iraq from
Its Oil." Foreign Affairs 83(4): 77–89.

Birdsall, Nancy, Stijn Claessens, and Ishac Diwan. 2003. "Policy
Selectivity Forgone: Debt and Donor Behavior in Africa." World Bank
Economic Review 17(3): 409–35.

Böhning, W. R., and M.-L. Schloeter-Paredes. 1994. Aid in Place
of Migration? Selected Contributions to an ILO-UNHCR Meeting.
Geneva: International Labour Organization.

Bourguignon, François. 2000. "Can Redistribution Accelerate Growth
and Development?" Paper presented at the Annual World Bank
Conference on Development Economics-Europe, 26–28 June,
Paris. [http://www.worldbank.org/research/abcde/eu_2000/
pdffiles/bourguignon.pdf]. May 2005.

Bourguignon, François, and Christian Morrisson. 1999. "The Size
Distribution of Income among World Citizens: 1820–1990." Ecole
Normale Supérieure, Départment et Laboratoire d'Economie, and
Université Paris 1 Panthéon-Sorbonne, Paris. [http://are.berkeley.
edu/~harrison/globalpoverty/bourguignon.pdf]. May 2005.

Bourguignon, François, Francisco H. G. Ferreira, and Marta
Menéndez. 2003. "Inequality of Outcomes and Inequality of
Opportunities in Brazil." Policy Research Working Paper 3174. World
Bank, Washington, DC.

Boyce, James K. 2003. "Aid, Conditionality, and War Economies."
Working Paper 70. University of Massachusetts, Amherst, Political
Economy Research Institute. [http://www.umass.edu/peri/pdfs/
WP70.pdf]. April 2005.

Boyden, Jo, and Paul Ryder. 1996. "Implementing the Right to
Education in Areas of Armed Conflict." Oxford. [http://www.essex.
ac.uk/armedcon/story_id/000021.htm]. May 2005.

Brenton, Paul. 2003. "Integrating the Least Developed Countries into
the World Trading System: The Current Impact of European Union
Preferences under Everything But Arms." Journal of World Trade
37(3): 623–46.

Brenton, Paul, and Takaka Ikezuki. 2004. "The Initial and Potential
Impact of Preferential Access to the US Market under the African
Growth and Opportunity Act." Policy Research Working Paper 3262.
World Bank, Washington, DC.

Brown-Collier, Elba. 1998. "Johnson's Great Society: Its Legacy in the
1990s." Review of Social Economy 56(3): 259–76.

Brück, T., V. Fitzgerald, and A. Gringsby. 2000. "Enhancing the Private
Sector Contribution to Post-War Recovery in Poor Countries." QEH
Working Paper 45(2). Oxford University, Queen Elizabeth House,
Oxford. [http://www.qeh.ox.ac.uk/ftprc.html]. June 2005.

Bruns, Barbara, Alain Mingat, and Ramaharta Rakotomalala. 2003.
Achieving Universal Primary Education by 2015: A Chance for Every
Child. Washington, DC: World Bank.

Bulír, Ales, and Alfonso Javier Hamann. 2001. "How Volatile and
Unpredictable Are Aid Flows, and What Are the Policy Implications?"
IMF Working Paper WP/01/167. International Monetary Fund,
Washington, DC. [http://www.imf.org/external/pubs/ft/wp/2001/
wp01167.pdf]. March 2005.
————. 2003. "Aid Volatility: An Empirical Assessment." IMF Staff
Paper 50(1): 64–89. Washington, DC.

Burnham, Margaret. 1989. "Legacy of the 1960s: The Great Society
Didn't Fail." The Nation, 24 July.

Burfisher, Mary, and Jeffrey Hopkins. 2003. "Decoupled Payments:
Household Income Transfers in Contemporary U.S." US Department
of Agriculture, Economic Research Service, Market and Trade
Economics Division. Washington, DC. [http://www.ers.usda.
gov/publications/aer822/aer822.pdf]. May 2005.

Bush, George W. 2002. "President Proposes $5 Billion Plan to
Help Developing Nations." [http://www.whitehouse.gov/news/
releases/2002/03/20020314-7.html]. April 2005.

CAFOD (Catholic Agency for Overseas Development). 2005. "Working Conditions in PC Supply Chains: Mexico and China." London. [http://www.cafod.org.uk/policy_and_analysis/policy_papers/private_sector/clean_up_your_computer_report/part_iii]. May 2005.

Caplan, Richard. 2002. *New Trusteeship? The International Administration of War-Torn Territories*. Oxford: Oxford University Press.

Carey, David. 2002. "Xbox: PC Meets Console." *EE Times*. 26 March. [http://www.eetimes.com/news/latest/showArticle.jhtml?articleID=18306939]. May 2005.

Carlson, Beverley A. 2001. "Education and the Labour Market in Latin America: Why Measurement Is Important and What It Tells Us about Policies, Reforms, and Performance." Economic Commission for Latin America and the Caribbean, Santiago.

Carr-Hill, R. A. 2004. "HIV/AIDS, Poverty, and Educational Statistics in Africa: Evidence and Indication." United Nations Educational, Scientific and Cultural Organization, Institute for Statistics, Montreal, Canada.

Case, A., and A. Deaton. 1998. "Large Cash Transfers to the Elderly in South Africa." *Economic Journal* 108(450): 1330–61.

Cassen, Robert, Leela Visaria, and Tim Dyson, eds. 2004. *Twenty-first Century India: Population, Economy, Human Development, and the Environment*. Oxford: Oxford University Press.

Castro-Leal, F., J. Dayton, and K. Mehra. 2000. "Public Spending on Health Care in Africa: Do the Poor Benefit?" *Bulletin of the World Health Organization* 78(1): 66–74. [http://www.who.int/docstore/bulletin/pdf/2000/issue1/bu0201.pdf].

CEH (Comisión de Esclarecimiento Histórico). 1999. *Guatemala. Memoria del Silencio. Tomo IV. Consecuencias y Efectos de la Violencia*. Guatemala City: United Nations Office for Project Services, Servigráficos S.A.

Center for Global Development. 2004. "Why Global Development Matters for the U.S." Rich World, Poor World Brief, 24 April. Washington, DC. [http://www.cgdev.org/docs/rp_whymatters.pdf]. May 2005.

Centre for International Cooperation and Security, Department of Peace Studies. 2005. "The Impact of Armed Violence on Poverty and Development: Full Report to the Armed Violence and Poverty Initiative." Paper commissioned for UK Department for Investing in Development. University of Bradford, Bradford.

Cernat, Lucian, Sam Laird, and Alessandro Turrini. 2003. "Back to Basics: Market Access Issues in the Doha Agenda." United Nations Conference on Trade and Development, Geneva. [http://192.91.247.38/tab/pubs/itcdtabMisc9_en.pdf]. May 2005.

Chanda, Rupa. 1999. "Movement of Natural Persons and Trade in Services: Liberalising Temporary Movement of Labour Under the GATS." ICRIER Working Paper 51. Indian Council for Research on International Economic Relations, New Delhi.

Chauduri, Shubham, Pinelopi K. Goldberg, and Panle Jia. 2003. *The Effects of Extending Intellectual Property Rights Protection to Developing Countries: A Case Study of the Indian Pharmaceutical Market*. NBER Working Paper 10159. Cambridge, Mass.: National Bureau of Economic Research. [http://papers.nber.org/papers/w10159.pdf]. May 2005.

Chen, Shaohua, and Martin Ravallion. 2004. "How Have the World's Poorest Fared since the Early 1980s?" Policy Research Paper 3341. World Bank, Washington, DC.

Chen, Shaohua, and Yan Wang. 2001. "China's Growth and Poverty Reduction: Recent Trends between 1990 and 1999." Policy Research Working Paper 2651. Washington, DC.

Chesterman, Simon. 2001. *Just War or Just Peace? Humanitarian Intervention and International Law*. Oxford: Oxford University Press.

China, National Bureau of Statistics of. 2004. "China Statistical Yearbook 2004." Beijing. [http://www.stats.gov.cn/english/statisticaldata/yearlydata/yb2004-e/indexeh.htm]. June 2005.

CIDCM (Center for International Development and Conflict Management). 2005. *The Polity IV Project 2005: Political Regime Characteristics and Transitions, 1800–2003*. Database. University of Maryland, College Park.

Cilliers, Jakkie, and Kathryn Sturman. 2002. "The Right Intervention: Enforcement Challenges for the African Union." *African Security Review* 11(3): 29–39.

Claeson, Mariam, Eduard R. Bos, Tazim Mawji, and Indra Pathmanathan. 2000. "Reducing Child Mortality in India in the New Millennium." *Bulletin of the World Health Organization* 78(10): 1192–99. Geneva. [http://www.scielosp.org/pdf/bwho/v78n10/78n10a05.pdf]. May 2005.

Clark, Wesley K. 2003. *Winning Modern Wars: Iraq, Terrorism, and the American Empire*. New York: Public Affairs.

Clemens, Michael, Rikhil Bhavnani, and Steven Radelet. 2004. "Counting Chickens When They Hatch: The Short-Term Effect of Aid on Growth." Working Paper 44. Center for Global Development, Washington, DC. [http://econwpa.wustl.edu/eps/if/papers/0407/0407010.pdf]. May 2005.

Clemens, Michael, Charles Kenny, and Todd Moss. 2005. "The Trouble with the MDGs: Confronting Expectations of Aid and Development Success." Working Paper 40. Center for Global Development, Washington, DC. [http://econwpa.wustl.edu/eps/dev/papers/0405/0405011.pdf]. March 2005.

Coady, David, and Susan Parker. 2005. "A Cost-Effectiveness Analysis of Demand and Supply-Side Education Interventions: The Case of PROGRESA in Mexico." IFPRI Discussion Paper 127. International Food Policy Research Institute, Washington, DC.

Coady, David, Margaret Grosh, and John Hoddinott. 2004. *Targeting of Transfers in Developing Countries: Review of Lessons and Experience*. Washington, DC: World Bank.

Collier, Paul. 1999. "Aid Dependency: A Critique." *Journal of African Economies* 8(4): 528–45.

Collier, Paul, and Jan Dehn. 2001. "Aid, Shocks, and Growth." Policy Research Working Paper 2688. World Bank, Washington, DC. [http://wdsbeta.worldbank.org/external/default/WDSContentServer/IW3P/IB/2001/11/06/000094946_01102304052049/Rendered/PDF/multi0page.pdf]. May 2005.

Collier, Paul, and David Dollar. 2002a. "Aid Allocation and Poverty Reduction." *European Economic Review* 46(8): 1475–1500. [http://www.sciencedirect.com/science?_ob=MImg&_imagekey=B6V64-44B6VR3-1-32&_cdi=5804&_user=666074&_orig=browse&_coverDate=09%2F30%2F2002&_sk=999539991&view=c&wchp=dGLbVzz-zSkWA&md5=b0d4b7f87e8527420e35dd45dd046170&ie=/sdarticle.pdf]. March 2005.

———. 2002b. *Globalization, Growth, and Poverty: Building an Inclusive World Economy*. Washington, DC: World Bank and Oxford University Press

———. 2004. "Development Effectiveness: What Have We Learnt?" *The Economic Journal* 114(496): F244–F271.

Collier, Paul, and J. Gunning. 1999. "Explaining African Economic Performance." *Journal of Economic Literature* 37(1): 64–111.

Collier, Paul, and Anke Hoeffler. 2001. "Greed and Grievance in Civil War." World Bank, Washington, DC. [http://www.worldbank.org/research/conflict/papers/greedgrievance_23oct.pdf]. May 2005.

———. 2002. "Aid, Policy, and Growth in Post-Conflict Societies." Policy Research Working Paper 2902. World Bank, Washington, DC. [http://wdsbeta.worldbank.org/external/default/WDSContentServer/IW3P/IB/2002/11/01/000094946_02101904245026/Rendered/PDF/multi0page.pdf]. May 2005.

———. 2004a. "The Challenge of Reducing the Global Incidence of Civil War." Paper prepared for the Copenhagen Consensus Project. Oxford. [http://www.copenhagenconsensus.com/Files/Filer/CC/Papers/Conflicts_230404.pdf]. May 2005.

———. 2004b. "Conflicts." In Bjørn Lomborg, ed., *Global Crises, Global Solutions*. Cambridge: Cambridge University Press.

Collier, Paul, V. L. Elliot, Håvard Hegre, Anke Hoeffler, Marta Reynal-Querol, and Nicholas Sambanis. 2003. *Breaking the Conflict Trap: Civil War and Development Policy.* Washington, DC: World Bank and Oxford University Press. [http://web. worldbank.org/external/default/WDSContentServer/IW3P/ IB/2003/06/30/000094946_0306190405396/Rendered/PDF/ multi0page.pdf]. May 2005.

Commission for Africa. 2005. "Our Common Interest: Report of the Commission for Africa." London. [http://www.commissionforafrica. org/english/report/thereport/english/11-03-05_cr_report.pdf]. May 2005.

Commission on Human Security. 2003. *Human Security Now: Report of the Commission on Human Security.* New York. [http://www. humansecurity-chs.org/finalreport/FinalReport.pdf]. May 2005.

Commission on International Development. 1969. *Partners in Development: Report of the Commission on International Development.* New York: Praeger Publishers.

Commission on Macroeconomics and Health. 2001. "Macroeconomics and Health: Investing in Health for Economic Development." World Health Organization, Geneva. [http://www3. who.int/whosis/cmh/cmh_report/e/pdf/001-004.pdf]. May 2005.

Commission on Social Justice. 1993. *The Justice Gap.* London: Institute for Public Policy Research.

Commission on Weak States and US National Security. 2004. "On the Brink: Weak States and US National Security." Center for Global Development, Washington, DC. [http://www.cgdev.org/docs/ Full_Report.pdf].

Conflictsensitivity.org. 2004. "Conflict-Sensitive Approaches to Development, Humanitarian Assistance and Peacebuilding: A Resource Pack." [http://www.conflictsensitivity.org]. May 2005.

Corbacho, Ana, and Gerd Schwartz. 2002. "Mexico: Experiences with Pro-Poor Expenditure Policies." IMF Working Paper WP/02/12. International Monetary Fund, Washington, DC. [http://www.imf. org/external/pubs/ft/wp/2002/wp0212.pdf]. May 2005.

Cordella, Tito, and Giovanni Dell'Ariccia. 2003. "Budget Support versus Project Aid." IMF Working Paper WP/03/88. International Monetary Fund, Washington, DC. [http://www.imf.org/external/ pubs/ft/wp/2003/wp0388.pdf]. March 2005.

Cornejo, Luis Jorge. 2002. "Rules of Origin and Trade Preferences." In Bernard Hoekman, Aaditya Mattoo, and Philip English, eds., *Development, Trade, and the WTO: A Handbook.* Washington, DC: World Bank.

Cornia, Giovanni Andrea, ed. 2004. *Inequality, Growth, and Poverty in an Era of Liberalization and Globalization.* Oxford: Oxford University Press.

Cousens, Elizabeth. 2002. "From Missed Opportunities to Overcompensation: Implementing the Dayton Agreement on Bosnia." In Stephen J. Stedman, D. Rothchild, and Elizabeth Cousens, eds. *Ending Civil Wars: The Implementation of Peace Agreements.* Boulder, Colo.: Lynne Rienner.

Cousens, Simon, Joy E. Lawn, and Jelka Zupan. 2005. "Four Million Neonatal Deaths: When? Where? Why?" *The Lancet* 365(9462): 891–900.

Cragin, Kim, and Peter Chalk. 2003. "Terrorism and Development: Using Social and Economic Development to Inhibit a Resurgence of Terrorism." RAND Corporation, Santa Monica, Calif. [http://www. rand.org/publications/MR/MR1630/MR1630.pdf]. May 2005.

CTA (Technical Centre for Agricultural and Rural Cooperation ACP-EU). 2004. "EU Common Fisheries Policy and Its Implications for EU-ACP Relations." [http://agritrade.cta.int/fisheries/cfp/].

Daalder, Ivo H., and James M. Lindsay. 2003. *America Unbound: The Bush Revolution in Foreign Policy.* Washington, DC: Brookings Institution Press.

Dalgaard, Carl-Johan, Henrik Hansen, and Finn Tarp. 2004. "On the Empirics of Foreign Aid and Growth." *The Economic Journal* 114(496): F191–F216. [http://www.univ-paris12.fr/www/labos/ gratice/Hansen%20.pdf]. March 2005.

Dallaire, Lt. Gen. Roméo. 2003. *Shake Hands with the Devil: The Failure of Humanity in Rwanda.* New York: Carroll & Graf.

Das, Gurcharan. 2001. "India's Growing Middle Class." *The Globalist.* 5 November. [http://www.theglobalist.com/DBWeb/StoryId. aspx?StoryId=2195]. May 2005.

Datt, Gaurav, and Martin Ravallion. 2002. "Is India's Economic Growth Leaving the Poor Behind?" Policy Research Working Paper 2846. World Bank, Washington, DC.

de Córdoba, Santiago Fernandez, and David Vanzetti. 2005. "Coping with Trade Reforms: Implications of the WTO Industrial Tariff Negotiations for Developing Countries." United Nations Conference on Trade and Development, Geneva.

de Ferranti, David, Guillermo E. Perry, Francisco H.G. Ferreira, Michael Walton, David Coady, Wendy Cunningham, Leonardo Gasparini, Joyce Jacobsen, Yasuhiko Matsuda, James Robinson, Kenneth Sokoloff, and Quentin Wodon. 2003. *Inequality in Latin America and the Caribbean: Breaking With History?* Washington, DC: World Bank. [http://wbln0018.worldbank.org/ LAC/lacinfoclient.nsf/d29684951174975c85256735007fef12/ 32d7c0bacee5752a85256dba00545d3f/$FILE/Inequality%20in% 20Latin%20America%20-%20complete.pdf]. May 2005.

de Renzio, Paolo. 2005. "Can More Aid Be Spent in Africa?" *Opinions* 30. Overseas Development Institute, London. [http://www.odi.org. uk/publications/opinions/30_odi_opinions_aid_africa_jan05.pdf]. May 2005.

de Renzio, Paolo, David Booth, Andrew Rogerson, and Zaza Curran. 2004. "Incentives for Harmonisation in Aid Agencies: A Report to the DAC Working Party on Aid Effectivenss." Overseas Development Institute, London. [http://www.oecd. org/dataoecd/58/27/34373869.pdf]. March 2005.

de Waal, Alex. 1997. *Famine Crimes: Politics and the Disaster Relief Industry in Africa.* London: African Rights and the International African Institute.

Deaton, Angus. 2002. "Policy Implications of the Gradient of Health and Wealth: An Economist Asks Would Redistributing Income Improve Population Health?" *Health Affairs* 21(2): 13–30.

———. 2003. "Health, Inequality, and Economic Development." *Journal of Economic Literature* 41(March): 113–58. [http://www.wcfia. harvard.edu/conferences/socialcapital/Happiness%20Readings/ DeatonNew.pdf]. May 2005.

———. 2004. "Health in an Age of Globalization." Paper prepared for the Brookings Trade Forum, 13–14 May, Washington, DC. [http://www.wws.princeton.edu/~rpds/downloads/deaton_ healthglobalage.pdf]. May 2005.

Deaton, Angus, and Jean Drèze. 2002. "Poverty and Inequality in India: A Re-Examination." *Economic and Political Weekly* 37(35): 3729–48.

Deaton, Angus, and Valerie Kozel. 2004. "Data and Dogma: The Great Indian Poverty Debate." Princeton University, Research Program in Development Studies, and World Bank, Washington, DC. [http://poverty2.forumone.com/files/15168_deaton_kozel_2004. pdf]. May 2005.

Deininger, Klaus, and Paul Mpuga. 2004. "Economic and Welfare Effects of the Abolition of Health User Fees: Evidence from Uganda." Policy Research Working Paper 3276. World Bank, Washington, DC. [http://wdsbeta.worldbank.org/external/default/WDSContentServer/ IW3P/IB/2004/05/21/000009486_20040521105433/Rendered/ PDF/wps3276health.pdf]. May 2005.

DeLong, Bradford, and Barry Eichengreen. 1991. "The Marshall Plan: History's Most Successful Structural Adjustment Program." Centre for Economic Performance, the Anglo-German Foundations, and Landeszentralbank Hamburg. Paper presented at the conference on Post–World War II European Reconstruction, 5–7 September, Hamburg, Germany.

Demombynes, Gabriel, and Johannes Hoogeveen. 2004. "Growth, Inequality, and Simulated Poverty Paths for Tanzania, 1992–2002." Policy Research Working Paper 3432. World Bank, Washington, DC.

Dev, Mahendra. 2002. "Pro-Poor Growth in India: What Do We Know about the Employment Effects of Growth 1980–2000?" Working Paper 161. Overseas Development Institute, London. [http://www.odi.org.uk/publications/wp161.pdf]. May 2005.

Devarajan, Shantayanan, and Ritva Reinikka. 2003. "Making Services Work for Poor People." Finance & Development 40(3): 48–51. [http://www.imf.org/external/pubs/ft/fandd/2003/09/pdf/devaraja.pdf]. May 2005.

Devarajan, Shantayanan, Margaret Miller, and Eric Swanson. 2002. "Goals for Development: History, Prospects, and Costs." Policy Research Working Paper 2819. World Bank, Washington, DC. [http://econ.worldbank.org/files/13269_wps2819.pdf]. March 2005.

Development Initiatives. 2005d. Correspondence on official development assistance. May. London.

DFID (UK Department for International Development). 2003. "Standards as Barriers to Trade: Issues for Development." Background Briefing. London. [http://www.dfid.gov.uk/pubs/files/tradebrief-standards.pdf]. May 2005.

———. 2004a. "Nepal Country Assistance Plan 2004." London. [http://www.dfid.gov.uk/pubs/files/capnepal.pdf]. May 2005.

———. 2004b. "What Is Pro-poor Growth and Why Do We Need to Know?" Pro-Poor Growth Briefing Note 1. London.

———. 2005. "Why We Need to Work More Effectively in Fragile States." London. [http://www.dfid.gov.uk/pubs/files/fragilestates-paper.pdf].

DFID (UK Department for International Development), Foreign and Commonwealth Office, and UK (United Kingdom), HM Treasury. 2005. "Partnerships for Poverty Reduction: Rethinking Conditionality." London. [http://www.dfid.gov.uk/pubs/files/conditionality.pdf]. May 2005.

Diao, Xinshen, and Peter Hazell. 2003. "Africa: Exploring Market Opportunities for African Smallholders." 2020 Africa Conference Brief 6. International Food Policy Research Institute, Washington, DC. [http://www.ifpri.org/pubs/ib/ib22.pdf]. May 2005.

Diao, Xinshen, Eugenio Diaz-Bonilla, and Sherman Robinson. 2003. "How Much Does It Hurt: The Impact of Agricultural Trade Policies on Developing Countries." International Food Policy Research Institute, Washington, DC.

Diao, Xinshen, Eugenio Diaz-Bonilla, Sherman Robinson, and David Orden. 2005. "Tell Me Where It Hurts, an' I'll Tell You Who to Call: Industrialized Countries' Agricultural Policies and Developing Countries." MTID Discussion Paper 84. International Food Policy Research Institute, Markets, Trade, and Institutions Divisions, Washington, DC. [http://www.ifpri.org/divs/mtid/dp/papers/mtidp84.pdf]. May 2005.

Dodge, C. P. 1990. "Health Implications of War in Uganda and Sudan." Social Science & Medicine 31(6): 691–98.

Dollar, David. 2004. "Reform, Growth and Poverty." In Paul Glewwe, Nisha Agrawal, and David Dollar, eds., Economic Growth, Poverty and Household Welfare in Vietnam. Washington, DC: World Bank. [http://www-wds.worldbank.org/servlet/WDSContentServer/WDSP/IB/2004/06/09/000012009_20040609161332/Rendered/PDF/290860rev.pdf]. May 2005.

Dollar, David, and Craig Burnside. 2000. "Aid, Policies, and Growth." American Economic Review 90(4): 847–68.

Dollar, David, and Aart Kraay. 2001a. "Growth Is Good for the Poor." World Bank, Development Research Group, Washington, DC. [http://www.worldbank.org/research/growth/pdfiles/growthgoodforpoor.pdf]. May 2005.

———. 2001b. "Trade, Growth, and Poverty." World Bank, Development Research Group, Washington, DC. [http://www.worldbank.org/research/growth/pdfiles/Trade5.pdf]. May 2005.

Dollar, David, and Victoria Levin. 2004. "The Increasing Selectivity of Aid, 1984–2002." Policy Research Working Paper 3299. World Bank, Washington, DC.

Dorosh, Paul. 2002. "Trade Liberalization and Food Security in Bangladesh." ICRIER-ICAR-IFPRI Conference on Economic Reforms and Food Security: The Role of Trade and Technology, 24–25 April, New Delhi.

Doyle, Michael W. 2001. "War-Making and Peace-Making: The United Nations' Post-Cold War Record." In Chester A. Crocker, Fen Osler Hampson, and Pamela Aall, eds., Turbulent Peace: The Challenges of Managing International Conflict. Washington, DC: United States Institute of Peace Press.

Drahos, Peter. 2001. "BITs and BIPs: Bilateralism in Intellectual Property." Journal of World Intellectual Property 4(6): 791–808.

Drahos, Peter, and John Braithwaite. 2002. Information Feudalism: Who Owns the Knowledge Economy? London: Earthscan.

Drèze, Jean. 2004. "Bangladesh Shows the Way." The Hindu, 17 September.

Drèze, Jean, and Mamta Murthi. 2001. "Fertility, Education, and Development: Evidence from India." Population and Development Review 27(1): 33–63.

Duffield, Mark. 1994. "The Political Economy of Internal War: Asset Transfer, Complex Emergencies and International Aid." In Joanna Macrae and Anthony Zwi, eds., War and Hunger: Rethinking International Responses. London: Zed Press.

———. 1998. "Aid Policy and Post Modern Conflict: A Critical Review." Occasional Paper 19. University of Birmingham, School of Public Policy, Birmingham, United Kingdom.

Duncan, Brack. 2004. "Trade, Aid and Security: Introduction, Background and Conceptual Framework." Second draft. Winnipeg, Canada. [http://www.iisd.org/pdf/2005/security_trade_aid_sec.pdf]. May 2005.

Dunning, John. 2003. Making Globalization Good: The Moral Challenges of Global Capitalism. Oxford: Oxford University Press.

The Economist. 2004a. "The Best Use of Aid?" 26 April.

———. 2004b. "A Question of Justice." 11 March.

Edsforth, Ronald. 2000. The New Deal: America's Response to the Great Depression. Oxford: Blackwell.

Egerter, Susan, Kristen Marchi, Catherine Cubbin, Paula Braveman, Alina Salganicoff, and Usha R. Ranji. 2004. "Disparities in Maternal and Infant Health: Are We Making Progress? Lessons from California." The Henry J. Kaiser Family Foundation, Washington, DC. [http://www.kff.org/womenshealth/loader.cfm?url=/commonspot/security/getfile.cfm&PageID=47306]. May 2005.

Elbadawi, Ibrahim. 1999. "External Aid: Help or Hindrance to Export Orientation in Africa?" Journal of African Economies 8(4): 578–616.

Elliott, Kimberly Ann. 2000. "(Mis)Managing Diversity: Worker Rights and US Trade Policy." International Negotiation 5: 97–127. [http://www.iie.com/publications/papers/elliott0900.pdf]. May 2005.

Environmental Working Group. 2005. Farm Subsidy Database. Database. Washington, DC. [http://www.ewg.org/farm/progdetail.php?fips=00000&progcode=total&page=states]. May 2005.

EORG (The European Opinion Research Group). 2003. "L'aide aux pays en développement." Eurobarometer 58.2. Commission Européenne, Direction Générale Développement Brussels. [http://europa.eu.int/comm/development/body/tmp_docs/EB58.pdf]. March 2005.

Evans, P. 2005. "Transferable Lessons? Re-examining the Institutional Pre-requisites of East Asian Economic Policies." Journal of Development Studies 34(6): 66–86.

FAO (Food and Agricultural Organization). 2004a. "Cotton: Impact of Support Policies on Developing Countries—Why Do the Numbers Vary?" FAO Trade Policy Brief on Issues Related to the WTO Negotiations on Agriculture 1. Rome.

———. 2004b. The State of Food Insecurity in the World 2004. Rome. [http://www.fao.org/documents/show_cdr.asp?url_file=/docrep/007/y5650e/y5650e00.htm]. May 2005.

———. 2005. *FAO Statistical Databases.* Rome. [http://faostat.fao. org/]. June 2005.

Farmer, Paul. 2004. *Pathologies of Power: Health, Human Rights, and the New War on the Poor.* Berkeley: University of California Press.

FBI (Federal Bureau of Investigation). Various years. "Uniform Crime Reports." Washington, DC. [http://www.fbi.gov/ucr/ucr. htm]. May 2005.

Fearon, James, and David Laitin. 2003. "Ethnicity, Insurgency, and Civil War." *American Political Science Review* 97(1): 75–90.

Fedelino, Annalisa, and Alina Kudina. 2003. "Fiscal Sustainability in African HIPC Countries: A Policy Dilemma?" IMF Working Paper WP/03/187. International Monetary Fund, Washington, DC. [http://www.imf.org/external/pubs/ft/wp/2003/wp03187.pdf]. March 2005.

Feinstein, Lee, and Anne-Marie Slaughter. 2004. "A Duty to Prevent." *Foreign Affairs* 83(1): 136–50.

Firebaugh, Glenn. 2003. *The New Geography of Global Income Inequality.* Cambridge, Mass.: Harvard University Press.

Fiszbein, Ariel, Paula Inés Giovagnoli, and Isidro Adúriz. 2002. "Argentina's Crisis and Its Impact on Household Welfare." Working Paper 1/02. World Bank Office for Argentina, Chile, Paraguay and Uruguay, Washington, DC. [http://wbln0018.worldbank. org/lac/lacinfoclient.nsf/5996dfbf9847f67d85256736005dc67c/ 1c506119f270f43a85256d5d00531139/$FILE/ESW01-02_ bienestar_eng.pdf]. May 2005.

Foster, Mick, and Adrian Fozzard. 2000. "Aid and Public Expenditure: A Guide." Working Paper 141. Overseas Development Institute, Centre for Aid and Public Expenditure, London. [http://www.odi.org. uk/publications/wp141.pdf]. March 2005.

Foster, Mick, and Andrew Keith. 2003a. *The Case for Increased Aid: Final Report to the Department for International Development. Volume 1: Main Report.* Essex, United Kingdom: Mick Foster Economics Ltd. [http://www.dfid.gov.uk/pubs/files/caseforaid-vol1. pdf]. March 2005.

———. 2003b. *The Case for Increased Aid: Final Report to the Department for International Development. Volume 2: Country Case Studies.* Essex, United Kingdom: Mick Foster Economics Ltd. [http://www.dfid.gov.uk/pubs/files/caseforaid-vol2.pdf]. March 2005.

Freedman, Lawrence. 1993. "Weak States and the West: Warfare Has a Future." *The Economist*, 11 September.

Frum, David, and Richard Perle. 2003. *An End to Evil: How to Win the War on Terror.* New York: Random House.

Frye, Isobel. 2002. Statement made on behalf of the Black Sash at the Commission on Human Security public hearings on human security, Global Civil Society Forum of the World Summit on Sustainable Development, 27 August, Johannesburg.

Fuentes, Juan Alberto. 2005b. Personal communication: "Colombia Budget Analysis." April. Guatemala City.

G-8 (Group of Eight). 2005. "G-8 Gleneagle 2005." [http://www. g8.gov.uk]. July 2005.

Galeano, Eduardo. 1973. *Open Veins of Latin America: Five Centuries of the Pillage of a Continent.* New York: Monthly Review Press.

GAVI (Global Alliance for Vaccines and Immunization) and The Vaccine Fund. 2005a. "GAVI/The Vaccine Fund—Progress and Achievements." Geneva and Washington, DC. [http://gavi. elca-services.com/resources/FS_Progress___Achievements_en_ Jan05.pdf]. May 2005.

———. 2005b. "Progress and Challenges 2004." Geneva and Washington, DC. [http://www.vaccinealliance.org/resources/gavi_ pandc2004.pdf]. May 2005.

Gelb, Stephen. 2004. "Inequality in South Africa: Nature, Causes and Responses." African Development and Poverty Reduction: The Macro-Micro Linkage, 13–15 October, Somerset West, South Africa. [http://www.commerce.uct.ac.za/dpru/dpruconference2004/ Papers/Gelb_Inequality_in_SouthAfrica.pdf]. May 2005.

Gemmell, Norman, and Mark McGillivray. 1998. "Aid and Tax Instability and the Government Budget Constraints in Developing Countries." Research Paper 98/1. CREDIT (Centre for Research in Economic Development and International Trade). University of Nottingham, Nottingham, United Kingdom.

Ghobarah, Hazem Adam, Paul Huth, and Bruce Russett. 2004. "The Post-War Public Health Effects of Civil Conflict." *Social Science & Medicine* 59(4): 869–84.

Gibbon, Peter. 2003. "Value-chain Governance, Public Regulation and Entry Barriers in the Global Fresh Fruit and Vegetable Chain into the EU." *Development Policy Review* 21(5-6): 615–25.

Gilbert, Christopher L. 1996. "International Commodity Agreements: An Obituary." *World Development* 24(1): 1–19.

Gillespie, Stuart, and Suneetha Kadiyala. 2005. "HIV/AIDS and Food and Nutrition Security: From Evidence to Action." IFPRI Food Policy Review 7. International Food Policy Research Instutute, Washington, DC. [http://www.ifpri.org/pubs/fpreview/pv07/pv07.pdf]. May 2005.

Ginifer, Jeremy. 2005. "Armed Violence and Poverty in Sierra Leone." Case study for the Armed Violence and Poverty Initiative. University of Bradford, Center for International Cooperation and Security, Bradford, United Kingdom.

Global Campaign for Education. 2005. "Universal Primary Education by 2015." Brussels. [http://www.campaignforeducation.org/]. May 2005.

Global IDP Project. 2003. "Precarious Health Situation Prevailing in Chechnya." Geneva. [http://www.db.idpproject. org/Sites/IdpProjectDb/idpSurvey.nsf/wViewCountries/ 053B0FBFC11AA8D5C1256E01005A0ABF]. May 2005.

———. 2005a. *Internal Displacement: Global Overview of Trends and Developments in 2004.* Geneva. [http://www.idpproject. org/publications/2005/Global_overview_%202004_final.pdf]. May 2005

———. 2005b. "War in Darfur Has Displaced Close to Two Million People Since February 2003." Geneva. [http://www.db.idpproject. org/Sites/IdpProjectDb/idpSurvey.nsf/wViewCountries/ 8E0D7B571AC744F2C1256CDE0038F23A]. May 2005.

Global Witness. 2004. "Broken Vows: Exposing the 'Loupe' Holes in the Diamond Industry's Efforts to Prevent the Trade in Conflict Diamonds." London. [http://www.globalwitness.org/reports/ download.php/00126.pdf]. April 2005.

Goldberg, Jörg. 2005. "The Pilot Social Cash Transfer Scheme: Kalomo District—Zambia." Third Forum on Human Development, 17–19 January, Paris. [http://hdr.undp.org/docs/events/global_ forum/2005/papers/Jorg_Goldberg.pdf]. May 2005.

Goldstone, Jack. 2005. "Population and Security: How Demographic Change Can Lead to Violent Conflict." *Journal of International Affairs* 56(1): 283–302.

Goodhand, Jonathan, and Philippa Atkinson. 2001. "Conflict and Aid: Enhancing the Peacebuilding Impact of International Engagement: A Synthesis of Findings from Afghanistan, Liberia and Sri Lanka." International Alert, London. [http://www.international- alert.org/pdf/pubdev/Synthrep.pdf]. April 2005.

Gordillo, Gustavo, Alain de Janvry, Jean-Philippe Platteau, and Elisabeth Sadoulet, eds. 2001. *Access to Land, Rural Poverty and Public Action.* Oxford: Oxford University Press.

Graham, Wendy J. 2004. "Exploring the Links between Maternal Death and Poverty." *In Focus* (May) 6–8 [http://www.undp. org/povertycentre/newsletters/infocus3may04eng.pdf].

Gray, S. J. 2000. "A Memory of Loss: Ecological Politics, Local History, and the Evolution of Karimojong Violence." *Human Organization* 59(4): 401–18.

Gunter, Bernhard G. 2004. "The Social Dimension of Globalization: A Review of the Literature." *International Labour Review* 143(1–2): 7–43.

Gupta, Geeta Rao, Daniel Whelan, and Keera Allendorf. 2003. "Integrating Gender Into HIV/AIDS Programmes: A Review Paper."

World Health Organization, Geneva. [http://www.who.int/gender/hiv_aids/en/Integrating%5b258KB%5d.pdf]. May 2005.

Gupta, Sanjeev, Benedict Clements, Alexander Pivovarsky, and Erwin R. Tiongson. 2003. "Foreign Aid and Revenue Response: Does the Composition of Aid Matter?" IMF Working Paper WP/03/176. International Monetary Fund, Washington, DC. [http://www.imf.org/external/pubs/ft/wp/2003/wp03176.pdf]. March 2005.

Gwatkin, Davidson, Shea Rutstein, Kiersten Johnson, Eldaw Abdalla Suliman, Adam Wagstaff, and Agbessi Amouzou. Forthcoming. *Socioeconomic Differences in Health, Nutrition and Population*. Washington, DC: World Bank.

Hansen, Henrik, and Finn Tarp. 2000. "Aid Effectiveness Disputed." In F. Tarp and P. Hjertholm, eds., *Foreign Aid and Development: Lessons Learnt and Directions for the Future*. London: Routledge. [http://www.econ.ku.dk/derg/papers/Aid_Effectiveness_Disputed.pdf]. February 2005.

Hausmann, Ricardo, and Dani Rodrik. 2002. *Economic Development as Self-Discovery*. NBER Working Paper 8952. Cambridge, Mass.: National Bureau of Economic Research. [http://papers.nber.org/papers/w8952.pdf]. May 2005.

Hausmann, Ricardo, Lant Pritchett, and Dani Rodrik. 2004. "Growth Accelerations." NBER Working Paper 10566. Cambridge, Mass.: National Bureau of Economic Research.

Hegarty, David. 2003. "Peace Interventions in the South Pacific: Lessons from Bougainville and Solomon Islands." Asia-Pacific Center for Security Studies Conference—Island State Security: Oceania at the Crossroads, 15–17 July, Honolulu, Hawaii. [http://rspas.anu.edu.au/papers/conflict/hegarty_interventions.pdf]. April 2005.

Hegre, Håvard, Tanja Ellingsen, Scott Gates, and Nils Petter Gleditsch. 2001. "Toward a Democratic Civil Peace? Democracy, Political Change, and Civil War, 1816–1992." *American Political Science Review* 95(1): 33–48.

The Henry Kaiser Family Foundation. 2005. "Child Death Rate per 100,000 Population." [http://www.statehealthfacts.org]. May 2005.

High-Level Forum on the Health MDGs. 2004. "Achieving the Health Millennium Development Goals in Fragile States." Abuja.

Hills, John. 2004. *Inequality and the State*. Oxford: Oxford University Press.

Hocking, Brian, and Steven McGuire. 1999. *Trade Politics*. London: Routledge.

Hoekman, Bernard. 2002. "The WTO: Functions and Basic Principles." In Bernard Hoekman, Aaditya Mattoo, and Philip English, eds., *Development, Trade, and the WTO: A Handbook*. Washington, DC: World Bank.

———. 2005. "Operationalizing the Concept of Policy Space in the WTO: Beyond Special and Differential Treatment of Developing Countries." In Ernst-Ulrich Petersmann, ed., *Reforming the World Trading System Rule-making, Trade Negotiations, and Dispute Settlement*. Oxford: Oxford University Press.

Hoekman, Bernard, and Will Martin. 2001. *Developing Countries and the WTO: A Pro-active Agenda*. Oxford: Blackwell Publishers.

Hoekman, Bernard, Michael Kostecki, and M. M. Kostecki. 1995. *The Political Economy of the World Trading System: From GATT to WTO*. Oxford: Oxford University Press.

Hoekman, Bernard, Aaditya Mattoo, and Philip English, eds. 2002. *Development, Trade and the WTO: A Handbook*. Washington, DC: World Bank.

Holsti, Kalevi J. 2000. "Political Causes of Humanitarian Emergencies." In Wayne E. Nafziger, Frances Stewart, and Raimo Vayrynen, eds., *War, Hunger, and Displacement: The Origins of Humanitarian Emergencies. Volume 1: Analysis*. Oxford: Oxford University Press.

Horn, Karen, Dani Rodrik, and Margaret McMillan. 2003. *When Economic Reform Goes Wrong: Cashews in Mozambique*. NBER Working Paper 9117. Cambridge, Mass.: National Bureau of Economic Research. [http://www.nber.org/papers/W9117]. May 2005.

Horton, R. 1993. "On the Brink of Humanitarian Disaster." *The Lancet* 343(8905): 1053.

Human Rights Watch. 2004a. "D.R. Congo: Civilians at Risk During Disarmament Operations." Backgrounder. New York. [http://www.hrw.org/backgrounder/africa/drc1204/]. May 2005.

———. 2004b. "Human Rights Abuses of Civilians by Armed Groups in Walungu." Backgrounder. New York. [http://www.hrw.org/backgrounder/africa/drc1204/2.htm#_Toc92019547]. May 2005.

Humphreys, Macartan. 2003. "Economics and Violent Conflict." Cambridge, Mass. [http://www.preventconflict.org/portal/economics/Essay.pdf]. May 2005.

Humphreys, Macartan, and Ashutosh Varshney. 2004. "Violent Conflict and the Millennium Development Goals: Diagnosis and Recommendations." Paper prepared for the meeting of the Millennium Development Goals Poverty Task Force Workshop, June, Bangkok.

IADB (Inter-American Development Bank). 2004. *Good Jobs Wanted: Labor Markets in Latin America*. Washington, DC.

ICG (International Crisis Group). 2001a. "Bosnia's Precarious Economy: Still Not Open for Business." ICG Balkans Report 115. Sarajevo. [http://www.crisisgroup.org/library/documents/report_archive/A400375_07082001.pdf]. April 2005.

———. 2001b. "Bosnia: Reshaping the International Machinery." ICG Balkans Report 121. Sarajevo. [http://www.crisisgroup.org/library/documents/report_archive/A400499_29112001-1.pdf]. May 2005.

———. 2002. "Liberia: The Key to Ending Regional Instability." ICG Africa Report 43. Brussels. [http://www.crisisgroup.org/library/documents/report_archive/A400627_24042002.pdf]. May 2005.

———. 2003. "Sierra Leone: The State of Security and Governance." ICG Africa Report 67. Brussels. [http://www.crisisgroup.org/library/documents/report_archive/A401113_02092003.pdf]. May 2005.

———. 2004a. "Bolivia's Divisions: Too Deep to Heal?" ICG Latin America Report 7. Brussels. [http://www.crisisgroup.org/library/documents/latin_america/07___bolivias_divisions.pdf]. May 2005.

———. 2004b. "Liberia and Sierra Leone: Rebuilding Failed States." ICG Africa Report 87. Brussels. [http://www.crisisgroup.org/library/documents/africa/west_africa/087_liberia_and_sierra_leone_rebuilding_failed_states.pdf]. May 2005.

ICISS (International Commission on Intervention and State Sovereignty). 2001. "The Responsibility to Protect: Report of the International Commission on Intervention and State Sovereignty." Ottawa. [http://www.idrc.org.sg/en/ev-9436-201-1-DO_TOPIC.html]. April 2005.

IFPRI (International Food Policy Research Institute). 2005. "Women: Still the Key to Food and Nutrition Security." Washington, DC. [http://www.ifpri.org/pubs/ib/ib33.pdf]. May 2005.

IIPS (International Institute for Population Studies) and ORC Macro. 2000. "National Family Health Survey (NFHS-2)." Mumbai, India and Calverton, Md. [http://www.nfhsindia.org/india2.html]. June 2005.

IMF (International Monetary Fund). 2001. "Conditionality in Fund-Supported Programs—Policy Issues." Policy Development and review Department, Washington, DC. [http://www.imf.org/external/np/pdr/cond/2001/eng/policy/021601.pdf]. May 2005.

———. 2002. "Aid and Fiscal Management." IMF Conference on Macroeconomics and Poverty, 14–15 March, Washington, DC.

———. 2003a. "Financing of Losses from Preference Erosion, Note on Issues Raised by Developing Countries in the Doha Round." Communication to the WTO WT/TF/COH/14. Washington, DC.

———. 2003b. "Vietnam, Selected Issues." IMF Country Report 03/381. Washington, DC. [http://www.imf.org/external/pubs/ft/scr/2003/cr03381.pdf]. May 2005.

———. 2004a. "Argentina: First Review under the Stand-By Arrangement and Request for Waiver of Nonobservance and

Applicability of Performance Criteria." IMF Country Report 04/194. Washington, DC. [http://www.imf.org/external/pubs/ft/scr/2004/cr04194.pdf]. May 2005.

————. 2004b. "Fund Support for Trade-Related Balance of Payments Adjustments." Policy Development and Review Department, Washington, DC. [http://www.imf.org/external/np/pdr/tim/2004/eng/022704.pdf]. May 2005.

————. 2005a. "Burkina Faso: Second and Third Reviews under the Three-Year Arrangement Under the Poverty Reduction and Growth Facility and Requests for Waiver of Nonobservance of Performance Criteria and Extension of Commitment Period." IMF Country Report 05/95. Washington, DC. [http://www.imf.org/external/pubs/ft/scr/2005/cr0595.pdf]. May 2005.

————. 2005b. World Economic Outlook. Washington, DC.

IMF (International Monetary Fund) and World Bank. 2001. "Market Access for Developing Country Exports: Selected Issues." Washington, DC. [http://www.worldbank.org/economics/marketaccess.pdf]. May 2005.

India, Ministry of Statistics and Programme Implementation. 2002a. "Selected Socio-Economic Statistics India." New Delhi. [http://mospi.nic.in/cso_rept_pubn.htm]. May 2005.

————. 2002b. "Women and Men in India." New Delhi. [http://mospi.nic.in/cso_rept_pubn.htm]. May 2005.

Indiatogether.org. 2004. "Interview with Jean Drèze, National Advisory Council Member." [http://www.indiatogether.org/2004/sep/pov-nrega.htm]. May 2005.

Integrated Framework for Trade-Related Technical Assistance to Least Developed Countries. 2003. "Senegal: Diagnostic Trade Integration Study." Vol 1. Washington, DC. [http://www.integratedframework.org/files/Senegal_dtis_en.pdf]. May 2005.

Intel. 2005. "Intel's Worldwide Manufacturing Operations." [http://www.intel.com/pressroom/kits/manufacturing/manufacturing_qa.htm#1]. May 2005.

International Cotton Advisory Committee. 2005. Correspondence on cotton prices and production. April. Washington, DC.

Inyega, Hellen Nasimiuyh, and Patricia Nyawira Mbugua. 2005. "Education Technology in Kenya Today and Tomorrow." In M. Orey, T. Amiel, and J. McClendon, eds., The World Almanac of Education Technologies. [http://www.waet.uga.edu/kenya/kenya.htm]. May 2005.

IRC (International Rescue Committee). 2004. "Mortality in the Democratic Republic of Congo: Results from a Nationwide Survey." New York. [http://www.theirc.org/pdf/DRC_MortalitySurvey2004_RB_8Dec04.pdf]. May 2005.

ISMEA (Istituto di Servizi per il Mercato Agricolo Alimentare). 2003. "Bandi gara Agea: Forniture alimentari ai paesi in via di sviluppo." Fornitura di riso a grana lunga all'Afghanistan: Bando di gara prot. N. 37/DIR del 17/01/2003. [http://www.ismea.it/RPrincipale_n.asp?FT=TRUE&area=4&sottoarea=3&sottoarea2=2]. May 2005.

Jaffee, Steven. 2003. "From Challenge to Opportunity: Transforming Kenya's Fresh Vegetable Trade in the Context of Emerging Food Safety and other Standards in Europe." Agriculture and Rural Development Discussion Paper 2. World Bank, Washington, DC. [http://www-wds.worldbank.org/servlet/WDSContentServer/WDSP/IB/2005/01/24/000112742_20050124135734/Rendered/PDF/310100revised0ARD1DP11KE.pdf]. May 2005.

————. 2005. "Delivering and Taking the Heat: Indian Spices and Evolving Product and Process Standards." World Bank, Washington, DC. [http://siteresources.worldbank.org/INTRANETTRADE/Resources/Topics/Standards/IndiaSpicesF.pdf]. May 2005.

James, E. 2001. The End of Globalisation: Lessons from the Great Depression. Cambridge, Mass.: Harvard University Press.

Jank, Marcos Sawaya, Maristela Franco Paes Leme, André Meloni Nassar, and Paulo Faveret Filho. 2001. "Concentration and Internationalization of Brazilian Agribusiness Exporters."

International Food and Agribusiness Management Review 2(3/4): 359–74.

Jepma, Catrinus J. 1991. "The Tying of Aid." Organisation for Economic Co-operation and Development, Paris.

Jha, P., and A. Mills. 2002. "Improving Health Outcomes of the Poor." Report of Working Group 5 of the Commission on Macroeconomics and Health. World Health Organization, Geneva.

Jha, Veena. 2005. "Trade Adjustment Study: India." United Nations Conference on Trade and Development, Geneva. [http://192.91.247.38/tab/namameeting/Draft%20with%20Tables-after%20final4.pdf]. June 2005.

Johnson, Lyndon B. 1964. "Great Society." University of Michigan commencement speech, 22 May, Ann Arbor. [http://www.cnn.com/SPECIALS/cold.war/episodes/13/documents/lbj/]. May 2005.

Johnson, Alison, Matthew Martin, and Hannah Bargawi. 2004. "The Effectiveness of Aid to Africa Since the HIPC Initiative: Issues, Evidence and Possible Areas for Action." Development Finance International, London. [http://www.dri.org.uk/pdfs/DFI_Aid_Effectiveness.pdf]. March 2005.

Johnson, Robert, Steven Woolf, George Fryer, George Rust, and David Satcher. 2004. "The Health Impact of Resolving Racial Disparities: An Analysis of US Mortality Data." American Journal of Public Health 94(12): 2078–81.

Joint Learning Initiative. 2004. Human Resources for Health: Overcoming the Crisis. Cambridge, Mass.: Harvard University Press. [http://www.globalhealthtrust.org/report/Human_Resources_for_Health.pdf].

Jones, Gareth Stedman. 2004. An End to Poverty? A Historical Debate. London: Profile Books Ltd.

Joshi, Vijay. 2004. "Myth of India's Outsourcing Boom." Financial Times, 16 November.

Juma, Monica, and Aida Mengistu. 2002. "The Infrastructure of Peace in Africa: Assessing the Peacebuilding Capacity of African Institutions." International Peace Academy, New York. [http://www.ipacademy.org/Publications/Publications.htm]. May 2005.

Justino, Patricia, Julie Litchfield, and Joko Niimi. 2004. "Multidimensional Inequality: An Empirical Application to Brazil." PRUS Working Paper 24. Poverty Research Unit at Sussex, Brighton, United Kingdom. [http://www.sussex.ac.uk/Units/PRU/wps/wp24.pdf]. May 2005.

Justino, Patricia, Julie Litchfield, and Laurence Whitehead. 2003. "The Impact of Inequality in Latin America." PRUS Working Paper 21. Poverty Research Unit at Sussex, Brighton, United Kingdom.

Kaczynski, V. M. and D. L. Fluharty. 2002. "European Policies in West Africa: Who Benefits from Fisheries Agreements?" Marine Policy 26(2): 75–93.

Kagan, Robert. 2002. "Power and Weakness." World Policy Review 113. [http://www.policyreview.org/JUN02/kagan.html]. May 2005.

Kagwanja, Peter. 2004. "Darfur: An African Union Peace-Keeping Crucible?" Center for International Political Studies. Paper presented at "Keeping Peace in Tough Neighborhoods: The Challenges Confronting Peacekeepers in Africa," 14 September, Pretoria. [http://www.up.ac.za/academic/cips/Publications/KTP_Dr_Peter_Kagwanja_ICG.pdf]. April 2005.

Kakwani, Nanak. 2004. "Poverty Measurement Matters: An Indian Story." United Nations Development Programme, International Poverty Centre, Brasília.

Kakwani, Nanak, Shahid Khandker, and Hyun H. Son. 2004. "Pro-Poor Growth: Concepts and Measurements with Country Case Studies." Working Paper 1. United Nations Development Programme, International Poverty Centre, Brasília.

Kaldor, Mary. 2001. New and Old Wars: Organized Violence in a Global Era. Stanford, Calif.: Stanford University Press.

Kalipeni, E., and J. Oppong. 1998. "The Refugee Crisis in Africa and Implications for Health and Disease: A Political Ecology Approach." Social Science & Medicine 46(12): 1637–53.

Kanbur, Ravi. 2005. "Pareto's Revenge." Paper prepared for the Workshop on Ethics, Globalization, and Hunger, Cornell University, Ithaca, NY. [http://www.he.cornell.edu/cfnpp/images/wp182.pdf]. May 2005.

Kasterine, Alexander. 2004. "Agriculture, Rural Development and Pro-Poor Growth." UK Department for International Development, London.

Kattan, Raja Bentaouet, and Nicholas Burnett. 2004. "User Fees in Primary Education." World Bank, Human Development Network, Education Sector, Washington, DC. [http://www1.worldbank.org/education/pdf/EFAcase_userfees.pdf]. March 2005.

Keen, David. 1998. *The Economic Functions of Violence in Civil Wars*. Adelphi Paper 320. Oxford: Oxford University Press.

Kelch, David, and Mary Anne Normile. 2004. "CAP Reform of 2003–2004." Report WRS-04-07. US Department of Agriculture, Washington, DC. [http://www.ers.usda.gov/publications/WRS0407/wrs0407.pdf]. May 2005.

Kenya, Ministry of Planning and National Development. 2003. *Millennium Development Goals: Progress Report for Kenya 2003*. Nairobi. [http://www.undp.org/mdg/kenya.pdf]. March 2005.

———. 2004. "Investment Programme for the Economic Recovery Strategy for Wealth and Employment Creation: 2003–2007." Poverty Reduction Strategy Paper. World Bank, Washington, DC. [http://povlibrary.worldbank.org/files/cr0511.pdf]. March 2005.

Keynes, John Maynard. 1980. "The International Control of Raw Material Prices [1946]." In John Maynard Keynes, ed., *The Collected Writings of John Maynard Keynes*. Vol. 27. London: Macmillan.

Khor, M. 2001. *Rethinking Globalisation: Critical Issues and Policy Choices*. London and New York: Zed Press.

Kibria, N. 2001. "Becoming the Garment Worker: The Mobilisation of Women into the Garment Factories of Bangladesh." In N. S. Khundker, ed., *Globalisation and Gender: Changing Patterns of Women's Employment in Bangladesh*. Dhaka: University Press.

Kijima, Yoko, and Peter Lanjouw. 2003. "Poverty in India During the 1990s: A Regional Perspective." Policy Research Working Paper 3141. World Bank, Washington, DC.

Killick, Tony. 2001. "Globalisation and the Rural Poor." *Development Policy Review* 19(2): 155–80.

———. 2002a. "Responding to Inequality." Inequality Briefing Paper 3. Overseas development Institute, London. [http://www.odi.org.uk/pppg/publications/briefings/inequality_briefings/03.pdf]. May 2005.

———. 2002b. "The 'Streamlining' of IMF Conditionality: Aspirations, Reality and Repercussions." Overseas Development Institute, London. [http://www.odi.org.uk/iedg/Projects/imf_conditionality.pdf]. May 2005.

———. 2004. "Politics, Evidence and the New Aid Agenda." *Development Policy Review* 22(1): 5–29.

The Kimberley Process. 2004. "Chair's Report to Plenary." Kimberley Process Plenary Meeting, 27–29 October, Gatineau, Canada. [http://www.kimberleyprocess.com:8080/site/www_docs/plenary_meetings20/chair_report_to_plenary.pdf]. April 2005.

King, Betty. 1998. "U.S. Representative to the United Nations Economic and Social Council Statement in the Economic and Social Council on Coordinated Follow-Up to and the Implementation of the Vienna Declaration and Program of Action." USUN Press Release 129(98). 17 July. [http://www.un.int/usa/98_129.htm]. June 2005.

King, Gary, and Lisa L. Martin. 2001. "The Human Costs of Military Conflict." Conference on Military Conflict as a Public Health Problem, 29 June, Cambridge, Mass. [http://www.iq.harvard.edu/NewsEvents/Past/PHS/papers/humancosts.pdf]. April 2005.

King, Martin Luther, Jr. 1963. "I Have a Dream." Speech, 28 August, Washington, DC. [http://www.usconstitution.net/dream.html]. May 2005.

Kingdon, Geeta Gandhi, Robert Cassen, Kirsty McNay, and Leela Visaria. 2004. "Education and Literacy." In Robert Cassen, Tim Dyson, and Leela Visaria, eds., *Twenty-First Century India: Population, Economy, Human Development, and the Environment*. Oxford: Oxford University Press.

Klare, Michael T. 2001. *Resource Wars: The New Landscape of Global Conflict*. New York: Metropolitan Books.

———. 2005. "Oil Curse Stalks Africa's New Petro-State." *Financial Times*, 27 January.

Klump, Rainer, and Thomas Bonschab. 2004. "'Operationalising Pro-poor Growth': A Country Case Study on Vietnam." Agence Française de Développement, Bundesministerium für Wirtschaftliche Zusammenarbeit, Deutsche Gesellschaft für Technische Zusammenarbeit GmbH, KfW Entwicklungsbank, UK Department for International Development London, and World Bank. [http://www.dfid.gov.uk/pubs/files/oppgvietnam]. May 2005.

Knack, Stephen, and Aminur Rahman. 2004. "Donor Fragmentation and Bureaucratic Quality in Aid Recipients." Policy Research Working Paper 3186. World Bank, Washington, DC.

Kroll, Luisa, and Lea Goldman, eds. 2005. "Special Report: The World's Billionaires." Forbes.com. [http://www.forbes.com/worldsrichest].

Krug, Etienne G., Linda L. Dahlberg, James A. Mercy, Anthony B. Zwi, and Rafael Lozano. 2002. "World Report on Violence and Health." World Health Organization, Geneva. [http://www.who.int/violence_injury_prevention/violence/world_report/en/full_en.pdf]. May 2005.

Laird, Sam. 2002. "Market Access Issues and the WTO: An Overview." In Bernard Hoekman, Aaditya Mattoo, and Philip English, eds., *Development, Trade and the WTO*. Washington, DC: World Bank.

Laird, Sam, Santiago Fernandez de Córdoba, and David Vanzetti. 2004. "Trick or Treat? Development Opportunities and Challenges in the WTO Negotiations on Industrial Tariffs." University of Nottingham, Centre for Research in Economic Development and International Trade, United Kingdom. [http://www.nottingham.ac.uk/economics/credit/research/papers/cp.04.03.pdf]. May 2005.

Laird, Sam, Ralf Peters, and David Vanzetti. 2004. "Southern Discomfort: Agricultural Policies, Trade and Poverty." CREDIT Research Paper 04/02. University of Nottingham, Centre for Research in Economic Development and International Trade, United Kingdom.

Lall, Sanjaya. 2000. "The Technological Structure and Performance of Developing Country Manufactured Exports: 1985–1998." QEH Working Paper 44. University of Oxford, Queen Elizabeth House, Oxford. [http://www2.qeh.ox.ac.uk/RePEc/qeh/qehwps/qehwps44.pdf]. May 2005.

———. 2001. *Competitiveness, Technology and Skills*. Cheltenham, United Kingdom: Edward Elgar.

———. 2004. "Reinventing Industrial Strategy: The Role of Government Policy in Building Competitiveness." G-24 Discussion Paper Series 28. United Nations Conference on Trade and Development, Geneva. [http://www.unctad.org/en/docs/gdsmdpbg2420044_en.pdf]. May 2005.

Lall, Sanjaya, and Carlo Pietrobelli. 2002. *Failing to Compete: Technology Development and Technology Systems in Africa*. Cheltenham, United Kingdom: Edward Elgar.

Landes, David S. 1998. *The Wealth and Poverty of Nations: Why Some Are So Rich and Some So Poor*. London: Abacus.

Lang, Tim. 2003. "Food Industralization and Food Power: Implications for Food Governance." *Development Policy Review* 21(5-6): 555–568.

Lanjouw, J. 2001. "New Pills For Poor People? Empirical Evidence after GATT." *World Development* 29(2): 265–89.

Larsen, Marianne Nylandsted. 2003. "Quality Standard-Setting in the Global Cotton Chain and Cotton Sector Reforms in Sub-Saharan Africa." DIIS/GI Kongevej Working Paper 03.7. Institute for International Studies, Copenhagen. [http://www.cdr.dk/working_papers/wp-03-7.pdf]. May 2005.

Le Billon, Philippe. 2001. "The Political Ecology of War: Natural Resources and Armed Conflicts." *Political Geography* 20(5): 561–84.

Lensink, Robert, and Oliver Morrisey. 2000. "Aid Instability as a Measure of Uncertainty and the Positive Impact of Aid on Growth." *Journal of Development Studies* 36(3): 31–49.

Levin, Victoria, and David Dollar. 2005. "The Forgotten States: Aid Volumes and Volatility in Difficult Partnership Countries (1992–2002)." Summary paper for Development Assistance Committee Learning and Advisory Process on Difficult Partnerships. Paris. [http://www.oecd.org/dataoecd/32/44/34687926.pdf]. May 2005.

Levine, Ruth, and the What Works Working Group. 2004. *Millions Saved: Proven Successes in Global Health*. Washington, DC: Center for Global Development.

Lim, Meng-Kin, Hui Yang, Tuohong Zhang, Wen Feng, and Zijun Zhou. 2004. "Public Perceptions of Private Health Care In Socialist China." *Health Affairs* 23(6): 222–34.

Lindert, Peter H. 2005. *Growing Public: Social Spending and Economic Growth since the Eighteenth Century*. Cambridge: Cambridge University Press.

Lindert, Peter H., and Jeffrey G. Williamson. 2001a. "Does Globalization Make the World More Unequal." Harvard University, Cambridge, Mass. [http://post.economics.harvard.edu/faculty/jwilliam/papers/GlobalUnequal_10_25.pdf]. May 2005.

———. 2001b. "Globalisation and Inequality: A Long History." Annual World Bank Conference of Development Economics, 25–27 June, Barcelona, Spain. [http://wbln0018.worldbank.org/eurvp/web.nsf/Pages/Williamson/$File/WILLIAMSON-FINAL.PDF]. May 2005.

Liu, A. 1996. "Welfare Changes in China During the Economic Reforms." Research Paper 26. World Institute for Development Economics Research, Helsinki.

Liu, G., X. Liu, and Q. Meng. 1994. "Privatization of the Medical Market in Socialist China: A Historical Approach." *Health Policy* 27(2): 157–74.

Lockhart, Clare. 2004. "Case Study on Afghanistan: Five Mental Models of Reconstruction and State-Building." UNDP Draft Paper. United Nations Development Programme, Kabul.

Lomborg, Bjørn. 2004. *Global Crises, Global Solutions*. Cambridge: Cambridge University Press.

Lopez, Humberto. 2003. "The Economic and Social Costs of Armed Conflict in El Salvador." Dissemination Notes 8. World Bank, Conflict Prevention and Reconstruction Unit, Washington, DC.

Lula da Silva, Luiz Inácio. 2004. "Address by His Excellency Luiz Inácio Lula da Silva." Shanghai Conference on Scaling Up Poverty, 25–27 May, Shanghai. [http://www.worldbank.org/wbi/reducingpoverty/docs/confDocs/Lula%20Speech.pdf]. May 2005.

Lund, Frances. 2002. "Crowding in Care, Security and Micro-enterprise Formation: Revisiting the Role of the State in Poverty Reduction and in Development." *Journal of International Development* 14(6): 681–94.

———. 2004. "Informal Workers' Access to Social Security Protection." Background paper prepared for UNRISD, *Gender Equality: Striving for Justice in an Unequal World*. United Nations Research Institute for Social Development, Geneva.

Lustig, Nora Claudia, and Miguel Szekely. 1998. "Economic Trends, Poverty and Inequality in Mexico." POV-103. Inter-American Development Bank, Washington, DC.

Luther, N. Y. 1998. "Mother's Tetanus Immunisation Is Associated Not Only with Lower Neonatal Mortality but Also with Lower Early-Childhood Mortality." *National Family Health Survey Bulletin* 10:1–4.

Mackenzie, Regina Burns, and Margie Buchanan-Smith. 2005. "Armed Violence and Poverty in Southern Sudan: A Case Study for the Armed Violence and Poverty Initiative." Pact Sudan and University of Bradford, Centre for International Cooperation and Security, Bradford, United Kingdom.

Macrae, Joanna, Andrew Shepherd, Oliver Morrissey, Adele Harmer, Ed Anderson, Laure-Hélène Piron, Andy McKay, Diana Cammack, and Nambusi Kyegombe. 2004. "Aid to 'Poorly Performing' Countries: A Critical Review of Debates and Issues." Overseas Development Institute, London. [http://www.odi.org.uk/publications/poorly_performing_countries/Aid_to_PPCs.pdf]. March 2005.

Maddison, Angus. 2001. *Monitoring the World Economy 1820–1922*. Paris: Organisation for Economic Co-operation and Development.

Mainuddin, K. 2000. "Case of the Garment Industry in Dhaka, Bangladesh." Urban Development Papers Background Series 6. World Bank, Washington, DC.

Maison, J. B., A. T. Bailes, and K. E. Mason. 2003. "Drought, AIDS and Child Malnutrition in Southern Africa: Preliminar Analysis of Nutritional Data on the Humanitarian Crisis." Tulane University, New Orleans, La.

Maizels, A. 2000. "The Manufacturers' Terms of Trade of Developing Countries with the United States, 1981-97." QEH Working Paper 36. Oxford University, Queen Elizabeth House, Oxford.

Malan, Mark, Sarah Meek, Thusi Thokozani, Jeremy Ginifer, and Patrick Coker. 2003. *Sierra Leone: Building a Road to Recovery*. Capetown: Institute for Security Studies. [http://www.iss.co.za/Pubs/Monographs/No80/Content.html]. May 2005.

Malyutina, Sofia, Martin Bobak, Svetlana Kurilovitch, Valery Gafarov, Galina Simonova, Yuri Nikitin, and Michael Marmot. 2002. "Relation between Heavy Binge Drinking and All-Cause and Cardiovascular Mortality in Novosibirsk, Russia: A Prospective Cohort Study." *The Lancet* 360(9344): 1448–54.

Mann, Jonathan, Ernest Drucker, Daniel Tarantola, and Mary Pat McCabe. 1994. "Bosnia: The War Against Public Health." *Medicine and Global Survival* 1(3): 130–46.

Marshall, Monty G. 2005. "Major Episodes of Political Violence 1946–2004." Center for Systemic Peace, Severn, Md. [http://members.aol.com/cspmgm/warlist.htm]. May 2005.

Martin, Matthew, and Hannah Bargawi. 2004. "The Role of the IMF in Low-Income Countries." Study for Swedish Ministries of Finance and Foreign Affairs, Stockholm. [http://www.dri.org.uk/pdfs/DRI_Sweden_IMF_LICs.pdf]. May 2005.

Martin, Matthew, Alison Johnson, Hannah Bargawi, and Rose-Innes Cleo. 2004. "Long-Term Debt Sustainability for Africa." Background paper prepared for Commission for Africa (Secretariat), London. [http://www.commissionforafrica.org/english/report/background/martin_et_al_background.pdf]. May 2005.

Martin, Will. 2004. "Market Access in Agriculture: Beyond the Blender." Trade Note 17. World Bank, Washington, DC.

Maskus, Keith. 2000. *Intellectual Property Rights in the Global Economy*. Washington, DC: Institute for International Economics.

———. 2004. "Encouraging International Technology Transfer." Issue Paper 7. International Centre for Trade and sustainable Development and United Nations Conference on Trade and Development, Geneva.

McCulloch, Neil, Alan Winters, and Xavier Cirera. 2002. *Trade Liberalization and Poverty: A Handbook*. London: Centre for Economic Policy Research. [http://www.ids.ac.uk/ids/global/pdfs/tlpov.pdf]. May 2005.

McKay, Andrew. 2002. "Defining and Measuring Inequality." ODI Briefing Paper 1. Overseas Development Institute, London. [http://www.odi.org.uk/PPPG/publications/briefings/inequality_briefings/01.pdf]. May 2005.

McKay, Andrew, and Ernest Aryeetey. 2004. "Operationalising Pro-Poor Growth: A Country Case Study on Ghana." Agence Française de Développement, Bundesministerium für Wirtschaftliche Zusammenarbeit, Deutsche Gesellschaft für Technische Zusammenarbeit GmbH, KfW Entwicklungsbank, UK Department for International Development London, and World Bank. [http://www.dfid.gov.uk/pubs/files/oppgghana.pdf]. May 2005.

Measure DHS. 2005. "Demographic and Health Surveys." [http://www.measuredhs.com/]. May 2005.

Men, Tamara, Paul Brennan, Paolo Boffetta, and David Zaridze. 2003. "Russian Mortality Trends for 1991–2001: Analysis by Cause and Region." *British Medical Journal* 327(7421): 964.

Mexico, INEGI (Instituto Nacional de Estadístic Geografía e Informática). 2005. *Informació estadística*. Database. Mexico City [http://www.inegi.gob.mx/est/default.asp?c=715]. June 2005.

Mexico, Secretaría de Desarrollo Social. 2005. "Oportunidades: Información general: Histórico de la cobertura de municipios, localidades y familias beneficiarias." Colonia Juárez, Mexico. [http://www.progresa.gob.mx/informacion_general/mpios_locs_historico.pdf]. May 2005.

Milanovic, Branko. 2001. "World Income Inequality in the Second Half of the 20th Century." Paper presented at the Annual World Bank Conference on Development Economics, 10–11 May, Washington, DC.

———. 2003. "The Two Faces of Globalization: Against Globalization As We Know It." *World Development* 31(4): 667–83.

Millennium Challenge Corporation. 2005a. "The Millennium Challenge Account." Washington, DC. [http://www.mca.gov/about_us/overview/index.shtml]. April 2005.

———. 2005b. "Millennium Challenge Corporation Board Approves First Compact with Madagascar." Press release, 14 March, Washington, DC. [http://www.mca.gov/public_affairs/press_releases/pr_031405.shtml]. May 2005.

Mills, Anne, and Sam Shilcutt. 2004. "Communicable Diseases." In Bjørn Lomborg, ed., *Global Crises, Global Solutions*. Cambridge: Cambridge University Press.

Minot, N., and L. Daniels. 2002. "Impact of Global Cotton Markets on Rural Poverty in Benin." MSSD Discussion Paper 48. International Food Policy Research Institute, Markets and Structural Studies Division, Washington, DC. [http://www.ifpri.org/divs/mtid/dp/papers/mssdp48.pdf].

Miovic, Peter. 2004. "Poverty Reduction Support Credits in Uganda: Results of a Stocktaking Study." World Bank, Washington, DC.

MIPT (National Memorial Institute for the Prevention of Terrorism). 2005. "Terrorism Knowledge Base." Washington, DC. [http://www.tkb.org/IncidentRegionModule.jsp]. May 2005.

Mlachila, Montfort, and Yongzheng Yang. 2004. "The End of Textile Quotas: A Case Study of the Impact on Bangladesh." IMF Working Paper WP/04/108. International Monetary Fund, Washington, DC.

Morley, Samuel. 2001. *The Income Distribution Problem in Latin America and the Caribbean*. Santiago, Chile: United Nations. [http://www.eclac.cl/publicaciones/DesarrolloEconomico/7/LCG2127P/lcg2127i.pdf]. May 2005.

———. 2002. "Slower Growth and Rising Poverty: Latin America in the New Millennium." International Food Policy Research Institute, Policy Seminar, 24 October, Washington, DC.

Mosley, Paul, John Hudson, and Arjan Verschoor. 2004. "Aid, Poverty Reduction and the 'New Conditionality.'" *The Economic Journal* 114(496): F217–F243.

Muggah, Robert. 2001. "Globalization and Insecurity: The Direct and Indirect Effects of Small Arms Availability." *IDS Bulletin* 32(2): 70–78. [http://www.ids.ac.uk/ids/news/Archive2001/muggah.pdf]. April 2005.

Muggah, Robert, and Peter Batchelor. 2002. "Development Held Hostage: Assessing the Effects of Small Arms Availability." United Nations Development Programme, Bureau of Crisis Prevention and Recovery, New York. [http://www.undp.org/bcpr/smallarms/docs/development_held_hostage.pdf]. April 2005.

Munnell, Alicia H., Robert E. Hatch, and James G. Lee. 2004. "Why is Life Expectancy So Low in the United States?" Issues in Brief 21. Centre for Retirement Research at Boston College, Chestnut Hill, Mass. [http://www.bc.edu/centers/crr/issues/ib_21.pdf]. May 2005.

Mwaura, Ciru, and Susanne Schmeidl, eds. 2001. *Early Warning and Conflict Management in the Horn of Africa*. Asmara: Red Sea Press.

Naschold, Felix. 2002. "Why Inequality Matters for Poverty." ODI Inequality Briefing Paper 2. Overseas Development Institute, London.

Ng, Francis. 2001. "Eliminating Excessive Tariffs on Exports of Least Developed Countries." Policy Research Working Paper 2604. World Bank, Washington, DC.

Ng, Francis, Bernard Hoekman, and Marcelo Olarreaga. 2001. "Tariff Peaks in the Quad and Least Developed Country Exports." Discussion Paper DP2747. Centre for Economic Policy Research, London. [www.cepr.org/pubs/dps/DP2747.asp]. May 2005.

Nguyen, Kim Phuong, and Afsaar Akal. 2003. "Recent Advances in Social Health Insurance in Vietnam: A comprehensive Review of Recent Health Insurance Regulations." WHO Health Financing Mast Plan Technical Paper Series 1. World Health Organization, Ha Noi.

Nicaragua, Government of. 2001. "Strengthened Growth and Poverty Reduction Strategy." Managua, Nicaragua.

Nkusu, Mwanza. 2004. "Aid and the Dutch Disease in Low-Income Countries: Informed Diagnoses for Prudent Prognoses." IMF Working Paper WP/04/49. International Monetary Fund, Washington, DC. [http://www.imf.org/external/pubs/ft/wp/2004/wp0449.pdf]. March 2005.

Nogues, Julio. 2003. "Agricultural Protectionism: Debt Problems and the Doha Round." *Development Outreach* 5(2): 13–15.

Nyoni, T. S. 1998. "Foreign Aid and Economic Performance in Tanzania." *World Development* 26(7): 1235–40.

O'Brien, Maureen. 2004. "Public Attitudes Towards Development: Knowledge and Attitudes Concerning Poverty in Developing Countries." UK Department for International Development, London. [http://www.dfid.gov.uk/pubs/files/omnibus2004.pdf]. May 2005.

Odhiambo, Michael. 2004. "Oxfam Karamoja Conflict Study: A Report." Oxfam International, Oxford.

ODI (Overseas Development Institute). 2004. "Inequality in Middle Income Countries: Synthesis Paper." Poverty and Public Policy Group, London. [http://www.odi.org.uk/PPPG/activities/country_level/mic/workshop/MIC-Ineq-SynthesisPaper.pdf]. May 2005.

OECD (Organisation for Economic Co-Operation and Development). 2000. *Agricultural Trade Liberalisation: The Perspective of Emerging and Transition Economies*. Paris. [http://www.oecd.org/dataoecd/49/23/1911073.pdf]. May 2005.

———. 2001a. *The DAC Guidelines: Helping Prevent Violent Conflict*. Paris. [http://www.oecd.org/dataoecd/15/54/1886146.pdf]. May 2005.

———. 2001b. "The Development Dimensions of Trade." OECD Policy Brief. Paris.

———. 2001c. "Untying Aid to the Least Developed Countries." OECD Policy Brief. Paris. [http://www.oecd.org/dataoecd/16/24/2002959.pdf]. March 2005.

———. 2003a. *Agricultural Trade and Poverty: Making Policy Analysis Count*. Paris.

———. 2003b. "Trade Capacity Building: Critical for Development." OECD Policy Brief. Paris.

———. 2004a. *Agricultural Policies in OECD Countries: At a Glance—2004 Edition*. Paris.

———. 2004b. "Agricultural Support: How Is It Measured and What does It Mean?" OECD Policy Brief. Paris.

———. 2004c. "Analysis of the 2003 CAP Reform." Working Party on Agricultural Policies and Markets, Directorate for Food, Agriculture, and Fisheries, Paris

———. 2004d. "Impact of Changes in Tariffs on Developing Countries' Government Revenue." OECD Trade Policy Working Paper 18. Paris.

———. 2005. "Agricultural Policies in OECD Countries: Monitoring and Evaluation 2005. Highlights." Paris. [http://www.oecd.org/dataoecd/33/27/35016763.pdf]. June 2005.

OECD/DAC (Organisation for Economic Co-Operation and Development/Development Assistance Committee). 1997a. "Conflict, Peace and Development Co-operation on the Threshold

of the 21st Century." Policy Statement. Paris. [http://www.oecd.
org/dataoecd/31/41/2755386.pdf]. May 2005.

———. 1997b. "OECD Development Assistance Committee Guidelines
on Conflict, Peace and Development Cooperation." Paris.

———. 2002. "Canada, DAC Peer Review: Main Findings
and Recommendations." Paris. [http://www.oecd.org/
dataoecd/46/38/2409572.pdf]. March 2005.

———. 2003a. A Development Co-operation Lens on Terrorism
Prevention: Key Entry Points for Action. DAC Guidelines
and References Series. Paris. [http://www.oecd.org/
dataoecd/17/4/16085708.pdf]. May 2005.

———. 2003b. Harmonising Donor Practices for Effective Aid Delivery.
DAC Guidelines and Reference Series. Paris. [http://www.oecd.
org/dataoecd/0/48/20896122.pdf]. March 2005.

———. 2004a. The DAC Journal: Development Cooperation Report
2003. Paris. [http://213.253.134.29/oecd/pdfs/browseit/
4304311E.pdf]. March 2005.

———. 2004b. "Implementing the 2001 DAC Recommendations on
Untying Official Development Assistance to the Least Developed
Countries: 2004 Progress Report." Paris.

———. 2004c. "The Second High-level Forum on Harmonization and
Alignment for Aid Effectiveness." Concept Note. Paris. [http://www.
developmentgateway.org/download/244504/Harmonization_--
_HLF_II_concept_note_05-24-04_kh_clean.pdf]. March 2005.

———. 2004d. "Security System Reform and Governance." Paris.
[http://www.oecd.org/dataoecd/8/39/31785288.pdf]. May 2005.

———. 2004e. Survey on Harmonisation and Alignment: Measuring Aid
Harmonisation and Alignment in 14 Partner Countries. Preliminary
Edition. Paris. [http://www.oecd.org/dataoecd/31/37/33981948.
pdf]. May 2005.

———. 2005a. "DAC Chair's Summary." UK Department for
International Development. Senior Level Forum on Development
Effectiveness in Fragile States, 13–14 January, London.

———. 2005b. The DAC Journal: Development Cooperation Report
2004. Paris. [http://213.253.134.29/oecd/pdfs/browseit/
4305011E.PDF]. May 2005.

———. 2005c. "Geographical Distribution of Financial Flows to Aid
Recipients 1999–2003." Paris.

———. 2005d. "Harmonization, Alignment, Results: Report on
Progress, Challenges, and Opportunities." OECD-DAC Working
Party on Aid Effectiveness. Prepared for the Joint Progress Toward
Enhanced Effectiveness High Level Forum, 28 February–2 March,
Paris.

———. 2005e. "Implementing the 2001 DAC Recommendation on
Untying Official Development Assistance to the Least Developed
Countries: 2005 Progress Report." Paris.

———. 2005f. "International Development Statistics (IDS) Online:
Databases on Aid and Other Resource Flows." Paris. [http://www.
oecd.org/dataoecd/50/17/5037721.htm]. March 2005.

———. 2005g. "United States: Development Co-operation Review:
Main Findings and Recommendations." Paris. [http://www.oecd.
org/dataoecd/16/28/1836463.pdf]. March 2005.

O'Hanlon, Michael E., and Susan E. Rice. 2004. "To Avoid Calamities,
Boost African Intervention Force." Los Angeles Times, 5 April.

Okediji, Ruth L. 2004. "Development in the Information Age: Issues in
the Regulation of Intellectual Property Rights, Computer Software
and Electronic Commerce." UNCTAD Issue Paper 9. United Nations
Conference on Trade and Development, Geneva. [http://www.
iprsonline.org/unctadictsd/docs/CS_Okediji.pdf]. May 2005.

Olarreaga, Marcelo, and Francis Ng. 2002. "Tariff Peaks and
Preferences." In Bernard Hoekman, Aaditya Mattoo, and Philip
English, eds., Development, Trade and the WTO: A Handbook.
Washington, DC: World Bank.

Omitoogun, Wuyi. 2003. Military Expenditure Data in Africa: A Survey
of Cameroon, Ethiopia, Ghana, Kenya, Nigeria and Uganda. Oxford:
Oxford University Press.

Orden, David. 2003. "US Agricultural Policy: The 2002 Farm Bill
and WTO Doha Round Proposal." IFPRI Discussion Paper 109.
International Food Policy Research Institute, Washington, DC.

Osorio, Nestor. 2004. "Lessons from the World Coffee Crisis: A
Serious Problem for Sustainable Development." International Coffee
Organization, London. [http://www.ico.org/electdocs/archives/
cy2003-04/English/ed/ed1922.pdf]. May 2005.

Østby, Gudrun. 2003. "Horizontal Inequalities and Civil War: Do Ethnic
Group Inequalities Influence the Risk of Domestic Armed Conflict?"
Norwegian University of Science and Technology, Department of
Sociology, Trondheim and Political Science and Centre for the Study
of Civil War, International Peace Research Institute, Oslo.

Otunnu, Olara. 2005. "'Era of Application' Instituting a Compliance and
Enforcement Regime for CAAC." United Nations. Statement to the
Security Council, Security Council Meeting on Children and Armed
Conflict, 23 February, New York.

Oxfam GB. 2003. "Oxfam GB-Funded Peacebuilding Initiatives in the
Arid Districts of Kenya: Lessons and Challenges." Oxford. [http://
www.oxfam.org.uk/what_we_do/issues/pastoralism/downloads/
peacebuildingkenyafinal2004.pdf]. April 2005.

———. 2004. "Programme Impact Report: Oxfam GB's Work With
Partners and Allies Around the World." Oxford. [http://www.oxfam.
org.uk/what_we_do/issues/evaluation/downloads/impact_report_
2004.pdf]. March 2005.

Oxfam GB, Save the Children, and Christian Aid. 2001. "No End
in Sight: The Human Tragedy of the Conflict in the Democratic
Republic of Congo." Oxford. [http://www.oxfam.org.uk/what_we_
do/issues/conflict_disasters/downloads/noend_drc.pdf]. May
2005.

Oxfam International. 2002a. "The Great EU Sugar Scam: How
Europe's Sugar Regime is Devastating Livelihoods in the Developing
World." Oxfam Briefing Paper 27. Oxford.

———. 2002b. Rigged Rules and Double Standards: Trade,
Globalisation and the Fight Against Poverty. Oxford. [http://www.
maketradefair.com/assets/english/report_english.pdf]. May 2005.

———. 2003a. "Beyond the Headlines: An agenda to Protect Civilians
in Neglected Conflicts." Oxford. [http://www.oxfaminternational.
org/eng/pdfs/pp030916_headlines.pdf].

———. 2003b. "Dumping Without Borders: How US Agricultural
Policies are Destroying the Livelihoods of Mexican Corn Farmers."
Oxfam Briefing Paper 50. Oxford. [http://www.oxfam.org/eng/pdfs/
pp030827_corn_dumping.pdf]. May 2005.

———. 2004a. "Dumping On the World: How EU Sugar Policies Hurt
Poor Countries." Oxfam Briefing Paper 61. Oxford.

———. 2004b. "Extortion at the Gate: Will Viet Nam Join the WTO
on Pro-Development Terms?" Oxfam Briefing Paper 67. Oxford.
[http://www.oxfam.org/eng/pdfs/bp67_Viet_%20Nam_041004.
pdf]. May 2005.

———. 2004c. "Spotlight on Subsidies: Cereal Injustice under the CAP
in Britain." Oxfam Briefing Paper 55. Oxford. [http://www.oxfam.
org.uk/what_we_do/issues/trade/downloads/bp55_subsidies.
pdf]. May 2005.

———. 2004d. "Stitched Up: How Rich-Country Protectionism in
Textiles and Clothing Trade Prevents Poverty Alleviation." Oxfam
Briefing Paper 60. Oxford. [http://www.oxfam.org.uk/what_we_do/
issues/trade/downloads/bp60_textiles.pdf]. May 2005.

———. 2004e. Trading Away Our Rights: Women Working in Global
Supply Chains. Oxford. [http://www.oxfam.org.uk/what_we_do/
issues/trade/downloads/trading_rights.pdf]. May 2005.

———. 2005a. "Kicking Down the Door: How Upcoming WTO Talks
Threaten Farmers in Poor Countries." Oxfam Briefing Paper 72.
Oxford. [http://www.oxfam.org.uk/what_we_do/issues/trade/
downloads/bp72_rice.pdf]. June 2005.

———. 2005b. Paying the Price: Why Rich Countries Must Invest Now
in a War on Poverty. Oxford. [http://www.oxfam.org.uk/what_we_
do/issues/debt_aid/downloads/mdgs_price.pdf]. March 2005.

Oxfam International, CARE, Save the Children, IRC (International Rescue Committee), Tearfund, and Christian Aid. 2002. "The Key to Peace: Unlocking the Human Potential of Sudan." Oxford. [http://www.oxfam.org.uk/what_we_do/issues/conflict_disasters/downloads/peace_sudan.pdf]. May 2005.

Page, Sheila. 2005. "A Preference Erosion Compensation Fund: A New Proposal to Protect Countries from the Negative Effects of Trade Liberalisation." ODI Opinions 35. Overseas Development Institute, London. [http://www.odi.org.uk/publications/opinions/35_preference_erosion_jan05.pdf]. May 2005.

Page, Sheila, and Peter Kleen. 2004. "Special and Differential Treatment of Developing Countries in the World Trade Organization." Report for the Ministry of Foreign Affairs, Sweden. London. [http://www.egdi.gov.se/word/SDT%2016Augustdraft.doc]. May 2005.

Pakistan, Statistics Division. 2002. "Pakistan Integrated Household Survey (PIHS) Round IV: 2001–2002." Karachi. [http://www.statpak.gov.pk/depts/fbs/statistics/pihs2000-2001/pihs2001-02_2.pdf]. June 2005.

Pallage, Stéphane ,and Michel A. Robe. 2001. "Foreign Aid and the Business Cycle." Review of International Economics 9(4): 636–67.

Parikh, Vaibhav. 2002. "Movement of Natural Persons Under the GATS in Computer and Related Services." Presentation to the Joint WTO–World Bank Symposium on "The Movement of Natural Persons (Mode4) Under the GATS," 11–12 April, Geneva. [http://www.wto.org/english/tratop_e/serv_e/symp_apr_02_parikh_e.ppt]. May 2005.

Partnership Africa Canada. 2005. "Kimberley Process Monitoring: Good System Marred by Holdouts." Other Facets 16(2): 1. [http://www.pacweb.org/e/images/stories/of16_v2.pdf]. April 2005.

Pedersen, Duncan. 2002. "Political Violence, Ethnic Conflict, and Contemporary Wars: Broad Implications for Health and Social Well-Being." Social Science & Medicine 55(2): 175–90.

Peimani, Hooman. 2005. "Armed Violence and Poverty in Chechnya: Mini Case Study for the Armed Violence and Poverty Initiative." University of Bradford, Center for International Cooperation and Security, Bradford, United Kingdom.

Pelletier, D. L., E. A. Frongillo, D. G. Schroeder, and J. P. Habicht. 1995. "The Effects of Malnutrition on Child Mortality in Developing Countries." Bulletin of the World Health Organization 73(4): 443–48.

Petras, James. 2004. "Bolivia: Between Colonization and Revolution." Canadian Dimension January/February. [http://www.canadiandimension.mb.ca/v38/v38_1jp.htm]. May 2005.

Physicians for Human Rights. 2002. War-Related Sexual Violence in Sierra Leone: A Population-Based Assessment. Boston, Mass. [http://www.phrusa.org/research/sierra_leone/]. June 2005.

Picciotto, Robert. 2004. "Policy Coherence and Development Evaluation—Concepts, Issues and Possible Approaches." Background paper for OECD Workshop: Policy Coherence for Development, 18–19 May, Paris. [http://www.oecd.org/dataoecd/43/35/31659358.pdf]. May 2005.

Pillay, Rajeev. 2002. "Halting the Downward Spiral: Returning Countries with Special Development Needs to Sustainable Growth and Development." United Nations Development Programme, Institutional Development Group of the Bureau for Development Statistics, New York.

PIPA (Program on International Policy Attitudes). 2001. "Americans on Foreign Aid and World Hunger. A Study of U.S. Public Attitudes." Washington, DC. [http://www.pipa.org/OnlineReports/BFW/toc.html]. March 2005.

———. 2004. "Americans on Globalization, Trade and Farm Subsidies." Washington, DC. [http://www.pipa.org/OnlineReports/Globalization/pdf/IntTradeRep_1_22_04.pdf].

Plato. [360 BC] 2000. Laws. Book V. Translated by Benjamin Jowett. The Classical Library, HTML Edition. [http://www.classicallibrary.org/plato/dialogues/laws/book5.htm]. May 2005.

Ponte, Stefano. 2001. "The 'Latte Revolution'? Winners and Losers in the Re-Structuring of the Global Coffee Marketing Chain."

CDR Working Paper 01.3. Centre for Development Research, Copenhagen. [http://www.cdr.dk/working_papers/wp-01-3.pdf]. May 2005.

Ponzio, Richard. 2005a. "Solomon Islands: The UN and Intervention by Coalitions of the Willing." International Peacekeeping 12(2): 173–88.

———. 2005b. Personal communication. Comments on draft chapter. January. Oxford.

Potbury, T. 2000. "US and EU Agricultural Support: Who Does it Benefit?" ABARE Current Issues. Australian Bureau of Agricultural and Resource Economics, Canberra.

Prati, Alessandro, Ratna Sahai, and Thierry Tressel. 2003. "Is There a Case for Sterilizing Foreign Aid Inflows?" Prepared for the International Monetary Fund Research Workshop Macroeconomic Challenges in Low Income Countries, 23–24 October, Washington, DC. [http://www.imf.org/external/np/res/seminars/2003/lic/pdf/tt.pdf]. May 2005.

Prime Minister's Strategy Unit. 2005. "Investing in Prevention: An International Strategy to Manage Risks of Instability and Improve Crisis Response." London. [http://www.strategy.gov.uk/downloads/work_areas/countries_at_risk/cri_report.pdf]. April 2005.

Proctor, Bernadette, and Joseph Dalaker. 2003. "Poverty in the United States: 2002." US Census Bureau, Washington, DC. [http://www.census.gov/prod/2003pubs/p60-222.pdf]. May 2005.

Radelet, Steven. 2003a. Challenging Foreign Aid: A Policymaker's Guide to the Millennium Challenge Account. Washington, DC: Center for Global Development.

———. 2003b. "Will the Millennium Challenge Account Be Different?" The Washington Quarterly 26(2): 171–87. [http://www.twq.com/03spring/docs/03spring_radelet.pdf]. March 2005.

Ramcharan, Rodney. 2002. "How Does Conditional Aid (Not) Work?" IMF Working Paper WP/02/183. International Monetary Fund, Washington, DC. [http://www.imf.org/external/pubs/ft/wp/2002/wp02183.pdf]. March 2005.

Ravallion, Martin. 2005. "Pro-Poor Growth: A Primer." Policy Research Working Paper 3242. World Bank, Development Research Group, Washington, DC.

Ravallion, Martin, and Shaohua Chen. 2004. "China's (Uneven) Progress Against Poverty." Policy Research Working Paper 3408. World Bank, Washington, DC. [http://wdsbeta.worldbank.org/external/default/WDSContentServer/IW3P/IB/2004/10/08/000012009_20041008125921/Rendered/PDF/WPS3408.pdf]. May 2005.

Reardon, Thomas, and Julio A. Berdegue. 2002. "The Rapid Rise of Supermarkets in Latin America: Challenges and Opportunities for Development." Development Policy Review 20(4): 371–88.

Reardon, Thomas, C. Peter Timmer, and Julio A. Berdegue. 2003. "The Rise of Supermarkets and Private Standards in Developing Countries: Illustrations from the Produce Sector and Hypothesized Implications for Trade." Paper presented at the Agricultural Policy Reform and the WTO: Where Are We Heading? 23–26 June, Capri, Italy.

Reardon, Thomas, C. Peter Timmer, Christopher B. Berrett, and Julio A. Berdegue. 2003. "The Rise of Supermarkets in Africa, Asia and Latin America." American Journal of Agricultural Economics 85(5): 1140–46.

Reddy, Sanjay G., and Camelia Minoiu. 2005. "Real Income Stagnation of Countries, 1960–2001." Columbia University, New York. [http://www.columbia.edu/~cm2036/stagnation.pdf]. May 2005.

Reddy, Sanjay G., and Thomas W. Pogge. 2003. "How Not to Count the Poor." Columbia University, New York. [http://www.columbia.edu/~sr793/count.pdf]. May 2005.

Reilly, Benjamin. 2002. "Post-Conflict Elections: Constraints and Dangers." International Peacekeeping 9(2): 118–120.

Reisen, Helmut. 2004. "Innovative Approaches to Funding the Millennium Development Goals." Policy Brief 24. Organisation for

Economic Co-operation and Development/Development Cooperation Directorate, Paris.

Riascos, Alvaro, and Juan Vargas. 2004. "Violence and Growth in Colombia: A Brief Review of the Literature." Webpondo Edición 11. Webpondo. [http://www.webpondo.org/files_ene_mar04/rgc.pdf]. May 2005.

Rodriguez, Francisco and Dani Rodrik. 2000. "Trade Policy and Economic Growth: A Skeptic's Guide to the Cross-National Evidence." University of Maryland, Department of Economics, College Park, Md. and Harvard University, John F. Kennedy School of Government, Cambridge, Mass. [http://ksghome.harvard.edu/~drodrik/skepti1299.pdf]. May 2005.

Rodrik, Dani. 2000. "Comments on 'Trade, Growth, and Poverty,' By D. Dollar and A. Kraay." Harvard University, Cambridge, Mass.

———. 2001a. "Comments at the Conference on 'Immigration Policy and the Welfare State.'" Immigration Policy and the Welfare State, 23 June, Trieste, Italy.

———. 2001b. "The Global Governance of Trade as If Development Really Mattered." Paper prepared for United Nations Development Programme, New York. [http://www.servicesforall.org/html/Governance/Rodrik-Trade%20&%20Development.pdf]. May 2005.

———. 2001c. "Trading in Illusions." Foreign Policy, March/April.

———. 2003. In Search of Prosperity: Analytic Narratives on Economic Growth. Princeton, N.J.: Princeton University Press.

———. 2004. "Industrial Policy for the Twenty-First Century." Harvard University, John F. Kennedy School of Government, Cambridge, Mass. [http://ksghome.harvard.edu/~drodrik/UNIDOSep.pdf%20]. May 2005.

Rodrik, Dani, and Arvind Subramanian. 2004. From 'Hindu Growth' to Productivity Surge: The Mystery of the Indian Growth Transition. NBER Working Paper 10376. National Bureau of Economic Research, Cambridge, Mass. [http://www.imf.org/External/Pubs/FT/staffp/2004/00-00/rodrik.pdf]. May 2005.

Rogerson, Andrew. 2005. "Giving, Forgiving, and Taking Back: Why Continue to Make Soft Loans to Very Poor Countries?" ODI Opinions 29. Overseas Development Institute, London. [http://www.odi.org.uk/publications/opinions/29_odi_opinions_soft_loans_jan05.pdf]. May 2005.

Rogerson, Andrew, and Paolo De Renzio. 2005. "The Seven Habits of Effective Aid: Best Practices, Challenges and Open Questions." ODI Opinions 36. Overseas Development Institute, London. [http://www.odi.org.uk/publications/opinions/36_effective_aid_feb05.pdf]. May 2005.

Rogerson, Andrew, Adrian Hewitt, and David Waldenburg. 2004. "The International Aid System 2005–2010: Forces For and Against Change." Working Paper 235. Overseas Development Institute, London. [http://www.odi.org.uk/publications/working_papers/wp235.pdf]. March 2005.

Roodman, David. 2004. "An Index of Donor Performance." Working Paper 42. Center for Global Development, Washington, DC. [http://www.cgdev.org/docs/cgd_wp042.pdf]. March 2005.

Roosevelt, Franklin D. 1937. "Second Inaugural Address." 20 January, Washington, DC. [http://www.bartleby.com/124/pres50.html].

Rosen, Howard. 2002. "Congress' Penny-Wise, Pound-Foolish Trade Strategy." CNP PolicyWire. Center for National Policy, Washington, DC. [http://www.cnponline.org/Issue%20Briefs/PolicyWires/policy0702.htm]. May 2005.

Rotberg, Robert I., ed. 2004. When States Fail: Cause and Consequences. Princeton, N.J.: Princeton University Press.

Roy, Davesh. 2000. "Financial Services and the WTO: Liberalisation Commitments of the Developing and Transition Economies." World Economy 23(3): 351–86.

———. 2001. "The African Growth and Opportunity Act: Rules of Origin and the Impact on Market Access." International Monetary Fund, Washington, DC.

Rubin, Barnett R., Abby Stoddard, Humayun Hamidzada, and Adib Farhadi. 2005. "Building a New Afghanistan: The Value of Success, the Cost of Failure." Center for International Cooperation, New York University, New York. [http://www.cic.nyu.edu/pdf/Building.pdf]. May 2005.

Sachs, Jeffrey, and Gro Harlem Brundtland. 2001. "Macroeconomics and Health: Investing in Health for Economic Development." Commission on Macroeconomics and Health, Geneva. [http://www3.who.int/whosis/cmh/cmh_report/e/pdf/001-004.pdf]. May 2005.

Sagasti, Francisco, Keith Bezanson, and Fernando Prada. 2005. "The Future of Development Financing: Challenges and Strategic Choices." Global Development Studies Series 1. Expert Group on Development Issues, Stockholm.

Sandler, Todd, and Daniel Arce. 2005. "A Conceptual Framework for Understanding Global and Transnational Goods for Health." Paper WG2: 1. Commission on Macroeconomics and Health, Cambridge, Mass. [http://www.cmhealth.org/docs/wg2_paper1.pdf]. March 2005.

Sanford, Jonathan E. 2004. "IMF Gold and the World Bank's Unfunded HIPC Initiative." Development Policy Review 22(1): 31–40.

Schenkenberg van Mierop, Edward. 2004. "The Humanitarian Response in Liberia: Some Observations by the ICVA Coordinator." International Council of Voluntary Agencies, Geneva.

Seagate. 2003. "Seagate Lifts Lid on Factory System." 10 December. [http://www.seagate.com/cda/newsinfo/newsroom/coverage/article/1,1113,1924,00.html]. May 2005.

Sen, Amartya. 1992. Inequality Re-Examined. Oxford: Clarendon Press.

———. 1999. Development as Freedom. Oxford: Oxford University Press.

———. 2004. "Passage to China." The New York Review of Books 51(19).

Sen, Amartya, and Jean Drèze. 1997. Indian Development: Selected Regional Perspectives. Oxford: Oxford University Press.

Sen, Binayak, Mustafa K. Mujeri, and Shahabuddin Quazi. 2004. "Operationalising Pro-Poor Growth: A Country Case Study on Bangladesh." Agence Française de Développement, Bundesministerium Für Wirtschaftliche Zusammenarbeit, Deutsche Gesellschaft für Technische Zusammenarbeit GmbH, KfW Entwicklungsbank, UK Department for International Development London, and World Bank. [http://www.dfid.gov.uk/pubs/files/oppgbangladesh.pdf]. May 2005.

Sethi, R. 1958. Last Phase of British Sovereignty in India, 1919–1947. Vol. 2. Delhi, India: S. Chand.

Shah, Anup. 2005. "The US and Foreign Aid Assistance." Global Issues. [http://www.globalissues.org/TradeRelated/Debt/USAid.asp]. March 2005.

Shkolnikov, Vladimir, and Giovanni Andrea Cornia. 2000. "Population Crisis and Rising Mortality in Transitional Russia." In Giovanni Andrea Cornia and Renato Paniccià, eds., Mortality Crisis in Transitional Economies. Oxford: Oxford University Press.

SIPRI (Stockholm International Peace Research Institute). 2004. "SIPRI Yearbook 2004: Armaments, Disarmament and International Security." Oxford.

Sivard, Ruth Leger. 1991. World Military and Social Expenditures. Washington, DC: World Priorities.

———. 1996. World Military and Social Expenditures. Washington, DC: World Priorities.

Small Arms Survey. 2002. Small Arms Survey 2002: Counting the Human Cost. Oxford: Oxford University Press.

Smith, Adam. [1776] 1976. An Inquiry into the Nature and Causes of the Wealth of Nations. Oxford: Oxford University Press.

Sommers, Marc. 2002. "Children, Education and War: Reaching Education for All (EFA) Objectives in Countries Affected by Conflict." Working Paper 1. World Bank, Conflict Prevention and Reconstruction Unit and Education Team, Human Development Network, Washington, DC. [http://www-wds.worldbank.org/servlet/WDSContentServer/WDSP/IB/2002/10/12/000094946_02091704130527/Rendered/PDF/multi0page.pdf]. May 2005.

Ssewanyana, N. S., A. J. Okidi, D. Angemi, and V. Barungi. 2004. "Understanding the Detriments of Income Inequality in Uganda." Paper 223. Centre for the Study of African Economies, Oxford University. [http://www.bepress.com/cgi/viewcontent.cgi?article=1229&context=csae].

Stern, Nicholas. 2002. "Making Trade Work for Poor People." Speech delivered at National Council of Applied Economic Research, 28 November, New Delhi.

Stevens, Christopher, and Jane Kennan. 2002. "How Far will Doha Reduce Tariff Peaks?" Institute for Development Studies, Brighton.

———. 2004a. "Making Trade Preferences More Effective." IDS Briefing. Institute for Development Studies, Brighton. [http://www.ids.ac.uk/ids/global/pdfs/CSJKTradePreferences.pdf]. May 2005.

———. 2004b. "The Utilisation of EU Preferences to the ACP." World Trade Organization. Paper presented at the Technical Seminar on Tariff Preferences and Their Utilisation, 31 March, Geneva.

———. 2005a. "EU-ACP Economic Partnership Agreements: the Effects of Reciprocity." Institute for Development Studies, Brighton.

———. 2005b. "Preparing for Economic Partnership Agreements." Institute for Development Studies, Brighton.

Stewart, Frances. 2002. "Horizontal Inequalities: A Neglected Dimension of Development." QEH Working Paper 81. Oxford University, Queen Elizabeth House, Oxford. [http://www.qeh.ox.ac.uk/pdf/qehwp/qehwps81.pdf]. May 2005.

———. 2005. "Policies towards Horizontal Inequalities in Post-Conflict Reconstruction." CRISE Working Paper 7. Centre for Research on Inequality, Human Security and Ethnicity, Queen Elizabeth House, Oxford University. [http://www.crise.ox.ac.uk/pubs/workingpaper7.pdf]. April 2005.

Stewart, Frances, and Valpy Fitzgerald. 2001. War and Underdevelopment. Volume I: The Economic and Social Consequences of Conflict. Oxford: Oxford University Press.

Stewart, Frances, Graham Brown, and Luca Mancini. 2005. "Why Horizontal Inequalities Matter: Some Implications for Measurement." Paper prepared for the International Meeting on Gini and Lorenz in Commemoration of their Centenary Scientific Research, 23–26 May, Siena, Italy.

Stewart, Patrick. 2000. "The Donor Community and the Challenge of Postconflict Recovery." In Forman Shepard and Patrick Stewart, eds., Good Intensions: Pledges of Aid for Postconflict Recovery. Boulder, Colo.: Lynne Rienner.

Story, Alan. 2004. "Intellectual Property and Computer Software: A Battle of Competing Use and Access Visions for Countries of the South." ICTSD-UNCTAD Issue Paper 10. International Centre for Trade and Sustainable Development and United Nations Conference on Trade and Development, Geneva. [http://www.iprsonline.org/unctadictsd/docs/CS_Story.pdf]. May 2005.

Strand, Håvard, Lars Wilhelmsen, and Nils Petter Gleditsch. 2004. Armed Conflict Data Project 2004: Armed Conflict Database Codebook. Version 3.0. Oslo: PRIO (International Peace Research Institute).

———. 2005. "Armed Conflict Data Project 2004: Armed Conflict Database." PRIO (International Peace Research Institute), Oslo. [http://www.prio.no/cwp/armedconflict/current/armedconflicts.xls]. May 2005.

Sundberg, Mark, Hans Lofgren, and François Bourguignon. 2005. "Absorptive Capacity and Achieving the MDGs: The Case of Ethiopia." World Bank, Development Economics Department, Washington, DC.

Sutton, John. 2004. "The Auto-Component Supply Chain in China and India: A Benchmarking Study." London School of Economics and Political Science, London. [http://sticerd.lse.ac.uk/dps/ei/ei34.pdf]. May 2005.

Swaziland, Ministry of Agriculture and Co-operatives and Business. 2002. "Impact of HIV/AIDS on Agriculture and the Private Sector in Swaziland." Mbabane. [http://www.sahims.net/doclibrary/Sahims_Documents/Impact%20of%20HIVAIDS%20on%20agriculture%20&%20private%20sector%20in%20Swaziland.pdf]. May 2005.

Sykes, Michael, ed. 2004. Understanding Economic Growth. Paris: Organisation for Economic Co-operation and Development.

Tangermann, Stefan. 2003. "Cutting Support Can Help Farmers to Prosper." Financial Times, 22 August.

Tanzania, Government of. 2004. "Poverty Reduction Strategy: The Third Progress Report 2002/03." Dar es Salaam. [http://www.tanzania.go.tz/pdf/THE%20THIRD%20PRSP%20Progress%20Report%202003.pdf]. May 2005.

Teal, Francis, and Marcella Vigneri. 2004. "Production Changes in Ghana Cocoa Farming Households Under Market Reforms." CSAE WPS/2004-16. Centre for the Study of African Economies, Oxford University. [http://www.csae.ox.ac.uk/workingpapers/pdfs/2004-16text.pdf]. May 2005.

Tewari, Meenu. 2003. "Engaging the New Global Interlocutors: Foreign Direct Investment and the Re-Shaping of local productive Capabilities in Tamil Nadu's Automotive Supply Sector." University of North Carolina, Chapel Hill. [http://www.ids.ac.uk/globalvaluechains/publications/AutoLoraine2003-FINAL.pdf]. May 2005.

Thakur, Ramesh, and Albrecht Schnabel. 2001. United Nations Peacekeeping Operations: Ad Hoc Missions, Permanent Engagement. Tokyo: United Nations University Press.

Thurlow, James, and Peter Wobst. 2004. "The Road to Pro-Poor Growth in Zambia." DSGC Discussion Paper 16. International Food Policy Research Institute, Development Strategy and Governance Division, Washington, DC. [http://www.ifpri.org/divs/dsgd/dp/papers/dsgdp16.pdf]. May 2005.

Toole, M. J., and R. J. Waldman. 1997. "The Public Health Aspects of Complex Emergencies and Refugee Situations." Annual Review of Public Health 18: 283–312.

Torvik, Ragnar. 2001. "Learning By Doing and the Dutch Disease." European Economic Review 45(2): 285–306.

Tussie, Diana, and Miguel Lengyel. 2002. "Developing Countries: Turning Participation Into Influence." In Bernard Hoekman, Aaditya Mattoo, and Philip English, eds., Development, Trade and the WTO: A Handbook. Washington, DC: World Bank.

Uganda, Ministry of Finance, Planning and Economic Development. 2003. "Task Force Report on Infant and Maternal Mortality in Uganda." Kampala.

ul Haq, Mahbub. 1995. Reflections on Human Development. New York: Oxford University Press.

UK (United Kingdom), HM Treasury. 2003. "International Finance Facility Proposal. January 2003." London. [http://www.hm-treasury.gov.uk/documents/international_issues/international_development/development_iff.cfm]. April 2005.

UN (United Nations). 1992. "An Agenda for Peace: Preventive Diplomacy, Peacemaking and Peace-Keeping." Report of the Secretary-General pursuant to the Statement adopted by the Summit Meeting of the Security Council on 31 January 1992. New York. [http://www.un.org/Docs/SG/agpeace.html]. April 2005.

———. 2000a. "Millennium Declaration." A/RES/55/2, 18 September. New York.

———. 2000b. "Report of the Panel on United Nations Peace Operations: A Far-Reaching Report by an Independent Panel." A/55/305-S/2000/809. New York.

———. 2000c. "Security Council Discusses Exit Strategies for Peacekeeping Operations." Press Release SC/6951. [http://www.un.org/News/Press/docs/2000/20001115.sc6951.doc.html]. May 2005.

———. 2003. World Population Prospects 1950–2050: The 2002 Revision. Database. Department of Economics and Social Affairs, Population Division, New York

————. 2004a. *Millennium Development Goals: China's Progress: 2003.* Office of the United Nations Resident Coordinator, Beijing. [http://www.undp.org/mdg/chinaMDG.pdf]. May 2005.

————. 2004b. *A More Secure World: Our Shared Responsibility.* Report of the UN Secretary-General's High-level Panel on Threats, Challenges and Change. New York: United Nations Department of Information. [http://www.un.org/secureworld/report2.pdf]. March 2005.

————. 2005a. "An Agenda for Peace: Position Paper of the Secretary-General on the occasion of the Fiftieth Anniversary of the United Nations." Report of the Secretary-General on the work of the organization. New York. [http://www.un.org/Docs/SG/agsupp.html]. April 2005.

————. 2005b. "Millennium Indicators Database." Department of Economic and Social Affairs, Statistics Division, New York. [http://millenniumindicators.un.org/unsd/mi/mi_goals.asp]. March 2005.

————. 2005c. "UN Commodity Trade Statistics Database (UN Comtrade)." New York. [http://unstats.un.org/unsd/comtrade/]. June 2005.

————. 2005d. *World Population Prospects 1950–2050: The 2004 Revision.* Department of Economic and Social Affairs, Population Division, New York

UNAIDS (Joint United Nations Programme on HIV/AIDS). 2003. "HIV/AIDS and Conflict." Office on AIDS, Security, and Humanitarian Response, Copenhagen. [http://www.unaids.org/NetTools/Misc/DocInfo.aspx?LANG=en&href=http://gva-doc-owl/WEBcontent/Documents/pub/Topics/Security/FS_Conflict_en.pdf]. April 2005.

————. 2004a. "Care, Women and AIDS." Fact Sheet. Geneva. [http://www.unaids.org/html/pub/una-docs/gcwa_care_02feb04_en_pdf.pdf]. May 2005.

————. 2004b. "Report on the Global AIDS Epidemic." Geneva. [http://www.unaids.org/bangkok2004/GAR2004_pdf/UNAIDSGlobalReport2004_en.pdf]. May 2005.

————. 2005a. "HIV and AIDS Statistics and Features, Fnd of 2002 and 2004: Asia." Geneva. [http://www.unaids.org/wad2004/EPIupdate2004_html_en/epi04_07_en.htm#TopOfPage]. May 2005.

————. 2005b. "HIV and AIDS Statistics and Features, End of 2002 and 2004: Eastern Europe and Central Asia." Geneva. [http://www.unaids.org/wad2004/EPIupdate2004_html_en/epi04_08_en.htm#TopOfPage]. May 2005.

UNCTAD (United Nations Conference on Trade and Development). 2000. *The Competitiveness Challenge: Transnational Corporations and Industrial Restructuring in Developing Countries.* Geneva.

————. 2003. "Economic Development in Africa: Trade Performance and Commodity Dependence." Geneva. [http://www.unctad.org/en/docs/gdsafrica20031_en.pdf]. May 2005.

————. 2004a. "The Least Developed Countries Report 2004: Linking International Trade with Poverty Reduction." Geneva. [http://www.unctad.org/en/docs/ldc2004_en.pdf]. May 2005.

————. 2004b. "Trade and Development Report 2004: Policy Coherence, Development Strategies and Integration into the World Economy." Geneva. [http://www.unctad.org/en/docs/tdr2004_en.pdf]. May 2005.

UNCTAD (United Nations Conference on Trade and Development) and World Bank. 2005. *WITS/TRAINS (World Integrated Trade Solution/Trade Analysis and Information System).* Database. Geneva. [http://192.91.247.38/tab/WITS.asp]. May 2005.

UNDP (United Nations Development Programme). 1990. *Human Development Report 1990: Concept and Measurement of Human Development.* New York: Oxford University Press.

————. 1994. *Human Development Report 1994: New Dimensions of Human Security.* New York: Oxford University Press. [http://hdr.undp.org/reports/global/1994/en/]. May 2005.

————. 2000. "Aid Transaction Costs in Viet Nam." Department for International Development, Ha Noi. [http://www.undp.org.vn/undp/docs/2000/aid/aidtransacte.pdf]. March 2005.

————. 2001. *Nepal National Human Development Report 2001: Poverty Reduction and Governance.* New York: Oxford University Press.

————. 2002. *China National Human Development Report 2002—Making Green Development: A Choice.* New York: Oxford University Press.

————. 2003a. *El conflicto, callejón con salida: Informe Nacional de Desarrollo Humano para Colombia—2003.* Bogotá. [http://www.pnud.org.co/2003/Informe_2003_completo_v2.pdf]. May 2005.

————. 2003b. "Ghana Millennium Development Goals Report 2003." New York. [http://www.undp.org/mdg/ghana_report.pdf]. May 2005.

————. 2003c. *Human Development Report 2003: Millennium Development Goals: A Compact among Nations to End Poverty.* New York: Oxford University Press.

————. 2003d. *Pakistan National Human Development Report 2003: Poverty, Growth, and Governance.* New York: Oxford University Press.

————. 2003e. "Synthesis of Work Done since the July Workshop on Defining Democratic Dialogue." Regional Bureau for Latin America, Democratic Dialogue Project, New York.

————. 2003f. *Tajikistan National Human Development Report 2003: Tapping the Potential: Improving Water Governance.* New York: Oxford University Press.

————. 2004a. *Afghanistan National Human Development Report 2004: Security with a Human Face: Challenges and Responsibilities.* New York: Oxford University Press.

————. 2004b. "Review of Aid Management Systems: Summary and Lessons Learned." New York. [http://www.devaid.org/indexAction.cfm?module=Library&action=GetFile&DocumentID=4201]. June 2005.

————. 2005a. "Afghanistan's Future Holds Promise and Peril." News Bulletin. 21 February. [http://www.undp.org/dpa/pressrelease/releases/2005/february/pr21feb05.html]. May 2005.

————. 2005b. *Nepal Human Development Report 2004: Empowerment and Poverty Reduction.* New York: Oxford University Press.

————. 2005c. "UNDP Regional Bureau for Latin America Democratic Dialogue Project." New York. [http://www.democraticdialoguenetwork.org/english/]. April 2005.

UNEP (United Nations Environment Programme). 1999. "Environmental Impacts of Trade Liberalization and Policies for Sustainable Management of Natural Resources: A Case Study on Bangladesh's Shrimp Farming Industry." UNEP/99/3. New York and Geneva. [http://www.unep.ch/etu/etp/acts/capbld/rdone/bangladesh.pdf]. May 2005.

————. 2002. *Integrated Assessment of Trade Liberalization and Trade-Related Policies: A Country Study on the Fisheries Sector in Senegal.* New York and Geneva.

UNESCO (United Nations Educational, Scientific and Cultural Organization). 2005. *Education for All Global Monitoring Report: Education for All: The Quality Imperative.* Paris. [http://www.unesco.org/education/gmr_download/chapter6.pdf]. May 2005.

UNESCO (United Nations Educational, Scientific and Cultural Organization) Institute of Statistics. 2005. Correspondence on gross and net enrolment ratios and children reaching grade 5. April. Montreal, Canada.

UNHCR (United Nations High Commissioner for Refugees). 2004. "2003 Global Refugees Trends: Overview of Refugee Populations, New Arrivals, Durable Solutions, Asylum-Seekers, and Other Persons of Concern to UNHCR." Population Data Unit/PGDS, Division of Operational Support, Geneva. [http://www.unhcr.ch/cgi-bin/texis/vtx/statistics/opendoc.pdf?tbl=STATISTICS&id=40d015fb4]. May 2005.

UNICEF (United Nations Children's Fund). 2000. "From Survival to Thrival: Children and Women in the Southern Part of Sudan." New York.

————. 2001a. "Progress since the World Summit for Children: A Statistical Review." New York. [http://www.unicef.org/publications/files/pub_wethechildren_stats_en.pdf]. February 2005.

————. 2001b. *State of the World's Children 2001.* New York.

————. 2005a. "Child Poverty in Rich Countries 2005: The Proportion of Children Living in Poverty Has Risen in a Majority of the World's Developed Economies." Innocenti Report Card No. 6. Florence. [http://www.unicef-icdc.org/publications/index.html]. May 2005.

————. 2005b. Correspondence on under-five mortality. May. New York.

————. 2005c. "Monitoring the Situation of Children and Women." [www.childinfo.org]. May 2005.

————. 2005d. "Progress for Children: A Report Card on Gender Parity and Primary Education." Number 2. New York.

————. 2005e. *State of the World's Children 2005.* New York. [http://www.unicef.org/sowc05/english/sowc05.pdf]. May 2005.

UNIDO (United Nations Industrial Development Organization). 2002. *Industrial Development Report 2002/2003: Competing through Innovation and Learning.* Vienna. [http://www.unido.org/userfiles/hartmany/12IDR_full_report.pdf]. May 2005.

————. 2004. *Industrial Development Report 2004: Industrialization, Environment, and the Millennium Development Goals in Sub-Saharan Africa: The New Frontier in the Fight Against Poverty.* Vienna.

University of California, Berkeley, and Max Planck Institute for Demographic Research. 2005. *Human Mortality Database.* Database. Berkeley and Munich. [http://www.mortality.org]. June 2005.

UN Millennium Project. 2005a. *Combating AIDS in the Developing World.* Task Force on HIV/AIDS, Malaria, TB, and Access to Essential Medicines, Working Group on HIV/AIDS. London: Earthscan.

————. 2005b. *Coming to Grips with Malaria in the New Millennium.* Task Force on HIV/AIDS, Malaria, TB, and Access to Essential Medicines, Working Group on Malaria. London: Earthscan.

————. 2005c. *Halving Hunger: It Can Be Done.* Task Force on Hunger. London: Earthscan.

————. 2005d. *Health, Dignity, and Development: What Will It Take?* Task Force on Water and Sanitation. London: Earthscan.

————. 2005e. *Investing in Development: A Practical Plan to Achieve the Millennium Development Goals.* London: Earthscan.

————. 2005f. *Toward Universal Primary Education: Investments, Incentives, and Institutions.* Task Force on Education and Gender Equality. London: Earthscan.

————. 2005g. *Trade for Development.* Task Force on Trade. London: Earthscan.

————. 2005h. *Who's Got the Power? Transforming Health Systems for Women and Children.* Task Force on Child Health and Maternal Health. London: Earthscan.

UN News Centre. 2004. "Annan Calls for Overhaul in Security Structure to Better Protect UN Personnel." 11 October. [http://www.un.org/apps/news/storyAr.asp?NewsID=12186&Cr=security&Cr1=]. May 2005.

UN OCHA (United Nations Office for the Coordination of Humanitarian Affairs). 2002. "Democratic Republic of the Congo 2002: Consolidated Appeals Process (CAP)." Geneva.

————. 2004a. "Democratic Republic of the Congo 2004: Consolidated Appeals Process (CAP)." Geneva. [http://ochadms.unog.ch/quickplace/cap/main.nsf/h_Index/CAP_2004_DRCongo/$FILE/CAP_2004_DRCongo_SCREEN.PDF?OpenElement]. May 2005.

————. 2004b. "Occupied Palestinian Territory 2004: Consolidated Appeals Process (CAP)." Geneva. [http://ochadms.unog.ch/quickplace/cap/main.nsf/h_Index/CAP_2004_oPt/$FILE/CAP_2004_oPt_SCREEN.PDF?OpenElement]. May 2005.

UN (United Nations) Viet Nam. 2002. "Vietnam: Bringing the MDGs Closer to the People." New York. [http://www.undp.org/mdg/vietnam2002.pdf]. May 2005.

US Department of Agriculture, Economic Research Service. 2002. "Agricultural Outlook: Statistical Indicators." [http://www.ers.usda.gov/publications/Agoutlook/AOTables/]. May 2005.

————. 2005a. "Farm and Commodity Policy: Government Payments and the Farm Sector." Briefing Room. Washington, DC. [http://www.ers.usda.gov/Briefing/FarmPolicy/gov-pay.htm]. May 2005.

————. 2005b. "WTO: Uruguay Round Agreement on Agriculture." Briefing Room. Washington, DC. [http://www.ers.usda.gov/Briefing/WTO/domesticSupportPillar.htm]. May 2005.

US Department of Agriculture, Foreign Agricultural Service. 2005. "United States-Central America-Dominican Republic: Free Trade Agreement." Commodity Fact Sheets. [http://www.fas.usda.gov/info/factsheets/CAFTA/foodgrains.html]. May 2005.

US Department of State. 1999. "Patterns of Global Terrorism: 1998." Department of State publication 10610. Office of the Secretary of State, Office of the Coordinator of Counterterrorism, Washington, DC.

————. 2004. "The Prevention and Combating of Terrorism in Africa." Washington, DC. [http://www.state.gov/s/ct/rls/rm/2004/37230.htm]. May 2005.

USITC (United States International Trade Commission). 2005. "Interactive Tariff and Trade Dataweb." Washington, DC. [http://dataweb.usitc.gov/]. May 2005.

Uvin, Peter. 1998. *Aiding Conflict: The Development Enterprise in Rwanda.* West Hartford: Kumarian Press.

Vakis, Renos, Diana Kruger, and Andrew D. Mason. 2004. "Shocks and Coffee: Lessons from Nicaragua." Social Protection Discussion Paper 30164. World Bank, Washington, DC.

van der Gaag, Jacques. 2004. "Alternative Perspectives 2.2." In Bjørn Lomborg, ed., *Global Crises, Global Solutions.* Cambridge: Cambridge University Press.

Victora, Cesar G., Adam Wagstaff, Joanna Armstrong Schellenberg, Davidson Gwatkin, Mariam Claeson, and Jean-Pierre Habicht. 2003. "Applying an Equity Lens to Child Health and Mortality: More of the Same Is Not Enough." *The Lancet* 362(9379): 233–41. [http://www.sciencedirect.com/science?_ob=MImg&_imagekey=B6T1B-4938BXH-Y-1&_cdi=4886&_user=666074&_orig=browse&_coverDate=07%2F19%2F2003&_sk=996370620&view=c&wchp=dGLbVtz-zSkWA&md5=112639e83039a42aef6a9ce24009d7fd&ie=/sdarticle.pdf]. February 2005.

Viet Nam, Government of. 2004. "Vietnam: The Comprehensive Poverty Reduction and Growth Strategy." IMF Country Report 04/25. Washington, DC. [http://www.imf.org/external/pubs/ft/scr/2004/cr0425.pdf]. May 2005.

Visaria, Leela. 2004a. "The Continuing Fertility Transition." In Tim Dyson, Robert Cassen, and Leela Visaria, eds., *Twenty-First Century India: Population, Economy, Human Development, and the Environment.* Oxford: Oxford University Press.

————. 2004b. "Mortality Trends and the Health Transition." In Tim Dyson, Robert Cassen, and Leela Visaria, eds., *Twenty-First Century India: Population, Economy, Human Development, and the Environment.* Oxford: Oxford University Press.

Vorley, Bill. 2003. "Food, Inc.: Corporate Concentration from Farm to Consumer." UK Food Group, London. [http://www.ukfg.org.uk/docs/UKFG-Foodinc-Nov03.pdf]. June 2005.

Wade, Robert. 2005. "Is Globalization Reducing Poverty and Inequality?" *World Development* 32(4): 567–89.

Wagstaff, Adam. 2000. "Socioeconomic Inequalities in Child Mortality: Comparisons Across Nine Developing Countries." *Bulletin of the World Health Organization* 78(1): 19–29.

Wagstaff, Adam, and Mariam Claeson. 2004. *The Millennium Development Goals for Health: Rising to the Challenges.* Washington, DC: World Bank. [http://www-wds.worldbank.org/servlet/WDSContentServer/WDSP/IB/2004/07/15/000009486_20040715130626/Rendered/PDF/296730PAPER0Mi1ent0goals0for0health.pdf]. May 2005.

Wagstaff, Adam, and Eddy van Doorslaer. 2003. "Catastrophe and Impoverishment in Paying for Health Care: With Applications to Vietnam 1993–98." *Health Economics* 12(11): 921–33.

Waldman, Ronald. 2005. "Public Health in War." *Harvard International Review* 27(1).

Walker, A., and C. Walker, eds. 1987. *The Growing Divide: A Social Audit 1979–1987*. London: CPAG Ltd.

Watal, Jayashree. 2002. "Implementing the TRIPS Agreement." In Bernard Hoekman, Aaditya Mattoo, and Philip English, eds., *Development, Trade and the WTO*. Washington, DC: World Bank.

Watkins, Kevin. 2000. *The Oxfam Education Report*. Oxford: Oxfam International.

———. 2003a. "Farm Fallacies That Hurt the Poor." *Development Outreach* 5(2):10–12.

———. 2003b. "Northern Agricultural Policies and World Poverty: Will the Doha 'Development Round' Make a Difference?" Paper presented at the Annual World Bank Conference on Development Economics, World Bank, 15–16 May, Paris. [http://wbln0018.worldbank.org/eurvp/web.nsf/Pages/Paper+by+Watkins/$File/WATKINS.PDF]. May 2005.

Welsh, Jennifer M. 2002. "From Right to Responsibility: Humanitarian Intervention and International Society." *Global Governance* 8(4): 503–21.

White, David. 2005. "Progress Relies on Donors' Pledges." *Financial Times*, 14 February.

White, Howard, and Geske Dijkstra. 2003. *Programme Aid and Development: Beyond Conditionality*. London and New York: Routledge.

The White House. 2002. "Expand the Circle of Development by Opening Societies and Building the Infrastructure of Democracy." In *The National Security Strategy of the United States of America*. Washington, DC. [http://www.whitehouse.gov/nsc/nss.pdf].

WHO (World Health Organization). 2004a. "Retrospective Mortality Survey among the Internally Displaced Population, Greater Darfur, Sudan." Geneva. [http://www.who.int/disasters/repo/14656.pdf]. May 2005.

———. 2004b. *The World Health Report 2004: Changing History*. Geneva. [http://www.who.int/whr/2004/en/report04_en.pdf]. May 2005.

WHO (World Health Organization) and UNICEF (United Nations Children's Fund). 2003. *The Africa Malaria Report 2003*. Geneva. [http://www.unicef.org/publications/files/pub_africa_malaria_report_en.pdf]. May 2005.

Winters, L. Alan. 2002. "The Economic Implications of Liberalising Mode 4 Trade." Joint WTO-World Bank Symposium on "The Movement of Natural Persons (Mode4) Under the GATS," 11–12 April, Geneva. [http://www.tessproject.com/guide/pubs/mode4/Economic_Implications_of%20Lib_Mode4_Trade.pdf]. May 2005.

Winters, L. Alan, Neil McCulloch, and Andrew McKay. 2004. "Trade Liberalization and Poverty: The Evidence So Far." *Journal of Economic Literature* 42(1):72–115.

Wolf, Martin. 2005. "Asia's Giants Take Different Routes." *Financial Times*, 22 February.

Wolfensohn, James, and François Bourguignon. 2004. "Development and Poverty Reduction: Looking Back, Looking Ahead." Prepared for the 2004 Annual Meetings of the World Bank and IMF. World Bank, Washington, DC. [http://www.worldbank.org/ambc/lookingbacklookingahead.pdf]. May 2005.

Woods, Ngaire. 2005. "The Shifting Politics of Foreign Aid." *International Affairs* 81(2): 393–409.

Woods, Ngaire, and research team. 2004. "Reconciling Effective Aid and Global Security: Implications for the Emerging International Development Architecture." Global Economic Governance Programme, University College, Oxford. [http://users.ox.ac.uk/~ntwoods/IDAFinalDraft2(26Nov2004).pdf]. March 2005.

Woodward, Llewellyn. 1963. *The Age of Reform 1815–1870*. Oxford: Oxford University Press.

Woodward, Susan. 2002. "Economic Priorities for Successful Peace Implementation." In Stephen John Stedman, Donald Rothchild, and Elizabeth Cousens, eds., *Ending Civil Wars: The Implementation of Peace Agreements*. Boulder: Lynne Rienner.

Working Group on New International Financial Contributions, Office of the President of the French Republic. 2004. "New International Financial Contributions." A report by the working group chaired by Jean-Pierre Landau. Report to Jacques Chirac, President of the French Republic. Paris.

World Bank. 1998. *Assessing Aid: What Works, What Doesn't, and Why*. Washington, DC: Oxford University Press.

———. 2001. "Tanzania: World Bank Approves Primary Education Project." News Release 2002/096/AFR. Washington, DC.

———. 2002. "Corruption, Poverty, and Inequality." Washington, DC. [http://www1.worldbank.org/publicsector/anticorrupt/corpov.htm]. June 2005.

———. 2003a. "Benin: Second Poverty Reduction Support Credit." Environmental Assessment E1083. Washington, DC.

———. 2003b. *Brazil: Equitable, Competitive, Sustainable—Contributions for Debate*. Washington, DC.

———. 2003c. *Poverty in Guatemala*. Washington, DC.

———. 2003d. *Rural Poverty Alleviation in Brazil: Toward an Integrated Strategy*. Washington, DC.

———. 2003e. *World Development Report 2004: Making Services Work for Poor People*. New York: Oxford University Press.

———. 2004a. *2003 Annual Review of Development Effectiveness: The Effectiveness of Bank Support for Policy Reform*. Washington, DC. [http://lnweb18.worldbank.org/oed/oeddoclib.nsf/DocUNIDViewForJavaSearch/3D82DE51D6B462DA85256E69006BD181/$file/arde_2003.pdf]. March 2005.

———. 2004b. "Books, Buildings, and Learning Outcomes: An Impact Evaluation of World Bank Support to Basic Education in Ghana." Report 28779. Operations Evaluation Department, Washington, DC. [http://lnweb18.worldbank.org/oed/oeddoclib.nsf/0/928a136deb347b3485256e8a0061bc8d/$FILE/report_28779_basic_education.pdf]. May 2005.

———. 2004c. *Global Economic Prospects 2005: Trade, Regionalism, and Development*. Washington, DC.

———. 2004d. "Opportunities and Challenges for Developing High-Value Agricultural Exports in Ethiopia." April draft. Africa Region, Country Department for Ethiopia, Washington, DC.

———. 2004e. *World Development Indicators 2004*. Washington, DC.

———. 2004f. *Inequality and Economic Development in Brazil*. Washington, DC.

———. 2005a. "2004 Annual Review of Development Effectiveness: The Bank's Contributions to Poverty Reduction." Operations Evaluation Department. Washington, DC. [http://lnweb18.worldbank.org/oed/oeddoclib.nsf/24cc3bb1f94ae11c85256808006a0046/efbce22c91b5796685256ff10057bb6c/$FILE/2004_ARDE.pdf]. June 2005.

———. 2005b. "China's Progress towards the Health MDGs." World Bank Rural Health in China: Briefing Note 2. Washington, DC.

———. 2005c. "Conditionality Review: Conditionality and Policy Based Lending—Trends." Washington, DC.

———. 2005d. "PovcalNet." [http://iresearch.worldbank.org/PovcalNet/jsp/index.jsp]. June 2005.

———. 2005e. "Russian Federation: Reducing Poverty through Growth and Social Policy Reform." Report 28923-RU. Europe and Central Asia Region, Poverty Reduction and Economic Management Unit, Washington, DC. [http://www-wds.worldbank.org/servlet/WDSContentServer/WDSP/IB/2005/03/17/000012009_20050317113145/Rendered/PDF/289230RU.pdf]. May 2005.

———. 2005f. *World Development Indicators 2005 CD-ROM (Single User)*. Washington, DC.

World Bank and IMF (International Monetary Fund). 2003. "Supporting Sound Policies with Adequate and Appropriate Financing." DC2003-0016. Background paper for Development Committee (Joint Ministerial Committee of the Boards of Governors of the Bank and the Fund on the Real Resources to Developing Countries, "Item I of the Provision Agenda." Washington, DC. [http://siteresources.worldbank.org/DEVCOMMINT/Documentation/20127712/DC2003-0016(E)-Financing.pdf].

———. 2004a. "Financing Modalities toward the Millennium Development Goals: Progress Note." DC2004-003. Background paper for Development Committee (Joint Ministerial Committee of the Boards of Governors of the Bank and the Fund on the Real Resources to Developing Countries, "Item I of the Provision Agenda." Washington, DC. [http://siteresources.worldbank.org/DEVCOMMINT/Documentation/20191435/DC2004-0003(E)-FinMod.pdf]. May 2005.

———. 2004b. *Global Monitoring Report 2004: Policies and Actions for Achieving the Millennium Development Goals and Related Outcomes*. Washington, DC. [http://siteresources.worldbank.org/GLOBALMONITORINGEXT/Resources/0821358596.pdf].

———. 2004c. "Heavily Indebted Poor Countries (HIPC) Initiative: Status of Implementation." Washington, DC. [http://www.imf.org/external/NP/hipc/2004/082004.pdf]. May 2005.

———. 2005a. *Global Monitoring Report 2005: Millennium Development Goals: From Consensus to Momentum*. Washington, DC. [http://siteresources.worldbank.org/GLOBALMONITORINGEXT/Resources/complete.pdf]. May 2005.

———. 2005b. "Heavily Indebted Poor Countries (HIPCs) Initiative—Statistical Update." Washington, DC. [http://www.imf.org/external/np/hipc/2005/040405.pdf]. May 2005.

———. 2005c. "Moving Forward: Financing Modalities Toward the MDGs." DC2005-0008/Add. 1. Background paper for Development Committee (Joint Ministerial Committee of the Boards of Governors of the Bank and the Fund on the Real Resources to Developing Countries, "Item II of the Provision Agenda." Washington, DC. [http://siteresources.worldbank.org/DEVCOMMINT/Documentation/20449410/DC2005-0008(E)-FinMod%20Add1.pdf]. May 2005.

World Bank and Palestinian Central Bureau of Statistics. 2004. "Deep Palestinian Poverty in the Midst of Economic Crisis." Working Paper 30751. Washington, DC. [http://www-wds.worldbank.org/servlet/WDSContentServer/WDSP/IB/2004/11/24/000112742_20041124094109/Rendered/PDF/307510arabic.pdf]. May 2005.

World Bank and the Republic of Kenya. 2004. "Kenya Public Expenditure Review 2004: Report on the Structure and Management of Public Funding." Report 29421-KE. Africa Region, Country Department for Kenya, Washington, DC. [http://www-wds.worldbank.org/servlet/WDSContentServer/WDSP/IB/2005/03/17/000012009_20050317111633/Rendered/PDF/294210KE.pdf]. May 2005.

WTO (World Trade Organization). 2004a. "Background Statistical Information with Respect to Trade in Textiles and Clothing." WTO Document G/L/692. Geneva.

———. 2004b. "International Trade Statistics 2004." Geneva. [http://www.wto.org/english/res_e/statis_e/its2004_e/its2004_e.pdf]. May 2005.

———. 2004c. "Market Access Issues Related to Products of Export Interest Originating from Least Developed Countries: Note by the Secretariat." Washington, DC.

———. 2005. "Trade Topics: Agriculture Gateway." Geneva. [http://www.wto.org/english/tratop_e/agric_e/agric_e.htm]. June 2005.

Yamano, T., and T. S. Jayne. 2004. "Measuring the Impact of Working Age Adult Mortality on Small-Scale Farm Households in Kenya." *World Development* 32(1): 91–119.

Yunker, James A. 2004. "Could a Global Marshall Plan be Successful? An Investigation Using The WEEP Simulation Model." *World Development* 32(7): 1109–37. [http://www.sciencedirect.com/science?_ob=MImg&_imagekey=B6VC6-4CGM6SP-1-3P&_cdi=5946&_user=666074&_orig=na&_coverDate=07%2F31%2F2004&_sk=999679992&view=c&wchp=dGLbVtz-zSkWA&md5=10d919d5a9c240234cbb00895899fc80&ie=/sdarticle.pdf]. March 2005.

Yunus, Muhammad. 2004. "Grameen Bank, Microcredit and Millennium Development Goals." *Economic and Political Weekly* 39(36): 4077–80.

Human development indicators

Readers guide

Human development indicator tables

The human development indicator tables provide a global assessment of country achievements in different areas of human development. Many of the Millennium Development Goal indicators are incorporated in these tables (see *Index to indicators* and *Index to Millennium Development Goal indicators in the indicator tables*). Data for these indicators provide a statistical reference for assessing the progress in each country towards the Millennium Development Goals and their targets.

The main tables are organized thematically as described by the running titles at the top of each table. The tables include data for 175 UN member countries along with Hong Kong, China (SAR), and the Occupied Palestinian Territories—all those for which the human development index (HDI) can be calculated. Because of lack of data, 16 UN member countries are not included in the HDI this year. Basic human development indicators for these countries are presented in table 33.

In the tables countries and areas are ranked in descending order by their HDI value. To locate a country in these tables, refer to *Key to countries* on the back cover flap, which lists countries alphabetically with their HDI rank.

Most of the data in the tables are for 2003 and are those available to the Human Development Report Office as of 16 May 2005, unless otherwise specified.

Sources and definitions

The Human Development Report Office is primarily a user, not a producer, of statistics. It relies on international data agencies with the resources and expertise to collect and compile international data on specific statistical indicators. Sources for all data used in compiling the indicator tables

are given in short citations at the end of each table. These correspond to full references in *Statistical references*. When an agency provides data that it has collected from another source, both sources are credited in the table notes. But when an agency has built on the work of many other contributors, only that agency is given as the source. The source notes also show the original data components used in any calculations by the Human Development Report Office to ensure that all calculations can be easily replicated.

Indicators for which short, meaningful definitions can be given are included in *Definitions of statistical terms*. All other relevant information appears in the notes at the end of each table. For more detailed technical information about these indicators, please consult the relevant Web sites of the source agencies through the *Human Development Report* Web site at http://hdr.undp.org/statistics/understanding/resources.cfm.

Inconsistencies between national and international estimates

When compiling international data series, international data agencies often apply international standards and harmonization procedures to improve comparability across countries. When international data are based on national statistics, as they usually are, national data may need to be adjusted. When data for a country are missing, an international agency may produce an estimate if other relevant information can be used. And because of the difficulties in coordination between national and international data agencies, international data series may not incorporate the most recent national data. All these factors can lead to significant inconsistencies between national and international estimates (see *Note on statistics*).

This Report has often brought such inconsistencies to light. The Human Development Report Office advocates for improvements in international data and plays an active role in supporting efforts to enhance data quality. When data inconsistencies have arisen, we have helped to link national and international data authorities to address those inconsistencies. In many cases this has led to better statistics in the Report. The Human Development Report Office is working with national agencies and international bodies to improve data consistency through more systematic reporting and monitoring of data quality.

Comparability over time

Because of periodic revisions of data or changes in methodology by international agencies, statistics presented in different editions of the Report may not be comparable. For this reason the Human Development Report Office strongly advises against constructing trend analyses based on data from different editions.

HDI values and ranks similarly are not comparable across editions of the Report. For trend analysis based on consistent data and methodology, refer to table 2 (Human development index trends). The HDI values and ranks recalculated for 2003 based on data comparable to this year's Report and country coverage are available at the Human Development Report Office Web site (http://hdr.undp.org/statistics).

Country classifications

Countries are classified in four ways: by human development level, by income, by major world aggregates and by region (see *Classification of countries*). These designations do not necessarily express a judgement about the development stage of a particular country or area. The term *country* as used in the text and tables refers, as appropriate, to territories or areas.

Human development classifications. All countries included in the HDI are classified into three clusters by achievement in human development: high human development (with an HDI of 0.800 or above), medium human development (HDI of 0.500–0.799) and low human development (HDI of less than 0.500).

Income classifications. All countries are grouped by income using World Bank classifications: high income (gross national income per capita of $9,386 or more in 2003), middle income ($766–$9,385) and low income ($765 or less).

Major world classifications. The three global groups are *developing countries, Central and Eastern Europe and the CIS* and *OECD.* These groups are not mutually exclusive. (Replacing the OECD group with the high-income OECD group and excluding the Republic of Korea would produce mutually exclusive groups.) Unless otherwise specified, the classification *world* represents the universe of 193 countries and areas covered—191 UN member countries plus Hong Kong, China (SAR), and the Occupied Palestinian Territories.

Regional classifications. Developing countries are further classified into the following regions: Arab States, East Asia and the Pacific, Latin America and the Caribbean (including Mexico), South Asia, Southern Europe and Sub-Saharan Africa. These regional classifications are consistent with the Regional Bureaux of the United Nations Development Programme. An additional classification is *least developed countries,* as defined by the United Nations (UN-OHRLLS 2005).

Aggregates and growth rates

Aggregates. Aggregates for the classifications described above are presented at the end of tables where it is analytically meaningful to do so and data are sufficient. Aggregates that are the total for the classification (such as for population) are indicated by a T. Because of rounding, world totals may not always equal the sum of the totals for subgroups. All other aggregates are weighted averages.

In general, an aggregate is shown for a classification only when data are available for half the countries and represent at least two-thirds of the available weight in that classification. The Human Development Report Office does not fill in missing data for the purpose of aggregation. Therefore, unless otherwise specified, aggregates for each classification represent only the countries for which data are available, refer to the year or period specified and refer only to data from the primary sources listed. Aggregates are not shown where appropriate weighting procedures were unavailable.

Aggregates for indices, growth rates and indicators covering more than one point in time are based only on countries for which data exist for all necessary points in time. When no aggregate is shown for one or more regions, aggregates are not always shown for the *world* classification, which refers only to the universe of 193 countries and areas.

Aggregates in this Report will not always conform to those in other publications because of differences in country classifications and methodology. Where indicated, aggregates are calculated by the statistical agency providing the data for the indicator.

Growth rates. Multiyear growth rates are expressed as average annual rates of change. In calculations of rates by the Human Development Report Office only the beginning and end points are used. Year-to-year growth rates are expressed as annual percentage changes.

Country notes
Unless otherwise indicated, data for China do not include Hong Kong, China (SAR), Macau, China (SAR), or Taiwan Province of China.

In most cases data for Eritrea before 1992 are included in the data for Ethiopia. Data for Germany refer to the unified Germany, unless otherwise noted. Data for Indonesia include Timor-Leste through 1999, unless otherwise noted. Data for Jordan refer to the East Bank only. Economic data for Tanzania cover the mainland only. Data for Sudan are often based on information collected from the northern part of the country. And data for the Republic of Yemen refer to that country from 1990 onward, while data for earlier years refer to aggregated data for the former People's Democratic Republic of Yemen and the former Yemen Arab Republic.

Symbols
In the absence of the words *annual, annual rate* or *growth rate,* a dash between two years, such as in 1995–2000, indicates that the data were collected during one of the years shown. A slash between two years, such as in 1998/2001, indicates an average for the years shown unless otherwise specified. The following symbols are used:

..   Data not available.
(.)   Less than half the unit shown.
<   Less than.
—   Not applicable.
T   Total.

Note to table 1: about this year's human development index

The human development index (HDI) is a composite index that measures the average achievements in a country in three basic dimensions of human development: a long and healthy life, as measured by life expectancy at birth; knowledge, as measured by the adult literacy rate and the combined gross enrolment ratio for primary, secondary and tertiary schools; and a decent standard of living, as measured by GDP per capita in purchasing power parity (PPP) US dollars. The index is constructed from indicators that are currently available globally using a methodology that is simple and transparent (see *Technical note 1*).

While the concept of human development is much broader than any single composite index can measure, the HDI offers a powerful alternative to income as a summary measure of human well-being. It provides a useful entry point into the rich information contained in the subsequent indicator tables on different aspects of human development.

Data availability determines HDI country coverage

The HDI in this Report refers to 2003. It covers 175 UN member countries, along with Hong Kong, China (SAR), and the Occupied Palestinian Territories. Because of a lack of comparable data, 16 UN member countries cannot not be included in the HDI this year. Basic human development indicators for these countries are presented in table 33.

To enable cross-country comparisons, the HDI is, to the extent possible, calculated based on data from leading international data agencies available at the time the Report was prepared (see *Primary international data sources* below). But for a number of countries data are missing from these agencies for one or more of the four HDI components.

In response to the desire of countries to be included in the HDI table, and striving to include as many UN member countries as possible, the Human Development Report Office has made special efforts to obtain estimates from other international, regional or national sources when data are lacking from the primary international data agencies for one or two of the HDI components for a country. In a very few cases the Human Development Report Office has produced an estimate. These estimates from sources other than the primary international agencies are clearly documented in the notes to table 1. They are of varying quality and reliability and are not presented in other indicator tables showing similar data.

Primary international data sources

Life expectancy at birth. The life expectancy at birth estimates are from the *2004 Revision* of *World Population Prospects* (UN 2005), the official source of UN population estimates and projections. They are prepared biannually by the Population Division of the United Nations Department of Economic and Social Affairs on the basis of data from national vital registration systems, population censuses and surveys.

In the *2004 Revision* the United Nations Population Division incorporated national data available through the end of 2004. For assessing the impact of HIV/AIDS, the latest HIV prevalence estimates prepared by the Joint United Nations Programme on HIV/AIDS are combined with a series of assumptions about the demographic trends and mortality of both the infected and non-infected people in each of the 60 countries for which the impact of the disease is explicitly modelled.

The volatile dynamics of major infectious diseases like HIV/AIDS pose serious challenges for population estimates and projections. The availability of new empirical evidence on the HIV/AIDS epidemic and demographic trends often requires adjustment to earlier estimates. For example, while the most recent HIV prevalence estimate is similar to earlier estimates for most countries, it is notably lower for Cameroon, Côte d'Ivoire, Ethiopia, Kenya, Rwanda, Zambia and Zimbabwe and higher for Equatorial Guinea and Senegal. These changes are the result mainly of reassessments of input data and estimation methods rather than a reflection of real changes. Similarly, a significant decrease in life expectancy estimates for some Sub-Saharan African countries (such as Botswana, Nigeria and São Tomé and Principe) and many transition economies (such as Azerbaijan, Kazakhstan and Russian Federation) are based on more recent and accurate data that imply higher levels of mortality than previously estimated.

The life expectancy estimates published by the United Nations Population Division are usually five-year averages. This year, for the first time, the United Nations Population Division produced annual life expectancy estimates and projections through interpolation based on these five-year averages. The life expectancy estimates for 2003 shown in table 1 and those underlying table 2 are from these interpolated data (UN 2005c). For details on the *2004 Revision* of *World Population Prospects* (UN 2005h), see www.un.org/esa/population/unpop.htm.

Adult literacy rate. Data on the adult literacy rate are usually collected during national population censuses, generally conducted every 5 or 10 years, or from household surveys.

This Report uses data on adult literacy rates from the United Nations Educational, Scientific and Cultural Organization (UNESCO) Institute for Statistics (UIS) April 2005 Assessment (UNESCO Institute for Statistics 2005a), which combines direct national estimates with UIS estimates. The national estimates, made available through targeted efforts by UIS to collect recent literacy data from countries, are obtained from national censuses or surveys between 2000 and 2004 (with the exception of a few cases referring to 1995–99).

The UIS estimates, produced in July 2002, were based mostly on national data collected before 1995. For details on these literacy estimates, see www.uis.unesco.org.

Many high-income countries, having attained high levels of literacy, no longer collect literacy statistics in national population censuses or household surveys and thus are not included in the UNESCO data. In calculating the HDI, a literacy rate of 99.0% is applied for these countries.

In collecting literacy data, many countries estimate the number of literate people based on self-reported data. Some use educational attainment data as a proxy, but measures of school attendance or grade completion may differ. Because definitions and data collection methods vary across countries, literacy estimates should be used with caution.

The UIS, in collaboration with other partner agencies, is actively pursuing an alternative methodology for measuring literacy, the Literacy Assessment and Monitoring Programme (LAMP). LAMP seeks to go beyond the current simple categories of literate and illiterate by providing information on a continuum of literacy skills.

Combined gross enrolment ratio for primary, secondary and tertiary schools. Gross enrolment ratios are produced by the UIS based on enrolment data collected from national governments (usually from administrative sources) and population data from the United Nations Population Division's *2002 Revision* of *World Population Prospects* (UN 2003). The ratios are calculated by dividing the number of students enrolled in all levels of schooling by the total population in the official age group corresponding to these levels. The tertiary age group is set to five cohorts immediately following on the end of upper secondary school in all countries.

Countries are asked to report numbers of students enrolled at the beginning of the academic year in each level of education as defined by the International Standard Classification of Education (ISCED). A revised version of ISCED was introduced in 1997 that led to some changes in the classifications of national programmes of education. These changes, however, have less impact on the estimation of combined gross enrolment ratios for primary, secondary and tertiary schools. For details on enrolment data and the ISCED, see www.uis. unesco.org.

Though intended as a proxy for educational attainment, combined gross enrolment ratios do not reflect the quality of education outcomes. Even when used to capture access to education opportunities, combined gross enrolment ratios can hide important differences among countries because of differences in the age range corresponding to a level of education and in the duration of education programmes. Grade repetition and dropout rates can also distort the data. Measures such as the mean years of schooling of a population or school life expectancy could more adequately capture education attainment and should ideally supplant the gross enrolment ratio in the HDI. However, such data are not yet regularly available for a sufficient number of countries.

As currently defined, the combined gross enrolment ratio does not take into account students enrolled in other countries. Current data for many smaller countries where many people pursue tertiary education abroad could significantly underrepresent access to education or the educational attainment of a population and thus lead to a lower HDI value.

GDP per capita (PPP US$). In comparing standards of living across countries, economic statistics must be converted into PPP terms to eliminate differences in national price levels. The GDP per capita (PPP US$) data for the HDI are provided for 164 countries by the World Bank based on price data from the latest International Comparison Program (ICP) surveys and GDP in local currency from national accounts data. The last round of ICP surveys covered 118 countries, for which PPPs have been estimated directly by extrapolating from the latest benchmark results. For countries not included in the benchmark surveys, estimates are derived through econometric regression. For countries not covered by the World Bank, PPP estimates provided by the Penn World Tables of

the University of Pennsylvania (Aten, Heston and Summers 2001, 2002) are used.

In a limited number of cases where reliable PPP estimates are not available from the two international sources, the Human Development Report Office has worked with regional and national agencies to obtain a PPP estimate for a country. For example, in the case of Cuba, a technical team of national and international experts has been formed to explore different methodologies for obtaining a better PPP estimate. The results of this effort will be reflected in future Reports.

Though much progress has been made in recent decades, the current PPP data set suffers from several deficiencies, including lack of universal coverage, of timeliness of the data and of uniformity in the quality of results from different regions and countries. Filling gaps in country coverage with econometric regression requires strong assumptions, while extrapolation over time implies that the results become weaker as the distance lengthens between the reference survey year and the current year.

The importance of PPPs in economic analysis underlines the need for improvement in PPP data. A new Millennium Round of the ICP has been established and promises much improved PPP data for economic policy analysis, including international poverty assessment. For details on the ICP and the PPP methodology, see the ICP Web site at www.worldbank.org/data/icp.

Comparisons over time and across editions of the Report

The HDI is an important tool for monitoring long-term trends in human development. To facilitate trend analyses across countries, the HDI is calculated at five-year intervals for the period 1975–2003. These estimates, presented in table 2, are based on a consistent methodology and on comparable trend data available when the Report is prepared.

As international data agencies continually improve their data series, including updating historical data periodically, the year-to-year changes in the HDI values and rankings across editions of the *Human Development Report* often reflect revisions to data—both specific to a country and relative to other countries—rather than real changes in a country. In addition, occasional changes in country coverage could also affect the HDI ranking of a country, even when consistent methodology is used to calculate the HDI. As a result, a country's HDI rank could drop considerably between two consecutive Reports, but when comparable, revised data are used to reconstruct the HDI for recent years, the HDI rank and value may actually show an improvement.

For these reasons HDI trend analyses should not be based on data from different editions of the Report. Table 2 provides up-to-date HDI trend data based on consistent data and methodology. For HDI values and ranks recalculated for 2002 (the reference year of the HDI in *Human Development Report 2004*) based on data and country coverage comparable to this year's Report, please visit http://hdr.undp.org/statistics.

HDI for high human development countries

The HDI in this Report is constructed to compare country achievements across all levels of human development. The indicators currently used in the index yield very small differences among the top HDI countries, and thus the top of the HDI ranking often reflects only the very small differences in these underlying indicators. For these high-income countries, an alternative index—the human poverty index (shown in table 4)—can better reflect the extent of human deprivation that still exist among the populations and help direct the focus of public policies.

For further discussions on the use and limitations of the HDI and its component indicators, see http://hdr.undp.org/statistics.

Human development index

HDI rank[a]		Human development index (HDI) value 2003	Life expectancy at birth (years) 2003	Adult literacy rate (% ages 15 and above) 2003[b]	Combined gross enrolment ratio for primary, secondary and tertiary schools (%) 2002/03[c]	GDP per capita (PPP US$) 2003	Life expectancy index	Education index	GDP index	GDP per capita (PPP US$) rank minus HDI rank[d]
HIGH HUMAN DEVELOPMENT										
1	Norway	0.963	79.4	.. [e]	101 [f]	37,670	0.91	0.99	0.99	2
2	Iceland	0.956	80.7	.. [e]	96	31,243	0.93	0.98	0.96	4
3	Australia	0.955	80.3	.. [e]	116 [f]	29,632	0.92	0.99	0.95	7
4	Luxembourg	0.949	78.5	.. [e]	88 [g]	62,298 [h]	0.89	0.95	1.00	−3
5	Canada	0.949	80.0	.. [e]	94 [i, j]	30,677	0.92	0.97	0.96	2
6	Sweden	0.949	80.2	.. [e]	114 [f]	26,750	0.92	0.99	0.93	14
7	Switzerland	0.947	80.5	.. [e]	90	30,552	0.93	0.96	0.96	1
8	Ireland	0.946	77.7	.. [e]	93	37,738	0.88	0.97	0.99	−6
9	Belgium	0.945	78.9	.. [e]	114 [f]	28,335	0.90	0.99	0.94	3
10	United States	0.944	77.4	.. [e]	93	37,562	0.87	0.97	0.99	−6
11	Japan	0.943	82.0	.. [e]	84	27,967	0.95	0.94	0.94	2
12	Netherlands	0.943	78.4	.. [e]	99	29,371	0.89	0.99	0.95	−1
13	Finland	0.941	78.5	.. [e]	108 [f]	27,619	0.89	0.99	0.94	3
14	Denmark	0.941	77.2	.. [e]	102 [f]	31,465	0.87	0.99	0.96	−9
15	United Kingdom	0.939	78.4	.. [e]	123 [f, i]	27,147	0.89	0.99	0.94	3
16	France	0.938	79.5	.. [e]	92	27,677	0.91	0.97	0.94	−1
17	Austria	0.936	79.0	.. [e]	89	30,094	0.90	0.96	0.95	−8
18	Italy	0.934	80.1	98.5 [e, k, l]	87	27,119	0.92	0.95	0.94	1
19	New Zealand	0.933	79.1	.. [e]	106 [f]	22,582	0.90	0.99	0.90	3
20	Germany	0.930	78.7	.. [e]	89	27,756	0.90	0.96	0.94	−6
21	Spain	0.928	79.5	97.7 [e, k, l]	94	22,391	0.91	0.97	0.90	3
22	Hong Kong, China (SAR)	0.916	81.6	93.5 [k, l]	74	27,179	0.94	0.87	0.94	−5
23	Israel	0.915	79.7	96.9	91	20,033	0.91	0.95	0.88	2
24	Greece	0.912	78.3	91.0 [e]	92	19,954	0.89	0.97	0.88	2
25	Singapore	0.907	78.7	92.5	87 [m]	24,481	0.89	0.91	0.92	−4
26	Slovenia	0.904	76.4	99.7 [e, k]	95	19,150	0.86	0.98	0.88	4
27	Portugal	0.904	77.2	92.5 [e, k, l]	94	18,126	0.87	0.97	0.87	5
28	Korea, Rep. of	0.901	77.0	97.9 [e, k, l]	93	17,971	0.87	0.97	0.87	6
29	Cyprus	0.891	78.6	96.8	78	18,776 [j]	0.89	0.91	0.87	2
30	Barbados	0.878	75.0	99.7 [e, k]	89 [j]	15,720	0.83	0.96	0.84	9
31	Czech Republic	0.874	75.6	.. [e]	80	16,357	0.84	0.93	0.85	7
32	Malta	0.867	78.4	87.9 [n]	79	17,633	0.89	0.85	0.86	3
33	Brunei Darussalam	0.866	76.4	92.7	74	19,210 [j, o]	0.86	0.86	0.88	−4
34	Argentina	0.863	74.5	97.2	95	12,106	0.82	0.96	0.80	12
35	Hungary	0.862	72.7	99.3	89	14,584	0.80	0.96	0.83	5
36	Poland	0.858	74.3	99.7 [e, k, l]	90	11,379	0.82	0.96	0.79	12
37	Chile	0.854	77.9	95.7	81	10,274	0.88	0.91	0.77	17
38	Estonia	0.853	71.3	99.8	92	13,539	0.77	0.97	0.82	4
39	Lithuania	0.852	72.3	99.6	94	11,702	0.79	0.97	0.79	8
40	Qatar	0.849	72.8	89.2 [n]	82	19,844 [j, p]	0.80	0.87	0.88	−13
41	United Arab Emirates	0.849	78.0	77.3 [k]	74 [i]	22,420 [j, q]	0.88	0.76	0.90	−18
42	Slovakia	0.849	74.0	99.6	75	13,494	0.82	0.91	0.82	1
43	Bahrain	0.846	74.3	87.7	81	17,479 [j]	0.82	0.86	0.86	−7
44	Kuwait	0.844	76.9	82.9 [k]	74 [i]	18,047 [q]	0.87	0.80	0.87	−11
45	Croatia	0.841	75.0	98.1	75	11,080	0.83	0.90	0.79	5
46	Uruguay	0.840	75.4	97.7 [k]	88 [i]	8,280	0.84	0.94	0.74	16
47	Costa Rica	0.838	78.2	95.8 [k]	68	9,606 [q]	0.89	0.87	0.76	10
48	Latvia	0.836	71.6	99.7	90	10,270	0.78	0.96	0.77	7
49	Saint Kitts and Nevis	0.834	70.0 [j, m, r]	97.8 [j, m, r]	89 [i]	12,404	0.75	0.95	0.80	−4
50	Bahamas	0.832	69.7	95.5 [k, l]	77	17,159 [j]	0.75	0.89	0.86	−13
51	Seychelles	0.821	72.7 [j, m]	91.9	85	10,232 [j, p]	0.80	0.89	0.77	5
52	Cuba	0.817	77.3	96.9 [k]	80	.. [s]	0.87	0.91	0.67	40
53	Mexico	0.814	75.1	90.3	75	9,168	0.83	0.85	0.75	7

Human development indicators

TABLE 1

Human development index

HDI rank [a]		Human development index (HDI) value 2003	Life expectancy at birth (years) 2003	Adult literacy rate (% ages 15 and above) 2003 [b]	Combined gross enrolment ratio for primary, secondary and tertiary schools (%) 2002/03 [c]	GDP per capita (PPP US$) 2003	Life expectancy index	Education index	GDP index	GDP per capita (PPP US$) rank minus HDI rank [d]
54	Tonga	0.810	72.2	98.9 [n]	83 [i]	6,992 [q]	0.79	0.93	0.71	17
55	Bulgaria	0.808	72.2	98.2	78	7,731	0.79	0.91	0.73	10
56	Panama	0.804	74.8	91.9	79	6,854	0.83	0.88	0.71	17
57	Trinidad and Tobago	0.801	69.9	98.5 [k]	66 [i]	10,766	0.75	0.88	0.78	−6
MEDIUM HUMAN DEVELOPMENT										
58	Libyan Arab Jamahiriya	0.799	73.6	81.7 [k]	96 [i]	.. [j, t]	0.81	0.86	0.72	9
59	Macedonia, TFYR	0.797	73.8	96.1	70	6,794	0.81	0.87	0.70	16
60	Antigua and Barbuda	0.797	73.9 [j, m, r]	85.8 [j, u]	69 [j, m, r]	10,294	0.82	0.80	0.77	−7
61	Malaysia	0.796	73.2	88.7	71	9,512	0.80	0.83	0.76	−3
62	Russian Federation	0.795	65.3	99.4	90	9,230	0.67	0.96	0.76	−3
63	Brazil	0.792	70.5	88.4	91	7,790	0.76	0.89	0.73	1
64	Romania	0.792	71.3	97.3	72	7,277	0.77	0.89	0.72	4
65	Mauritius	0.791	72.2	84.3	71 [i]	11,287	0.79	0.80	0.79	−16
66	Grenada	0.787	65.3 [j, u]	96.0 [j, u]	96	7,959	0.67	0.96	0.73	−3
67	Belarus	0.786	68.1	99.6 [e, n]	88	6,052	0.72	0.95	0.68	17
68	Bosnia and Herzegovina	0.786	74.2	94.6	67 [v]	5,967	0.82	0.86	0.68	17
69	Colombia	0.785	72.4	94.2	71	6,702 [q]	0.79	0.86	0.70	8
70	Dominica	0.783	75.6 [j, u]	88.0 [j, u]	75	5,448	0.84	0.84	0.67	21
71	Oman	0.781	74.1	74.4 [k]	63 [i]	13,584 [j]	0.82	0.71	0.82	−30
72	Albania	0.780	73.8	98.7	69	4,584	0.81	0.89	0.64	30
73	Thailand	0.778	70.0	92.6	73 [i]	7,595	0.75	0.86	0.72	−7
74	Samoa (Western)	0.776	70.2	98.7 [k]	71 [i]	5,854 [q]	0.75	0.89	0.68	14
75	Venezuela	0.772	72.9	93.0	75 [i]	4,919	0.80	0.87	0.65	22
76	Saint Lucia	0.772	72.4	90.1	75 [i]	5,709	0.79	0.85	0.68	13
77	Saudi Arabia	0.772	71.8	79.4	57 [i]	13,226 [q]	0.78	0.72	0.82	−33
78	Ukraine	0.766	66.1	99.4	86	5,491	0.69	0.95	0.67	12
79	Peru	0.762	70.0	87.7	87 [i]	5,260	0.75	0.88	0.66	14
80	Kazakhstan	0.761	63.2	99.5 [e, n]	85	6,671	0.64	0.94	0.70	−2
81	Lebanon	0.759	72.0	86.5 [k, l]	79 [i]	5,074	0.78	0.84	0.66	14
82	Ecuador	0.759	74.3	91.0	.. [w]	3,641	0.82	0.86	0.60	30
83	Armenia	0.759	71.5	99.4	72	3,671	0.77	0.90	0.60	28
84	Philippines	0.758	70.4	92.6	82	4,321	0.76	0.89	0.63	19
85	China	0.755	71.6	90.9	69	5,003 [x]	0.78	0.84	0.65	11
86	Suriname	0.755	69.1	88.0	73 [i]	.. [y]	0.74	0.83	0.70	−7
87	Saint Vincent and the Grenadines	0.755	71.1	88.1 [j, u]	67	6,123	0.77	0.81	0.69	−5
88	Paraguay	0.755	71.0	91.6	73 [i]	4,684 [q]	0.77	0.86	0.64	13
89	Tunisia	0.753	73.3	74.3	74	7,161	0.80	0.74	0.71	−20
90	Jordan	0.753	71.3	89.9	78	4,320	0.77	0.86	0.63	14
91	Belize	0.753	71.9	76.9	77 [i]	6,950	0.78	0.77	0.71	−19
92	Fiji	0.752	67.8	92.9 [n]	73 [k, i]	5,880	0.71	0.86	0.68	−5
93	Sri Lanka	0.751	74.0	90.4 [z]	69 [i]	3,778	0.82	0.83	0.61	17
94	Turkey	0.750	68.7	88.3	68 [i]	6,772	0.73	0.82	0.70	−18
95	Dominican Republic	0.749	67.2	87.7	76 [i]	6,823 [q]	0.70	0.84	0.70	−21
96	Maldives	0.745	66.6	97.2 [k]	75 [i]	.. [j, y]	0.69	0.90	0.65	2
97	Turkmenistan	0.738	62.4	98.8 [n]	.. [w]	5,938	0.62	0.91	0.68	−11
98	Jamaica	0.738	70.8	87.6 [k]	74 [i]	4,104	0.76	0.83	0.62	9
99	Iran, Islamic Rep. of	0.736	70.4	77.0	69 [i]	6,995	0.76	0.74	0.71	−29
100	Georgia	0.732	70.5	100.0 [e, z, aa]	71	2,588	0.76	0.90	0.54	21
101	Azerbaijan	0.729	66.9	98.8 [n]	69	3,617	0.70	0.89	0.60	12
102	Occupied Palestinian Territories	0.729	72.5	91.9	80 [i]	.. [ab]	0.79	0.88	0.52	26
103	Algeria	0.722	71.1	69.8	74 [i]	6,107 [q]	0.77	0.71	0.69	−20
104	El Salvador	0.722	70.9	79.7 [k]	68	4,781 [q]	0.76	0.76	0.65	−5
105	Cape Verde	0.721	70.4	75.7 [k]	73	5,214 [q]	0.76	0.75	0.66	−11
106	Syrian Arab Republic	0.721	73.3	82.9	62 [i]	3,576	0.81	0.76	0.60	8

Human development indicators

TABLE 1

HDI rank [a]		Human development index (HDI) value 2003	Life expectancy at birth (years) 2003	Adult literacy rate (% ages 15 and above) 2003 [b]	Combined gross enrolment ratio for primary, secondary and tertiary schools (%) 2002/03 [c]	GDP per capita (PPP US$) 2003	Life expectancy index	Education index	GDP index	GDP per capita (PPP US$) rank minus HDI rank [d]
107	Guyana	0.720	63.1	96.5 [j, u]	77 [i]	4,230 [q]	0.63	0.90	0.63	−2
108	Viet Nam	0.704	70.5	90.3 [n]	64 [i]	2,490	0.76	0.82	0.54	16
109	Kyrgyzstan	0.702	66.8	98.7 [n]	82	1,751	0.70	0.93	0.48	33
110	Indonesia	0.697	66.8	87.9 [k]	66	3,361	0.70	0.81	0.59	5
111	Uzbekistan	0.694	66.5	99.3 [e, k]	76	1,744	0.69	0.91	0.48	32
112	Nicaragua	0.690	69.7	76.7	69	3,262 [q]	0.75	0.74	0.58	4
113	Bolivia	0.687	64.1	86.5	87 [i]	2,587	0.65	0.87	0.54	9
114	Mongolia	0.679	64.0	97.8	74	1,850	0.65	0.90	0.49	23
115	Moldova, Rep. of	0.671	67.7	96.2	62	1,510	0.71	0.85	0.45	33
116	Honduras	0.667	67.8	80.0	62 [i]	2,665 [q]	0.71	0.74	0.55	3
117	Guatemala	0.663	67.3	69.1	61	4,148 [q]	0.70	0.66	0.62	−11
118	Vanuatu	0.659	68.6	74.0 [n]	58	2,944 [q]	0.73	0.69	0.56	−1
119	Egypt	0.659	69.8	55.6 [n]	74 [i]	3,950	0.75	0.62	0.61	−10
120	South Africa	0.658	48.4	82.4 [n]	78 [i]	10,346 [q]	0.39	0.81	0.77	−68
121	Equatorial Guinea	0.655	43.3	84.2	65 [i]	19,780 [j, q]	0.30	0.78	0.88	−93
122	Tajikistan	0.652	63.6	99.5	76	1,106	0.64	0.91	0.40	36
123	Gabon	0.635	54.5	71.0 [aa]	74 [i, j]	6,397	0.49	0.72	0.69	−43
124	Morocco	0.631	69.7	50.7 [k]	58	4,004	0.75	0.53	0.62	−16
125	Namibia	0.627	48.3	85.0	71 [i]	6,180 [q]	0.39	0.80	0.69	−44
126	São Tomé and Principe	0.604	63.0	83.1 [j, m]	62 [i, j]	1,231 [j, p]	0.63	0.76	0.42	27
127	India	0.602	63.3	61.0 [z]	60	2,892 [q]	0.64	0.61	0.56	−9
128	Solomon Islands	0.594	62.3	76.6 [j, m]	52	1,753 [q]	0.62	0.68	0.48	13
129	Myanmar	0.578	60.2	89.7	48 [i]	.. [j, t]	0.59	0.76	0.39	34
130	Cambodia	0.571	56.2	73.6	59	2,078 [q]	0.52	0.69	0.51	3
131	Botswana	0.565	36.3	78.9 [k]	70 [i]	8,714	0.19	0.76	0.75	−70
132	Comoros	0.547	63.2	56.2 [k]	47 [i]	1,714 [q]	0.64	0.53	0.47	13
133	Lao People's Dem. Rep.	0.545	54.7	68.7	61	1,759	0.49	0.66	0.48	7
134	Bhutan	0.536	62.9	47.0 [aa]	.. [w]	1,969 [j, p]	0.63	0.48	0.50	0
135	Pakistan	0.527	63.0	48.7	35	2,097	0.63	0.44	0.51	−5
136	Nepal	0.526	61.6	48.6	61	1,420	0.61	0.53	0.44	15
137	Papua New Guinea	0.523	55.3	57.3	41 [i]	2,619 [q]	0.50	0.52	0.55	−17
138	Ghana	0.520	56.8	54.1	46 [i]	2,238 [q]	0.53	0.51	0.52	−11
139	Bangladesh	0.520	62.8	41.1 [k]	53	1,770	0.63	0.45	0.48	−1
140	Timor-Leste	0.513	55.5	58.6 [m]	75 [j, m]	.. [ac]	0.51	0.64	0.39	22
141	Sudan	0.512	56.4	59.0 [z]	38 [i]	1,910 [q]	0.52	0.52	0.49	−6
142	Congo	0.512	52.0	82.8 [k]	47	965	0.45	0.71	0.38	23
143	Togo	0.512	54.3	53.0	66	1,696 [q]	0.49	0.57	0.47	3
144	Uganda	0.508	47.3	68.9 [k]	74 [i]	1,457 [q]	0.37	0.71	0.45	6
145	Zimbabwe	0.505	36.9	90.0 [k]	55 [i]	2,443 [j]	0.20	0.78	0.53	−20
LOW HUMAN DEVELOPMENT										
146	Madagascar	0.499	55.4	70.6	51	809	0.51	0.64	0.35	24
147	Swaziland	0.498	32.5	79.2	60 [i]	4,726	0.12	0.73	0.64	−47
148	Cameroon	0.497	45.8	67.9	55 [i]	2,118	0.35	0.64	0.51	−19
149	Lesotho	0.497	36.3	81.4	66 [i]	2,561 [q]	0.19	0.76	0.54	−26
150	Djibouti	0.495	52.8	65.5 [k, l]	24 [i]	2,086 [q]	0.46	0.52	0.51	−18
151	Yemen	0.489	60.6	49.0 [k]	55 [i]	889	0.59	0.51	0.36	15
152	Mauritania	0.477	52.7	51.2	45 [i]	1,766 [q]	0.46	0.49	0.48	−13
153	Haiti	0.475	51.6	51.9 [k]	.. [w]	1,742 [q]	0.44	0.50	0.48	−9
154	Kenya	0.474	47.2	73.6	52 [i]	1,037	0.37	0.66	0.39	7
155	Gambia	0.470	55.7	37.8 [k, l]	48 [i]	1,859 [q]	0.51	0.41	0.49	−19
156	Guinea	0.466	53.7	41.0 [aa]	41 [i]	2,097	0.48	0.41	0.51	−26
157	Senegal	0.458	55.7	39.3	40 [i]	1,648	0.51	0.39	0.47	−10
158	Nigeria	0.453	43.4	66.8 [k]	64 [i]	1,050	0.31	0.66	0.39	2
159	Rwanda	0.450	43.9	64.0	55	1,268 [q]	0.31	0.61	0.42	−7

TABLE 1

Human development index

HDI rank [a]	Human development index (HDI) value 2003	Life expectancy at birth (years) 2003	Adult literacy rate (% ages 15 and above) 2003 [b]	Combined gross enrolment ratio for primary, secondary and tertiary schools (%) 2002/03 [c]	GDP per capita (PPP US$) 2003	Life expectancy index	Education index	GDP index	GDP per capita (PPP US$) rank minus HDI rank [d]
160 Angola	0.445	40.8	66.8	30 [i,j]	2,344 [q]	0.26	0.54	0.53	−34
161 Eritrea	0.444	53.8	56.7 [k,l]	35 [i]	849 [q]	0.48	0.49	0.36	7
162 Benin	0.431	54.0	33.6	55 [i]	1,115	0.48	0.41	0.40	−5
163 Côte d'Ivoire	0.420	45.9	48.1	42 [i,j]	1,476	0.35	0.46	0.45	−14
164 Tanzania, U. Rep. of	0.418	46.0	69.4	41 [i]	621	0.35	0.60	0.30	11
165 Malawi	0.404	39.7	64.1 [n]	72 [i]	605	0.24	0.67	0.30	11
166 Zambia	0.394	37.5	67.9 [n]	48 [i]	877	0.21	0.61	0.36	1
167 Congo, Dem. Rep. of the	0.385	43.1	65.3	28 [i,j]	697	0.30	0.53	0.32	6
168 Mozambique	0.379	41.9	46.5 [k]	43 [i]	1,117 [q]	0.28	0.45	0.40	−12
169 Burundi	0.378	43.6	58.9	35 [i]	648 [q]	0.31	0.51	0.31	5
170 Ethiopia	0.367	47.6	41.5 [k]	36 [i]	711 [q]	0.38	0.40	0.33	1
171 Central African Republic	0.355	39.3	48.6	31	1,089 [q]	0.24	0.43	0.40	−12
172 Guinea-Bissau	0.348	44.7	39.6 [k,l]	37 [i,j]	711 [q]	0.33	0.39	0.33	−1
173 Chad	0.341	43.6	25.5	38 [i]	1,210 [q]	0.31	0.30	0.42	−19
174 Mali	0.333	47.9	19.0 [n]	32 [i]	994	0.38	0.23	0.38	−10
175 Burkina Faso	0.317	47.5	12.8 [n]	24 [i]	1,174 [q]	0.38	0.16	0.41	−20
176 Sierra Leone	0.298	40.8	29.6	45 [i]	548	0.26	0.35	0.28	1
177 Niger	0.281	44.4	14.4	21 [i]	835 [q]	0.32	0.17	0.35	−8
Developing countries	0.694	65.0	76.6	63	4,359	0.67	0.72	0.70	..
Least developed countries	0.518	52.2	54.2	45	1,328	0.45	0.50	0.60	..
Arab States	0.679	67.0	64.1	62	5,685	0.70	0.61	0.72	..
East Asia and the Pacific	0.768	70.5	90.4	69	5,100	0.76	0.83	0.71	..
Latin America and the Caribbean	0.797	71.9	89.6	81	7,404	0.78	0.87	0.74	..
South Asia	0.628	63.4	58.9	56	2,897	0.64	0.58	0.67	..
Sub-Saharan Africa	0.515	46.1	61.3	50	1,856	0.35	0.56	0.63	..
Central and Eastern Europe and the CIS	0.802	68.1	99.2	83	7,939	0.72	0.94	0.75	..
OECD	0.892	77.7	..	89	25,915	0.88	0.95	0.85	..
High-income OECD	0.911	78.9	..	95	30,181	0.90	0.98	0.86	..
High human development	0.895	78.0	..	91	25,665	0.88	0.96	0.85	..
Medium human development	0.718	67.2	79.4	66	4,474	0.70	0.75	0.70	..
Low human development	0.486	46.0	57.5	46	1,046	0.35	0.53	0.58	..
High income	0.910	78.8	..	94	29,898	0.90	0.97	0.86	..
Middle income	0.774	70.3	89.6	73	6,104	0.75	0.84	0.73	..
Low income	0.593	58.4	60.8	54	2,168	0.56	0.58	0.64	..
World	0.741	67.1	..	67	8,229	0.70	0.77	0.75	..

NOTES

Aggregates in column 7 are based on aggregates of gross enrolment data calculated by the United Nations Educational, Scientific and Cultural Organization (UNESCO) Institute for Statistics and literacy data as used to calculate the HDI.

a The HDI rank is detemined using HDI values to the fifth decimal point.

b Data refer to national literacy estimates from censuses or surveys conducted between 2000 and 2004, unless otherwise noted. Due to differences in methodology and timeliness of underlying data, comparisons across countries and over time should be made with caution. For more details, see www.uis.unesco.org/ev.php?ID=4930_201&ID2=DO_TOPIC.

c Data refer to the school year 2002/03, unless otherwise noted. Data for some countries may refer to national or UNESCO Institute for Statistics estimates.

d A positive figure indicates that the HDI rank is higher than the GDP per capita (PPP US$) rank, a negative the opposite.

e For purposes of calculating the HDI, a value of 99.0% was applied.

f For purposes of calculating the HDI, a value of 100% was applied.

g Statec 2005. Data refer to nationals enrolled both in the country and abroad and thus differ from the standard definition.

h For purposes of calculating the HDI, a value of $40,000 (PPP US$) was applied.

i Preliminary UNESCO Institute for Statistics estimate, subject to further revision.

j Data refer to year other than that specified.

k Estimate produced by UNESCO Institute for Statistics in July 2002.

l UNESCO Institute for Statistics 2003a. Estimates are based on outdated census or household survey information and should be interpreted with caution.

m Data are from national sources.

n Data refer to a year between 1995 and 1999.

o World Bank 2003c.

p Aten, Heston and Summers 2002. Data differ from the standard definition.

q Estimate based on regression.

r Data are from the Secretariat of the Organization of Eastern Caribbean States, based on national sources.

s Efforts to produce a more accurate and recent estimate are ongoing (see *Note to table 1: About this year's human development index*). A preliminary estimate of $5,400 (PPP US$) was used.

t Aten, Heston and Summers 2001. Data differ from the standard definition.

u Data are from the Secretariat of the Caribbean Community, based on national sources.

v UNDP 2003.

w Because the combined gross enrolment ratio was unavailable, the following Human Development Report Office estimates were used: Bhutan 49%, Ecuador 75%, Haiti 48%, and Turkmenistan 75%.

x Estimate based on a bilateral comparison between China and the United States (Ren and Kai 1995).

y In the absence of an official estimate of GDP per capita (PPP US$), preliminary World Bank estimates, subject to further revision, were used as follows: Maldives $4,798; and Suriname $6,552.

z Data refer to a year or period other than that specified, differ from the standard definition or refer to only part of a country.

aa UNICEF 2004.

ab In the absence of an estimate of GDP per capita (PPP US$), the Human Development Report Office estimate of $2,302, derived using the value of GDP in US dollars and the weighted average ratio of PPP US dollars to US dollars in the Arab States, was used.

ac A national estimate of $1,033 (PPP US$) was used.

ad Estimates are based primarily on information for Northern Sudan.

SOURCES

Column 1: calculated on the basis of data in columns 6–8; see *Technical note 1* for details.

Column 2: UN 2005c, unless otherwise noted.

Columns 3 and 4: UNESCO Institute for Statistics 2005c, unless otherwise noted.

Column 5: World Bank 2005c, unless otherwise noted; aggregates calculated for the Human Development Report Office by the World Bank.

Column 6: calculated on the basis of data in column 2.

Column 7: calculated on the basis of data in columns 3 and 4.

Column 8: calculated on the basis of data in column 5.

Column 9: calculated on the basis of data in columns 1 and 5.

Human development index trends

HDI rank	1975	1980	1985	1990	1995	2000	2003
HIGH HUMAN DEVELOPMENT							
1 Norway	0.868	0.888	0.898	0.912	0.936	0.956	0.963
2 Iceland	0.863	0.886	0.896	0.915	0.919	0.943	0.956
3 Australia	0.848	0.866	0.879	0.893	0.933	0.960	0.955
4 Luxembourg	0.840	0.851	0.858	0.884	0.911	0.929	0.949
5 Canada	0.869	0.886	0.909	0.929	0.934	..	0.949
6 Sweden	0.864	0.874	0.886	0.897	0.929	0.958	0.949
7 Switzerland	0.879	0.890	0.896	0.910	0.921	0.940	0.947
8 Ireland	0.811	0.826	0.845	0.870	0.894	0.929	0.946
9 Belgium	0.846	0.863	0.878	0.899	0.929	0.949	0.945
10 United States	0.867	0.887	0.901	0.916	0.929	0.938	0.944
11 Japan	0.857	0.882	0.895	0.911	0.925	0.936	0.943
12 Netherlands	0.867	0.879	0.893	0.908	0.928	0.939	0.943
13 Finland	0.841	0.861	0.879	0.901	0.914	0.940	0.941
14 Denmark	0.874	0.882	0.890	0.898	0.913	0.932	0.941
15 United Kingdom	0.845	0.854	0.863	0.883	0.921	0.948	0.939
16 France	0.853	0.869	0.881	0.903	0.921	0.932	0.938
17 Austria	0.843	0.858	0.871	0.894	0.914	0.933	0.936
18 Italy	0.842	0.858	0.866	0.889	0.907	0.921	0.934
19 New Zealand	0.848	0.854	0.868	0.875	0.905	0.924	0.933
20 Germany	..	0.861	0.869	0.888	0.913	0.927	0.930
21 Spain	0.837	0.854	0.868	0.886	0.904	0.918	0.928
22 Hong Kong, China (SAR)	0.761	0.800	0.827	0.862	0.882	..	0.916
23 Israel	0.795	0.819	0.840	0.858	0.880	0.909	0.915
24 Greece	0.835	0.850	0.864	0.872	0.876	0.895	0.912
25 Singapore	0.725	0.761	0.784	0.822	0.861	..	0.907
26 Slovenia	..	..	..	..	0.853	0.884	0.904
27 Portugal	0.787	0.802	0.826	0.849	0.878	0.898	0.904
28 Korea, Rep. of	0.707	0.741	0.780	0.818	0.855	0.884	0.901
29 Cyprus	..	0.793	0.813	0.836	0.858	0.883	0.891
30 Barbados	0.805	0.828	0.839	0.850	0.852	0.877	0.878
31 Czech Republic	..	..	..	..	0.843	0.857	0.874
32 Malta	0.727	0.764	0.791	0.825	0.852	0.874	0.867
33 Brunei Darussalam	..	..	..	..	..	..	0.866
34 Argentina	0.784	0.799	0.808	0.810	0.833	0.856	0.863
35 Hungary	0.779	0.795	0.808	0.807	0.812	0.843	0.862
36 Poland	..	..	..	0.803	0.816	0.845	0.858
37 Chile	0.704	0.739	0.763	0.785	0.816	0.843	0.854
38 Estonia	..	..	..	0.814	0.795	0.833	0.853
39 Lithuania	..	..	..	0.823	0.787	0.828	0.852
40 Qatar	..	..	..	..	..	..	0.849
41 United Arab Emirates	0.734	0.769	0.787	0.812	0.814	..	0.849
42 Slovakia	..	..	..	..	..	..	0.849
43 Bahrain	..	0.747	0.780	0.809	0.826	0.838	0.846
44 Kuwait	0.763	0.777	0.780	..	0.813	0.837	0.844
45 Croatia	..	..	..	0.806	0.799	0.826	0.841
46 Uruguay	0.759	0.780	0.787	0.804	0.817	..	0.840
47 Costa Rica	0.746	0.772	0.776	0.792	0.811	0.832	0.838
48 Latvia	..	0.792	0.805	0.799	0.765	0.812	0.836
49 Saint Kitts and Nevis	..	..	..	..	..	..	0.834
50 Bahamas	..	0.809	0.819	0.821	0.810	..	0.832
51 Seychelles	..	..	..	..	..	..	0.821
52 Cuba	..	..	..	..	..	..	0.817
53 Mexico	0.689	0.735	0.755	0.764	0.782	0.809	0.814

Human development indicators

TABLE 2

Human development index trends

HDI rank	1975	1980	1985	1990	1995	2000	2003
54 Tonga	..	..	..	..	..	..	0.810
55 Bulgaria	..	0.769	0.789	0.795	0.784	0.795	0.808
56 Panama	0.710	0.737	0.747	0.749	0.772	0.794	0.804
57 Trinidad and Tobago	0.749	0.781	0.788	0.792	0.789	0.800	0.801
MEDIUM HUMAN DEVELOPMENT							
58 Libyan Arab Jamahiriya	..	..	..	..	..	..	0.799
59 Macedonia, TFYR	..	..	..	..	..	..	0.797
60 Antigua and Barbuda	..	..	..	..	..	..	0.797
61 Malaysia	0.615	0.659	0.695	0.721	0.760	0.790	0.796
62 Russian Federation	..	..	..	0.817	0.770	..	0.795
63 Brazil	0.645	0.682	0.698	0.719	0.747	0.783	0.792
64 Romania	..	..	..	0.772	0.768	0.773	0.792
65 Mauritius	..	0.659	0.690	0.724	0.747	0.776	0.791
66 Grenada	..	..	..	..	..	..	0.787
67 Belarus	..	..	..	0.787	0.751	0.774	0.786
68 Bosnia and Herzegovina	..	..	..	..	..	..	0.786
69 Colombia	0.662	0.691	0.708	0.727	0.752	0.773	0.785
70 Dominica	..	..	..	..	..	..	0.783
71 Oman	0.494	0.547	0.641	0.699	0.738	0.769	0.781
72 Albania	..	..	0.693	0.703	0.702	0.736	0.780
73 Thailand	0.614	0.652	0.678	0.714	0.749	..	0.778
74 Samoa (Western)	..	..	0.723	0.732	0.742	0.763	0.776
75 Venezuela	0.718	0.732	0.740	0.759	0.767	0.772	0.772
76 Saint Lucia	..	..	..	..	..	..	0.772
77 Saudi Arabia	0.603	0.659	0.673	0.708	0.741	0.762	0.772
78 Ukraine	..	..	..	0.799	0.747	0.754	0.766
79 Peru	0.643	0.674	0.698	0.707	0.734	..	0.762
80 Kazakhstan	..	..	..	0.767	0.721	0.731	0.761
81 Lebanon	..	..	..	0.677	0.727	0.742	0.759
82 Ecuador	0.630	0.674	0.698	0.715	0.730	..	0.759
83 Armenia	..	..	..	0.737	0.698	0.735	0.759
84 Philippines	0.654	0.687	0.693	0.720	0.736	..	0.758
85 China	0.525	0.558	0.594	0.627	0.683	..	0.755
86 Suriname	..	..	..	..	..	..	0.755
87 Saint Vincent and the Grenadines	..	..	..	..	..	..	0.755
88 Paraguay	0.668	0.702	0.709	0.720	0.739	0.753	0.755
89 Tunisia	0.514	0.570	0.622	0.657	0.698	0.738	0.753
90 Jordan	..	0.641	0.664	0.683	0.708	0.742	0.753
91 Belize	..	0.707	0.717	0.747	0.768	0.779	0.753
92 Fiji	0.663	0.686	0.702	0.724	0.741	..	0.752
93 Sri Lanka	0.607	0.649	0.681	0.705	0.727	..	0.751
94 Turkey	0.587	0.610	0.646	0.678	0.709	..	0.750
95 Dominican Republic	0.619	0.650	0.672	0.679	0.700	0.732	0.749
96 Maldives	..	..	..	..	..	..	0.745
97 Turkmenistan	..	..	..	..	..	..	0.738
98 Jamaica	0.688	0.696	0.699	0.719	0.723	0.730	0.738
99 Iran, Islamic Rep. of	0.566	0.570	0.610	0.650	0.694	0.721	0.736
100 Georgia	..	..	..	..	..	..	0.732
101 Azerbaijan	..	..	..	..	..	..	0.729
102 Occupied Palestinian Territories	..	..	..	..	..	..	0.729
103 Algeria	0.506	0.558	0.610	0.649	0.671	..	0.722
104 El Salvador	0.592	0.588	0.609	0.650	0.689	0.715	0.722
105 Cape Verde	..	..	..	0.625	0.677	..	0.721
106 Syrian Arab Republic	0.540	0.587	0.623	0.646	0.672	0.692	0.721

Human development indicators

TABLE 2

HDI rank	1975	1980	1985	1990	1995	2000	2003
107 Guyana	0.678	0.684	0.677	0.683	0.685	0.714	0.720
108 Viet Nam	..	..	..	0.617	0.660	0.695	0.704
109 Kyrgyzstan	..	..	..	..	..	..	0.702
110 Indonesia	0.468	0.530	0.583	0.625	0.663	0.680	0.697
111 Uzbekistan	..	..	..	..	0.679	..	0.694
112 Nicaragua	0.587	0.596	0.604	0.610	0.641	0.659	0.690
113 Bolivia	0.512	0.549	0.580	0.604	0.636	0.672	0.687
114 Mongolia	..	..	0.668	0.673	0.633	0.657	0.679
115 Moldova, Rep. of	..	..	..	0.739	0.682	0.665	0.671
116 Honduras	0.518	0.569	0.601	0.623	0.640	..	0.667
117 Guatemala	0.512	0.546	0.562	0.586	0.617	0.650	0.663
118 Vanuatu	..	..	..	..	..	..	0.659
119 Egypt	0.439	0.487	0.540	0.579	0.611	..	0.659
120 South Africa	0.655	0.674	0.702	0.735	0.742	0.696	0.658
121 Equatorial Guinea	..	..	0.483	0.500	0.518	0.641	0.655
122 Tajikistan	..	..	0.699	0.696	0.629	0.630	0.652
123 Gabon	..	..	..	..	..	..	0.635
124 Morocco	0.429	0.478	0.515	0.548	0.579	0.610	0.631
125 Namibia	..	..	..	..	0.693	0.649	0.627
126 São Tomé and Principe	..	..	..	..	..	..	0.604
127 India	0.412	0.438	0.476	0.513	0.546	0.577	0.602
128 Solomon Islands	..	..	..	..	..	..	0.594
129 Myanmar	..	..	..	..	..	..	0.578
130 Cambodia	..	..	..	..	0.533	0.541	0.571
131 Botswana	0.503	0.577	0.638	0.681	0.659	0.596	0.565
132 Comoros	..	0.480	0.498	0.504	0.517	0.533	0.547
133 Lao People's Dem. Rep.	..	..	0.423	0.450	0.487	0.522	0.545
134 Bhutan	..	..	..	..	..	..	0.536
135 Pakistan	0.363	0.386	0.419	0.462	0.492	..	0.527
136 Nepal	0.296	0.333	0.376	0.423	0.466	0.499	0.526
137 Papua New Guinea	0.425	0.445	0.467	0.481	0.515	0.529	0.523
138 Ghana	0.439	0.468	0.482	0.511	0.531	0.556	0.520
139 Bangladesh	0.345	0.364	0.389	0.419	0.452	0.506	0.520
140 Timor-Leste	..	..	..	..	..	..	0.513
141 Sudan	0.349	0.376	0.396	0.428	0.465	0.500	0.512
142 Congo	0.452	0.499	0.540	0.526	0.531	..	0.512
143 Togo	0.423	0.475	0.474	0.500	0.510	0.519	0.512
144 Uganda	..	..	0.412	0.409	0.412	0.474	0.508
145 Zimbabwe	0.546	0.574	0.640	0.637	0.589	0.527	0.505
LOW HUMAN DEVELOPMENT							
146 Madagascar	0.400	0.437	0.436	0.446	0.458	..	0.499
147 Swaziland	0.530	0.562	0.584	0.624	0.603	0.534	0.498
148 Cameroon	0.416	0.463	0.505	0.514	0.494	0.500	0.497
149 Lesotho	0.461	0.510	0.534	0.571	0.573	0.520	0.497
150 Djibouti	..	..	..	..	0.477	0.487	0.495
151 Yemen	..	..	..	0.393	0.436	0.470	0.489
152 Mauritania	0.340	0.363	0.384	0.388	0.424	0.444	0.477
153 Haiti	..	0.449	0.458	0.446	0.450	..	0.475
154 Kenya	0.461	0.509	0.530	0.546	0.524	0.499	0.474
155 Gambia	0.284	..	..	..	0.424	0.457	0.470
156 Guinea	..	..	..	..	..	..	0.466
157 Senegal	0.311	0.339	0.375	0.403	0.421	0.444	0.458
158 Nigeria	0.318	0.376	0.386	0.406	0.418	..	0.453
159 Rwanda	0.342	0.388	0.401	0.340	0.335	0.435	0.450

Human development indicators

TABLE 2

Human development index trends

HDI rank	1975	1980	1985	1990	1995	2000	2003
160 Angola	..	..	..	..	..	..	0.445
161 Eritrea	..	..	..	..	0.409	0.428	0.444
162 Benin	0.304	0.336	0.362	0.368	0.395	0.422	0.431
163 Côte d'Ivoire	0.409	0.441	0.448	0.442	0.427	0.428	0.420
164 Tanzania, U. Rep. of	..	..	..	0.435	0.422	0.416	0.418
165 Malawi	0.320	0.351	0.362	0.371	0.412	0.402	0.404
166 Zambia	0.468	0.475	0.484	0.462	0.424	0.409	0.394
167 Congo, Dem. Rep. of the	0.414	0.423	0.431	0.422	0.393	..	0.385
168 Mozambique	..	0.299	0.287	0.311	0.328	0.360	0.379
169 Burundi	0.285	0.311	0.345	0.353	0.324	..	0.378
170 Ethiopia	..	..	0.291	0.311	0.323	0.352	0.367
171 Central African Republic	0.343	0.364	0.386	0.383	0.367	..	0.355
172 Guinea-Bissau	0.255	0.262	0.283	0.313	0.341	0.353	0.348
173 Chad	0.269	0.271	0.311	0.335	0.344	0.359	0.341
174 Mali	0.230	0.256	0.263	0.283	0.307	0.330	0.333
175 Burkina Faso	0.253	0.273	0.297	0.305	0.311	0.328	0.317
176 Sierra Leone	..	..	..	..	..	..	0.298
177 Niger	0.236	0.252	0.242	0.249	0.256	0.271	0.281

NOTES

The human development index values in this table were calculated using a consistent methodology and data series. They are not strictly comparable with those in earlier *Human Development Reports*. For detailed discussion, see *Note to table 1: About this year's human development index.*

SOURCES

Columns 1–6: calculated on the basis of data on life expectancy from UN 2005c, data on adult literacy rates from UNESCO Institute for Statistics 2003a, 2005a, data on combined gross enrolment ratios from UNESCO Institute for Statistics 1999, 2005c, and data on GDP per capita (2000 PPP US$) and GDP per capita (PPP US$) from World Bank 2005c.
Column 7: column 1 of indicator table 1.

Human and income poverty: developing countries

HDI rank	Human poverty index (HPI-1) Rank	Human poverty index (HPI-1) Value (%)	Probability at birth of not surviving to age 40 [a,t] (% of cohort) 2000–05	Adult illiteracy rate [b,t] (% ages 15 and above) 2003	Population without sustainable access to an improved water source [t] (%) 2002	MDG Children under weight for age [t] (% under age 5) 1995–2003[c]	MDG Population below income poverty line (%) $1 a day 1990–2003[c]	$2 a day 1990–2003[c]	National poverty line 1990–2002[c]	HPI-1 rank minus income poverty rank [d]
HIGH HUMAN DEVELOPMENT										
22 Hong Kong, China (SAR)	..	..	1.5	6.5 e,f	..	..	..	..	..	..
25 Singapore	6	6.3	1.8	7.5	0 g	14 h	..	..	..	..
28 Korea, Rep. of	..	..	2.7	2.1 e,f	8	..	<2	<2	..	..
29 Cyprus	..	..	2.8	3.2	0	..	..	..	..	..
30 Barbados	4	4.5	6.3	0.3 e	0	6 h	..	..	..	..
33 Brunei Darussalam	..	..	2.8	7.3	..	..	..	..	..	..
34 Argentina	..	..	5.0	2.8	..	5	3.3	14.3	..	..
37 Chile	2	3.7	3.5	4.3	5	1	<2	9.6	17.0	1
40 Qatar	10	7.8	4.7	10.8	0	6	..	..	..	..
41 United Arab Emirates	..	..	2.2	22.7 e	..	14	..	..	..	..
43 Bahrain	..	..	3.8	12.3	..	9	..	..	..	..
44 Kuwait	..	..	2.5	17.1 e	..	10	..	..	..	..
46 Uruguay	1	3.6	4.4	2.3 e	2	5	<2	3.9	..	0
47 Costa Rica	3	4.0	3.7	4.2 e	3	5	2.0	9.5	22.0	−10
49 Saint Kitts and Nevis	..	..	..	..	1	..	..	..	..	..
50 Bahamas	..	..	13.4	4.5 e,f	3	..	..	..	..	..
51 Seychelles	..	..	..	8.1	13	6 h	..	..	..	..
52 Cuba	5	4.8	3.2	3.1 e	9	4	..	..	..	..
53 Mexico	13	8.4	6.0	9.7	9	8	9.9	26.3	10.1 j	−13
54 Tonga	..	..	5.0	1.1 i	0	..	..	..	..	..
56 Panama	9	7.7	6.8	8.1	9	7	7.2	17.6	37.3	−10
57 Trinidad and Tobago	15	8.8	11.6	1.5 e	9	7 h	12.4	39.0	21.0	−14
MEDIUM HUMAN DEVELOPMENT										
58 Libyan Arab Jamahiriya	33	15.3	4.2	18.3 e	28	5	..	..	..	..
60 Antigua and Barbuda	..	..	..	..	9	10 h	..	..	..	..
61 Malaysia	16	8.9	4.3	11.3	5	12	<2	9.3	15.5 j	9
63 Brazil	20	10.3	10.3	11.6	11	6	8.2	22.4	17.4	−5
65 Mauritius	24	11.4	5.0	15.7	0	15	..	..	10.6	..
66 Grenada	..	..	..	..	5	..	..	..	..	..
69 Colombia	8	7.4	8.3	5.8	8	7	8.2	22.6	64.0	−15
70 Dominica	..	..	..	..	3	5 h	..	..	..	..
71 Oman	46	21.1	3.9	25.6 e	21	24	..	..	..	..
73 Thailand	28	12.8	9.9	7.4	15	19 h	<2	32.5	13.1	18
74 Samoa (Western)	..	..	6.5	1.3 e	12	..	..	..	..	..
75 Venezuela	14	8.8	8.2	7.0	17	4	15.0	32.0	31.3 j	−19
76 Saint Lucia	12	8.3	5.9	9.9	2	14 h	..	..	..	..
77 Saudi Arabia	32	14.9	5.8	20.6	5 g	14	..	..	..	..
79 Peru	26	12.0	10.3	12.3	19	7	18.1	37.7	49.0	−17
81 Lebanon	18	9.6	5.7	13.5 e,f	0	3	..	..	..	..
82 Ecuador	22	10.6	8.6	9.0	14	12	17.7	40.8	35.0	−18
84 Philippines	35	16.3	7.2	7.4	15	31	14.6	46.4	36.8	−4
85 China	27	12.3	6.9	9.1	23	10	16.6	46.7	4.6	−13
86 Suriname	23	10.9	10.1	12.0	8	13	..	..	..	..
87 Saint Vincent and the Grenadines	..	..	6.6	..	..	..	..	..	..	..
88 Paraguay	17	9.4	8.1	8.4	17	5	16.4	33.2	21.8	−19
89 Tunisia	43	18.3	4.7	25.7	18	4	<2	6.6	7.6	27
90 Jordan	11	8.1	6.4	10.1	9	4	<2	7.4	11.7	5
91 Belize	38	16.7	10.6	23.1	9	6 h	..	..	..	..
92 Fiji	49	21.3	7.0	7.1 i	53 g	8 h	..	..	..	..
93 Sri Lanka	42	18.0	4.3	9.6 h	22	29	7.6	50.7	25.0	10
94 Turkey	19	9.7	8.9	11.7	7	8	<2	10.3	..	11
95 Dominican Republic	25	11.8	14.1	12.3	7	5	<2	<2	28.6	15
96 Maldives	37	16.6	11.4	2.8 e	16	30	..	..	..	..

TABLE 3

Human and income poverty: developing countries

HDI rank	Human poverty index (HPI-1) Rank	Human poverty index (HPI-1) Value (%)	Probability at birth of not surviving to age 40 [a,†] (% of cohort) 2000–05	Adult illiteracy rate [b,†] (% ages 15 and above) 2003	Population without sustainable access to an improved water source [†] (%) 2002	MDG Children under weight for age [†] (% under age 5) 1995–2003 [c]	MDG Population below income poverty line (%) $1 a day 1990–2003 [c]	$2 a day 1990–2003 [c]	National poverty line 1990–2002 [c]	HPI-1 rank minus income poverty rank [d]
98 Jamaica	21	10.5	11.3	12.4 [e]	7	4	<2	13.3	18.7	13
99 Iran, Islamic Rep. of	36	16.4	7.2	23.0	7	11	<2	7.3	..	22
102 Occupied Palestinian Territories	7	6.5	5.3	8.1	6	4	..	..	..	..
103 Algeria	48	21.3	7.8	30.2	13	6	<2	15.1	12.2	29
104 El Salvador	34	15.9	9.9	20.3 [e]	18	10	31.1	58.0	48.3	−23
105 Cape Verde	45	18.7	7.6	24.3 [e]	20	14 [h]	..	..	..	..
106 Syrian Arab Republic	29	13.8	4.6	17.1	21	7	..	..	..	..
107 Guyana	31	14.8	18.2	1.4 [k, l]	17	14	..	..	35.0	..
108 Viet Nam	47	21.2	9.4	9.7 [i]	27	33	..	..	50.9	..
110 Indonesia	41	17.8	11.2	12.1 [e]	22	26	7.5	52.4	27.1	10
112 Nicaragua	40	17.7	10.1	23.3	19	10	45.1	79.9	47.9	−30
113 Bolivia	30	13.9	16.0	13.5	15	8	14.4	34.3	62.7	−5
114 Mongolia	44	18.5	13.3	2.2	38	13	27.0	74.9	36.3	−14
116 Honduras	39	16.9	15.8	20.0	10	17	20.7	44.0	53.0	−12
117 Guatemala	51	22.9	15.9	30.9	5	23	16.0	37.4	56.2	2
118 Vanuatu	52	24.7	8.9	26.0 [i]	40	20 [h]	..	..	..	..
119 Egypt	55	30.9	7.8	44.4 [i]	2	9	3.1	43.9	16.7	18
120 South Africa	56	30.9	43.3	17.6 [i]	13	12	10.7	34.1	..	12
121 Equatorial Guinea	71	38.1	47.7	15.8	56	19	..	..	..	..
123 Gabon	..	..	32.6	..	13	12	..	..	..	..
124 Morocco	61	34.5	8.6	49.3 [e]	20	9	<2	14.3	19.0	35
125 Namibia	60	33.0	45.4	15.0	20	24	34.9	55.8	..	−12
126 São Tomé and Príncipe	..	..	17.1	..	21	13	..	..	..	..
127 India	58	31.3	16.6	39.0	14	47	34.7	79.9	28.6	−12
128 Solomon Islands	..	..	14.1	..	30	21 [h]	..	..	..	..
129 Myanmar	50	21.9	21.2	10.3	20	35	..	..	..	..
130 Cambodia	81	41.3	28.3	26.4	66	45	34.1	77.7	36.1	5
131 Botswana	94	48.4	69.1	21.1 [e]	5	13	23.5	50.1	..	22
132 Comoros	57	31.2	15.5	43.8 [e]	6	25	..	..	..	..
133 Lao People's Dem. Rep.	72	38.2	28.0	31.3	57	40	26.3	73.2	38.6	2
134 Bhutan	..	..	18.0	..	38	19	..	..	..	..
135 Pakistan	68	37.1	16.1	51.3	10	38	13.4	65.6	32.6	18
136 Nepal	74	38.7	17.6	51.4	16	48	37.7	82.5	42.0	−5
137 Papua New Guinea	78	40.5	22.4	42.7	61	35 [h]	..	..	37.5	..
138 Ghana	62	35.1	27.7	45.9	21	25	44.8	78.5	39.5	−16
139 Bangladesh	86	44.1	15.9	58.9 [e]	25	48	36.0	82.8	49.8	5
140 Timor-Leste	..	..	25.5	..	48	43	..	..	..	..
141 Sudan	59	32.4	27.0	41.0 [h]	31	17	..	..	..	..
142 Congo	54	30.1	33.6	17.2 [e]	54	14	..	..	..	..
143 Togo	76	39.5	31.0	47.0	49	25	..	..	32.3 [i]	..
144 Uganda	66	36.0	41.6	31.1 [e]	44	23	..	..	55.0	..
145 Zimbabwe	89	45.9	65.9	10.0 [e]	17	13	56.1	83.0	34.9	−1
LOW HUMAN DEVELOPMENT										
146 Madagascar	63	35.3	27.8	29.4	55	33	61.0	85.1	71.3	−23
147 Swaziland	97	52.9	74.3	20.8	48	10	..	..	40.0	..
148 Cameroon	67	36.2	43.9	32.1	37	21	17.1	50.6	40.2	9
149 Lesotho	91	47.6	67.6	18.6	24	18	36.4	56.1	49.2	9
150 Djibouti	53	29.5	30.6	34.5 [e, f]	20	18	..	..	45.1	..
151 Yemen	77	40.3	18.8	51.0 [e]	31	46	15.7	45.2	41.8	19
152 Mauritania	79	40.5	30.5	48.8	44	32	25.9	63.1	46.3	9
153 Haiti	70	38.0	34.4	48.1 [e]	29	17	..	..	65.0 [i]	..
154 Kenya	64	35.4	44.8	26.4	38	20	22.8	58.3	42.0	2
155 Gambia	88	44.7	27.8	62.2 [e, f]	18	17	59.3	82.9	64.0	−5
156 Guinea	..	..	30.0	..	49	23	..	..	40.0	..

Human development indicators

TABLE 3

HDI rank	Human poverty index (HPI-1) Rank	Human poverty index (HPI-1) Value (%)	Probability at birth of not surviving to age 40 [a],† (% of cohort) 2000–05	Adult illiteracy rate [b],† (% ages 15 and above) 2003	Population without sustainable access to an improved water source† (%) 2002	MDG Children under weight for age† (% under age 5) 1995–2003 [c]	MDG Population below income poverty line (%) $1 a day 1990–2003 [c]	$2 a day 1990–2003 [c]	National poverty line 1990–2002 [c]	HPI-1 rank minus income poverty rank [d]
157 Senegal	87	44.2	26.6	60.7	28	23	26.3	67.8	33.4	14
158 Nigeria	75	38.8	46.0	33.2[e]	40	29	70.2	90.8	34.1	−19
159 Rwanda	69	37.7	45.5	36.0	27	27	51.7	83.7	51.2	−13
160 Angola	83	41.5	48.1	33.2	50	31	..	..	..	..
161 Eritrea	73	38.7	27.6	43.3[e, f]	43	40	..	..	53.0	..
162 Benin	95	48.4	30.0	66.4	32	23	..	..	33.0	..
163 Côte d'Ivoire	84	41.9	42.3	51.9	16	21	10.8	38.4	36.8	29
164 Tanzania, U. Rep. of	65	35.8	44.4	30.6	27	29	19.9	59.7	35.7	5
165 Malawi	85	43.4	56.3	35.9[i]	33	22	41.7	76.1	65.3	0
166 Zambia	90	46.4	60.1	32.1[i]	45	28	63.7	87.4	72.9	−6
167 Congo, Dem. Rep. of the	82	41.4	45.4	34.7	54	31	..	..	..	..
168 Mozambique	96	49.1	50.9	53.5[e]	58	24	37.9	78.4	69.4	10
169 Burundi	80	40.9	46.3	41.1	21	45	58.4	89.2	..	−10
170 Ethiopia	99	55.3	39.5	58.5[e]	78	47	26.3	80.7	44.2	23
171 Central African Republic	92	47.8	56.2	51.4	25	24	66.6	84.0	..	−5
172 Guinea-Bissau	93	48.2	42.9	60.4[e, f]	41	25	..	..	48.7	..
173 Chad	100	58.8	45.2	74.5	66	28	..	..	64.0	..
174 Mali	101	60.3	37.3	81.0[i]	52	33	72.3	90.6	63.8	−2
175 Burkina Faso	102	64.2	38.9	87.2[i]	49	34	44.9	81.0	45.3	11
176 Sierra Leone	98	54.9	47.0	70.4	43	27	57.0	74.5	68.0	4
177 Niger	103	64.4	41.4	85.6	54	40	61.4	85.3	63.0[i]	4

NOTES

† Denotes indicators used to calculate the human poverty index (HPI-1). For further details, see Technical note 1.

a Data refer to the probability at birth of not surviving to age 40, multiplied by 100.

b Data refer to national literacy estimates from censuses or surveys conducted between 2000 and 2004, unless otherwise noted. Due to differences in methodology and timeliness of underlying data, comparisons across countries and over time should be made with caution. For more details, see www.uis.unesco.org/ev.php?ID=4930_201&ID2=DO_TOPIC.

c Data refer to the most recent year available during the period specified.

d Income poverty refers to the share of the population living on less than $1 a day. All countries with an income poverty rate of less than 2% were given equal rank. The rankings are based on countries for which data are available for both indicators. A positive figure indicates that the country performs better in income poverty than in human poverty, a negative the opposite.

e Estimate produced by the United Nations Educational, Scientific and Cultural Organization Institute for Statistics in July 2002.

f UNESCO Institute for Statistics 2003a. Estimates are based on outdated census or household survey information and should be interpreted with caution.

g UNICEF 2004. Data refer to 2000.

h UNICEF 2004. Data refer to a year or period other than that specified, differ from the standard definition or refer to only part of a country.

i Data refer to a year between 1995 and 1999.

j Data refer to a period other than that specified.

k Data refer to year other than that specified.

l Data are from the Secretariat of the Caribbean Community, based on national sources.

SOURCES

Column 1: determined on the basis of the HPI-1 values in column 2.

Column 2: calculated on the basis of data in columns 3–6; see Technical note 1 for details.

Column 3: UN 2005h.

Column 4: calculated on the basis of data on adult literacy from UNESCO Institute for Statistics 2005a.

Columns 5 and 6: UN 2005f.

Columns 7–9: World Bank 2005c.

Column 10: calculated on the basis of data in columns 1 and 7.

HPI-1 ranks for 103 developing countries and areas

1 Uruguay	21 Jamaica	42 Sri Lanka	63 Madagascar	84 Côte d'Ivoire
2 Chile	22 Ecuador	43 Tunisia	64 Kenya	85 Malawi
3 Costa Rica	23 Suriname	44 Mongolia	65 Tanzania, U. Rep. of	86 Bangladesh
4 Barbados	24 Mauritius	45 Cape Verde	66 Uganda	87 Senegal
5 Cuba	25 Dominican Republic	46 Oman	67 Cameroon	88 Gambia
6 Singapore	26 Peru	47 Viet Nam	68 Pakistan	89 Zimbabwe
7 Occupied Palestinian Territories	27 China	48 Algeria	69 Rwanda	90 Zambia
8 Colombia	28 Thailand	49 Fiji	70 Haiti	91 Lesotho
9 Panama	29 Syrian Arab Republic	50 Myanmar	71 Equatorial Guinea	92 Central African Republic
10 Qatar	30 Bolivia	51 Guatemala	72 Lao People's Dem. Rep.	93 Guinea-Bissau
11 Jordan	31 Guyana	52 Vanuatu	73 Eritrea	94 Botswana
12 Saint Lucia	32 Saudi Arabia	53 Djibouti	74 Nepal	95 Benin
13 Mexico	33 Libyan Arab Jamahiriya	54 Congo	75 Nigeria	96 Mozambique
14 Venezuela	34 El Salvador	55 Egypt	76 Togo	97 Swaziland
15 Trinidad and Tobago	35 Philippines	56 South Africa	77 Yemen	98 Sierra Leone
16 Malaysia	36 Iran, Islamic Rep. of	57 Comoros	78 Papua New Guinea	99 Ethiopia
17 Paraguay	37 Maldives	58 India	79 Mauritania	100 Chad
18 Lebanon	38 Belize	59 Sudan	80 Burundi	101 Mali
19 Turkey	39 Honduras	60 Namibia	81 Cambodia	102 Burkina Faso
20 Brazil	40 Nicaragua	61 Morocco	82 Congo, Dem. Rep. of the	103 Niger
	41 Indonesia	62 Ghana	83 Angola	

Human development indicators

Human and income poverty: OECD countries, Eastern Europe and the CIS

HDI rank	Human poverty index (HPI-2) [a] Rank	Human poverty index (HPI-2) [a] Value (%)	Probability at birth of not surviving to age 60 [b,†] (% of cohort) 2000–05	Population lacking functional literacy skills [c,†] (% ages 16–65) 1994–2003	Long-term unemployment [†] (% of labour force) 2003	Population below income poverty line (%) 50% of median income [†] 1999–2000 [e]	Population below income poverty line (%) $11 a day 1994–95 [e]	Population below income poverty line (%) $4 a day 1996–99 [e]	HPI-2 rank minus income poverty rank [d]
HIGH HUMAN DEVELOPMENT									
1 Norway	2	7.0	8.4	7.9	0.3	6.4	4.3	..	−1
2 Iceland	..	..	6.8	..	0.4 [f]	..	..	..	..
3 Australia	14	12.8	7.7	17.0 [g]	1.4	14.3	17.6	..	−3
4 Luxembourg	8	11.1	9.7	.. [h]	1.0 [f,g]	6.0	0.3	..	6
5 Canada	9	11.3	8.1	14.6	0.8	12.8	7.4	..	−7
6 Sweden	1	6.5	7.2	7.5 [g]	0.9	6.5	6.3	..	−3
7 Switzerland	7	11.0	7.8	15.9	1.1	9.3	..	..	−3
8 Ireland	16	15.2	8.7	22.6 [g]	1.6	12.3	..	..	3
9 Belgium	13	12.4	9.4	18.4 [g,j]	3.7	8.0	..	..	7
10 United States	17	15.4	11.8	20.0	0.7	17.0	13.6	..	−1
11 Japan	12	11.7	7.1	.. [h]	1.8	11.8 [k]	..	..	0
12 Netherlands	3	8.2	8.7	10.5 [i]	1.2	7.3	7.1	..	−2
13 Finland	4	8.2	9.7	10.4 [i]	2.2	5.4	4.8	..	3
14 Denmark	5	8.9	10.4	9.6 [i]	1.1	9.2	..	..	−4
15 United Kingdom	15	14.8	8.7	21.8 [i]	1.2	12.5	15.7	..	1
16 France	10	11.4	9.8	.. [h]	4.2	8.0	9.9	..	4
17 Austria	..	..	9.1	..	1.4	8.0	..	..	..
18 Italy	18	29.9	7.8	47.0	5.1	12.7	..	..	3
19 New Zealand	..	..	8.9	18.4 [i]	0.6	..	..	..	..
20 Germany	6	10.3	8.8	14.4 [i]	4.6	8.3	7.3	..	−2
21 Spain	11	11.6	8.7	.. [h]	4.5	10.1	..	..	0
23 Israel	..	..	7.7	..	..	13.5	..	..	..
24 Greece	..	..	9.2	..	5.4	..	..	..	..
26 Slovenia	..	..	11.8	..	..	8.2	..	<1	..
27 Portugal	..	..	10.3	..	2.0	..	..	..	..
31 Czech Republic	..	..	12.1	..	3.9	4.9	..	<1	..
32 Malta	..	..	7.7	..	..	..	..	..	..
35 Hungary	..	..	18.3	..	2.5	6.7	..	<1	..
36 Poland	..	..	15.1	..	9.8	8.6	..	10	..
38 Estonia	..	..	21.7	..	..	12.4	..	18	..
39 Lithuania	..	..	20.6	..	..	..	..	17	..
42 Slovakia	..	..	14.9	..	10.7	7.0	..	8	..
45 Croatia	..	..	13.1	..	..	..	..	..	..
48 Latvia	..	..	21.5	..	..	..	..	28	..
55 Bulgaria	..	..	16.6	..	..	..	..	22	..

TABLE 4

HDI rank	Human poverty index (HPI-2) [a] Rank	Human poverty index (HPI-2) [a] Value (%)	Probability at birth of not surviving to age 60 [b,†] (% of cohort) 2000–05	Population lacking functional literacy skills [c,†] (% ages 16–65) 1994–2003	Long-term unemployment[†] (% of labour force) 2003	Population below income poverty line (%) 50% of median income[†] 1999–2000[e]	Population below income poverty line (%) $11 a day 1994–95[e]	Population below income poverty line (%) $4 a day 1996–99[e]	HPI-2 rank minus income poverty rank [d]
MEDIUM HUMAN DEVELOPMENT									
59 Macedonia, TFYR	..	..	13.3	..	..	..	..	..	..
62 Russian Federation	..	..	31.6	..	..	18.8	..	53	..
64 Romania	..	..	19.0	..	..	8.1	..	23	..
67 Belarus	..	..	26.7	..	..	..	..	..	..
68 Bosnia and Herzegovina	..	..	13.6	..	..	..	..	..	..
72 Albania	..	..	11.4	..	..	..	..	..	..
78 Ukraine	..	..	31.0	..	..	..	..	25	..
80 Kazakhstan	..	..	32.0	..	..	..	..	62	..
83 Armenia	..	..	18.0	..	..	..	..	..	..
97 Turkmenistan	..	..	32.0	..	..	..	..	..	..
100 Georgia	..	..	18.9	..	..	..	..	..	..
101 Azerbaijan	..	..	24.9	..	..	..	..	..	..
109 Kyrgyzstan	..	..	26.0	..	..	..	..	88	..
111 Uzbekistan	..	..	26.3	..	..	..	..	..	..
115 Moldova, Rep. of	..	..	25.5	..	..	..	..	82	..
122 Tajikistan	..	..	29.0	..	..	..	..	..	..

NOTES

This table includes Israel and Malta, which are not Organisation for Economic Co-operation and Development (OECD) member countries, but excludes the Republic of Korea, Mexico and Turkey, which are. For the human poverty index and related indicators for these countries, see table 3.

† Denotes indicators used to calculate the human poverty index (HPI-2). For further details, see *Technical note 1*.

a The human poverty index (HPI-2) is calculated for selected high-income OECD countries only.

b Data refer to the probability at birth of not surviving to age 60, multiplied by 100.

c Based on scoring at level 1 on the prose literacy scale of the International Adult Literacy Survey. Data refer to the most recent year available during the period specified.

d Income poverty refers to the share of the population living on less than 50% of the median adjusted disposable household income. A positive figure indicates that the country performs better in income poverty than in human poverty, a negative the opposite.

e Data refer to the most recent year available during the period specified.

f Data refer to 2002.

g Based on OECD and Statistics Canada 2000.

h For purposes of calculating the HPI-2 an estimate of 16.4%, the unweighted average of countries with available data, was applied.

i Data are based on small sample sizes and should be treated with caution.

j Data refer to Flanders.

k Smeeding 1997.

SOURCES

Column 1: determined on the basis of HPI-2 values in column 2.

Column 2: calculated on the basis of data in columns 3–6; see *Technical note 1* for details.

Column 3: calculated on the basis of survival data from UN 2005h.

Column 4: OECD and Statistics Canada 2005, unless otherwise noted.

Column 5: calculated on the basis of data on youth long-term unemployment and labour force from OECD 2005d.

Column 6: LIS 2005.

Column 7: Smeeding, Rainwater and Burtless 2000.

Column 8: Milanovic 2002.

Column 9: calculated on the basis of data in columns 1 and 6.

HPI-2 ranks for 18 selected OECD countries

1	Sweden	7	Switzerland	13	Belgium
2	Norway	8	Luxembourg	14	Australia
3	Netherlands	9	Canada	15	United Kingdom
4	Finland	10	France	16	Ireland
5	Denmark	11	Spain	17	United States
6	Germany	12	Japan	18	Italy

Human development indicators

TABLE 5

... to lead a long and healthy life ...

Demographic trends

		Total population (millions)			Annual population growth rate (%)		Urban population (% of total) [a]			Population under age 15 (% of total)		Population ages 65 and above (% of total)		Total fertility rate (births per woman)	
HDI rank		1975	2003	2015[b]	1975–2003	2003–15[b]	1975	2003[b]	2015[b]	2003	2015[b]	2003	2015[b]	1970–75[c]	2000–05[c]
HIGH HUMAN DEVELOPMENT															
1	Norway	4.0	4.6	4.8	0.5	0.5	68.2	78.6	86.4	19.9	17.5	13.3	17.5	2.2	1.8
2	Iceland	0.2	0.3	0.3	1.0	0.8	86.6	92.8	94.1	22.5	19.4	10.1	14.0	2.8	2.0
3	Australia	13.6	19.7	22.2	1.3	1.0	85.9	91.9	94.9	20.3	17.7	10.7	15.5	2.5	1.7
4	Luxembourg	0.4	0.5	0.5	0.8	1.2	73.7	91.8	94.1	19.0	17.6	11.9	14.3	2.0	1.7
5	Canada	23.1	31.6	35.1	1.1	0.9	75.6	80.4	84.0	18.2	15.3	11.1	16.2	2.0	1.5
6	Sweden	8.2	9.0	9.3	0.3	0.3	82.7	83.4	84.3	17.9	16.4	15.0	20.4	1.9	1.6
7	Switzerland	6.3	7.2	7.3	0.5	0.1	55.7	67.6	68.7	17.0	14.1	13.5	19.8	1.8	1.4
8	Ireland	3.2	4.0	4.7	0.8	1.3	53.6	59.9	63.6	20.6	20.2	9.3	12.6	3.8	1.9
9	Belgium	9.8	10.4	10.5	0.2	0.1	94.5	97.2	97.5	17.1	15.5	15.1	19.4	1.9	1.7
10	United States	220.2	292.6	325.7	1.0	0.9	73.7	80.1	83.6	21.1	19.7	10.7	14.1	2.0	2.0
11	Japan	111.5	127.7	128.0	0.5	(.)	56.8	65.5	67.7	14.2	13.3	16.0	26.0	2.1	1.3
12	Netherlands	13.7	16.1	16.8	0.6	0.3	56.9	65.8	71.4	18.4	16.4	11.9	17.5	2.1	1.7
13	Finland	4.7	5.2	5.4	0.4	0.2	58.3	61.0	62.1	17.7	15.8	13.4	20.3	1.6	1.7
14	Denmark	5.1	5.4	5.6	0.2	0.2	82.1	85.4	86.8	18.8	17.0	12.8	18.4	2.0	1.8
15	United Kingdom	55.4	59.3	61.4	0.2	0.3	82.7	89.1	90.2	18.4	16.4	13.8	18.1	2.0	1.7
16	France	52.7	60.0	62.3	0.5	0.3	72.9	76.3	79.0	18.3	17.6	14.5	19.0	2.3	1.9
17	Austria	7.6	8.1	8.3	0.3	0.1	65.3	65.8	67.2	16.0	13.4	14.0	19.6	2.0	1.4
18	Italy	55.4	58.0	57.8	0.2	(.)	65.6	67.4	69.2	14.1	13.2	16.7	23.0	2.3	1.3
19	New Zealand	3.1	3.9	4.3	0.9	0.7	82.8	85.9	87.0	22.0	18.9	10.4	15.0	2.8	2.0
20	Germany	78.7	82.6	82.5	0.2	(.)	81.2	88.1	90.0	14.8	12.9	15.0	20.7	1.6	1.3
21	Spain	35.6	42.1	44.4	0.6	0.4	69.0	76.5	78.1	14.3	15.3	14.5	18.0	2.9	1.3
22	Hong Kong, China (SAR)	4.4	6.9	7.8	1.6	1.0	89.7	100.0	100.0	15.2	12.7	9.8	14.4	2.9	0.9
23	Israel	3.4	6.5	7.8	2.3	1.6	86.6	91.6	92.4	28.0	25.8	8.7	11.5	3.8	2.9
24	Greece	9.0	11.1	11.2	0.7	0.1	55.3	60.9	65.2	14.6	13.5	15.2	19.3	2.3	1.3
25	Singapore	2.3	4.2	4.8	2.2	1.1	100.0	100.0	100.0	20.7	13.2	6.5	13.3	2.6	1.4
26	Slovenia	1.7	2.0	1.9	0.4	−0.1	42.4	50.8	52.6	14.5	13.0	12.9	18.1	2.2	1.2
27	Portugal	9.1	10.4	10.8	0.5	0.3	27.7	54.6	60.9	16.0	15.1	14.4	18.9	2.7	1.5
28	Korea, Rep. of	35.3	47.5	49.1	1.1	0.3	48.0	80.3	83.0	19.5	13.9	7.0	13.2	4.3	1.2
29	Cyprus	0.6	0.8	0.9	1.0	1.1	45.2	69.2	71.6	20.9	17.2	10.0	14.2	2.5	1.6
30	Barbados	0.2	0.3	0.3	0.3	0.2	40.8	51.7	59.1	19.6	16.7	9.0	11.5	2.7	1.5
31	Czech Republic	10.0	10.2	10.1	0.1	−0.1	63.7	74.3	75.7	15.3	13.4	12.2	18.4	2.2	1.2
32	Malta	0.3	0.4	0.4	1.0	0.4	80.4	91.6	93.7	18.5	15.2	11.1	18.3	2.1	1.5
33	Brunei Darussalam	0.2	0.4	0.5	2.9	2.0	62.0	76.1	82.8	30.3	25.8	2.4	4.3	5.4	2.5
34	Argentina	26.0	38.0	42.7	1.3	1.0	81.0	90.1	92.2	27.1	23.9	8.7	11.1	3.1	2.4
35	Hungary	10.5	10.2	9.8	−0.1	−0.3	52.8	65.2	70.0	16.2	14.0	13.1	17.5	2.1	1.3
36	Poland	34.0	38.6	38.1	0.5	−0.1	55.4	61.9	64.0	17.3	14.3	10.9	14.9	2.3	1.3
37	Chile	10.4	16.0	17.9	1.5	1.0	78.4	87.0	90.2	26.1	20.9	6.6	10.5	3.6	2.0
38	Estonia	1.4	1.3	1.3	−0.2	−0.3	67.6	69.5	71.4	16.2	15.7	13.9	17.4	2.2	1.4
39	Lithuania	3.3	3.5	3.3	0.2	−0.4	55.7	66.8	67.5	18.0	13.8	13.0	16.7	2.3	1.3
40	Qatar	0.2	0.7	1.0	5.2	2.3	84.8	92.0	93.6	23.1	21.8	0.9	2.0	6.8	3.0
41	United Arab Emirates	0.5	4.0	5.6	7.2	2.7	83.6	85.1	87.2	22.8	19.8	0.8	1.4	6.4	2.5
42	Slovakia	4.7	5.4	5.4	0.5	(.)	46.3	57.5	60.8	17.8	14.0	10.1	14.1	2.5	1.2
43	Bahrain	0.3	0.7	0.9	3.4	1.6	85.8	90.0	91.4	27.7	21.7	2.3	4.4	5.9	2.5
44	Kuwait	1.0	2.5	3.4	3.3	2.4	83.8	96.2	96.9	24.8	23.2	1.1	3.1	6.9	2.4
45	Croatia	4.3	4.5	4.5	0.2	−0.1	45.1	59.0	64.6	16.1	13.9	14.2	18.7	2.0	1.3
46	Uruguay	2.8	3.4	3.7	0.7	0.6	83.4	92.5	94.4	24.5	22.4	11.5	13.8	3.0	2.3
47	Costa Rica	2.1	4.2	5.0	2.5	1.5	42.5	60.6	66.8	29.7	23.8	4.7	7.4	4.3	2.3
48	Latvia	2.5	2.3	2.2	−0.2	−0.5	65.4	66.3	66.3	15.9	14.1	14.2	18.3	2.0	1.3
49	Saint Kitts and Nevis	(.)	(.)	(.)	−0.2	1.1	35.0	32.2	32.5	..	..	..	..	..	..
50	Bahamas	0.2	0.3	0.4	1.8	1.3	73.4	89.4	91.6	28.9	24.7	4.9	8.2	3.4	2.3
51	Seychelles	0.1	0.1	0.1	1.0	0.9	33.3	50.0	53.3	..	..	..	..	..	..
52	Cuba	9.3	11.2	11.4	0.7	0.2	64.2	75.7	78.1	19.9	16.6	8.6	14.4	3.5	1.6
53	Mexico	59.3	104.3	119.1	2.0	1.1	62.8	75.5	78.8	32.1	25.5	4.2	7.1	6.6	2.4

Human development indicators

TABLE 5

HDI rank	Total population (millions) 1975	2003	2015[b]	Annual population growth rate (%) 1975–2003	2003–15[b]	Urban population (% of total)[a] 1975	2003[b]	2015[b]	Population under age 15 (% of total) 2003	2015[b]	Population ages 65 and above (% of total) 2003	2015[b]	Total fertility rate (births per woman) 1970–75[c]	2000–05[c]
54 Tonga	0.1	0.1	0.1	0.4	0.2	24.4	33.5	38.2	36.5	30.7	4.6	6.9	5.5	3.5
55 Bulgaria	8.7	7.8	7.2	−0.4	−0.8	57.5	69.8	74.0	14.4	13.1	14.3	18.6	2.2	1.2
56 Panama	1.7	3.1	3.8	2.1	1.6	49.0	57.2	61.7	30.9	27.2	4.8	7.5	4.9	2.7
57 Trinidad and Tobago	1.0	1.3	1.3	0.9	0.3	63.0	75.4	79.7	22.7	20.2	5.9	9.9	3.5	1.6
MEDIUM HUMAN DEVELOPMENT														
58 Libyan Arab Jamahiriya	2.4	5.6	7.0	3.0	1.8	60.9	86.2	89.0	30.8	28.9	2.9	5.6	7.6	3.0
59 Macedonia, TFYR	1.7	2.0	2.1	0.7	0.1	50.6	59.6	62.0	20.6	16.6	8.8	12.9	3.0	1.5
60 Antigua and Barbuda	0.1	0.1	0.1	0.9	1.2	34.2	37.8	43.4	..	..	..	..	..	..
61 Malaysia	12.3	24.4	29.6	2.5	1.6	37.7	63.8	71.0	33.0	27.2	3.5	6.1	5.2	2.9
62 Russian Federation	134.2	144.6	136.7	0.3	−0.5	66.4	73.3	74.3	16.2	16.4	11.5	13.3	2.0	1.3
63 Brazil	108.1	181.4	209.4	1.8	1.2	61.2	83.0	88.4	28.4	25.4	4.9	7.8	4.7	2.3
64 Romania	21.2	21.9	20.9	0.1	−0.4	42.8	54.6	56.4	16.5	14.4	12.1	15.5	2.6	1.3
65 Mauritius	0.9	1.2	1.3	1.1	0.8	43.4	43.3	47.3	25.1	21.3	5.4	8.3	3.2	2.0
66 Grenada	0.1	0.1	0.1	0.4	1.3	32.6	40.7	49.5	..	..	..	..	..	..
67 Belarus	9.4	9.9	9.2	0.2	−0.6	50.3	70.9	75.2	16.4	14.5	12.5	13.5	2.3	1.2
68 Bosnia and Herzegovina	3.7	3.9	3.9	0.2	−0.1	31.3	44.4	51.1	17.4	14.0	10.3	16.7	2.6	1.3
69 Colombia	25.4	44.2	52.1	2.0	1.4	60.0	76.4	81.3	31.8	26.8	4.2	6.5	5.0	2.6
70 Dominica	0.1	0.1	0.1	0.3	0.9	55.3	72.0	76.2	..	..	..	..	..	..
71 Oman	0.9	2.5	3.2	3.6	1.9	19.6	77.6	82.6	35.2	30.6	1.8	3.4	7.2	3.8
72 Albania	2.4	3.1	3.3	0.9	0.6	32.7	43.8	51.2	28.3	23.1	6.3	9.9	4.7	2.3
73 Thailand	41.3	63.1	69.1	1.5	0.7	23.8	32.0	36.7	24.5	21.2	5.4	9.3	5.0	1.9
74 Samoa (Western)	0.2	0.2	0.2	0.7	0.3	21.1	22.3	24.7	41.0	34.2	3.7	5.0	5.7	4.4
75 Venezuela	12.7	25.8	31.3	2.5	1.6	75.8	87.6	90.0	32.1	27.8	4.0	6.8	4.9	2.7
76 Saint Lucia	0.1	0.2	0.2	1.3	0.8	23.6	30.5	36.8	29.9	25.4	6.1	7.3	5.7	2.2
77 Saudi Arabia	7.3	23.3	30.8	4.2	2.3	58.3	87.6	91.1	38.2	32.3	2.1	3.5	7.3	4.1
78 Ukraine	49.0	47.5	41.8	−0.1	−1.1	58.3	67.3	68.9	16.0	13.5	13.1	16.4	2.2	1.1
79 Peru	15.2	27.2	32.2	2.1	1.4	61.5	73.9	78.0	33.2	27.9	4.1	6.5	6.0	2.9
80 Kazakhstan	14.1	14.9	14.9	0.2	(.)	52.2	55.9	58.2	24.8	21.3	6.6	8.0	3.5	2.0
81 Lebanon	2.7	3.5	4.0	1.0	1.0	67.0	87.5	90.1	29.5	24.4	5.9	7.7	4.8	2.3
82 Ecuador	6.9	12.9	15.1	2.2	1.4	42.4	61.8	67.6	33.2	28.1	4.6	7.3	6.0	2.8
83 Armenia	2.8	3.0	3.0	0.3	−0.2	63.0	64.5	64.2	22.8	17.4	9.6	11.0	3.0	1.3
84 Philippines	42.0	80.2	96.8	2.3	1.6	35.6	61.0	69.2	36.1	30.0	3.0	4.9	6.0	3.2
85 China	927.8[d]	1,300.0[d]	1,393.0[d]	1.2[d]	0.6[d]	17.4	38.6	49.5	22.7	18.5	5.9	9.6	4.9	1.7
86 Suriname	0.4	0.4	0.5	0.7	0.5	49.5	76.0	81.6	30.9	26.7	5.1	7.2	5.3	2.6
87 Saint Vincent and the Grenadines	0.1	0.1	0.1	0.7	0.4	27.0	58.2	68.6	30.5	26.5	5.5	7.1	5.5	2.3
88 Paraguay	2.7	5.9	7.6	2.8	2.2	39.0	57.2	64.3	38.4	33.9	3.0	4.3	5.7	3.9
89 Tunisia	5.7	9.9	11.1	2.0	1.0	49.9	63.7	68.1	27.5	21.9	5.0	6.8	6.2	2.0
90 Jordan	1.9	5.4	7.0	3.7	2.1	57.8	79.1	81.1	38.0	31.7	2.3	4.0	7.8	3.5
91 Belize	0.1	0.3	0.3	2.4	1.8	50.2	48.4	51.8	37.9	31.2	3.5	4.7	6.3	3.2
92 Fiji	0.6	0.8	0.9	1.3	0.7	36.7	51.7	60.1	32.3	27.6	2.9	5.4	4.2	2.9
93 Sri Lanka	14.0	20.4	22.3	1.3	0.7	22.0	21.1	22.5	24.8	21.4	5.8	9.3	4.1	2.0
94 Turkey	41.2	71.3	82.6	2.0	1.2	41.6	66.3	71.9	29.7	25.8	4.3	6.2	5.3	2.5
95 Dominican Republic	5.1	8.6	10.1	1.9	1.3	45.7	59.3	64.6	33.6	29.5	3.2	5.3	5.6	2.7
96 Maldives	0.1	0.3	0.4	2.9	2.4	18.1	28.8	35.2	42.0	35.7	2.7	3.3	7.0	4.3
97 Turkmenistan	2.5	4.7	5.5	2.2	1.3	47.6	45.4	50.0	33.5	27.0	3.8	4.4	6.2	2.8
98 Jamaica	2.0	2.6	2.7	1.0	0.4	44.1	52.2	54.2	32.1	26.7	6.6	8.2	5.0	2.4
99 Iran, Islamic Rep. of	33.3	68.2	79.9	2.6	1.3	45.8	66.6	73.9	31.0	25.6	3.7	4.9	6.4	2.1
100 Georgia	4.9	4.6	4.2	−0.3	−0.7	49.5	52.0	51.6	20.0	15.8	11.5	14.4	2.6	1.5
101 Azerbaijan	5.7	8.3	9.1	1.3	0.7	51.5	50.1	51.3	27.9	21.2	5.5	6.7	4.3	1.9
102 Occupied Palestinian Territories	1.3	3.5	5.0	3.6	3.0	59.6	71.1	75.6	46.0	41.6	2.7	3.0	7.7	5.6
103 Algeria	16.0	31.9	38.1	2.5	1.5	40.3	58.8	65.3	31.2	26.7	3.6	5.0	7.4	2.5
104 El Salvador	4.1	6.6	8.0	1.7	1.6	41.5	59.4	64.2	34.7	29.8	4.4	6.2	6.1	2.9
105 Cape Verde	0.3	0.5	0.6	2.0	2.2	21.4	55.9	64.8	40.7	35.6	3.7	3.3	7.0	3.8
106 Syrian Arab Republic	7.5	18.1	23.8	3.1	2.3	45.1	50.2	52.4	38.0	33.2	2.5	3.6	7.5	3.5

Human development indicators

TABLE 5

Demographic trends

		Total population (millions)			Annual population growth rate (%)		Urban population (% of total) [a]			Population under age 15 (% of total)		Population ages 65 and above (% of total)		Total fertility rate (births per woman)	
HDI rank		1975	2003	2015 [b]	1975–2003	2003–15 [b]	1975	2003 [b]	2015 [b]	2003	2015 [b]	2003	2015 [b]	1970–75 [c]	2000–05 [c]
107	Guyana	0.7	0.7	0.7	0.1	−0.1	30.0	37.6	44.2	29.8	24.8	4.4	6.6	4.9	2.3
108	Viet Nam	48.0	82.0	95.0	1.9	1.2	18.9	25.8	32.4	31.1	25.0	4.6	5.6	6.7	2.3
109	Kyrgyzstan	3.3	5.1	5.9	1.6	1.1	37.9	34.0	35.4	32.8	27.5	5.0	5.5	4.7	2.7
110	Indonesia	134.4	217.4	246.8	1.7	1.1	19.3	45.5	57.8	29.0	25.2	4.2	6.4	5.2	2.4
111	Uzbekistan	14.0	25.8	30.7	2.2	1.4	39.1	36.7	37.0	34.8	28.3	3.8	4.4	6.3	2.7
112	Nicaragua	2.6	5.3	6.6	2.5	1.9	48.9	57.3	62.8	40.2	33.4	2.7	3.9	6.8	3.3
113	Bolivia	4.8	8.8	10.9	2.2	1.7	41.3	63.4	69.0	38.8	33.5	3.6	5.2	6.5	4.0
114	Mongolia	1.4	2.6	3.0	2.1	1.2	48.7	56.8	59.5	32.2	26.3	3.1	4.1	7.3	2.4
115	Moldova, Rep. of	3.8	4.2	4.1	0.3	−0.2	35.8	46.1	50.0	20.0	15.2	8.4	10.9	2.6	1.2
116	Honduras	3.0	6.9	8.8	3.0	2.0	32.1	45.6	51.3	40.3	33.8	3.1	4.5	7.1	3.7
117	Guatemala	6.2	12.0	15.9	2.4	2.3	36.7	46.3	51.9	43.6	39.7	3.5	4.7	6.2	4.6
118	Vanuatu	0.1	0.2	0.3	2.5	1.8	15.7	22.9	28.6	40.8	35.5	2.6	4.0	6.1	4.2
119	Egypt	39.3	71.3	88.2	2.1	1.8	43.5	42.2	44.9	34.3	31.4	3.8	5.5	5.7	3.3
120	South Africa	25.9	46.9	47.9	2.1	0.2	48.0	56.9	62.7	32.9	30.2	3.2	6.1	5.5	2.8
121	Equatorial Guinea	0.2	0.5	0.6	2.7	2.2	27.1	48.0	58.2	44.2	45.6	3.2	3.8	5.7	5.9
122	Tajikistan	3.4	6.4	7.6	2.2	1.5	35.5	24.8	24.4	40.4	33.0	3.0	3.5	6.8	3.8
123	Gabon	0.6	1.3	1.6	2.9	1.5	40.0	83.7	89.1	40.9	35.5	3.8	4.4	5.3	4.0
124	Morocco	17.3	30.6	36.2	2.0	1.4	37.8	57.4	64.8	31.9	28.4	3.9	5.2	6.9	2.8
125	Namibia	0.9	2.0	2.2	2.9	1.0	20.6	32.4	39.8	42.6	34.7	2.8	4.2	6.6	4.0
126	São Tomé and Principe	0.1	0.1	0.2	2.1	2.1	27.3	37.8	40.3	40.1	36.4	3.5	3.4	6.5	4.1
127	India	620.7	1,070.8	1,260.4	1.9	1.4	21.3	28.3	32.2	32.9	28.0	4.1	6.2	5.4	3.1
128	Solomon Islands	0.2	0.5	0.6	3.1	2.3	9.1	16.5	20.9	41.3	36.4	1.8	2.8	7.2	4.3
129	Myanmar	30.1	49.5	55.0	1.8	0.9	23.9	29.5	37.6	30.8	23.6	4.0	6.4	5.8	2.5
130	Cambodia	7.1	13.5	17.1	2.3	1.9	10.3	18.6	26.1	38.3	34.1	2.8	4.4	5.5	4.1
131	Botswana	0.9	1.8	1.7	2.5	−0.4	12.8	51.6	57.5	38.2	34.7	2.6	4.8	6.8	3.2
132	Comoros	0.3	0.8	1.0	3.1	2.5	21.2	35.0	43.0	42.4	38.5	2.1	3.1	7.1	4.9
133	Lao People's Dem. Rep.	3.0	5.7	7.3	2.2	2.1	11.1	20.7	27.4	41.7	37.1	2.9	3.7	6.2	4.8
134	Bhutan	1.2	2.1	2.7	2.1	2.2	3.5	8.5	12.6	39.5	34.7	3.6	5.1	5.9	4.4
135	Pakistan	68.3	151.8	193.4	2.9	2.0	26.4	34.1	39.5	39.5	34.1	3.0	4.2	6.6	4.3
136	Nepal	13.5	26.1	32.7	2.3	1.9	5.0	15.0	20.5	39.9	33.9	2.9	4.2	5.8	3.7
137	Papua New Guinea	2.9	5.7	7.0	2.4	1.8	11.9	13.2	14.5	41.0	34.0	1.8	2.7	6.1	4.1
138	Ghana	10.2	21.2	26.6	2.6	1.9	30.1	45.4	51.1	39.9	35.2	2.8	4.3	6.7	4.4
139	Bangladesh	73.2	136.6	168.2	2.2	1.7	9.9	24.3	29.6	36.3	31.4	2.8	4.2	6.2	3.2
140	Timor-Leste	0.7	0.8	1.5	0.7	4.9	8.9	7.7	9.5	42.5	46.7	2.2	3.0	6.2	7.8
141	Sudan	17.1	34.9	44.0	2.6	1.9	18.9	38.9	49.3	39.7	35.6	2.8	4.3	6.7	4.4
142	Congo	1.5	3.8	5.4	3.2	3.1	34.8	53.5	59.3	46.9	47.4	2.4	2.7	6.3	6.3
143	Togo	2.4	5.8	7.8	3.1	2.5	16.3	35.2	43.3	43.9	40.2	2.5	3.4	7.1	5.4
144	Uganda	10.8	26.9	41.9	3.3	3.7	8.3	12.3	14.2	50.4	50.8	2.1	2.2	7.1	7.1
145	Zimbabwe	6.2	12.9	13.8	2.6	0.6	19.6	35.0	41.4	41.0	36.6	2.9	4.1	7.7	3.6
LOW HUMAN DEVELOPMENT															
146	Madagascar	7.9	17.6	23.8	2.9	2.5	16.4	26.6	30.7	44.4	40.7	2.5	3.3	6.7	5.4
147	Swaziland	0.5	1.0	1.0	2.4	−0.3	14.0	23.6	27.0	42.1	37.2	2.7	4.6	6.9	4.0
148	Cameroon	7.6	15.7	19.0	2.6	1.6	26.9	51.4	59.9	41.9	37.2	2.9	3.9	6.3	4.6
149	Lesotho	1.1	1.8	1.7	1.6	−0.3	10.8	18.0	21.0	39.3	36.6	4.2	5.8	5.7	3.6
150	Djibouti	0.2	0.8	0.9	4.4	1.6	61.6	83.6	87.6	42.1	37.3	2.2	3.4	7.2	5.1
151	Yemen	7.0	19.7	28.5	3.7	3.1	14.8	25.7	31.3	47.1	43.4	1.8	2.4	8.5	6.2
152	Mauritania	1.4	2.9	4.0	2.5	2.7	20.3	61.7	73.9	43.1	41.7	2.7	3.4	6.5	5.8
153	Haiti	4.9	8.3	9.8	1.9	1.4	21.7	37.5	45.5	38.6	34.9	3.2	4.5	5.8	4.0
154	Kenya	13.5	32.7	44.2	3.2	2.5	12.9	39.3	51.8	43.1	42.6	2.3	2.8	8.0	5.0
155	Gambia	0.6	1.4	1.9	3.4	2.3	17.0	26.2	27.8	40.6	36.8	2.9	4.4	6.5	4.7
156	Guinea	4.2	9.0	11.9	2.7	2.3	16.3	34.9	44.2	43.9	42.0	2.8	3.9	6.9	5.9
157	Senegal	5.3	11.1	14.5	2.7	2.2	34.2	49.6	57.9	43.4	38.8	2.5	3.4	7.0	5.0
158	Nigeria	58.9	125.9	160.9	2.7	2.0	23.4	46.6	55.5	44.7	41.3	2.4	3.2	6.9	5.8
159	Rwanda	4.4	8.8	11.3	2.5	2.1	4.0	18.5	40.5	44.9	41.6	1.9	2.6	8.3	5.7

Human development indicators

TABLE 5

HDI rank	Total population (millions)			Annual population growth rate (%)		Urban population (% of total) [a]			Population under age 15 (% of total)		Population ages 65 and above (% of total)		Total fertility rate (births per woman)	
	1975	2003	2015 [b]	1975–2003	2003–15 [b]	1975	2003 [b]	2015 [b]	2003	2015 [b]	2003	2015 [b]	1970–75 [c]	2000–05 [c]
160 Angola	6.8	15.0	20.9	2.8	2.8	17.4	35.7	44.9	46.7	45.5	2.0	2.4	7.2	6.8
161 Eritrea	2.1	4.1	5.8	2.4	3.0	12.7	20.0	26.5	44.9	42.6	1.9	2.6	6.5	5.5
162 Benin	3.2	7.9	11.2	3.2	2.9	21.9	44.6	53.5	44.8	42.0	2.2	3.0	7.1	5.9
163 Côte d'Ivoire	6.6	17.6	21.6	3.5	1.7	32.1	44.9	51.0	42.4	38.2	2.4	3.7	7.4	5.1
164 Tanzania, U. Rep. of	16.0	36.9	45.6	3.0	1.8	10.1	35.4	46.8	43.2	38.9	2.5	3.7	6.8	5.0
165 Malawi	5.2	12.3	16.0	3.1	2.2	7.7	16.3	22.2	47.1	44.9	2.4	3.2	7.4	6.1
166 Zambia	5.2	11.3	13.8	2.8	1.7	34.8	35.9	40.8	46.1	43.7	2.4	3.2	7.8	5.7
167 Congo, Dem. Rep. of the	23.9	54.2	78.0	2.9	3.0	29.5	31.8	39.7	47.1	48.0	2.2	2.6	6.5	6.7
168 Mozambique	10.6	19.1	23.5	2.1	1.8	8.7	35.6	48.5	44.1	41.6	2.7	3.6	6.6	5.5
169 Burundi	3.7	7.0	10.6	2.3	3.4	3.2	10.0	14.6	46.2	46.4	2.3	2.5	6.8	6.8
170 Ethiopia	34.1	73.8	97.2	2.8	2.3	9.5	15.7	19.8	45.0	41.7	2.3	3.2	6.8	5.9
171 Central African Republic	2.1	3.9	4.6	2.3	1.4	33.7	42.7	50.3	43.2	40.6	3.3	4.0	5.7	5.0
172 Guinea-Bissau	0.7	1.5	2.1	3.0	3.0	16.0	34.0	43.5	47.2	48.0	2.5	2.8	7.1	7.1
173 Chad	4.2	9.1	12.8	2.8	2.8	15.6	25.0	31.1	47.1	47.7	2.5	2.7	6.7	6.7
174 Mali	6.2	12.7	18.1	2.6	2.9	16.2	32.3	40.9	48.3	46.7	2.2	2.4	7.6	6.9
175 Burkina Faso	5.9	12.4	17.7	2.6	2.9	6.3	17.8	23.2	47.7	45.7	2.3	2.6	7.8	6.7
176 Sierra Leone	2.9	5.1	6.9	2.0	2.5	21.4	38.8	47.6	42.8	42.8	2.6	3.3	6.5	6.5
177 Niger	5.3	13.1	19.3	3.2	3.3	10.6	22.2	29.7	49.0	47.9	1.6	2.0	8.1	7.9
Developing countries	2,967.1 T	5,022.4 T	5,885.6 T	1.9	1.3	26.4	42.0	48.6	31.6	28.0	4.3	6.5	5.5	2.9
Least developed countries	355.2 T	723.2 T	950.1 T	2.5	2.3	14.8	26.7	33.5	42.2	39.5	2.6	3.5	6.6	5.0
Arab States	144.6 T	303.9 T	386.0 T	2.7	2.0	41.7	54.7	59.1	36.3	32.5	3.1	4.4	6.7	3.7
East Asia and the Pacific	1,310.4 T	1,928.1 T	2,108.9 T	1.4	0.7	20.4	41.0	51.0	24.9	20.7	5.4	8.7	5.0	1.9
Latin America and the Caribbean	318.4 T	540.7 T	628.3 T	1.9	1.3	61.1	76.7	80.9	30.8	26.5	4.9	7.5	5.1	2.5
South Asia	838.7 T	1,503.4 T	1,801.4 T	2.1	1.5	21.3	29.8	34.2	34.1	29.3	3.8	5.7	5.6	3.2
Sub-Saharan Africa	313.1 T	674.2 T	877.4 T	2.7	2.2	21.0	35.6	42.4	44.0	42.0	2.5	3.3	6.8	5.5
Central and Eastern Europe and the CIS	366.6 T	406.3 T	396.8 T	0.4	-0.2	56.8	62.9	63.8	19.1	17.3	10.6	12.9	2.5	1.5
OECD	925.7 T	1,157.3 T	1,233.6 T	0.8	0.5	67.2	75.9	78.9	19.8	17.8	11.6	16.1	2.6	1.8
High-income OECD	765.9 T	917.4 T	968.5 T	0.6	0.5	69.9	77.5	80.4	17.9	16.4	13.0	18.0	2.2	1.6
High human development	972.2 T	1,211.5 T	1,289.2 T	0.8	0.5	68.7	77.2	80.1	19.6	17.6	11.7	16.2	2.5	1.7
Medium human development	2,678.2 T	4,205.8 T	4,753.6 T	1.6	1.0	27.9	42.2	48.6	29.2	25.3	4.9	7.2	5.0	2.5
Low human development	359.5 T	788.7 T	1,038.5 T	2.8	2.3	18.2	34.0	41.7	44.9	42.6	2.4	3.1	7.0	5.8
High income	781.8 T	948.3 T	1,005.6 T	0.7	0.5	70.1	78.0	80.8	18.0	16.5	12.8	17.7	2.2	1.7
Middle income	1,849.6 T	2,748.6 T	3,028.6 T	1.4	0.8	34.8	52.9	60.7	25.9	22.3	5.8	8.6	4.5	2.1
Low income	1,440.9 T	2,614.5 T	3,182.5 T	2.1	1.6	20.7	30.2	35.7	37.2	33.3	3.4	4.9	6.0	3.9
World	4,073.7 T [e]	6,313.8 T [e]	7,219.4 T [e]	1.6	1.1	37.2	48.3	53.5	28.9	25.9	6.0	8.4	4.5	2.6

NOTES

a Because data are based on national definitions of what constitutes a city or metropolitan area, cross-country comparisons should be made with caution.

b Data refer to medium-variant projections.

c Data refer to estimates for the period specified.

d Population estimates include Taiwan, province of China.

e Data refer to the total world population according to UN 2005h. The total population of the 177 countries included in the main indicator tables was estimated to be 4,068.1 million in 1975, 6,305.6 million in 2003 and projected to be 7,210.3 in 2015.

SOURCES

Columns 1-3, 13 and 14: UN 2005h.

Columns 4 and 5: calculated on the basis of columns 1 and 2.

Columns 6-8: UN 2004.

Columns 9 and 10: calculated on the basis of data on population under age 15 and total population from UN 2005h.

Columns 11 and 12: calculated on the basis of data on population ages 65 and above and total population from UN 2005h.

Human development indicators

TABLE 6

. . . to lead a long and healthy life . . .

Commitment to health: resources, access and services

	Health expenditure			One-year-olds fully immunized		MDG Children with diarrhoea receiving oral rehydration and continued feeding	Contraceptive prevalence rate[a]	MDG Births attended by skilled health personnel	Physicians (per 100,000 people)
HDI rank	Public (% of GDP) 2002	Private (% of GDP) 2002	Per capita (PPP US$) 2002	Against tuberculosis (%) 2003	Against measles (%) 2003	(% under age 5) 1994–2003[b]	(%) 1995–2003[b]	(%) 1995–2003[b]	1990–2004[b]
HIGH HUMAN DEVELOPMENT									
1 Norway	8.0	1.6	3,409	..	84	..	74	100[c]	356
2 Iceland	8.3	1.6	2,802	..	93	..	..	..	347
3 Australia	6.5	3.0	2,699	..	93	..	76	100	249
4 Luxembourg	5.3	0.9	3,066	..	91	..	..	100[c]	255
5 Canada	6.7	2.9	2,931	..	95	..	75	98	209
6 Sweden	7.8	1.4	2,512	16[d]	94	..	78	100[c]	305
7 Switzerland	6.5	4.7	3,446	..	82	..	82	..	352
8 Ireland	5.5	1.8	2,367	90	78	..	..	100	237
9 Belgium	6.5	2.6	2,515	..	75	..	78	100[c]	418
10 United States	6.6	8.0	5,274	..	93	..	76	99	549
11 Japan	6.5	1.4	2,133	..	99	..	56	100	201
12 Netherlands	5.8	3.0	2,564	..	96	..	79	100	329
13 Finland	5.5	1.8	1,943	98	97	..	77	100[c]	311
14 Denmark	7.3	1.5	2,583	..	96	..	78	100[c]	366
15 United Kingdom	6.4	1.3	2,160	..	80	..	84[e]	99	166
16 France	7.4	2.3	2,736	85	86	..	75	99[c]	329
17 Austria	5.4	2.3	2,220	..	79	..	51	100[c]	324
18 Italy	6.4	2.1	2,166	..	83	..	60	..	606
19 New Zealand	6.6	1.9	1,857	..	85	..	75	100	223
20 Germany	8.6	2.3	2,817	..	92	..	75	100[c]	362
21 Spain	5.4	2.2	1,640	..	97	..	81	..	320
22 Hong Kong, China (SAR)	..	..	..	..	..	..	86	..	..
23 Israel	6.0	3.1	1,890	..	95	..	68	99[c]	391
24 Greece	5.0	4.5	1,814	88	88	..	..	..	440
25 Singapore	1.3	3.0	1,105	97	88	..	62	100	140
26 Slovenia	6.2	2.1	1,547	98	94	..	74	100[c]	219
27 Portugal	6.6	2.7	1,702	81	96	..	66	100	324
28 Korea, Rep. of	2.6	2.4	982	87	96	..	81	100	181
29 Cyprus	2.9	4.1	883	..	86	..	..	100[c]	298
30 Barbados	4.7	2.2	1,018	..	90	..	55	91	121
31 Czech Republic	6.4	0.6	1,118	98	99	..	72	99	343
32 Malta	7.0	2.7	965	..	90	..	..	98[c]	293
33 Brunei Darussalam	2.7	0.8	653	99	99	..	..	99	101
34 Argentina	4.5	4.4	956	99	97	..	..	99	301
35 Hungary	5.5	2.3	1,078	99	99	..	77	..	316
36 Poland	4.4	1.7	657	94	97	..	49	99[c]	220
37 Chile	2.6	3.2	642	94	99	..	..	100	109
38 Estonia	3.9	1.2	604	99	95	..	70	..	316
39 Lithuania	4.3	1.6	549	99	98	..	47	..	403
40 Qatar	2.4	0.7	894	99	93	..	43	98	221
41 United Arab Emirates	2.3	0.8	750	98	94	..	28	96	202
42 Slovakia	5.3	0.6	723	98	99	..	74	..	325
43 Bahrain	3.2	1.2	792	..	100	..	62	98	160
44 Kuwait	2.9	0.9	552	..	97	..	50	98	153
45 Croatia	5.9	1.4	630	98	95	..	..	100	237
46 Uruguay	2.9	7.1	805	99	95	..	..	100	365
47 Costa Rica	6.1	3.2	743	87	89	..	80	98	173
48 Latvia	3.3	1.8	477	99	99	..	48	100	291
49 Saint Kitts and Nevis	3.4	2.1	667	99	98	..	41	99	118
50 Bahamas	3.4	3.5	1,074	..	90	..	62	99[c]	106
51 Seychelles	3.9	1.3	557	99	99	..	..	..	132
52 Cuba	6.5	1.0	236	99	99	..	73	100	591
53 Mexico	2.7	3.4	550	99	96	..	68	86	171

Human development indicators

TABLE 6

HDI rank	Health expenditure Public (% of GDP) 2002	Health expenditure Private (% of GDP) 2002	Per capita (PPP US$) 2002	One-year-olds fully immunized Against tuberculosis (%) 2003	MDG One-year-olds fully immunized Against measles (%) 2003	Children with diarrhoea receiving oral rehydration and continued feeding (% under age 5) 1994–2003 [b]	Contraceptive prevalence rate [a] (%) 1995–2003 [b]	MDG Births attended by skilled health personnel (%) 1995–2003 [b]	Physicians (per 100,000 people) 1990–2004 [b]
54 Tonga	5.1	1.8	292	99	99	..	..	92	34
55 Bulgaria	4.0	3.4	499	98	96	..	42	..	338
56 Panama	6.4	2.5	576	87	83	..	58	90	168
57 Trinidad and Tobago	1.4	2.3	428	..	88	31	38	96	79
MEDIUM HUMAN DEVELOPMENT									
58 Libyan Arab Jamahiriya	1.6	1.7	222	99	91	..	45	94	129
59 Macedonia, TFYR	..	..	..	..	96	..	..	..	..
60 Antigua and Barbuda	3.3	1.5	527	..	99	..	53	100	17
61 Malaysia	2.0	1.8	349	99	92	..	55	97	70
62 Russian Federation	3.5	2.7	535	97	96	..	73	99	417
63 Brazil	3.6	4.3	611	99	99	28	77	88	206
64 Romania	4.2	2.1	469	99	97	..	64	98	189
65 Mauritius	2.2	0.7	317	92	94	..	75	99	85
66 Grenada	4.0	1.7	465	..	99	..	54	99	50
67 Belarus	4.7	1.7	583	99	99	..	50	100	450
68 Bosnia and Herzegovina	4.6	4.6	322	94	84	23	48	100	134
69 Colombia	6.7	1.4	536	96	92	44	77	86	135
70 Dominica	4.6	1.8	310	99	99	42	50	100	49
71 Oman	2.8	0.6	379	98	98	..	24	95	126
72 Albania	2.4	3.7	302	95	93	51	75	94	139
73 Thailand	3.1	1.3	321	99	94	..	72	99	30
74 Samoa (Western)	4.7	1.5	238	73	99	..	..	100	70
75 Venezuela	2.3	2.6	272	91	82	51	49	94	194
76 Saint Lucia	3.4	1.6	306	95	90	..	47	100	518
77 Saudi Arabia	3.3	1.0	534	94	96	..	32	91	140
78 Ukraine	3.3	1.4	210	98	99	..	68	100	297
79 Peru	2.2	2.2	226	94	95	46	69	59	117
80 Kazakhstan	1.9	1.6	261	99	99	22	66	99	330
81 Lebanon	3.5	8.0	697	..	96	..	61	89	325
82 Ecuador	1.7	3.1	197	99	99	..	66	69	148
83 Armenia	1.3	4.5	232	92	94	48	61	97	353
84 Philippines	1.1	1.8	153	91	80	37	49	60	116
85 China	2.0	3.8	261	93	84	..	84	97	164
86 Suriname	3.6	5.0	385	..	71	43	42	85	45
87 Saint Vincent and the Grenadines	3.9	2.0	340	87	94	..	58	100	88
88 Paraguay	3.2	5.2	343	70	91	..	73	71	117
89 Tunisia	2.9	2.9	415	93	90	..	63	90	70
90 Jordan	4.3	5.0	418	67	96	..	56	100	205
91 Belize	2.5	2.7	300	99	96	..	47	83	105
92 Fiji	2.7	1.5	240	99	91	..	41	100	34
93 Sri Lanka	1.8	1.9	131	99	99	..	70	97	43
94 Turkey	4.3	2.2	420	89	75	19	64	81	124
95 Dominican Republic	2.2	3.9	295	90	79	53	70	99	188
96 Maldives	5.1	0.7	307	98	96	..	42	70	78
97 Turkmenistan	3.0	1.3	182	99	97	..	62	97	317
98 Jamaica	3.4	2.6	234	88	78	21	66	95	85
99 Iran, Islamic Rep. of	2.9	3.1	432	99	99	..	73	90	105
100 Georgia	1.0	2.8	123	87	73	..	41	96	391
101 Azerbaijan	0.8	2.9	120	99	98	40	55	84	354
102 Occupied Palestinian Territories	..	..	..	99	..	..	..	97	84
103 Algeria	3.2	1.1	182	98	84	..	64	92	85
104 El Salvador	3.6	4.4	372	90	99	..	67	69	124
105 Cape Verde	3.8	1.2	193	78	68	..	53	89	17
106 Syrian Arab Republic	2.3	2.8	109	99	98	..	40	76 [c]	140

Human development indicators

TABLE 6

Commitment to health: resources, access and services

HDI rank		Public (% of GDP) 2002	Private (% of GDP) 2002	Per capita (PPP US$) 2002	Against tuberculosis (%) 2003	MDG Against measles (%) 2003	Children with diarrhoea receiving oral rehydration and continued feeding (% under age 5) 1994–2003 [b]	Contraceptive prevalence rate [a] (%) 1995–2003 [b]	MDG Births attended by skilled health personnel (%) 1995–2003 [b]	Physicians (per 100,000 people) 1990–2004 [b]
		Health expenditure			**One-year-olds fully immunized**					
107	Guyana	4.3	1.3	227	95	89	40	37	86	48
108	Viet Nam	1.5	3.7	148	98	93	24	79	85	53
109	Kyrgyzstan	2.2	2.1	117	99	99	16	60	98	268
110	Indonesia	1.2	2.0	110	82	72	61	60	68	16
111	Uzbekistan	2.5	3.0	143	98	99	33	68	96	289
112	Nicaragua	3.9	4.0	206	94	93	49	69	67	164
113	Bolivia	4.2	2.8	179	94	64	59	53	65	73
114	Mongolia	4.6	2.0	128	98	98	66	67	99	267
115	Moldova, Rep. of	4.1	2.9	151	98	96	52	62	99	269
116	Honduras	3.2	3.0	156	91	95	..	62	56	83
117	Guatemala	2.3	2.5	199	97	75	22	43	41	90
118	Vanuatu	2.8	1.0	121	63	48	..	..	89	11
119	Egypt	1.8	3.1	192	98	98	29	60	69	212
120	South Africa	3.5	5.2	689	97	83	37	56	84	69
121	Equatorial Guinea	1.3	0.5	139	73	51	36	..	65	25
122	Tajikistan	0.9	2.4	47	99	89	29	34	71	218
123	Gabon	1.8	2.5	248	89	55	44	33	86	29
124	Morocco	1.5	3.1	186	92	90	..	50	40	48
125	Namibia	4.7	2.0	331	92	70	39	29	78	30
126	São Tomé and Principe	9.7	1.4	108	99	87	44	29	79	47
127	India	1.3	4.8	96	81	67	22	48 [f]	43	51
128	Solomon Islands	4.5	0.3	83	76	78	..	..	85	13
129	Myanmar	0.4	1.8	30	79	75	48	37	56	30
130	Cambodia	2.1	9.9	192	76	65	..	24	32	16
131	Botswana	3.7	2.3	387	99	90	7	40	94	29
132	Comoros	1.7	1.2	27	75	63	31	26	62	7
133	Lao People's Dem. Rep.	1.5	1.4	49	65	42	37	32	19	59
134	Bhutan	4.1	0.4	76	93	88	..	19	24	5
135	Pakistan	1.1	2.1	62	82	61	33 [c]	28	23	66
136	Nepal	1.4	3.8	64	91	75	43	39	11	5
137	Papua New Guinea	3.8	0.5	136	60	49	..	26	53	5
138	Ghana	2.3	3.3	73	92	80	24	25	44	9
139	Bangladesh	0.8	2.3	54	95	77	35	58	14	23
140	Timor-Leste	6.2	3.5	195	80	60	..	10	24	..
141	Sudan	1.0	3.9	58	53	57	38	10	86 [c]	16
142	Congo	1.5	0.7	25	60	50	..	..	..	25
143	Togo	1.1	9.4	163	84	58	25	26	49	6
144	Uganda	2.1	5.3	77	96	82	29	23	39	5
145	Zimbabwe	4.4	4.1	152	92	80	80	54	73	6
LOW HUMAN DEVELOPMENT										
146	Madagascar	1.2	0.9	18	72	55	47	27	46	9
147	Swaziland	3.6	2.4	309	97	94	24	28	70	18
148	Cameroon	1.2	3.4	68	82	61	33	19	60	7
149	Lesotho	5.3	0.9	119	83	70	29	30	60	5
150	Djibouti	3.3	3.0	78	63	66	..	..	61	13
151	Yemen	1.0	2.7	58	67	66	23 [c]	21	22	22
152	Mauritania	2.9	1.0	54	84	71	..	8	57	14
153	Haiti	3.0	4.6	83	71	53	41	27	24	25
154	Kenya	2.2	2.7	70	87	72	15	39	41	13
155	Gambia	3.3	4.0	83	99	90	38	10	55	4
156	Guinea	0.9	4.9	105	78	52	29	6	35	9
157	Senegal	2.3	2.8	62	77	60	33	11	58	8
158	Nigeria	1.2	3.5	43	48	35	28	13	35	27
159	Rwanda	3.1	2.4	48	88	90	16	13	31	2

TABLE 6

	Health expenditure			One-year-olds fully immunized		MDG Children with diarrhoea receiving oral rehydration and continued feeding	Contraceptive prevalence rate[a]	MDG Births attended by skilled health personnel	Physicians (per 100,000 people)
	Public (% of GDP)	**Private** (% of GDP)	**Per capita** (PPP US$)	**Against tuberculosis** (%)	**Against measles** (%)	(% under age 5)	(%)	(%)	
HDI rank	2002	2002	2002	2003	2003	1994–2003[b]	1995–2003[b]	1995–2003[b]	1990–2004[b]
160 Angola	2.1	2.9	92	62	62	32	6	45	8
161 Eritrea	3.2	1.9	36	91	84	..	8	28	3
162 Benin	2.1	2.6	44	99	83	42	19	66	6
163 Côte d'Ivoire	1.4	4.8	107	66	56	34	15	63	9
164 Tanzania, U. Rep. of	2.7	2.2	31	91	97	38	25	36	2
165 Malawi	4.0	5.8	48	91	77	51	31	61	1
166 Zambia	3.1	2.7	51	94	84	24	34	43	7
167 Congo, Dem. Rep. of the	1.2	2.9	15	68	54	17	31	61	7
168 Mozambique	4.1	1.7	50	87	77	33	6	48	2
169 Burundi	0.6	2.4	16	84	75	16	16	25	5
170 Ethiopia	2.6	3.1	21	76	52	38	8	6	3
171 Central African Republic	1.6	2.3	50	70	35	47	28	44	4
172 Guinea-Bissau	3.0	3.3	38	84	61	23	8	35	17
173 Chad	2.7	3.8	47	72	61	50	8	16	3
174 Mali	2.3	2.2	33	63	68	45	8	41	4
175 Burkina Faso	2.0	2.3	38	83	76	..	14	31	4
176 Sierra Leone	1.7	1.2	27	87	73	39	4	42	7
177 Niger	2.0	2.0	27	64	64	43	14	16	3
Developing countries	..	..	..	85	75	..	..	59	..
Least developed countries	..	..	..	79	67	..	..	34	..
Arab States	..	..	..	86	84	..	..	70	..
East Asia and the Pacific	..	..	..	91	82	..	..	86	..
Latin America and the Caribbean	..	..	..	96	93	..	..	82	..
South Asia	..	..	..	83	68	..	..	38	..
Sub-Saharan Africa	..	..	..	75	62	..	..	41	..
Central and Eastern Europe and the CIS	..	..	..	97	97	..	..	97	..
OECD	..	..	..	..	91	..	..	95	..
High-income OECD	..	..	..	..	92	..	..	99	..
High human development	..	..	..	..	93	..	..	97	..
Medium human development	..	..	..	89	79	..	..	68	..
Low human development	..	..	..	75	61	..	..	35	..
High income	..	..	..	..	92	..	..	99	..
Middle income	..	..	..	95	89	..	..	88	..
Low income	..	..	..	79	66	..	..	42	..
World	..	..	..	85[g]	77[g]	..	..	62[g]	

NOTES

a Data usually refer to married women ages 15–49; the actual age range covered may vary across countries.

b Data refer to the most recent year available during the period specified.

c Data refer to a year or period other than that specified, differ from the standard definition or refer to only part of a country.

d Only high-risk children.

e Excluding Northern Ireland.

f Excluding the state of Tripura.

g Data refer to the world aggregate from UNICEF 2004.

SOURCES

Columns 1–3: WHO 2005a.

Columns 4 and 6: UNICEF 2004.

Columns 5 and 8: UN 2005f, based on a joint effort by the United Nations Children's Fund and the World Health Organization.

Column 7: UN 2005e.

Column 9: WHO 2005b.

TABLE 7 . . . to lead a long and healthy life . . .

Water, sanitation and nutritional status

HDI rank		MDG Population with sustainable access to improved sanitation (%)		MDG Population with sustainable access to an improved water source (%)		MDG Population undernourished (% of total)		MDG Children under weight for age (% under age 5)	Children under height for age (% under age 5)	Infants with low birthweight (%)
		1990	2002	1990	2002	1990/92[a]	2000/02[a]	1995–2003[b]	1995–2003[b]	1998–2003[b]
HIGH HUMAN DEVELOPMENT										
1	Norway	..	..	100	100	..	..	..	..	5
2	Iceland	..	..	100	100	..	..	..	..	4
3	Australia	100	100	100	100	..	..	..	..	7
4	Luxembourg	..	..	100	100	..	..	..	..	8
5	Canada	100	100	100	100	..	..	..	..	6
6	Sweden	100	100	100	100	..	..	..	..	4
7	Switzerland	100	100	100	100	..	..	..	..	6
8	Ireland	..	..	..	..	..	..	..	..	6
9	Belgium	..	..	..	..	..	..	..	..	8[c]
10	United States	100	100	100	100	..	..	1[d]	2[c]	8
11	Japan	100	100	100	100	..	..	..	..	8
12	Netherlands	100	100	100	100	..	..	..	..	..
13	Finland	100	100	100	100	..	..	..	..	4
14	Denmark	..	..	100	100	..	..	..	..	5
15	United Kingdom	..	..	..	..	..	..	..	..	8
16	France	..	..	..	..	..	..	..	..	7
17	Austria	100	100	100	100	..	..	..	..	7
18	Italy	..	..	..	..	..	..	..	..	6
19	New Zealand	..	..	97	..	..	..	..	..	6
20	Germany	..	..	100	100	..	..	..	..	7
21	Spain	..	..	..	..	..	..	..	..	6[c]
22	Hong Kong, China (SAR)	..	..	..	..	..	..	..	..	..
23	Israel	..	..	100	100	..	..	..	..	8
24	Greece	..	..	..	..	..	..	..	..	8
25	Singapore	..	..	..	..	..	..	14[d]	11[c]	8
26	Slovenia	..	..	..	..	..	3	..	..	6
27	Portugal	..	..	..	..	..	..	..	..	8
28	Korea, Rep. of	..	..	..	92	2	2	..	..	4
29	Cyprus	100	100	100	100	..	..	..	..	..
30	Barbados	100	99	100	100	..	..	6[d]	7[c]	10[c]
31	Czech Republic	..	..	..	..	..	2	1[d]	2[c]	7
32	Malta	..	..	100	100	..	..	..	..	6
33	Brunei Darussalam	..	..	..	..	..	..	..	..	10
34	Argentina	82	..	94	..	2	2	5	12	7
35	Hungary	..	95	99	99	..	1	2[d]	3[c]	9
36	Poland	..	..	..	..	..	1	..	..	6
37	Chile	85	92	90	95	8	4	1	2	5
38	Estonia	..	..	..	..	..	5	..	..	4
39	Lithuania	..	..	..	..	..	1	..	..	4
40	Qatar	100	100	100	100	..	..	6	8	10
41	United Arab Emirates	100	100	..	..	4	2	14	17	15[c]
42	Slovakia	100	100	100	100	..	5	..	..	7
43	Bahrain	..	..	..	..	..	..	9	10	8
44	Kuwait	..	..	..	..	23	5	10	24	7
45	Croatia	..	..	..	..	..	7	1	1	6
46	Uruguay	..	94	..	98	6	4	5	8	8
47	Costa Rica	..	92	..	97	6	4	5	6	7
48	Latvia	..	..	..	..	..	4	..	..	5
49	Saint Kitts and Nevis	96	96	99	99	..	..	..	..	9
50	Bahamas	100	100	..	97	..	..	..	..	7
51	Seychelles	..	..	..	87	..	..	6[d]	5[c]	..
52	Cuba	98	98	..	91	8	3	4	5	6
53	Mexico	66	77	80	91	5	5	8	18	9

Human development indicators

TABLE 7

HDI rank	Population with sustainable access to improved sanitation (%)		Population with sustainable access to an improved water source (%)		Population undernourished (% of total)		Children under weight for age (% under age 5)	Children under height for age (% under age 5)	Infants with low birthweight (%)
	MDG		**MDG**		**MDG**		**MDG**		
	1990	2002	1990	2002	1990/92[a]	2000/02[a]	1995–2003[b]	1995–2003[b]	1998–2003[b]
54 Tonga	97	97	100	100	..	..	..	..	0
55 Bulgaria	100	100	100	100	..	11	..	..	10
56 Panama	..	72	..	91	21	26	7	14	10[c]
57 Trinidad and Tobago	100	100	92	91	13	12	7[d]	5[c]	23
MEDIUM HUMAN DEVELOPMENT									
58 Libyan Arab Jamahiriya	97	97	71	72	1	1	5	15	7[c]
59 Macedonia, TFYR	..	..	..	..	..	11	6	7	5
60 Antigua and Barbuda	..	95	..	91	..	..	10[d]	7[c]	8
61 Malaysia	96	..	..	95	3	2	12	..	10
62 Russian Federation	87	87	94	96	..	4	3	13	6
63 Brazil	70	75	83	89	12	9	6	11	10[c]
64 Romania	..	51	..	57	..	1	6[d]	8[c]	9
65 Mauritius	99	99	100	100	6	6	15	10	13
66 Grenada	97	97	..	95	..	..	..	..	9
67 Belarus	..	..	100	100	..	2	..	..	5
68 Bosnia and Herzegovina	..	93	98	98	..	8	4	10	4
69 Colombia	82	86	92	92	17	13	7	14	9
70 Dominica	..	83	..	97	..	..	5[d]	6[c]	10
71 Oman	83	89	77	79	..	..	24	23	8
72 Albania	..	89	97	97	..	6	14	32	3
73 Thailand	80	99	81	85	28	20	19[d]	16[c]	9
74 Samoa (Western)	98	100	91	88	..	..	..	..	4[c]
75 Venezuela	..	68	..	83	11	17	4	13[c]	7
76 Saint Lucia	..	89	98	98	..	..	14[d]	11[c]	8
77 Saudi Arabia	..	..	90	..	4	3	14	20	11[c]
78 Ukraine	99	99	..	98	..	3	3	15	5
79 Peru	52	62	74	81	42	13	7	25	11[c]
80 Kazakhstan	72	72	86	86	..	13	4	10	8
81 Lebanon	..	98	100	100	3	3	3	12	6
82 Ecuador	56	72	69	86	8	4	12	26	16
83 Armenia	..	84	..	92	..	34	3	13	7
84 Philippines	54	73	87	85	26	22	31	31	20
85 China	23	44	70	77	16	11	10	14	6
86 Suriname	..	93	..	92	13	11	13	10	13
87 Saint Vincent and the Grenadines	..	..	..	..	..	..	..	..	10
88 Paraguay	58	78	62	83	18	14	5	..	9[c]
89 Tunisia	75	80	77	82	1	1	4	12	7
90 Jordan	..	93	98	91	4	7	4	9	10[c]
91 Belize	..	47	..	91	..	..	6[d]	..	6
92 Fiji	98	98	..	..	..	..	8[d]	3[c]	10
93 Sri Lanka	70	91	68	78	28	22	29	14	22
94 Turkey	84	83	81	93	2	3	8	16	16
95 Dominican Republic	48	57	86	93	27	25	5	9	11
96 Maldives	..	58	99	84	..	..	30	25	22
97 Turkmenistan	..	62	..	71	..	9	12	22	6
98 Jamaica	75	80	92	93	14	10	4	5	9
99 Iran, Islamic Rep. of	83	84	91	93	4	4	11	15	7[c]
100 Georgia	..	83	..	76	..	27	3	12	6
101 Azerbaijan	..	55	66	77	..	15	7	13	11
102 Occupied Palestinian Territories	..	76	..	94	..	..	4	9	9
103 Algeria	88	92	95	87	5	5	6	18	7
104 El Salvador	51	63	67	82	12	11	10	19	13
105 Cape Verde	..	42	..	80	..	..	14[d]	16[c]	13
106 Syrian Arab Republic	76	77	79	79	5	4	7	18	6

Human development indicators

TABLE 7

Water, sanitation and nutritional status

Human development indicators

		MDG Population with sustainable access to improved sanitation (%)		MDG Population with sustainable access to an improved water source (%)		MDG Population undernourished (% of total)		MDG Children under weight for age (% under age 5)	Children under height for age (% under age 5)	Infants with low birthweight (%)
HDI rank		1990	2002	1990	2002	1990/92[a]	2000/02[a]	1995–2003[b]	1995–2003[b]	1998–2003[b]
107	Guyana	..	70	..	83	21	9	14	11	12
108	Viet Nam	22	41	72	73	31	19	33	36	9
109	Kyrgyzstan	..	60	..	76	..	6	11	25	7 c
110	Indonesia	46	52	71	78	9	6	26	..	9
111	Uzbekistan	58	57	89	89	..	26	8	21	7
112	Nicaragua	47	66	69	81	30	27	10	20	12
113	Bolivia	33	45	72	85	28	21	8	27	9
114	Mongolia	..	59	62	62	34	28	13	25	8
115	Moldova, Rep. of	..	68	..	92	..	11	3	10	5
116	Honduras	49	68	83	90	23	22	17	29	14
117	Guatemala	50	61	77	95	16	24	23	49	13
118	Vanuatu	..	..	60	60	..	..	20 d	19 c	6
119	Egypt	54	68	94	98	4	3	9	16	12
120	South Africa	63	67	83	87	..	..	12	25	15
121	Equatorial Guinea	..	53	..	44	..	..	19	39	13
122	Tajikistan	..	53	..	58	..	61	..	36	15
123	Gabon	..	36	..	87	10	6	12	21	14
124	Morocco	57	61	75	80	6	7	9	24	11 c
125	Namibia	24	30	58	80	35	22	24	24	14
126	São Tomé and Principe	..	24	..	79	..	..	13	29	..
127	India	12	30	68	86	25	21	47	46	30
128	Solomon Islands	..	31	..	70	..	..	21 d	27 c	13 c
129	Myanmar	21	73	48	80	10	6	35	34	15
130	Cambodia	..	16	..	34	43	33	45	45	11
131	Botswana	38	41	93	95	23	32	13	23	10
132	Comoros	23	23	89	94	..	..	25	42	25
133	Lao People's Dem. Rep.	..	24	..	43	29	22	40	41	14
134	Bhutan	..	70	..	62	..	..	19	40	15
135	Pakistan	38	54	83	90	24	20	38	37	19 c
136	Nepal	12	27	69	84	20	17	48	51	21
137	Papua New Guinea	45	45	39	39	..	..	35 d	..	11 c
138	Ghana	43	58	54	79	37	13	25	26	11
139	Bangladesh	23	48	71	75	35	30	48	45	30
140	Timor-Leste	..	33	..	52	..	..	43	47	10
141	Sudan	33	34	64	69	32	27	17	..	31
142	Congo	..	9	..	46	54	37	14	19	..
143	Togo	37	34	49	51	33	26	25	22	15
144	Uganda	43	41	44	56	24	19	23	39	12
145	Zimbabwe	49	57	77	83	45	44	13	27	11
LOW HUMAN DEVELOPMENT										
146	Madagascar	12	33	40	45	35	37	33	49	14
147	Swaziland	..	52	..	52	14	19	10	30	9
148	Cameroon	21	48	50	63	33	25	21	35	11
149	Lesotho	37	37	..	76	17	12	18	46	14
150	Djibouti	48	50	78	80	..	..	18	26	..
151	Yemen	21	30	69	69	34	36	46	53	32 c
152	Mauritania	28	42	41	56	15	10	32	35	..
153	Haiti	15	34	53	71	65	47	17	23	21
154	Kenya	42	48	45	62	44	33	20	31	11
155	Gambia	..	53	..	82	22	27	17	19	17
156	Guinea	17	13	42	51	39	26	23	26	12
157	Senegal	35	52	66	72	23	24	23	25	18
158	Nigeria	39	38	49	60	13	9	29	38 c	14
159	Rwanda	37	41	58	73	44	37	27	41	9

TABLE 7

HDI rank	MDG Population with sustainable access to improved sanitation (%)		MDG Population with sustainable access to an improved water source (%)		MDG Population undernourished (% of total)		MDG Children under weight for age (% under age 5)	Children under height for age (% under age 5)	Infants with low birthweight (%)
	1990	2002	1990	2002	1990/92 [a]	2000/02 [a]	1995–2003 [b]	1995–2003 [b]	1998–2003 [b]
160 Angola	30	30	32	50	58	40	31	45	12
161 Eritrea	8	9	40	57	..	73	40	38	21 [c]
162 Benin	11	32	60	68	20	15	23	31	16
163 Côte d'Ivoire	31	40	69	84	18	14	21	25	17
164 Tanzania, U. Rep. of	47	46	38	73	37	44	29	44	13
165 Malawi	36	46	41	67	50	33	22	45	16
166 Zambia	41	45	50	55	48	49	28	47	12
167 Congo, Dem. Rep. of the	18	29	43	46	32	71	31	38	12
168 Mozambique	..	27	..	42	66	47	24	41	14 [c]
169 Burundi	44	36	69	79	48	68	45	57	16
170 Ethiopia	4	6	25	22	..	46	47	52	15
171 Central African Republic	23	27	48	75	50	43	24	39	14
172 Guinea-Bissau	..	34	..	59	..	..	25	30	22
173 Chad	6	8	20	34	58	34	28	29	17 [c]
174 Mali	36	45	34	48	29	29	33	38	23
175 Burkina Faso	13	12	39	51	21	19	34	37	19
176 Sierra Leone	..	39	..	57	46	50	27	34	..
177 Niger	7	12	40	46	41	34	40	40	17
Developing countries	33	48	70	79	19	16	..	..	..
Least developed countries	23	35	51	61	34	33	..	..	..
Arab States	61	66	83	84	10	9	..	..	..
East Asia and the Pacific	30	49	71	78	..	..	..	..	..
Latin America and the Caribbean	68	75	81	89	13	10	..	..	..
South Asia	20	37	71	86	25	21	..	..	..
Sub-Saharan Africa	32	36	48	58	32	30	..	..	..
Central and Eastern Europe and the CIS	..	82	..	..	..	..	..	..	..
OECD	..	..	96	98	..	..	..	..	..
High-income OECD	..	..	..	100	..	..	..	..	..
High human development	..	..	..	..	..	..	..	..	..
Medium human development	36	51	74	83	19	15	..	..	..
Low human development	27	32	44	55	32	32	..	..	..
High income	..	..	..	..	..	..	..	..	..
Middle income	48	61	77	83	..	..	..	..	..
Low income	20	35	64	77	27	24	..	..	..
World	43	58 [e]	75	83 [e]	..	..	..	..	..

NOTES

a Data refer to the average for the years specified.
b Data refer to the most recent year available during the period specified.
c Data refer to a year or period other than that specified, differ from the standard definition or refer to only part of a country.
d Data from UNICEF 2004. Data refer to a year or period other than that specified, differ from the standard definition or refer to only part of a country.
e Data refer to the world aggregate from UNICEF 2004.

SOURCES

Columns 1–4 and 7: UN 2005f, based on a joint effort by the United Nation's Children's Fund (UNICEF) and the World Health Organization (WHO).
Columns 5 and 6: UN 2005f, based on estimates from FAO 2005.
Columns 8 and 9: UNICEF 2004, based on a joint effort by UNICEF and the WHO.

TABLE 8

... to lead a long and healthy life ...

Inequalities in maternal and child health

HDI rank	Survey year	Births attended by skilled health personnel (%)		One-year-olds fully immunized [a] (%)		Children under height for age (% under age 5)		Infant mortality rate [b] (per 1,000 live births)		Under-five mortality rate [b] (per 1,000 live births)	
		Poorest 20%	Richest 20%	Poorest 20%	Richest 20%	Poorest 20%	Richest 20%	Poorest 20%	Richest 20%	Poorest 20%	Richest 20%
MEDIUM HUMAN DEVELOPMENT											
63 Brazil	1996	71.6	98.6	56.6	73.8	16.8	2.0	83.2	28.6	98.9	33.3
69 Colombia	1995	60.6	98.1	57.7	77.3	16.7	4.5	40.8	16.2	52.1	23.6
72 Albania	2000	93.3	100.0	66.2	68.0	15.7	7.9	52.3	27.3	60.9	29.6
79 Peru	2000	13.0	87.5	57.9	81.1	29.4	4.2	63.5	13.9	92.6	17.6
80 Kazakhstan	1999	99.2	98.5	68.7	62.3 [c]	13.2	3.7	67.6	42.3	81.9	44.8
84 Philippines	1998	21.2	91.9	59.8	86.5	..	..	48.8	20.9	79.8	29.2
88 Paraguay	1990	41.2	98.1	20.2	53.0	16.7	3.0	42.9	15.7	57.2	20.1
90 Jordan	1997	91.2	99.3	21.3	17.1	10.5	4.5	35.4	23.4	42.1	25.2
94 Turkey	1998	53.4	98.2	27.7	69.7	14.8	3.2	68.3	29.8	85.0	32.6
95 Dominican Republic	1996	88.9	97.8	34.4	46.5	14.2	1.7	66.7	23.4	89.9	26.6
97 Turkmenistan	2000	96.8	98.3	85.0	77.5	16.9	11.4	89.3	58.4	105.5	69.8
108 Viet Nam	2000	58.1	99.7	44.3	92.3	..	..	39.3	13.8	52.9	15.8
109 Kyrgyzstan	1997	96.0	100.0	69.3	73.1	27.9	11.6	83.3	45.8	96.4	49.3
110 Indonesia	1997	21.3	89.2	42.9	72.1	..	..	78.1	23.3	109.0	29.2
111 Uzbekistan	1996	91.7	100.0	80.9	77.5	19.5	16.0	54.4	45.9	70.3	50.4
112 Nicaragua	2001	77.5	99.3	63.6	71.0	22.4	4.1	49.6	16.3	64.3	19.2
113 Bolivia	1998	19.8	97.9	21.8	30.6	25.4	3.9	106.5	25.5	146.5	32.0
117 Guatemala	1998	8.8	91.9	66.3	56.0	30.0	7.2	58.0	39.2	77.6	39.3
119 Egypt	2000	31.4	94.2	91.2	92.0	16.4	7.9	75.6	29.6	97.9	33.7
120 South Africa	1998	67.8	98.1	51.3	70.2	..	..	61.6	17.0	87.4	21.9
123 Gabon	2000	67.2	97.1	5.5	23.5	20.7	8.8	57.0	35.9	93.1	55.4
124 Morocco	1992	5.1	77.9	53.7	95.2	23.3	6.6	79.7	35.1	111.6	39.2
125 Namibia	2000	55.4	97.1	59.5	68.2	18.4	9.1	35.8	22.7	55.4	31.4
127 India	1998	16.4	84.4	21.3	63.8	25.0	17.4	96.5	38.1	141.3	45.5
130 Cambodia	2000	14.7	81.2	28.6	67.7	26.9	13.5	109.7	50.3	154.8	63.6
132 Comoros	1996	26.2	84.8	39.8	82.0	23.4	17.8	87.2	64.6	128.9	86.6 [c]
135 Pakistan	1990	4.6	55.2	22.5	54.7	25.2	16.8	88.7	62.5	124.5	73.8
136 Nepal	2001	3.6	45.1	54.2	81.6	32.7	24.6	85.5	53.2	129.9	67.7
138 Ghana	1998	17.9	86.1	49.6	79.3	20.3	9.1	72.7	26.0	138.8	52.2
139 Bangladesh	1999	3.5	42.1	50.3	74.9	..	..	92.9	57.9	139.7	72.4
143 Togo	1998	25.1	91.2	22.2	52.0	19.0	10.1	84.1	65.8	167.7	97.0
144 Uganda	2000	19.7	77.3	26.5	42.6	25.1	18.0	105.7	60.2	191.8	106.4
145 Zimbabwe	1999	56.7	93.5	63.9	64.1	19.2	13.1	59.1	44.3	99.5	62.2

Human development indicators

TABLE 8

HDI rank	Survey year	Births attended by skilled health personnel (%)		One-year-olds fully immunized[a] (%)		Children under height for age (% under age 5)		Infant mortality rate[b] (per 1,000 live births)		Under-five mortality rate[b] (per 1,000 live births)	
		Poorest 20%	Richest 20%	Poorest 20%	Richest 20%	Poorest 20%	Richest 20%	Poorest 20%	Richest 20%	Poorest 20%	Richest 20%
LOW HUMAN DEVELOPMENT											
146 Madagascar	1997	29.6	88.5	22.0	66.0	24.7	25.2	119.1	57.5	195.0	101.4
148 Cameroon	1991	32.0	94.7	27.4	63.5	18.9	7.9	103.9	51.2	200.7	81.7
151 Yemen	1997	6.8	49.7	7.8	55.7	26.4	22.0	108.5	60.0	163.1	73.0
152 Mauritania	2000	14.7	92.8	15.6	45.3	18.1	14.7	60.8	62.3	98.1	78.5
153 Haiti	2000	4.1	70.0	25.4	42.3	18.2	5.1	99.5	97.2	163.9	108.7
154 Kenya	1998	23.2	79.6	48.1	59.9	26.7	10.5	95.8	40.2	136.2	60.7
156 Guinea	1999	12.1	81.5	17.2	51.8	18.8	11.6	118.9	70.2	229.9	133.0
157 Senegal	1997	20.3	86.2	..	..	..	..	84.5	44.9	181.0	69.6
158 Nigeria	1990	12.2	70.0	13.9	58.1	22.2	19.2	102.2	68.6	239.6	119.8
159 Rwanda	2000	17.3	59.6	71.3	78.8	27.0	15.7	138.7	87.9	246.4	154.1
161 Eritrea	1995	5.0	74.3	25.0	83.8	22.7	14.6	74.0	67.5	152.2	103.5
162 Benin	1996	34.4	97.5	37.8	73.6	17.0	12.1	119.4	63.3	208.3	110.1
164 Tanzania, U. Rep. of	1999	28.9	82.8	53.1	78.4	28.5	16.3	114.8	91.9	160.0	135.2
165 Malawi	2000	43.0	83.0	65.4	81.4	25.8	22.6	131.5	86.4	230.8	149.0
166 Zambia	2001	19.7	91.1	63.9	80.0	26.9	19.5	115.2	56.7	191.7	92.4
168 Mozambique	1997	18.1	82.1	19.7	85.3	22.4	14.4	187.7	94.7	277.5	144.6
170 Ethiopia	2000	0.9	25.3	7.0	33.5	25.7	23.3	92.8	95.1	159.2	147.1
173 Chad	1996	2.6	47.4	4.0	23.0	23.0	18.4	79.8	89.3	170.6	172.0
174 Mali	2001	8.1	81.9	19.5	56.0	19.7	12.2	137.2	89.9	247.8	148.1
175 Burkina Faso	1998	17.9	75.0	21.4	52.1	20.9	15.0	106.2	76.7	239.2	154.5
177 Niger	1998	4.2	62.8	4.6	50.9	21.2	20.9	131.1	85.8	281.8	183.7

NOTES

This table presents data for developing countries based on the Demographic and Health Surveys conducted since 1995. Quintiles are defined by socio-economic status in terms of assets or wealth, rather than in terms of income or consumption. For details, see Gwatkin and others forthcoming.

a Includes tuberculosis (BCG), measles, and diphteria, pertussis and tetanus (DPT) vaccination.
b Based on births in the 10 years preceding the survey.
c Large sampling error due to small number of cases.

SOURCE

All columns: Gwatkin and others forthcoming.

TABLE 9
. . . to lead a long and healthy life . . .

Leading global health crises and risks

HDI rank	HIV prevalence[a] (% ages 15–49) 2003	MDG Condom use at last high-risk sex[b] (% ages 15–24) Women 1998–2003[h]	Men 1998–2003[h]	MDG Malaria cases[c] (per 100,000 people) 2000	MDG Children under age 5 With insecticide-treated bednets (%) 1999–2003[h]	With fever treated with anti-malarial drugs (%) 1999–2003[h]	MDG Tuberculosis cases Per 100,000 people[d] 2003	Detected under DOTS[e] (%) 2003	Cured under DOTS[f] (%) 2003	Prevalence of smoking[g] (% of adults) Women 2000–02[h]	Men 2000–02[h]
HIGH HUMAN DEVELOPMENT											
1 Norway	0.1 [0.0–0.2]	..	..	..	..	..	5	46	80	32	31
2 Iceland	0.2 [0.1–0.3]	..	..	..	..	..	3	28	100	23	25
3 Australia	0.1 [0.1–0.2]	..	..	..	..	..	6	9	78	18	21
4 Luxembourg	0.2 [0.1–0.4]	..	..	..	..	..	10	126	..	..	..
5 Canada	0.3 [0.2–0.5]	..	..	..	..	..	4	76	81	20	24
6 Sweden	0.1 [0.0–0.2]	..	..	..	..	..	4	62	73	20	17
7 Switzerland	0.4 [0.2–0.6]	..	..	..	..	..	7	0	..	24	27
8 Ireland	0.1 [0.0–0.3]	..	..	..	..	..	12	0	..	..	..
9 Belgium	0.2 [0.1–0.3]	..	..	..	..	..	12	57	69	20	28
10 United States	0.6 [0.3–1.1]	..	..	..	..	..	3	89	70	21	26
11 Japan	<0.1 [<0.2]	..	..	..	..	..	42	40	76	12	47
12 Netherlands	0.2 [0.1–0.4]	..	..	..	..	..	6	50	68	25	32
13 Finland	<0.1 [<0.2]	..	..	..	..	..	10	0	..	20	27
14 Denmark	0.2 [0.1–0.3]	..	..	..	..	..	6	75	77	29	32
15 United Kingdom	0.1 [0.1–0.2]	..	..	..	..	..	12	..	..	26	28
16 France	0.4 [0.2–0.7]	..	..	..	..	..	12	0	..	21	33
17 Austria	0.3 [0.1–0.4]	..	..	..	..	..	12	..	..	..	..
18 Italy	0.5 [0.2–0.8]	..	..	..	..	..	6	79	79	22	31
19 New Zealand	<0.1 [<0.2]	..	..	..	..	..	11	57	60	25	25
20 Germany	0.1 [0.1–0.2]	..	..	..	..	..	7	55	69	31	39
21 Spain	0.7 [0.3–1.1]	..	..	..	..	..	27	0	..	25	39
22 Hong Kong, China (SAR)	0.1 [<0.2]	..	..	..	..	..	79	58	79	4	25
23 Israel	0.1 [0.1–0.2]	..	..	..	..	..	8	55	81	22	39
24 Greece	0.2 [0.1–0.3]	..	..	..	..	..	22	0	..	29	47
25 Singapore	0.2 [0.1–0.5]	..	..	..	..	..	42	44	87	4	24
26 Slovenia	<0.1 [<0.2]	..	..	..	..	..	22	70	85	20	28
27 Portugal	0.4 [0.2–0.7]	..	..	..	..	..	37	87	82	..	..
28 Korea, Rep. of	<0.1 [<0.2]	..	..	9	..	..	118	23	83	..	..
29 Cyprus	..	..	..	..	..	..	4	91	75	..	..
30 Barbados	1.5 [0.4–5.4]	..	..	..	..	..	14	..	..	..	..
31 Czech Republic	0.1 [<0.2]	..	..	..	..	..	12	63	73	22	36
32 Malta	0.2 [0.1–0.3]	..	..	..	..	..	6	19	60	..	..
33 Brunei Darussalam	<0.1 [<0.2]	..	..	..	..	..	61	138	84	..	..
34 Argentina	0.7 [0.3–1.1]	..	..	1	..	..	55	65	58	..	..
35 Hungary	0.1 [0.0–0.2]	..	..	..	..	..	33	41	55	..	..
36 Poland	0.1 [0.0–0.2]	..	..	..	..	..	34	56	86	..	..
37 Chile	0.3 [0.2–0.5]	..	..	..	..	..	17	115	86	34	44
38 Estonia	1.1 [0.4–2.1]	..	..	..	..	..	53	69	67	20	44
39 Lithuania	0.1 [<0.2]	..	..	..	..	..	73	85	72	16	51
40 Qatar	..	..	..	..	..	..	72	57	75	..	..
41 United Arab Emirates	..	..	..	..	..	..	26	32	79	..	..
42 Slovakia	<0.1 [<0.2]	..	..	..	..	..	29	34	85	..	..
43 Bahrain	0.2 [0.1–0.3]	..	..	..	..	..	52	49	88	3	17
44 Kuwait	..	..	..	..	..	..	31	67	55	..	..
45 Croatia	<0.1 [<0.2]	..	..	..	..	..	68	0	..	27	34
46 Uruguay	0.3 [0.2–0.5]	..	..	..	..	..	33	80	82	..	..
47 Costa Rica	0.6 [0.3–1.0]	..	..	42	..	..	18	117	85	10	29
48 Latvia	0.6 [0.3–1.0]	..	..	..	..	..	78	83	76	..	..
49 Saint Kitts and Nevis	..	..	..	..	..	..	16	..	0	..	..
50 Bahamas	3.0 [1.8–4.9]	..	..	..	..	..	52	52	59	..	..
51 Seychelles	..	..	..	..	..	..	65	40	45	..	..
52 Cuba	0.1 [<0.2]	..	..	..	..	..	13	93	92	..	..
53 Mexico	0.3 [0.1–0.4]	..	..	8	..	..	45	81	84	..	..

Human development indicators

TABLE 9

HDI rank	HIV prevalence[a] (% ages 15–49) 2003	MDG Condom use at last high-risk sex[b] (% ages 15–24) Women 1998–2003[h]	Men 1998–2003[h]	MDG Malaria cases[c] (per 100,000 people) 2000	MDG Children under age 5 With insecticide-treated bednets (%) 1999–2003[h]	With fever treated with anti-malarial drugs (%) 1999–2003[h]	MDG Tuberculosis cases Per 100,000 people[d] 2003	Detected under DOTS[e] (%) 2003	Cured under DOTS[f] (%) 2003	Prevalence of smoking[g] (% of adults) Women 2000–02[h]	Men 2000–02[h]
54 Tonga	..	..	..	..	..	..	44	80	83	..	..
55 Bulgaria	<0.1 [<0.2]	..	..	..	..	..	47	81	86	..	..
56 Panama	0.9 [0.5–1.5]	..	..	36	..	..	52	92	73	..	..
57 Trinidad and Tobago	3.2 [1.2–8.3]	..	..	1	..	..	13	..	..	..	..
MEDIUM HUMAN DEVELOPMENT											
58 Libyan Arab Jamahiriya	0.3 [0.1–0.6]	..	..	2	..	..	21	147	61	..	..
59 Macedonia, TFYR	<0.1 [<0.2]	..	..	..	..	..	37	49	79	..	..
60 Antigua and Barbuda	..	..	..	..	..	..	10	45	100	..	..
61 Malaysia	0.4 [0.2–0.7]	..	..	57	..	..	135	69	76	..	..
62 Russian Federation	1.1 [0.6–1.9]	..	..	1	..	..	157	9	67	..	..
63 Brazil	0.7 [0.3–1.1]	..	..	344	..	..	91	18	75	27	35
64 Romania	<0.1 [<0.2]	..	..	..	..	..	194	38	76	..	..
65 Mauritius	..	..	..	1	..	..	136	28	92	..	..
66 Grenada	..	..	..	..	..	..	8	..	..	..	..
67 Belarus	0.5 [0.2–0.8]	..	..	..	..	..	59	44	..	9	53
68 Bosnia and Herzegovina	<0.1 [<0.2]	..	..	..	..	..	63	48	95	..	..
69 Colombia	0.7 [0.4–1.2]	29	..	250	1	..	80	7	84	..	..
70 Dominica	..	..	..	..	..	..	23	..	..	..	..
71 Oman	0.1 [0.0–0.2]	..	..	27	..	..	12	81	92	..	..
72 Albania	..	..	..	..	..	..	33	29	90	18	60
73 Thailand	1.5 [0.8–2.8]	..	..	130	..	..	203	72	74	2	39
74 Samoa (Western)	..	..	..	..	..	..	44	51	84	..	..
75 Venezuela	0.7 [0.4–1.2]	..	..	94	..	..	52	80	82	..	..
76 Saint Lucia	..	..	..	..	..	..	22	71	25	..	..
77 Saudi Arabia	..	..	..	32	..	..	57	38	76	8	19
78 Ukraine	1.4 [0.7–2.3]	..	..	..	..	..	133	..	..	10	57
79 Peru	0.5 [0.3–0.9]	19	..	258	..	..	231	81	92	..	..
80 Kazakhstan	0.2 [0.1–0.3]	32	65	(.)	..	..	152	86	78	..	..
81 Lebanon	0.1 [0.0–0.2]	..	..	..	..	..	13	67	91	..	..
82 Ecuador	0.3 [0.1–0.5]	..	..	728	..	..	209	37	84	..	..
83 Armenia	0.1 [0.1–0.2]	..	44	4	..	..	89	43	79	3	68
84 Philippines	<0.1 [<0.2]	..	..	15	..	..	458	68	88	8	51
85 China	0.1 [0.1–0.2]	..	..	1	..	..	245	43	93	..	..
86 Suriname	1.7 [0.5–5.8]	..	..	2,954	3	..	102	..	..	..	..
87 Saint Vincent and the Grenadines	..	..	..	..	..	..	40	38	..	..	..
88 Paraguay	0.5 [0.2–0.8]	..	..	124	..	..	105	18	92	..	..
89 Tunisia	<0.1 [<0.2]	..	..	1	..	..	24	91	92	..	..
90 Jordan	..	..	..	3	..	..	5	89	89	..	..
91 Belize	2.4 [0.8–6.9]	..	..	657	..	..	56	98	85	..	..
92 Fiji	0.1 [0.0–0.2]	..	..	..	..	..	38	63	85	..	..
93 Sri Lanka	<0.1 [<0.2]	..	..	1,110	..	..	89	70	81	2	26
94 Turkey	<0.1 [<0.2]	..	..	17	..	..	40	..	..	..	..
95 Dominican Republic	1.7 [0.9–3.0]	29	52	6	..	..	123	65	78	..	..
96 Maldives	..	..	..	..	..	..	39	106	95	15	37
97 Turkmenistan	<0.1 [<0.2]	..	..	1	..	..	83	49	77	..	..
98 Jamaica	1.2 [0.6–2.2]	..	..	..	..	..	9	90	49	..	..
99 Iran, Islamic Rep. of	0.1 [0.0–0.2]	..	..	27	..	..	36	59	85	2	22
100 Georgia	0.2 [0.1–0.4]	..	..	5	..	..	95	52	65	..	..
101 Azerbaijan	<0.1 [<0.2]	..	..	19	1	1	109	28	84	..	..
102 Occupied Palestinian Territories	..	..	..	..	..	..	37	4	100	..	..
103 Algeria	0.1 [<0.2]	..	..	2[i]	..	..	53	113	89	..	..
104 El Salvador	0.7 [0.3–1.1]	..	..	11	..	..	78	53	88	15	42
105 Cape Verde	..	..	..	..	..	..	328	..	..	..	..
106 Syrian Arab Republic	<0.1 [<0.2]	..	..	(.)	..	..	52	45	87	..	..

TABLE 9

Leading global health crises and risks

HDI rank	HIV prevalence[a] (% ages 15–49) 2003	MDG Condom use at last high-risk sex[b] (% ages 15–24) Women 1998–2003[h]	Men 1998–2003[h]	MDG Malaria cases[c] (per 100,000 people) 2000	MDG Children under age 5 With insecticide-treated bednets (%) 1999–2003[h]	With fever treated with anti-malarial drugs (%) 1999–2003[h]	MDG Tuberculosis cases Per 100,000 people[d] 2003	Detected under DOTS[e] (%) 2003	Cured under DOTS[f] (%) 2003	Prevalence of smoking[g] (% of adults) Women 2000–02[h]	Men 2000–02[h]
107 Guyana	2.5 [0.8–7.7]	..	..	3,074	6	3	178	31	85	..	..
108 Viet Nam	0.4 [0.2–0.8]	..	..	95	16	7	238	86	92	..	..
109 Kyrgyzstan	0.1 [<0.2]	..	..	(.)			140	57	82	..	..
110 Indonesia	0.1 [0.0–0.2]	..	..	920	0	1	674	33	86	3	69
111 Uzbekistan	0.1 [0.0–0.2]	..	50	1	..	..	156	20	80	..	..
112 Nicaragua	0.2 [0.1–0.3]	17	..	402	..	2	78	91	82	..	..
113 Bolivia	0.1 [0.0–0.2]	..	..	378	..	..	301	71	84	..	..
114 Mongolia	<0.1 [<0.2]	..	..	..	..	..	237	68	87	26	68
115 Moldova, Rep. of	0.2 [0.1–0.3]	..	..	..	..	..	177	39	61	..	..
116 Honduras	1.8 [1.0–3.2]	..	..	541	..	..	102	78	87	..	..
117 Guatemala	1.1 [0.6–1.8]	..	..	386	1	..	104	44	84	..	..
118 Vanuatu	..	..	..	..	..	..	71	70	79	..	..
119 Egypt	<0.1 [<0.2]	..	..	(.)	..	..	36	56	88	18	40
120 South Africa	21.5 [18.5–24.9]	20	..	143	..	..	341	118	68	12	44
121 Equatorial Guinea	..	..	..	..	1	49	351	..	..	..	..
122 Tajikistan	<0.1 [<0.2]	..	..	303	2	69	267	..	79	..	..
123 Gabon	8.1 [4.1–15.3]	33	48	2,148	..	..	242	93	47	..	..
124 Morocco	0.1 [0.0–0.2]	..	..	(.)	..	..	105	83	89	2	35
125 Namibia	21.3 [18.2–24.7]	48	69	1,502	3	..	477	86	62	..	..
126 São Tomé and Principe	..	..	..	..	23	61	256	..	..	..	..
127 India	[0.4–1.3]	51	59	7	..	..	287	47	87	..	..
128 Solomon Islands	..	..	..	15,172	..	..	60	107	90	..	..
129 Myanmar	1.2 [0.6–2.2]	..	..	224	..	..	183	73	81	22	43
130 Cambodia	2.6 [1.5–4.4]	..	..	476	..	..	742	60	92	..	..
131 Botswana	37.3 [35.5–39.1]	75	88	48,704	..	..	342	68	71	..	..
132 Comoros	..	..	..	1,930	9	63	103	37	96	..	..
133 Lao People's Dem. Rep.	0.1 [<0.2]	..	..	759	..	..	327	47	78	..	..
134 Bhutan	..	..	..	285	..	..	194	32	86	..	..
135 Pakistan	0.1 [0.0–0.2]	..	..	58	..	..	358	17	77	..	..
136 Nepal	0.3 [0.2–0.5]	..	..	33	..	..	316	60	86	24	40
137 Papua New Guinea	0.6 [0.3–1.0]	..	..	1,688	..	..	527	15	53	..	..
138 Ghana	3.1 [1.9–5.0]	33	52	15,344	5	61	369	40	60	..	..
139 Bangladesh	[<0.2]	..	..	40	..	..	490	33	84	21	48
140 Timor-Leste	..	..	..	..	8	47	753	53	81	..	..
141 Sudan	2.3 [0.7–7.2]	..	..	13,934	0	50	355	34	78	..	..
142 Congo	4.9 [2.1–11.0]	..	..	5,880	..	..	489	57	71	..	..
143 Togo	4.1 [2.7–6.4]	22	41	7,701	2	60	673	17	68	..	..
144 Uganda	4.1 [2.8–6.6]	44	62	46	0	..	621	44	60	..	..
145 Zimbabwe	24.6 [21.7–27.8]	42	69	5,410	..	..	500	42	67	..	..
LOW HUMAN DEVELOPMENT											
146 Madagascar	1.7 [0.8–2.7]	..	..	..	0	61	325	77	74	..	..
147 Swaziland	38.8 [37.2–40.4]	..	..	2,835	0	26	683	35	47	..	..
148 Cameroon	6.9 [4.8–9.8]	16	31	2,900	1	66	221	86	70	..	..
149 Lesotho	28.9 [26.3–31.7]	..	..	0	..	..	390	70	52	..	..
150 Djibouti	..	..	..	715	..	..	988	53	82	..	..
151 Yemen	0.1 [0.0–0.2]	..	..	15,160	..	..	151	43	82	..	..
152 Mauritania	0.6 [0.3–1.1]	..	..	11,150	..	..	664	..	..	..	..
153 Haiti	5.6 [2.5–11.9]	19	30	15	..	12	386	46	78	..	..
154 Kenya	6.7 [4.7–9.6]	25	47	545	5	27	821	46	79	32	67
155 Gambia	1.2 [0.3–4.2]	..	..	17,340	15	55	337	70	74	..	..
156 Guinea	3.2 [1.2–8.2]	17	32	75,386	..	..	394	51	72	..	..
157 Senegal	0.8 [0.4–1.7]	..	..	11,925	2	36	429	59	66	..	..
158 Nigeria	5.4 [3.6–8.0]	24	46	30	1	34	518	18	79	..	..
159 Rwanda	5.1 [3.4–7.6]	23	55	6,510	5	13	628	27	58	..	..

Human development indicators

TABLE 9

HDI rank	HIV prevalence [a] (% ages 15–49) 2003	MDG Condom use at last high-risk sex [b] (% ages 15–24) Women 1998–2003 [h]	Men 1998–2003 [h]	MDG Malaria cases [c] (per 100,000 people) 2000	MDG Children under age 5 With insecticide-treated bednets (%) 1999–2003 [h]	With fever treated with anti-malarial drugs (%) 1999–2003 [h]	MDG Tuberculosis cases Per 100,000 people [d] 2003	Detected under DOTS [e] (%) 2003	Cured under DOTS [f] (%) 2003	Prevalence of smoking [g] (% of adults) Women 2000–02 [h]	Men 2000–02 [h]
160 Angola	3.9 [1.6–9.4]	..	..	8,773	2	63	256	118	74	..	..
161 Eritrea	2.7 [0.9–7.3]	..	..	3,479	4	4	431	18	82	..	..
162 Benin	1.9 [1.1–3.3]	19	34	10,697 [k]	7	60	141	94	80	..	..
163 Côte d'Ivoire	7.0 [4.9–10.0]	25	56	12,152	1	58	618	39	67	..	..
164 Tanzania, U. Rep. of	8.8 [6.4–11.9]	21	31	1,207 [i]	2	53	476	43	80	..	..
165 Malawi	14.2 [11.3–17.7]	32	38	25,948	3	27	469	35	72	..	..
166 Zambia	16.5 [13.5–20.0]	33	42	34,204	7	52	508	65	83	..	..
167 Congo, Dem. Rep. of the	4.2 [1.7–9.9]	..	..	2,960 [i]	1	45	537	63	78	..	..
168 Mozambique	12.2 [9.4–15.7]	29	33	18,115	..	..	557	45	78	..	..
169 Burundi	6.0 [4.1–8.8]	..	..	48,098	1	31	519	30	79	..	..
170 Ethiopia	4.4 [2.8–6.7]	17	30	..	..	3	507	36	76	..	..
171 Central African Republic	13.5 [8.3–21.2]	..	..	..	2	69	493	6	..	..	..
172 Guinea-Bissau	..	..	..	2,421 [i]	7	58	300	55	48	..	..
173 Chad	4.8 [3.1–7.2]	..	..	197 [i]	1	32	439	11	72	..	..
174 Mali	1.9 [0.6–5.9]	14	30	4,008 [j]	8	38	582	18	50	..	..
175 Burkina Faso	4.2 [2.7–6.5]	41	55	619	7	50	303	18	64	..	..
176 Sierra Leone	..	..	..	..	2	61	794	33	81	..	..
177 Niger	1.2 [0.7–2.3]	7	30	1,693 [i]	6	48	272	54	..	..	..
Developing countries	1.3 [1.1–1.4]	..	..	..	..	..	289	..	..	..	..
Least developed countries	3.2 [2.9–3.8]	..	..	..	..	..	452	..	..	..	..
Arab States	0.3 [0.2–0.9]	..	..	..	..	..	128	..	..	..	..
East Asia and the Pacific	0.2 [0.2–0.3]	..	..	..	..	..	298	..	..	..	..
Latin America and the Caribbean	0.7 [0.6–0.9]	..	..	..	..	..	90	..	..	..	..
South Asia	0.7 [0.3–1.1]	..	..	..	..	..	306	..	..	..	..
Sub-Saharan Africa	7.3 [6.8–8.2]	..	..	..	..	..	487	..	..	..	..
Central and Eastern Europe and the CIS	0.7 [0.4–1.0]	..	..	..	..	..	122	..	..	..	..
OECD	0.3 [0.2–0.4]	..	..	..	..	..	23	..	..	..	..
High-income OECD	0.4 [0.2–0.5]	..	..	..	..	..	18	..	..	..	..
High human development	0.3 [0.2–0.4]	..	..	..	..	..	24	..	..	..	..
Medium human development	0.8 [0.7–1.0]	..	..	..	..	..	264	..	..	..	..
Low human development	5.6 [5.1–6.6]	..	..	..	..	..	485	..	..	..	..
High income	0.3 [0.2–0.5]	..	..	..	..	..	19	..	..	..	..
Middle income	0.7 [0.6–0.7]	..	..	..	..	..	215	..	..	..	..
Low income	2.0 [1.8–2.4]	..	..	..	..	..	362	..	..	..	..
World	1.1 [1.0–1.3]	..	..	..	..	..	240	..	..	..	..

NOTES

a Data refer to point and range estimates based on new estimation models developed by the Joint United Nations Programme on HIV/AIDS (UNAIDS). Range estimates are presented in square brackets. Regional aggregates refer to 2004.

b Because of data limitations, comparisons across countries should be made with caution. Data for some countries may refer to only part of the country or differ from the standard definition.

c Data refer to malaria cases reported to the World Health Organization (WHO) and may represent only a fraction of the true number in a country.

d Data refer to the prevalence of all forms of tuberculosis.

e WHO 2003. Calculated by dividing the new smear-positive cases of tuberculosis detected under the directly observed treatment, short course (DOTS) case detection and treatment strategy by the estimated annual incidence of new smear-positive cases. Values can exceed 100% because of intense case detection in an area with a backlog or

chronic cases, overreporting (for example, double counting), overdiagnosis or underestimation of incidence.

f Data refer to the share of new smear-positive cases registered for treatment under the DOTS case detection and treatment strategy in 2001 that were successfully treated.

g The age range varies among countries but in most is 18 and older or 15 and older.

h Data refer to the most recent year available during the period specified.

i Data refer to 1999.

j Data refer to 1998.

k Data refer to 1997.

SOURCES

Column 1: UNAIDS 2005; aggregates were calculated for the Human Development Report Office by the Joint United Nations Programme on HIV/AIDS (UNAIDS).

Columns 2 and 3: UN 2005f, based on a data from a joint effort by the United Nation's Children's Fund (UNICEF), UNAIDS and the World Health Organization (WHO).

Columns 4–9: UN 2005f, based on data from UNICEF and the WHO.

Columns 10 and 11: World Bank 2005c, based on data from the WHO and the National Tobacco Information Online System.

Human development indicators

TABLE 10

... to lead a long and healthy life ...

Survival: progress and setbacks

	Life expectancy at birth (years)		MDG Infant mortality rate (per 1,000 live births)		MDG Under-five mortality rate (per 1,000 live births)		Probability at birth of surviving to age 65 [a] (% of cohort)		MDG Maternal mortality ratio (per 100,000 live births)	
HDI rank	1970–75 [d]	2000–05 [d]	1970	2003	1970	2003	Female 2000–05 [d]	Male 2000–05 [d]	Reported [b] 1985–2003 [e]	Adjusted [c] 2000
HIGH HUMAN DEVELOPMENT										
1 Norway	74.4	79.3	13	3	15	4	90.6	84.7	6	16
2 Iceland	74.3	80.6	13	3	14	4	91.4	87.4	..	0
3 Australia	71.7	80.2	17	6	20	6	91.5	85.7	..	8
4 Luxembourg	70.7	78.4	19	5	26	5	89.9	82.6	0	28
5 Canada	73.2	79.9	19	5	23	6	90.7	85.0	..	6
6 Sweden	74.7	80.1	11	3	15	3	91.5	86.4	5	2
7 Switzerland	73.8	80.5	15	4	18	5	91.9	85.4	5	7
8 Ireland	71.3	77.7	20	6	27	6	89.7	83.1	6	5
9 Belgium	71.4	78.8	21	4	29	5	90.4	82.5	..	10
10 United States	71.5	77.3	20	7	26	8	86.7	79.1	8	17
11 Japan	73.3	81.9	14	3	21	4	93.3	85.7	8	10
12 Netherlands	74.0	78.3	13	5	15	5	89.7	83.5	7	16
13 Finland	70.7	78.4	13	4	16	5	91.2	80.9	6	6
14 Denmark	73.6	77.1	14	3	19	4	87.0	81.0	10	5
15 United Kingdom	72.0	78.3	18	5	23	6	89.4	83.6	7	13
16 France	72.4	79.4	18	4	24	5	91.2	80.9	10	17
17 Austria	70.6	78.9	26	4	33	5	91.0	82.4	..	4
18 Italy	72.1	80.0	30	4	33	4	92.2	84.6	7	5
19 New Zealand	71.7	79.0	17	5	20	6	89.1	84.1	15	7
20 Germany	71.0	78.7	22	4	26	5	90.5	82.3	8	8
21 Spain	72.9	79.5	27	4	34	4	92.0	82.l	6	4
22 Hong Kong, China (SAR)	72.0	81.5	..	..	..	..	93.7	86.4	..	..
23 Israel	71.6	79.7	24	5	27	6	91.5	85.5	5	17
24 Greece	72.3	78.2	38	4	54	5	91.5	82.0	1	9
25 Singapore	69.5	78.6	22	3	27	3	90.7	84.5	6	30
26 Slovenia	69.8	76.3	25	4	29	4	88.9	76.1	17	17
27 Portugal	68.0	77.2	53	4	62	5	90.2	79.8	8	5
28 Korea, Rep. of	62.6	76.9	43	5	54	5	90.2	76.9	20	20
29 Cyprus	71.4	78.5	29	4	33	5	91.6	84.3	0	47
30 Barbados	69.4	74.9	40	11	54	13	86.7	74.8	0	95
31 Czech Republic	70.1	75.5	21	4	24	4	88.2	75.2	3	9
32 Malta	70.7	78.3	25	5	32	6	90.3	85.4	..	21
33 Brunei Darussalam	68.3	76.3	58	5	78	6	87.9	84.7	0	37
34 Argentina	67.1	74.3	59	17	71	20	84.9	72.1	46	82
35 Hungary	69.3	72.6	36	7	39	8	83.7	64.7	5	16
36 Poland	70.5	74.3	32	6	36	7	87.0	69.7	4	13
37 Chile	63.4	77.9	78	8	98	9	88.5	79.1	17	31
38 Estonia	70.5	71.2	21	8	26	9	83.9	57.2	46	63
39 Lithuania	71.3	72.2	23	8	28	11	85.2	60.5	13	13
40 Qatar	62.1	72.7	45	11	65	15	81.2	74.0	10	7
41 United Arab Emirates	62.2	77.9	61	7	83	8	90.2	85.0	3	54
42 Slovakia	70.0	74.0	25	7	29	8	86.8	69.3	16	3
43 Bahrain	63.3	74.2	55	12	75	15	84.6	78.9	46	28
44 Kuwait	67.0	76.8	49	8	59	9	87.9	82.7	5	5
45 Croatia	69.6	74.9	34	6	42	7	88.1	73.2	2	8
46 Uruguay	68.7	75.3	48	12	57	14	85.9	73.3	26	27
47 Costa Rica	67.9	78.1	62	8	83	10	88.4	81.2	29	43
48 Latvia	70.1	71.4	21	10	26	12	81.9	60.1	25	42
49 Saint Kitts and Nevis	..	..	..	19	..	22	..	..	250	..
50 Bahamas	66.5	69.5	38	11	49	14	73.6	61.4	..	60
51 Seychelles	..	..	..	11	..	15	..	..	..	..
52 Cuba	70.7	77.2	34	6	43	8	86.2	80.0	34	33
53 Mexico	62.4	74.9	79	23	110	28	84.0	75.2	63	83

Human development indicators

TABLE 10

| | Life expectancy at birth (years) | | MDG Infant mortality rate (per 1,000 live births) | | MDG Under-five mortality rate (per 1,000 live births) | | Probability at birth of surviving to age 65 [a] (% of cohort) | | MDG Maternal mortality ratio (per 100,000 live births) | |
| | | | | | | | Female | Male | Reported [b] | Adjusted [c] |
HDI rank	1970–75 [d]	2000–05 [d]	1970	2003	1970	2003	2000–05 [d]	2000–05 [d]	1985–2003 [e]	2000
54 Tonga	65.6	72.1	..	15	..	19	78.2	73.4	..	..
55 Bulgaria	71.0	72.1	28	14	32	15	84.5	68.2	15	32
56 Panama	66.2	74.7	46	18	68	24	85.1	76.3	70	160
57 Trinidad and Tobago	65.9	69.9	49	17	57	20	76.1	64.5	45	160
MEDIUM HUMAN DEVELOPMENT										
58 Libyan Arab Jamahiriya	52.8	73.4	105	13	160	16	82.5	74.6	77	97
59 Macedonia, TFYR	67.5	73.7	85	10	120	11	84.6	75.4	11	23
60 Antigua and Barbuda	..	..	..	11	..	12	..	..	65	..
61 Malaysia	63.0	73.0	46	7	63	7	83.5	73.4	50	41
62 Russian Federation	69.7	65.4	29	16	36	21	76.3	44.7	37	67
63 Brazil	59.5	70.3	95	33	135	35	77.7	62.7	75	260
64 Romania	69.2	71.3	46	18	57	20	82.9	65.3	34	49
65 Mauritius	62.9	72.1	64	16	86	18	80.9	66.9	21	24
66 Grenada	..	..	..	18	..	23	..	..	1	..
67 Belarus	71.5	68.1	22	13	27	17	79.3	50.6	18	35
68 Bosnia and Herzegovina	67.5	74.1	60	14	82	17	85.2	74.2	10	31
69 Colombia	61.6	72.2	69	18	108	21	81.0	71.0	78	130
70 Dominica	..	..	..	12	..	14	..	..	67	..
71 Oman	52.1	74.0	126	10	200	12	84.2	78.8	23	87
72 Albania	67.7	73.7	68	18	82	21	87.6	80.0	20	55
73 Thailand	61.0	69.7	74	23	102	26	80.3	64.5	36	44
74 Samoa (Western)	56.1	70.0	106	19	160	24	78.4	65.5	..	130
75 Venezuela	65.7	72.8	47	18	61	21	82.8	71.7	60	96
76 Saint Lucia	65.3	72.3	..	16	..	18	77.0	71.3	35	..
77 Saudi Arabia	53.9	71.6	118	22	185	26	81.2	73.4	..	23
78 Ukraine	70.1	66.1	22	15	27	20	76.4	46.6	22	35
79 Peru	55.5	69.8	115	26	178	34	77.1	68.1	190	410
80 Kazakhstan	63.2	63.2	..	63	..	73	71.9	48.0	50	210
81 Lebanon	66.4	71.9	45	27	54	31	81.7	73.0	100	150
82 Ecuador	58.8	74.2	87	24	140	27	82.6	72.7	80	130
83 Armenia	70.8	71.4	..	30	..	33	81.7	66.4	22	55
84 Philippines	58.1	70.2	60	27	90	36	78.6	70.1	170	200
85 China	63.2	71.5	85	30	120	37	81.3	74.2	50	56
86 Suriname	64.0	69.0	..	30	..	39	77.3	63.1	150	110
87 Saint Vincent and the Grenadines	61.6	71.0	..	23	..	27	81.3	70.3	93	..
88 Paraguay	65.9	70.9	57	25	76	29	79.8	71.3	180	170
89 Tunisia	55.6	73.1	135	19	201	24	84.9	75.7	69	120
90 Jordan	56.5	71.2	77	23	107	28	77.7	71.6	41	41
91 Belize	67.6	71.9	56	33	77	39	80.9	71.7	140	140
92 Fiji	60.6	67.8	50	16	61	20	72.2	62.0	38	75
93 Sri Lanka	63.1	73.9	65	13	100	15	85.6	76.1	92	92
94 Turkey	57.0	68.6	150	33	201	39	77.9	67.3	130	70
95 Dominican Republic	59.7	67.1	91	29	128	35	75.1	60.8	180	150
96 Maldives	51.4	66.3	157	55	255	72	67.5	67.8	140	110
97 Turkmenistan	59.2	62.4	..	79	..	102	69.8	52.1	9	31
98 Jamaica	69.0	70.7	49	17	64	20	73.4	67.9	110	87
99 Iran, Islamic Rep. of	55.2	70.2	122	33	191	39	79.2	71.7	37	76
100 Georgia	68.2	70.5	36	41	46	45	83.0	66.3	67	32
101 Azerbaijan	65.6	66.9	..	75	..	91	76.0	60.3	25	94
102 Occupied Palestinian Territories	56.6	72.4	..	22	..	24	81.4	75.0	..	100
103 Algeria	54.5	71.0	143	35	234	41	78.4	75.2	140	140
104 El Salvador	58.2	70.7	111	32	162	36	77.7	67.3	170	150
105 Cape Verde	57.5	70.2	..	26	..	35	79.8	67.7	76	150
106 Syrian Arab Republic	57.4	73.2	90	16	129	18	83.2	76.3	65	160

Human development indicators

TABLE 10

Survival: progress and setbacks

		Life expectancy at birth (years)		MDG Infant mortality rate (per 1,000 live births)		MDG Under-five mortality rate (per 1,000 live births)		Probability at birth of surviving to age 65 [a] (% of cohort)		MDG Maternal mortality ratio (per 100,000 live births)	
HDI rank		1970–75 [d]	2000–05 [d]	1970	2003	1970	2003	Female 2000–05 [d]	Male 2000–05 [d]	Reported [b] 1985–2003 [e]	Adjusted [c] 2000
107	Guyana	60.0	62.9	81	52	101	69	65.7	54.2	190	170
108	Viet Nam	50.3	70.4	55	19	87	23	78.4	71.0	95	130
109	Kyrgyzstan	61.2	66.8	111	59	146	68	76.0	58.6	44	110
110	Indonesia	49.2	66.5	104	31	172	41	72.1	63.8	310	230
111	Uzbekistan	63.6	66.5	..	57	..	69	72.9	59.9	34	24
112	Nicaragua	55.2	69.5	113	30	165	38	74.9	66.1	97	230
113	Bolivia	46.7	63.9	147	53	243	66	68.0	60.0	390	420
114	Mongolia	53.8	63.9	..	56	..	68	67.6	57.9	110	110
115	Moldova, Rep. of	64.8	67.5	46	26	61	32	74.3	56.5	44	36
116	Honduras	53.9	67.6	116	32	170	41	70.1	63.5	110	110
117	Guatemala	53.7	67.1	115	35	168	47	73.5	59.7	150	240
118	Vanuatu	54.0	68.4	107	31	160	38	75.2	67.6	68	130
119	Egypt	52.1	69.6	157	33	235	39	79.3	69.3	84	84
120	South Africa	53.7	49.0	..	53	..	66	38.1	28.9	150	230
121	Equatorial Guinea	40.5	43.5	165	97	281	146	33.0	30.6	..	880
122	Tajikistan	60.9	63.5	78	92	111	118	69.4	59.3	45	100
123	Gabon	48.7	54.6	..	60	..	91	48.9	45.6	520	420
124	Morocco	52.9	69.5	119	36	184	39	78.9	70.3	230	220
125	Namibia	53.9	48.6	104	48	155	65	36.7	31.6	270	300
126	São Tomé and Principe	56.5	62.9	..	75	..	118	68.6	63.1	100	..
127	India	50.3	63.1	127	63	202	87	67.4	59.2	540	540
128	Solomon Islands	55.6	62.2	71	19	99	22	62.0	59.0	550	130
129	Myanmar	49.2	60.1	122	76	179	107	63.5	52.7	230	360
130	Cambodia	40.3	56.0	..	97	..	140	61.5	45.0	440	450
131	Botswana	56.1	36.6	99	82	142	112	16.5	13.1	330	100
132	Comoros	48.9	63.0	159	54	215	73	66.5	57.8	520	480
133	Lao People's Dem.Rep.	40.4	54.5	145	82	218	91	53.1	47.8	530	650
134	Bhutan	41.5	62.7	156	70	267	85	65.3	60.2	260	420
135	Pakistan	51.9	62.9	120	81	181	103	65.6	62.7	530	500
136	Nepal	44.0	61.4	165	61	250	82	61.0	57.9	540	740
137	Papua New Guinea	44.7	55.1	106	69	147	93	46.6	41.5	370	300
138	Ghana	49.9	56.7	111	59	186	95	52.9	50.4	210	540
139	Bangladesh	45.2	62.6	145	46	239	69	63.7	59.3	380	380
140	Timor-Leste	40.0	55.2	..	87	..	124	52.7	47.3	..	660
141	Sudan	45.1	56.3	104	63	172	93	55.4	49.6	550	590
142	Congo	54.9	51.9	100	81	160	108	43.5	38.6	..	510
143	Togo	49.8	54.2	128	78	216	140	53.8	45.2	480	570
144	Uganda	51.1	46.8	100	81	170	140	34.4	32.9	510	880
145	Zimbabwe	55.6	37.2	86	78	138	126	15.5	15.7	700	1,100
LOW HUMAN DEVELOPMENT											
146	Madagascar	44.9	55.3	109	78	180	126	54.1	48.7	490	550
147	Swaziland	49.6	33.0	132	105	196	153	12.0	9.3	230	370
148	Cameroon	45.7	45.8	127	95	215	166	36.1	33.1	430	730
149	Lesotho	49.8	36.7	128	63	190	84	18.6	11.6	..	550
150	Djibouti	44.4	52.7	160	97	241	138	48.1	42.9	74	730
151	Yemen	39.9	60.3	202	82	303	113	61.0	54.9	350	570
152	Mauritania	43.4	52.5	150	120	250	183	50.7	44.5	750	1,000
153	Haiti	48.5	51.5	148	76	221	118	41.3	38.2	520	680
154	Kenya	53.6	47.0	96	79	156	123	31.8	35.0	590	1,000
155	Gambia	38.0	55.5	183	90	319	123	54.3	48.7	730	540
156	Guinea	39.3	53.6	197	104	345	160	52.6	49.1	530	740
157	Senegal	40.1	55.6	164	78	279	137	54.6	49.4	560	690
158	Nigeria	42.8	43.3	140	98	265	198	33.2	31.6	..	800
159	Rwanda	44.6	43.6	124	118	209	203	35.5	29.6	1,100	1,400

TABLE 10

HDI rank	Life expectancy at birth (years)		MDG Infant mortality rate (per 1,000 live births)		MDG Under-five mortality rate (per 1,000 live births)		Probability at birth of surviving to age 65[a] (% of cohort)		MDG Maternal mortality ratio (per 100,000 live births)	
							Female	Male	Reported[b]	Adjusted[c]
	1970–75[d]	2000–05[d]	1970	2003	1970	2003	2000–05[d]	2000–05[d]	1985–2003[e]	2000
160 Angola	37.9	40.7	180	154	300	260	33.0	27.8	..	1,700
161 Eritrea	44.3	53.5	..	45	..	85	45.5	35.9	1,000	630
162 Benin	47.0	53.8	149	91	252	154	52.9	48.4	500	850
163 Côte d'Ivoire	49.8	46.0	158	117	239	192	38.5	34.8	600	690
164 Tanzania, U. Rep. of	49.5	46.0	129	104	218	165	35.8	33.4	530	1,500
165 Malawi	41.8	39.6	189	112	330	178	24.5	23.2	1,100	1,800
166 Zambia	50.2	37.4	109	102	181	182	18.5	20.0	730	750
167 Congo, Dem. Rep. of the	46.0	43.1	148	129	245	205	34.4	30.8	950	990
168 Mozambique	40.7	41.9	163	109	278	158	30.5	26.7	1,100	1,000
169 Burundi	44.1	43.5	138	114	233	190	33.1	29.7	..	1,000
170 Ethiopia	43.5	47.6	160	112	239	169	40.7	36.6	870	850
171 Central African Republic	43.5	39.4	149	115	248	180	24.5	21.9	1,100	1,100
172 Guinea-Bissau	36.5	44.6	..	126	..	204	38.8	33.2	910	1,100
173 Chad	40.6	43.6	..	117	..	200	35.1	31.2	830	1,100
174 Mali	38.0	47.8	225	122	400	220	44.8	40.8	580	1,200
175 Burkina Faso	43.8	47.4	163	107	290	207	41.7	37.9	480	1,000
176 Sierra Leone	35.4	40.6	206	166	363	284	36.2	30.7	1,800	2,000
177 Niger	38.4	44.3	197	154	330	262	40.2	37.8	590	1,600
Developing countries	55.6	64.9	109	60	167	88	69.6	62.3	..	..
Least developed countries	44.5	52.0	151	99	244	156	47.9	43.5	..	..
Arab States	52.1	66.9	129	48	197	61	73.3	66.3	..	..
East Asia and the Pacific	60.5	70.4	84	31	122	39	79.2	71.3	..	..
Latin America and the Caribbean	61.1	71.7	86	27	123	32	79.7	68.2	..	..
South Asia	50.1	63.2	130	66	206	91	67.1	60.0	..	..
Sub-Saharan Africa	45.8	46.1	143	105	243	179	37.0	33.8	..	..
Central and Eastern Europe and the CIS	69.0	68.1	34	20	42	24	78.8	55.4	..	..
OECD	70.3	77.6	40	11	53	13	88.4	79.6	..	..
High-income OECD	71.6	78.8	22	5	28	6	89.9	81.8	..	..
High human development	70.7	77.9	32	9	42	10	88.9	80.0	..	..
Medium human development	57.6	67.0	102	46	155	61	73.7	64.6	..	..
Low human development	44.1	46.0	150	108	254	183	37.5	34.6	..	..
High income	71.6	78.8	22	5	28	6	89.9	81.8	..	..
Middle income	62.0	70.1	86	29	125	36	79.0	68.7	..	..
Low income	48.8	58.2	130	80	209	124	58.3	52.4	..	..
World	59.9	67.0	96	54	147	80	73.1	64.5	..	..

NOTES
a Data refer to the probability at birth of surviving to age 65, multiplied by 100.
b Data reported by national authorities.
c Data adjusted based on reviews by the United Nations Children's Fund (UNICEF), World Health Organization (WHO) and United Nations Population Fund to account for well documented problems of underreporting and misclassifications.
d Data refer to estimates for the period specified.
e Data refer to the most recent year available during the period specified.

SOURCES
Columns 1, 2, 7 and 8: UN 2005h.
Columns 3–6 and 10: UN 2005f, based on data from a joint effort by UNICEF and the WHO.
Column 9: UNICEF 2004.

Human development indicators

TABLE 11

... to acquire knowledge ...

Commitment to education: public spending

		Public expenditure on education				Public expenditure on education by level [a] (% of all levels)					
		As % of GDP		As % of total government expenditure		Pre-primary and primary		Secondary		Tertiary	
HDI rank		1990	2000–02 [b]	1990	2000–02 [b]	1990	2000–02 [b]	1990	2000–02 [b]	1990	2000–02 [b]
HIGH HUMAN DEVELOPMENT											
1	Norway	7.0	7.6	14.6	16.2	39.5	36.5	24.7	33.0 [c]	15.2	27.5
2	Iceland	5.4	6.0 [c]	..	..	59.5	38.4 [d]	25.6	39.1 [c]	14.9	17.8 [c]
3	Australia	4.9	4.9	14.8	13.3	2.2	35.0	57.4	38.8	32.0	24.2
4	Luxembourg	3.1	..	10.4	..	..	..	..	..	..	..
5	Canada	6.5	5.2	14.2	12.7	..	..	62.2	..	28.6	36.2
6	Sweden	7.1	7.7	13.8	12.8	47.7	34.8	19.6	36.4	13.2	28.3
7	Switzerland	4.9	5.8 [c]	18.7	15.1	49.9	34.7	25.1	38.2 [c]	19.7	24.2 [c]
8	Ireland	4.8	5.5	10.2	13.5	37.8	32.6	40.1	34.4	20.4	27.6
9	Belgium	5.0	6.3	..	..	23.3	31.6	42.9	44.5	16.5	21.7
10	United States	5.1	5.7	12.3	17.1	..	39.5	..	35.3	..	25.2
11	Japan	..	3.6	..	10.5	..	38.2	..	39.8	..	14.9
12	Netherlands	5.7	5.1	14.8	10.7	21.5	35.5	37.7	39.2	32.1	25.2
13	Finland	5.5	6.4	11.9	12.7	27.9	27.0	39.4	40.6	23.9	32.5
14	Denmark	..	8.5	..	15.4	..	31.1	..	34.3	..	32.0
15	United Kingdom	4.8	5.3	..	11.5	29.7	32.2	43.8	47.1	19.6	20.6
16	France	5.3	5.6	..	11.4	27.3	31.3	40.7	49.7	13.8	17.7
17	Austria	5.3	5.7	7.6	11.1	23.7	27.6	46.6	45.7	19.1	22.6
18	Italy	3.1	4.7	..	10.3	33.0	34.4	63.2	46.1	..	18.5
19	New Zealand	6.1	6.7	..	15.1	30.5	28.6	25.3	40.5	37.4	24.9
20	Germany	..	4.6	..	9.5	..	22.8	..	49.0	..	24.5
21	Spain	4.2	4.5	9.4	11.3	29.3	35.8	45.0	41.4	15.4	22.8
22	Hong Kong, China (SAR)	2.8	4.4	17.4	23.3	26.6	25.1	38.8	32.8	30.8	32.6
23	Israel	6.3	7.5	11.3	..	43.0	46.3	31.3	29.8	16.2	16.7
24	Greece	2.4	4.0	..	..	34.1	27.5	45.1	34.1	19.5	32.4
25	Singapore	3.1	..	18.2	..	29.6	..	36.5	..	29.3	..
26	Slovenia	..	6.1	..	..	..	..	..	..	..	..
27	Portugal	4.0	5.8	..	12.7	44.6	36.9	32.5	42.2	16.3	17.2
28	Korea, Rep. of	3.3	4.2	22.4	15.5	44.4	35.2	34.1	43.4	7.4	8.1
29	Cyprus	3.5	6.3	11.3	..	38.5	35.3	50.3	50.0	3.8	14.4
30	Barbados	7.8	7.6	22.2	17.3	37.5	33.7	37.6	35.0	19.2	28.6
31	Czech Republic	..	4.4	..	9.6	..	25.8	..	50.8	..	20.0
32	Malta	4.3	..	8.3	..	25.1	..	44.7	..	14.6	..
33	Brunei Darussalam	3.9	9.1	..	9.1 [c]	24.1	..	26.1	..	9.5	..
34	Argentina	..	4.0	..	13.8	3.4	43.3	44.9	39.2	46.7	17.5
35	Hungary	5.8	5.5	7.8	14.1	55.4	30.9	23.9	38.6	15.2	22.8
36	Poland	..	5.6	..	12.8	42.8	41.6	17.5	37.9	22.0	19.5
37	Chile	2.5	4.2	10.4	18.7	60.1	50.7	17.3	35.3	20.3	14.0
38	Estonia	..	5.7	..	..	..	33.2	..	40.9	..	19.7
39	Lithuania	4.6	5.9	13.8	..	..	..	..	..	..	..
40	Qatar	3.5	..	..	..	..	..	..	..	..	..
41	United Arab Emirates	1.8	1.6 [c]	14.6	22.5 [c]	..	45.6	..	50.4 [c]	..	2.4 [c]
42	Slovakia	5.1	4.4	..	7.5	..	24.4	..	53.2	..	20.2
43	Bahrain	4.1	..	14.6	..	..	..	45.8	..	..	..
44	Kuwait	4.8	..	3.4	..	53.4	..	13.6	..	16.0	..
45	Croatia	7.2	4.5	..	10.0	..	32.3	..	46.7 [c]	..	19.1
46	Uruguay	2.7	2.6	15.9	9.6	37.5	44.1	30.3	34.4	22.6	21.5
47	Costa Rica	4.4	5.1	20.8	22.4	..	49.3	..	31.9	..	18.8
48	Latvia	3.8	5.8	10.8	..	11.2	30.2	56.3	52.9	11.6	15.4
49	Saint Kitts and Nevis	2.6	7.6	..	19.0	..	28.5	..	31.5	..	21.2
50	Bahamas	4.0	..	17.8	..	..	..	..	..	..	..
51	Seychelles	7.8	5.2	14.8	..	28.2	42.5	40.7	26.1 [c]	9.5	17.4
52	Cuba	8.9	18.7	12.3	18.7	25.7	43.0	39.0	36.8	14.4	17.5
53	Mexico	3.6	5.3	12.8	24.3	32.3	49.1	29.6	28.7	16.5	19.6

Human development indicators

TABLE 11

	Public expenditure on education				Public expenditure on education by level [a] (% of all levels)					
	As % of GDP		As % of total government expenditure		Pre-primary and primary		Secondary		Tertiary	
HDI rank	1990	2000–02 [b]	1990	2000–02 [b]	1990	2000–02 [b]	1990	2000–02 [b]	1990	2000–02 [b]
54 Tonga	..	4.9 [c]	..	13.2 [c]	..	49.2 [d]	..	28.9 [c]	..	..
55 Bulgaria	5.2	3.5	..	..	70.7	37.2	..	46.7	13.9	15.8
56 Panama	4.7	4.5	20.9	7.7	37.0	34.2	23.3	29.2	21.3	28.1
57 Trinidad and Tobago	3.7	4.3 [c]	11.6	13.4	42.5	..	36.8	..	11.9	..
MEDIUM HUMAN DEVELOPMENT										
58 Libyan Arab Jamahiriya	..	..	..	..	..	..	..	..	..	..
59 Macedonia, TFYR	..	3.5	..	..	..	61.0	..	24.0	..	15.0
60 Antigua and Barbuda	..	3.8	..	..	..	30.7	..	35.2	..	6.7
61 Malaysia	5.1	8.1	18.3	20.3	34.3	32.0	34.4	33.5	19.9	33.3
62 Russian Federation	3.5	3.8	..	11.5	..	..	..	..	..	..
63 Brazil	..	4.2	..	12.0	..	38.3	..	40.1	..	21.6
64 Romania	2.8	3.5	7.3	..	52.1	..	22.1	..	9.6	..
65 Mauritius	3.8	4.7	11.8	13.3	37.7	32.0	36.4	38.3	16.6	15.6
66 Grenada	5.1	5.1	13.2	12.9	64.1	42.1	31.7	35.8	0.0	9.8
67 Belarus	4.8	6.0 [c]	..	..	57.7	..	16.2	..	14.4	..
68 Bosnia and Herzegovina	..	..	..	..	..	..	..	..	..	..
69 Colombia	2.4	5.2	15.4	15.6	39.3	42.1	30.9	29.4	20.7	13.3
70 Dominica	..	..	..	..	..	..	..	..	..	..
71 Oman	3.1	4.6 [c]	11.1	..	54.1	35.9	37.0	47.4 [c]	7.4	9.2 [c]
72 Albania	5.9	..	..	..	..	..	..	..	..	..
73 Thailand	3.5	5.2	20.0	28.3	56.2	42.3	21.6	20.5	14.6	21.7
74 Samoa (Western)	3.2	4.8 [c]	10.7	14.6 [c]	52.6	43.0	25.2	23.8 [c]	0.0	33.2 [c]
75 Venezuela	3.0	..	12.0	..	23.5	..	4.5	..	40.7	..
76 Saint Lucia	..	7.7 [c]	..	..	48.2	59.5 [d]	23.3	..	12.8	..
77 Saudi Arabia	5.8	..	17.8	..	78.8	..	..	..	21.2	..
78 Ukraine	5.1	5.4	19.7	20.3	54.9	20.0	15.0	31.4 [c]	15.1	34.0
79 Peru	2.8	3.0	..	17.1	..	42.6	..	27.7	..	14.6
80 Kazakhstan	3.2	3.0	17.6	..	..	22.9	..	56.0 [c]	..	13.1
81 Lebanon	..	2.7 [c]	..	12.3	..	..	..	..	..	28.5
82 Ecuador	4.3	1.0 [c]	17.2	8.0 [c]	34.4	41.1	34.2	36.1 [c]	18.3	5.2
83 Armenia	7.0	3.2 [c]	20.5	..	..	21.7	..	43.4 [c]	..	29.8 [c]
84 Philippines	2.9	3.1	10.1	17.8	..	57.6	..	22.2	..	14.0
85 China	2.3	..	12.8	..	..	..	..	..	..	..
86 Suriname	6.4	..	..	..	60.5	..	14.5	..	8.8	..
87 Saint Vincent and the Grenadines	..	10.0	..	20.3	..	..	..	..	..	..
88 Paraguay	1.1	4.4	9.1	11.4	..	55.1	22.6	28.3	25.8	16.5
89 Tunisia	6.0	6.4	13.5	18.2	39.8	32.9	36.4	44.4 [c]	18.5	22.8
90 Jordan	8.1	..	17.1	..	..	..	62.4	..	35.1	..
91 Belize	4.6	5.2	18.5	18.1	61.0	50.9	20.2	26.3	8.1	19.6
92 Fiji	4.7	5.6 [c]	..	19.4 [c]	..	35.0 [d]	..	48.9 [c]	..	16.0 [c]
93 Sri Lanka	2.7	..	8.1	..	..	..	84.3	..	13.4	..
94 Turkey	2.2	3.7 [c]	..	..	58.1	37.7	29.4	30.1 [c]	..	32.2
95 Dominican Republic	..	2.3	..	12.4	..	46.3	..	18.9 [c]	..	10.9
96 Maldives	3.8	..	10.0	..	..	..	..	..	..	..
97 Turkmenistan	4.3	..	21.0	..	..	..	..	..	..	..
98 Jamaica	4.5	6.1	12.8	12.3	37.4	36.8	33.2	33.8	21.1	19.2
99 Iran, Islamic Rep. of	4.1	4.9	22.4	17.7	33.2	25.1	39.2	36.0	13.6	17.1
100 Georgia	..	2.2	..	11.8	..	..	..	..	..	..
101 Azerbaijan	7.7	3.2	23.5	20.7	..	25.9	..	53.7 [c]	..	5.8
102 Occupied Palestinian Territories	..	..	..	..	..	..	..	..	..	..
103 Algeria	5.3	..	21.1	..	..	..	..	..	..	..
104 El Salvador	1.9	2.9	16.6	20.0	..	61.0	..	23.6 [c]	..	6.6
105 Cape Verde	..	7.9	..	17.0	..	43.8 [d]	..	29.8	..	17.5
106 Syrian Arab Republic	4.0	..	17.3	..	38.5	..	28.2	..	21.3	..

Human development indicators

TABLE 11

Commitment to education: public spending

| | | Public expenditure on education | | | Public expenditure on education by level [a] (% of all levels) | | | | | |
| | As % of GDP | | As % of total government expenditure | | Pre-primary and primary | | Secondary | | Tertiary | |
HDI rank	1990	2000–02 [b]	1990	2000–02 [b]	1990	2000–02 [b]	1990	2000–02 [b]	1990	2000–02 [b]
107 Guyana	3.4	8.4	4.4	18.4	..	54.7	..	23.5	..	4.9
108 Viet Nam	2.0	..	7.5	..	..	..	..	..	..	..
109 Kyrgyzstan	8.4	3.1 c	22.5	18.6	8.5	23.0	57.9	48.0 c	10.0	18.0 c
110 Indonesia	1.0	1.2	..	9.0 c	..	37.1	..	39.3	..	23.6
111 Uzbekistan	9.5	..	20.4	..	..	..	..	..	..	..
112 Nicaragua	3.4	3.1	9.7	15.0	..	50.3	..	12.0	..	37.7
113 Bolivia	2.3	6.3	..	19.7	..	46.9	..	23.4	..	25.1
114 Mongolia	12.3	9.0	17.6	..	13.9	53.8	48.8	26.4	14.5	15.5
115 Moldova, Rep. of	5.6	4.9	17.2	21.4	..	37.3	..	52.0 c	..	10.7
116 Honduras	..	..	..	..	..	..	..	..	..	..
117 Guatemala	1.4	..	11.8	..	31.1	..	12.9	..	21.2	..
118 Vanuatu	4.7	11.0 c	19.2	28.1 c	59.8	27.9	26.6	57.5 c	3.4	10.5 c
119 Egypt	3.9	..	..	..	..	..	..	..	..	..
120 South Africa	5.9	5.3 c	..	18.5	75.6	47.8	..	31.3 c	21.5	14.6 c
121 Equatorial Guinea	..	0.6	..	1.6	..	34.4	..	18.1 c	..	34.9
122 Tajikistan	..	2.8	24.7	17.8	6.9	30.8	57.0	47.7 c	9.1	12.1
123 Gabon	..	3.9 c	..	..	..	..	..	..	..	..
124 Morocco	5.3	6.5	26.1	26.4	34.8	39.8	48.9	43.5	16.2	16.3
125 Namibia	7.9	7.2	..	..	..	65.4	..	24.5	..	8.7
126 São Tomé and Principe	..	..	..	..	..	..	..	..	..	..
127 India	3.7	4.1	12.2	12.7	38.9	38.4	27.0	40.1	14.9	20.3
128 Solomon Islands	..	3.4 c	..	..	..	..	..	..	..	..
129 Myanmar	..	..	..	..	..	..	..	..	..	..
130 Cambodia	..	1.8	..	15.3	..	65.6	..	..	..	..
131 Botswana	6.2	2.2	17.0	25.6	..	53.2 d	..	23.8	..	18.6
132 Comoros	..	3.9	..	24.1	42.4	45.7	28.2	40.1 c	17.3	7.7 c
133 Lao People's Dem. Rep.	..	2.8 c	..	11.0 c	..	47.0	..	19.0	..	12.6
134 Bhutan	..	5.2	..	12.9	..	..	..	..	..	..
135 Pakistan	2.6	1.8 c	7.4	7.8 c	..	..	..	..	..	..
136 Nepal	2.0	3.4	8.5	14.9	48.2	61.5	15.7	22.1	23.3	10.3
137 Papua New Guinea	..	2.3 c	..	17.5 c	..	71.4	..	24.3 c	..	4.3 c
138 Ghana	3.2	..	24.3	..	29.2	..	34.3	..	11.0	..
139 Bangladesh	1.5	2.4	10.3	15.5	45.6	45.4 d	42.2	45.5	8.7	9.1
140 Timor-Leste	..	..	..	..	..	..	..	..	..	..
141 Sudan	6.0	..	2.8	..	..	..	..	..	..	..
142 Congo	5.0	3.2 c	14.4	12.6	..	36.1	..	30.2 c	..	25.5 c
143 Togo	5.5	2.6	26.4	13.6	30.4	44.8	25.8	27.1 c	29.0	19.4
144 Uganda	1.5	..	11.5	..	..	..	..	..	..	..
145 Zimbabwe	7.7	4.7 c	..	..	54.1	54.9	28.6	28.6 c	12.3	16.6 c
LOW HUMAN DEVELOPMENT										
146 Madagascar	2.1	2.9 c	..	..	49.1	42.1	35.6	29.0 c	..	12.2 c
147 Swaziland	5.8	7.1	19.5	..	31.2	31.8	24.5	41.1 c	26.0	25.5
148 Cameroon	3.2	3.8	19.6	17.3	70.5	..	..	..	29.5	..
149 Lesotho	6.2	10.4 c	12.2	18.4	..	53.2 d	..	23.8 c	..	18.6 c
150 Djibouti	3.5	..	10.5	..	58.0	..	21.7	..	11.5	..
151 Yemen	..	9.5 c	..	32.8	..	..	..	..	..	..
152 Mauritania	..	..	..	..	33.3	..	37.7	..	24.9	..
153 Haiti	1.5	..	20.0	..	53.1	..	19.0	..	9.1	..
154 Kenya	6.7	7.0	17.0	22.1	50.3	..	18.8	..	21.6	..
155 Gambia	3.8	2.8	14.6	8.9	41.6	54.7 d	21.2	21.1 c	17.8	14.0 c
156 Guinea	..	1.8 c	..	25.6 c	..	52.1 d	..	..	..	..
157 Senegal	3.9	3.6	26.9	..	43.9	..	25.7	..	24.0	..
158 Nigeria	0.9	..	..	..	..	..	..	..	..	..
159 Rwanda	..	2.8 c	..	..	..	48.2 d	..	16.7 c	..	34.7 c

TABLE 11

		Public expenditure on education			Public expenditure on education by level [a] (% of all levels)					
		As % of GDP		As % of total government expenditure		Pre-primary and primary		Secondary		Tertiary	
HDI rank		1990	2000–02 [b]	1990	2000–02 [b]	1990	2000–02 [b]	1990	2000–02 [b]	1990	2000–02 [b]
160	Angola	3.9	2.8 [c]	10.7	..	96.3	..	..	..	3.7	..
161	Eritrea	..	4.1	..	..	..	26.0	..	35.4	..	14.9
162	Benin	..	3.3 [c]	..	..	..	57.4	..	25.5 [c]	..	16.4 [c]
163	Côte d'Ivoire	..	4.6 [c]	..	21.5	..	42.2	..	32.5 [c]	..	25.1 [c]
164	Tanzania, U. Rep. of	2.8	..	11.4	..	..	..	..	..	..	..
165	Malawi	3.2	6.0	11.1	..	44.7	54.9 [d]	13.1	21.1	20.2	18.3
166	Zambia	2.4	2.0 [c]	8.7	..	..	54.8 [d]	..	25.8	..	19.4
167	Congo, Dem. Rep. of the	..	..	..	..	..	..	..	..	..	..
168	Mozambique	3.1	..	12.0	..	49.8	..	15.7	..	9.9	..
169	Burundi	3.4	3.9	16.7	21.8	46.8	43.1	29.1	32.0	22.0	24.9
170	Ethiopia	3.4	4.6 [c]	9.4	13.8	53.9	..	28.1	..	12.1	..
171	Central African Republic	2.2		..	..	..	..	..	..	..	..
172	Guinea-Bissau	..	..	..	..	..	..	..	..	..	..
173	Chad	..	..	..	..	..	..	..	..	..	..
174	Mali	..	..	..	..	..	..	..	..	..	..
175	Burkina Faso	2.4	..	..	..	..	..	..	..	..	..
176	Sierra Leone	..	3.7	..	..	..	..	..	..	..	..
177	Niger	3.2	2.3 [c]	18.6	..	..	51.5	..	24.4 [c]	..	16.2 [c]

NOTES

As a result of limitations in the data and metholodogical changes, comparisons of education expenditure data across countries and over time must be made with caution. For detailed notes on the data see www.uis.unesco.org.

a Expenditures by level may not sum to 100 as a result of rounding or the omission of the categories expenditures in post-secondary education and expenditures not allocated by level.

b Data refer to the most recent year available during the period specified.

c Data refer to a United Nations Educational, Scientific and Cultural Organization Institute for Statistics estimate where no national estimate is available.

d Data refer to primary school expenditure only.

SOURCES

Columns 1–5 and 7–10: UNESCO Institute for Statistics 2005b.

Column 6: calculated on the basis of data on public expenditure on education by pre-primary and primary levels from UNESCO Institute for Statistics 2005b.

Human development indicators

TABLE 12

... to acquire knowledge ...

Literacy and enrolment

		Adult literacy rate [a] (% ages 15 and above)		Youth literacy rate [a] (% ages 15–24)		MDG Net primary enrolment ratio [b] (%)		Net secondary enrolment ratio [b, c] (%)		MDG Children reaching grade 5 (% of grade 1 students)		Tertiary students in science, math and engineering (% of all tertiary students)
HDI rank		1990	2003	1990	2003	1990/91	2002/03 [d]	1990/91	2002/03 [d]	1990/91	2001/02 [d]	1998–2003 [e]
HIGH HUMAN DEVELOPMENT												
1	Norway	..	..	..	..	100	100	88	96	100	100	18
2	Iceland	..	..	..	..	100	100	..	86	..	100	17
3	Australia	..	..	..	..	99	97	79	88 [f]	..	..	24
4	Luxembourg	..	..	..	..	81	90	..	80	..	99 [g]	18
5	Canada	..	..	..	..	98	100 [f, g]	89	98 [f, g]	..	..	20 [h]
6	Sweden	..	..	..	..	100	100	85	100	100	..	27
7	Switzerland	..	..	..	..	84	99	80	87	80	..	25
8	Ireland	..	..	..	..	90	96	80	83	100	99	25 [h]
9	Belgium	..	..	..	..	96	100	87	97	..	..	19
10	United States	..	..	..	..	97	92	85	88	..	..	..
11	Japan	..	..	..	..	100	100	97	101 [f]	100	..	20
12	Netherlands	..	..	..	..	95	99	84	89	..	100	16
13	Finland	..	..	..	..	98	100	93	95	100	100	38
14	Denmark	..	..	..	..	98	100	87	96	94	100 [i]	20
15	United Kingdom	..	..	..	..	98	100	81	95	..	..	21 [h]
16	France	..	..	..	..	100	99	..	94	96	98 [i]	..
17	Austria	..	..	..	..	88	90	..	89	..	..	25
18	Italy	97.7	..	99.8	..	100	100	..	91	..	96 [g]	24
19	New Zealand	..	..	..	..	100	100 [f]	85	93	92	..	19
20	Germany	..	..	..	..	84	83	..	88	..	..	29
21	Spain	96.3	..	99.6	..	100	100	..	96	..	..	31
22	Hong Kong, China (SAR)	..	..	98.2	..	..	98 [i]	..	74 [f]	100	100	30 [h]
23	Israel	91.4	96.9	98.7	99.6	92	99	..	89	..	85	31
24	Greece	94.9	91.0	99.5	99.5	95	99	83	86	100	..	30
25	Singapore	88.8	92.5	99.0	99.5	96	..	..	..	..	..	..
26	Slovenia	99.6	99.7 [k]	99.8	99.8 [k]	100	93	..	93	..	..	22
27	Portugal	87.2	..	99.5	..	100	100	..	85	..	..	29
28	Korea, Rep. of	..	..	99.8	..	100	100 [i]	86	88 [i]	99	100	41
29	Cyprus	94.3	96.8	99.7	99.8	87	96	69	93	100	99	17
30	Barbados	99.4	99.7 [k]	99.8	99.8 [k]	80	100	..	90	..	99	..
31	Czech Republic	..	..	..	..	87	87	..	91	..	98	31
32	Malta	88.4	87.9 [m]	97.5	96.0 [m]	97	96	78	87	99	99	13
33	Brunei Darussalam	85.5	92.7	97.9	98.9	90	..	..	..	..	93 [g]	8
34	Argentina	95.7	97.2	98.2	98.9	94	..	..	81	..	92	15 [h]
35	Hungary	99.1	99.3	99.7	99.5	91	91	75	94	98	..	21
36	Poland	99.6	..	99.8	..	97	98	76	83	98	99	20
37	Chile	94.0	95.7	98.1	99.0	88	85 [i]	55	81 [i]	..	99 [n]	31
38	Estonia	99.8	99.8	99.8	99.8	99	95	..	88	..	98	22
39	Lithuania	99.3	99.6	99.8	99.7	..	91	..	94	..	..	26
40	Qatar	77.0	89.2 [m]	90.3	98.6 [m]	89	95	70	82 [f]	64	..	16
41	United Arab Emirates	71.0	77.3 [k]	84.7	91.4 [k]	99	83	58	71	80	93	..
42	Slovakia	..	99.6	..	99.6	..	86	..	88	..	..	27
43	Bahrain	82.1	87.7	95.6	99.3	99	90	85	87	89	99	21
44	Kuwait	76.7	82.9 [k]	87.5	93.1 [k]	49	83	..	77 [f, o]	..	..	24
45	Croatia	96.9	98.1	99.6	99.6	74	89	57	87	..	..	24
46	Uruguay	96.5	97.7 [k]	98.7	99.1 [k]	92	90	..	73	94	93	..
47	Costa Rica	93.9	95.8 [k]	97.4	98.4 [k]	87	90	37	53	82	92	26
48	Latvia	99.8	99.7	99.8	99.7	92	86	..	88	..	..	17
49	Saint Kitts and Nevis	..	..	..	..	..	100	..	95	..	..	..
50	Bahamas	..	..	96.5	..	90	86 [f]	..	76 [f]	..	75	..
51	Seychelles	..	91.9	..	99.1	..	100	..	100	..	99	..
52	Cuba	95.1	96.9 [k]	99.3	99.8 [k]	92	94	69	86	92	98	..
53	Mexico	87.3	90.3	95.2	97.6	99	99	45	63	80	93	31

Human development indicators

TABLE 12

HDI rank	Adult literacy rate [a] (% ages 15 and above)		MDG Youth literacy rate [a] (% ages 15–24)		MDG Net primary enrolment ratio [b] (%)		Net secondary enrolment ratio [b, c] (%)		MDG Children reaching grade 5 (% of grade 1 students)		Tertiary students in science, math and engineering (% of all tertiary students)
	1990	2003	1990	2003	1990/91	2002/03 [d]	1990/91	2002/03 [d]	1990/91	2001/02 [d]	1998–2003 [e]
54 Tonga	..	98.9 [m]	..	99.3 [m]	92	100 [o]	83	72 [f, o]	90	..	..
55 Bulgaria	97.2	98.2	99.4	98.2	86	90	63	88	91	..	27
56 Panama	89.0	91.9	95.3	96.1	92	100	50	63 [f]	..	90	22
57 Trinidad and Tobago	96.8	98.5 [k]	99.6	99.8 [k]	91	91	..	72 [f]	..	71 [g]	35
MEDIUM HUMAN DEVELOPMENT											
58 Libyan Arab Jamahiriya	68.1	81.7 [k]	91.0	97.0 [k]	96	..	..	..	..	..	31
59 Macedonia, TFYR	..	96.1	..	98.7	94	91	..	81 [f, o]	..	..	27
60 Antigua and Barbuda	..	..	..	..	..	..	..	..	..	..	..
61 Malaysia	80.7	88.7	94.8	97.2	94	93	..	70	98	87	40
62 Russian Federation	99.2	99.4	99.8	99.7	99	90 [f]	..	..	..	..	..
63 Brazil	82.0	88.4	91.8	96.6	86	97	15	75	..	..	..
64 Romania	97.1	97.3	99.3	97.8	81	89	..	81	..	..	27
65 Mauritius	79.8	84.3	91.1	94.5	95	97	..	74 [f]	98	99	25
66 Grenada	..	..	..	..	..	84 [f, g]	..	104 [f]	..	79	..
67 Belarus	99.5	99.6 [m]	99.8	99.8 [m]	86	94	..	85	..	..	..
68 Bosnia and Herzegovina	..	94.6	..	99.6	..	..	..	..	..	..	..
69 Colombia	88.4	94.2	94.9	97.6	68	87	..	55 [f]	62	69	32
70 Dominica	..	..	..	..	..	81	..	92 [f]	..	84	..
71 Oman	54.7	74.4 [k]	85.6	98.5 [k]	69	72	..	69	97	98	..
72 Albania	77.0	98.7	94.8	99.4	95	95	..	77	..	..	11
73 Thailand	92.4	92.6	98.1	98.0	76	85 [f]	..	..	..	94 [i]	..
74 Samoa (Western)	98.0	98.7 [k]	99.0	99.5 [k]	..	98 [f]	..	62 [f]	..	94 [g]	14
75 Venezuela	88.9	93.0	96.0	97.2	88	91	19	59	86	84	..
76 Saint Lucia	..	90.1	..	95.4	95	99	..	76 [f]	..	97 [g]	..
77 Saudi Arabia	66.2	79.4	85.4	95.9	59	54	31	53 [f]	83	91	17
78 Ukraine	99.4	99.4	99.8	99.8	80	84	..	85	98	..	27
79 Peru	85.5	87.7	94.5	96.8	88	100	..	69	..	84	..
80 Kazakhstan	98.8	99.5 [m]	99.8	99.8 [m]	88	92	..	87	..	..	..
81 Lebanon	..	..	92.1	..	78	91	..	..	..	92	28
82 Ecuador	87.6	91.0	95.5	96.4	98	100	..	50	..	74	..
83 Armenia	97.5	99.4	99.5	99.8	..	94	..	83	..	..	7 [h]
84 Philippines	91.7	92.6	97.3	95.1	96	94	..	59	..	76	25
85 China	78.3	90.9	95.3	98.9	97	..	..	..	86	99	..
86 Suriname	..	88.0	..	93.5	78	97 [f]	..	64 [f]	..	..	19
87 Saint Vincent and the Grenadines	..	..	..	..	..	90	..	58	..	88	..
88 Paraguay	90.3	91.6	95.6	96.3	93	89	26	51	70	70	..
89 Tunisia	59.1	74.3	84.1	94.3	94	97	..	65	87	96	31 [h]
90 Jordan	81.5	89.9	96.7	99.1	94	92	..	80	..	97	30
91 Belize	89.1	76.9	96.0	84.2	94	99	31	69 [f]	67	81 [p]	..
92 Fiji	88.6	92.9 [m]	97.8	99.3 [m]	100	100 [f, o]	..	76 [f, o]	..	88 [g]	..
93 Sri Lanka	88.7	90.4 [q]	95.1	95.6 [q]	90	..	..	..	94	98 [n]	..
94 Turkey	77.9	88.3	92.7	96.6	89	86	42	..	98	..	21 [h]
95 Dominican Republic	79.4	87.7	87.5	94.0	58	96	..	36 [f]	..	69	..
96 Maldives	94.8	97.2 [k]	98.1	99.2 [k]	87	92	..	51 [f]	..	..	..
97 Turkmenistan	..	98.8 [m]	..	99.8 [m]	..	..	..	..	..	..	..
98 Jamaica	82.2	87.6 [k]	91.2	94.5 [k]	96	95	64	75 [f]	..	90	..
99 Iran, Islamic Rep. of	63.2	77.0	86.3	..	92	86	..	..	90	95	..
100 Georgia	..	..	..	..	97	89	..	61	..	..	28
101 Azerbaijan	..	98.8 [m]	..	99.9 [m]	100	80	..	76	..	..	..
102 Occupied Palestinian Territories	..	91.9	..	98.7	..	91	..	84	..	..	19
103 Algeria	52.9	69.8	77.3	90.1	93	95	54	67 [f]	95	97	..
104 El Salvador	72.4	79.7 [k]	83.8	88.9 [k]	73	90	..	49 [f]	..	69	22
105 Cape Verde	63.8	75.7 [k]	81.5	89.1 [k]	94	99	..	58	..	88	..
106 Syrian Arab Republic	64.8	82.9	79.9	95.2	92	98	43	43	96	91	..

TABLE 12

Literacy and enrolment

HDI rank	Adult literacy rate [a] (% ages 15 and above)		MDG Youth literacy rate [a] (% ages 15–24)		MDG Net primary enrolment ratio [b] (%)		Net secondary enrolment ratio [b,c] (%)		MDG Children reaching grade 5 (% of grade 1 students)		Tertiary students in science, math and engineering (% of all tertiary students)
	1990	2003	1990	2003	1990/91	2002/03 [d]	1990/91	2002/03 [d]	1990/91	2001/02 [d]	1998–2003 [e]
107 Guyana	97.2	..	99.8	..	89	99 [f]	67	76 [f,g]	93	77 [p]	..
108 Viet Nam	90.4	90.3 [m]	94.1	..	90	94 [f,o]	..	65 [f,o]	..	87	20
109 Kyrgyzstan	..	98.7 [m]	..	99.7 [m]	92	89	..	..	..	..	16
110 Indonesia	79.5	87.9 [k]	95.0	98.0 [k]	97	92	39	54	84	89	..
111 Uzbekistan	98.7	99.3 [k]	99.6	99.7 [k]	78	..	..	..	..	..	..
112 Nicaragua	62.7	76.7	68.2	86.2	72	86	..	39	46	65	..
113 Bolivia	78.1	86.5	92.6	97.3	91	95	29	71 [f]	..	84	..
114 Mongolia	97.8	97.8	98.9	97.7	90	79	..	77	..	..	26
115 Moldova, Rep. of	97.5	96.2	99.8	98.7	89	79	..	69	..	..	..
116 Honduras	68.1	80.0	79.7	88.9	90	87 [f,o]	..	..	..	..	..
117 Guatemala	61.0	69.1	73.4	82.2	64	87	..	30	..	65	19 [h]
118 Vanuatu	..	74.0 [m]	..	..	71	94 [f]	..	28 [o]	..	72 [p]	..
119 Egypt	47.1	55.6 [m]	61.3	73.2 [m]	84	91 [f]	..	81 [f,o]	..	98	..
120 South Africa	81.2	82.4 [m]	88.5	93.9 [m]	88	89	..	66 [f]	75	65 [p]	17
121 Equatorial Guinea	73.3	84.2	92.7	93.8	91	85 [o]	..	26 [f,p]	..	29 [g]	..
122 Tajikistan	98.2	99.5	99.8	99.8	77	94 [i]	..	83 [f]	..	..	18
123 Gabon	..	..	..	..	86	78 [f,g]	..	..	..	69	..
124 Morocco	38.7	50.7 [k]	55.3	69.5 [k]	57	90	..	36 [f]	75	81	19
125 Namibia	74.9	85.0	87.4	92.3	83	78	..	44	..	95	8
126 São Tomé and Principe	..	..	..	..	..	97 [f,o]	..	29 [f,o]	..	61 [g]	..
127 India	49.3	61.0 [q]	64.3	76.4 [i]	..	87	..	..	..	84	20 [h]
128 Solomon Islands	..	..	..	..	83	..	..	..	85	..	..
129 Myanmar	80.7	89.7	88.2	94.4	98	84	..	35	..	65	42
130 Cambodia	62.0	73.6	73.5	83.4	67	93	..	24 [f]	..	61	17
131 Botswana	68.1	78.9 [k]	83.3	89.1 [k]	85	81 [f]	29	54 [f]	97	88	19
132 Comoros	53.8	56.2 [k]	56.7	59.0 [k]	57	55 [f,p]	..	..	..	72 [p]	11
133 Lao People's Dem. Rep.	56.5	68.7	70.1	78.5	63	85	..	35	..	64	8 [h]
134 Bhutan	..	..	..	..	..	..	..	..	..	91 [g]	..
135 Pakistan	35.4	48.7	47.4	64.5	35	59 [f,g]	..	..	..	..	..
136 Nepal	30.4	48.6	46.6	70.1	81	71 [f,g]	..	..	..	65	..
137 Papua New Guinea	56.6	57.3	68.6	66.7	66	73 [f,o]	..	24 [f,o]	59	51 [g]	..
138 Ghana	58.5	54.1	81.8	..	52	59 [l]	..	36 [f,l]	80	63	26
139 Bangladesh	34.2	41.1 [k]	42.0	49.7 [k]	71	84	19	45	..	54	13
140 Timor-Leste	..	..	..	..	..	..	..	20 [f,g]	..	..	..
141 Sudan	45.8	59.0 [q]	65.0	74.6 [q]	43	46 [f,p]	..	..	94	84	..
142 Congo	67.1	82.8 [k]	92.5	97.8 [k]	79	54	..	..	63	66	11 [h]
143 Togo	44.2	53.0	63.5	74.0	75	91	18	27 [f,p]	51	69	8
144 Uganda	56.1	68.9 [k]	70.1	80.2 [k]	53	..	..	17 [f]	..	64	8
145 Zimbabwe	80.7	90.0 [k]	93.9	97.6 [k]	86	79 [l]	..	34 [l]	..	..	..
LOW HUMAN DEVELOPMENT											
146 Madagascar	58.0	70.6	72.2	70.1	65	79	..	12 [f,i]	22	53	20
147 Swaziland	71.6	79.2	85.1	88.1	77	75	..	32 [f]	76	73	11
148 Cameroon	57.9	67.9	81.1	..	74	..	..	..	..	64	..
149 Lesotho	78.0	81.4	87.2	..	73	86	..	23 [f]	71	73	6 [h]
150 Djibouti	..	..	73.2	..	31	36 [l]	..	21 [f,l]	87	80	22
151 Yemen	32.7	49.0 [k]	50.0	67.9 [k]	52	72	..	35 [f,p]	..	76	..
152 Mauritania	34.8	51.2	45.8	61.3	35	68	..	16 [f]	75	61	10
153 Haiti	39.7	51.9 [k]	54.8	66.2 [k]	22	..	..	..	..	..	..
154 Kenya	70.8	73.6	89.8	80.3	74	67	..	25 [f]	..	59	29
155 Gambia	..	..	42.2	..	48	79 [f]	..	33 [f]	..	..	..
156 Guinea	..	..	..	..	25	66	..	21 [f]	59	..	..
157 Senegal	28.4	39.3	40.1	49.1	47	58 [f]	..	..	85	80	..
158 Nigeria	48.7	66.8 [k]	73.6	88.6 [k]	60	67 [f]	..	29	..	..	..
159 Rwanda	53.3	64.0	72.7	76.5	67	87	7	..	60	47	..

Human development indicators

TABLE 12

HDI rank	Adult literacy rate[a] (% ages 15 and above)		MDG Youth literacy rate[a] (% ages 15–24)		MDG Net primary enrolment ratio[b] (%)		Net secondary enrolment ratio[b, c] (%)		MDG Children reaching grade 5 (% of grade 1 students)		Tertiary students in science, math and engineering (% of all tertiary students)
	1990	2003	1990	2003	1990/91	2002/03[d]	1990/91	2002/03[d]	1990/91	2001/02[d]	1998–2003[e]
160 Angola	..	66.8	..	71.4	58	61[f, i]	..	..	..	..	18
161 Eritrea	..	..	60.9	..	16	45	..	22	..	86	17
162 Benin	26.4	33.6	40.4	44.4	45	58[f, p]	..	20[f, g]	55	68	25
163 Côte d'Ivoire	38.5	48.1	52.6	59.8	46	61[j]	..	21[f, o]	73	69[j]	..
164 Tanzania, U. Rep. of	62.9	69.4	83.1	78.4	50	82[f]	..	..	79	88	22
165 Malawi	51.8	64.1[m]	63.2	76.3[m]	50	..	..	29[f]	64	44	33
166 Zambia	68.2	67.9[m]	81.2	69.4[m]	79	68	..	23[f]	..	81[p]	30
167 Congo, Dem. Rep. of the	47.5	65.3	68.9	68.7	54	..	..	..	55	..	..
168 Mozambique	33.5	46.5[k]	48.8	62.8[k]	45	55	..	12	33	49	..
169 Burundi	37.0	58.9	51.6	72.3	53	57	..	9[f]	62	68	10[h]
170 Ethiopia	28.6	41.5[k]	43.0	57.4[k]	23	51[f]	..	18[f, l]	..	62	19
171 Central African Republic	33.2	48.6	52.1	58.5	53	..	..	..	24	..	15
172 Guinea-Bissau	..	..	44.1	..	38	45[p]	..	9[f, p]	..	38[j]	..
173 Chad	27.7	25.5	48.0	37.3	36	63[f]	..	10[f]	53	60[g]	..
174 Mali	18.8	19.0[m]	27.6	24.2[m]	20	45	5	..	73	75	..
175 Burkina Faso	..	12.8[m]	..	19.4[m]	26	36	..	9	70	66	..
176 Sierra Leone	..	29.6	..	38.2	41	..	..	..	..	..	8
177 Niger	11.4	14.4	17.0	19.8	24	38	6	6	62	69	..
Developing countries	67.0	76.6	81.1	85.2	..	..	..	..	..	..	..
Least developed countries	44.2	54.2	57.2	64.2	..	..	..	..	..	..	..
Arab States	50.8	64.1	68.4	81.3	..	..	..	..	..	..	..
East Asia and the Pacific	79.7	90.4	95.0	98.0	..	..	..	..	..	..	..
Latin America and the Caribbean	85.1	89.6	92.7	95.9	..	..	..	..	..	..	..
South Asia	47.7	58.9	61.7	72.2	..	..	..	..	..	..	..
Sub-Saharan Africa	51.1	61.3	68.5	73.7	..	..	..	..	..	..	..
Central and Eastern Europe and the CIS	98.7	99.2	99.7	99.5	..	..	..	..	..	..	..
OECD	..	..	..	..	..	..	..	..	..	..	..
High-income OECD	..	..	..	..	..	..	..	..	..	..	..
High human development	..	..	..	..	..	..	..	..	..	..	..
Medium human development	70.6	79.4	83.2	87.5	..	..	..	..	..	..	..
Low human development	45.1	57.5	63.7	70.1	..	..	..	..	..	..	..
High income	..	..	..	..	..	..	..	..	..	..	..
Middle income	81.2	89.6	93.6	96.8	..	..	..	..	..	..	..
Low income	50.2	60.8	64.4	73.0	..	..	..	..	..	..	..
World	..	..	..	..	..	..	..	..	..	..	..

NOTES

a Data for 1990 refer to estimates produced by United Nations Educational, Scientific and Cultural Organization (UNESCO) Institute for Statistics based on data prior to 1990; data for 2003 refer to national literacy estimates from censuses or surveys conducted between 2000 and 2004, unless otherwise noted. Due to differences in methodology and timeliness of underlying data, comparisons across countries and over time should be made with caution. For more details, see www.uis.unesco.org/ev.php?ID=4930_201&ID2=DO_TOPIC.

b The net enrolment ratio is the ratio of enrolled children of the official age for the education level indicated to the total population of that age. Net enrolment ratios exceeding 100% reflect discrepancies between these two data sets.

c Enrolment ratios are based on the new International Standard Classification of Education, adopted in 1997 (UNESCO 1997), and so may not be strictly comparable with those for earlier years.

d Data on net enrolment ratios refer to the 2002/03 school year, and data on children reaching grade 5 to the 2001/02 school year, unless otherwise specified. Data for some countries may refer to national or UNESCO Institute for Statistics estimates. For details, see www.uis.unesco.org. Because data are from different sources, comparisons across countries should be made with caution.

e Data refer to the most recent year available during the period specified.

f Preliminary UNESCO Institute for Statistics estimate, subject to further revision.

g Data refer to the 2000/01 school year.

h Figure should be treated with caution due to the fact that the reported number of enrolled pupils in "Not known or unspecified" category represents more than 10% of the total enrolment.

i Data refer to the 1998/99 school year.

j National estimates.

k Estimate produced by UNESCO Institute for Statistics in July 2002.

l Data refer to the 2003/04 school year.

m Data refer to a year between 1995 and 1999.

n Data refer to the 2002/03 school year.

o Data refer to the 2001/02 school year.

p Data refer to the 1999/2000 school year.

q Data refer to a year or period other than that specified, differ from the standard definition or refer to only part of a country.

r Data refer to the 2004/05 school year.

SOURCES

Columns 1 and 3: UNESCO Institute for Statistics 2003a.

Columns 2 and 4: UNESCO Institute for Statistics 2005a.

Columns 5–10: UNESCO Institute for Statistics 2005c.

Column 11: UNESCO Institute for Statistics 2005d.

Human development indicators

TABLE 13

... to acquire knowledge ...

Technology: diffusion and creation

		MDG Telephone mainlines[a] (per 1,000 people)		MDG Cellular subscribers[a] (per 1,000 people)		MDG Internet users (per 1,000 people)		Patents granted to residents (per million people)	Receipts of royalties and licence fees (US$ per person)	Research and development (R&D) expenditures (% of GDP)	Researchers in R&D (per million people)
HDI rank		1990	2003	1990	2003	1990	2003	2002	2003	1997–2002[b]	1990–2003[b]
HIGH HUMAN DEVELOPMENT											
1	Norway	502	713	46	909	7	346	0	42.9	1.7	4,442
2	Iceland	510	660	39	966	0	675	7	0.0	3.1	6,592
3	Australia	456	542	11	719	6	567	85	20.1	1.5	3,446
4	Luxembourg	481	797	2	1,194	0	377	234	267.3	1.7	3,757
5	Canada	565	651	22	419	4	..	40	81.5	1.9	3,487
6	Sweden	681	..	54	980	6	..	317	261.8	4.3	5,171
7	Switzerland	574	727	18	843	6	398	279	..	2.6	3,594
8	Ireland	281	491	7	880	0	317	110	52.4	1.1	2,315
9	Belgium	393	489	4	793	(.)	386	72	..	2.2	3,180
10	United States	547	624	21	546	8	556	302	167.2	2.7	4,526
11	Japan	441	472	7	679	(.)	483	852	96.3	3.1	5,085
12	Netherlands	464	614	5	768	3	522	186	116.8	1.9	2,826
13	Finland	534	492	52	910	4	534	35	96.5	3.5	7,431
14	Denmark	567	669	29	883	1	541	90	..	2.5	4,822
15	United Kingdom	441	..	19	912	1	..	88	173.0	1.9	2,691
16	France	495	566	5	696	1	366	183	66.3	2.3	3,134
17	Austria	418	481	10	879	1	462	196	19.2	2.2	2,346
18	Italy	388	484	5	1,018	(.)	337	22	9.1	1.1	1,156
19	New Zealand	434	448	16	648	0	526	70	30.0	1.2	2,593
20	Germany	441	657	4	785	1	473	274	51.7	2.5	3,222
21	Spain	316	429	1	916	(.)	239	29	13.2	1.0	2,036
22	Hong Kong, China (SAR)	450	559	24	1,079	0	472	3	..	0.6	1,568
23	Israel	343	458	3	961	1	..	35	64.7	5.1	1,570
24	Greece	389	454	0	902	0	150	30	1.7	0.6	1,357
25	Singapore	346	450	17	852	0	509	58	47.3	2.2	4,352
26	Slovenia	211	407	0	871	0	401	123	5.4	1.5	2,364
27	Portugal	243	411	1	898	0	..	3	3.5	0.9	1,745
28	Korea, Rep. of	306	538	2	701	(.)	610	633	27.8	2.5	2,979
29	Cyprus	419	572	5	744	0	337	1	19.9	0.3	569
30	Barbados	281	497	0	519	0	371	0	3.2	..	..
31	Czech Republic	158	360	0	965	0	308	24	4.9	1.2	1,467
32	Malta	360	521	0	725	0	..	45	(.)	..	..
33	Brunei Darussalam	136	..	7	..	0	..	..	..	..	282
34	Argentina	93	..	(.)	..	0	..	..	0.9	0.4	715
35	Hungary	96	349	(.)	769	0	232	21	30.8	1.0	1,473
36	Poland	86	307	0	451	0	232	22	0.7	0.6	1,469
37	Chile	66	221	1	511	0	272	..	2.9	0.5	419
38	Estonia	204	341	0	777	0	444	8	3.5	0.7	2,253
39	Lithuania	212	239	0	630	0	202	15	0.1	0.7	1,824
40	Qatar	220	261	9	533	0	199	..	..	..	..
41	United Arab Emirates	224	281	19	736	0	275	0	..	..	..
42	Slovakia	135	241	0	684	0	256	13	9.2	0.6	1,707
43	Bahrain	191	268	10	638	0	216	..	..	..	..
44	Kuwait	188	196	12	572	0	228	..	0.0[c]	0.2	73
45	Croatia	172	..	(.)	584	0	232	20	7.8	1.1	1,920
46	Uruguay	134	..	0	..	0	..	1	0.0[c]	0.2	370
47	Costa Rica	101	278	0	181	0	288	0	0.1	0.4	533
48	Latvia	234	285	0	526	0	404	0	1.9	0.4	1,476
49	Saint Kitts and Nevis	237	..	0	..	0	..	..	0.0[c]	..	..
50	Bahamas	274	415	8	367	0	265	..	0.0	..	..
51	Seychelles	124	256	0	595	0	..	0	..	0.1	452
52	Cuba	31	64	0	3	0	9	0	..	0.5	538
53	Mexico	65	160	1	295	0	120	1	0.8	0.4	259

TABLE 13

Human development indicators

HDI rank	MDG Telephone mainlines[a] (per 1,000 people)		MDG Cellular subscribers[a] (per 1,000 people)		MDG Internet users (per 1,000 people)		Patents granted to residents (per million people)	Receipts of royalties and licence fees (US$ per person)	Research and development (R&D) expenditures (% of GDP)	Researchers in R&D (per million people)
	1990	2003	1990	2003	1990	2003	2002	2003	1997–2002[b]	1990–2003[b]
54 Tonga	46	..	0	..	0	..	..	..	..	..
55 Bulgaria	242	380	0	466	0	206	16	0.6	0.5	1,158
56 Panama	93	122	0	268	0	62	..	0.0c	0.4	95
57 Trinidad and Tobago	141	..	0	399	0	..	0	..	0.1	347
MEDIUM HUMAN DEVELOPMENT										
58 Libyan Arab Jamahiriya	48	136	0	23	0	29	..	..	..	361
59 Macedonia, TFYR	148	252	0	372	0	60	13	1.1	0.3	500
60 Antigua and Barbuda	253	..	0	..	0	..	0	0.0c	..	..
61 Malaysia	89	182	5	442	0	344	..	0.8	0.7	294
62 Russian Federation	140	253	0	249	0	..	105	1.2	1.2	3,415
63 Brazil	65	223	(.)	264	0	..	4	0.6	1.0	324
64 Romania	102	199	0	324	0	184	26	0.1c	0.4	910
65 Mauritius	52	285	2	267	0	123	..	0.0c	0.3	..
66 Grenada	177	290	2	376	0	169	0	0.0c	..	..
67 Belarus	154	311	0	113	0	141	54	0.1	0.6	1,870
68 Bosnia and Herzegovina	..	245	0	274	0	..	0	..	..	..
69 Colombia	69	179	0	141	0	53	(.)	0.1	0.1	81
70 Dominica	164	..	0	..	0	..	0	0.0c	..	..
71 Oman	60	88	2	228	0	..	0	..	..	..
72 Albania	13	83	0	358	0	10	..	1.7	..	..
73 Thailand	24	105	1	394	0	111	..	0.1	0.2	289
74 Samoa (Western)	26	73	0	58	0	..	..	..	..	..
75 Venezuela	76	111	(.)	273	0	60	..	0.0c	0.4	222
76 Saint Lucia	129	..	0	..	0	..	0	..	..	481
77 Saudi Arabia	77	155	1	321	0	67	(.)	0.0c	..	..
78 Ukraine	136	233	0	136	0	..	0	0.3	1.2	1,749
79 Peru	26	67	(.)	106	0	104	..	0.1	0.1	225
80 Kazakhstan	80	141	0	..	0	..	0	(.)	0.3	744
81 Lebanon	155	200	0	234	0	143	..	..	..	..
82 Ecuador	48	122	0	189	0	46	(.)	0.0c	0.1	84
83 Armenia	157	148	0	30	0	37	42	..	0.3	1,606
84 Philippines	10	41	0	270	0	..	0	(.)	..	..
85 China	6	209	(.)	215	0	63	5	0.1	1.2	633
86 Suriname	92	152	0	320	0	44	..	..	..	..
87 Saint Vincent and the Grenadines	124	273	0	529	0	..	0	0.0c	0.2	179
88 Paraguay	27	46	0	299	0	20	..	35.1	0.1	83
89 Tunisia	37	118	(.)	197	0	64	0	1.8	0.6	1,013
90 Jordan	72	114	(.)	242	0	81	..	..	..	1,977
91 Belize	92	113	0	205	0	..	0	0.0c	..	..
92 Fiji	58	124	0	133	0	67	..	..	..	..
93 Sri Lanka	7	49	(.)	73	0	13	0	..	..	197
94 Turkey	121	268	1	394	0	85	1	0.0c	0.7	345
95 Dominican Republic	48	115	(.)	272	0	102	..	0.0c	..	..
96 Maldives	29	..	0	..	0	..	..	20.7	..	..
97 Turkmenistan	60	77	0	..	0	..	0	..	..	..
98 Jamaica	45	..	0	680	0	..	1	4.6	..	..
99 Iran, Islamic Rep. of	40	220	0	51	0	72	..	..	..	484
100 Georgia	99	134	0	145	0	24	27	1.2	0.3	2,317
101 Azerbaijan	86	114	0	128	0	..	0	..	0.3	1,248
102 Occupied Palestinian Territories	..	87	0	133	0	40	..	..	..	..
103 Algeria	32	69	(.)	45	0	..	(.)	..	..	..
104 El Salvador	24	113	0	173	0	83	..	(.)	(.)	47
105 Cape Verde	24	156	0	116	0	44	..	0.2	(.)	131
106 Syrian Arab Republic	41	..	0	68	0	35	0	..	0.2	29

TABLE 13

Technology: diffusion and creation

HDI rank	MDG Telephone mainlines[a] (per 1,000 people)		MDG Cellular subscribers[a] (per 1,000 people)		MDG Internet users (per 1,000 people)		Patents granted to residents (per million people)	Receipts of royalties and licence fees (US$ per person)	Research and development (R&D) expenditures (% of GDP)	Researchers in R&D (per million people)
	1990	2003	1990	2003	1990	2003	2002	2003	1997–2002[b]	1990–2003[b]
107 Guyana	20	..	0	..	0	..	..	41.9	..	..
108 Viet Nam	1	54	0	34	0	43	0	..	..	..
109 Kyrgyzstan	72	76	0	27	0	38	10	0.4	0.2	413
110 Indonesia	6	39	(.)	87	0	38	0	..	..	..
111 Uzbekistan	69	67	0	13	0	19	17	..	..	..
112 Nicaragua	13	37	0	85	0	..	0	0.0[c]	0.1	73
113 Bolivia	28	72	0	152	0	..	..	0.2	0.3	118
114 Mongolia	32	56	0	130	0	58	31	..	0.3	710
115 Moldova, Rep. of	106	219	0	132	0	80	48	0.3	..	171
116 Honduras	17	49	0	55	0	40	1	0.0[c]	0.1	74
117 Guatemala	21	77	(.)	165	0	..	..	0.0[c]	..	..
118 Vanuatu	18	31	0	38	0	36	..	..	..	..
119 Egypt	30	127	(.)	84	0	44	2	1.8	0.2	..
120 South Africa	93	..	(.)	364	0	..	0	1.1	0.7	192
121 Equatorial Guinea	4	18	0	76	0	..	..	..	..	..
122 Tajikistan	45	37	0	7	0	1	3	0.1	..	..
123 Gabon	22	29	0	224	0	26	..	..	..	..
124 Morocco	16	40	(.)	244	0	33	0	0.9	..	..
125 Namibia	39	66	0	116	0	34	..	0.0	..	..
126 São Tomé and Principe	19	46	0	32	0	99	..	..	..	..
127 India	6	46	0	25	0	17	0	(.)[c]	0.8	120
128 Solomon Islands	15	13	0	3	0	5	..	..	..	..
129 Myanmar	2	7	0	1	0	1	..	0.0[c]	..	..
130 Cambodia	(.)	3	0	35	0	2	..	..	..	..
131 Botswana	21	75	0	297	0	..	0	0.3[c]	..	..
132 Comoros	8	17	0	3	0	6	..	..	..	..
133 Lao People's Dem. Rep.	2	12	0	20	0	3	..	..	..	..
134 Bhutan	4	34	0	11	0	20	..	..	..	..
135 Pakistan	8	27	(.)	18	0	..	..	0.1	0.2	88
136 Nepal	3	16	0	2	0	..	..	..	0.7	62
137 Papua New Guinea	8	..	0	..	0	..	0	..	..	..
138 Ghana	3	13	0	36	0	..	0	0.0[c]	..	..
139 Bangladesh	2	5	0	10	0	2	..	(.)	..	..
140 Timor-Leste	..	..	0	..	0	..	..	..	..	..
141 Sudan	3	27	0	20	0	9	0	..	..	..
142 Congo	7	2	0	94	0	4	..	..	..	29
143 Togo	3	12	0	44	0	42	..	0.0[c]	..	..
144 Uganda	2	2	0	30	0	5	0	0.2	0.8	25
145 Zimbabwe	13	..	0	..	0	..	0	..	..	..
LOW HUMAN DEVELOPMENT										
146 Madagascar	3	4	0	17	0	4	(.)	0.1	0.1	15
147 Swaziland	17	44	0	84	0	26	0	0.1[c]	..	..
148 Cameroon	3	..	0	66	0	..	..	..	..	..
149 Lesotho	7	16	0	47	0	14	0	5.9[c]	..	42
150 Djibouti	11	15	0	34	0	10	..	..	..	..
151 Yemen	11	..	0	35	0	..	..	..	..	..
152 Mauritania	3	14	0	127	0	4	..	..	..	..
153 Haiti	7	17	0	38	0	18	..	0.0[c]	..	..
154 Kenya	8	10	0	50	0	..	0	0.4	..	..
155 Gambia	7	..	0	..	0	..	0	..	..	..
156 Guinea	2	3	0	14	0	5	..	(.)	..	286
157 Senegal	6	22	0	56	0	22	..	(.)[c]	..	..
158 Nigeria	3	7	0	26	0	6	..	..	..	..
159 Rwanda	2	..	0	16	0	..	..	0.0[c]	..	..

Human development indicators

TABLE 13

HDI rank	MDG Telephone mainlines[a] (per 1,000 people)		MDG Cellular subscribers[a] (per 1,000 people)		MDG Internet users (per 1,000 people)		Patents granted to residents (per million people)	Receipts of royalties and licence fees (US$ per person)	Research and development (R&D) expenditures (% of GDP)	Researchers in R&D (per million people)
	1990	2003	1990	2003	1990	2003	2002	2003	1997–2002[b]	1990–2003[b]
160 Angola	8	7	0	..	0	..	..	..	..	..
161 Eritrea	..	9	0	0	0	7	..	..	..	..
162 Benin	3	9	0	34	0	10	..	..	..	..
163 Côte d'Ivoire	6	14	0	77	0	14	..	0.0c	..	..
164 Tanzania, U. Rep. of	3	4	0	25	0	7	0	0.0c	..	..
165 Malawi	3	8	0	13	0	3	0	0.0c	..	..
166 Zambia	8	8	0	22	0	6	0	..	(.)	47
167 Congo, Dem. Rep. of the	1	..	0	19	0	..	..	..	..	..
168 Mozambique	3	..	0	23	0	..	0	0.8	..	..
169 Burundi	1	3	0	9	0	2	..	0.0c	..	..
170 Ethiopia	3	6	0	1	0	1	..	0.0c	..	..
171 Central African Republic	2	..	0	10	0	1	..	..	..	47
172 Guinea-Bissau	6	8	0	1	0	15	..	..	..	..
173 Chad	1	..	0	8	0	..	..	..	..	..
174 Mali	1	..	0	23	0	..	..	(.)c	..	..
175 Burkina Faso	2	5	0	19	0	4	..	..	0.2	17
176 Sierra Leone	3	..	0	0	0	..	0	(.)	..	..
177 Niger	1	..	0	6	0	..	..	..	..	..
Developing countries	29	113	(.)	134	(.)	53	..	0.6	0.9	400
Least developed countries	3	8	0	16	0	4	..	..	..	..
Arab States	79	94	4	118	0	49	..	..	..	..
East Asia and the Pacific	18	172	(.)	212	(.)	80	..	..	1.5	706
Latin America and the Caribbean	89	165	(.)	239	0	..	2	1.0	0.6	293
South Asia	7	47	(.)	24	0	18	..	..	0.7	135
Sub-Saharan Africa	5	9	(.)	54	0	..	..	..	..	..
Central and Eastern Europe and the CIS	120	232	(.)	287	0	..	48	2.0	1.0	2,213
OECD	365	494	7	644	3	403	248	80.6	2.5	3,046
High-income OECD	439	567	9	705	3	480	310	101.3	2.6	3,676
High human development	289	495	6	652	2	414	250	79.2	2.5	3,004
Medium human development	22	123	(.)	138	0	46	7	0.3	0.8	521
Low human development	3	8	0	25	0	..	..	..	..	..
High income	420	562	9	710	3	477	302	100.1	2.5	3,630
Middle income	46	180	(.)	224	0	77	10	0.6	0.7	760
Low income	6	32	(.)	24	0	14	..	..	..	..
World	81	184	1	226	1	120	62	17.9	2.4	1,146

NOTES

a Telephone mainlines and cellular subscribers combined form an indicator for Millennium Development Goal 8; see *Index to Millennium Development Goal Indicators in the indicator tables.*

b Data refer to the most recent year available during the period specified.

c Data refer to 2002.

SOURCES

Columns 1–6: ITU 2005.

Column 7: calculated on the basis of data on patents granted to residents from WIPO 2004 and data on population from UN 2005h.

Column 8: calculated on the basis of data on receipts of royalties and licence fees from World Bank 2005c, based on data from the International Monetary Fund, and data on population from UN 2005h.

Columns 9 and 10: World Bank 2005c, based on data from the United Nations Educational, Scientific and Cultural Organization; aggregates calculated for the Human Development Report Office by the World Bank.

Human development indicators

TABLE 14

... to have access to the resources needed for a decent standard of living ...

Economic performance

		GDP		GDP per capita		GDP per capita — Annual growth rate (%)		Highest value during 1975–2003	Year of highest	Average annual change in consumer price index (%)	
HDI rank		US$ billions 2003	PPP US$ billions 2003	US$ 2003	PPP US$ 2003	1975–2003	1990–2003	(PPP US$)	value	1990–2003	2002–03
HIGH HUMAN DEVELOPMENT											
1	Norway	220.9	171.9	48,412	37,670	2.8	2.9	37,911	2001	2.3	2.5
2	Iceland	10.5	9.0	36,377	31,243	1.7	2.1	31,243	2003	3.2	2.1
3	Australia	522.4	589.1	26,275	29,632	1.9	2.6	29,632	2003	2.4	2.8
4	Luxembourg	26.5	27.9	59,143	62,298	3.9	3.6	62,298	2003	2.0	2.0
5	Canada	856.5	970.3	27,079	30,677	1.6	2.3	30,677	2003	1.8	2.8
6	Sweden	301.6	239.6	33,676	26,750	1.6	2.0	26,750	2003	1.7	1.9
7	Switzerland	320.1	224.6	43,553	30,552	1.0	0.5	31,098	2001	1.3	0.6
8	Ireland	153.7	150.7	38,487	37,738	4.5	6.7	37,738	2003	2.7	3.5
9	Belgium	301.9	294.0	29,096	28,335	1.9	1.8	28,335	2003	1.9	1.6
10	United States	10,948.5	10,923.4 [a]	37,648	37,562	2.0	2.1	37,562	2003	2.6	2.3
11	Japan	4,300.9	3,567.8	33,713	27,967	2.4	1.0	27,967	2003	0.4	−0.3
12	Netherlands	511.5	476.5	31,532	29,371	1.8	2.1	29,568	2002	2.6	2.1
13	Finland	161.9	144.0	31,058	27,619	2.0	2.5	27,619	2003	1.6	0.9
14	Denmark	211.9	169.5	39,332	31,465	1.6	1.9	31,471	2002	2.2	2.1
15	United Kingdom	1,794.9	1,610.6	30,253	27,147	2.1	2.5	27,147	2003	2.7	2.9
16	France	1,757.6	1,654.0	29,410	27,677	1.7	1.6	27,677	2003	1.6	2.1
17	Austria	253.1	243.5	31,289	30,094	2.1	1.8	30,094	2003	2.1	1.4
18	Italy	1,468.3	1,563.3	25,471	27,119	2.0	1.5	27,119	2003	3.3	2.7
19	New Zealand	79.6	90.5	19,847	22,582	1.0	2.1	22,582	2003	1.9	1.8
20	Germany	2,403.2	2,291.0	29,115	27,756	2.0	1.3	27,769	2001	1.8	1.0
21	Spain	838.7	920.3	20,404	22,391	2.2	2.4	22,391	2003	3.5	3.0
22	Hong Kong, China (SAR)	156.7	185.3	22,987	27,179	4.3	2.1	27,294	2000	3.5	−2.6
23	Israel	110.2	134.0	16,481	20,033	1.9	1.6	21,822	2000	7.7	0.7
24	Greece	172.2	220.2	15,608	19,954	1.0	2.1	19,954	2003	7.2	3.5
25	Singapore	91.3	104.0	21,492	24,481	4.9	3.5	24,870	2000	1.3	0.5
26	Slovenia	27.7	38.2	13,909	19,150	..	3.1	19,150 [b]	2003	10.3	5.6
27	Portugal	147.9	189.3	14,161	18,126	2.8	2.2	18,597	2001	4.0	3.3
28	Korea, Rep. of	605.3	861.0	12,634	17,971	6.1	4.6	17,971	2003	4.5	3.6
29	Cyprus	11.4	14.3 [c]	14,786	18,776 [c]	4.6	3.2	18,776 [b]	2001	3.4	4.1
30	Barbados	2.6	4.3	9,708	15,720	1.2	1.4	16,220	2000	2.3	1.6
31	Czech Republic	89.7	166.9	8,794	16,357	..	1.5	16,357 [b]	2003	6.1	0.1
32	Malta	4.9	7.0	12,157	17,633	4.3	3.3	18,908	2000	2.8	0.5
33	Brunei Darussalam	..	..	..	..	..	..	..	..	..	..
34	Argentina	129.6	445.2	3,524	12,106	0.4	1.3	13,757	1998	7.2	13.4
35	Hungary	82.7	147.7	8,169	14,584	1.1	2.6	14,584	2003	16.9	4.6
36	Poland	209.6	434.6	5,487	11,379	..	4.2	11,379 [b]	2003	19.1	0.7
37	Chile	72.4	162.1	4,591	10,274	4.0	4.1	10,274	2003	7.2	2.8
38	Estonia	9.1	18.3	6,713	13,539	0.4 [b]	3.3	13,539 [b]	2003	14.8	1.3
39	Lithuania	18.2	40.4	5,274	11,702	..	0.5	12,075 [b]	1990	19.3	−1.2
40	Qatar	.. [d]	..	.. [d]	..	..	..	..	..	2.5	2.3
41	United Arab Emirates	.. [d]	..	.. [d]	..	−3.3 [b]	−2.1 [b]	49,432 [b, e]	1975	..	..
42	Slovakia	32.5	72.7	6,033	13,494	0.5 [b]	2.4	13,494 [b]	2003	8.1	8.6
43	Bahrain	.. [d]	12.2 [d]	.. [d]	17,479 [d]	1.1 [b]	1.5 [b]	17,479 [b]	2002	0.7	..
44	Kuwait	41.7	43.2 [e]	17,421	18,047 [e]	−1.2 [b]	−2.3 [b]	29,760 [b, e]	1975	1.9	1.0
45	Croatia	28.8	49.2	6,479	11,080	..	2.1	11,080 [b]	2003	52.8	0.1
46	Uruguay	11.2	28.0	3,308	8,280	1.2	0.9	9,858	1998	25.5	19.4
47	Costa Rica	17.4	38.5 [e]	4,352	9,606 [e]	1.3	2.6	9,836 [e]	1999	14.1	9.4
48	Latvia	11.1	23.8	4,771	10,270	(.)	2.2	10,482 [b]	1989	19.0	2.9
49	Saint Kitts and Nevis	0.3	0.6	7,397	12,404	5.1 [b]	3.1	12,413 [b]	2002	3.2	2.2
50	Bahamas	5.3	5.4 [d]	16,571	17,159 [d]	1.3 [b]	0.3 [b]	18,260 [b]	1989	2.0	3.0
51	Seychelles	0.7	..	8,610	..	2.9	2.2	..	..	2.4	3.3
52	Cuba	..	..	..	..	..	3.5 [b]	..	..	..	..
53	Mexico	626.1	937.8	6,121	9,168	0.9	1.4	9,442	2000	16.7	4.5

Human development indicators

TABLE 14

	GDP		GDP per capita		GDP per capita				Average annual change in consumer price index	
					Annual growth rate (%)		Highest value during 1975–2003	Year of highest	(%)	
	US$ billions	PPP US$ billions	US$	PPP US$			(PPP US$)	value		
HDI rank	2003	2003	2003	2003	1975–2003	1990–2003			1990–2003	2002–03
54 Tonga	0.2	0.7 e	1,603	6,992 e	1.8 b	2.0	6,992 b, e	2003	4.3	11.6
55 Bulgaria	19.9	60.5	2,539	7,731	0.3 b	0.6	7,968 b	1988	83.8	2.2
56 Panama	12.9	20.5	4,319	6,854	1.0	2.4	6,854	2003	1.1	1.4
57 Trinidad and Tobago	10.5	14.1	8,007	10,766	(.)	3.2	10,766	2003	5.2	3.8
MEDIUM HUMAN DEVELOPMENT										
58 Libyan Arab Jamahiriya	.. d	..	.. d	..	..	..	..	..	3.5	..
59 Macedonia, TFYR	4.7	13.9	2,277	6,794	..	−0.7	8,115 b	1990	7.1	1.1
60 Antigua and Barbuda	0.8	0.8	9,629	10,294	3.8 b	1.6	10,469 b	1999	..	..
61 Malaysia	103.7	235.7	4,187	9,512	3.9	3.4	9,512	2003	3.1	1.1
62 Russian Federation	432.9	1,323.8	3,018	9,230	−2.1 b	−1.5	11,269 b	1989	66.6	13.7
63 Brazil	492.3	1,375.7	2,788	7,790	0.8	1.2	7,918	2002	114.0	14.7
64 Romania	57.0	158.2	2,619	7,277	−0.8 b	0.6	7,277 b	2003	78.7	15.3
65 Mauritius	5.2	13.8	4,274	11,287	4.6 b	4.0	11,287 b	2003	6.5	3.9
66 Grenada	0.4	0.8	4,199	7,959	3.2 b	2.4	7,977 b	2000	2.0	..
67 Belarus	17.5	59.8	1,770	6,052	..	0.9	6,052 b	2003	185.8	28.4
68 Bosnia and Herzegovina	7.0	24.7	1,684	5,967	..	11.9 b	.. b	..	..	..
69 Colombia	78.7	298.8 e	1,764	6,702 e	1.4	0.4	6,852 e	1997	17.0	7.1
70 Dominica	0.3	0.4	3,639	5,448	3.2 b	1.2	6,278 b	2000	1.6	1.6
71 Oman	.. d	34.5 d	.. d	13,584 d	2.2 b	0.9 b	13,965 b	2001	0.2	−0.4
72 Albania	6.1	14.5	1,933	4,584	0.3 b	5.1	4,584 b	2003	19.2	0.5
73 Thailand	143.0	471.0	2,305	7,595	5.1	2.8	7,595	2003	4.1	1.8
74 Samoa (Western)	0.3	1.0 e	1,505	5,854 e	0.8 b	2.4	5,978 b, e	1986	3.6	0.1
75 Venezuela	85.4	126.3	3,326	4,919	−1.1	−1.5	8,038	1977	41.1	31.1
76 Saint Lucia	0.7	0.9	4,314	5,709	3.6 b	0.3	5,996 b	1999	2.5	0.9
77 Saudi Arabia	214.7	298.0 e	9,532	13,226 e	−2.4	−0.6	24,461 e	1977	0.5	0.6
78 Ukraine	49.5	265.5	1,024	5,491	−5.7 b	−4.7	9,755 b	1989	85.8	5.2
79 Peru	60.6	142.8	2,231	5,260	−0.5	2.1	5,845	1981	18.5	2.3
80 Kazakhstan	29.7	99.3	2,000	6,671	..	0.4	6,671 b	2003	38.8	6.4
81 Lebanon	19.0	22.8	4,224	5,074	3.4 b	2.9	5,074 b	2003	..	..
82 Ecuador	27.2	47.4	2,091	3,641	0.1	0.1	3,763	1988	37.7	7.9
83 Armenia	2.8	11.2	918	3,671	..	2.8	3,671 b	2003	36.9	4.8
84 Philippines	80.6	352.2	989	4,321	0.3	1.2	4,539	1982	7.3	3.0
85 China	1,417.0	6,445.9 f	1,100	5,003 f	8.2	8.5	5,003 f	2003	6.0	1.2
86 Suriname	1.2	..	2,635	..	−0.6	0.9	..	..	67.7	23.0
87 Saint Vincent and the Grenadines	0.4	0.7	3,403	6,123	3.4	1.8	6,123	2003	1.9	0.3
88 Paraguay	6.0	26.4 e	1,069	4,684 e	0.6	−0.6	5,380 e	1981	11.8	14.2
89 Tunisia	25.0	70.9	2,530	7,161	2.1	3.1	7,161	2003	3.9	2.7
90 Jordan	9.9	22.9	1,858	4,320	0.3	0.9	5,195	1987	3.0	2.3
91 Belize	1.0	1.9	3,612	6,950	3.1	2.2	6,950	2003	1.7	2.6
92 Fiji	2.0	4.9	2,438	5,880	0.7	1.8	5,880	2003	3.1	4.2
93 Sri Lanka	18.2	72.7	948	3,778	3.4	3.3	3,778	2003	9.7	6.3
94 Turkey	240.4	478.9	3,399	6,772	1.8	1.3	6,772	2003	72.4	25.3
95 Dominican Republic	16.5	59.6 e	1,893	6,823 e	2.0	4.0	6,823 e	2003	8.7	27.4
96 Maldives	0.7	..	2,441	..	..	4.7 b	..	..	5.0	−2.9
97 Turkmenistan	6.2	28.9	1,275	5,938	−3.0 b	−1.3	6,589 b	1988	..	..
98 Jamaica	8.1	10.8	3,083	4,104	0.4	(.)	4,125	1991	18.3	10.3
99 Iran, Islamic Rep. of	137.1	464.4	2,066	6,995	−0.3	2.1	8,443	1976	22.8	16.5
100 Georgia	4.0	13.3	778	2,588	−4.9	−2.7	7,065 b	1985	17.7	..
101 Azerbaijan	7.1	29.8	867	3,617	..	−2.6	3,617 b	2003	109.1	..
102 Occupied Palestinian Territories	3.5	..	1,026	..	..	−6.0 b	..	..	..	..
103 Algeria	66.5	194.4 e	2,090	6,107 e	−0.1	0.6	6,319 e	1985	12.7	2.6
104 El Salvador	14.9	31.2 e	2,277	4,781 e	0.2	2.1	5,456 e	1978	6.6	2.1
105 Cape Verde	0.8	2.4 e	1,698	5,214 e	3.0 b	3.3	5,214 b, e	2003	4.8	..
106 Syrian Arab Republic	21.5	62.2	1,237	3,576	0.9	1.4	3,696	1998	4.9	..

TABLE 14

Economic performance

		GDP		GDP per capita		GDP per capita				Average annual change in consumer price index	
		US$ billions	PPP US$ billions	US$	PPP US$	Annual growth rate (%)		Highest value during 1975–2003	Year of highest	(%)	
HDI rank		2003	2003	2003	2003	1975–2003	1990–2003	(PPP US$)	value	1990–2003	2002–03
107	Guyana	0.7	3.3e	965	4,230e	0.7	3.6	4,482e	1997	5.8	..
108	Viet Nam	39.2	202.5	482	2,490	5.0b	5.9	2,490b	2003	2.8	3.1
109	Kyrgyzstan	1.9	8.8	378	1,751	−3.1b	−2.4	2,586b	1990	16.5	3.5
110	Indonesia	208.3	721.5	970	3,361	4.1	2.0	3,493	1997	13.9	6.6
111	Uzbekistan	9.9	44.6	389	1,744	−1.2b	−0.5	1,744b	2003	..	..
112	Nicaragua	4.1	17.9e	745	3,262e	−2.8	0.9	7,602e	1977	22.3	5.1
113	Bolivia	7.9	22.8	892	2,587	−0.3	1.3	2,690	1977	7.0	3.3
114	Mongolia	1.3	4.6	514	1,850	−2.0b	−2.5	2,888b	1988	29.5	5.1
115	Moldova, Rep. of	2.0	6.4	463	1,510	−5.1b	−5.7	3,974b	1990	17.8	11.7
116	Honduras	7.0	18.6e	1,001	2,665e	0.1	0.2	2,876e	1979	16.4	7.7
117	Guatemala	24.7	51.0e	2,009	4,148e	0.2	1.1	4,255e	1980	9.1	5.5
118	Vanuatu	0.3	0.6e	1,348	2,944e	0.2b	−0.3	3,935b, e	1984	2.7	3.0
119	Egypt	82.4	266.9	1,220	3,950	2.7	2.5	3,950	2003	7.0	4.5
120	South Africa	159.9	474.1e	3,489	10,346e	−0.6	0.1	12,663e	1981	8.0	5.9
121	Equatorial Guinea	2.9	9.3c	5,900	19,780c, e	11.2b	16.8	19,780b, e	2001	..	..
122	Tajikistan	1.6	7.0	246	1,106	−8.1b	−6.5	2,790b	1988	..	..
123	Gabon	6.1	8.6	4,505	6,397	−1.5	−0.4	11,767	1976	4.6	..
124	Morocco	43.7	120.6	1,452	4,004	1.3	1.0	4,004	2003	3.1	1.2
125	Namibia	4.3	12.4e	2,120	6,180e	−0.1b	0.9	8,462b, e	1980	9.4	7.2
126	São Tomé and Principe	0.1	..	378	..	−0.5b	−0.2	..	..	..	..
127	India	600.6	3,078.2e	564	2,892e	3.3	4.0	2,892e	2003	7.9	3.8
128	Solomon Islands	0.3	0.8e	553	1,753e	1.4	−2.5	2,713e	1996	9.9	10.0
129	Myanmar	..	..	..	..	1.8b	5.7b	..	..	25.9	36.6
130	Cambodia	4.2	27.9e	315	2,078e	..	4.0b	2,078b, e	2003	4.3	1.2
131	Botswana	7.5	15.0	4,372	8,714	5.1	2.7	9,182	2002	9.6	9.2
132	Comoros	0.3	1.0e	538	1,714e	−1.0b	−1.3	2,177b, e	1985	..	..
133	Lao People's Dem. Rep.	2.1	10.0	375	1,759	3.3b	3.7	1,759b	2003	29.7	15.5
134	Bhutan	0.7	..	797	..	4.0b	3.6	..	..	7.7	1.6
135	Pakistan	82.3	311.3	555	2,097	2.5	1.1	2,097	2003	8.1	2.9
136	Nepal	5.9	35.0	237	1,420	2.1	2.2	1,444	2001	7.4	5.7
137	Papua New Guinea	3.2	14.4e	578	2,619e	0.4	0.2	2,900e	1994	10.3	14.7
138	Ghana	7.6	46.3e	369	2,238e	0.4	1.8	2,238e	2003	27.0	26.7
139	Bangladesh	51.9	244.4	376	1,770	1.9	3.1	1,770	2003	5.0	5.7
140	Timor-Leste	0.3	..	389	..	..	..	..	..	..	..
141	Sudan	17.8	64.1e	530	1,910e	1.1	3.3	1,910e	2003	63.6	..
142	Congo	3.6	3.6	949	965	−0.1	−1.4	1,318	1996	7.3	−0.8
143	Togo	1.8	8.2e	362	1,696e	−0.8	0.4	2,227e	1980	6.6	−1.0
144	Uganda	6.3	36.8e	249	1,457e	2.6b	3.9	1,457b, e	2003	7.9	7.8
145	Zimbabwe	..d	31.4c	..d	2,443c	(.)b	−0.8b	3,112b	1998	36.1	..
LOW HUMAN DEVELOPMENT											
146	Madagascar	5.5	13.7	324	809	−1.6	−0.9	1,274	1975	15.8	−1.2
147	Swaziland	1.8	5.2	1,669	4,726	1.8	0.2	4,777	1998	9.2	7.3
148	Cameroon	12.5	34.1	776	2,118	−0.5	0.2	2,865	1986	5.5	..
149	Lesotho	1.1	4.6e	635	2,561e	3.1	2.3	2,561e	2003	9.0	6.7
150	Djibouti	0.6	1.5e	886	2,086e	−4.2b	−3.3	..b, e	..	..	..
151	Yemen	10.8	17.0	565	889	..	2.4	889b	2003	20.8	10.8
152	Mauritania	1.1	5.0e	384	1,766e	0.4	1.6	1,827e	1976	5.6	5.2
153	Haiti	2.9	14.7e	346	1,742e	−2.3	−2.8	3,309e	1980	19.7	39.3
154	Kenya	14.4	33.1	450	1,037	0.2	−0.6	1,204	1990	12.6	9.8
155	Gambia	0.4	2.6e	278	1,859e	−0.2	−0.1	2,108e	1986	4.0	..
156	Guinea	3.6	16.6	459	2,097	1.4b	1.6	2,122b	2002	..	..
157	Senegal	6.5	16.9	634	1,648	(.)	1.3	1,669	1976	4.3	(.)
158	Nigeria	58.4	143.3	428	1,050	−0.5	(.)	1,086	1977	26.0	14.0
159	Rwanda	1.6	10.6e	195	1,268e	−0.5	0.7	1,446e	1983	12.3	6.9

Human development indicators

TABLE 14

	GDP		GDP per capita		GDP per capita				Average annual change in consumer price index	
					Annual growth rate (%)		Highest value during 1975–2003	Year of highest value	(%)	
	US$ billions	PPP US$ billions	US$	PPP US$						
HDI rank	2003	2003	2003	2003	1975–2003	1990–2003	(PPP US$)	value	1990–2003	2002–03
160 Angola	13.2	31.7 e	975	2,344 e	−1.1 b	0.4	2,910 b, e	1992	500.8	98.2
161 Eritrea	0.8	3.7 e	171	849 e	..	1.0 b	999 b, e	1998	..	..
162 Benin	3.5	7.5	517	1,115	0.7	2.2	1,115	2003	6.5	1.5
163 Côte d'Ivoire	13.7	24.8	816	1,476	−1.9	−0.4	2,726	1978	6.0	3.3
164 Tanzania, U. Rep. of	10.3	22.3	287	621	0.8 b	1.0	621 b	2003	16.2	3.5
165 Malawi	1.7	6.6	156	605	0.2	0.9	653	1979	31.0	9.6
166 Zambia	4.3	9.1	417	877	−1.9	−0.9	1,496	1976	48.4	..
167 Congo, Dem. Rep. of the	5.7	..	107	..	−4.9	−6.3	2,452	1975	0.0	..
168 Mozambique	4.3	21.0 e	230	1,117 e	2.3 b	4.6	1,117 b, e	2003	24.8	13.4
169 Burundi	0.6	4.7 e	83	648 e	−0.9	−3.5	952 e	1991	14.6	16.0
170 Ethiopia	6.7	48.8 e	97	711 e	0.1 b	2.0	752 b, e	2002	4.0	17.8
171 Central African Republic	1.2	4.2 e	309	1,089 e	−1.5	−0.4	1,707 e	1977	4.4	3.1
172 Guinea-Bissau	0.2	1.1 e	160	711 e	−0.4	−2.4	1,091 e	1997	24.6	−3.5
173 Chad	2.6	10.4 e	304	1,210 e	0.1	(.)	1,210 e	2003	7.2	−1.9
174 Mali	4.3	11.6	371	994	(.)	2.4	995 b	2002	4.3	−1.3
175 Burkina Faso	4.2	14.2 e	345	1,174 e	1.2	1.7	1,174 e	2003	4.6	2.0
176 Sierra Leone	0.8	2.9	149	548	−3.3	−5.3	1,139	1982	22.4	7.6
177 Niger	2.7	9.8 e	232	835 e	−1.8	−0.6	1,383 e	1979	5.0	−1.6
Developing countries	6,981.9 T	21,525.4 T	1,414	4,359	2.3	2.9	..	..	..	..
Least developed countries	221.4 T	895.1 T	329	1,328	0.7	2.0	..	..	..	..
Arab States	773.4 T	1,683.6 T	2,611	5,685	0.2	1.0	..	..	..	..
East Asia and the Pacific	2,893.6 T	9,762.2 T	1,512	5,100	6.0	5.6	..	..	..	..
Latin America and the Caribbean	1,745.9 T	3,947.0 T	3,275	7,404	0.6	1.1	..	..	..	..
South Asia	902.2 T	4,235.9 T	617	2,897	2.6	3.5	..	..	..	..
Sub-Saharan Africa	418.5 T	1,227.4 T	633	1,856	−0.7	0.1	..	..	..	..
Central and Eastern Europe and the CIS	1,189.9 T	3,203.5 T	2,949	7,939	..	0.3	..	..	..	..
OECD	29,650.5 T	29,840.6 T	25,750	25,915	2.0	1.8	..	..	..	..
High-income OECD	28,369.5 T	27,601.9 T	31,020	30,181	2.2	1.9	..	..	..	..
High human development	30,341.0 T	30,941.3 T	25,167	25,665	2.2	1.8	..	..	..	..
Medium human development	5,414.8 T	19,581.1 T	1,237	4,474	1.7	2.4	..	..	..	..
Low human development	202.2 T	590.4 T	358	1,046	2.0 g	2.8 g	..	..	..	..
High income	29,052.4 T	28,396.0 T	30,589	29,898	2.0	1.8	..	..	..	..
Middle income	6,021.9 T	18,244.6 T	2,015	6,104	2.0	2.5	..	..	..	..
Low income	1,103.0 T	4,948.9 T	483	2,168	−0.8 g	0.1 g	..	..	..	..
World	36,058.3 T	51,150.6 T	5,801	8,229	1.4	1.4	..	..	..	..

NOTES

a In theory, for the United States the value of GDP in purchasing power parity (PPP) US dollars should be the same as that in US dollars, but practical issues arising in the calculation of the PPP US dollar GDP prevent this.

b Data refer to a period shorter than that specified.

c Data refer to 2001.

d Data refer to 2002.

e Estimates are based on regression.

f Estimate based on a bilateral comparison between China and the United States (Ruoen and Kai 1995).

g India's growth rate accounts for most of the difference in average annual growth rates of low-income and low human development countries.

SOURCES

Columns 1 and 2: World Bank 2005c; aggregates calculated for the Human Development Report Office by the World Bank.

Columns 3 and 4: calculated on the basis of GDP and population data from World Bank 2005c; aggregates calculated for the Human Development Report Office by the World Bank.

Columns 5 and 6: World Bank 2005a; aggregates calculated for the Human Development Report Office by the World Bank using least squares method.

Columns 7 and 8: based on GDP per capita PPP US$ time series from World Bank 2005c.

Columns 9 and 10: calculated on the basis of data on the consumer price index from World Bank 2005c.

Human development indicators

TABLE 15

... to have access to the resources needed for a decent standard of living ...

Inequality in income or consumption

			MDG Share of income or consumption (%)				Inequality measures		
HDI rank	Survey year	Poorest 10%	Poorest 20%	Richest 20%	Richest 10%	Richest 10% to poorest 10% [a]	Richest 20% to poorest 20% [a]	Gini index [b]
HIGH HUMAN DEVELOPMENT									
1 Norway	2000 [c]	3.9	9.6	37.2	23.4	6.1	3.9	25.8
2 Iceland	..	..	..	..	..	..	..	..
3 Australia	1994 [c]	2.0	5.9	41.3	25.4	12.5	7.0	35.2
4 Luxembourg	..	..	..	..	..	..	..	..
5 Canada	1998 [c]	2.5	7.0	40.4	25.0	10.1	5.8	33.1
6 Sweden	2000 [c]	3.6	9.1	36.6	22.2	6.2	4.0	25.0
7 Switzerland	1992 [c]	2.6	6.9	40.3	25.2	9.9	5.8	33.1
8 Ireland	1996 [c]	2.8	7.1	43.3	27.6	9.7	6.1	35.9
9 Belgium	1996 [c]	2.9	8.3	37.3	22.6	7.8	4.5	25.0
10 United States	2000 [c]	1.9	5.4	45.8	29.9	15.9	8.4	40.8
11 Japan	1993 [c]	4.8	10.6	35.7	21.7	4.5	3.4	24.9
12 Netherlands	1999 [c]	2.5	7.6	38.7	22.9	9.2	5.1	30.9
13 Finland	2000 [c]	4.0	9.6	36.7	22.6	5.6	3.8	26.9
14 Denmark	1997 [c]	2.6	8.3	35.8	21.3	8.1	4.3	24.7
15 United Kingdom	1999 [c]	2.1	6.1	44.0	28.5	13.8	7.2	36.0
16 France	1995 [c]	2.8	7.2	40.2	25.1	9.1	5.6	32.7
17 Austria	1997 [c]	3.1	8.1	38.5	23.5	7.6	4.7	30.0
18 Italy	2000 [c]	2.3	6.5	42.0	26.8	11.6	6.5	36.0
19 New Zealand	1997 [c]	2.2	6.4	43.8	27.8	12.5	6.8	36.2
20 Germany	2000 [c]	3.2	8.5	36.9	22.1	6.9	4.3	28.3
21 Spain	1990 [c]	2.8	7.5	40.3	25.2	9.0	5.4	32.5
22 Hong Kong, China (SAR)	1996 [c]	2.0	5.3	50.7	34.9	17.8	9.7	43.4
23 Israel	1997 [c]	2.4	6.9	44.3	28.2	11.7	6.4	35.5
24 Greece	1998 [c]	2.9	7.1	43.6	28.5	10.0	6.2	35.4
25 Singapore	1998 [c]	1.9	5.0	49.0	32.8	17.7	9.7	42.5
26 Slovenia	1998 [c]	3.6	9.1	35.7	21.4	5.9	3.9	28.4
27 Portugal	1997 [c]	2.0	5.8	45.9	29.8	15.0	8.0	38.5
28 Korea, Rep. of	1998 [c]	2.9	7.9	37.5	22.5	7.8	4.7	31.6
29 Cyprus	..	..	..	..	..	..	..	..
30 Barbados	..	..	..	..	..	..	..	..
31 Czech Republic	1996 [c]	4.3	10.3	35.9	22.4	5.2	3.5	25.4
32 Malta	..	..	..	..	..	..	..	..
33 Brunei Darussalam	..	..	..	..	..	..	..	..
34 Argentina [d]	2001	1.0	3.1	56.4	38.9	39.1	18.1	52.2
35 Hungary	2002 [e]	4.0	9.5	36.5	22.2	5.5	3.8	26.9
36 Poland	2002 [e]	3.1	7.6	41.9	26.7	8.6	5.5	34.1
37 Chile	2000 [c]	1.2	3.3	62.2	47.0	40.6	18.7	57.1
38 Estonia	2000 [c]	1.9	6.1	44.0	28.5	14.9	7.2	37.2
39 Lithuania	2000 [e]	3.2	7.9	40.0	24.9	7.9	5.1	31.9
40 Qatar	..	..	..	..	..	..	..	..
41 United Arab Emirates	..	..	..	..	`	..	..	..
42 Slovakia	1996 [c]	3.1	8.8	34.8	20.9	6.7	4.0	25.8
43 Bahrain	..	..	..	..	..	..	..	..
44 Kuwait	..	..	..	..	..	..	..	..
45 Croatia	2001 [e]	3.4	8.3	39.6	24.5	7.3	4.8	29.0
46 Uruguay [d]	2000	1.8	4.8	50.1	33.5	18.9	10.4	44.6
47 Costa Rica	2000 [c]	1.4	4.2	51.5	34.8	25.1	12.3	46.5
48 Latvia	1998 [c]	2.8	7.3	41.1	26.1	9.2	5.6	33.6
49 Saint Kitts and Nevis	..	..	..	..	..	..	..	..
50 Bahamas	..	..	..	..	..	..	..	..
51 Seychelles	..	..	..	..	..	..	..	..
52 Cuba	..	..	..	..	..	..	..	..
53 Mexico	2000 [e]	1.0	3.1	59.1	43.1	45.0	19.3	54.6

Human development indicators

TABLE 15

HDI rank	Survey year	MDG Share of income or consumption (%)				Inequality measures		
		Poorest 10%	Poorest 20%	Richest 20%	Richest 10%	Richest 10% to poorest 10% [a]	Richest 20% to poorest 20% [a]	Gini index [b]
54 Tonga	..	..	..	..	..	..	..	..
55 Bulgaria	2001 [c]	2.4	6.7	38.9	23.7	9.9	5.8	31.9
56 Panama	2000 [c]	0.7	2.4	60.3	43.3	62.3	24.7	56.4
57 Trinidad and Tobago	1992 [c]	2.1	5.5	45.9	29.9	14.4	8.3	40.3
MEDIUM HUMAN DEVELOPMENT								
58 Libyan Arab Jamahiriya	..	..	..	..	..	..	..	..
59 Macedonia, TFYR	1998 [e]	3.3	8.4	36.7	22.1	6.8	4.4	28.2
60 Antigua and Barbuda	..	..	..	..	..	..	..	..
61 Malaysia	1997 [c]	1.7	4.4	54.3	38.4	22.1	12.4	49.2
62 Russian Federation	2002 [e]	3.3	8.2	39.3	23.8	7.1	4.8	31.0
63 Brazil	2001 [c]	0.7	2.4	63.2	46.9	68.0	26.4	59.3
64 Romania	2002 [e]	3.2	7.9	41.0	26.1	8.1	5.2	30.3
65 Mauritius	..	..	..	..	..	..	..	..
66 Grenada	..	..	..	..	..	..	..	..
67 Belarus	2000 [e]	3.5	8.4	39.1	24.1	6.9	4.6	30.4
68 Bosnia and Herzegovina	2001 [e]	3.9	9.5	35.8	21.4	5.4	3.8	26.2
69 Colombia	1999 [c]	0.8	2.7	61.8	46.5	57.8	22.9	57.6
70 Dominica	..	..	..	..	..	..	..	..
71 Oman	..	..	..	..	..	..	..	..
72 Albania	2002 [e]	3.8	9.1	37.4	22.4	5.9	4.1	28.2
73 Thailand	2000 [e]	2.5	6.1	50.0	33.8	13.4	8.3	43.2
74 Samoa (Western)	..	..	..	..	..	..	..	..
75 Venezuela	1998 [c]	0.6	3.0	53.4	36.3	62.9	17.9	49.1
76 Saint Lucia	..	..	..	..	..	..	..	..
77 Saudi Arabia	..	..	..	..	..	..	..	..
78 Ukraine	1999 [e]	3.7	8.8	37.8	23.2	6.4	4.3	29.0
79 Peru	2000 [c]	0.7	2.9	53.2	37.2	49.9	18.4	49.8
80 Kazakhstan	2003 [e]	3.2	7.8	40.0	24.4	7.5	5.1	32.3
81 Lebanon	..	..	..	..	..	..	..	..
82 Ecuador	1998 [e]	0.9	3.3	58.0	41.6	44.9	17.3	43.7
83 Armenia	1998 [e]	2.6	6.7	45.1	29.7	11.5	6.8	37.9
84 Philippines	2000 [e]	2.2	5.4	52.3	36.3	16.5	9.7	46.1
85 China	2001 [e]	1.8	4.7	50.0	33.1	18.4	10.7	44.7
86 Suriname	..	..	..	..	..	..	..	..
87 Saint Vincent and the Grenadines	..	..	..	..	..	..	..	..
88 Paraguay	2002 [c]	0.6	2.2	61.3	45.4	73.4	27.8	57.8
89 Tunisia	2000 [e]	2.3	6.0	47.3	31.5	13.4	7.9	39.8
90 Jordan	1997 [e]	3.3	7.6	44.4	29.8	9.1	5.9	36.4
91 Belize	..	..	..	..	..	..	..	..
92 Fiji	..	..	..	..	..	..	..	..
93 Sri Lanka	1999 [e]	3.4	8.3	42.2	27.8	8.1	5.1	33.2
94 Turkey	2000 [e]	2.3	6.1	46.7	30.7	13.3	7.7	40.0
95 Dominican Republic	1998 [c]	2.1	5.1	53.3	37.9	17.7	10.5	47.4
96 Maldives	..	..	..	..	..	..	..	..
97 Turkmenistan	1998 [e]	2.6	6.1	47.5	31.7	12.3	7.7	40.8
98 Jamaica	2000 [e]	2.7	6.7	46.0	30.3	11.4	6.9	37.9
99 Iran, Islamic Rep. of	1998 [e]	2.0	5.1	49.9	33.7	17.2	9.7	43.0
100 Georgia	2001 [e]	2.3	6.4	43.6	27.9	12.0	6.8	36.9
101 Azerbaijan	2001 [e]	3.1	7.4	44.5	29.5	9.7	6.0	36.5
102 Occupied Palestinian Territories	..	..	..	..	..	..	..	..
103 Algeria	1995 [e]	2.8	7.0	42.6	26.8	9.6	6.1	35.3
104 El Salvador	2000 [c]	0.9	2.9	57.1	40.6	47.4	19.8	53.2
105 Cape Verde	..	..	..	..	..	..	..	..
106 Syrian Arab Republic	..	..	..	..	..	..	..	..

Human development indicators

TABLE 15

Inequality in income or consumption

			MDG Share of income or consumption (%)				Inequality measures		
HDI rank		Survey year	Poorest 10%	Poorest 20%	Richest 20%	Richest 10%	Richest 10% to poorest 10% [a]	Richest 20% to poorest 20% [a]	Gini index [b]
107	Guyana	..	..	..	..	..	..	..	..
108	Viet Nam	2002 [e]	3.2	7.5	45.4	29.9	9.4	6.0	37.0
109	Kyrgyzstan	2002 [e]	3.2	7.7	43.0	27.9	8.6	5.5	34.8
110	Indonesia	2002 [e]	3.6	8.4	43.3	28.5	7.8	5.2	34.3
111	Uzbekistan	2000 [e]	3.6	9.2	36.3	22.0	6.1	4.0	26.8
112	Nicaragua	2001 [e]	2.2	5.6	49.3	33.8	15.5	8.8	43.1
113	Bolivia	1999 [e]	1.3	4.0	49.1	32.0	24.6	12.3	44.7
114	Mongolia	1998 [e]	2.1	5.6	51.2	37.0	17.8	9.1	30.3
115	Moldova, Rep. of	2002 [e]	2.7	6.8	44.1	28.4	10.3	6.5	36.9
116	Honduras	1999 [c]	0.9	2.7	58.9	42.2	49.1	21.5	55.0
117	Guatemala	2000 [c]	0.9	2.6	64.1	48.3	55.1	24.4	59.9
118	Vanuatu	..	..	..	..	..	..	..	..
119	Egypt	1999 [e]	3.7	8.6	43.6	29.5	8.0	5.1	34.4
120	South Africa	2000 [e]	1.4	3.5	62.2	44.7	33.1	17.9	57.8
121	Equatorial Guinea	..	..	..	..	..	..	..	..
122	Tajikistan	2003 [e]	3.3	7.9	40.8	25.6	7.8	5.2	32.6
123	Gabon	..	..	..	..	..	..	..	..
124	Morocco	1998 [e]	2.6	6.5	46.6	30.9	11.7	7.2	39.5
125	Namibia	1993 [c]	0.5	1.4	78.7	64.5	128.8	56.1	70.7
126	São Tomé and Principe	..	..	..	..	..	..	..	..
127	India	1999 [e]	3.9	8.9	43.3	28.5	7.3	4.9	32.5
128	Solomon Islands	..	..	..	..	..	..	..	..
129	Myanmar	..	..	..	..	..	..	..	..
130	Cambodia	1997 [e]	2.9	6.9	47.6	33.8	11.6	6.9	40.4
131	Botswana	1993 [e]	0.7	2.2	70.3	56.6	77.6	31.5	63.0
132	Comoros	..	..	..	..	..	..	..	..
133	Lao People's Dem. Rep.	1997 [e]	3.2	7.6	45.0	30.6	9.7	6.0	37.0
134	Bhutan	..	..	..	..	..	..	..	..
135	Pakistan	1998 [e]	3.7	8.8	42.3	28.3	7.6	4.8	33.0
136	Nepal	1995 [e]	3.2	7.6	44.8	29.8	9.3	5.9	36.7
137	Papua New Guinea	1996 [e]	1.7	4.5	56.5	40.5	23.8	12.6	50.9
138	Ghana	1998 [e]	2.1	5.6	46.6	30.0	14.1	8.4	40.8
139	Bangladesh	2000 [e]	3.9	9.0	41.3	26.7	6.8	4.6	31.8
140	Timor-Leste	..	..	..	..	..	..	..	..
141	Sudan	..	..	..	..	..	..	..	..
142	Congo	..	..	..	..	..	..	..	..
143	Togo	..	..	..	..	..	..	..	..
144	Uganda	1999 [e]	2.3	5.9	49.7	34.9	14.9	8.4	43.0
145	Zimbabwe	1995 [e]	1.8	4.6	55.7	40.3	22.0	12.0	56.8
LOW HUMAN DEVELOPMENT									
146	Madagascar	2001 [e]	1.9	4.9	53.5	36.6	19.2	11.0	47.5
147	Swaziland	1994 [c]	1.0	2.7	64.4	50.2	49.7	23.8	60.9
148	Cameroon	2001 [e]	2.3	5.6	50.9	35.4	15.7	9.1	44.6
149	Lesotho	1995 [e]	0.5	1.5	66.5	48.3	105.0	44.2	63.2
150	Djibouti	..	..	..	..	..	..	..	..
151	Yemen	1998 [e]	3.0	7.4	41.2	25.9	8.6	5.6	33.4
152	Mauritania	2000 [e]	2.5	6.2	45.7	29.5	12.0	7.4	39.0
153	Haiti	..	..	..	..	..	..	..	..
154	Kenya	1997 [e]	2.5	6.0	49.1	33.9	13.6	8.2	42.5
155	Gambia	1998 [e]	1.8	4.8	53.4	37.0	20.2	11.2	47.5
156	Guinea	1994 [e]	2.6	6.4	47.2	32.0	12.3	7.3	40.3
157	Senegal	1995 [e]	2.6	6.4	48.2	33.5	12.8	7.5	41.3
158	Nigeria	1996 [e]	1.6	4.4	55.7	40.8	24.9	12.8	50.6
159	Rwanda	1983 [e]	4.2	9.7	39.1	24.2	5.8	4.0	28.9

Human development indicators

TABLE 15

| HDI rank | Survey year | MDG Share of income or consumption (%) | | | | Inequality measures | | |
		Poorest 10%	Poorest 20%	Richest 20%	Richest 10%	Richest 10% to poorest 10% [a]	Richest 20% to poorest 20% [a]	Gini index [b]
160 Angola	..	..	..	..	..	..	..	..
161 Eritrea	..	..	..	..	..	..	..	..
162 Benin	..	..	..	..	..	..	..	..
163 Côte d'Ivoire	2002 [e]	2.0	5.2	50.7	34.0	16.6	9.7	44.6
164 Tanzania, U. Rep. of	1993 [e]	2.8	6.8	45.5	30.1	10.8	6.7	38.2
165 Malawi	1997 [e]	1.9	4.9	56.1	42.2	22.7	11.6	50.3
166 Zambia	1998 [e]	1.0	3.3	56.6	41.0	41.8	17.2	52.6
167 Congo, Dem. Rep. of the	..	..	..	..	..	..	..	..
168 Mozambique	1996 [e]	2.5	6.5	46.5	31.7	12.5	7.2	39.6
169 Burundi	1998 [e]	1.7	5.1	48.0	32.8	19.3	9.5	33.3
170 Ethiopia	1999 [e]	3.9	9.1	39.4	25.5	6.6	4.3	30.0
171 Central African Republic	1993 [e]	0.7	2.0	65.0	47.7	69.2	32.7	61.3
172 Guinea-Bissau	1993 [e]	2.1	5.2	53.4	39.3	19.0	10.3	47.0
173 Chad	..	..	..	..	..	..	..	..
174 Mali	1994 [e]	1.8	4.6	56.2	40.4	23.1	12.2	50.5
175 Burkina Faso	1998 [e]	1.8	4.5	60.7	46.3	26.2	13.6	48.2
176 Sierra Leone	1989 [e]	0.5	1.1	63.4	43.6	87.2	57.6	62.9
177 Niger	1995 [e]	0.8	2.6	53.3	35.4	46.0	20.7	50.5

NOTES

Because the underlying household surveys differ in method and in the type of data collected, the distribution data are not strictly comparable across countries.

a Data show the ratio of the income or consumption share of the richest group to that of the poorest. Because of rounding, results may differ from ratios calculated using the income or consumption shares in columns 2–5.

b A value of 0 represents perfect equality, and a value of 100 perfect inequality.

c Survey based on income.

d Data refer to urban areas only.

e Survey based on consumption.

SOURCES

Columns 1–5 and 8: World Bank 2005b.

Column 6: calculated on the basis of data in columns 2 and 5.

Column 7: calculated on the basis of data in columns 3 and 4.

TABLE 16

... to have access to the resources needed for a decent standard of living ...

The structure of trade

HDI rank	Imports of goods and services (% of GDP)		Exports of goods and services (% of GDP)		Primary exports (% of merchandise exports)		Manufactured exports (% of merchandise exports)		High-technology exports (% of manufactured exports)		Terms of trade (1980=100)[a]
	1990	2003	1990	2003	1990	2003	1990	2003	1990	2003	2002
HIGH HUMAN DEVELOPMENT											
1 Norway	34	28	40	41	67	74	33	21	12	19	71
2 Iceland	33	39	34	35	91	85	8	15	10	6	..
3 Australia	17	22[b]	17	20[b]	73	61	24	30	8	14	87
4 Luxembourg	100	123	104	140	..	13	..	84	..	12	..
5 Canada	26	37[b]	26	42[b]	36	33	59	61	14	14	88
6 Sweden	29	37	30	44	16	13	83	81	13	15	110
7 Switzerland	34	37[b]	36	44[b]	6	7	94	93	12	22	..
8 Ireland	52	75[b]	57	94[b]	26	9	70	86	41	34	99
9 Belgium	69	80	71	82	..	17	..	80	..	8	105
10 United States	11	14[b]	10	10[b]	22	16	74	80	33	31	119
11 Japan	9	10	10	12	3	3	96	93	24	24	145
12 Netherlands	51	58[b]	54	63[b]	37	29	59	71	16	31	103
13 Finland	24	30	23	37	17	15	83	84	8	24	117
14 Denmark	31	37	36	43	35	30	60	66	15	20	110
15 United Kingdom	27	28	24	25	19	16	79	78	24	26	99
16 France	22	25	21	26	23	17	77	81	16	19	..
17 Austria	38	50	40	52	12	13	88	78	8	13	..
18 Italy	20	25	20	25	11	11	88	87	8	8	126
19 New Zealand	27	31[b]	27	32[b]	75	67	23	29	4	10	111
20 Germany	25	32	25	36	10	9	89	84	11	16	117
21 Spain	20	30	16	28	24	21	75	77	6	7	132
22 Hong Kong, China (SAR)	124	161	132	170	4	6	95	93	..	13	100
23 Israel	45	44	35	37	13	7	87	93	10	18	112
24 Greece	28	28	18	20	46	40	54	58	2	12	71
25 Singapore	..	..	..	..	27	12	72	85	40	59	77
26 Slovenia	..	60	..	60	..	10	..	90	..	6	..
27 Portugal	39	38[b]	33	30[b]	19	14	80	86	4	9	..
28 Korea, Rep. of	29	36	28	38	6	7	94	93	18	32	116
29 Cyprus	57	..	52	..	45	51	55	49	6	5	..
30 Barbados	52	55[b]	49	52[b]	55	46	43	52	..	14	..
31 Czech Republic	43	65	45	63	..	10	..	90	..	13	..
32 Malta	99	89[b]	85	88[b]	4	4[c]	96	96[c]	45	62[c]	..
33 Brunei Darussalam	..	..	..	..	100	94	(.)	6	..	(.)	..
34 Argentina	5	14	10	25	71	72	29	27	..	9	74
35 Hungary	29	68[b]	31	65[b]	35	11	63	87	..	26	89
36 Poland	22	26	29	21	36	17	59	81	..	3	317
37 Chile	31	33	35	36	87	81	11	16	5	3	52
38 Estonia	..	83	..	75	..	26	..	74	..	13	..
39 Lithuania	61	60	52	54	..	37	..	63	..	5	..
40 Qatar	..	..	..	..	84	89[b]	16	10[b]	..	(.)[b]	..
41 United Arab Emirates	40	..	65	..	54	96[c]	46	4[c]	..	2[c]	..
42 Slovakia	36	80	27	78	..	12	..	88	..	4	..
43 Bahrain	95	65[b]	116	81[b]	91	91	9	9	..	(.)	..
44 Kuwait	58	40[b]	45	48[b]	94	93[c]	6	7[c]	3	1[c]	..
45 Croatia	..	57	..	47	..	28	..	72	..	12	..
46 Uruguay	18	23	24	26	61	66	39	34	..	2	118
47 Costa Rica	41	49	35	47	66	34	27	66	..	45	124
48 Latvia	49	57	48	47	..	40	..	60	..	4	..
49 Saint Kitts and Nevis	83	56	52	37	..	27[c]	..	73[c]	..	(.)[c]	..
50 Bahamas	..	..	..	..	..	..	..	37[c]	..	1[c]	..
51 Seychelles	67	77	62	77	..	..	(.)	5[b]	..	..	..
52 Cuba	..	..	..	..	..	90[c]	..	10[c]	..	29[c]	..
53 Mexico	20	30	19	28	56	18	43	81	8	21	30

Human development indicators

TABLE 16

HDI rank	Imports of goods and services (% of GDP)		Exports of goods and services (% of GDP)		Primary exports (% of merchandise exports)		Manufactured exports (% of merchandise exports)		High-technology exports (% of manufactured exports)		Terms of trade (1980=100)[a]
	1990	2003	1990	2003	1990	2003	1990	2003	1990	2003	2002
54 Tonga	65	58[c]	34	13[c]	..	..	21	..	..	..	..
55 Bulgaria	37	63	33	53	..	29	..	66	..	4	..
56 Panama	79	58	87	59	78	89	21	11	..	1	85
57 Trinidad and Tobago	29	41	45	50	73	67[b]	27	33[b]	..	2[b]	..
MEDIUM HUMAN DEVELOPMENT											
58 Libyan Arab Jamahiriya	31	36[b]	40	48[b]	95	..	5	..	..	..	..
59 Macedonia, TFYR	36	53	26	35	..	28	..	72	..	1	..
60 Antigua and Barbuda	87	68[b]	89	60[b]	..	..	..	..	..	..	..
61 Malaysia	72	93	75	114	46	22	54	77	38	58	..
62 Russian Federation	18	21	18	32	..	65	..	21	..	19	..
63 Brazil	7	13	8	17	47	47	52	52	7	12	145
64 Romania	26	39	17	33	26	17	73	83	2	4	..
65 Mauritius	71	57	64	60	34	26	66	74	1	5	94
66 Grenada	63	57[b]	42	47[b]	..	82	20	18	..	1	..
67 Belarus	44	70	46	66	..	35	..	62	..	4	..
68 Bosnia and Herzegovina	..	59	..	25	..	..	..	..	..	..	..
69 Colombia	15	22	21	21	74	64	25	36	..	7	71
70 Dominica	81	62	55	54	..	..	32	60	..	7	..
71 Oman	31	35[b]	53	57[b]	94	85	5	14	2	2	..
72 Albania	23	42	15	19	..	16	..	84	..	1	..
73 Thailand	42	59	34	66	36	22	63	75	21	30	69
74 Samoa (Western)	..	..	..	..	..	19	4	81	..	(.)	..
75 Venezuela	20	15	39	31	90	87	10	13	4	4	37
76 Saint Lucia	84	69	73	56	..	76[b]	28	26	..	8	..
77 Saudi Arabia	32	24	41	47	93	90[b]	7	10[b]	..	(.)[b]	..
78 Ukraine	29	48	28	53	..	32[b]	..	67[b]	..	5[b]	..
79 Peru	14	18	16	18	82	78	18	22	..	2	50
80 Kazakhstan	..	44	..	50	..	82	..	18	..	9	..
81 Lebanon	100	39	18	13	..	31	..	68	..	2	..
82 Ecuador	32	29	33	24	98	88	2	12	(.)	6	36
83 Armenia	46	50	35	32	..	38	..	62	..	1	..
84 Philippines	33	51	28	48	31	10	38	90	..	74	85
85 China	14	32	18	34	27	9	72	91	..	27	..
86 Suriname	44	45[b]	42	21[b]	26	..	74	7[b]	..	(.)[c]	..
87 Saint Vincent and the Grenadines	77	65	66	47	..	91[b]	..	10	..	(.)[b]	..
88 Paraguay	39	47	33	32	..	86	10	14	(.)	6	175
89 Tunisia	51	47	44	43	31	19	69	81	2	4	85
90 Jordan	93	70	62	45	..	31	51	69	1	2	129
91 Belize	60	67	62	54	..	..	..	15	1[b]	(.)[b]	..
92 Fiji	67	66[c]	62	73[c]	63	55	36	44	12	1	..
93 Sri Lanka	38	42	29	36	42	25[b]	54	74[b]	1	1[b]	..
94 Turkey	18	31	13	28	32	15	68	84	1	2	94
95 Dominican Republic	44	54	34	52	..	60[c]	..	34[c]	..	1[c]	57
96 Maldives	64	66	24	85	..	..	..	32	..	..	..
97 Turkmenistan	..	42[c]	..	41[c]	..	..	..	..	..	..	..
98 Jamaica	52	59	48	41	31	36[b]	69	64[b]	..	(.)[b]	..
99 Iran, Islamic Rep. of	24	23	22	25	..	92	..	8	..	2	..
100 Georgia	46	46	40	32	..	69	..	31	..	24	..
101 Azerbaijan	39	67	44	43	..	93	..	6	..	5	..
102 Occupied Palestinian Territories	..	49	..	10	..	..	..	..	..	..	..
103 Algeria	25	24	23	39	97	98	3	2	..	2	31
104 El Salvador	31	43	19	27	62	43	38	57	..	5	123
105 Cape Verde	44	68	13	32	..	..	..	96[c]	..	1[c]	100
106 Syrian Arab Republic	28	33	28	40	64	89	36	11	..	1	..

TABLE 16

The structure of trade

HDI rank	Imports of goods and services (% of GDP)		Exports of goods and services (% of GDP)		Primary exports (% of merchandise exports)		Manufactured exports (% of merchandise exports)		High-technology exports (% of manufactured exports)		Terms of trade (1980=100) [a]
	1990	2003	1990	2003	1990	2003	1990	2003	1990	2003	2002
107 Guyana	80	106 [b]	63	93 [b]	..	75	..	24	..	1	..
108 Viet Nam	45	68	36	60	..	49 [b]	..	50 [b]	..	2 [b]	..
109 Kyrgyzstan	50	42	29	38	..	60	..	39	..	2	..
110 Indonesia	24	26	25	31	65	48	35	52	1	14	..
111 Uzbekistan	48	30	29	37	..	..	..	..	..	..	..
112 Nicaragua	46	51	25	24	92	87	8	13	..	4	71
113 Bolivia	24	25	23	24	95	83	5	17	..	8	47
114 Mongolia	53	80	24	68	..	62	..	38	..	(.)	..
115 Moldova, Rep. of	51	88	49	54	..	68	..	32	..	3	..
116 Honduras	40	54	36	36	91	79 [b]	9	21 [b]	..	(.) [b]	81
117 Guatemala	25	28	21	16	76	60	24	40	..	7	86
118 Vanuatu	77	..	49	..	..	..	13	..	20	..	..
119 Egypt	33	24	20	22	57	63	42	31	..	(.)	53
120 South Africa	19	26	24	28	..	42	..	58	..	5	86
121 Equatorial Guinea	70	..	32	..	..	..	..	..	..	..	..
122 Tajikistan	35	79	28	60	..	..	..	..	..	..	..
123 Gabon	31	41	46	62	..	..	..	..	..	..	58
124 Morocco	32	36	26	32	48	31	52	69	..	11	106
125 Namibia	67	47	52	39	..	58	..	41	..	3	..
126 São Tomé and Principe	72	83	14	38	..	..	..	..	..	..	..
127 India	9	16	7	14	28	22	71	77	2	5	131
128 Solomon Islands	73	33 [b]	47	31 [b]	..	..	..	..	..	..	..
129 Myanmar	5	..	3	..	..	..	..	..	..	..	..
130 Cambodia	13	71	6	62	..	99	..	1	..	..	..
131 Botswana	50	34	55	44	..	9 [c]	..	91 [c]	..	(.) [c]	106
132 Comoros	35	25	14	13	..	..	..	..	..	..	109
133 Lao People's Dem. Rep.	25	25	11	25	..	..	..	..	..	..	..
134 Bhutan	32	43 [b]	28	22 [b]	..	..	..	..	..	..	..
135 Pakistan	23	20	16	20	21	15	79	85	(.)	1	88
136 Nepal	22	29	11	17	..	..	83	..	..	..	..
137 Papua New Guinea	49	..	41	..	89	94	10	6	..	39	..
138 Ghana	26	52	17	40	..	84 [c]	..	16 [c]	..	3 [c]	58
139 Bangladesh	14	20	6	14	..	10	77	89	(.)	(.)	..
140 Timor-Leste	..	..	..	..	..	..	..	..	..	..	..
141 Sudan	..	12	..	16	..	97 [b]	..	3 [b]	..	7 [b]	91
142 Congo	46	53	54	78	..	..	..	..	..	..	51
143 Togo	45	47	33	34	89	42	9	58	..	1	87
144 Uganda	19	26	7	12	..	91	..	9	..	8	..
145 Zimbabwe	23	22 [b]	23	24 [b]	68	62 [b]	31	38 [b]	2	3 [b]	115
LOW HUMAN DEVELOPMENT											
146 Madagascar	28	32	17	21	85	61	14	38	8	(.)	108
147 Swaziland	76	94	77	84	..	23 [b]	..	76 [b]	..	1 [b]	100
148 Cameroon	17	25	20	26	91	93	9	7	3	2	108
149 Lesotho	122	95	17	41	..	..	..	..	..	..	76
150 Djibouti	..	..	..	..	44	..	8	..	..	..	..
151 Yemen	20	36	14	31	..	..	..	..	..	..	..
152 Mauritania	61	75	46	34	..	79	..	21	..	..	124
153 Haiti	20	37 [b]	18	13 [b]	15	..	85	..	14	..	50
154 Kenya	31	29	26	25	71	76	29	24	4	4	101
155 Gambia	72	45	60	41	..	..	..	..	..	..	55
156 Guinea	31	25	31	22	..	75 [b]	..	25 [b]	..	(.) [b]	..
157 Senegal	30	40	25	28	77	64	23	34	..	9	96
158 Nigeria	29	41	43	50	..	..	..	..	..	..	28
159 Rwanda	14	28	6	9	..	90	..	10	..	25	133

Human development indicators

TABLE 16

HDI rank	Imports of goods and services (% of GDP)		Exports of goods and services (% of GDP)		Primary exports (% of merchandise exports)		Manufactured exports (% of merchandise exports)		High-technology exports (% of manufactured exports)		Terms of trade (1980=100)[a]
	1990	2003	1990	2003	1990	2003	1990	2003	1990	2003	2002
160 Angola	21	67	39	71	100	..	(.)	..	..	..	..
161 Eritrea	..	99	..	14	..	..	..	..	..	..	..
162 Benin	26	27	14	14	..	92[b]	..	8[b]	..	2[b]	126
163 Côte d'Ivoire	27	34	32	47	..	78	..	20	..	8	103
164 Tanzania, U. Rep. of	37	27	13	18	..	82	..	18	..	2	..
165 Malawi	33	41	24	27	95	88	5	12	(.)	1	64
166 Zambia	37	28	36	21	..	86[b]	..	14[b]	..	2[b]	79
167 Congo, Dem. Rep. of the	29	22[b]	30	19[b]	..	..	..	10	..	..	104
168 Mozambique	36	39	8	23	..	91[c]	..	8[c]	..	3[c]	..
169 Burundi	28	18	8	7	..	..	..	2[b]	..	22[b]	58
170 Ethiopia	12	37	8	17	..	89	..	11	..	(.)	..
171 Central African Republic	28	31	15	24	..	51[b]	..	37	..	(.)	78
172 Guinea-Bissau	37	44	10	30	..	..	..	..	..	..	86
173 Chad	28	53	13	21	..	..	..	..	..	..	141
174 Mali	34	31	17	26	..	59[c]	2	40[c]	..	8[c]	95
175 Burkina Faso	24	23	11	9	..	82[b]	..	17[b]	..	2[b]	220
176 Sierra Leone	24	49	22	22	..	..	..	7[b]	..	31[b]	225
177 Niger	22	25	15	16	..	91	..	8	..	3	..
Developing countries	24	33	25	35	..	29	58	73	..	21	..
Least developed countries	22	30	13	22	..	..	..	..	..	..	..
Arab States	38	30[b]	38	36[b]	81	86[b]	16	20[b]	..	2	..
East Asia and the Pacific	32	48	33	52	..	13	75	86	..	29	..
Latin America and the Caribbean	15	21	17	24	65	44	36	55	7	14	..
South Asia	13	18	11	17	..	43	71	61	..	3	..
Sub-Saharan Africa	26	33	27	33	..	..	..	..	..	..	..
Central and Eastern Europe and the CIS	26	37	27	37	..	36	..	58	..	13	..
OECD	18	22[b]	17	21[b]	20	16	76	79	18	18	..
High-income OECD	18	21[b]	17	21[b]	19	16	78	79	18	18	..
High human development	19	23[b]	18	22[b]	21	18	76	79	18	17	..
Medium human development	20	28	20	31	..	36	51	63	..	21	..
Low human development	29	37	27	34	..	..	..	..	..	..	..
High income	19	22[b]	18	22[b]	20	17	78	80	18	18	..
Middle income	21	30	22	33	..	34	48	65	..	21	..
Low income	17	24	13	21	..	40[b]	..	60[b]	..	4	..
World	19	24[b]	19	24[b]	..	22	72	77	18	18	..

NOTES

a The ratio of the export price index to the import price index measured relative to the base year 1980. A value of more than 100 means that the price of exports has risen relative to the price of imports.

b Data refer to 2002.

c Data refer to 2001.

SOURCES

Columns 1–10: World Bank 2005c, based on data from United Nations Conference on Trade and Development.

Column 11: calculated on the basis of data on terms of trade from World Bank 2005c.

Human development indicators

Rich country responsibilities: aid

	MDG Net official development assistance (ODA) disbursed			MDG ODA per capita of donor country (2002 US$)		MDG ODA to least developed countries [b] (% of total)		MDG ODA to basic social services [c] (% of total allocable by sector)		MDG Untied bilateral ODA (% of total)	
	Total [a] (US$ millions)	As % of GNI									
HDI rank	2003	1990 [d]	2003	1990	2003	1990	2003	1996/97 [e]	2002/03 [e]	1990	2003
1 Norway	2,042	1.17	0.92	314	388	44	39	12.9	20.2	61	100
3 Australia	1,219	0.34	0.25	49	50	18	21	7.5	18.1	33	67
4 Luxembourg	194	0.21	0.81	73	354	39	34	..	..	..	..
5 Canada	2,031	0.44	0.24	80	55	30	31	5.7	27.8	47	53
6 Sweden	2,400	0.91	0.79	184	218	39	34	10.5	17.0	87	94
7 Switzerland	1,299	0.32	0.39	119	154	43	31	8.6	14.3	78	96
8 Ireland	504	0.16	0.39	19	103	37	53	0.5	30.6	..	100
9 Belgium	1,853	0.46	0.60	88	145	41	59	11.3	19.4	..	99
10 United States	16,254	0.21	0.15	58	55	19	28	22.7	23.4	..	..
11 Japan	8,880	0.31	0.20	83	66	19	22	3.0	5.0	89	96
12 Netherlands	3,981	0.92	0.80	179	199	33	32	12.4	19.9	56	..
13 Finland	558	0.65	0.35	131	89	38	33	6.5	13.4	32	86
14 Denmark	1,748	0.94	0.84	227	265	39	38	9.6	14.3	..	71
15 United Kingdom	6,282	0.27	0.34	55	95	32	36	23.5	28.9	..	100
16 France	7,253	0.60	0.41	119	100	32	41	..	10.3	64	93
17 Austria	505	0.11	0.20	21	51	63	33	5.0	7.1	32	51
18 Italy	2,433	0.31	0.17	54	34	41	45	7.2	20.0	22	..
19 New Zealand	165	0.23	0.23	27	32	19	27	..	14.8	100	81
20 Germany	6,784	0.42	0.28	96	68	28	37	9.8	11.5	62	95
21 Spain	1,961	0.20	0.23	23	37	20	17	13.9	12.4	..	56
24 Greece	362	..	0.21	..	26	..	15	16.9	18.4	..	94
27 Portugal	320	0.24	0.22	18	25	70	64	6.4	2.9	..	94
DAC	69,029 T	0.33	0.25	72	70	29	33	9	17	73	92

NOTES

This table presents data for members of the Development Assistance Committee (DAC) of the Organisation for Economic Co-operation and Development (OECD).

a Some non-DAC countries and areas also provide ODA. According to OECD 2005e, net ODA disbursed in 2003 by Czech Republic, Hungary, Iceland, Israel, Republic of Korea, Kuwait, Poland, Saudi Arabia, Slovak Republic, Turkey, United Arab Emirates and other small donors, including Estonia, Latvia and Lithuania, totalled $3,278 million. China also provides aid but does not disclose the amount.
b Includes imputed multilateral flows that make allowance for contributions through multilateral organizations. These are calculated using the geographic distribution of disbursements for the year specified.
c Data refer to the share of sector-allocable ODA; they exclude technical cooperation and administrative costs.
d Data for individual countries (but not the DAC average) include forgiveness of non-ODA claims.
e Data refer to the average for the years specified.

SOURCE

All columns: OECD 2005c; aggregates calculated for the Human Development Report Office by the OECD.

TABLE **18**

Rich country responsibilities: debt relief and trade

			Trade			
	Debt relief		Goods imports			
			From developing countries		From least developed countries	
	Bilateral pledges to the HIPC trust fund [a]	Gross bilateral debt forgiveness	Total	Share of total imports	Total	Share of total imports
	(US$ millions)	(US$ millions)	(US$ millions)	(%)	(US$ millions)	(%)
HDI rank	2004	1990–2003	2003	2003	2003	2003
1 Norway	127	237	5,260	13	81	0.2
3 Australia	14	83	34,143	40	148	0.2
4 Luxembourg	4	..	298	2	6	..
5 Canada	165	1,567	46,012	19	770	0.3
6 Sweden	109	286	7,556	9	169	0.2
7 Switzerland	93	340	8,142	8	118	0.1
8 Ireland	25	..	8,833	16	136	0.3
9 Belgium	64	1,468	29,066	12	2,181	0.9
10 United States	750	10,882	641,803	49	11,525	0.9
11 Japan	256	4,331	237,583	62	1,584	0.4
12 Netherlands	242	2,170	50,887	24	657	0.3
13 Finland	51	156	4,899	12	157	0.4
14 Denmark	80	377	6,815	12	168	0.3
15 United Kingdom	436	2,574	79,488	20	1,587	0.4
16 France	258	15,878	64,258	18	2,598	0.7
17 Austria	50	709	7,997	9	179	0.2
18 Italy	217	2,334	55,504	19	1,400	0.5
19 New Zealand	2	..	5,675	31	29	0.2
20 Germany	350	7,371	98,247	16	2,761	0.5
21 Spain	165	1,208	45,009	21	1,647	0.8
24 Greece	17	..	9,835	22	180	0.4
27 Portugal	24	476	5,943	13	234	0.5

Table **18b** OECD country support to domestic agriculture

% of GDP

	MDG	
	1990	2003 [a]
Australia	0.8	0.3
Canada	1.7	0.9
Czech Republic	..	1.5
European Union [b]	2.2	1.3
Hungary	..	2.4
Iceland	4.6	1.9
Japan	1.7	1.3
Korea	8.7	3.9
Mexico	2.9	1.1
New Zealand	0.5	0.4
Norway	3.2	1.5
Poland	..	0.7
Slovak Republic	..	1.5
Switzerland	3.3	2.0
Turkey	4.3	4.4
United States	1.2	0.9
OECD	1.8	1.2

NOTES

This table presents data for members of the Development Assistance Committee of the Organisation for Economic Co-operation and Development.

a The Debt Initiative for Heavily Indebted Poor Countries (HIPCs) is a mechanism for debt relief, jointly overseen by the International Monetary Fund and the World Bank. Bilateral and multilateral creditors have provided debt relief through this framework since 1996. Includes pledges through the European Union.

SOURCES

Column 1: IMF and IDA 2004.
Column 2: calculated on the basis of data on debt cancellation from OECD 2005f.
Columns 3–6: calculated on the basis of data from UN 2005a.

a. Provisional data.
b. No data are available for individual member countries of the European Union. The member countries in 2003 were Austria, Belgium, Denmark, Finland, France, Germany, Greece, Ireland, Italy, Luxembourg, the Netherlands, Portugal, Spain, Sweden and the United Kingdom. Austria, Finland and Sweden joined in 1995 and thus are not included in the data for 1990.
Source: OECD 2005a; aggregates calculated for the Human Development Report Office by the Organisation for Economic Co-operation and Development.

TABLE 19

... to have access to the resources needed for a decent standard of living ...

Flows of aid, private capital and debt

		Official development assistance (ODA) received [a] (net disbursements)				Net foreign direct investment inflows [b] (% of GDP)		Other private flows [b, c] (% of GDP)		Total debt service			
		Total (US$ millions)	Per capita (US$)	As % of GDP						As % of GDP		MDG As % of exports of goods, services and net income from abroad	
HDI rank		2003	2003	1990	2003	1990	2003	1990	2003	1990	2003	1990	2003
HIGH HUMAN DEVELOPMENT													
22	Hong Kong, China (SAR)	5.0	0.7	0.1	(.)	..	8.6	..	..	..	..	..	..
23	Israel	440.0	65.8	2.6	0.4	0.3	3.3	..	..	..	..	..	..
25	Singapore	7.1	1.7	(.)	(.)	15.1	12.5						
26	Slovenia	65.9	33.6	..	0.2	..	1.2	..	..	..	..	..	..
28	Korea, Rep. of	−457.7	−9.6	(.)	−0.1	0.3	0.5	..	..	..	..	..	..
29	Cyprus	18.7	24.2	0.7	0.2	2.3	9.0	..	..	..	..	..	..
30	Barbados	19.9	73.4	0.2	0.8	6.5	2.2	−0.8	3.1	8.2	3.2	14.6	5.6
31	Czech Republic	263.3	25.8	(.)	0.3	0.0	2.8	..	3.2	..	6.1	..	3.0
32	Malta	10.1	25.3	0.2	0.2	..	..	..	..	..	..	..	..
33	Brunei Darussalam	0.5	1.3	..	..	..	..	..	..	..	..	..	..
34	Argentina	109.4	2.9	0.1	0.1	1.3	0.8	−1.5	0.1	4.4	10.8	34.7	34.7
35	Hungary	248.4	24.5	0.2	0.3	0.9	3.0	−1.4	3.2	12.8	18.3	33.4	6.8
36	Poland	1,191.5	31.2	2.2	0.6	0.2	2.0	(.)	1.4	1.6	9.1	4.4	6.5
37	Chile	75.6	4.8	0.3	0.1	2.2	4.1	5.1	1.2	9.1	11.7	18.1	5.5
38	Estonia	84.5	62.6	..	0.9	0.0	9.8	..	14.1	..	13.4	..	0.9
39	Lithuania	372.0	107.7	..	2.0	0.0	1.0	..	−1.8	..	36.4	..	11.3
40	Qatar	2.0	3.2	(.)	..	..	..	..	..	..	..	..	..
41	United Arab Emirates	5.2	1.3	(.)	..	..	..	..	..	..	..	..	..
42	Slovakia	159.9	29.7	(.)	0.5	0.0	1.8	..	2.9	..	10.7	..	6.9
43	Bahrain	37.5	52.7	3.2	..	..	..	..	..	..	..	..	..
44	Kuwait	4.4	1.9	(.)	(.)	0.0	−0.2	..	..	..	..	..	..
45	Croatia	120.6	27.1	..	0.4	0.0	6.9	..	20.9	..	11.8	..	7.9
46	Uruguay	16.8	5.0	0.6	0.1	0.0	2.5	−2.1	−2.1	10.6	7.8	35.2	23.1
47	Costa Rica	28.3	7.1	4.0	0.2	2.8	3.3	−2.5	1.5	8.8	4.8	22.0	8.9
48	Latvia	113.7	49.0	..	1.0	0.0	2.7	..	2.4	..	8.4	..	4.0
49	Saint Kitts and Nevis	(.)	−0.2	5.1	(.)	30.7	15.2	−0.3	12.0	1.9	12.6	3.4	34.9
50	Bahamas	3.9	12.3	0.1	0.1	−0.6	2.8	..	..	..	..	..	..
51	Seychelles	9.2	110.1	9.8	1.3	5.5	8.1	−1.7	−5.1	5.9	11.0	7.8	13.6
52	Cuba	70.0	6.2	..	..	..	..	..	..	..	..	..	..
53	Mexico	103.2	1.0	0.1	(.)	1.0	1.7	2.7	−0.2	4.3	6.5	18.3	11.3
54	Tonga	27.5	269.2	26.3	16.9	0.2	1.7	−0.1	0.0	1.7	2.3	3.5	5.8 [d]
55	Bulgaria	414.4	53.0	0.1	2.1	0.0	7.1	..	1.2	..	5.8	18.6	7.6
56	Panama	30.5	10.2	1.9	0.2	2.6	6.1	−0.1	2.2	6.5	7.4	4.1	9.2
57	Trinidad and Tobago	−2.3	−1.8	0.4	(.)	2.2	5.9	−3.5	0.0	8.9	2.4	15.6	3.6
MEDIUM HUMAN DEVELOPMENT													
58	Libyan Arab Jamahiriya	10.0	1.8	0.1	..	..	..	..	..	..	..	..	..
59	Macedonia, TFYR	233.5	114.0	..	5.0	0.0	2.0	..	−0.1	..	5.2	..	8.7
60	Antigua and Barbuda	5.0	64.1	1.2	0.7	..	..	..	..	..	..	..	..
61	Malaysia	109.1	4.4	1.1	0.1	5.3	2.4	−4.2	−0.3	9.8	9.1	10.6	4.7
62	Russian Federation	1,254.8	8.8	(.)	0.3	0.0	1.8	..	1.8	..	4.4	..	8.3
63	Brazil	296.0	1.7	(.)	0.1	0.2	2.1	−0.1	0.7	1.8	11.5	18.5	38.6
64	Romania	601.2	27.1	0.6	1.1	0.0	3.2	(.)	3.6	(.)	6.4	0.0	10.4
65	Mauritius	−15.1	−12.4	3.7	−0.3	1.7	1.2	1.9	0.5	6.5	4.5	7.3	4.7
66	Grenada	11.7	111.9	6.3	2.7	5.8	0.0	0.1	0.9	1.5	7.0	3.1	17.5
67	Belarus	31.9	3.2	..	0.2	0.0	1.0	..	−0.3	..	1.4	..	1.7
68	Bosnia and Herzegovina	538.8	130.1	..	7.7	..	5.5	..	0.3	..	2.6	..	6.4
69	Colombia	802.1	18.1	0.2	1.0	1.2	2.2	−0.4	−3.7	9.7	10.7	34.5	34.6
70	Dominica	10.9	153.8	11.9	4.2	7.7	0.0	−0.3	−0.3	3.5	6.5	6.0	13.4
71	Oman	44.5	17.1	0.6	..	1.4	..	−3.8	−5.5	7.0	8.6 [d]	12.0	5.3
72	Albania	342.3	108.0	0.5	5.6	0.0	2.9	..	(.)	..	0.9	0.9	3.6
73	Thailand	−966.3	−15.6	0.9	−0.7	2.9	1.4	2.3	−0.6	6.2	10.5	11.4	8.0
74	Samoa (Western)	33.0	185.6	23.7	12.3	3.3	−0.1	0.0	0.0	2.7	4.9	10.6	..
75	Venezuela	82.2	3.2	0.2	0.1	0.9	3.0	−1.2	1.2	10.3	10.4	..	..

TABLE 19

		Official development assistance (ODA) received[a] (net disbursements)			Net foreign direct investment inflows[b] (% of GDP)		Other private flows[b, c] (% of GDP)		Total debt service		MDG As % of exports of goods, services and net income from abroad	
		Total (US$ millions)	Per capita (US$)	As % of GDP						As % of GDP			
HDI rank		2003	2003	1990	2003	1990	2003	1990	2003	1990	2003	1990	2003
76	Saint Lucia	14.8	92.3	3.1	2.1	11.3	4.6	−0.2	1.3	1.6	4.7	2.1	7.4
77	Saudi Arabia	21.9	1.0	(.)	(.)	..	..	..	..	..	..	..	..
78	Ukraine	322.9	6.7	0.4	0.7	0.0	2.9	..	0.3	..	7.4	..	5.5
79	Peru	500.2	18.4	1.5	0.8	0.2	2.3	0.1	2.0	1.8	4.2	7.3	20.8
80	Kazakhstan	268.4	18.0	..	0.9	0.0	7.0	..	12.1	..	17.8	..	3.0
81	Lebanon	228.3	50.8	8.9	1.2	0.2	1.9	0.2	0.2	3.5	17.1	3.2	81.5
82	Ecuador	176.2	13.5	1.6	0.6	1.2	5.7	0.6	2.2	10.5	8.9	31.0	19.7
83	Armenia	247.4	81.0	..	8.8	0.0	4.3	..	−0.2	..	3.4	..	8.7
84	Philippines	737.2	9.1	2.9	0.9	1.2	0.4	0.2	1.3	8.1	12.8	25.6	13.8
85	China	1,324.6	1.0	0.6	0.1	1.0	3.8	1.3	0.4	2.0	2.6	10.6	2.8
86	Suriname	10.9	24.9	15.5	0.9	..	..	..	..	..	..	..	..
87	Saint Vincent and the Grenadines	6.3	58.0	7.8	1.7	3.9	10.1	0.0	5.5	2.2	3.9	3.1	6.7[d]
88	Paraguay	50.7	9.0	1.1	0.8	1.5	1.5	−0.2	0.5	6.2	5.1	11.5	6.6
89	Tunisia	305.5	30.9	3.2	1.2	0.6	2.2	−1.6	3.1	11.6	6.4	25.6	13.7
90	Jordan	1,234.3	232.5	22.1	12.5	0.9	3.8	5.3	−5.4	15.6	11.7	22.1	22.6
91	Belize	12.1	46.5	7.4	1.2	4.2	4.0	1.4	18.0	4.9	13.6	7.0	24.9
92	Fiji	51.1	61.2	3.7	2.5	6.8	1.0	−1.2	−0.1	7.8	1.4	9.0	..
93	Sri Lanka	671.9	35.0	9.1	3.7	0.5	1.3	0.1	(.)	4.8	3.3	14.8	7.8
94	Turkey	165.8	2.4	0.8	0.1	0.5	0.6	0.8	0.5	4.9	11.7	29.9	20.3
95	Dominican Republic	69.0	7.9	1.4	0.4	1.9	1.9	(.)	4.9	3.3	5.6	10.7	7.4
96	Maldives	18.0	61.3	9.8	2.5	2.6	1.9	0.5	1.4	4.1	3.0	4.0	3.5
97	Turkmenistan	27.2	5.6	..	0.4	0.0	1.6	..	..	..	..	..	5.7
98	Jamaica	3.4	1.3	5.9	(.)	3.0	8.8	−1.0	−2.6	14.4	10.1	27.0	21.4
99	Iran, Islamic Rep. of	133.1	2.0	0.1	0.1	−0.3	0.1	(.)	0.8	0.5	1.2	1.3	3.6
100	Georgia	219.8	42.9	..	5.5	0.0	8.5	..	−0.4	..	4.5	..	10.0
101	Azerbaijan	296.7	36.0	..	4.2	0.0	46.0	..	−0.7	..	3.4	..	6.0
102	Occupied Palestinian Territories	971.6	288.6	..	28.1	..	..	..	..	..	..	..	..
103	Algeria	232.2	7.3	0.2	0.3	(.)	1.0	−0.7	−0.1	14.2	6.5	63.7	..
104	El Salvador	191.8	29.4	7.2	1.3	(.)	0.6	0.1	2.1	4.3	3.7	18.2	11.7
105	Cape Verde	143.7	305.7	31.8	18.0	0.1	1.9	(.)	0.2	1.7	2.7	8.9	7.2
106	Syrian Arab Republic	160.3	9.2	5.6	0.7	0.6	0.7	−0.1	(.)	9.7	1.6	20.3	3.0
107	Guyana	86.6	112.6	42.6	11.7	2.0	3.5	−4.1	−0.2	74.5	7.8	..	9.5[e, f]
108	Viet Nam	1,768.6	21.8	2.9	4.5	2.8	3.7	0.0	−0.7	2.7	2.1	..	3.3
109	Kyrgyzstan	197.7	39.1	..	10.4	0.0	2.4	..	−3.0	..	7.1	..	7.7
110	Indonesia	1,743.5	8.1	1.5	0.8	1.0	−0.3	1.6	−1.5	8.7	8.9	25.6	12.8
111	Uzbekistan	194.4	7.6	..	2.0	0.0	0.7	..	0.1	..	8.2	..	19.6
112	Nicaragua	833.2	152.1	32.9	20.4	0.0	4.9	2.0	0.7	1.6	5.0	2.4	11.7[e, f]
113	Bolivia	929.7	103.5	11.2	11.8	0.6	2.1	−0.5	1.6	7.9	5.4	33.5	20.1[e, f]
114	Mongolia	247.1	99.7	..	19.4	..	10.3	..	(.)	..	22.6	0.3	4.4
115	Moldova, Rep. of	116.6	27.5	..	5.9	0.0	3.0	..	1.3	..	8.1	..	6.6
116	Honduras	389.0	55.8	14.7	5.6	1.4	2.8	1.0	−0.8	12.8	5.9	33.0	9.5[e, g]
117	Guatemala	247.0	20.1	2.6	1.0	0.6	0.5	−0.1	−0.2	2.8	1.9	11.6	9.8
118	Vanuatu	32.4	154.4	33.0	11.4	8.7	6.7	−0.1	0.0	1.6	0.7	1.6	1.2
119	Egypt	893.8	13.2	12.6	1.1	1.7	0.3	−0.2	−0.7	7.1	3.4	..	..
120	South Africa	624.9	13.8	..	0.4	−0.1	0.5	..	2.1	..	2.7	0.0	4.3
121	Equatorial Guinea	21.3	43.1	46.0	0.7	8.4	49.1	0.0	0.0	3.9	0.3	11.5	..
122	Tajikistan	144.1	22.9	..	9.3	0.0	2.0	..	−1.6	..	5.7	..	7.7
123	Gabon	−10.7	−8.0	2.2	−0.2	1.2	0.9	0.5	−1.2	3.0	6.2	4.8	..
124	Morocco	522.8	17.4	4.1	1.2	0.6	5.2	1.2	0.3	6.9	9.8	27.9	25.7
125	Namibia	146.1	72.5	5.2	3.4	..	..	..	..	..	..	..	..
126	São Tomé and Principe	37.7	239.9	95.0	63.3	0.0	16.8	−0.2	0.0	4.9	11.1	28.7	24.6[e, g]
127	India	942.2	0.9	0.4	0.2	0.1	0.7	0.5	1.1	2.6	3.4	29.3	18.1
128	Solomon Islands	60.2	131.8	21.7	23.8	4.9	−0.8	−1.5	−1.0	5.5	3.7	11.3	..
129	Myanmar	125.8	2.6	..	..	..	..	..	..	..	..	18.3	3.8[e, h]

Human development indicators

TABLE 19

Flows of aid, private capital and debt

		Official development assistance (ODA) received [a] (net disbursements)				Net foreign direct investment inflows [b] (% of GDP)		Other private flows [b, c] (% of GDP)		MDG Total debt service			
		Total (US$ millions)	Per capita (US$)	As % of GDP						As % of GDP		As % of exports of goods, services and net income from abroad	
HDI rank		2003	2003	1990	2003	1990	2003	1990	2003	1990	2003	1990	2003
130	Cambodia	508.0	37.9	3.7	12.0	0.0	2.1	0.0	0.0	2.7	0.6	..	0.9
131	Botswana	30.1	17.5	3.9	0.4	2.5	1.1	−0.5	(.)	2.8	0.7	4.3	1.3
132	Comoros	24.5	40.8	17.3	7.6	0.2	0.3	0.0	0.0	0.4	0.8	2.5	.. e, h
133	Lao People's Dem. Rep.	298.6	52.8	17.4	14.1	0.7	0.9	0.0	0.0	1.1	2.3	8.6	10.3 e, h
134	Bhutan	77.0	88.1	16.5	11.1	0.6	(.)	−0.9	0.0	1.8	1.0	5.3	4.7 d
135	Pakistan	1,068.4	7.2	2.8	1.3	0.6	0.6	−0.2	−0.5	4.8	3.7	22.9	16.8
136	Nepal	466.7	18.9	11.7	8.0	0.0	0.3	−0.4	(.)	1.9	1.9	15.2	10.0
137	Papua New Guinea	220.8	40.1	12.8	6.9	4.8	3.2	1.5	−3.1	17.2	9.3	18.4	7.3
138	Ghana	906.7	44.4	9.6	11.9	0.3	1.8	−0.3	−4.0	6.2	6.3	36.3	5.2 e, f
139	Bangladesh	1,393.4	10.1	7.0	2.7	(.)	0.2	0.2	(.)	2.5	1.3	34.8	8.3
140	Timor-Leste	150.8	186.1	..	44.2	..	..	..	..	..	..	..	..
141	Sudan	621.3	18.5	6.2	3.5	0.0	7.6	0.0	0.0	0.4	0.2	4.8	1.3 e, h
142	Congo	69.8	18.6	7.8	2.0	0.8	5.6	−3.6	0.0	19.0	1.7	32.2	3.8 e, h
143	Togo	44.8	9.2	16.0	2.5	1.1	1.1	0.3	0.0	5.3	0.9	11.5	1.9 e, h
144	Uganda	959.4	38.0	15.5	15.2	0.0	3.1	0.4	0.1	3.4	1.3	78.6	7.8 e, f
145	Zimbabwe	186.4	14.2	3.9	..	−0.1	..	1.1	−0.3	5.4	0.6 d	19.4	..
LOW HUMAN DEVELOPMENT													
146	Madagascar	539.5	31.9	12.9	9.9	0.7	0.2	−0.5	(.)	7.2	1.3	44.4	4.7 e, f
147	Swaziland	27.1	24.5	6.3	1.5	3.5	2.4	−0.5	0.0	5.4	1.5	5.6	1.6
148	Cameroon	883.9	55.0	4.0	7.1	−1.0	1.7	−0.1	−0.5	4.6	3.6	13.1	8.7 e, g
149	Lesotho	79.0	44.1	23.0	6.9	2.8	3.7	(.)	−0.5	3.8	5.9	4.2	8.9
150	Djibouti	77.8	110.4	46.4	12.5	(.)	1.8	−0.1	0.0	3.6	2.5	..	..
151	Yemen	243.1	12.7	8.4	2.2	−2.7	−0.8	3.3	0.0	3.5	1.6	7.1	4.0
152	Mauritania	242.7	90.1	23.3	22.2	0.7	19.6	−0.1	0.3	14.3	5.0	28.8	15.7 e, f
153	Haiti	199.8	23.7	5.9	6.8	0.0	0.3	0.0	0.0	1.2	1.8	9.0	10.8
154	Kenya	483.5	15.2	13.9	3.4	0.7	0.6	0.8	0.8	9.2	4.0	28.6	14.5
155	Gambia	59.8	42.1	31.3	15.1	0.0	15.2	−2.4	0.0	11.9	5.0	21.8	14.0 e, g
156	Guinea	237.5	30.0	10.4	6.5	0.6	2.2	−0.7	0.0	6.0	3.6	19.6	10.7 e, g
157	Senegal	449.6	44.7	14.4	6.9	1.0	1.2	−0.2	(.)	5.7	3.8	18.3	23.4 e, f
158	Nigeria	317.6	2.3	0.9	0.5	2.1	2.1	−0.4	−0.4	11.7	2.8	22.3	..
159	Rwanda	331.6	40.2	11.3	20.3	0.3	0.3	−0.1	0.0	0.8	1.3	10.7	10.0 e, g
160	Angola	498.7	36.9	2.6	3.8	−3.3	10.7	5.6	3.7	3.2	10.1	7.1	14.8
161	Eritrea	307.3	70.0	..	40.9	..	2.9	..	0.0	..	1.6	..	13.0
162	Benin	293.7	43.7	14.5	8.5	3.4	1.5	(.)	0.0	2.1	1.7	9.2	6.3 e, f
163	Côte d'Ivoire	252.1	15.0	6.4	1.8	0.4	1.3	0.1	−0.8	11.7	4.2	..	.. e, g
164	Tanzania, U. Rep. of	1,669.3	46.5	27.5	16.2	0.0	2.4	0.1	0.2	4.2	0.9	31.3	5.8 e, f
165	Malawi	497.9	45.4	26.8	29.1	1.2	1.3	0.1	0.0	7.1	2.1	28.0	23.1 e, g
166	Zambia	560.1	53.8	14.6	12.9	6.2	2.3	−0.3	−0.2	6.2	9.0	14.6	14.1 e, g
167	Congo, Dem. Rep. of the	5,381.0	101.2	9.6	94.9	−0.2	2.8	−0.1	0.5	3.7	2.6	..	8.9 e, g
168	Mozambique	1,032.8	55.0	40.7	23.9	0.4	7.8	1.0	−0.5	3.2	2.0	17.3	3.9 e, f
169	Burundi	224.2	31.1	23.3	37.6	0.1	(.)	−0.5	1.3	3.7	4.9	41.7	63.6 e, h
170	Ethiopia	1,504.4	21.9	11.8	22.6	0.1	0.9	−0.7	−0.1	2.7	1.4	37.6	7.3 e, f
171	Central African Republic	49.9	12.9	16.8	4.2	(.)	0.3	(.)	0.0	2.0	0.1	12.5	.. e, h
172	Guinea-Bissau	145.2	97.5	52.7	60.8	0.8	0.9	(.)	0.0	3.4	6.4	22.1	9.4 e, g
173	Chad	246.9	28.8	18.0	9.5	0.5	32.1	(.)	0.0	0.7	1.8	3.8	5.4 e, g
174	Mali	527.6	45.3	19.9	12.2	0.2	3.0	(.)	0.0	2.8	1.8	14.7	5.8 d, e, f
175	Burkina Faso	451.1	37.3	10.6	10.8	(.)	0.3	(.)	(.)	1.1	1.2	7.8	12.5 e, f
176	Sierra Leone	297.4	55.7	9.4	37.5	5.0	0.4	0.6	−0.1	3.3	3.2	10.1	10.9 e, g
177	Niger	453.3	38.5	16.0	16.6	1.6	1.1	0.4	−0.3	4.0	1.2	6.6	6.4 e, f

Human development indicators

TABLE 19

HDI rank	Official development assistance (ODA) received [a] (net disbursements) Total (US$ millions) 2003	Per capita (US$) 2003	As % of GDP 1990	As % of GDP 2003	Net foreign direct investment inflows [b] (% of GDP) 1990	(% of GDP) 2003	Other private flows [b, c] (% of GDP) 1990	(% of GDP) 2003	Total debt service As % of GDP 1990	As % of GDP 2003	MDG As % of exports of goods, services and net income from abroad 1990	2003
Developing countries	65,401.3 T	9.7	2.7	3.0	0.9	2.3	0.4	0.3	3.5	4.7	21.9	17.6
Least developed countries	23,457.4 T	33.4	13.0	18.7	0.1	3.6	0.4	0.2	2.8	2.1	16.2	7.5
Arab States	8,320.3 T	27.5	6.8	1.6	0.5	1.7	−0.1	−0.1	4.1	2.5	..	15.5
East Asia and the Pacific	7,231.9 T	3.4	1.0	0.5	1.7	3.1	0.6	0.1	3.0	3.2	17.9	10.5
Latin America and the Caribbean	6,090.4 T	9.9	1.3	0.8	0.8	2.1	0.5	0.3	4.0	8.6	23.7	30.7
South Asia	6,623.8 T	4.3	1.6	0.7	(.)	0.6	0.3	0.8	2.6	2.9	19.5	13.5
Sub-Saharan Africa	22,691.8 T	32.9	12.0	18.6	0.4	2.2	0.3	0.7	3.8	2.9	..	9.6
Central and Eastern Europe and the CIS	4,885.9 T	24.0	..	..	(.)	2.9	(.)	2.6	0.5	7.7	13.5	17.3
OECD	269.0 T	..	..	..	1.0	1.4	..	..	..	..	..	..
High-income OECD	.. T	..	..	..	1.0	1.4	..	..	..	..	..	..
High human development	646.1 T	..	..	..	1.0	1.5	..	..	..	..	..	..
Medium human development	27,342.9 T	6.5	1.6	0.9	0.5	2.2	0.3	0.6	2.9	5.3	21.3	16.2
Low human development	18,565.3 T	27.9	11.7	18.7	0.5	2.8	0.4	0.1	6.4	3.3	20.6	10.2
High income	37.5 T	..	..	..	1.0	1.5	..	..	..	..	..	..
Middle income	18,969.6 T	8.4	1.2	0.4	0.6	2.4	0.4	0.7	3.1	6.4	20.8	17.9
Low income	32,128.3 T	13.7	4.6	6.1	0.3	1.5	0.4	0.5	3.6	3.1	24.9	13.5
World	69,783.7 T	10.9	..	..	0.9	1.6	..	..	..	..	..	..

NOTES

This table presents data for countries included in Parts I and II of the Development Assistance Committee's (DAC) list of aid recipients (OECD 2005e). The denominator conventionally used when comparing official development assistance and total debt service to the size of the economy is GNI, not GDP (see *Definitions of statistical terms*). GDP is used here, however, to allow comparability throughout the table. With few exceptions the denominators produce similar results.

a ODA receipts are total net ODA flows from DAC countries as well as Czech Republic, Hungary, Iceland, Israel, Republic of Korea, Kuwait, Poland, Saudi Arabia, Slovak Republic, Turkey, United Arab Emirates, other small donors, including Estonia, Israel, Latvia and Lithuania, and concessional lending from multilateral organizations.

b A negative value indicates that the capital flowing out of the country exceeds that flowing in.

c Other private flows combine non-debt-creating portfolio equity investment flows, portfolio debt flows and bank and trade-related lending.

d Data refer to 2002.

e Country included in the Debt Initiative for Heavily Indebted Poor Countries (HIPCs).

f Completion point reached under the HIPC Initiative.

g Decision point reached under the HIPC Initiative.

h Decision and completion points not yet reached under the HIPC Initiative.

SOURCES

Column 1: OECD 2005f; aggregates calculated for the Human Development Report Office by the Organisation for Economic Co-operation and Development.

Columns 2–4: OECD 2005f.

Columns 5 and 6: World Bank 2005c; aggregates calculated for the Human Development Report Office by the World Bank.

Columns 7 and 8: calculated on the basis of data on portfolio investment (bonds and equity), bank and trade-related lending and GDP data from World Bank 2005c.

Columns 9 and 10: calculated on the basis of data on total debt service and GDP from World Bank 2005c.

Columns 11 and 12: UN 2005f, based on a joint effort by the International Monetary Fund and the World Bank.

Human development indicators

TABLE

20

. . . to have access to the resources needed for a decent standard of living . . .

Priorities in public spending

HDI rank	Public expenditure on education (% of GDP)		Public expenditure on health (% of GDP)		Military expenditure[a] (% of GDP)		Total debt service[b] (% of GDP)	
	1990[c]	2000–02[d]	1990	2002	1990	2003	1990	2003
HIGH HUMAN DEVELOPMENT								
1 Norway	7.0	7.6	8.0	8.0	2.9	2.0	..	..
2 Iceland	5.4	6.0[e]	8.3	8.3	0.0	0.0	..	..
3 Australia	4.9	4.9	6.5	6.5	2.1	1.9	..	..
4 Luxembourg	3.1	..	5.3	5.3	0.9	0.9	..	..
5 Canada	6.5	5.2	6.7	6.7	2.0	1.2	..	..
6 Sweden	7.1	7.7	7.8	7.8	2.6	1.8	..	..
7 Switzerland	4.9	5.8[e]	6.5	6.5	1.8	1.0	..	..
8 Ireland	4.8	5.5	5.5	5.5	1.2	0.7	..	..
9 Belgium	5.0	6.3	6.5	6.5	2.4	1.3	..	..
10 United States	5.1	5.7	6.6	6.6	5.3	3.8	..	..
11 Japan	..	3.6	6.5	6.5	0.9	1.0	..	..
12 Netherlands	5.7	5.1	5.8	5.8	2.5	1.6	..	..
13 Finland	5.5	6.4	5.5	5.5	1.6	1.2	..	..
14 Denmark	..	8.5	7.3	7.3	2.0	1.5	..	..
15 United Kingdom	4.8	5.3	6.4	6.4	4.0	2.8	..	..
16 France	5.3	5.6	7.4	7.4	3.5	2.6	..	..
17 Austria	5.3	5.7	5.4	5.4	1.0	0.8	..	..
18 Italy	3.1	4.7	6.4	6.4	2.1	1.9	..	..
19 New Zealand	6.1	6.7	6.6	6.6	1.9	1.1	..	..
20 Germany	..	4.6	8.6	8.6	2.8[f]	1.4	..	..
21 Spain	4.2	4.5	5.4	5.4	1.8	1.2	..	..
22 Hong Kong, China (SAR)	2.8	4.4	..	..	..	..	..	..
23 Israel	6.3	7.5	6.0	6.0	12.4	9.1	..	..
24 Greece	2.4	4.0	5.0	5.0	4.7	4.1	..	..
25 Singapore	3.1	..	1.3	1.3	4.9	5.2	..	..
26 Slovenia	..	6.1	6.2	6.2	..	1.5	..	..
27 Portugal	4.0	5.8	6.6	6.6	2.7	2.1	..	..
28 Korea, Rep. of	3.3	4.2	2.6	2.6	3.7	2.5	..	..
29 Cyprus	3.5	6.3	2.9	2.9	5.0	1.5	..	..
30 Barbados	7.8	7.6	4.7	4.7	..	..	8.2	3.2
31 Czech Republic	..	4.4	6.4	6.4	..	2.2	..	6.1
32 Malta	4.3	..	7.0	7.0	0.9	0.8	..	..
33 Brunei Darussalam	3.9	..	2.7	2.7	..	..	..	..
34 Argentina	..	4.0	4.5	4.5	1.2	1.2	4.4	10.8
35 Hungary	5.8	5.5	5.5	5.5	2.8	1.8	12.8	18.3
36 Poland	..	5.6	4.4	4.4	2.7	2.0	1.6	9.1
37 Chile	2.5	4.2	2.6	2.6	4.3	3.5	9.1	11.7
38 Estonia	..	5.7	3.9	3.9	..	1.9	..	13.4
39 Lithuania	4.6	5.9	4.3	4.3	..	1.6	..	36.4
40 Qatar	3.5	..	2.4	2.4	..	..	..	..
41 United Arab Emirates	1.8	1.6[e]	2.3	2.3	6.2	3.1	..	..
42 Slovakia	5.1	4.4	5.3	5.3	..	1.9	..	10.7
43 Bahrain	4.1	..	3.2	3.2	5.1	5.1	..	..
44 Kuwait	4.8	..	2.9	2.9	48.5	9.0	..	..
45 Croatia	7.2	4.5	5.9	5.9	..	2.1	..	11.8
46 Uruguay	2.7	2.6	2.9	2.9	2.5	1.6	10.6	7.8
47 Costa Rica	4.4	5.1	6.1	6.1	0.0	0.0	8.8	4.8
48 Latvia	3.8	5.8	3.3	3.3	..	1.7	..	8.4
49 Saint Kitts and Nevis	2.6	7.6	3.4	3.4	..	..	1.9	12.6
50 Bahamas	4.0	..	3.4	3.4	..	..	..	..
51 Seychelles	7.8	5.2	3.9	3.9	4.0	1.7	5.9	11.0
52 Cuba	8.9	9.0	6.5	6.5	..	..	..	..
53 Mexico	3.6	5.3	2.7	2.7	0.5	0.5	4.3	6.5

Human development indicators

TABLE 20

HDI rank	Public expenditure on education (% of GDP)		Public expenditure on health (% of GDP)		Military expenditure[a] (% of GDP)		Total debt service[b] (% of GDP)	
	1990[c]	2000–02[d]	1990	2002	1990	2003	1990	2003
54 Tonga	..	4.9[e]	5.1	5.1	..	..	1.7	2.3
55 Bulgaria	5.2	3.5	4.4	4.4	3.5	2.6	..	5.8
56 Panama	4.7	4.5	6.4	6.4	1.3	..	6.5	7.4
57 Trinidad and Tobago	3.7	4.3[e]	1.4	1.4	..	..	8.9	2.4
MEDIUM HUMAN DEVELOPMENT								
58 Libyan Arab Jamahiriya	..	..	1.6	1.6	..	2.0	..	..
59 Macedonia, TFYR	..	3.5	5.8	5.8	..	2.5	..	5.2
60 Antigua and Barbuda	..	3.8	3.3	3.3	..	..	..	..
61 Malaysia	5.1	8.1	2.0	2.0	2.6	2.8	9.8	9.1
62 Russian Federation	3.5	3.8	3.5	3.5	12.3	4.3	..	4.4
63 Brazil	..	4.2	3.6	3.6	2.5	1.6	1.8	11.5
64 Romania	2.8	3.5	4.2	4.2	4.6	2.4	(.)	6.4
65 Mauritius	3.8	4.7	2.2	2.2	0.3	0.2	6.5	4.5
66 Grenada	5.1	5.1	4.0	4.0	..	..	1.5	7.0
67 Belarus	4.8	6.0[e]	4.7	4.7	..	1.3	..	1.4
68 Bosnia and Herzegovina	..	..	4.6	4.6	..	2.9	..	2.6
69 Colombia	2.4	5.2	6.7	6.7	2.2	4.4	9.7	10.7
70 Dominica	..	..	4.6	4.6	..	..	3.5	6.5
71 Oman	3.1	4.6[e]	2.8	2.8	16.5	12.2	7.0	0.0
72 Albania	5.9	..	2.4	2.4	5.9	1.2	..	0.9
73 Thailand	3.5	5.2	3.1	3.1	2.6	1.3	6.2	10.5
74 Samoa (Western)	3.2	4.8[e]	4.7	4.7	..	..	2.7	4.9
75 Venezuela	3.0	..	2.3	2.3	..	1.3	10.3	10.4
76 Saint Lucia	..	7.7[e]	3.4	3.4	..	..	1.6	4.7
77 Saudi Arabia	5.8	..	3.3	3.3	12.8	8.7	..	..
78 Ukraine	5.1	5.4	3.3	3.3	..	2.9	..	7.4
79 Peru	2.8	3.0	2.2	2.2	0.1	1.3	1.8	4.2
80 Kazakhstan	3.2	3.0	1.9	1.9	..	1.1	..	17.8
81 Lebanon	..	2.7	3.5	3.5	7.6	4.3	3.5	17.1
82 Ecuador	4.3	1.0[e]	1.7	1.7	1.9	2.4	10.5	8.9
83 Armenia	7.0	3.2[e]	1.3	1.3	..	2.7	..	3.4
84 Philippines	2.9	3.1	1.1	1.1	1.4	0.9	8.1	12.8
85 China	2.3	..	2.0	2.0	2.7	2.3	2.0	2.6
86 Suriname	6.4	..	5.2	5.2	..	..	..	..
87 Saint Vincent and the Grenadines	..	10.0	3.9	3.9	..	..	2.2	3.9
88 Paraguay	1.1	4.4	3.2	3.2	1.0	0.9	6.2	5.1
89 Tunisia	6.0	6.4	2.9	2.9	2.0	1.6	11.6	6.4
90 Jordan	8.1	..	4.3	4.3	9.9	8.9	15.6	11.7
91 Belize	4.6	5.2	2.5	2.5	1.2	..	4.9	13.6
92 Fiji	4.7	5.6[e]	2.7	2.7	2.3	1.6	7.8	1.4
93 Sri Lanka	2.7	..	1.8	1.8	2.1	2.7	4.8	3.3
94 Turkey	2.2	3.7	4.3	4.3	3.5	4.9	4.9	11.7
95 Dominican Republic	..	2.3	2.2	2.2	..	..	3.3	5.6
96 Maldives	3.8	..	4.0	4.0[g]	..	..	4.1	3.0
97 Turkmenistan	4.3	..	3.0	3.0	..	..	..	..
98 Jamaica	4.5	6.1	3.4	3.4	..	..	14.4	10.1
99 Iran, Islamic Rep. of	4.1	4.9	2.9	2.9	2.9	3.8	0.5	1.2
100 Georgia	..	2.2	1.0	1.0	..	1.1	..	4.5
101 Azerbaijan	7.7	3.2	0.8	0.8	..	1.9	..	3.4
102 Occupied Palestinian Territories	..	..	..	..	..	..	..	..
103 Algeria	5.3	..	3.2	3.2	1.5	3.3	14.2	6.5
104 El Salvador	1.9	2.9	3.6	3.6	2.7	0.7	4.3	3.7
105 Cape Verde	..	7.9	3.8	3.8	..	0.7	1.7	2.7
106 Syrian Arab Republic	4.0	..	2.3	2.3	6.9	7.1	9.7	1.6

Human development indicators

TABLE 20

Priorities in public spending

HDI rank	Public expenditure on education (% of GDP)		Public expenditure on health (% of GDP)		Military expenditure [a] (% of GDP)		Total debt service [b] (% of GDP)	
	1990 [c]	2000–02 [d]	1990	2002	1990	2003	1990	2003
107 Guyana	3.4	8.4	4.3	4.3	0.9	..	74.5	7.8
108 Viet Nam	2.0	..	1.5	1.5	7.9	..	2.7	2.1
109 Kyrgyzstan	8.4	3.1 [e]	2.2	2.2	..	2.9	..	7.1
110 Indonesia	1.0	1.2	1.2	1.2	1.8	1.5	8.7	8.9
111 Uzbekistan	9.5	..	2.5	2.5	..	0.5	..	8.2
112 Nicaragua	3.4	3.1	3.9	3.9	10.6	0.9	1.6	5.0
113 Bolivia	2.3	6.3	4.2	4.2	2.4	1.7	7.9	5.4
114 Mongolia	12.3	9.0	4.6	4.6	5.7	..	..	22.6
115 Moldova, Rep. of	5.6	4.9	4.1	4.1	..	0.4	..	8.1
116 Honduras	..	..	3.2	3.2	..	0.4	12.8	5.9
117 Guatemala	1.4	..	2.3	2.3	1.5	0.5	2.8	1.9
118 Vanuatu	4.7	11.0 [e]	2.8	2.8	..	..	1.6	0.7
119 Egypt	3.9	..	1.8	1.8	3.9	2.6	7.1	3.4
120 South Africa	5.9	5.3 [e]	3.5	3.5	3.8	1.6	..	2.7
121 Equatorial Guinea	..	0.6	1.3	1.3	..	..	3.9	0.3
122 Tajikistan	..	2.8	0.9	0.9	..	2.2	..	5.7
123 Gabon	..	3.9 [e]	1.8	1.8	..	..	3.0	6.2
124 Morocco	5.3	6.5	1.5	1.5	4.1	4.2	6.9	9.8
125 Namibia	7.9	7.2	4.7	4.7	..	2.8	..	..
126 São Tomé and Principe	..	..	9.7	9.7	..	..	4.9	11.1
127 India	3.7	4.1	1.3	1.3	2.7	2.1	2.6	3.4
128 Solomon Islands	..	3.4 [e]	4.5	4.5	..	..	5.5	3.7
129 Myanmar	..	..	0.4	0.4	3.4	..	0.0	0.0
130 Cambodia	..	1.8	2.1	2.1	3.1	2.5	2.7	0.6
131 Botswana	6.2	2.2	3.7	3.7	4.1	4.1	2.8	0.7
132 Comoros	..	3.9	1.7	1.7	..	..	0.4	0.8
133 Lao People's Dem. Rep.	..	2.8 [e]	1.5	1.5	..	..	1.1	2.3
134 Bhutan	..	5.2	4.1	4.1	..	..	1.8	1.0
135 Pakistan	2.6	1.8 [e]	1.1	1.1	5.8	4.4	4.8	3.7
136 Nepal	2.0	3.4	1.4	1.4	0.9	1.6	1.9	1.9
137 Papua New Guinea	..	2.3 [e]	3.8	3.8	2.1	0.6	17.2	9.3
138 Ghana	3.2	..	2.3	2.3	0.4	0.7	6.2	6.3
139 Bangladesh	1.5	2.4	0.8	0.8	1.0	1.2	2.5	1.3
140 Timor-Leste	..	..	6.2	6.2	..	..	..	..
141 Sudan	6.0	..	1.0	1.0	3.6	2.4	0.4	0.2
142 Congo	5.0	3.2 [e]	1.5	1.5	..	1.4	19.0	1.7
143 Togo	5.5	2.6	5.1	5.1	3.1	1.6	5.3	0.9
144 Uganda	1.5	..	2.1	2.1	3.0	2.3	3.4	1.3
145 Zimbabwe	7.7	4.7 [e]	4.4	4.4	4.5	2.1	5.4	0.0
LOW HUMAN DEVELOPMENT								
146 Madagascar	2.1	2.9 [e]	1.2	1.2	1.2	..	7.2	1.3
147 Swaziland	5.8	7.1	3.6	3.6	2.1	..	5.4	1.5
148 Cameroon	3.2	3.8	1.2	1.2	1.5	1.5	4.6	3.6
149 Lesotho	6.2	10.4 [e]	5.3	5.3	4.5	2.6	3.8	5.9
150 Djibouti	3.5	..	3.3	3.3	6.3	..	3.6	2.5
151 Yemen	..	9.5 [e]	1.0	1.0	7.9	7.1	3.5	1.6
152 Mauritania	..	..	2.9	2.9	3.8	1.6	14.3	5.0
153 Haiti	1.5	..	3.0	3.0	..	..	1.2	1.8
154 Kenya	6.7	7.0	2.2	2.2	2.9	1.7	9.2	4.0
155 Gambia	3.8	2.8	3.3	3.3	1.1	0.5	11.9	5.0
156 Guinea	..	1.8 [e]	0.9	0.9	..	..	6.0	3.6
157 Senegal	3.9	3.6	2.3	2.3	2.0	1.5	5.7	3.8
158 Nigeria	0.9	..	1.2	1.2	0.9	1.2	11.7	2.8
159 Rwanda	..	2.8 [e]	3.1	3.1	3.7	2.8	0.8	1.3

TABLE 20

		Public expenditure on education (% of GDP)		Public expenditure on health (% of GDP)		Military expenditure[a] (% of GDP)		Total debt service[b] (% of GDP)	
HDI rank		1990[c]	2000–02[d]	1990	2002	1990	2003	1990	2003
160	Angola	3.9	2.8[e]	2.1	2.1	5.8	4.7	3.2	10.1
161	Eritrea	..	4.1	3.2	3.2	..	19.4	..	1.6
162	Benin	..	3.3[e]	2.1	2.1	1.8	..	2.1	1.7
163	Côte d'Ivoire	..	4.6[e]	1.4	1.4	1.3	1.5	11.7	4.2
164	Tanzania, U. Rep. of	2.8	..	2.7	2.7	..	2.1	4.2	0.9
165	Malawi	3.2	6.0	4.0	4.0	1.3	..	7.1	2.1
166	Zambia	2.4	2.0[e]	3.1	3.1	3.7	..	6.2	9.0
167	Congo, Dem. Rep. of the	..	..	1.1	1.1[g]	..	..	3.7	2.6
168	Mozambique	3.1	..	4.1	4.1	5.9	1.3	3.2	2.0
169	Burundi	3.4	3.9	0.6	0.6	3.4	5.9	3.7	4.9
170	Ethiopia	3.4	4.6[e]	2.6	2.6	8.5	4.3	2.7	1.4
171	Central African Republic	2.2	..	1.6	1.6	..	1.3	2.0	0.1
172	Guinea-Bissau	..	..	3.0	3.0	..	..	3.4	6.4
173	Chad	..	..	2.7	2.7	..	1.5	0.7	1.8
174	Mali	..	..	2.3	2.3	2.1	1.9	2.8	1.8
175	Burkina Faso	2.4	..	2.0	2.0	3.0	1.3	1.1	1.2
176	Sierra Leone	..	3.7	1.7	1.7	1.4	1.7	3.3	3.2
177	Niger	3.2	2.3[e]	2.0	2.0	..	..	4.0	1.2

NOTES

a As a result of a number of limitations in the data, comparisons of military expenditure data over time and across countries should be made with caution. For detailed notes on the data see SIPRI 2004.
b For aggregates, see table 19.
c Data may not be comparable across countries as a result of differences in methods of data collection.
d Data refer to the most recent year available during the period specified.
e Data refer to United Nations Educational, Scientific and Cultural Organization Institute for Statistics estimate when national estimate is not available.
f Data refer to the Federal Republic of Germany before reunification.
g Data differ slightly from data presented in table 6 from WHO 2005a.

SOURCES

Column 1: calculated on the basis of GDP and public expenditure data from UNESCO Institute for Statistics 2005b.
Column 2: UNESCO Institute for Statistics 2005b.
Columns 3 and 4: World Bank 2005c.
Columns 5 and 6: SIPRI 2005a.
Columns 7 and 8: calculated on the basis of data on GDP and total debt service from World Bank 2005c.

Human development indicators

TABLE 21

... to have access to the resources needed for a decent standard of living ...

Unemployment in OECD countries

		Unemployment rate			MDG Youth unemployment rate		Long-term unemployment (% of total unemployment)	
	Unemployed people (thousands)	Total (% of labour force)	Average annual (% of labour force)	Female (% of male rate)	Total (% of labour force ages 15–24) [a]	Female (% of male rate)	Women	Men
HDI rank	2003	2003	1993–2003	2003	2003	2003	2003	2003
HIGH HUMAN DEVELOPMENT								
1 Norway	106.7	4.5	4.3	81	11.7	84	5.4	7.1
2 Iceland	5.5	3.4	3.5	82 [b]	7.2 [b]	46 [b]	13.3 [b]	9.5 [b]
3 Australia	607.4	6.0	7.7	104	11.6	92	17.0	27.1
4 Luxembourg	7.6	3.8	3.0	188 [b]	7.0 [b]	168	26.5 [b, c]	28.6 [b, c]
5 Canada	1,302.2	7.6	8.6	91	13.8	76	8.4	11.4
6 Sweden	217.0	4.9	6.3	83	13.8	86	15.3	19.6
7 Switzerland	174.9	4.0	3.4	117	8.6	104	32.6	21.6
8 Ireland	88.0	4.6	8.5	81	7.6	75	26.0	40.9
9 Belgium	361.7	7.9	8.5	107	19.0	87	48.2	44.8
10 United States	8,776.6	6.0	5.3	90	12.4	86	11.0	12.5
11 Japan	3,504.0	5.3	4.0	89	10.1	75	24.6	38.9
12 Netherlands	353.8	4.1	4.8	105	7.8	98	28.1	30.1
13 Finland	234.4	9.1	12.2	97	21.6	99	21.4	27.7
14 Denmark	161.6	5.6	5.8	113	9.8	84	17.9	21.8
15 United Kingdom	1,485.5	5.0	7.0	75	11.5	72	17.1	26.5
16 France	2,648.2	9.7	10.7	126	20.8	110	42.8	43.1
17 Austria	244.9	5.7	5.4	96	6.5	97	23.9	25.0
18 Italy	2,096.5	8.8	10.7	172	26.3	134	58.9	57.5
19 New Zealand	94.8	4.6	6.5	113	10.2	103	11.0	15.5
20 Germany	3,838.0	9.1	8.1	92	10.6	69	52.3	48.3
21 Spain	2,127.4	11.3	14.5	195	22.7	140	43.9	34.3
24 Greece	417.1	9.5	10.2	238	25.1	191	61.0	49.2
27 Portugal	342.3	6.3	5.7	132	14.6	134	32.7	31.2
28 Korea, Rep. of	776.7	3.4	3.6	86	9.6	75	0.3	0.7
31 Czech Republic	399.1	7.8	6.3	162	17.6	113	51.9	47.4
35 Hungary	244.5	5.9	8.3	91	13.4	94	42.2	42.2
36 Poland	3,328.5	19.6	14.9	108	43.0	105	50.8	48.6
42 Slovakia	459.3	17.5	15.3 [d]	102	33.1	92	62.1	60.2
53 Mexico	1,033.6	2.5	3.1	106	5.3	126	0.8	1.1
MEDIUM HUMAN DEVELOPMENT								
94 Turkey	2,494.0	10.3	7.9	94	20.5	88	30.9	22.1
OECD [e]	37,931.6 T	6.9	6.8	105	13.6	94	31.9	30.2

NOTES

a The age range for the youth labour force may be 16–24 for some countries.

b Data refer to 2002.

c Data are based on a small sample and must be treated with caution.

d Data refer to the average annual rate in 1994–2003.

e Aggregates for the Organisation for Economic Co-operation and Development are from OECD 2005b, d.

SOURCES

Columns 1, 2 and 5 : OECD 2005b.

Columns 3, 4 and 6 : calculated on the basis of data on male and female unemployment rates from OECD 2005b.

Columns 7 and 8: OECD 2005d.

Human development indicators

TABLE 22

... while preserving it for future generations ...

Energy and the environment

HDI rank	Traditional fuel consumption (% of total energy requirements) 2002	Electricity consumption per capita (kilowatt-hours) 1980	2002	MDG GDP per unit of energy use (2000 PPP US$ per kg of oil equivalent) 1980	2002	MDG Carbon dioxide emissions Per capita (metric tons) 1980	2002	Share of world total (%) 2000	Cartagena Protocol on Biosafety	Framework Convention on Climate Change	Kyoto Protocol to the Framework Convention on Climate Change	Convention on Biological Diversity
HIGH HUMAN DEVELOPMENT												
1 Norway	..	22,400[b]	26,640[b]	4.6	6.1	10.6	12.2	0.2	●	●	●	●
2 Iceland	0.0	13,838	29,247	3.1	2.4	8.2	7.7	(.)	○	●	●	●
3 Australia	9.5	6,599	11,299	3.7	4.8	13.9	18.3	1.5		●	○	●
4 Luxembourg	..	10,879	10,547	2.3	6.3	29.1	21.1	(.)	●	●	●	●
5 Canada	4.6	14,243	18,541	2.5	3.6	17.2	16.5	1.9	○	●	●	●
6 Sweden	19.4	11,700	16,996	3.6	4.4	8.6	5.8	0.2	●	●	●	●
7 Switzerland	7.7[c]	5,878[c]	8,483[c]	7.6	7.8	6.5	5.7	0.2	●	●	●	●
8 Ireland	1.1	3,106	6,560	4.1	9.1	7.7	11.0	0.2	●	●	●	●
9 Belgium	1.0	5,177	8,749	4.0	4.8	13.3	6.8	0.4	●	●	●	●
10 United States	3.6	10,336	13,456	2.8	4.4	20.0	20.1	24.4		●	○	○
11 Japan	0.2	4,944	8,612	5.7	6.4	7.9	9.4	5.2	●	●	●	●
12 Netherlands	..	4,560	6,958	4.0	5.8	10.9	9.4	0.6	●	●	●	●
13 Finland	6.2	8,372	16,694	3.2	3.7	11.9	12.0	0.2	●	●	●	●
14 Denmark	12.7	5,059	6,925	5.3	8.1	12.3	8.9	0.2	●	●	●	●
15 United Kingdom	0.5	5,022	6,614	4.5	6.6	10.5	9.2	2.5	●	●	●	●
16 France	4.7[d]	4,633[d]	8,123[d]	5.0	5.8	9.0	6.2	1.6[d]	●	●	●	●
17 Austria	3.7	4,988	7,845	6.0	7.5	6.9	7.8	0.3	●	●	●	●
18 Italy	1.7[e]	3,364[e]	5,840[e]	7.0	8.5	6.6	7.5	1.9[e]	●	●	●	●
19 New Zealand	2.2	7,270	10,301	5.1	4.6	5.6	8.7	0.1	●	●	●	●
20 Germany	..	...	6,989	3.9	6.2	..	9.8	3.4	●	●	●	●
21 Spain	0.6	2,906	6,154	6.8	6.5	5.3	7.3	1.2	●	●	●	●
22 Hong Kong, China (SAR)		2,449	6,237	11.1	10.6	3.2	5.2	0.1				
23 Israel	0.0	3,187	6,698	6.1	6.0	5.6	11.0	0.3		●	●	●
24 Greece	4.1	2,413	5,247	8.4	6.8	5.4	8.5	0.4	●	●	●	●
25 Singapore	0.2	2,836	7,961	3.9	3.8	12.5	13.8	0.3		●	●	●
26 Slovenia	7.3	...	6,791	..	5.1	..	7.8	0.1	●	●	●	●
27 Portugal	..	1,750	4,647	9.6	6.9	2.8	6.0	0.3	●	●	●	●
28 Korea, Rep. of	..	1,051	7,058	4.2	3.9	3.3	9.4	1.9	○	●	●	●
29 Cyprus	0.0	1,692	5,323	4.9	..	5.2	8.3	(.)	●	●	●	●
30 Barbados	6.3	1,333	3,193	..	..	2.7	4.6	(.)	●	●	●	●
31 Czech Republic	2.4	...	6,368	..	3.7	..	11.2	0.5	●	●	●	●
32 Malta	..	1,627	4,939	6.5	7.6	3.1	7.5	(.)	●	●	●	●
33 Brunei Darussalam	0.0	2,430	8,903	..	..	35.6	17.7	(.)		●	●	●
34 Argentina	3.2	1,413	2,383	7.7	6.9	3.8	3.5	0.6	○	●	●	●
35 Hungary	3.2	2,920	3,972	3.5	5.3	7.7	5.6	0.2	●	●	●	●
36 Poland	5.5	3,419	3,549	..	4.4	12.8	7.7	1.3	●	●	●	●
37 Chile	12.5	1,054	2,918	5.3	6.0	2.5	3.6	0.3	○	●	●	●
38 Estonia	17.7	...	5,767	..	3.6	..	11.8	0.1	●	●	●	●
39 Lithuania	13.9	...	3,239	..	4.0	..	3.6	0.1	●	●	●	●
40 Qatar	0.0	10,616	17,489	..	..	56.3	53.1	0.2		●	●	●
41 United Arab Emirates	..	6,204	14,215	7.5	..	35.8	25.1	0.3		●	●	●
42 Slovakia	1.6	...	5,256	..	3.6	..	6.8	0.2	●	●	●	●
43 Bahrain	..	4,784	10,830	1.6	1.7	22.6	30.6	0.1		●	●	●
44 Kuwait	0.0	6,849	16,544	1.8	1.7	19.7	24.6	0.2		●	●	●
45 Croatia	5.4	...	3,558	..	5.3	..	4.7	0.1	●	●	○	●
46 Uruguay	35.4	1,163	2,456	8.5	10.0	2.0	1.2	(.)	○	●	●	●
47 Costa Rica	24.9	964	1,765	10.2	9.4	1.1	1.4	(.)	○	●	●	●
48 Latvia	47.4	...	2,703	33.3	4.9	..	2.7	(.)	●	●	●	●
49 Saint Kitts and Nevis	..	...	2,619	..	..	1.2	2.8	(.)	●	●		●
50 Bahamas	..	4,062	6,084	..	..	38.1	6.7	(.)	●	●	●	●
51 Seychelles	..	794	2,704	..	..	1.5	6.8	(.)	●	●	●	●
52 Cuba	33.8	1,029	1,395	..	..	3.2	2.1	0.1	●	●	●	●
53 Mexico	8.0	999	2,280	5.4	5.6	4.2	3.7	1.8	●	●	●	●

Ratification of environmental treaties[a]

Human development indicators

TABLE 22

Energy and the environment

HDI rank	Traditional fuel consumption (% of total energy requirements) 2002	Electricity consumption per capita (kilowatt-hours) 1980	Electricity consumption per capita (kilowatt-hours) 2002	MDG GDP per unit of energy use (2000 PPP US$ per kg of oil equivalent) 1980	MDG GDP per unit of energy use (2000 PPP US$ per kg of oil equivalent) 2002	MDG Carbon dioxide emissions Per capita (metric tons) 1980	MDG Carbon dioxide emissions Per capita (metric tons) 2002	Share of world total (%) 2000	Cartagena Protocol on Biosafety	Framework Convention on Climate Change	Kyoto Protocol to the Framework Convention on Climate Change	Convention on Biological Diversity
54 Tonga	..	109	340	..	..	0.4	1.1	(.)	●	●		●
55 Bulgaria	6.2	4,371	4,624	1.6	2.9	8.5	5.3	0.2	●	●	●	●
56 Panama	17.8	930	1,654	7.2	5.9	1.8	2.0	(.)	●	●	●	●
57 Trinidad and Tobago	0.4	1,900	4,422	2.7	1.3	15.4	31.9	0.1	●	●	●	●
MEDIUM HUMAN DEVELOPMENT												
58 Libyan Arab Jamahiriya	0.9	1,588	3,915	..	..	8.9	9.1	0.2		●		●
59 Macedonia, TFYR	8.9	..	3,363	..	..	..	5.1	(.)		●		●
60 Antigua and Barbuda	..	984	1,438	..	..	2.2	4.7	(.)	●	●	●	●
61 Malaysia	1.5	740	3,234	4.6	4.1	2.0	6.3	0.6	●	●	●	●
62 Russian Federation	2.9	..	6,062	..	1.9	..	9.9	6.2		●		●
63 Brazil	26.7	1,145	2,183	7.4	6.8	1.5	1.8	1.3	●	●	●	●
64 Romania	11.8	3,061	2,385	..	3.8	8.7	4.0	0.4	●	●	●	●
65 Mauritius	..	482	1,631	..	..	0.6	2.6	(.)	●	●	●	●
66 Grenada	0.0	281	1,913	..	..	0.5	2.3	(.)	●	●	●	●
67 Belarus	5.5	..	3,326	..	2.1	..	6.0	0.3	●	●	●	●
68 Bosnia and Herzegovina	7.7	..	2,527	..	5.3	..	4.8	0.1		●		●
69 Colombia	16.0	726	1,019	7.2	9.8	1.4	1.3	0.3	●	●		●
70 Dominica	..	149	1,197	..	..	0.5	1.5	(.)	●	●	●	●
71 Oman	0.0	847	5,219	8.2	3.0	5.0	12.1	0.1	●	●	●	●
72 Albania	5.1	1,204	1,844	..	6.7	1.8	0.8	(.)	●	●	●	●
73 Thailand	13.6	340	1,860	5.1	5.0	0.9	3.7	0.9	●	●	●	●
74 Samoa (Western)	..	252	597	..	..	0.6	0.8	(.)	●	●	●	●
75 Venezuela	2.8	2,379	3,484	2.9	2.4	5.8	4.3	0.7		●	●	●
76 Saint Lucia	..	504	1,698	..	..	0.9	2.4	(.)		●	●	●
77 Saudi Arabia	..	1,969	6,620	6.8	2.1	14.9	15.0	1.6		●	●	●
78 Ukraine	1.0	..	3,525	..	1.8	..	6.4	1.5	●	●	●	●
79 Peru	20.6	579	907	8.0	10.7	1.4	1.0	0.1	●	●	●	●
80 Kazakhstan	0.2	..	4,030	..	1.8	..	9.9	0.5		●	○	●
81 Lebanon	0.5	1,056	2,834	..	3.8	2.3	4.7	0.1		●	●	●
82 Ecuador	17.5	423	943	5.2	4.8	1.7	2.0	0.1	●	●	●	●
83 Armenia	0.0	..	1,554	..	4.8	..	1.0	(.)	●	●	●	●
84 Philippines	12.8	373	610	9.8	7.6	0.8	0.9	0.3	○	●	●	●
85 China	5.3	307	1,484	1.2	4.6	1.5	2.7	12.1	○	●	●	●
86 Suriname	3.3	4,442	4,447	..	..	6.7	5.1	(.)		●		●
87 Saint Vincent and the Grenadines	..	276	1,000	..	..	0.4	1.6	(.)	●	●	●	●
88 Paraguay	45.7	233	1,129	7.2	6.3	0.5	0.7	(.)	●	●	●	●
89 Tunisia	7.8	434	1,205	6.9	7.7	1.5	2.3	0.1	●	●	●	●
90 Jordan	1.4	366	1,585	5.5	3.9	2.1	3.2	0.1	●	●	●	●
91 Belize	..	370	713	..	..	1.3	3.1	(.)	●	●	●	●
92 Fiji	..	489	625	..	..	1.2	1.6	(.)	●	●	●	●
93 Sri Lanka	41.6	113	366	5.5	8.0	0.2	0.5	(.)	●	●	●	●
94 Turkey	10.5	554	1,904	5.6	5.7	1.7	3.0	1.0	●	●		●
95 Dominican Republic	7.2	582	1,326	6.3	6.8	1.1	2.5	0.1	●	●	●	●
96 Maldives	0.0	25	448	..	..	0.3	3.4	(.)	●	●	●	●
97 Turkmenistan	..	..	2,126	..	1.4	..	9.1	0.2		●	●	●
98 Jamaica	6.5	834	2,640	3.0	2.5	4.0	4.1	(.)	○	●	●	●
99 Iran, Islamic Rep. of	0.1	570	2,075	4.9	3.1	3.0	5.3	1.4	●	●	●	●
100 Georgia	25.2	..	1,508	6.4	4.4	..	0.7	(.)	●	●	●	●
101 Azerbaijan	0.0	..	2,579	..	2.2	..	3.4	0.1	●	●	●	●
102 Occupied Palestinian Territories	..	..	..	..	..	..	..	..				
103 Algeria	6.0	381	881	8.5	5.6	3.5	2.9	0.4	●	●	●	●
104 El Salvador	32.8	336	665	7.7	7.1	0.5	1.0	(.)	●	●	●	●
105 Cape Verde	..	55	99	..	..	0.4	0.3	(.)		●		●
106 Syrian Arab Republic	0.0	433	1,570	4.5	3.2	2.2	2.8	0.2	●	●		●

Human development indicators

TABLE 22

HDI rank	Traditional fuel consumption (% of total energy requirements) 2002	Electricity consumption per capita (kilowatt-hours) 1980	2002	MDG GDP per unit of energy use (2000 PPP US$ per kg of oil equivalent) 1980	2002	MDG Carbon dioxide emissions Per capita (metric tons) 1980	2002	Share of world total (%) 2000	Cartagena Protocol on Biosafety	Framework Convention on Climate Change	Kyoto Protocol to the Framework Convention on Climate Change	Convention on Biological Diversity
107 Guyana	42.5	545	1,195	..	..	2.3	2.2	(.)		●	●	●
108 Viet Nam	25.3	78	392	..	4.2	0.3	0.8	0.3	●	●	●	●
109 Kyrgyzstan	0.0	...	2,252	..	3.1	..	1.0	(.)		●	●	●
110 Indonesia	17.6	94	463	3.9	4.1	0.6	1.4	1.2	●	●	●	●
111 Uzbekistan	0.0	...	2,008	..	0.8	..	4.8	0.5		●	●	●
112 Nicaragua	47.9	363	496	8.7	5.7	0.7	0.7	(.)	●	●	●	●
113 Bolivia	..	292	485	5.4	4.8	0.8	1.2	(.)	●	●	●	●
114 Mongolia	2.1	1,119	1,318	..	..	4.1	3.3	(.)	●	●	●	●
115 Moldova, Rep. of	2.2	...	1,314	..	2.0	..	1.6	(.)	●	●	●	●
116 Honduras	52.8	259	696	5.0	5.0	0.6	0.9	(.)	○	●	●	●
117 Guatemala	58.6	245	660	7.1	6.4	0.6	0.9	(.)	●	●	●	●
118 Vanuatu	..	171	208	..	..	0.5	0.4	(.)		●	●	●
119 Egypt	9.2	433	1,287	5.9	4.6	1.0	2.1	0.6	●	●	●	●
120 South Africa	11.8 f	3,181 f	4,715 f	4.8	3.9	7.2	7.4	1.4	●	●	●	●
121 Equatorial Guinea	57.1	83	54	..	..	0.3	0.4	(.)		●	●	●
122 Tajikistan	..	...	2,559	..	1.8	..	0.7	(.)	●	●	●	●
123 Gabon	..	766	1,226	3.5	5.1	8.9	2.6	(.)		●	●	●
124 Morocco	2.2	254	560	11.4	10.1	0.8	1.4	0.2	○	●	●	●
125 Namibia	.. g	.. g	.. g	..	10.2	..	1.1	(.)	●	●	●	●
126 São Tomé and Principe	..	96	115	..	..	0.4	0.6	(.)		●		●
127 India	20.0	173	569	3.3	5.0	0.5	1.2	4.7	●	●	●	●
128 Solomon Islands	..	93	69	..	..	0.4	0.4	(.)		●		●
129 Myanmar	74.1	44	135	..	..	0.1	0.2	(.)	○	●	●	●
130 Cambodia	92.3	15	10	..	..	(.)	(.)	(.)	●	●	●	●
131 Botswana	.. g	.. g	.. g	..	..	0.9	2.3	(.)	●	●	●	●
132 Comoros	..	26	25	..	..	0.1	0.1	(.)		●		●
133 Lao People's Dem. Rep.	77.3	68	133	..	..	0.1	0.2	(.)	●	●	●	●
134 Bhutan	87.8	17	236	..	..	(.)	0.2	(.)	●	●	●	●
135 Pakistan	..	176	469	3.5	4.3	0.4	0.7	0.5	○	●	●	●
136 Nepal	..	17	62	2.6	3.8	(.)	0.2	(.)	○	●	●	●
137 Papua New Guinea	61.9	406	249	..	..	0.6	0.4	(.)		●	●	●
138 Ghana	82.5	450	416	4.9	5.0	0.2	0.4	(.)	●	●	●	●
139 Bangladesh	61.6	30	119	11.1	10.5	0.1	0.3	0.1	●	●	●	●
140 Timor-Leste	..	..	..	..	..	..	..	..				
141 Sudan	73.7	47	89	2.5	3.6	0.2	0.3	(.)		●	●	●
142 Congo	72.2	98	210	1.6	3.7	0.2	0.6	(.)	○	●	●	●
143 Togo	83.3	74	120	7.4	4.9	0.2	0.3	(.)	●	●	●	●
144 Uganda	93.4	28	61	..	..	0.1	0.1	(.)	●	●	●	●
145 Zimbabwe	66.2	1,020	981	2.7	..	1.3	1.0	0.1	●	●		●
LOW HUMAN DEVELOPMENT												
146 Madagascar	81.5	49	42	..	..	0.2	0.1	(.)		●	●	●
147 Swaziland	.. g	.. g	.. g	..	..	0.8	0.9	(.)		●	●	●
148 Cameroon	66.9	168	207	5.4	4.7	0.4	0.2	(.)	●	●	●	●
149 Lesotho	.. g	.. g	.. g	..	..	..	..	..		●	●	●
150 Djibouti	..	416	296	..	..	0.9	0.5	(.)	●	●	●	●
151 Yemen	2.3	...	159	..	3.8	..	0.7	(.)		●	●	●
152 Mauritania	..	60	58	..	..	0.4	1.1	(.)		●	●	●
153 Haiti	45.5	58	73	8.0	6.6	0.1	0.2	(.)	○	●	●	●
154 Kenya	64.9	109	155	1.8	2.0	0.4	0.2	(.)	●	●	●	●
155 Gambia	63.6	70	96	..	..	0.2	0.2	(.)	●	●	●	●
156 Guinea	87.8	85	95	..	..	0.2	0.1	(.)	○	●	●	●
157 Senegal	72.1	115	141	3.9	4.8	0.6	0.4	(.)	●	●	●	●
158 Nigeria	46.4	108	148	1.4	1.3	1.0	0.4	0.2	●	●	●	●
159 Rwanda	90.4	32	23	..	..	0.1	0.1	(.)	●	●	●	●

Human development indicators

TABLE 22

Energy and the environment

	Traditional fuel consumption (% of total energy requirements)	Electricity consumption per capita (kilowatt-hours)		MDG GDP per unit of energy use (2000 PPP US$ per kg of oil equivalent)		MDG Carbon dioxide emissions Per capita (metric tons)		Share of world total (%)	Ratification of environmental treaties [a] Cartagena Protocol on Biosafety	Framework Convention on Climate Change	Kyoto Protocol to the Framework Convention on Climate Change	Convention on Biological Diversity
HDI rank	2002	1980	2002	1980	2002	1980	2002	2000				
160 Angola	32.0	214	135	..	3.2	0.7	0.5	(.)		●		●
161 Eritrea	75.0	...	66	..	..	..	0.2	(.)	●	●		●
162 Benin	72.7	37	92	2.1	3.0	0.1	0.3	(.)	●	●	●	●
163 Côte d'Ivoire	72.7	220	197	4.9	3.7	0.7	0.4	(.)	●	●		●
164 Tanzania, U. Rep. of	82.6	41	83	..	1.4	0.1	0.1	(.)	●	●	●	●
165 Malawi	85.0	66	80	..	..	0.1	0.1	(.)	○	●	●	●
166 Zambia	87.3	1,125	603	1.4	1.3	0.6	0.2	(.)	●	●	○	●
167 Congo, Dem. Rep. of the	94.9	161	91	6.1	2.2	0.1	(.)	(.)	●	●	●	●
168 Mozambique	80.3	364	378	1.0	2.3	0.3	0.1	(.)	●	●	●	●
169 Burundi	95.6	12	25	..	..	(.)	(.)	(.)		●	●	●
170 Ethiopia	93.3	...	32	..	2.4	(.)	0.1	(.)	●	●	●	●
171 Central African Republic	83.3	29	28	..	..	(.)	0.1	(.)	○	●		●
172 Guinea-Bissau	50.0	18	41	..	..	0.2	0.2	(.)		●		●
173 Chad	97.2	10	12	..	..	(.)	(.)	(.)	○	●		●
174 Mali	85.0	15	33	..	..	0.1	(.)	(.)	●	●	●	●
175 Burkina Faso	89.4	16	32	..	..	0.1	0.1	(.)	●	●	●	●
176 Sierra Leone	91.2	62	54	..	..	0.2	0.1	(.)	●	●	●	●
177 Niger	85.3	39	40	..	..	0.1	0.1	(.)	●	●	●	●
Developing countries	24.5	388	1,155	3.7	4.6	1.3	2.0	36.9	..	..	..	..
Least developed countries	75.9	83	106	..	4.0	0.1	0.2	0.4	..	..	..	..
Arab States	18.0	626	1,946	5.8	3.5	3.1	4.1	4.5	..	..	..	..
East Asia and the Pacific	11.0	329	1,439	2.1	4.6	1.4	2.6	17.6	..	..	..	..
Latin America and the Caribbean	19.8	1,019	1,927	6.3	6.1	2.4	2.4	5.6	..	..	..	..
South Asia	24.5	171	566	3.8	4.8	0.5	1.2	6.3	..	..	..	..
Sub-Saharan Africa	70.6	434	536	3.3	2.7	1.0	0.8	1.9	..	..	..	..
Central and Eastern Europe and the CIS	4.1	3,284	3,328	..	2.4	10.1	5.9	12.2	..	..	..	..
OECD	4.1	5,761	8,615	3.9	5.1	11.0	11.2	51.0	..	..	..	..
High-income OECD	3.0	6,698	10,262	3.8	5.2	12.2	13.0	46.2	..	..	..	..
High human development	4.5	5,676	8,586	3.8	5.2	10.9	11.2	53.0	..	..	..	..
Medium human development	17.0	368	1,121	3.5	4.1	1.2	2.0	39.0	..	..	..	..
Low human development	71.1	135	133	3.3	4.1	0.4	0.2	0.5	..	..	..	..
High income	2.9	6,616	10,198	3.9	5.1	12.1	13.0	47.8	..	..	..	..
Middle income	9.2	623	1,653	3.7	4.1	2.1	2.9	38.9	..	..	..	..
Low income	42.2	174	399	2.3	2.0	0.5	0.8	7.3	..	..	..	..
World	7.6 [h]	1,573	2,465	3.8	4.6	3.4	3.6	100.0 [i]	..	..	..	..

● Ratification, acceptance, approval, accession or succession.
○ Signature.

NOTES

a Information is as of 15 April 2005. The Cartagena Protocol on Biosafety was signed in Cartagena in 2000, the United Nations Framework Convention on Climate Change in New York in 1992, the Kyoto Protocol to the United Nations Framework Convention on Climate Change in Kyoto in 1997 and the Convention on Biological Diversity in Rio de Janeiro in 1992.

b Includes Svalbard and Jan Mayen Islands.

c Includes Liechtenstein.

d Includes Monaco.

e Includes San Marino.

f Data refer to the South African Customs Union, which includes Botswana, Lesotho, Namibia and Swaziland.

g Included in data for South Africa.

h Data refer to the world aggregate from UN 2005d.

i Data refer to the world aggregate from CDIAC 2005. Data refer to total carbon dioxide emissions, including those of countries not shown in the main indicator tables as well as emissions not included in national totals, such as those from bunker fuels and oxidation of non-fuel hydrocarbon products.

SOURCES

Column 1: calculated on the basis of data on traditional fuel consumption and total energy requirements from UN 2005d.

Columns 2 and 3: UN 2005b.

Columns 4 and 5: World Bank 2005c, based on data from the International Energy Agency; aggregates calculated for the Human Development Report Office by the World Bank.

Columns 6 and 7: UN 2005f, based on data from the Carbon Dioxide Information Analysis Center.

Column 8: CDIAC 2005.

Columns 9–12: UN 2005g.

TABLE 23

... protecting personal security ...

Refugees and armaments

HDI rank	Internally displaced people[a] (thousands) 2004[e]	Refugees By country of asylum (thousands) 2004[e]	Refugees By country of origin[c] (thousands) 2004[e]	Conventional arms transfers[b] (1990 prices) Imports (US$ millions) 1994	Imports (US$ millions) 2004	Exports US$ millions 2004	Exports Share[d] (%) 2000–04	Total armed forces Thousands 2003	Total armed forces Index (1985=100) 2003
HIGH HUMAN DEVELOPMENT									
1 Norway	..	46	(.)	99	1	51	(.)	27	72
2 Iceland		(.)	(.)	..	..	0	(.)	..	..
3 Australia	..	56	(.)	263	334	52	(.)	52	74
4 Luxembourg		1	..	0	0	..	..	1	129
5 Canada	..	133	(.)	333	340	543	2	52	63
6 Sweden	..	112	(.)	258	13	260	2	28	42
7 Switzerland	..	50	(.)	113	125	154	(.)	27	137
8 Ireland	..	6	(.)	48	25	..	..	10	76
9 Belgium	..	13	(.)	52	12	0	(.)	41	45
10 United States	..	453	(.)	625	533	5,453	31	1,434	67
11 Japan	..	2	(.)	585	195	0	(.)	240	99
12 Netherlands	..	141	(.)	143	183	211	1	53	50
13 Finland	..	11	(.)	174	57	17	(.)	27	74
14 Denmark	..	70	(.)	66	194	6	(.)	21	72
15 United Kingdom	..	277	(.)	538	171	985	5	208	62
16 France	..	131	(.)	6	89	2,122	8	259	56
17 Austria	..	16	(.)	36	46	1	(.)	35	64
18 Italy	..	12	(.)	146	317	261	1	194	50
19 New Zealand	..	6	(.)	16	42	1	(.)	9	69
20 Germany	..	960	1	..	..	..	..	285	60
21 Spain	..	6	(.)	636	261	75	1	151	47
22 Hong Kong, China (SAR)	..	2	(.)	..	..	..	..	..	..
23 Israel	150–300[f]	4	1	793	724	283	1	168	118
24 Greece	..	3	(.)	1,215	1,434	0	(.)	171	85
25 Singapore	..	(.)	(.)	117	456	70	(.)	73	132
26 Slovenia	..	2	1	11	14	..	..	7	..
27 Portugal	..	(.)	(.)	433	59	0	(.)	45	62
28 Korea, Rep. of	..	(.)	(.)	668	737	50	(.)	688	115
29 Cyprus	210	(.)	(.)	46	0	0	(.)	10	100
30 Barbados	..	..	(.)	..	..	..	..	1	60
31 Czech Republic	..	2	7	0	18	0	(.)	45	22
32 Malta	..	(.)	(.)	0	0	10	(.)	2	263
33 Brunei Darussalam	..	..	(.)	0	0	..	..	7	171
34 Argentina	..	3	1	177	129	0	(.)	71	66
35 Hungary	..	7	3	4	15	0	(.)	32	30
36 Poland	..	2	15	8	256	86	(.)	142	44
37 Chile	..	(.)	2	113	43	0	(.)	78	77
38 Estonia	..	(.)	1	15	5	0	(.)	5	..
39 Lithuania	..	(.)	2	0	31	0	(.)	14	..
40 Qatar	..	(.)	(.)	10	0	0	(.)	12	207
41 United Arab Emirates	..	(.)	(.)	554	1,246	3	(.)	51	117
42 Slovakia	..	(.)	1	30	0	0	(.)	20	..
43 Bahrain	..	0	(.)	7	10	0	(.)	11	400
44 Kuwait	..	2	1	37	0	0	(.)	16	129
45 Croatia	10	4	230	57	8	0	(.)	21	..
46 Uruguay	..	(.)	(.)	8	0	0	(.)	24	75
47 Costa Rica	..	14	(.)	0	0	..	..	..	..
48 Latvia	..	(.)	3	12	14	0	(.)	5	..
49 Saint Kitts and Nevis	..	..	(.)	..	..	..	..	..	..
50 Bahamas	..	..	(.)	0	0	..	..	1	180
51 Seychelles	..	..	(.)	0	0	..	..	1	42
52 Cuba	..	1	16	0	0	..	..	49	30
53 Mexico	10–12	6	2	120	265	..	..	193	149

Human development indicators

TABLE 23

Refugees and armaments

		Refugees		Conventional arms transfers[b] (1990 prices)				Total armed forces	
	Internally displaced people[a]	By country of asylum	By country of origin	Imports (US$ millions)		Exports			Index
						US$ millions	Share[d] (%)	Thousands	(1985=100)
HDI rank	(thousands) 2004[e]	(thousands) 2004[e]	(thousands) 2004[e]	1994	2004	2004	2000–04	2003	2003
54 Tonga	..	..	(.)	0	0	..	..	..	..
55 Bulgaria	..	4	3	0	12	0	(.)	51	34
56 Panama	..	1	(.)	0	0	..	..	..	..
57 Trinidad and Tobago	..	..	(.)	0	0	..	..	3	129
MEDIUM HUMAN DEVELOPMENT									
58 Libyan Arab Jamahiriya	..	12	2	0	74	0	(.)	76	104
59 Macedonia, TFYR	2	(.)	6	27	0	29	(.)	11	..
60 Antigua and Barbuda	..	..	(.)	..	..	..	..	(.)	200
61 Malaysia	..	(.)	(.)	375	277	0	(.)	110	100
62 Russian Federation	339[f]	10	96	40	0	6,197	32	1,212	23
63 Brazil	..	3	(.)	226	38	100	(.)	303	110
64 Romania	..	2	8	25	276	0	(.)	97	51
65 Mauritius	..	0	(.)	0	0	..	..	..	..
66 Grenada	..	..	(.)	..	..	..	..	..	..
67 Belarus	..	1	8	0	0	50	1	73	..
68 Bosnia and Herzegovina	309	23	300	3	0	0	(.)	25	..
69 Colombia	1,575–3,410[g]	(.)	38	39	17	..	..	207	313
70 Dominica	..	..	(.)	..	..	..	..	..	..
71 Oman	..	..	(.)	168	123	0	(.)	42	143
72 Albania	..	(.)	10	0	6	..	..	22	53
73 Thailand	..	119	(.)	627	105	5	(.)	307	130
74 Samoa (Western)	..	..	0	..	..	..	..	..	..
75 Venezuela	..	(.)	1	1	12	1	(.)	82	168
76 Saint Lucia	..	..	(.)	..	..	..	..	..	..
77 Saudi Arabia	..	241	(.)	982	838	0	(.)	200	319
78 Ukraine	..	3	94	0	29	452	3	273	..
79 Peru	60	1	6	133	14	5	(.)	80	63
80 Kazakhstan	..	16	7	0	27	5	(.)	66	..
81 Lebanon	50–600	3	25	12	0	0	(.)	72	414
82 Ecuador	..	6	1	0	22	..	..	47	109
83 Armenia	8	239	13	310	68	..	..	45	..
84 Philippines	60	(.)	(.)	71	59	..	..	106	92
85 China	..	299	132	142	2,238	125	2	2,255	58
86 Suriname	..	0	(.)	0	0	..	..	2	90
87 Saint Vincent and the Grenadines	..	..	(.)	..	..	..	..	..	..
88 Paraguay	..	(.)	(.)	0	4	..	..	10	70
89 Tunisia	..	(.)	3	32	0	..	..	35	100
90 Jordan	..	1	1	5	132	72	(.)	101	143
91 Belize	..	1	(.)	0	0	..	..	1	183
92 Fiji	..	..	1	4	0	..	..	4	130
93 Sri Lanka	352	(.)	122	53	6	..	..	151	699
94 Turkey	230–1,000+	2	186	1,215	418	18	(.)	515	82
95 Dominican Republic	..	..	(.)	0	21	..	..	25	110
96 Maldives	..	..	(.)	0	0	..	..	..	..
97 Turkmenistan	..	14	1	0	20	..	..	26	..
98 Jamaica	..	..	(.)	0	0	..	..	3	133
99 Iran, Islamic Rep. of	..	985	132	389	283	1	(.)	540	89
100 Georgia	240	4	12	0	0	20	(.)	18	..
101 Azerbaijan	575	(.)	253	25	0	..	..	67	..
102 Occupied Palestinian Territories	21–50[h]	0	428	5	0	..	..	..	..
103 Algeria	1,000[i]	169	12	156	282	..	..	128	75
104 El Salvador	..	(.)	6	0	0	0	(.)	16	37
105 Cape Verde	..	..	(.)	0	0	..	..	1	16
106 Syrian Arab Republic	305	4	20	44	0	0	(.)	297	74

TABLE 23

HDI rank	Internally displaced people [a] (thousands) 2004 [e]	Refugees By country of asylum (thousands) 2004 [e]	Refugees By country of origin [c] (thousands) 2004 [e]	Conventional arms transfers [b] (1990 prices) Imports (US$ millions) 1994	Imports 2004	Exports US$ millions 2004	Exports Share [d] (%) 2000–04	Total armed forces Thousands 2003	Total armed forces Index (1985=100) 2003
107 Guyana	..	..	(.)	0	0	..	..	2	24
108 Viet Nam	..	15	363	0	247	..	..	484	47
109 Kyrgyzstan	..	6	3	0	5	0	(.)	13	..
110 Indonesia	600	(.)	13	559	85	50	(.)	302	109
111 Uzbekistan	3	45	7	0	0	170	1	52	..
112 Nicaragua	..	(.)	4	0	0	0	(.)	14	22
113 Bolivia	..	1	(.)	7	1	..	..	32	114
114 Mongolia	..	0	(.)	..	..	..	..	9	26
115 Moldova, Rep. of	..	(.)	11	2	0	0	(.)	7	..
116 Honduras	..	(.)	1	0	0	..	..	12	72
117 Guatemala	242	1	7	3	0	..	..	29	92
118 Vanuatu	..	..	..	..	..	..	..	..	..
119 Egypt	..	89	6	1,944	398	0	(.)	450	101
120 South Africa	..	27	(.)	19	8	35	(.)	56	52
121 Equatorial Guinea	..	..	1	0	0	..	..	1	59
122 Tajikistan	..	3	59	24	0	..	..	8	..
123 Gabon	..	14	(.)	0	0	..	..	5	196
124 Morocco	..	2	1	131	0	..	..	196	132
125 Namibia	..	20	1	3	53	..	..	9	..
126 São Tomé and Principe	..	0	(.)	..	..	..	..	..	..
127 India	600	165	14	565	2,375	22	(.)	1,325	105
128 Solomon Islands	..	..	(.)	0	0	..	..	..	..
129 Myanmar	526 [f]	0	147	3	65	..	..	378	203
130 Cambodia	..	(.)	31	71	0	0	(.)	124	355
131 Botswana	..	3	(.)	0	10	..	..	9	225
132 Comoros	..	0	(.)	..	..	..	..	..	..
133 Lao People's Dem. Rep.	..	0	10	0	0	..	..	29	54
134 Bhutan	..	..	104	0	0	..	..	..	..
135 Pakistan	30 [f]	1,124	24	755	344	10	(.)	619	128
136 Nepal	100–150	124	1	0	32	..	..	72	288
137 Papua New Guinea	..	7	(.)	1	0	..	..	..	..
138 Ghana	..	44	16	10	27	..	..	7	46
139 Bangladesh	500	20	6	50	26	..	..	126	137
140 Timor-Leste	..	(.)	(.)	..	..	..	..	..	..
141 Sudan	6,000	138	606	0	270	..	..	105	185
142 Congo	100	91	29	0	0	..	..	10	115
143 Togo	..	12	11	3	0	..	..	9	236
144 Uganda	1,400 [f]	231	35	0	19	..	..	50	250
145 Zimbabwe	150	13	7	0	0	..	..	29	71
LOW HUMAN DEVELOPMENT									
146 Madagascar	..	0	(.)	0	0	..	..	14	64
147 Swaziland	..	1	(.)	0	0	..	..	..	..
148 Cameroon	..	59	6	0	0	..	..	23	316
149 Lesotho	..	0	(.)	0	1	..	..	2	100
150 Djibouti	..	27	1	0	0	..	..	10	327
151 Yemen	..	62	2	4	309	..	..	67	104
152 Mauritania	..	(.)	31	27	0	..	..	16	185
153 Haiti	..	..	8	..	..	..	..	..	..
154 Kenya	360	238	3	12	0	..	..	24	176
155 Gambia	..	7	1	0	0	..	..	1	160
156 Guinea	82	184	4	0	0	..	..	10	98
157 Senegal	64	21	8	1	0	..	..	14	135
158 Nigeria	200	9	24	73	10	0	(.)	79	84
159 Rwanda	..	37	75	0	0	..	..	51	981

Human development indicators

TABLE 23

Refugees and armaments

		Refugees		Conventional arms transfers [b] (1990 prices)					Total armed forces	
	Internally displaced people [a]	By country of asylum	By country of origin [c]	Imports (US$ millions)		Exports				Index
						US$ millions	Share [d] (%)		Thousands	(1985=100)
	(thousands)	(thousands)	(thousands)							
HDI rank	2004 [e]	2004 [e]	2004 [e]	1994	2004	2004	2000–04		2003	2003
160 Angola	40–340 [f]	13	324	96	5	0	(.)		108	219
161 Eritrea	59	4	124	16	382	0	(.)		202	..
162 Benin	..	5	(.)	0	0	..	..		5	102
163 Côte d'Ivoire	500	76	34	0	14	..	..		17	129
164 Tanzania, U. Rep. of	..	650	1	2	0	..	..		27	67
165 Malawi	..	3	(.)	1	0	0	(.)		5	100
166 Zambia	..	227	(.)	0	0	0	(.)		18	112
167 Congo, Dem. Rep. of the	2,330	234	453	0	0	..	..		65	135
168 Mozambique	..	(.)	(.)	0	0	..	..		10	65
169 Burundi	170	41	532	0	0	..	..		51	971
170 Ethiopia	132	130	63	0	162	..	..		183	84
171 Central African Republic	..	45	35	0	0	..	..		3	113
172 Guinea-Bissau	..	8	1	0	0	..	..		7	84
173 Chad	..	146	52	8	0	..	..		30	248
174 Mali	..	10	(.)	0	0	..	..		7	151
175 Burkina Faso	..	(.)	1	0	0	..	..		11	270
176 Sierra Leone	..	61	71	1	0	..	..		13	419
177 Niger	..	(.)	1	0	0	..	..		5	241
Developing countries	..	6,484 T	..	..	..	..	..		12,670 T	81
Least developed countries	..	2,476 T	..	..	..	..	..		1,933 T	165
Arab States	..	883 T	..	..	..	..	..		1,866 T	69
East Asia and the Pacific	..	444 T	..	..	..	..	..		4,874 T	65
Latin America and the Caribbean	..	38 T	..	..	..	..	..		1,282 T	95
South Asia	..	2,417 T	..	..	..	..	..		2,923 T	115
Sub-Saharan Africa	..	2,698 T	..	..	..	..	..		1,200 T	142
Central and Eastern Europe and the CIS	..	678 T	..	..	..	..	..		2,352 T	36
OECD	..	2,524 T	..	..	..	..	..		5,002 T	69
High-income OECD	..	2,505 T	..	..	..	..	..		4,055 T	69
High human development	..	2,560 T	..	..	..	..	..		5,165 T	69
Medium human development	..	4,353 T	..	..	..	..	..		12,215 T	71
Low human development	..	2,299 T	..	..	..	..	..		1,076 T	154
High income	..	2,516 T	..	..	..	..	..		4,412 T	72
Middle income	..	2,812 T	..	..	..	..	..		10,614 T	65
Low income	..	4,344 T	..	..	..	..	..		4,640 T	92
World	25,300 [i]	9,672 T	..	19,501 T [k]	19,162 T [k]	19,156 T [k]	..		18,560 T	67

NOTES

a Refers to estimates maintained by the Global IDP Project based on various sources. Estimates are associated with high levels of uncertainty.

b Data are as of 16 February 2005 and are trend indicator values, which are an indicator only of the volume of international arm transfers, not of the actual financial value of such transfers. Published reports of arms transfers provide partial information, as not all transfers are fully reported. The estimates presented are conservative and may understate actual transfers of conventional weapons.

c The country of origin for many refugees is unavailable or unreported. These data may therefore be underestimates.

d Calculated using the 2000–04 totals for all countries and non-state actors with exports of major conventional weapons as defined in SIPRI 2005b.

e Data refer to the end of 2004 unless otherwise specified.

f Estimate excludes certain parts of the country or some groups of internally displaced persons.

g Lower estimate accumulated since 1994. Higher figure accumulated since 1985.

h Lower estimate only includes internally displaced persons evicted mainly by house demolitions since 2000. Higher figure cumulative since 1967.

i Figures accumulated since 1992.

j Aggregate provided by the Global IDP Project.

k Data refer to the world aggregate from SIPRI 2005c and include all countries and non-state actors with transfers of major conventional weapons as defined therein.

SOURCES

Column 1: Global IDP Project 2005.
Columns 2 and 3: UNHCR 2005.
Columns 4–6: SIPRI 2005c.
Column 7: calculated on the basis of data on weapons transfers from SIPRI 2005c.
Column 8: IISS 2004.
Column 9: calculated on the basis of data on armed forces from IISS 2004.

TABLE 24 ... protecting personal security ...

Victims of crime

		Population victimized by crime [a] (% of total)					
	Year [b]	Total crime [c]	Property crime [d]	Robbery	Sexual assault [e]	Assault	Bribery (corruption) [f]
NATIONAL							
Australia	1999	30.1	13.9	1.2	1.0	2.4	0.3
Austria	1995	18.8	3.1	0.2	1.2	0.8	0.7
Belgium	1999	21.4	7.7	1.0	0.3	1.2	0.3
Canada	1999	23.8	10.4	0.9	0.8	2.3	0.4
Denmark	1999	23.0	7.6	0.7	0.4	1.4	0.3
England and Wales	1999	26.4	12.2	1.2	0.9	2.8	0.1
Finland	1999	19.1	4.4	0.6	1.1	2.1	0.2
France	1999	21.4	8.7	1.1	0.7	1.4	1.3
Italy	1991	24.6	12.7	1.3	0.6	0.2	..
Japan	1999	15.2	3.4	0.1	0.1	0.1	(.)
Malta	1996	23.1	10.9	0.4	0.1	1.1	4.0
Netherlands	1999	25.2	7.4	0.8	0.8	1.0	0.4
New Zealand	1991	29.4	14.8	0.7	1.3	2.4	..
Northern Ireland	1999	15.0	6.2	0.1	0.1	2.1	0.2
Poland	1999	22.7	9.0	1.8	0.2	1.1	5.1
Portugal	1999	15.5	7.5	1.1	0.2	0.4	1.4
Scotland	1999	23.2	7.6	0.7	0.3	3.0	..
Slovenia	2000	21.2	7.7	1.1	0.8	1.1	2.1
Sweden	1999	24.7	8.4	0.9	1.1	1.2	0.1
Switzerland	1999	18.2	4.5	0.7	0.6	1.0	0.2 [g]
United States	1999	21.1	10.0	0.6	0.4	1.2	0.2
MAJOR CITY							
Asunción (Paraguay)	1995	34.4	16.7	6.3	1.7	0.9	13.3
Baku (Azerbaijan)	1999	8.3	2.4	1.6	0.0	0.4	20.8
Beijing (China)	1991	19.0	2.2	0.5	0.6	0.6	..
Bishkek (Kyrgyzstan)	1995	27.8	11.3	1.6	2.2	2.1	19.3
Bogotá (Colombia)	1996	54.6	27.0	11.5	4.8	2.5	19.5
Bratislava (Slovakia)	1996	36.0	20.8	1.2	0.4	0.5	13.5
Bucharest (Romania)	1999	25.4	10.8	1.8	0.4	0.6	19.2
Budapest (Hungary)	1999	32.1	15.6	1.8	0.9	0.8	9.8
Buenos Aires (Argentina)	1995	61.1	30.8	6.4	6.4	2.3	30.2
Cairo (Egypt)	1991	28.7	12.1	2.2	1.8	1.1	..
Dar es Salaam (Tanzania, U. Rep. of)	1991	..	23.1	8.2	6.1	1.7	..
Gaborone (Botswana)	1996	31.7	19.7	2.0	0.7	3.2	2.8
Jakarta (Indonesia)	1995	20.9	9.4	0.7	1.3	0.5	29.9
Johannesburg (South Africa)	1995	38.0	18.3	4.7	2.7	4.6	6.9
Kampala (Uganda)	1995	40.9	20.6	2.3	5.1	1.7	19.5
Kiev (Ukraine)	1999	29.1	8.9	2.5	1.2	1.5	16.2
La Paz (Bolivia)	1995	39.8	18.1	5.8	1.5	2.0	24.4
Manila (Philippines)	1995	10.6	3.3	1.5	0.1	0.1	4.3
Maputo (Mozambique)	2001	40.6	29.3	7.6	2.2	3.2	30.5
Minsk (Belarus)	1999	23.6	11.1	1.4	1.4	1.3	20.6
Moscow (Russian Federation)	1999	26.3	10.9	2.4	1.2	1.1	16.6
Mumbai (India)	1995	31.8	6.7	1.3	3.5	0.8	22.9
New Delhi (India)	1995	30.5	6.1	1.0	1.7	0.8	21.0
Prague (Czech Republic)	1999	34.1	21.6	0.5	0.9	1.1	5.7
Rïga (Latvia)	1999	26.5	9.4	2.8	0.5	1.9	14.3
Rio de Janeiro (Brazil)	1995	44.0	14.7	12.2	7.5	3.4	17.1
San José (Costa Rica)	1995	40.4	21.7	8.9	3.5	1.7	9.2
Skopje (Macedonia, TFYR)	1995	21.1	9.4	1.1	0.3	0.7	7.4
Sofia (Bulgaria)	1999	27.2	16.1	1.5	0.1	0.6	16.4
Tallinn (Estonia)	1999	41.2	22.5	6.3	3.3	3.7	9.3
Tbjlisi (Georgia)	1999	23.6	11.1	1.8	0.4	0.9	16.6

Human development indicators

TABLE
24

Victims of crime

	Year[b]	Total crime[c]	Property crime[d]	Robbery	Sexual assault[e]	Assault	Bribery (corruption)[f]
				Population victimized by crime[a] (% of total)			
Tirana (Albania)	1999	31.7	11.2	2.9	1.2	0.7	59.1
Tunis (Tunisia)	1991	37.5	20.1	5.4	1.5	0.4	..
Ulaanbaatar (Mongolia)	1999	41.8	20.0	4.5	1.4	2.1	21.3
Vilnius (Lithuania)	1999	31.0	17.8	3.2	2.0	1.4	22.9
Zagreb (Croatia)	1999	14.3	4.4	0.5	0.8	0.5	9.5

NOTES

a Data refer to victimization as reported in the International Crime Victims Survey.

b Surveys were conducted in 1992, 1995, 1996–97 and 2000–01. Data refer to the year preceding the survey.

c Data refer to people victimized by 1 or more of 11 crimes recorded in the survey: robbery, burglary, attempted burglary, car theft, car vandalism, bicycle theft, sexual assault, theft from car, theft of personal property, assault and threats, and theft of motorcycle or moped.

d Includes car theft, theft from car, burglary with entry and attempted burglary.

e Data refer to women only.

f Data refer to people who have been asked or expected to pay a bribe by a government official.

g Data refer to 1995.

SOURCE

All columns: UNODC 2004.

TABLE 25

. . . and achieving equality for all women and men

Gender-related development index

HDI rank	Gender-related development index (GDI)		Life expectancy at birth (years) 2003		Adult literacy rate[a] (% ages 15 and above) 2003		Combined gross enrolment ratio for primary, secondary and tertiary schools[b] (%) 2002/03		Estimated earned income[c] (PPP US$) 2003		HDI rank minus GDI rank[d]
	Rank	Value	Female	Male	Female	Male	Female	Male	Female	Male	
HIGH HUMAN DEVELOPMENT											
1 Norway	1	0.960	81.9	76.8	..[e]	..[e]	106	97	32,272	43,148	0
2 Iceland	3	0.953	82.6	78.7	..[e]	..[e]	102	91	25,411	36,908	−1
3 Australia	2	0.954	82.8	77.7	..[e]	..[e]	117	114	24,827	34,446	1
4 Luxembourg	7	0.944	81.5	75.2	..[e]	..[e]	89[f]	88[f]	34,890	89,883[g]	−3
5 Canada	5	0.946	82.4	77.4	..[e]	..[e]	96[h, i]	92[h, i]	23,922	37,572	0
6 Sweden	4	0.947	82.4	77.9	..[e]	..[e]	124	105	21,842	31,722	2
7 Switzerland	6	0.946	83.2	77.6	..[e]	..[e]	88	92	28,972	32,149	1
8 Ireland	11	0.939	80.3	75.1	..[e]	..[e]	97	89	22,125	53,549	−3
9 Belgium	9	0.941	82.0	75.7	..[e]	..[e]	119	110	19,951	37,019	0
10 United States	8	0.942	80.0	74.6	..[e]	..[e]	97	89	29,017	46,456	2
11 Japan	14	0.937	85.4	78.4	..[e]	..[e]	83	85	17,795	38,612	−3
12 Netherlands	12	0.939	81.1	75.7	..[e]	..[e]	99	99	20,512	38,389	0
13 Finland	10	0.940	81.7	75.1	..[e]	..[e]	112	103	23,211	32,250	3
14 Denmark	13	0.938	79.4	74.8	..[e]	..[e]	106	97	26,587	36,430	1
15 United Kingdom	15	0.937	80.6	76.0	..[e]	..[e]	133[h]	113[h]	20,790	33,713	0
16 France	16	0.935	83.0	75.9	..[e]	..[e]	94	90	20,642	35,123	0
17 Austria	19	0.926	81.8	76.0	..[e]	..[e]	90	88	15,878	45,174	−2
18 Italy	18	0.928	83.1	76.9	..[e]	..[e]	89	85	17,176	37,670	0
19 New Zealand	17	0.929	81.3	76.8	..[e]	..[e]	104	94	18,379	26,960	2
20 Germany	20	0.926	81.5	75.7	..[e]	..[e]	88	90	19,534	36,258	0
21 Spain	21	0.922	83.2	75.9	..[e]	..[e]	96	91	13,854	31,322	0
22 Hong Kong, China (SAR)	22	0.912	84.6	78.7	89.6	96.9	73	74	19,593	35,037	0
23 Israel	23	0.911	81.7	77.6	95.6	98.3	93	89	14,159	25,969	0
24 Greece	24	0.907	80.9	75.6	88.3[e]	94.0[e]	93	91	12,531	27,591	0
25 Singapore	..	..	80.6	76.7	88.6	96.6	..	..	16,489	32,089	..
26 Slovenia	25	0.901	80.0	72.7	99.6[e]	99.7[e]	99	92	14,751	23,779	0
27 Portugal	26	0.900	80.6	73.9	..[e]	..[e]	97	90	12,853	23,829	0
28 Korea, Rep. of	27	0.896	80.6	73.3	..[e]	..[e]	87	100	11,698	24,167	0
29 Cyprus	28	0.884	81.1	76.1	95.1	98.6	79	78	11,864	25,260	0
30 Barbados	29	0.876	78.5	71.4	99.7[e]	99.7[e]	94[i]	84[i]	11,976	19,687	0
31 Czech Republic	30	0.872	78.7	72.3	..	..	81	80	12,843	20,051	0
32 Malta	32	0.858	80.8	75.9	89.2[j]	86.4[j]	80	78	9,893	25,525	−1
33 Brunei Darussalam	..	..	79.0	74.3	90.2	95.2	75	72	..	..	..
34 Argentina	34	0.854	78.2	70.7	97.2	97.2	99	91	6,635	17,800	−2
35 Hungary	31	0.860	76.8	68.6	99.3[e]	99.4[e]	92	87	11,287	18,183	2
36 Poland	33	0.856	78.4	70.3	99.7[e]	99.8[e]	93	88	8,769	14,147	1
37 Chile	38	0.846	80.9	74.8	95.6	95.8	81	82	5,753	14,872	−3
38 Estonia	35	0.852	77.0	65.6	99.8[e]	99.8[e]	99	87	10,745	16,750	1
39 Lithuania	36	0.851	77.8	66.6	99.6[e]	99.6[e]	98	90	9,595	14,064	1
40 Qatar	..	..	76.0	71.2	..	0.0	84	80	..	..	..
41 United Arab Emirates	..	..	80.8	76.4	80.7[k]	75.6[k]	79[h]	69[h]	..	..	..
42 Slovakia	37	0.847	77.9	70.1	99.6[e]	99.7[e]	76	74	10,681	16,463	1
43 Bahrain	41	0.837	75.9	73.1	83.0	92.5	85	77	7,685	24,909	−2
44 Kuwait	39	0.843	79.5	75.2	81.0[k]	84.7[k]	85[h]	75[h]	8,448	24,204	1
45 Croatia	40	0.837	78.4	71.4	97.1	99.3[e]	76	74	8,047	14,351	1
46 Uruguay	42	0.836	79.0	71.7	98.1[k]	97.3[k]	93[h]	83[h]	5,763	10,950	0
47 Costa Rica	44	0.829	80.6	75.9	95.9[k]	95.7[k]	69	67	5,236	14,000	−1
48 Latvia	43	0.834	77.0	65.8	99.7[e]	99.8[e]	95	84	8,050	12,886	1
49 Saint Kitts and Nevis	..	..	..	..	..	..	94[h]	83[h]	..	..	..
50 Bahamas	..	..	73.0	66.5	96.3	94.6	..	..	13,357	20,723	..
51 Seychelles	..	..	..	..	92.3	91.4	85	85	..	..	..
52 Cuba	..	..	79.2	75.5	96.8[k]	97.0[k]	81	79	..	..	..
53 Mexico	46	0.804	77.5	72.6	88.7	92.0	76	74	5,068	13,506	−1

TABLE 25

Gender-related development index

HDI rank		Gender-related development index (GDI)		Life expectancy at birth (years) 2003		Adult literacy rate [a] (% ages 15 and above) 2003		Combined gross enrolment ratio for primary, secondary and tertiary schools [b] (%) 2002/03		Estimated earned income [c] (PPP US$) 2003		HDI rank minus GDI rank [d]
		Rank	Value	Female	Male	Female	Male	Female	Male	Female	Male	
54	Tonga	..	..	73.5	71.0	99.0 [i]	98.8 [i]	84 [h]	82 [h]	..	..	..
55	Bulgaria	45	0.807	75.6	68.9	97.7	98.7	78	77	6,212	9,334	1
56	Panama	47	0.800	77.4	72.3	91.2	92.5	82	76	4,597	9,069	0
57	Trinidad and Tobago	48	0.796	73.0	66.9	97.9 [k]	99.0 [k]	67 [h]	64 [h]	6,792	14,807	0
MEDIUM HUMAN DEVELOPMENT												
58	Libyan Arab Jamahiriya	..	..	76.2	71.6	70.7 [k]	91.8 [k]	100 [h]	93 [h]	..	..	..
59	Macedonia, TFYR	49	0.794	76.3	71.3	94.1	98.2	71	69	4,861	8,725	0
60	Antigua and Barbuda	..	..	..	..	..	..	..	..	..	..	..
61	Malaysia	50	0.791	75.6	70.9	85.4	92.0	73	68	6,075	12,869	0
62	Russian Federation	..	..	72.1	59.0	99.2 [e]	99.7 [e]	..	..	7,302	11,429	..
63	Brazil	52	0.786	74.6	66.6	88.6	88.3	93	89	4,704	10,963	−1
64	Romania	51	0.789	75.0	67.8	96.3	98.4	73	70	5,391	9,261	1
65	Mauritius	54	0.781	75.7	68.8	80.5	88.2	71 [h]	71 [h]	6,084	16,606	−1
66	Grenada	..	..	..	..	..	..	96	96	..	..	..
67	Belarus	53	0.785	74.0	62.4	99.4 [e,j]	99.8 [e,j]	91	86	4,842	7,418	1
68	Bosnia and Herzegovina	..	..	76.8	71.4	91.1	98.4	..	..	3,759	8,229	..
69	Colombia	55	0.780	75.4	69.3	94.6	93.7	72	69	4,557	8,892	0
70	Dominica	..	..	..	..	..	..	78	73	..	..	..
71	Oman	60	0.759	75.7	72.8	65.4 [k]	82.0 [k]	63 [h]	63 [h]	4,013	21,614	−4
72	Albania	56	0.776	76.7	71.0	98.3	99.2 [e]	70	68	3,266	5,836	1
73	Thailand	57	0.774	73.8	66.3	90.5	94.9	72 [h]	72 [h]	5,784	9,452	1
74	Samoa (Western)	..	..	73.7	67.2	98.4 [k]	98.9 [k]	72 [h]	70 [h]	..	..	..
75	Venezuela	58	0.765	75.9	70.0	92.7	93.3	76 [h]	73 [h]	2,890	6,929	1
76	Saint Lucia	..	..	73.9	70.9	90.6	89.5	78 [h]	72 [h]	..	..	..
77	Saudi Arabia	65	0.749	73.9	70.1	69.3	87.1	57 [h]	58 [h]	4,440	20,717	−5
78	Ukraine	59	0.763	72.5	60.1	99.2 [e]	99.7 [e]	87	84	3,891	7,329	2
79	Peru	67	0.745	72.6	67.5	82.1	93.5	88 [h]	87 [h]	2,231	8,256	−5
80	Kazakhstan	61	0.759	69.0	57.8	99.3 [e,j]	99.8 [e,j]	87	83	5,221	8,217	2
81	Lebanon	68	0.745	74.2	69.8	81.0	92.4	80 [h]	77 [h]	2,430	7,789	−4
82	Ecuador	..	..	77.3	71.4	89.7	92.3	..	..	1,696	5,569	..
83	Armenia	62	0.756	74.7	68.0	99.2 [e]	99.7 [e]	74	69	3,026	4,352	3
84	Philippines	63	0.755	72.5	68.3	92.7	92.5	83	80	3,213	5,409	3
85	China	64	0.754	73.5	69.9	86.5	95.1	68	70	3,961	5,976	3
86	Suriname	..	..	72.6	65.9	84.1	92.3	78 [h]	69 [h]	..	..	..
87	Saint Vincent and the Grenadines	..	..	73.9	68.3	..	..	68	65	..	..	..
88	Paraguay	72	0.742	73.2	68.7	90.2	93.1	74 [h]	73 [h]	2,316	7,000	−4
89	Tunisia	69	0.743	75.4	71.2	65.3	83.4	76	73	3,840	10,420	0
90	Jordan	73	0.740	72.9	69.9	84.7	95.1	79	77	2,004	6,491	−3
91	Belize	76	0.734	74.5	69.5	77.1	76.7	78 [h]	76 [h]	2,695	11,143	−5
92	Fiji	71	0.742	70.1	65.7	91.4 [j]	94.5 [j]	73 [h,i]	73 [h,i]	3,146	8,525	1
93	Sri Lanka	66	0.747	76.8	71.5	88.6 [i]	92.2 [i]	69 [h]	67 [h]	2,579	5,009	7
94	Turkey	70	0.742	71.1	66.5	81.1	95.7	62 [h]	74 [h]	4,276	9,286	4
95	Dominican Republic	74	0.739	71.0	63.9	87.3	88.0	81 [h]	71 [h]	3,608	9,949	1
96	Maldives	..	..	66.1	67.1	97.2 [k]	97.3 [k]	75 [h]	74 [h]	..	..	..
97	Turkmenistan	..	..	66.8	58.3	98.3 [j]	99.3 [e,j]	..	..	4,603	7,305	..
98	Jamaica	75	0.736	72.5	69.0	91.4 [k]	83.8 [k]	77 [h]	71 [h]	3,279	4,944	1
99	Iran, Islamic Rep. of	78	0.719	71.9	69.0	70.4	83.5	65 [h]	72 [h]	3,094	10,856	−1
100	Georgia	..	..	74.3	66.6	..	..	71	70	1,566	3,715	..
101	Azerbaijan	77	0.725	70.5	63.2	98.2 [j]	99.5 [e,j]	68	71	2,683	4,591	1
102	Occupied Palestinian Territories	..	..	74.0	70.9	87.4	96.3	81 [h]	78 [h]	..	..	..
103	Algeria	82	0.706	72.4	69.8	60.1	79.5	72 [h]	76 [h]	2,896	9,244	−3
104	El Salvador	80	0.715	73.9	67.8	77.1 [k]	82.4 [k]	67	68	2,939	6,689	0
105	Cape Verde	81	0.714	73.2	67.0	68.0 [k]	85.4 [k]	73	73	3,392	7,136	0
106	Syrian Arab Republic	84	0.702	75.1	71.6	74.2	91.0	60 [h]	65 [h]	1,584	5,534	−2

TABLE 25

HDI rank	Gender-related development index (GDI) Rank	Value	Life expectancy at birth (years) 2003 Female	Male	Adult literacy rate[a] (% ages 15 and above) 2003 Female	Male	Combined gross enrolment ratio for primary, secondary and tertiary schools[b] (%) 2002/03 Female	Male	Estimated earned income[c] (PPP US$) 2003 Female	Male	HDI rank minus GDI rank[d]
107 Guyana	79	0.716	66.1	60.0	98.2	99.0	78[h]	77[h]	2,426	6,152	4
108 Viet Nam	83	0.702	72.6	68.6	86.9[j]	93.9[j]	61[h]	67[h]	2,026	2,964	1
109 Kyrgyzstan	85	0.700	71.1	62.7	98.1[j]	99.3[e,j]	83	81	1,388	2,128	0
110 Indonesia	87	0.691	68.8	64.9	83.4[k]	92.5[k]	65	67	2,289	4,434	−1
111 Uzbekistan	86	0.692	69.8	63.4	98.9[k]	99.6[k]	74	77	1,385	2,099	1
112 Nicaragua	88	0.683	72.1	67.3	76.6	76.8	71	68	2,018	4,512	0
113 Bolivia	89	0.679	66.2	62.0	80.4	92.9	84[h]	90[h]	1,615	3,573	0
114 Mongolia	90	0.677	66.1	62.1	97.5	98.0	80	69	1,478	2,227	0
115 Moldova, Rep. of	91	0.668	71.3	63.9	95.0	97.5	64	60	1,200	1,850	0
116 Honduras	..	..	69.9	65.8	80.2	79.8	..	..	1,447	3,877	..
117 Guatemala	94	0.649	71.0	63.6	63.3	75.4	59	63	2,073	6,197	−2
118 Vanuatu	..	..	70.6	66.9	..	..	58	59	..	..	..
119 Egypt	..	..	72.1	67.7	43.6[j]	67.2[j]	..	..	1,614	6,203	..
120 South Africa	92	0.652	50.2	46.8	80.9[j]	84.1[j]	78[h]	78[h]	6,505	14,326	1
121 Equatorial Guinea	95	0.641	43.9	42.6	76.4	92.1	60[h]	71[h]	10,771	27,053	−1
122 Tajikistan	93	0.650	66.3	61.0	99.3[e]	99.7[e]	69	82	854	1,367	2
123 Gabon	..	..	55.2	53.7	..	..	70[h,i]	74[h,i]	4,765	8,054	..
124 Morocco	97	0.616	71.9	67.5	38.3[k]	63.3[k]	54	62	2,299	5,699	−1
125 Namibia	96	0.621	49.0	47.6	83.5	86.8	72[h]	70[h]	4,201	8,234	1
126 São Tomé and Principe	..	..	64.0	62.0	..	..	59[h,i]	64[h,i]	..	..	..
127 India	98	0.586	65.0	61.8	47.8	73.4	56	64	1,569	4,130	0
128 Solomon Islands	..	..	63.0	61.6	..	..	..	..	1,391	2,107	..
129 Myanmar	..	..	63.1	57.5	86.2	93.7	49[h]	48[h]	..	..	..
130 Cambodia	99	0.567	59.8	52.4	64.1	84.7	54	64	1,807	2,368	0
131 Botswana	100	0.559	36.7	35.9	81.5[k]	76.1[k]	71[h]	70[h]	6,617	10,816	0
132 Comoros	101	0.541	65.4	61.1	49.1[k]	63.5[k]	42[h]	51[h]	1,216	2,206	0
133 Lao People's Dem. Rep.	102	0.540	55.9	53.4	60.9	77.0	55	67	1,391	2,129	0
134 Bhutan	..	..	64.2	61.7	..	..	14	16	..	..	..
135 Pakistan	107	0.508	63.2	62.8	35.2	61.7	31	43	1,050	3,082	−4
136 Nepal	106	0.511	62.0	61.2	34.9	62.7	55	66	949	1,868	−2
137 Papua New Guinea	103	0.518	56.0	54.9	50.9	63.4	37[h]	44[h]	1,896	3,305	2
138 Ghana	104	0.517	57.3	56.3	45.7	62.9	43[h]	48[h]	1,915	2,567	2
139 Bangladesh	105	0.514	63.7	62.1	31.4[k]	50.3[k]	54	52	1,245	2,289	2
140 Timor-Leste	..	..	56.6	54.5	..	..	..	..	..	..	..
141 Sudan	110	0.495	57.9	54.9	49.9[j]	69.2[j]	35[h]	41[h]	918	2,890	−2
142 Congo	108	0.507	53.2	50.7	77.1[k]	88.9[k]	44	52	689	1,238	1
143 Togo	112	0.491	56.3	52.4	38.3	68.5	52	76	1,092	2,318	−2
144 Uganda	109	0.502	47.6	46.9	59.2[k]	78.8[k]	72[h]	75[h]	1,169	1,751	2
145 Zimbabwe	111	0.493	36.5	37.3	86.3[k]	93.8[k]	51[h]	54[h]	1,751	3,042	1
LOW HUMAN DEVELOPMENT											
146 Madagascar	116	0.483	56.8	54.1	65.2	76.4	40	41	603	1,017	−3
147 Swaziland	115	0.485	32.9	32.1	78.1	80.4	58[h]	61[h]	2,669	6,927	−1
148 Cameroon	113	0.487	46.5	45.1	59.8	77.0	50[h]	60[h]	1,310	2,940	2
149 Lesotho	114	0.487	37.7	34.6	90.3	73.7	67[h]	65[h]	1,480	3,759	2
150 Djibouti	..	..	54.0	51.6	..	..	23[h]	31[h]	..	..	..
151 Yemen	121	0.448	61.9	59.3	28.5[k]	69.5[k]	41[h]	69[h]	413	1,349	−4
152 Mauritania	118	0.471	54.3	51.1	43.4	59.5	43[h]	47[h]	1,269	2,284	0
153 Haiti	..	..	52.4	50.8	50.0[k]	53.8[k]	..	..	1,250	2,247	..
154 Kenya	117	0.472	46.3	48.1	70.2	77.7	50[h]	53[h]	1,001	1,078	1
155 Gambia	119	0.464	57.1	54.3	30.9	45.0	45[h]	50[h]	1,391	2,339	1
156 Guinea	..	..	54.1	53.4	..	..	34[h]	49[h]	1,692	2,503	..
157 Senegal	120	0.449	56.9	54.5	29.2	51.1	37[h]	43[h]	1,175	2,131	1
158 Nigeria	123	0.439	43.6	43.1	59.4[k]	74.4[k]	57[h]	71[h]	614	1,495	−1
159 Rwanda	122	0.447	45.6	42.1	58.8	70.5	53	58	985	1,583	1

TABLE 25

Gender-related development index

HDI rank	Gender-related development index (GDI)		Life expectancy at birth (years) 2003		Adult literacy rate [a] (% ages 15 and above) 2003		Combined gross enrolment ratio for primary, secondary and tertiary schools [b] (%) 2002/03		Estimated earned income [c] (PPP US$) 2003		HDI rank minus GDI rank [d]
	Rank	Value	Female	Male	Female	Male	Female	Male	Female	Male	
160 Angola	124	0.438	42.3	39.3	53.8	82.1	27 [h,i]	32 [h,i]	1,797	2,897	0
161 Eritrea	125	0.431	55.7	51.8	45.6	68.2	30 [h]	40 [h]	579	1,125	0
162 Benin	126	0.419	54.7	53.2	22.6	46.4	43 [h]	66 [h]	910	1,316	0
163 Côte d'Ivoire	128	0.403	46.7	45.2	38.2	60.1	34 [h,i]	50 [h,i]	792	2,142	−1
164 Tanzania, U. Rep. of	127	0.414	46.3	45.5	62.2	77.5	40 [h]	42 [h]	516	725	1
165 Malawi	129	0.396	39.6	39.8	54.0 [i]	74.9 [i]	69 [h]	75 [h]	486	717	0
166 Zambia	130	0.383	36.9	37.9	59.7 [i]	76.1 [i]	45 [h]	50 [h]	629	1,130	0
167 Congo, Dem. Rep. of the	131	0.373	44.1	42.1	51.9	79.8	24 [h,i]	31 [h,i]	500	903	0
168 Mozambique	133	0.365	42.7	41.1	31.4 [k]	62.3 [k]	38 [h]	48 [h]	910	1,341	−1
169 Burundi	132	0.373	44.5	42.6	51.9	66.8	31 [h]	40 [h]	545	758	1
170 Ethiopia	134	0.355	48.7	46.6	33.8 [k]	49.2 [k]	29 [h]	42 [h]	487	931	0
171 Central African Republic	..	..	40.1	38.4	33.5	64.8	..	..	829	1,366	..
172 Guinea-Bissau	135	0.326	46.2	43.2	24.7	55.2	29 [h,i]	45 [h,i]	466	960	0
173 Chad	137	0.322	44.7	42.5	12.7	40.6	28 [h]	48 [h]	902	1,525	−1
174 Mali	136	0.323	48.5	47.2	11.9 [i]	26.7 [i]	27 [h]	38 [h]	742	1,247	1
175 Burkina Faso	138	0.311	48.2	46.8	8.1 [i]	18.5 [i]	20 [h]	27 [h]	986	1,357	0
176 Sierra Leone	139	0.279	42.1	39.4	20.5	39.8	38 [i]	52 [i]	325	783	0
177 Niger	140	0.271	44.4	44.3	9.4	19.6	17 [h]	25 [h]	601	1,056	0

NOTES

a Data refer to national literacy estimates from censuses or surveys conducted between 2000 and 2004, unless otherwise noted. Due to differences in methodology and timeliness of underlying data, comparisons across countries and over time should be made with caution. For more details, see www.uis.unesco.org/ev.php?ID=4930_201&ID2=DO_TOPIC.

b Data refer to the 2002/03 school year. Data for some countries may refer to national or United Nations Educational, Scientific and Cultural Organization (UNESCO) Institute for Statistics estimates. For details, see www.uis.unesco.org. Because data are from different sources, comparisons across countries should be made with caution.

c Because of the lack of gender-disaggregated income data, female and male earned income are crudely estimated on the basis of data on the ratio of the female non-agricultural wage to the male non-agricultural wage, the female and male shares of the economically active population, the total female and male population and GDP per capita (PPP US$) (see Technical note 1). Estimates are based on data for the most recent year available during 1991–2003, unless otherwise specified.

d The HDI ranks used in this column are those recalculated for the 140 countries with a GDI value. A positive figure indicates that the GDI rank is higher than the HDI rank, a negative the opposite.

e For purposes of calculating the GDI, a value of 99.0% was applied.

f Statec 2005.

g For purposes of calculating the GDI, a value of $40,000 (PPP US$) was applied.

h Preliminary UNESCO Institute for Statistics estimate, subject to further revision.

i Data refer to year other than that specified.

j Data refer to a year between 1995 and 1999.

k Estimate produced by UNESCO Institute for Statistics in July 2002.

l Data refer to a year or period other than that specified, differ from the standard definition or refer to only part of a country.

SOURCES

Column 1: determined on the basis of the GDI values in column 2

Column 2: calculated on the basis of data in columns 3–10; see Technical note 1 for details.

Columns 3 and 4: UN 2005c, unless otherwise noted.

Columns 5 and 6: UNESCO Institute for Statistics 2005a, unless otherwise noted.

Columns 7 and 8: UNESCO Institute for Statistics 2005c.

Columns 9 and 10: calculated on the basis of data on GDP per capita (PPP US$) and population from World Bank 2005c, data on wages from ILO 2005b; data on the economically active population from ILO 2002, unless otherwise noted.

Column 11: calculated on the basis the recalculated HDI ranks on the GDI ranks in column 1.

GDI ranks for 140 countries and areas

1 Norway	29 Barbados	57 Thailand	85 Kyrgyzstan	113 Cameroon
2 Australia	30 Czech Republic	58 Venezuela	86 Uzbekistan	114 Lesotho
3 Iceland	31 Hungary	59 Ukraine	87 Indonesia	115 Swaziland
4 Sweden	32 Malta	60 Oman	88 Nicaragua	116 Madagascar
5 Canada	33 Poland	61 Kazakhstan	89 Bolivia	117 Kenya
6 Switzerland	34 Argentina	62 Armenia	90 Mongolia	118 Mauritania
7 Luxembourg	35 Estonia	63 Philippines	91 Moldova, Rep. of	119 Gambia
8 United States	36 Lithuania	64 China	92 South Africa	120 Senegal
9 Belgium	37 Slovakia	65 Saudi Arabia	93 Tajikistan	121 Yemen
10 Finland	38 Chile	66 Sri Lanka	94 Guatemala	122 Rwanda
11 Ireland	39 Kuwait	67 Peru	95 Equatorial Guinea	123 Nigeria
12 Netherlands	40 Croatia	68 Lebanon	96 Namibia	124 Angola
13 Denmark	41 Bahrain	69 Tunisia	97 Morocco	125 Eritrea
14 Japan	42 Uruguay	70 Turkey	98 India	126 Benin
15 United Kingdom	43 Latvia	71 Fiji	99 Cambodia	127 Tanzania, U. Rep. of
16 France	44 Costa Rica	72 Paraguay	100 Botswana	128 Côte d'Ivoire
17 New Zealand	45 Bulgaria	73 Jordan	101 Comoros	129 Malawi
18 Italy	46 Mexico	74 Dominican Republic	102 Lao People's Dem. Rep.	130 Zambia
19 Austria	47 Panama	75 Jamaica	103 Papua New Guinea	131 Congo, Dem. Rep. of the
20 Germany	48 Trinidad and Tobago	76 Belize	104 Ghana	132 Burundi
21 Spain	49 Macedonia, TFYR	77 Azerbaijan	105 Bangladesh	133 Mozambique
22 Hong Kong, China (SAR)	50 Malaysia	78 Iran, Islamic Rep. of	106 Nepal	134 Ethiopia
23 Israel	51 Romania	79 Guyana	107 Pakistan	135 Guinea-Bissau
24 Greece	52 Brazil	80 El Salvador	108 Congo	136 Mali
25 Slovenia	53 Belarus	81 Cape Verde	109 Uganda	137 Chad
26 Portugal	54 Mauritius	82 Algeria	110 Sudan	138 Burkina Faso
27 Korea, Rep. of	55 Colombia	83 Viet Nam	111 Zimbabwe	139 Sierra Leone
28 Cyprus	56 Albania	84 Syrian Arab Republic	112 Togo	140 Niger

Human development indicators

TABLE 26

... and achieving equality for all women and men

Gender empowerment measure

HDI rank	Gender empowerment measure (GEM)		Seats in parliament held by women[a] (% of total)	Female legislators, senior officials and managers[b] (% of total)	Female professional and technical workers[b] (% of total)	Ratio of estimated female to male earned income[c]
	Rank	Value				
HIGH HUMAN DEVELOPMENT						
1 Norway	1	0.928	38.2	30	50	0.75
2 Iceland	4	0.834	30.2	29	55	0.69
3 Australia	7	0.826	28.3[d]	36	55	0.72
4 Luxembourg	..	..	23.3	..	..	0.39
5 Canada	10	0.807	24.7	35	54	0.64
6 Sweden	3	0.852	45.3	30	51	0.69
7 Switzerland	11	0.795	24.8	28	45	0.90
8 Ireland	16	0.724	14.2	29	50	0.41
9 Belgium	6	0.828	35.7	31	48	0.54
10 United States	12	0.793	14.8	46	55	0.62
11 Japan	43	0.534	9.3	10	46	0.46
12 Netherlands	8	0.814	34.2	26	48	0.53
13 Finland	5	0.833	37.5	28	53	0.72
14 Denmark	2	0.860	36.9	26	51	0.73
15 United Kingdom	18	0.716	17.9	33	45	0.62
16 France	..	..	13.9	..	..	0.59
17 Austria	13	0.779	32.2	27	49	0.35
18 Italy	37	0.589	10.4	21	45	0.46
19 New Zealand	14	0.769	28.3	36	52	0.68
20 Germany	9	0.813	31.3	36	50	0.54
21 Spain	15	0.745	30.5	30	47	0.44
22 Hong Kong, China (SAR)	..	..	..	26	39	0.56
23 Israel	24	0.622	15.0	29	54	0.55
24 Greece	36	0.594	14.0	26	48	0.45
25 Singapore	22	0.654	16.0	26	45	0.51
26 Slovenia	30	0.603	12.2	33	56	0.62
27 Portugal	21	0.656	20.0	32	52	0.54
28 Korea, Rep. of	59	0.479	13.0	6	39	0.48
29 Cyprus	39	0.571	16.1	18	47	0.47
30 Barbados	25	0.615	17.6	45	71	0.61
31 Czech Republic	34	0.595	15.7	26	52	0.64
32 Malta	58	0.486	9.2	18	39	0.39
33 Brunei Darussalam	..	..	—[e]	..	..	..
34 Argentina	20	0.665	33.6	25	55	0.37
35 Hungary	44	0.528	9.1	34	61	0.62
36 Poland	27	0.612	20.7	34	61	0.62
37 Chile	61	0.475	10.1	24	52	0.39
38 Estonia	35	0.595	18.8	35	69	0.64
39 Lithuania	26	0.614	22.0	39	70	0.68
40 Qatar	..	..	—[e]	..	..	..
41 United Arab Emirates	..	..	0.0	8	25	..
42 Slovakia	33	0.597	16.7	35	61	0.65
43 Bahrain	68	0.393	7.5[f]	10	19	0.31
44 Kuwait	..	..	0.0[g]	..	..	0.35
45 Croatia	32	0.599	21.7	26	52	0.56
46 Uruguay	50	0.504	10.8	35	53	0.53
47 Costa Rica	19	0.668	35.1	29	40	0.37
48 Latvia	28	0.606	21.0	40	64	0.62
49 Saint Kitts and Nevis	..	..	0.0	..	..	..
50 Bahamas	17	0.719	26.8	40	51	0.64
51 Seychelles	..	..	29.4	..	..	..
52 Cuba	..	..	36.0	..	..	..
53 Mexico	38	0.583	23.7	25	40	0.38

Human development indicators

TABLE 26

Gender empowerment measure

HDI rank	Gender empowerment measure (GEM)		Seats in parliament held by women[a] (% of total)	Female legislators, senior officials and managers[b] (% of total)	Female professional and technical workers[b] (% of total)	Ratio of estimated female to male earned income[c]
	Rank	Value				
54 Tonga	..	..	0.0	..	..	..
55 Bulgaria	29	0.604	26.3	30	34	0.67
56 Panama	40	0.563	16.7	40	50	0.51
57 Trinidad and Tobago	23	0.650	25.4	38	54	0.46
MEDIUM HUMAN DEVELOPMENT						
58 Libyan Arab Jamahiriya	..	..	..	..	..	..
59 Macedonia, TFYR	41	0.555	19.2	27	51	0.56
60 Antigua and Barbuda	..	..	13.9	..	..	..
61 Malaysia	51	0.502	13.1	23	40	0.47
62 Russian Federation	60	0.477	8.0	39	64	0.64
63 Brazil	..	..	9.1	..	62	0.43
64 Romania	56	0.488	10.9	31	57	0.58
65 Mauritius	..	..	5.7	..	..	0.37
66 Grenada	..	..	32.1	..	..	..
67 Belarus	..	..	30.1	..	..	0.65
68 Bosnia and Herzegovina	..	..	12.3	..	..	0.46
69 Colombia	52	0.500	10.8	38	50	0.51
70 Dominica	..	..	19.4	..	..	..
71 Oman	..	..	7.8	..	..	0.19
72 Albania	..	..	6.4	..	..	0.56
73 Thailand	63	0.452	8.1	26	52	0.61
74 Samoa (Western)	..	..	6.1	..	..	..
75 Venezuela	64	0.441	9.7	27	61	0.42
76 Saint Lucia	..	..	20.7	..	..	..
77 Saudi Arabia	78	0.253	0.0	31	6	0.21
78 Ukraine	66	0.417	5.3	39	63	0.53
79 Peru	48	0.511	18.3	23	47	0.27
80 Kazakhstan	..	..	9.5	..	..	0.64
81 Lebanon	..	..	2.3	..	..	0.31
82 Ecuador	55	0.490	16.0	26	40	0.30
83 Armenia	..	..	5.3	..	..	0.70
84 Philippines	46	0.526	15.4	58	62	0.59
85 China	..	..	20.2	..	..	0.66
86 Suriname	..	..	19.6	28	51	..
87 Saint Vincent and the Grenadines	..	..	22.7	..	..	..
88 Paraguay	65	0.427	9.6	23	54	0.33
89 Tunisia	..	..	22.8	..	..	0.37
90 Jordan	..	..	7.9	..	..	0.31
91 Belize	57	0.486	11.9	31	52	0.24
92 Fiji	70	0.381	9.7	51	9	0.37
93 Sri Lanka	72	0.370	4.9	21	46	0.51
94 Turkey	76	0.285	4.4	6	30	0.46
95 Dominican Republic	45	0.527	15.4	31	49	0.36
96 Maldives	..	..	4.8	15	40	..
97 Turkmenistan	..	..	16.0	..	..	0.63
98 Jamaica	..	..	13.6	..	..	0.66
99 Iran, Islamic Rep. of	75	0.316	4.1	13	33	0.28
100 Georgia	67	0.416	9.4	28	63	0.42
101 Azerbaijan	..	..	10.5	..	..	0.58
102 Occupied Palestinian Territories	..	..	..	12	34	..
103 Algeria	..	..	5.3	..	..	0.31
104 El Salvador	62	0.467	10.7	32	44	0.44
105 Cape Verde	..	..	11.1	..	..	0.48
106 Syrian Arab Republic	..	..	12.0	..	..	0.29

TABLE 26

HDI rank	Gender empowerment measure (GEM)		Seats in parliament held by women [a] (% of total)	Female legislators, senior officials and managers [b] (% of total)	Female professional and technical workers [b] (% of total)	Ratio of estimated female to male earned income [c]
	Rank	Value				
107 Guyana	..	..	30.8	..	..	0.39
108 Viet Nam	..	..	27.3	..	..	0.68
109 Kyrgyzstan	..	..	..	..	..	0.65
110 Indonesia	..	..	11.3	..	..	0.52
111 Uzbekistan	..	..	16.4	..	..	0.66
112 Nicaragua	..	..	20.7	..	..	0.45
113 Bolivia	47	0.525	17.8	36	40	0.45
114 Mongolia	69	0.388	6.7	30	66	0.66
115 Moldova, Rep. of	53	0.494	15.8	40	66	0.65
116 Honduras	74	0.356	5.5	22	36	0.37
117 Guatemala	..	..	8.2	..	..	0.33
118 Vanuatu	..	..	3.8	..	..	..
119 Egypt	77	0.274	4.3	9	31	0.26
120 South Africa	..	..	32.8 [h]	..	..	0.45
121 Equatorial Guinea	..	..	18.0	..	..	0.40
122 Tajikistan	..	..	..	..	..	0.62
123 Gabon	..	..	11.9	..	..	0.59
124 Morocco	..	..	6.4	..	..	0.40
125 Namibia	31	0.603	25.5	30	55	0.51
126 São Tomé and Principe	..	..	9.1	..	..	..
127 India	..	..	9.3	..	..	0.38
128 Solomon Islands	..	..	0.0	..	..	0.66
129 Myanmar	..	..	..	..	..	..
130 Cambodia	73	0.364	10.9	14	33	0.76
131 Botswana	49	0.505	11.1	31	53	0.61
132 Comoros	..	..	3.0	..	..	0.55
133 Lao People's Dem. Rep.	..	..	22.9	..	..	0.65
134 Bhutan	..	..	8.7	..	..	..
135 Pakistan	71	0.379	20.6	2	26	0.34
136 Nepal	..	..	6.4	..	..	0.51
137 Papua New Guinea	..	..	0.9	..	..	0.57
138 Ghana	..	..	10.9	..	..	0.75
139 Bangladesh	79	0.218	2.0	8	25	0.54
140 Timor-Leste	..	..	25.3 [i]	..	..	..
141 Sudan	..	..	9.7	..	..	0.32
142 Congo	..	..	10.6	..	..	0.56
143 Togo	..	..	6.2	..	..	0.47
144 Uganda	..	..	23.9	..	..	0.67
145 Zimbabwe	..	..	10.0	..	..	0.58
LOW HUMAN DEVELOPMENT						
146 Madagascar	..	..	8.4	..	..	0.59
147 Swaziland	54	0.492	16.8	24	61	0.39
148 Cameroon	..	..	8.9	..	..	0.45
149 Lesotho	..	..	17.0	..	..	0.39
150 Djibouti	..	..	10.8	..	..	..
151 Yemen	80	0.123	0.3	4	15	0.31
152 Mauritania	..	..	4.4	..	..	0.56
153 Haiti	..	..	9.1	..	..	0.56
154 Kenya	..	..	7.1	..	..	0.93
155 Gambia	..	..	13.2	..	..	0.59
156 Guinea	..	..	19.3	..	..	0.68
157 Senegal	..	..	19.2	..	..	0.55
158 Nigeria	..	..	5.8	..	..	0.41
159 Rwanda	..	..	45.3	..	..	0.62

Human development indicators

TABLE 26

Gender empowerment measure

	Gender empowerment measure (GEM)		Seats in parliament held by women[a]	Female legislators, senior officials and managers[b]	Female professional and technical workers[b]	Ratio of estimated female to male earned income[c]
HDI rank	Rank	Value	(% of total)	(% of total)	(% of total)	
160 Angola	..	..	15.0	..	..	0.62
161 Eritrea	..	..	22.0	..	..	0.51
162 Benin	..	..	7.2	..	..	0.69
163 Côte d'Ivoire	..	..	8.5	..	..	0.37
164 Tanzania, U. Rep. of	42	0.538	21.4	49	32	0.71
165 Malawi	..	..	14.0	..	..	0.68
166 Zambia	..	..	12.7	..	..	0.56
167 Congo, Dem. Rep. of the	..	..	10.2	..	..	0.55
168 Mozambique	..	..	34.8	..	..	0.68
169 Burundi	..	..	18.5	..	..	0.72
170 Ethiopia	..	..	7.8	..	..	0.52
171 Central African Republic	..	..	—[k]	..	..	0.61
172 Guinea-Bissau	..	..	14.0	..	..	0.49
173 Chad	..	..	6.5	..	..	0.59
174 Mali	..	..	10.2	..	..	0.60
175 Burkina Faso	..	..	11.7	..	..	0.73
176 Sierra Leone	..	..	14.5	..	..	0.42
177 Niger	..	..	12.4	..	..	0.57

NOTES

a Data are as of 1 March 2005. Where there are lower and upper houses, data refer to the weighted average of women's shares of seats in both houses.

b Data refer to the most recent year available during 1992–2003. Estimates for countries that have implemented the recent International Standard Classification of Occupations (ISCO-88) are not strictly comparable with those for countries using the previous classification (ISCO-68).

c Calculated on the basis of data in columns 9 and 10 in table 25. Estimates are based on data for the most recent year available during 1991–2003.

d The figure reflects the Senate composition until 1 July 2005.

e Brunei Darussalam and Qatar do not currently have a parliament. Elections for a new parliament in Qatar, according to the 2004 constitution, are scheduled to take place in late 2005 or early 2006.

f Women were allowed to vote in the referendum of 14–15 February 2001, which approved the National Action Charter. Subsequently, women exercised their full political rights as both voters and candidates in the 2002 national elections.

g On 16 May 2005 parliament passed a law granting women the right to vote and stand for election.

h Does not include the 36 upper house special rotation delegates appointed on an ad hoc basis. The shares given are therefore calculated on the basis of lower house seats and the 54 permanent seats in the upper house.

i The parliament elected in 1990 has never been convened nor authorized to sit, and many of its members were detained or forced into exile.

j The purpose of elections held on 30 August 2001 was to elect members of the Constituent Assembly of Timor-Leste. This body became the National Parliament on 20 May 2002, the date on which the country became independent, without any new elections.

k Parliament was suspended on 15 March 2003. May 2005 election results are not yet available.

SOURCES

Column 1: determined on the basis of GEM values in column 2.

Column 2: calculated on the basis of data in columns 3–6; see *Technical note 1* for details.

Column 3: calculated on the basis of data on parliamentary seats from IPU 2005a, d.

Columns 4 and 5: calculated on the basis of occupational data from ILO 2005b.

Column 6: calculated on the basis of data in columns 9 and 10 of table 25.

GEM ranks for 80 countries

1	Norway	17	Bahamas	33	Slovakia	49	Botswana
2	Denmark	18	United Kingdom	34	Czech Republic	50	Uruguay
3	Sweden	19	Costa Rica	35	Estonia	51	Malaysia
4	Iceland	20	Argentina	36	Greece	52	Colombia
5	Finland	21	Portugal	37	Italy	53	Moldova, Rep. of
6	Belgium	22	Singapore	38	Mexico	54	Swaziland
7	Australia	23	Trinidad and Tobago	39	Cyprus	55	Ecuador
8	Netherlands	24	Israel	40	Panama	56	Romania
9	Germany	25	Barbados	41	Macedonia, TFYR	57	Belize
10	Canada	26	Lithuania	42	Tanzania, U. Rep. of	58	Malta
11	Switzerland	27	Poland	43	Japan	59	Korea, Rep. of
12	United States	28	Latvia	44	Hungary	60	Russian Federation
13	Austria	29	Bulgaria	45	Dominican Republic	61	Chile
14	New Zealand	30	Slovenia	46	Philippines	62	El Salvador
15	Spain	31	Namibia	47	Bolivia	63	Thailand
16	Ireland	32	Croatia	48	Peru	64	Venezuela

65	Paraguay		
66	Ukraine		
67	Georgia		
68	Bahrain		
69	Mongolia		
70	Fiji		
71	Pakistan		
72	Sri Lanka		
73	Cambodia		
74	Honduras		
75	Iran, Islamic Rep. of		
76	Turkey		
77	Egypt		
78	Saudi Arabia		
79	Bangladesh		
80	Yemen		

TABLE 27

... and achieving equality for all women and men

Gender inequality in education

	HDI rank	Adult literacy[a]		Youth literacy[a]		MDG Net primary enrolment[b, c]		MDG Net secondary enrolment[b, c]		MDG Gross tertiary enrolment[c, d]	
		Female rate (% ages 15 and above)	Female rate as % of male rate	Female rate (% ages 15–24)	Female rate as % of male rate	Female ratio (%)	Ratio of female to male[e]	Female ratio (%)	Ratio of female to male[e]	Female ratio (%)	Ratio of female to male[e]
		2003	2003	2003	2003	2002/03	2002/03	2002/03	2002/03	2002/03	2002/03
HIGH HUMAN DEVELOPMENT											
1	Norway	..	..	..	..	100	1.00	97	1.01	99	1.55
2	Iceland	..	..	..	..	99	0.99	88	1.05	81	1.81
3	Australia	..	..	..	..	97	1.01	89[f]	1.02[f]	82	1.23
4	Luxembourg	..	..	..	..	91	1.01	83	1.07	13	1.17
5	Canada	..	..	..	..	100[f, g]	1.00[f, g]	98[f, g]	1.00[f, g]	66[f, h]	1.34[f, h]
6	Sweden	..	..	..	..	99	0.99	100	1.01	102	1.55
7	Switzerland	..	..	..	..	99	0.99	84	0.95	44	0.83
8	Ireland	..	..	..	..	97	1.02	87	1.08	59	1.32
9	Belgium	..	..	..	..	100	1.00	98	1.01	66	1.19
10	United States	..	..	..	..	93	1.01	89	1.01	96	1.37
11	Japan	..	..	..	..	100	1.00	101[f, i]	1.01[f, i]	47	0.88
12	Netherlands	..	..	..	..	99	0.99	89	1.01	61	1.09
13	Finland	..	..	..	..	100	1.00	95	1.01	96	1.20
14	Denmark	..	..	..	..	100	1.00	98	1.04	79	1.43
15	United Kingdom	..	..	..	..	100	1.00	97	1.03	72	1.27
16	France	..	..	..	..	99	1.00	95	1.02	63	1.28
17	Austria	..	..	..	..	91	1.02	89	0.99	53	1.20
18	Italy	..	..	..	..	99	0.99	92	1.01	65	1.34
19	New Zealand	..	..	..	..	99[f]	0.99[f]	94	1.03	90	1.53
20	Germany	..	..	..	..	84	1.02	88	1.00	51	1.00
21	Spain	..	..	..	..	99	0.99	98	1.04	67	1.19
22	Hong Kong, China (SAR)	..	..	..	..	97[j]	0.99[j]	75[f]	1.04[f]	31	0.99
23	Israel	95.6	97	99.4	100	99	1.00	89	1.00	66	1.33
24	Greece	88.3	94	99.5	100	99	1.00	87	1.02	78	1.10
25	Singapore	88.6	92	99.6	100	..	..	..	1.01	79	1.35
26	Slovenia	99.6[k]	100[k]	99.8[k]	100[k]	93	0.99	94	1.01	79	1.35
27	Portugal	..	..	..	..	99	0.99	89	1.11	64	1.35
28	Korea, Rep. of	..	..	..	..	100[l]	1.00[l]	88[l]	1.00[l]	64[l]	0.61[l]
29	Cyprus	95.1	96	99.8	100	96	1.00	94	1.03	33	1.03
30	Barbados	99.7[k]	100[k]	99.8[k]	100[k]	100	1.00	90	1.00	55[g]	2.47[g]
31	Czech Republic	..	..	..	..	87	1.00	92	1.03	37	1.07
32	Malta	89.2[m]	103[m]	97.8[m]	104[m]	96	0.99	88	1.02	35	1.40
33	Brunei Darussalam	90.2	95	98.9	100	..	..	..	..	17	1.76
34	Argentina	97.2	100	99.1	100	..	..	84	1.06	72	1.49
35	Hungary	99.3	100	99.6	100	90	1.00	94	1.00	59	1.37
36	Poland	..	..	..	..	98	1.00	83	0.99	71	1.42
37	Chile	95.6	100	99.2	100	84[l]	0.99[l]	81[l]	1.01[l]	44[l]	0.94[l]
38	Estonia	99.8	100	99.8	100	94	0.99	90	1.04	83	1.66
39	Lithuania	99.6	100	99.7	100	91	1.00	94	1.01	88	1.56
40	Qatar	..	..	..	..	94	1.00	85[f]	1.06[f]	32	2.71
41	United Arab Emirates	80.7[k]	107[k]	95.0[k]	108[k]	82	0.98	72	1.03	53[f]	2.55[f]
42	Slovakia	99.6	100	99.7	100	86	1.01	88	1.01	36	1.17
43	Bahrain	83.0	90	99.3	100	91	1.02	90	1.08	44	1.89
44	Kuwait	81.0[k]	96[k]	93.9[k]	102[k]	84	1.02	79[f, h]	1.05[f, h]	32[f, n]	2.58[f, n]
45	Croatia	97.1	98	99.7	100	89	0.99	87	1.02	43	1.18
46	Uruguay	98.1[k]	101[k]	99.4[k]	101[k]	91	1.00	77	1.10	50[f]	1.95[f]
47	Costa Rica	95.9[k]	100[k]	98.7[k]	101[k]	91	1.02	55	1.09	21	1.16
48	Latvia	99.7	100	99.8	100	85	0.99	88	1.01	91	1.66
49	Saint Kitts and Nevis	..	..	..	..	..	..	100[h]	1.06[h]	..	..
50	Bahamas	..	..	..	..	88[f]	1.03[f]	77[f]	1.04[f]	..	..
51	Seychelles	92.3	101	99.4	101	99	0.99	100	1.00	..	..
52	Cuba	96.8[k]	100[k]	99.8[k]	100[k]	93	0.99	86	1.00	39	1.34
53	Mexico	88.7	96	97.3	99	100	1.01	64	1.04	22	0.97

TABLE 27

Gender inequality in education

HDI rank		Adult literacy [a] Female rate (% ages 15 and above) 2003	Adult literacy [a] Female rate as % of male rate 2003	Youth literacy [a] Female rate (% ages 15–24) 2003	Youth literacy [a] Female rate as % of male rate 2003	MDG Net primary enrolment [b, c] Female ratio (%) 2002/03	MDG Net primary enrolment [b, c] Ratio of female to male [e] 2002/03	MDG Net secondary enrolment [b, c] Female ratio (%) 2002/03	MDG Net secondary enrolment [b, c] Ratio of female to male [e] 2002/03	MDG Gross tertiary enrolment [c, d] Female ratio (%) 2002/03	MDG Gross tertiary enrolment [c, d] Ratio of female to male [e] 2002/03
54	Tonga	99.0 [m]	100 [m]	99.4 [m]	100 [m]	100 [h]	1.00 [h]	77 [f, h]	1.14 [f, h]	4 [f, h]	1.40 [f, h]
55	Bulgaria	97.7	99	98.1	100	90	0.99	86	0.98	42	1.18
56	Panama	91.2	99	95.6	99	99	0.99	66 [f]	1.11 [f]	55	1.69
57	Trinidad and Tobago	97.9 [k]	99 [k]	99.8 [k]	100 [k]	90	0.99	75 [f]	1.08 [f]	11	1.59
MEDIUM HUMAN DEVELOPMENT											
58	Libyan Arab Jamahiriya	70.7 [k]	77 [k]	94.0 [k]	94 [k]	..	..	..	..	61 [f]	1.09 [f]
59	Macedonia, TFYR	94.1	96	98.5	99	91	1.00	80 [f, h]	0.97 [f, h]	32	1.34
60	Antigua and Barbuda	..	..	..	..	..	..	..	..	..	..
61	Malaysia	85.4	93	97.3	100	93	1.00	74	1.11	33	1.28
62	Russian Federation	99.2	100	99.8	100	90 [f]	1.02 [f]	..	..	79 [f]	1.31 [f]
63	Brazil	88.6	100	97.7	102	91 [g]	0.93 [g]	78	1.08	23	1.32
64	Romania	96.3	98	97.8	100	88	0.99	82	1.03	39	1.24
65	Mauritius	80.5	91	95.4	102	98	1.02	74 [f]	1.00 [f]	18	1.41
66	Grenada	..	..	..	..	80 [f, g]	0.90 [f, g]	..	..	..	..
67	Belarus	99.4 [m]	100 [m]	99.8 [m]	100 [m]	94 [f]	0.99 [f]	86 [f]	1.04 [f]	72	1.39
68	Bosnia and Herzegovina	91.1	93	99.7	100	..	..	..	..	..	..
69	Colombia	94.6	101	98.4	102	87 [f]	0.99 [f]	58 [f]	1.10 [f]	25	1.09
70	Dominica	..	..	..	..	79	0.95	98 [f]	1.14 [f]	..	..
71	Oman	65.4 [k]	80 [k]	97.3 [k]	98 [k]	72	1.01	70	1.01	10 [f, h]	1.67 [f, h]
72	Albania	98.3	99	99.5	100	94	0.98	78	1.02	21	1.78
73	Thailand	90.5	95	97.8	100	84 [f]	0.97 [f]	..	..	42 [f]	1.17 [f]
74	Samoa (Western)	98.4 [k]	99 [k]	99.5 [k]	100 [k]	96 [f]	0.98 [f]	65 [f]	1.11 [f]	6 [f, h]	0.90 [f, h]
75	Venezuela	92.7	99	98.1	102	91	1.01	64	1.16	42 [f]	1.08 [f]
76	Saint Lucia	90.6	101	95.9	101	100	1.01	85 [f]	1.25 [f]	..	..
77	Saudi Arabia	69.3	80	93.7	96	54	0.99	52 [f]	0.96 [f]	30	1.47
78	Ukraine	99.2	99	99.8	100	84 [f]	1.00 [f]	85 [f]	1.01 [f]	67 [j]	1.19 [j]
79	Peru	82.1	88	95.7	98	100	1.00	68	0.97	33 [f]	1.07 [f]
80	Kazakhstan	99.3 [m]	100 [m]	99.9 [m]	100 [m]	91	0.99	87	1.00	51	1.31
81	Lebanon	..	..	..	..	90	0.99	..	..	48	1.19
82	Ecuador	89.7	97	96.5	100	100	1.01	51	1.03	..	..
83	Armenia	99.2	99	99.9	100	93	0.98	85	1.03	31	1.26
84	Philippines	92.7	100	95.7	101	95	1.02	65	1.19	34	1.28
85	China	86.5	91	98.5	99	..	..	..	..	14	0.84
86	Suriname	84.1	91	92.1	97	98 [f]	1.02 [f]	74 [f]	1.38 [f]	15 [h]	1.69 [h]
87	Saint Vincent and the Grenadines	..	..	..	..	90	0.99	61	1.09	..	..
88	Paraguay	90.2	97	96.5	100	89	1.00	53	1.06	31 [f]	1.39 [f]
89	Tunisia	65.3	78	92.2	96	97	1.00	68	1.11	30	1.28
90	Jordan	84.7	89	98.9	100	93	1.02	81	1.03	37	1.10
91	Belize	77.1	101	84.5	101	100	1.02	71 [f]	1.05 [f]	3 [j]	1.91 [j]
92	Fiji	91.4 [m]	97 [m]	99.4 [m]	100 [m]	100 [f, h]	1.00 [f, h]	79 [f, h]	1.07 [f, h]	..	..
93	Sri Lanka	88.6 [o]	96 [o]	96.0 [o]	101 [o]	..	..	..	..	..	..
94	Turkey	81.1	85	94.8	96	84	0.94	..	..	24	0.76
95	Dominican Republic	87.3	99	95.0	102	94 [f]	0.95 [f]	41 [f]	1.34 [f]	43	1.67
96	Maldives	97.2 [k]	100 [k]	99.2 [k]	100 [k]	93	1.00	55 [f]	1.15 [f]	..	..
97	Turkmenistan	98.3 [m]	99 [m]	99.8 [m]	100 [m]	..	..	..	..	..	..
98	Jamaica	91.4 [k]	109 [k]	97.8 [k]	107 [k]	95	1.00	77 [f]	1.04 [f]	25 [f]	2.36 [f]
99	Iran, Islamic Rep. of	70.4	84	..	..	85	0.97	..	..	22	1.07
100	Georgia	..	..	..	..	88	0.98	61	0.98	38	0.98
101	Azerbaijan	98.2 [m]	99 [m]	99.9 [m]	100 [m]	79	0.97	75	0.98	14	0.78
102	Occupied Palestinian Territories	87.4	91	98.6	100	91	1.00	86	1.05	35	1.04
103	Algeria	60.1	76	86.1	92	94	0.97	69 [f]	1.05 [f]	..	..
104	El Salvador	77.1 [k]	94 [k]	88.1 [k]	98 [k]	90	1.00	49 [f]	1.02 [f]	19	1.21
105	Cape Verde	68.0 [k]	80 [k]	86.3 [k]	94 [k]	98	0.98	61	1.11	5	1.09
106	Syrian Arab Republic	74.2	82	93.0	96	96	0.96	41	0.93	..	..

TABLE 27

HDI rank	Adult literacy[a]		Youth literacy[a] MDG		Net primary enrolment[b,c] MDG		Net secondary enrolment[b,c] MDG		Gross tertiary enrolment[c,d] MDG	
	Female rate (% ages 15 and above) 2003	Female rate as % of male rate 2003	Female rate (% ages 15–24) 2003	Female rate as % of male rate 2003	Female ratio (%) 2002/03	Ratio of female to male[e] 2002/03	Female ratio (%) 2002/03	Ratio of female to male[e] 2002/03	Female ratio (%) 2002/03	Ratio of female to male[e] 2002/03
107 Guyana	..	..	..	..	98[f]	0.98[f]	78[f,g]	1.04[f,g]	7[f]	1.58[f]
108 Viet Nam	86.9[m]	93[m]	..	..	92[f,g]	0.94[f,g]	..	..	9[f]	0.76[f]
109 Kyrgyzstan	98.1[m]	99[m]	99.7[m]	100[m]	88	0.96	..	..	46	1.19
110 Indonesia	83.4[k]	90[k]	97.6[k]	99[k]	92	0.98	54	0.99	15	0.80
111 Uzbekistan	98.9[k]	99[k]	99.6[k]	100[k]	..	..	..	..	14	0.80
112 Nicaragua	76.6	100	88.8	106	85	1.00	42	1.18	19	1.10
113 Bolivia	80.4	87	96.1	98	95	1.00	71[f]	0.98[f]	22[f,n]	0.55[f,n]
114 Mongolia	97.5	100	98.4	101	80	1.03	83	1.16	47	1.69
115 Moldova, Rep. of	95.0	98	99.1	101	79	0.99	70	1.04	34	1.32
116 Honduras	80.2	101	90.9	105	88[f,h]	1.02[f,h]	..	..	17[f,h]	1.31[f,h]
117 Guatemala	63.3	84	78.4	91	86	0.97	29	0.95	8	0.78
118 Vanuatu	..	..	..	..	95[f]	1.02[f]	28[h]	1.01[h]	..	..
119 Egypt	43.6[m]	65[m]	66.9[m]	85[m]	90[f]	0.96[f]	79[f,h]	0.95[f,h]	..	..
120 South Africa	80.9[m]	96[m]	94.3[m]	101[m]	89	1.01	68[f]	1.09[f]	16	1.15
121 Equatorial Guinea	76.4	83	93.7	100	78[h]	0.85[h]	19[f,i]	0.58[f,i]	2[i]	0.43[i]
122 Tajikistan	99.3	100	99.8	100	91[n]	0.94[n]	76[f]	0.85[f]	8	0.34
123 Gabon	..	..	..	..	78[f,g]	0.99[f,g]	..	..	5[n]	0.54[n]
124 Morocco	38.3[k]	61[k]	61.3[k]	79[k]	87	0.94	33[f]	0.86[f]	10	0.84
125 Namibia	83.5	96	93.5	103	81	1.07	50	1.29	7	0.89
126 São Tomé and Principe	..	..	..	..	94[f,h]	0.94[f,h]	26[f,h]	0.83[f,h]	1[f,h]	0.56[f,h]
127 India	47.8	65	67.7	80	85	0.94	..	..	10	0.68
128 Solomon Islands	..	..	..	..	..	..	..	..	..	..
129 Myanmar	86.2	92	93.2	98	85	1.01	34	0.94	15[f,g]	1.75[f,g]
130 Cambodia	64.1	76	78.9	90	91	0.95	19[f]	0.64[f]	2[f]	0.40[f]
131 Botswana	81.5[k]	107[k]	92.8[k]	109[k]	83[f]	1.04[f]	57[f]	1.15[f]	4[f]	0.75[f]
132 Comoros	49.1[k]	77[k]	52.2[k]	79[k]	50[f,i]	0.84[f,i]	..	..	2	0.77
133 Lao People's Dem. Rep.	60.9	79	74.7	90	82	0.93	32	0.83	4	0.57
134 Bhutan	..	..	..	..	..	..	..	..	..	..
135 Pakistan	35.2	57	53.9	72	50[f,g]	0.74[f,g]	..	..	2	0.81
136 Nepal	34.9	56	60.1	75	66[f,g]	0.88[f,g]	..	..	3	0.34
137 Papua New Guinea	50.9	80	64.1	93	69[f,h]	0.90[f,h]	21[f,h]	0.79[f,h]	1[f]	0.54[n]
138 Ghana	45.7	73	..	..	53[i]	0.81[i]	33[f,i]	0.85[f,i]	2[i]	0.46[i]
139 Bangladesh	31.4[k]	62[k]	41.1[k]	71[k]	86	1.04	47	1.11	4	0.50
140 Timor-Leste	..	..	..	..	..	..	..	..	15[h,j]	1.58[h,j]
141 Sudan	49.9[o]	72[o]	69.2[o]	85[o]	42[f,i]	0.83[f,i]	..	..	6[f,i]	0.92[f,i]
142 Congo	77.1[k]	87[k]	97.3[k]	99[k]	53	0.96	..	..	1[f]	0.14[f]
143 Togo	38.3	56	63.3	76	83	0.84	17[f,i]	0.48[f,i]	1[i]	0.20[i]
144 Uganda	59.2[k]	75[k]	74.0[k]	86[k]	..	..	16[f]	0.90[f]	2[f]	0.52[f]
145 Zimbabwe	86.3[k]	92[k]	96.2[k]	97[k]	80[i]	1.02[i]	33[i]	0.93[i]	3[f,i]	0.63[f,i]
LOW HUMAN DEVELOPMENT										
146 Madagascar	65.2	85	68.1	94	79	1.00	12[f,n]	1.03[f,n]	2	0.83
147 Swaziland	78.1	97	89.4	103	75	1.00	36[f]	1.21[f]	5[f]	1.16[f]
148 Cameroon	59.8	78	..	..	..	..	..	..	4[f]	0.63[f]
149 Lesotho	90.3	123	..	..	89	1.07	27[f]	1.53[f]	4	1.48
150 Djibouti	..	..	..	..	32[i]	0.80[i]	17[f,i]	0.69[f,i]	2[i]	0.81[i]
151 Yemen	28.5[k]	41[k]	50.9[k]	60[k]	59	0.71	21[f,i]	0.46[f,i]	5[f,i]	0.28[f,i]
152 Mauritania	43.4	73	55.5	82	67	0.97	14[f]	0.77[f]	2[f]	0.27[f]
153 Haiti	50.0[k]	93[k]	66.5[k]	101[k]	..	..	..	..	..	..
154 Kenya	70.2	90	80.7	101	66	1.00	24[f]	0.98[f]	2[f,h]	0.53[f,h]
155 Gambia	..	..	..	..	78[f]	0.99[f]	27[f]	0.68[f]	1[n]	0.29[n]
156 Guinea	..	..	..	..	58	0.80	13[f]	0.48[f]	..	..
157 Senegal	29.2	57	41.0	70	54[f]	0.89[f]	..	..	..	..
158 Nigeria	59.4[k]	80[k]	86.5[k]	95[k]	60[f]	0.82[f]	26	0.80	7[f]	0.69[f]
159 Rwanda	58.8	84	75.9	98	88	1.04	..	..	2	0.46

Human development indicators

TABLE 27

Gender inequality in education

HDI rank	Adult literacy [a] Female rate (% ages 15 and above) 2003	Adult literacy [a] Female rate as % of male rate 2003	MDG Youth literacy [a] Female rate (% ages 15–24) 2003	MDG Youth literacy [a] Female rate as % of male rate 2003	MDG Net primary enrolment [b, c] Female ratio (%) 2002/03	MDG Net primary enrolment [b, c] Ratio of female to male [e] 2002/03	MDG Net secondary enrolment [b, c] Female ratio (%) 2002/03	MDG Net secondary enrolment [b, c] Ratio of female to male [e] 2002/03	MDG Gross tertiary enrolment [c, d] Female ratio (%) 2002/03	MDG Gross tertiary enrolment [c, d] Ratio of female to male [e] 2002/03
160 Angola	53.8	66	62.6	76	57 [f, n]	0.86 [f, n]	..	..	1 [j]	0.65 [j]
161 Eritrea	..	..	..	..	42	0.86	18	0.74	(.) [f]	0.15 [f]
162 Benin	22.6	49	32.5	56	47 [f, i]	0.69 [f, i]	13 [f, g]	0.48 [f, g]	1 [j]	0.24 [j]
163 Côte d'Ivoire	38.2	64	51.5	74	54 [j]	0.81 [j]	15 [f, h]	0.57 [f, h]	4 [n]	0.36 [n]
164 Tanzania, U. Rep. of	62.2	80	76.2	94	81 [p]	0.98 [p]	..	..	1	0.44
165 Malawi	54.0 [m]	72 [m]	70.7 [m]	86 [m]	..	..	26 [f]	0.81 [f]	(.)	0.41
166 Zambia	59.7 [m]	78 [m]	66.1 [m]	91 [m]	68	0.98	21 [f]	0.83 [f]	2 [f, g]	0.46 [f, g]
167 Congo, Dem. Rep. of the	51.9	65	61.1	80	..	..	..	..	..	..
168 Mozambique	31.4 [k]	50 [k]	49.2 [k]	64 [k]	53	0.91	10	0.70	(.) [f, i]	0.73 [f, i]
169 Burundi	51.9	78	69.5	92	52	0.84	8 [f]	0.78 [f]	1 [f]	0.45 [f]
170 Ethiopia	33.8 [k]	69 [k]	51.8 [k]	82 [k]	47 [l]	0.85 [l]	13 [f, l]	0.57 [f, l]	1 [l]	0.33 [l]
171 Central African Republic	33.5	52	46.8	67	..	..	..	..	1 [j]	0.19 [j]
172 Guinea-Bissau	..	..	..	..	38 [i]	0.71 [i]	6 [f, i]	0.55 [f, i]	(.) [j]	0.18 [j]
173 Chad	12.7	31	23.1	42	51 [f]	0.68 [f]	4 [f, g]	0.31 [f, g]	(.) [j]	0.17 [j]
174 Mali	11.9 [m]	44 [m]	16.9 [m]	52 [m]	39	0.77	..	..	..	..
175 Burkina Faso	8.1 [m]	44 [m]	14.0 [m]	55 [m]	31	0.73	7	0.67	1 [f]	0.34 [f]
176 Sierra Leone	20.5	52	29.9	64	..	..	..	..	1 [f, h]	0.40 [f, h]
177 Niger	9.4	48	14.2	54	31	0.69	5	0.67	1 [f, h]	0.34 [f, h]
Developing countries	69.6	84	81.2	92	..	..	..	..	..	..
Least developed countries	44.6	70	56.8	81	..	..	..	..	..	..
Arab States	53.1	71	75.8	87	..	..	..	..	..	..
East Asia and the Pacific	86.2	91	97.5	99	..	..	..	..	..	..
Latin America and the Caribbean	88.9	98	96.3	101	..	..	..	..	..	..
South Asia	46.6	66	63.3	79	..	..	..	..	..	..
Sub-Saharan Africa	52.6	76	67.9	88	..	..	..	..	..	..
Central and Eastern Europe and the CIS	98.6	99	99.6	100	..	..	..	..	..	..
OECD	..	..	..	..	..	..	..	..	..	..
High-income OECD	..	..	..	..	..	..	..	..	..	..
High human development	..	..	..	..	..	..	..	..	..	..
Medium human development	73.3	86	84.1	93	..	..	..	..	..	..
Low human development	47.9	73	63.6	86	..	..	..	..	..	..
High income	..	..	..	..	..	..	..	..	..	..
Middle income	86.2	93	96.3	99	..	..	..	..	..	..
Low income	49.9	70	65.4	82	..	..	..	..	..	..
World	..	..	..	..	..	..	..	..	..	..

NOTES

a Data refer to national literacy estimates from censuses or surveys conducted between 2000 and 2004, unless otherwise noted. Due to differences in methodology and timeliness of underlying data, comparisons across countries and over time should be made with caution. For more details, see www.uis.unesco.org/ev.php?ID=4930_201&ID2=DO_TOPIC.

b The net enrolment ratio is the ratio of enrolled children of the official age for the education level indicated to the total population at that age. Net enrolment ratios exceeding 100% reflect discrepancies between these two data sets.

c Data for some countries may refer to national or United Nations Educational, Scientific and Cultural Organization (UNESCO) Institute for Statistics estimates. For details, see www.uis.unesco.org. Because data are from different sources, comparisons across countries should be made with caution.

d Tertiary enrolment is generally calculated as a gross ratio.

e Calculated as the ratio of the female enrolment ratio to the male enrolment ratio.

f Preliminary UNESCO Institute for Statistics estimate, subject to further revision.

g Data refer to the 2000/01 school year.

h Data refer to the 2001/02 school year.

i Data refer to the 1999/2000 school year.

j National estimate.

k Estimate produced by UNESCO Institute for Statistics in July 2002.

l Data refer to the 2003/04 school year.

m Data refer to a year between 1995 and 1999.

n Data refer to the 1998/99 school year.

o Data refer to a year or period other than that specified, differ from the standard definition or refer to only part of a country.

p Data refer to the 2004/05 school year.

SOURCES

Columns 1 and 3: UNESCO Institute for Statistics 2005a.

Columns 2 and 4: calculated on the basis of data on adult literacy rates from UNESCO Institute for Statistics 2005a.

Columns 5, 7 and 9: UNESCO Institute for Statistics 2005c.

Columns 6, 8 and 10: calculated on the basis of data on net enrolment rates from UNESCO Institute for Statistics 2005c.

TABLE 28
... and achieving equality for all women and men

Gender inequality in economic activity

	Female economic activity (ages 15 and above)			Employment by economic activity (%)						Contributing family workers (%)	
				Agriculture		Industry		Services			
	Rate (%)	Index (1990=100)	As % of male rate	Women	Men	Women	Men	Women	Men	Women	Men
HDI rank	2003	2003	2003	1995–2002[a]	1995–2002[a]	1995–2002[a]	1995–2002[a]	1995–2002[a]	1995–2002[a]	1995–2003[a]	1995–2003[a]
HIGH HUMAN DEVELOPMENT											
1 Norway	60.3	111	86	2	6	9	33	88	58	63	38
2 Iceland	66.7	101	83	3	12	10	33	85	54	50	50
3 Australia	56.7	109	79	3	6	10	30	87	64	58	42
4 Luxembourg	38.3	104	58	..	..	..	..	..	..	..	..
5 Canada	60.7	105	83	2	4	11	33	87	64	65	35
6 Sweden	62.8	102	90	1	3	11	36	88	61	50	50
7 Switzerland	51.1	104	67	3	5	13	36	84	59	59	41
8 Ireland	38.3	119	54	2	11	14	39	83	50	53	47
9 Belgium	40.3	107	67	1	3	10	36	82	58	85	15
10 United States	59.6	107	83	1	3	12	32	87	65	63	37
11 Japan	51.2	104	68	5	5	21	37	73	57	81	19
12 Netherlands	46.0	107	68	2	4	9	31	86	64	80	20
13 Finland	56.8	98	87	4	7	14	40	82	53	42	58
14 Denmark	61.8	100	85	2	5	14	36	85	59	..	..
15 United Kingdom	53.5	106	76	1	2	11	36	88	62	68	32
16 France	49.3	108	78	1	2	13	34	86	64	..	..
17 Austria	44.2	103	66	6	5	14	43	80	52	67	33
18 Italy	39.0	108	60	5	6	20	39	75	55	54	46
19 New Zealand	58.4	111	81	6	12	12	32	82	56	61	39
20 Germany	48.0	101	71	2	3	18	44	80	52	78	22
21 Spain	38.5	114	58	5	8	15	42	81	51	63	37
22 Hong Kong, China (SAR)	51.2	105	66	(.)	(.)	10	27	90	73	87	13
23 Israel	49.5	116	69	1	3	12	34	86	62	76	24
24 Greece	38.7	109	60	18	15	12	30	70	56	69	31
25 Singapore	50.0	99	64	(.)	(.)	18	31	81	69	76	24
26 Slovenia	54.3	97	81	10	10	29	46	61	43	62	38
27 Portugal	51.8	105	72	14	12	23	44	63	44	70	30
28 Korea, Rep. of	54.4	113	71	12	9	19	34	70	57	88	12
29 Cyprus	49.3	103	63	4	5	13	31	83	58	84	16
30 Barbados	62.6	108	80	4	5	10	29	63	49	..	..
31 Czech Republic	61.3	100	83	3	6	28	50	68	44	86	14
32 Malta	26.5	114	38	1	3	21	36	78	61	..	..
33 Brunei Darussalam	51.0	113	64	..	..	..	..	..	..	..	..
34 Argentina	37.2	127	48	(.)	1	12	30	87	69	59	41
35 Hungary	48.7	102	72	4	9	26	42	71	49	70	30
36 Poland	57.0	99	81	19	19	18	40	63	40	58	42
37 Chile	39.0	122	50	5	18	13	29	83	53	..	..
38 Estonia	60.1	94	82	4	10	23	42	73	48	50	50
39 Lithuania	57.3	96	80	12	20	21	34	67	45	59	41
40 Qatar	42.6	129	47	..	..	..	..	..	..	..	..
41 United Arab Emirates	32.1	110	38	(.)	9	14	36	86	55	..	..
42 Slovakia	62.6	99	84	4	8	26	48	71	44	75	25
43 Bahrain	34.5	121	40	..	..	..	..	..	..	..	..
44 Kuwait	36.2	96	49	..	..	..	..	..	..	..	..
45 Croatia	49.0	102	74	15	16	21	37	63	47	73	27
46 Uruguay	48.9	110	68	2	6	14	32	85	62	74	25
47 Costa Rica	37.9	114	47	4	22	15	27	80	51	43	57
48 Latvia	59.0	94	80	12	18	16	35	72	47	50	50
49 Saint Kitts and Nevis	..	..	..	..	..	..	..	..	..	..	..
50 Bahamas	67.1	104	84	1	6	5	24	93	69	..	..
51 Seychelles	..	..	..	..	..	..	..	..	..	..	..
52 Cuba	51.5	122	67	..	..	..	..	..	..	..	..
53 Mexico	40.6	120	49	6	24	22	28	72	48	49	51

TABLE 28

Gender inequality in economic activity

	Female economic activity (ages 15 and above)			Employment by economic activity (%)						Contributing family workers (%)	
				Agriculture		Industry		Services			
HDI rank	Rate (%) 2003	Index (1990=100) 2003	As % of male rate 2003	Women 1995–2002[a]	Men 1995–2002[a]	Women 1995–2002[a]	Men 1995–2002[a]	Women 1995–2002[a]	Men 1995–2002[a]	Women 1995–2003[a]	Men 1995–2003[a]
54 Tonga	..	..	..	..	..	..	..	..	..	..	..
55 Bulgaria	55.8	93	85	..	..	..	..	..	..	..	..
56 Panama	44.3	114	56	6	29	10	20	85	51	36	64
57 Trinidad and Tobago	45.3	116	60	3	11	13	36	84	53	75	25
MEDIUM HUMAN DEVELOPMENT											
58 Libyan Arab Jamahiriya	25.9	126	35	..	..	..	..	..	..	..	..
59 Macedonia, TFYR	50.1	104	73	..	..	..	..	..	..	61	39
60 Antigua and Barbuda	..	..	..	..	..	..	..	..	..	..	..
61 Malaysia	49.2	110	62	14	21	29	34	57	45	..	..
62 Russian Federation	59.1	98	83	8	15	23	36	69	49	42	58
63 Brazil	43.7	98	52	16	24	10	27	74	49	..	..
64 Romania	50.3	97	76	45	40	22	30	33	30	71	29
65 Mauritius	38.7	112	49	13	15	43	39	45	46	..	..
66 Grenada	..	..	..	10	17	12	32	77	46	..	..
67 Belarus	59.0	97	82	..	..	..	..	..	..	..	..
68 Bosnia and Herzegovina	43.1	99	60	..	..	..	..	..	..	..	..
69 Colombia	49.3	116	62	7	33	17	19	76	48	58	42
70 Dominica	..	..	..	14	31	10	24	72	40	..	..
71 Oman	20.3	160	27	..	..	..	..	..	..	..	..
72 Albania	60.2	104	74	..	..	..	..	..	..	..	..
73 Thailand	72.9	97	85	48	50	17	20	35	30	66	34
74 Samoa (Western)	..	..	..	..	..	..	..	..	..	..	..
75 Venezuela	44.2	117	55	2	15	12	28	86	57	..	..
76 Saint Lucia	..	..	..	16	27	14	24	71	49	..	..
77 Saudi Arabia	22.4	150	29	..	..	..	..	..	..	..	..
78 Ukraine	55.3	98	80	17	22	22	39	55	33	60	40
79 Peru	35.6	121	45	6	11	10	24	84	65	66	34
80 Kazakhstan	61.2	101	82	..	..	..	..	..	..	..	..
81 Lebanon	30.7	126	40	..	..	..	..	..	..	..	..
82 Ecuador	33.7	121	40	4	10	16	30	79	60	64	36
83 Armenia	62.3	99	89	..	..	..	..	..	..	..	..
84 Philippines	50.1	107	62	25	45	12	18	63	37	..	..
85 China	72.4	98	86	..	..	..	..	..	..	..	..
86 Suriname	37.6	126	50	2	8	1	22	97	64	..	..
87 Saint Vincent and the Grenadines	..	..	..	..	..	..	..	..	..	..	..
88 Paraguay	37.5	111	44	20	39	10	21	69	40	..	..
89 Tunisia	37.7	115	48	..	..	..	..	..	..	..	..
90 Jordan	28.1	165	36	..	..	..	..	..	..	..	..
91 Belize	27.7	116	33	6	37	12	19	81	44	32	68
92 Fiji	39.5	149	49	..	..	..	..	..	..	..	..
93 Sri Lanka	43.5	108	56	49	38	22	23	27	37	56	44
94 Turkey	51.2	117	63	56	24	15	28	29	48	68	32
95 Dominican Republic	41.2	121	49	2	21	17	26	81	53	23	77
96 Maldives	65.4	101	80	5	18	24	16	39	55	57	43
97 Turkmenistan	62.7	105	82	..	..	..	..	..	..	..	..
98 Jamaica	67.3	101	86	10	30	9	26	81	45	66	34
99 Iran, Islamic Rep. of	30.5	141	39	..	..	..	..	..	..	46	54
100 Georgia	55.7	100	79	53	53	6	12	41	35	57	43
101 Azerbaijan	55.2	107	76	43	37	7	14	50	49	..	..
102 Occupied Palestinian Territories	9.6	153	14	26	9	11	32	62	58	46	54
103 Algeria	31.6	165	41	..	..	..	..	..	..	..	..
104 El Salvador	47.6	128	56	4	34	22	25	74	42	39	61
105 Cape Verde	46.9	110	54	..	..	..	..	..	..	..	..
106 Syrian Arab Republic	29.5	125	38	..	..	..	..	..	..	..	..

TABLE 28

	Female economic activity (ages 15 and above)			Employment by economic activity (%)						Contributing family workers (%)	
				Agriculture		Industry		Services			
	Rate (%)	Index (1990=100)	As % of male rate	Women	Men	Women	Men	Women	Men	Women	Men
HDI rank	2003	2003	2003	1995–2002[a]	1995–2002[a]	1995–2002[a]	1995–2002[a]	1995–2002[a]	1995–2002[a]	1995–2003[a]	1995–2003[a]
107 Guyana	41.9	117	51	..	..	..	..	..	..	..	..
108 Viet Nam	73.3	96	91	..	..	..	..	..	..	..	..
109 Kyrgyzstan	61.4	105	85	53	52	8	14	38	34	..	..
110 Indonesia	56.3	112	69	43	43	16	19	41	38	..	..
111 Uzbekistan	63.0	107	86	..	..	..	..	..	..	..	..
112 Nicaragua	48.5	120	58	..	..	..	..	..	..	..	..
113 Bolivia	48.6	107	58	3	6	14	39	82	55	63	37
114 Mongolia	73.9	103	88	..	..	..	..	..	..	70	30
115 Moldova, Rep. of	60.2	98	84	50	52	10	18	40	31	70	30
116 Honduras	41.6	123	49	9	50	25	21	67	30	40	60
117 Guatemala	37.7	134	44	18	50	23	18	56	27	..	..
118 Vanuatu	..	..	..	..	..	..	..	..	..	..	..
119 Egypt	36.0	119	46	39	27	7	25	54	48	33	67
120 South Africa	47.3	102	59	9	12	14	33	75	50	..	..
121 Equatorial Guinea	45.8	101	52	..	..	..	..	..	..	..	..
122 Tajikistan	58.9	113	81	..	..	..	..	..	..	..	..
123 Gabon	63.2	101	77	..	..	..	..	..	..	..	..
124 Morocco	41.9	108	53	6	6	40	32	54	63	19	81
125 Namibia	53.7	101	68	29	33	7	17	63	49	..	..
126 São Tomé and Principe	..	..	..	..	..	..	..	..	..	..	..
127 India	42.5	105	50	..	..	..	..	..	..	..	..
128 Solomon Islands	80.8	97	92	..	..	..	..	..	..	..	..
129 Myanmar	65.8	99	75	..	..	..	..	..	..	..	..
130 Cambodia	80.1	98	97	..	..	..	..	..	..	64	36
131 Botswana	62.4	95	76	17	22	14	26	67	51	45	55
132 Comoros	62.3	99	73	..	..	..	..	..	..	..	..
133 Lao People's Dem. Rep.	74.6	101	85	..	..	..	..	..	..	..	..
134 Bhutan	57.1	100	65	..	..	..	..	..	..	..	..
135 Pakistan	36.7	129	44	73	44	9	20	18	36	33	67
136 Nepal	56.9	101	67	..	..	..	..	..	..	..	..
137 Papua New Guinea	67.6	100	79	..	..	..	..	..	..	..	..
138 Ghana	79.8	98	98	..	..	..	..	..	..	..	..
139 Bangladesh	66.5	101	76	77	53	9	11	12	30	81	19
140 Timor-Leste	73.1	96	86	..	..	..	..	..	..	..	..
141 Sudan	35.7	116	42	..	..	..	..	..	..	..	..
142 Congo	58.4	100	71	..	..	..	..	..	..	..	..
143 Togo	53.5	101	62	..	..	..	..	..	..	..	..
144 Uganda	79.1	98	88	..	..	..	..	..	..	..	..
145 Zimbabwe	64.9	97	78	..	..	..	..	..	..	..	..
LOW HUMAN DEVELOPMENT											
146 Madagascar	68.9	99	78	..	..	..	..	..	..	..	..
147 Swaziland	42.1	107	52	..	..	..	..	..	..	..	..
148 Cameroon	49.7	105	59	..	..	..	..	..	..	..	..
149 Lesotho	47.7	103	56	..	..	..	..	..	..	..	..
150 Djibouti	..	..	..	..	..	..	..	..	..	..	..
151 Yemen	30.9	110	37	88	43	3	14	9	43	26	74
152 Mauritania	63.1	97	74	..	..	..	..	..	..	..	..
153 Haiti	55.6	97	70	37	63	6	15	57	23	..	..
154 Kenya	74.7	100	85	16	20	10	23	75	57	..	..
155 Gambia	69.8	101	78	..	..	..	..	..	..	..	..
156 Guinea	77.0	97	89	..	..	..	..	..	..	..	..
157 Senegal	61.8	101	72	..	..	..	..	..	..	..	..
158 Nigeria	47.8	102	56	2	4	11	30	87	67	..	..
159 Rwanda	82.3	98	88	..	..	..	..	..	..	..	..

Human development indicators

TABLE 28

Gender inequality in economic activity

HDI rank	Female economic activity (ages 15 and above)			Employment by economic activity (%)						Contributing family workers (%)	
	Rate (%) 2003	Index (1990=100) 2003	As % of male rate 2003	Agriculture Women 1995–2002[a]	Agriculture Men 1995–2002[a]	Industry Women 1995–2002[a]	Industry Men 1995–2002[a]	Services Women 1995–2002[a]	Services Men 1995–2002[a]	Women 1995–2003[a]	Men 1995–2003[a]
160 Angola	72.5	98	82	..	..	..	..	..	..	..	..
161 Eritrea	74.5	98	87	..	..	..	..	..	..	..	..
162 Benin	73.1	96	90	..	..	..	..	..	..	..	..
163 Côte d'Ivoire	44.0	102	51	..	..	..	..	..	..	..	..
164 Tanzania, U. Rep. of	81.4	97	93	..	..	..	..	..	..	..	..
165 Malawi	77.5	97	90	..	..	..	..	..	..	..	..
166 Zambia	63.9	98	74	..	..	..	..	..	..	..	..
167 Congo, Dem. Rep. of the	60.3	97	72	..	..	..	..	..	..	..	..
168 Mozambique	82.6	99	92	..	..	..	..	..	..	..	..
169 Burundi	81.7	98	89	..	..	..	..	..	..	..	..
170 Ethiopia	57.2	98	67	..	..	..	..	..	..	..	..
171 Central African Republic	67.1	96	78	..	..	..	..	..	..	..	..
172 Guinea-Bissau	57.0	100	63	..	..	..	..	..	..	..	..
173 Chad	67.4	102	77	..	..	..	..	..	..	..	..
174 Mali	69.6	97	79	..	..	..	..	..	..	..	..
175 Burkina Faso	74.6	97	85	..	..	..	..	..	..	..	..
176 Sierra Leone	45.2	107	55	..	..	..	..	..	..	..	..
177 Niger	69.3	99	75	..	..	..	..	..	..	..	..
Developing countries	56.0	102	67	..	..	..	..	..	..	..	..
Least developed countries	64.3	100	74	..	..	..	..	..	..	..	..
Arab States	33.3	119	42	..	..	..	..	..	..	..	..
East Asia and the Pacific	68.9	100	83	..	..	..	..	..	..	..	..
Latin America and the Caribbean	42.7	110	52	..	..	..	..	..	..	..	..
South Asia	44.1	107	52	..	..	..	..	..	..	..	..
Sub-Saharan Africa	62.3	99	73	..	..	..	..	..	..	..	..
Central and Eastern Europe and the CIS	57.5	99	81	..	..	..	..	..	..	..	..
OECD	51.8	107	72	..	..	..	..	..	..	..	..
High-income OECD	52.8	107	75	..	..	..	..	..	..	..	..
High human development	51.1	106	71	..	..	..	..	..	..	..	..
Medium human development	56.4	101	68	..	..	..	..	..	..	..	..
Low human development	61.3	99	71	..	..	..	..	..	..	..	..
High income	52.5	107	74	..	..	..	..	..	..	..	..
Middle income	59.5	102	73	..	..	..	..	..	..	..	..
Low income	51.2	103	61	..	..	..	..	..	..	..	..
World	55.6	103	69	..	..	..	..	..	..	..	..

NOTES

As a result of limitations in the data, comparisons of labour statistics over time and across countries should be made with caution. For detailed notes on the data, see ILO 2002, 2003, 2005b. The percentage shares of employment by economic activity may not sum to 100 because of rounding or the omission of activities not classified.

a Data refer to the most recent year available during the period specified.

SOURCES

Columns 1–3: calculated on the basis of data on the economically active population and total population from ILO 2002.

Columns 4–9: ILO 2003.

Columns 10 and 11: calculated on the basis of data on contributing family workers from ILO 2005b.

TABLE 29

... and achieving equality for all women and men

Gender, work and time allocation

		Total work time (minutes per day)		Female work time (% of male)	Time allocation (%)					
					Total work time		Time spent by women		Time spent by men	
HDI rank	Year	Women	Men		Market activities	Non-market activities	Market activities	Non-market activities	Market activities	Non-market activities
SELECTED DEVELOPING COUNTRIES										
URBAN AREAS										
Colombia	1983	399	356	112	49	51	24	76	77	23
Indonesia	1992	398	366	109	60	40	35	65	86	14
Kenya	1986	590	572	103	46	54	41	59	79	21
Nepal	1978	579	554	105	58	42	25	75	67	33
Venezuela	1983	440	416	106	59	41	30	70	87	13
Average [a]		**481**	**453**	**107**	**54**	**46**	**31**	**69**	**79**	**21**
RURAL AREAS										
Bangladesh	1990	545	496	110	52	48	35	65	70	30
Guatemala	1977	678	579	117	59	41	37	63	84	16
Kenya	1988	676	500	135	56	44	42	58	76	24
Nepal	1978	641	547	117	56	44	46	54	67	33
Highlands	1978	692	586	118	59	41	52	48	66	34
Mountains	1978	649	534	122	56	44	48	52	65	35
Rural Hills	1978	583	520	112	52	48	37	63	70	30
Philippines	1975–77	546	452	121	73	27	29	71	84	16
Average [a]		**617**	**515**	**120**	**59**	**41**	**38**	**62**	**76**	**24**
NATIONAL [b]										
India	2000	457	391	117	61	39	35	65	92	8
Mongolia	2000	545	501	109	61	39	49	51	75	25
South Africa	2000	332	273	122	51	49	35	65	70	30
Average [a]		**445**	**388**	**116**	**58**	**42**	**40**	**60**	**79**	**21**
SELECTED OECD COUNTRIES [c]										
Australia	1997	435	418	104	46	54	30	70	62	38
Austria [d]	1992	438	393	111	49	51	31	69	71	29
Canada	1998	420	429	98	53	47	41	59	65	35
Denmark [d]	1987	449	458	98	68	32	58	42	79	21
Finland [d]	1987–88	430	410	105	51	49	39	61	64	36
France	1999	391	363	108	46	54	33	67	60	40
Germany [d]	1991–92	440	441	100	44	56	30	70	61	39
Hungary	1999	432	445	97	51	49	41	59	60	40
Israel [d]	1991–92	375	377	99	51	49	29	71	74	26
Italy [d]	1988–89	470	367	128	45	55	22	78	77	23
Japan	1996	393	363	108	66	34	43	57	93	7
Korea, Rep. of	1999	431	373	116	64	36	45	55	88	12
Latvia	1996	535	481	111	46	54	35	65	58	42
Netherlands	1995	308	315	98	48	52	27	73	69	31
New Zealand	1999	420	417	101	46	54	32	68	60	40
Norway [d]	1990–91	445	412	108	50	50	38	62	64	36
United Kingdom [d]	1985	413	411	100	51	49	37	63	68	32
United States [d]	1985	453	428	106	50	50	37	63	63	37
Average [e]		**423**	**403**	**105**	**52**	**48**	**37**	**64**	**69**	**31**

NOTES

Data are estimates based on time use surveys available in time for publication. Time use data have also being collected in other countries, including Benin, Chad, Cuba, the Dominican Republic, Ecuador, Guatemala, the Lao People's Democratic Republic, Mali, Mexico, Morocco, Nepal, Nicaragua, Nigeria, Oman, the Philippines, Thailand and Viet Nam. Market activities refer to market-oriented production activities as defined by the 1993 revised

UN System of National Accounts; surveys before 1993 are not strictly comparable with those for later years.

a Refers to the unweighted average for countries or areas shown above.

b Classifications of market and non-market activities are not strictly based on the 1993 revised UN System of National Accounts, so comparisons between countries and areas must be made with caution.

c Includes Israel and Latvia although they are not Organisation for Economic Co-operation and Development (OECD) countries.

d Goldshmidt-Clermont and Aligisakis 1995.

e Refers to the unweighted average for the selected OECD countries above (excluding Israel and Latvia).

SOURCES

Columns 1–10: For urban and rural areas in selected developing countries, Harvey 1995; for national studies in selected developing countries, UN 2002; for OECD countries and Latvia, Harvey 2001, unless otherwise noted.

Human development indicators

TABLE 30

... and achieving equality for all women and men

Women's political participation

		Year women received right [a]		Year first woman elected (E) or appointed (A) to parliament	Women in government at ministerial level (% of total) [b] 2005	MDG Seats in parliament held by women (% of total) [c]		Upper house or senate
						Lower or single house		
HDI rank		To vote	To stand for election			1990	2005	2005
HIGH HUMAN DEVELOPMENT								
1	Norway	1907	1907, 1913	1911 A	44.4	36	38.2	..
2	Iceland	1915, 1920	1915, 1920	1922 E	27.3	21	30.2	..
3	Australia	1902, 1962	1902, 1962	1943 E	20.0	6	24.7	35.5
4	Luxembourg	1919	1919	1919 E	14.3	13	23.3	..
5	Canada	1917, 1960	1920, 1960	1921 E	23.1	13	21.1	37.1
6	Sweden	1862, 1921	1907, 1921	1921 E	52.4	38	45.3	..
7	Switzerland	1971	1971	1971 E	14.3	14	25.0	23.9
8	Ireland	1918, 1928	1918, 1928	1918 E	21.4	8	13.3	16.7
9	Belgium	1919, 1948	1921, 1948	1921 A	21.4	9	34.7	38.0
10	United States	1920, 1965	1788 [d]	1917 E	14.3	7	15.0	14.0
11	Japan	1945, 1947	1945, 1947	1946 E	12.5	1	7.1	13.6
12	Netherlands	1919	1917	1918 E	36.0	21	36.7	29.3
13	Finland	1906	1906	1907 E	47.1	32	37.5	..
14	Denmark	1915	1915	1918 E	33.3	31	36.9	..
15	United Kingdom	1918, 1928	1918, 1928	1918 E	28.6	6	18.1	17.8
16	France	1944	1944	1945 E	17.6	7	12.2	16.9
17	Austria	1918	1918	1919 E	35.3	12	33.9	27.4
18	Italy	1945	1945	1946 E	8.3	13	11.5	8.1
19	New Zealand	1893	1919	1933 E	23.1	14	28.3	..
20	Germany	1918	1918	1919 E	46.2	0	32.8	18.8
21	Spain	1931	1931	1931 E	50.0	15	36.0	23.2
22	Hong Kong, China (SAR)	..	..	..	..	..	..	..
23	Israel	1948	1948	1949 E	16.7	7	15.0	..
24	Greece	1949, 1952	1949, 1952	1952 E	5.6	7	14.0	..
25	Singapore	1947	1947	1963 E	0	5	16.0	..
26	Slovenia	1945	1945	1992 E [e]	6.3	0	12.2	..
27	Portugal	1931, 1976	1931, 1976	1934 E	16.7	8	19.1	..
28	Korea, Rep. of	1948	1948	1948 E	5.6	2	13.0	..
29	Cyprus	1960	1960	1963 E	0	2	16.1	..
30	Barbados	1950	1950	1966 A	29.4	4	13.3	23.8
31	Czech Republic	1920	1920	1992 E [e]	11.1	0	17.0	12.3
32	Malta	1947	1947	1966 E	15.4	3	9.2	..
33	Brunei Darussalam	—	—	—	9.1	..	.. [f]	.. [f]
34	Argentina	1947	1947	1951 E	8.3	6	33.7	33.3
35	Hungary	1918	1918	1920 E	11.8	21	9.1	..
36	Poland	1918	1918	1919 E	5.9	14	20.2	23.0
37	Chile	1931, 1949	1931, 1949	1951 E	16.7	0	12.5	4.2
38	Estonia	1918	1918	1919 E	15.4	0	18.8	..
39	Lithuania	1921	1921	1920 A	15.4	0	22.0	..
40	Qatar	—	—	—	7.7	..	.. [f]	.. [f]
41	United Arab Emirates	—	—	—	5.6	0	0.0	..
42	Slovakia	1920	1920	1992 E [e]	0	0	16.7	..
43	Bahrain	1973 [g]	1973 [g]	2002 A	8.7	0	0.0	15.0
44	Kuwait	—	—	—	0	0	0.0 [h]	.. [h]
45	Croatia	1945	1945	1992 E [e]	33.3	0	21.7	..
46	Uruguay	1932	1932	1942 E	0	6	12.1	9.7
47	Costa Rica	1949	1949	1953 E	25.0	11	35.1	..
48	Latvia	1918	1918	..	23.5	0	21.0	..
49	Saint Kitts and Nevis	1951	1951	1984 E	0	7	0.0	..
50	Bahamas	1961, 1964	1961, 1964	1977 A	26.7	4	20.0	43.8
51	Seychelles	1948	1948	1976 E+A	12.5	16	29.4	..
52	Cuba	1934	1934	1940 E	16.2	34	36.0	..
53	Mexico	1947	1953	1952 A	9.4	12	24.2	21.9

Human development indicators

TABLE 30

		Year women received right [a]		Year first woman elected (E) or appointed (A) to parliament	Women in government at ministerial level (% of total) [b]	MDG Seats in parliament held by women (% of total) [c]		
						Lower or single house		Upper house or senate
HDI rank		To vote	To stand for election		2005	1990	2005	2005
54	Tonga	..	..	..	..	0	0.0	..
55	Bulgaria	1944	1944	1945 E	23.8	21	26.3	..
56	Panama	1941, 1946	1941, 1946	1946 E	14.3	8	16.7	..
57	Trinidad and Tobago	1946	1946	1962 E+A	18.2	17	19.4	32.3
MEDIUM HUMAN DEVELOPMENT								
58	Libyan Arab Jamahiriya	1964	1964	..	..	..	..	..
59	Macedonia, TFYR	1946	1946	1990 E [e]	16.7	0	19.2	..
60	Antigua and Barbuda	1951	1951	1984 A	15.4	0	10.5	17.6
61	Malaysia	1957	1957	1959 E	9.1	5	9.1	25.7
62	Russian Federation	1918	1918	1993 E [e]	0	0	9.8	3.4
63	Brazil	1934	1934	1933 E	11.4	5	8.6	12.3
64	Romania	1929, 1946	1929, 1946	1946 E	12.5	34	11.1	9.5
65	Mauritius	1956	1956	1976 E	8.0	7	5.7	..
66	Grenada	1951	1951	1976 E+A	40.0	0	26.7	38.5
67	Belarus	1919	1919	1990 E [e]	10.0	0	29.4	31.6
68	Bosnia and Herzegovina	1946	1946	1990 E [e]	11.1	0	16.7	0.0
69	Colombia	1954	1954	1954 A	35.7	5	12.0	8.8
70	Dominica	1951	1951	1980 E	0	10	19.4	..
71	Oman	1994, 2003	1994, 2003	..	10.0	0	2.4	15.5
72	Albania	1920	1920	1945 E	5.3	29	6.4	..
73	Thailand	1932	1932	1948 A	7.7	3	10.6	10.5
74	Samoa (Western)	1948, 1990	1948, 1990	1976 A	7.7	0	6.1	..
75	Venezuela	1946	1946	1948 E	13.6	10	9.7	..
76	Saint Lucia	1951	1951	1979 A	8.3	0	11.1	36.4
77	Saudi Arabia	—	—	—	0	0	0.0	..
78	Ukraine	1919	1919	1990 E [e]	5.6	0	5.3	..
79	Peru	1955	1955	1956 E	11.8	6	18.3	..
80	Kazakhstan	1924	1924	1990 E [e]	17.6	0	10.4	7.7
81	Lebanon	1952	1952	1991 A	6.9	0	2.3	..
82	Ecuador	1929, 1967	1929, 1967	1956 E	14.3	5	16.0	..
83	Armenia	1921	1921	1990 E [e]	0	36	5.3	..
84	Philippines	1937	1937	1941 E	25.0	9	15.3	16.7
85	China	1949	1949	1954 E	6.3	21	20.2	..
86	Suriname	1948	1948	1975 E	11.8	8	19.6	..
87	Saint Vincent and the Grenadines	1951	1951	1979 E	20.0	10	22.7	..
88	Paraguay	1961	1961	1963 E	30.8	6	10.0	8.9
89	Tunisia	1957, 1959	1957, 1959	1959 E	7.1	4	22.8	..
90	Jordan	1974	1974	1989 A	10.7	0	5.5	12.7
91	Belize	1954	1954	1984 E+A	6.3	0	6.7	25.0
92	Fiji	1963	1963	1970 A	9.1	0	8.5	12.5
93	Sri Lanka	1931	1931	1947 E	10.3	5	4.9	..
94	Turkey	1930, 1934	1930, 1934	1935 A	4.3	1	4.4	..
95	Dominican Republic	1942	1942	1942 E	14.3	8	17.3	6.3
96	Maldives	1932	1932	1979 E	11.8	6	12.0	..
97	Turkmenistan	1927	1927	1990 E [e]	9.5	26	..	..
98	Jamaica	1944	1944	1944 E	17.6	5	11.7	19.0
99	Iran, Islamic Rep. of	1963	1963	1963 E+A	6.7	2	4.1	..
100	Georgia	1918, 1921	1918, 1921	1992 E [e]	22.2	0	9.4	..
101	Azerbaijan	1921	1921	1990 E [e]	15.0	0	10.5	..
102	Occupied Palestinian Territories	..	..	..	..	..	..	..
103	Algeria	1962	1962	1962 A	10.5	2	6.2	2.8
104	El Salvador	1939	1961	1961 E	35.3	12	10.7	..
105	Cape Verde	1975	1975	1975 E	18.8	12	11.1	..
106	Syrian Arab Republic	1949, 1953	1953	1973 E	6.3	9	12.0	..

Human development indicators

TABLE 30

Women's political participation

				MDG		
			Women in government at ministerial level	Seats in parliament held by women (% of total)[c]		
	Year women received right[a]				Lower or single house	Upper house or senate
HDI rank	To vote	To stand for election	Year first woman elected (E) or appointed (A) to parliament	(% of total)[b] 2005	1990	2005	2005
---	---	---	---	---	---	---	---
107 Guyana	1953	1945	1968 E	22.2	37	30.8	..
108 Viet Nam	1946	1946	1976 E	11.5	18	27.3	..
109 Kyrgyzstan	1918	1918	1990 E[e]	12.5	0	3.2	..
110 Indonesia	1945	1945	1950 A	10.8	12	11.3	..
111 Uzbekistan	1938	1938	1990 E[e]	3.6	0	17.5	15.0
112 Nicaragua	1955	1955	1972 E	14.3	15	20.7	..
113 Bolivia	1938, 1952	1938, 1952	1966 E	6.7	9	19.2	11.1
114 Mongolia	1924	1924	1951 E	5.9	25	6.7	..
115 Moldova, Rep. of	1978	1978	1990 E	11.1	0	15.8	..
116 Honduras	1955	1955	1957 E	14.3	10	5.5	..
117 Guatemala	1946, 1985	1946, 1965	1956 E	25.0	7	8.2	..
118 Vanuatu	1975, 1980	1975, 1980	1987 E	8.3	4	3.8	..
119 Egypt	1956	1956	1957 E	5.9	4	2.9	6.8
120 South Africa	1930, 1994	1930, 1994	1933 E	41.4	3	32.8	33.3[i]
121 Equatorial Guinea	1963	1963	1968 E	4.5	13	18.0	..
122 Tajikistan	1924	1924	1990 E[e]	3.1	0	..	11.8
123 Gabon	1956	1956	1961 E	11.8	13	9.2	15.4
124 Morocco	1963	1963	1993 E	5.9	0	10.8	1.1
125 Namibia	1989	1989	1989 E	19.0	7	25.0	26.9
126 São Tomé and Principe	1975	1975	1975 E	14.3	12	9.1	..
127 India	1950	1950	1952 E	3.4	5	8.3	11.6
128 Solomon Islands	1974	1974	1993 E	0	0	0.0	..
129 Myanmar	1935	1946	1947 E	..	..	..[j]	..[j]
130 Cambodia	1955	1955	1958 E	7.1	0	9.8	13.1
131 Botswana	1965	1965	1979 E	26.7	5	11.1	..
132 Comoros	1956	1956	1993 E	..	0	3.0	..
133 Lao People's Dem. Rep.	1958	1958	1958 E	0	6	22.9	..
134 Bhutan	1953	1953	1975 E	0	2	8.7	..
135 Pakistan	1947	1947	1973 E[e]	5.6	10	21.3	18.0
136 Nepal	1951	1951	1952 A	7.4	6	5.9	8.3
137 Papua New Guinea	1964	1963	1977 E	..	0	0.9	..
138 Ghana	1954	1954	1960	11.8	0	10.9	..
139 Bangladesh	1972	1972	1973 E	8.3	10	2.0	..
140 Timor-Leste	..	..	..	22.2	0	25.3[k]	..
141 Sudan	1964	1964	1964 E	2.6	0	9.7	..
142 Congo	1961	1961	1963 E	14.7	14	8.5	15.0
143 Togo	1945	1945	1961 E	20.0	5	6.2	..
144 Uganda	1962	1962	1962 A	23.4	12	23.9	..
145 Zimbabwe	1919, 1957	1919, 1978	1980 E+A	14.7	11	10.0	..
LOW HUMAN DEVELOPMENT							
146 Madagascar	1959	1959	1965 E	5.9	7	6.9	11.1
147 Swaziland	1968	1968	1972 E+A	13.3	4	10.8	30.0
148 Cameroon	1946	1946	1960 E	11.1	14	8.9	..
149 Lesotho	1965	1965	1965 A	27.8	0	11.7	36.4
150 Djibouti	1946	1986	2003 E	5.3	0	10.8	..
151 Yemen	1967, 1970	1967, 1970	1990 E[e]	2.9	4	0.3	..
152 Mauritania	1961	1961	1975 E	9.1	0	3.7	5.4
153 Haiti	1950	1957	1961 E	25.0	0	3.6	25.9
154 Kenya	1919, 1963	1919, 1963	1969 E+A	10.3	1	7.1	..
155 Gambia	1960	1960	1982 E	20.0	8	13.2	..
156 Guinea	1958	1958	1963 E	15.4	0	19.3	..
157 Senegal	1945	1945	1963 E	20.6	13	19.2	..
158 Nigeria	1958	1958	..	10.0	0	6.4	3.7
159 Rwanda	1961	1961	1981	35.7	17	48.8	34.6

Human development indicators

TABLE 30

HDI rank	Year women received right[a] To vote	Year women received right[a] To stand for election	Year first woman elected (E) or appointed (A) to parliament	Women in government at ministerial level (% of total)[b] 2005	MDG Seats in parliament held by women (% of total)[c] Lower or single house 1990	Lower or single house 2005	Upper house or senate 2005
160 Angola	1975	1975	1980 E	5.7	15	15.0	..
161 Eritrea	1955	1955	1994 E	17.6	0	22.0	..
162 Benin	1956	1956	1979 E	19.0	3	7.2	..
163 Côte d'Ivoire	1952	1952	1965 E	17.1	6	8.5	..
164 Tanzania, U. Rep. of	1959	1959	..	15.4	0	21.4	..
165 Malawi	1961	1961	1964 E	14.3	10	14.0	..
166 Zambia	1962	1962	1964 E+A	25.0	7	12.7	..
167 Congo, Dem. Rep. of the	1967	1970	1970 E	12.5	5	12.0	2.5
168 Mozambique	1975	1975	1977 E	13.0	16	34.8	..
169 Burundi	1961	1961	1982 E	10.7	0	18.4	18.9
170 Ethiopia	1955	1955	1957 E	5.9	0	7.7	8.3
171 Central African Republic	1986	1986	1987 E	10.0	4	..[l]	..[l]
172 Guinea-Bissau	1977	1977	1972 A	37.5	20	14.0	..
173 Chad	1958	1958	1962 E	11.5	0	6.5	..
174 Mali	1956	1956	1959 E	18.5	0	10.2	..
175 Burkina Faso	1958	1958	1978 E	14.8	0	11.7	..
176 Sierra Leone	1961	1961	..	13.0	0	14.5	..
177 Niger	1948	1948	1989 E	23.1	5	12.4	..

NOTES

a Data refer to the year in which right to vote or stand for election on a universal and equal basis was recognized. Where two years are shown, the first refers to the first partial recognition of the right to vote or stand for election.

b Data are as of 1 January 2005. The total includes deputy prime ministers and ministers. Prime ministers were also included when they held ministerial portfolios. Vice-presidents and heads of ministerial-level departments or agencies were also included when exercising a ministerial function in the government structure.

c Data are as of 1 March 2005 unless otherwise specified. The percentage was calculated using as a reference the number of total seats filled in parliament at that time.

d No information is available on the year all women received the right to stand for election. However, the constitution does not mention gender with regard to this right.

e Refers to the year women were elected to the current parliamentary system.

f Brunei Darussalam and Qatar do not currently have a parliament. Elections for a new parliament in Qatar, according to the 2004 constitution, are scheduled to take place in late 2005 or early 2006.

g According to the constitution in force (1973), all citizens are equal before the law; however, women were not able to exercise electoral rights in the first legislative elections held in 1973. The first legislature was dissolved by decree of the Emir on 26 August 1975. Women were allowed to vote in the referendum of 14–15 February 2001, which approved the National Action Charter. Subsequently, women exercised their full political rights as both voters and candidates in the 2002 national elections.

h On 16 May 2005 Parliament voted a law granting women the right to vote and stand for election.

i Data on the distribution of seats do not include the 36 special rotating delegates appointed on an ad hoc basis, and the percentages given are therefore calculated on the basis of the 54 permanent seats.

j The parliament elected in 1990 has never been convened nor authorized to sit, and many of its members were detained or forced into exile.

k The purpose of elections held on 30 August 2001 was to elect members of the Constituent Assembly of Timor-Leste. This body became the National Parliament on 20 May 2002, the date on which the country became independent, without any new elections.

l Parliament was suspended on 15 March 2003. May 2005 election results are yet to become available.

SOURCES
Columns 1–3: IPU 1995.
Column 4: IPU 2005a.
Column 5: UN 2005f.
Columns 6 and 7: IPU 2005d.

TABLE 31

Human and labour rights instruments

Status of major international human rights instruments

HDI rank	International Convention on the Prevention and Punishment of the Crime of Genocide 1948	International Convention on the Elimination of All Forms of Racial Discrimination 1965	International Covenant on Civil and Political Rights 1966	International Covenant on Economic, Social and Cultural Rights 1966	Convention on the Elimination of All Forms of Discrimination against Women 1979	Convention against Torture and Other Cruel, Inhuman or Degrading Treatment or Punishment 1984	Convention on the Rights of the Child 1989
HIGH HUMAN DEVELOPMENT							
1 Norway	●	●	●	●	●	●	●
2 Iceland	●	●	●	●	●	●	●
3 Australia	●	●	●	●	●	●	●
4 Luxembourg	●	●	●	●	●	●	●
5 Canada	●	●	●	●	●	●	●
6 Sweden	●	●	●	●	●	●	●
7 Switzerland	●	●	●	●	●	●	●
8 Ireland	●	●	●	●	●	●	●
9 Belgium	●	●	●	●	●	●	●
10 United States	●	●	●	○	○	●	○
11 Japan		●	●	●	●	●	●
12 Netherlands	●	●	●	●	●	●	●
13 Finland	●	●	●	●	●	●	●
14 Denmark	●	●	●	●	●	●	●
15 United Kingdom	●	●	●	●	●	●	●
16 France	●	●	●	●	●	●	●
17 Austria	●	●	●	●	●	●	●
18 Italy	●	●	●	●	●	●	●
19 New Zealand	●	●	●	●	●	●	●
20 Germany	●	●	●	●	●	●	●
21 Spain	●	●	●	●	●	●	●
23 Israel	●	●	●	●	●	●	●
24 Greece	●	●	●	●	●	●	●
25 Singapore					●		●
26 Slovenia	●	●	●	●	●	●	●
27 Portugal	●	●	●	●	●	●	●
28 Korea, Rep. of	●	●	●	●	●	●	●
29 Cyprus	●	●	●	●	●	●	●
30 Barbados		●	●	●	●		●
31 Czech Republic	●	●	●	●	●	●	●
32 Malta		●	●	●	●	●	●
33 Brunei Darussalam							●
34 Argentina	●	●	●	●	●	●	●
35 Hungary	●	●	●	●	●	●	●
36 Poland	●	●	●	●	●	●	●
37 Chile	●	●	●	●		●	●
38 Estonia	●	●	●	●	●	●	●
39 Lithuania	●	●	●	●	●	●	●
40 Qatar		●				●	●
41 United Arab Emirates		●					●
42 Slovakia	●	●	●	●	●	●	●
43 Bahrain	●	●			●	●	●
44 Kuwait	●	●	●	●	●	●	●
45 Croatia	●	●	●	●	●	●	●
46 Uruguay	●	●	●	●	●	●	●
47 Costa Rica	●	●	●	●	●	●	●
48 Latvia	●	●	●	●	●	●	●
49 Saint Kitts and Nevis					●		●
50 Bahamas	●	●			●		●
51 Seychelles	●	●	●	●	●	●	●
52 Cuba	●	●			●	●	●
53 Mexico	●	●	●	●	●	●	●
54 Tonga	●	●					●

Human development indicators

TABLE 31

HDI rank	International Convention on the Prevention and Punishment of the Crime of Genocide 1948	International Convention on the Elimination of All Forms of Racial Discrimination 1965	International Covenant on Civil and Political Rights 1966	International Covenant on Economic, Social and Cultural Rights 1966	Convention on the Elimination of All Forms of Discrimination against Women 1979	Convention against Torture and Other Cruel, Inhuman or Degrading Treatment or Punishment 1984	Convention on the Rights of the Child 1989
55 Bulgaria	●	●	●	●	●	●	●
56 Panama	●	●	●	●	●	●	●
57 Trinidad and Tobago	●	●	●	●	●		●
MEDIUM HUMAN DEVELOPMENT							
58 Libyan Arab Jamahiriya	●	●	●	●	●	●	●
59 Macedonia, TFYR	●	●	●	●	●	●	●
60 Antigua and Barbuda	●	●			●	●	●
61 Malaysia	●				●		●
62 Russian Federation	●	●	●	●	●	●	●
63 Brazil	●	●	●	●	●	●	●
64 Romania	●	●	●	●	●	●	●
65 Mauritius		●	●	●	●	●	●
66 Grenada		○	●	○	●		●
67 Belarus	●	●	●	●	●	●	●
68 Bosnia and Herzegovina	●	●	●	●	●	●	●
69 Colombia	●	●	●	●	●	●	●
70 Dominica			●	●	●		●
71 Oman					●		●
72 Albania	●	●	●	●	●	●	●
73 Thailand		●	●	●	●		●
74 Samoa (Western)					●		●
75 Venezuela	●	●	●	●	●	●	●
76 Saint Lucia		●			●		●
77 Saudi Arabia	●	●			●	●	●
78 Ukraine	●	●	●	●	●	●	●
79 Peru	●	●	●	●	●	●	●
80 Kazakhstan	●	●	●	○	●	●	●
81 Lebanon	●	●	●	●	●	●	●
82 Ecuador	●	●	●	●	●	●	●
83 Armenia	●	●	●	●	●	●	●
84 Philippines	●	●	●	●	●	●	●
85 China	●	●		●	●	●	●
86 Suriname		●	●	●	●		●
87 Saint Vincent and the Grenadines	●	●	●	●	●	●	●
88 Paraguay	●	●	●	●	●	●	●
89 Tunisia	●	●	●	●	●	●	●
90 Jordan	●	●	●	●	●	●	●
91 Belize	●	●	●	○	●	●	●
92 Fiji	●	●			●		●
93 Sri Lanka	●	●	●	●	●	●	●
94 Turkey	●	●	●	●	●	●	●
95 Dominican Republic	○	●	●	●	●		●
96 Maldives		●			●		●
97 Turkmenistan		●	●	●	●	●	●
98 Jamaica	●	●	●	●	●		●
99 Iran, Islamic Rep. of	●	●	●	●			●
100 Georgia	●	●	●	●	●	●	●
101 Azerbaijan	●	●	●	●	●	●	●
103 Algeria	●	●	●	●	●	●	●
104 El Salvador	●	●	●	●	●	●	●
105 Cape Verde		●	●	●	●	●	●
106 Syrian Arab Republic	●	●	●	●	●	●	●
107 Guyana		●	●	●	●	●	●
108 Viet Nam	●	●	●	●	●		●

Human development indicators

TABLE 31

Status of major international human rights instruments

HDI rank	International Convention on the Prevention and Punishment of the Crime of Genocide 1948	International Convention on the Elimination of All Forms of Racial Discrimination 1965	International Covenant on Civil and Political Rights 1966	International Covenant on Economic, Social and Cultural Rights 1966	Convention on the Elimination of All Forms of Discrimination against Women 1979	Convention against Torture and Other Cruel, Inhuman or Degrading Treatment or Punishment 1984	Convention on the Rights of the Child 1989
109 Kyrgyzstan	●	●	●	●	●	●	●
110 Indonesia		●	●		●	●	●
111 Uzbekistan	●	●	●	●	●	●	●
112 Nicaragua	●	●	●	●	●	●	●
113 Bolivia	○	●	●	●	●	●	●
114 Mongolia	●	●	●	●	●	●	●
115 Moldova, Rep. of	●	●	●	●	●	●	●
116 Honduras	●	●	●	●	●	●	●
117 Guatemala	●	●	●	●	●	●	●
118 Vanuatu					●		●
119 Egypt	●	●	●	●	●	●	●
120 South Africa	●	●	●	○	●	●	●
121 Equatorial Guinea	●	●	●	●	●	●	●
122 Tajikistan		●	●	●	●	●	●
123 Gabon	●	●	●	●	●	●	●
124 Morocco	●	●	●	●	●	●	●
125 Namibia	●	●	●	●	●	●	●
126 São Tomé and Principe		○	○	○	●	○	●
127 India	●	●	●	●	●		●
128 Solomon Islands		●	●	●	●		●
129 Myanmar	●				●		●
130 Cambodia	●	●	●	●	●	●	●
131 Botswana	●	●	●		●	●	●
132 Comoros	●	●			●	●	●
133 Lao People's Dem. Rep.	●	●	●	○	●	●	●
134 Bhutan		○	○		●		●
135 Pakistan	●	●	●	○	●		●
136 Nepal	●	●	●	●	●	●	●
137 Papua New Guinea	●	●			●	●	●
138 Ghana	●	●	●	●	●	●	●
139 Bangladesh	●	●	●	●	●	●	●
140 Timor-Leste		●	●	●	●	●	●
141 Sudan	●	●	●	●		●	●
142 Congo		●	●	●	●	●	●
143 Togo	●	●	●	●	●	●	●
144 Uganda	●	●	●	●	●	●	●
145 Zimbabwe	●	●	●	●	●		●
LOW HUMAN DEVELOPMENT							
146 Madagascar		●	●	●	●	○	●
147 Swaziland		●	●	●	●	●	●
148 Cameroon		●	●	●	●	●	●
149 Lesotho	●	●	●	●	●	●	●
150 Djibouti		●	●	●	●	●	●
151 Yemen	●	●	●	●	●	●	●
152 Mauritania	●	●			●	●	●
153 Haiti	●	●	●		●		●
154 Kenya	●		●	●	●	●	●
155 Gambia	●	●	●	●	●	●	●
156 Guinea	●	●	●	●	●	●	●
157 Senegal	●	●	●	●	●	●	●
158 Nigeria	●	●	●	●	●	●	●
159 Rwanda	●	●	●	●	●		●
160 Angola		●	●	●	●		●
161 Eritrea		●	●	●	●		●

Human development indicators

TABLE 31

HDI rank	International Convention on the Prevention and Punishment of the Crime of Genocide 1948	International Convention on the Elimination of All Forms of Racial Discrimination 1965	International Covenant on Civil and Political Rights 1966	International Covenant on Economic, Social and Cultural Rights 1966	Convention on the Elimination of All Forms of Discrimination against Women 1979	Convention against Torture and Other Cruel, Inhuman or Degrading Treatment or Punishment 1984	Convention on the Rights of the Child 1989
162 Benin		●	●	●	●	●	●
163 Côte d'Ivoire	●	●	●	●	●	●	●
164 Tanzania, U. Rep. of	●	●	●	●	●		●
165 Malawi		●	●	●	●	●	●
166 Zambia		●	●	●	●	●	●
167 Congo, Dem. Rep. of the	●	●	●	●	●	●	●
168 Mozambique	●	●	●		●	●	●
169 Burundi	●	●	●	●	●	●	●
170 Ethiopia	●	●	●	●	●	●	●
171 Central African Republic		●	●	●	●	●	●
172 Guinea-Bissau		○	○		●	●	●
173 Chad		●	●	●	●	●	●
174 Mali	●	●	●	●	●	●	●
175 Burkina Faso	●	●	●	●	●	●	●
176 Sierra Leone	●	●	●	●	●	●	●
177 Niger		●	●	●	●	●	●
OTHERS [a]							
Afghanistan	●	●	●	●	●	●	●
Andorra		○	○		●	○	●
Iraq	●	●	●	●	●		●
Kiribati							●
Korea, Dem. Rep.	●		●	●			●
Liberia	●	●	●	●	●	●	●
Liechtenstein	●	●	●	●	●	●	●
Marshall Islands					●		●
Micronesia, Fed. Sts.					●		●
Monaco	●	●	●	●	●	●	●
Nauru		○	○			○	●
Palau							●
San Marino		●	●	●	●	○	●
Somalia		●	●	●		●	○
Tuvalu					●		●
Serbia and Montenegro	●	●	●	●	●	●	●
Total states parties [b]	**136**	**170**	**170**	**151**	**180**	**146**	**192**
Signatures not yet followed by ratification	**2**	**6**	**6**	**7**	**1**	**5**	**2**

● Ratification, accession or succession.
○ Signature not yet followed by ratification.

NOTES
The table includes states that have signed or ratified at least one of the seven human rights instruments. Information is as of 1 May 2005.
a These are the countries or areas, in addition to the 177 countries or areas included in the main indicator tables, that have signed or ratified at least one of the seven human rights instruments.
b Refers to ratification, accession or succession.

SOURCE
All columns: UN 2005g.

TABLE 32

Human and labour rights instruments

Status of fundamental labour rights conventions

HDI rank	Freedom of association and collective bargaining		Elimination of forced and compulsory labour		Elimination of discrimination in respect of employment and occupation		Abolition of child labor	
	Convention 87 [a]	Convention 98 [b]	Convention 29 [c]	Convention 105 [d]	Convention 100 [e]	Convention 111 [f]	Convention 138 [g]	Convention 182 [h]
HIGH HUMAN DEVELOPMENT								
1 Norway	•	•	•	•	•	•	•	•
2 Iceland	•	•	•	•	•	•	•	•
3 Australia	•	•	•	•	•	•		•
4 Luxembourg	•	•	•	•	•	•	•	•
5 Canada	•			•	•	•		•
6 Sweden	•	•	•	•	•	•	•	•
7 Switzerland	•	•	•	•	•	•	•	•
8 Ireland	•	•	•	•	•	•	•	•
9 Belgium	•	•	•	•	•	•	•	•
10 United States				•				•
11 Japan	•	•	•		•		•	•
12 Netherlands	•	•	•	•	•	•	•	•
13 Finland	•	•	•	•	•	•	•	•
14 Denmark	•	•	•	•	•	•	•	•
15 United Kingdom	•	•	•	•	•	•	•	•
16 France	•	•	•	•	•	•	•	•
17 Austria	•	•	•	•	•	•	•	•
18 Italy	•	•	•	•	•	•	•	•
19 New Zealand		•	•	•	•	•	•	•
20 Germany	•	•	•	•	•	•	•	•
21 Spain	•	•	•	•	•	•	•	•
23 Israel	•	•	•	•	•	•	•	•
24 Greece	•	•	•	•	•	•	•	•
25 Singapore		•	•	▼	•		•	•
26 Slovenia	•	•	•	•	•	•	•	•
27 Portugal	•	•	•	•	•	•	•	•
28 Korea, Rep. of					•	•	•	•
29 Cyprus	•	•	•	•	•	•	•	•
30 Barbados	•	•	•	•	•	•		•
31 Czech Republic	•	•	•	•	•	•	•	•
32 Malta	•	•	•	•	•	•	•	•
33 Brunei Darussalam								•
34 Argentina	•	•	•	•	•	•	•	•
35 Hungary	•	•	•	•	•	•	•	•
36 Poland	•	•	•	•	•	•	•	•
37 Chile	•	•	•	•	•	•	•	•
38 Estonia	•	•	•	•	•	•		•
39 Lithuania	•	•	•	•	•	•	•	•
40 Qatar			•	•		•	•	•
41 United Arab Emirates			•	•	•	•	•	•
42 Slovakia	•	•	•	•	•	•	•	•
43 Bahrain			•	•		•		•
44 Kuwait	•		•	•		•	•	•
45 Croatia	•	•	•	•	•	•	•	•
46 Uruguay	•	•	•	•	•	•	•	•
47 Costa Rica	•	•	•	•	•	•	•	•
48 Latvia	•	•	•	•	•	•	•	•
49 Saint Kitts and Nevis	•	•	•	•	•	•		•
50 Bahamas	•	•	•	•	•	•		•
51 Seychelles	•	•	•	•	•	•	•	•
52 Cuba	•	•	•	•	•	•	•	•
53 Mexico	•		•	•	•	•		•
54 Tonga								

Human development indicators

TABLE 32

HDI rank	Freedom of association and collective bargaining		Elimination of forced and compulsory labour		Elimination of discrimination in respect of employment and occupation		Abolition of child labor	
	Convention 87 [a]	Convention 98 [b]	Convention 29 [c]	Convention 105 [d]	Convention 100 [e]	Convention 111 [f]	Convention 138 [g]	Convention 182 [h]
55 Bulgaria	●	●	●	●	●	●	●	●
56 Panama	●	●	●	●	●	●	●	●
57 Trinidad and Tobago	●	●	●	●	●	●	●	●
MEDIUM HUMAN DEVELOPMENT								
58 Libyan Arab Jamahiriya	●	●	●	●	●	●	●	●
59 Macedonia, TFYR	●	●	●	●	●	●	●	●
60 Antigua and Barbuda	●	●	●	●	●	●	●	●
61 Malaysia		●	●	◆	●		●	●
62 Russian Federation	●	●	●	●	●	●	●	●
63 Brazil		●	●	●	●	●	●	●
64 Romania	●	●	●	●	●	●	●	●
65 Mauritius		●	●	●	●	●	●	●
66 Grenada	●	●	●	●	●	●	●	●
67 Belarus	●	●	●	●	●	●	●	●
68 Bosnia and Herzegovina	●	●	●	●	●	●	●	●
69 Colombia	●	●	●	●	●	●	●	●
70 Dominica	●	●	●	●	●	●	●	●
71 Oman			●				●	●
72 Albania	●	●	●	●	●	●	●	●
73 Thailand			●	●	●		●	●
74 Samoa (Western)								
75 Venezuela	●	●	●	●	●	●	●	
76 Saint Lucia	●	●	●	●	●	●		●
77 Saudi Arabia			●	●	●	●		●
78 Ukraine	●	●	●	●	●	●	●	●
79 Peru	●	●	●	●	●	●	●	●
80 Kazakhstan	●	●	●	●	●	●	●	●
81 Lebanon		●	●	●	●	●	●	●
82 Ecuador	●	●	●	●	●	●	●	●
83 Armenia		●	●	●	●	●		●
84 Philippines	●	●	●	●	●	●	●	●
85 China					●		●	●
86 Suriname	●	●	●	●	●			●
87 Saint Vincent and the Grenadines	●	●	●	●	●			●
88 Paraguay	●	●	●	●	●	●	●	●
89 Tunisia	●	●	●		●	●	●	●
90 Jordan		●	●	●	●	●	●	●
91 Belize	●	●	●	●	●	●	●	●
92 Fiji	●	●	●	●	●	●	●	●
93 Sri Lanka	●	●	●	●	●	●	●	●
94 Turkey	●	●	●	●	●	●	●	●
95 Dominican Republic	●	●	●	●	●	●	●	●
96 Maldives								
97 Turkmenistan	●	●	●	●	●	●		
98 Jamaica	●	●	●	●	●	●		
99 Iran, Islamic Rep. of			●	●	●	●		●
100 Georgia	●	●	●	●	●	●	●	●
101 Azerbaijan	●	●	●	●	●	●	●	●
103 Algeria	●	●	●	●	●	●	●	●
104 El Salvador			●	●	●	●	●	●
105 Cape Verde	●	●	●	●	●	●	●	●
106 Syrian Arab Republic	●	●	●	●	●	●	●	●
107 Guyana	●	●	●	●	●	●	●	●
108 Viet Nam					●		●	●

Human development indicators

TABLE 32

Status of fundamental labour rights conventions

HDI rank	Freedom of association and collective bargaining		Elimination of forced and compulsory labour		Elimination of discrimination in respect of employment and occupation		Abolition of child labor	
	Convention 87[a]	Convention 98[b]	Convention 29[c]	Convention 105[d]	Convention 100[e]	Convention 111[f]	Convention 138[g]	Convention 182[h]
109 Kyrgyzstan	●	●	●	●	●	●	●	●
110 Indonesia	●	●	●	●	●	●	●	●
111 Uzbekistan		●	●	●	●	●		
112 Nicaragua	●	●	●	●	●	●	●	●
113 Bolivia	●	●		●	●	●	●	●
114 Mongolia	●	●			●	●	●	●
115 Moldova, Rep. of	●	●		●	●	●	●	●
116 Honduras	●	●	●	●	●	●	●	●
117 Guatemala	●	●	●	●	●	●	●	●
118 Vanuatu								
119 Egypt	●	●	●	●	●	●	●	●
120 South Africa	●	●	●	●	●	●	●	●
121 Equatorial Guinea		●	●	●	●	●	●	●
122 Tajikistan	●	●	●	●	●	●	●	●
123 Gabon	●	●	●	●	●	●	●	●
124 Morocco		●	●	●	●	●	●	●
125 Namibia	●	●	●	●	●	●	●	
126 São Tomé and Principe	●	●			●	●		
127 India			●	●	●	●		
128 Solomon Islands			●					
129 Myanmar	●		●					
130 Cambodia	●	●	●	●	●	●	●	●
131 Botswana	●	●	●	●	●	●	●	●
132 Comoros	●	●	●	●	●	●		●
133 Lao People's Dem. Rep.			●		●	●	●	●
134 Bhutan								
135 Pakistan	●	●	●	●	●	●		●
136 Nepal		●	●	●	●	●		●
137 Papua New Guinea	●	●	●	●	●	●	●	●
138 Ghana	●	●	●	●	●	●		●
139 Bangladesh	●	●	●	●	●	●		●
140 Timor-Leste								
141 Sudan			●	●	●	●	●	●
142 Congo	●	●	●	●	●	●	●	●
143 Togo	●	●	●	●	●	●	●	●
144 Uganda		●	●	●		●	●	●
145 Zimbabwe	●	●	●	●			●	●
LOW HUMAN DEVELOPMENT								
146 Madagascar	●	●	●		●	●	●	●
147 Swaziland	●	●	●	●	●	●	●	●
148 Cameroon	●	●	●	●	●	●	●	●
149 Lesotho	●	●	●	●	●	●	●	●
150 Djibouti	●	●	●	●	●	●	●	●
151 Yemen	●	●	●	●	●	●	●	●
152 Mauritania	●	●	●	●	●	●	●	●
153 Haiti	●	●	●	●	●	●		●
154 Kenya		●	●	●	●	●	●	●
155 Gambia	●	●	●	●	●	●	●	●
156 Guinea	●	●	●	●	●	●	●	●
157 Senegal	●	●	●	●	●	●	●	●
158 Nigeria	●	●	●	●	●	●	●	●
159 Rwanda	●	●	●	●	●	●	●	●
160 Angola	●	●	●	●	●	●	●	●
161 Eritrea	●	●	●	●	●	●	●	●

Human development indicators

TABLE 32

HDI rank	Freedom of association and collective bargaining		Elimination of forced and compulsory labour		Elimination of discrimination in respect of employment and occupation		Abolition of child labor	
	Convention 87 [a]	Convention 98 [b]	Convention 29 [c]	Convention 105 [d]	Convention 100 [e]	Convention 111 [f]	Convention 138 [g]	Convention 182 [h]
162 Benin	●	●	●	●	●	●	●	●
163 Côte d'Ivoire	●	●	●	●	●	●	●	●
164 Tanzania, U. Rep. of	●	●	●	●	●	●	●	●
165 Malawi	●	●	●	●	●	●	●	●
166 Zambia	●	●	●	●	●	●	●	●
167 Congo, Dem. Rep. of the	●	●	●	●	●	●	●	●
168 Mozambique	●	●	●	●	●	●	●	●
169 Burundi	●	●	●	●	●	●	●	●
170 Ethiopia	●	●	●	●	●	●	●	●
171 Central African Republic	●	●	●	●	●	●	●	●
172 Guinea-Bissau		●	●	●	●	●		●
173 Chad	●	●	●	●	●	●		●
174 Mali	●	●	●	●	●	●	●	●
175 Burkina Faso	●	●	●	●	●	●	●	●
176 Sierra Leone	●	●	●	●	●	●		●
177 Niger	●	●	●	●	●	●	●	●
OTHERS [i]								
Afghanistan				●	●	●		
Iraq		●	●	●	●	●	●	●
Kiribati	●	●	●	●				
Liberia	●	●	●	·			●	●
San Marino	●	●	●	●	●	●	●	●
Serbia and Montenegro	●	●	●	●	●	●	●	●
Somalia			●	●		●		
Total ratifications	142	154	164	160	161	161	135	152

● Convention ratified.
▼ Convention denounced.

NOTES

Table includes UN member states. Information is as of 1 May 2005.

a Freedom of Association and Protection of the Right to Organize Convention (1948).
b Right to Organize and Collective Bargaining Convention (1949).
c Forced Labour Convention (1930).
d Abolition of Forced Labour Convention (1957).
e Equal Remuneration Convention (1951).
f Discrimination (Employment and Occupation) Convention (1958).
g Minimum Age Convention (1973).
h Worst Forms of Child Labour Convention (1999).
i States not included in the human development index that have ratified at least one labour rights convention.

SOURCE
All columns: ILO 2005a.

Human development indicators

TABLE 33

Basic indicators for other UN member countries

	Human development index components			GDP per capita (PPP US$) 2003	Total population (thousands) 2003	Total fertility rate (births per woman) 2000–05 b	MDG Under-five mortality rate (per 1,000 live births) 2003	MDG Net primary enrolment ratio (%) 2002/03 c	HIV prevalence a (% ages 15–49) 2003	MDG Population under-nourished (% of total) 2000/02 e	MDG Population with sustainable access to an improved water source (%) 2002
	Life expectancy at birth (years) 2000–05 b	Adult literacy rate (% ages 15 and above) 2003 c	Combined gross enrolment ratio for primary, secondary and tertiary schools (%) 2002/03 d								
Afghanistan	46.0	..	39.4	..	27	7.5	257	..	..	..	13
Andorra	..	..	65.9	..	(.)	..	7	89	..	..	100
Iraq	58.8	..	63.0	..	27	4.8	125	91 f, g	<0.1 [<0.2]	..	81
Kiribati	..	..	84.9	..	(.)	..	66	..	..	..	64
Korea, Dem. Rep.	63.0	..	..	..	22	2.0	55	..	..	36	100
Liberia	42.5	55.9	61.2	..	3	6.8	235	70 h	5.9 [2.7–12.4]	46	62
Liechtenstein	..	..	..	..	(.)	..	11	..	..	..	..
Marshall Islands	..	..	74.3	..	(.)	..	61	84 i	..	..	85
Micronesia, Fed. Sts.	67.6	..	..	..	(.)	4.4	23	..	..	..	94
Monaco	..	..	..	..	(.)	..	4	..	..	..	..
Nauru	..	..	55.1	..	(.)	..	30	81 g, i	..	..	..
Palau	..	..	90.1	..	(.)	..	28	97 g, i	..	..	84
San Marino	..	..	..	..	(.)	..	5	..	..	..	..
Serbia and Montenegro	73.2	96.4	74.4	..	11	1.7	11	96 f	0.2 [0.1–0.4]	11	..
Somalia	46.2	..	..	..	8	6.4	225	..	..	..	29
Tuvalu	..	..	68.7	..	(.)	..	51	..	..	..	93

NOTES

This table presents data for UN member countries not included in the main indicator tables.

a Data refer to point and range estimates based on new estimation models developed by the Joint United Nations Programme on HIV/AIDS. Regional aggregates refer to 2004. Range estimates are presented in square brackets.

b Data refer to estimates for the period specified.

c Data refer to national literacy estimates from censuses or surveys conducted between 2000 and 2004. Due to differences in methodology and timeliness of underlying data, comparisons across countries and over time should be made with caution.

d Data on net enrolment ratios refer to the 2002/03 school year, unless otherwise specified. For details, see www.uis.unesco.org.

e Data refer to the average for the years specified.

f Data refer to the 2000/01 school year.

g Preliminary United Nations Educational, Scientific and Cultural Organization Institute for Statistics estimate, subject to further revision.

h Data refer to the 1999/2000 school year.

i Data refer to the 2001/02 school year.

j Data refer to the 1998/99 school year.

SOURCES

Column 1: UN 2005c.
Column 2: UNESCO Institute for Statistics 2005a.
Columns 3 and 8: UNESCO Institute for Statistics 2005b.
Column 4: World Bank 2005c.
Columns 5 and 6: UN 2005h.
Column 7: UNICEF 2004.
Column 9: UNAIDS 2005.
Column 10: FAO 2004.
Column 11: UN 2005f.

Note on statistics in the Human Development Report

The *Human Development Report* usually presents two types of statistical information: statistics in the human development indicator tables, which provide a global assessment of country achievements in different areas of human development, and statistical evidence on the thematic analysis in the chapters. This note outlines the principles that guide the selection, use and presentation of these statistics, and the efforts of the Human Development Report Office to achieve high standard of statistical rigour in the Report and to promote innovative use and development of better human development statistics.

Human Development Report Office as a user of statistics

The Human Development Report Office is primarily a user, not a producer, of statistics. It relies on international and national data agencies with the resources and expertise to collect and compile data on specific statistical indicators.

Human development indicator tables and human development index

To allow comparisons across countries and over time, the Human Development Report Office, to the extent possible, uses international data series produced by international data agencies or other specialized institutions in preparing the human development indicator tables (box 1).

Despite significant progress over recent years, many gaps still exist in the data, even in some very basic areas of human development. While advocating for improvements in human development data, as a principle—and for practical reasons—the Human Development Report Office does not collect data directly from countries or make estimates to fill these data gaps.

The one exception is the human development index (HDI). The Human Development Report Office strives to include as many UN member countries as possible in the HDI. For a country to be included, data ideally should be available from the relevant international data agencies for all four components of the index (see *Note to table 1: About this year's human development index*). But for a significant number of countries data are missing for one or more of these components. In response to the desire of countries to be included in the HDI, the Human Development Report Office makes every effort in these cases to identify other reasonable estimates, working with international data agencies, the UN Regional Commissions, national statistical offices and United Nations Development Programme (UNDP) country offices. In a few cases the Human Development Report Office has estimated missing components in consultation with regional and national statistical offices or other experts.

Millennium Development Goal indicators

The United Nations Statistics Division maintains the global Millennium Indicators Database (http://millenniumindicators.un.org) compiled from international data series provided by the responsible international data agencies. The database forms the statistical basis for the UN Secretary-General's annual report to the UN General Assembly on global and regional progress towards the Millennium Development Goals (MDGs) and their targets. It also feeds into other international reports presenting data on the MDG indicators across countries, such as this Report and the World Bank's annual World Development Indicators.

This year's Report incorporates many of the MDG indicators in the human development

| Box 1 | **Major sources of data used in the *Human Development Report*** |

By generously sharing data, the following organizations made it possible for the *Human Development Report* to publish the important human development statistics appearing in the indicator tables.

Carbon Dioxide Information Analysis Center (CDIAC) The CDIAC, a data and analysis centre of the US Department of Energy, focuses on the greenhouse effect and global climate change. It is the source of data on carbon dioxide emissions.

Food and Agriculture Organization (FAO) The FAO collects, analyses and disseminates data and information on food and agriculture. It is the source of data on food insecurity indicators.

Global IDP Project The Norwegian Refugee Council's Global IDP Project maintains an online database of information and analysis on conflict-induced internal displacement worldwide. The database is designated as the authoritative source of information on internally displaced persons by the United Nations and is presented in this year's Report for the first time.

International Institute for Strategic Studies (IISS) An independent centre for research, information and debate on the problems of conflicts, the IISS maintains an extensive military database. The data on armed forces are from its publication *The Military Balance*.

International Labour Organization (ILO) The ILO maintains an extensive statistical publication programme, with the *Yearbook of Labour Statistics* and the *Key Indicators of the Labour Market* its most comprehensive collection of labour market data. The ILO is the source of data on wages, employment and occupations and information on the ratification status of labour rights conventions.

International Monetary Fund (IMF) The IMF has an extensive programme for developing and compiling statistics on international financial transactions and balance of payments. Much of the financial data provided to the Human Development Report Office by other agencies originates from the IMF.

International Telecommunication Union (ITU) This specialized UN agency maintains an extensive collection of statistics on information and communications. The data on trends in telecommunications come from its *World Telecommunication Indicators* database.

Inter-Parliamentary Union (IPU) This organization provides data on trends in political participation and structures of democracy. The Human Development Report Office relies on the IPU for data relating to elections and information on women's political representation.

Joint United Nations Programme on HIV/AIDS (UNAIDS) This joint UN programme monitors the spread of HIV/AIDS and provides regular updates. The *Report on the Global HIV/AIDS Epidemic*, a joint publication of UNAIDS and the World Health Organization, is the primary source of data on HIV/AIDS.

Luxembourg Income Study (LIS) A cooperative research project with 25 member countries, the LIS focuses on poverty and policy issues. It is the source of income poverty estimates for many OECD countries.

Organisation for Economic Co-operation and Development (OECD) The OECD publishes data on a variety of social and economic trends in its member countries as well as on flows of aid. This year's Report presents data from the OECD on aid, energy, employment and education.

Stockholm International Peace Research Institute (SIPRI) SIPRI conducts research on international peace and security. The *SIPRI Yearbook: Armaments, Disarmament and International Security* is the published source of data on military expenditure and arms transfers.

United Nations Children's Fund (UNICEF) UNICEF monitors the well-being of children and provides a wide array of data. Its *State of the World's Children* is an important source of data for the Report.

United Nations Conference on Trade and Development (UNCTAD) UNCTAD provides trade and economic statistics through a number of publications, including the *World Investment Report*. It is the original source of data on investment flows that the Human Development Report Office receives from other agencies.

United Nations Educational, Scientific and Cultural Organization (UNESCO) The Institute for Statistics of this specialized UN agency is the source of data relating to education. The Human Development Report Office relies on data in UNESCO's statistical publications as well as data received directly from its Institute for Statistics.

United Nations High Commissioner for Refugees (UNHCR) This UN organization provides data on refugees through its *Statistical Yearbook* or other on-line statistical publications.

United Nations Office on Drugs and Crime (UNODC) This UN organization carries out international comparative research to support the fight against illicit drugs and international crime. It provides data on crime victims from the International Crime Victims Surveys.

United Nations Multilateral Treaties Deposited with the Secretary General (UN Treaty Section) The Human Development Report Office compiles information on the status of major international human rights instruments and environmental treaties based on the database maintained by this UN office.

United Nations Population Division (UNPOP) This specialized UN office produces international data on population trends. The Human Development Report Office relies on *World Population Prospects* and *World Urbanization Prospects,* two of the main publications of UNPOP, and its other publications and databases, for demographic estimates and projections.

United Nations Statistics Division (UNSD) The UNSD provides a wide range of statistical outputs and services. Much of the national accounts data provided to the Human Development Report Office by other agencies originates from the UNSD. This year's Report also presents UNSD data on trade and energy and draws on the global Millennium Indicators Database, maintained by the

UNSD, as the source of data for the Millennium Development Goal indicators.

World Bank The World Bank produces and compiles data on economic trends as well as a broad array of other indicators. Its *World Development Indicators* is the primary source for many indicators in the Report.

World Health Organization (WHO) This specialized agency maintains a large array of data series on health issues, the source for the health-related indicators in the Report.

World Intellectual Property Organization (WIPO) As a specialized UN agency, WIPO promotes the protection of intellectual property rights throughout the world through different kinds of cooperative efforts. It is the source of data relating to patents.

---

indicator tables (see *Index to the Millennium Development Goal indicators in the indicator tables*). Data for these indicators provide the statistical basis for assessments of progress and prospects in each country towards achieving the MDGs and their targets, as well as the potential benefits of achieving the MDGs by 2015 (see chapter 1).

Data for thematic analysis

The statistical evidence used in the thematic analysis in the Report is often drawn from the indicator tables. But a wide range of other sources are also used, including commissioned papers, government documents, national human development reports, reports of non-governmental organizations, and journal articles and other scholarly publications. Official statistics usually receive priority. Because of the cutting-edge nature of the issues discussed, relevant official statistics may not exist, so that non-official sources of information must be used. Nevertheless, the Human Development Report Office is committed to relying on data compiled through scholarly and scientific research and to ensuring impartiality in the sources of information and in its use in the analysis.

This year's Report draws on a wide range of international and national sources of data to address the issues of inequality in income

and non-income dimensions of human development, on aid, trade and conflicts, and their relationships to both the broad goals of human development and the specific objectives of the MDGs.

Where information from sources other than the Report's indicator tables is used in boxes or tables in the text, the source is shown and the full citation is given in the bibliography. In addition, a summary note for each chapter outlines the major sources for the chapter, and endnotes specify the sources of statistical information not drawn from the indicator tables.

Achieving high standards of statistical quality

Even though its direct role in international data production is limited, the Human Development Report Office fully acknowledges its distinct accountability in disseminating the international statistics produced by other data agencies through the Report. In particular, it recognizes that the Report's high profile imposes a special burden to be informed and responsible in the selection, use and presentation of statistics.

To achieve the highest standard of rigour and professionalism in the statistical work of the Report, the Human Development Report Office has sought to establish and strengthen a number of quality assurance procedures over the past few years. In addition to building stronger internal statistical capacity and establishing a streamlined production system, these procedures include a Statistical Advisory Panel, a statistical peer review process and continuing close collaboration and networking with other regional and international data agencies.

Since 2000 the Report has benefited greatly from the intellectual and technical advice and guidance of the Statistical Advisory Panel, comprising leading national and international statisticians and development economists. The panel usually meets twice a year, at the beginning and the final stages of Report production, to discuss issues related to the guiding principles of the Report's statistical work and to specific technical issues about data sources, methods of analysis or data presentation related to the Report's thematic content. Occasionally a small working group is formed to help tackle a particular issue and provide advice to the Report's team. The panel members usually serve a two-year term.

Annual production of the Report includes a statistical peer review, with contributors from leading international, regional and national statistical offices. These peer reviewers are responsible for reviewing an advance draft of the Report for statistical relevance, consistency and proper interpretation. This review takes place separately but concurrently with the peer reviews for the substantive content of the Report. The statistical peer reviews have contributed significantly to the continuing improvement in the Report's statistical quality over the years. Responsibility for the final content of the Report, however, rests with the *Human Development Report* team.

Through close collaborations with specialized regional and international data agencies and by participating actively in regional and international statistical forums, including the United Nations Statistical Commission, the Coordination Committee for Statistical Activities and other regional statistical conferences and interagency measurement task forces, the *Human Development Report* team strives continuingly to remain informed and

responsible in its selection and use of statistics in the Report.

Other mechanisms have also been used to guide and monitor the Report's statistical work. For example, the Human Development Report Office regularly consults with member states through informal consultation sessions with the United Nations Development Programme/United Nations Population Fund Executive Board. These consultations focus on the Report's statistical principles and practices, as well as proposed strategies to deal with specific statistical issues, such as inconsistencies between national and international data, that have wide implications for the Report's credibility and policy impact. Frequent feedback from national governments and other users of the Report has been another important means of quality assurance.

Promoting innovative use of statistics

Since its introduction the Report has been at the forefront of promoting the innovative use and development of human development statistics to assess achievements across countries and to facilitate policy debates on critical issues of human development. One of its important contributions is the HDI and other composite human development indices. Since the HDI was first published, it has gained wide recognition as a powerful tool for advocating for and monitoring human development. It has been explored and expanded, both in the Report itself and in other national and regional human development reports. This year, the Report explores two distinct new ways of using the HDI: to look at the relative contributions of its different components to HDI progress and to incorporate inequality by focusing on the difference between the poorest and the population as a whole in a country (box 2).

However, to be innovative and effective in using statistics to assess progress and enhance policy discussions, both the *Human Development Report* team and the readers of the Report need to understand and interpret the statistics properly. Unless the usefulness and limitations of the chosen measures and statistics are

The human development index (HDI) is a summary measure of three dimensions of human development: leading a long and healthy life, measured by life expectancy at birth; being knowledgeable, measured by literacy and school enrolment; and having a decent standard of living, measured by GDP per capita (PPP US$). This year, the Report explores two new ways of using the HDI. The first looks at relative contributions of the different HDI components to HDI progress. The second attempts to incorporate inequality by focusing on the difference between the poorest and the population as a whole in HDI scores.

Health, education and income—not always moving together. While the HDI provides a summary picture, taking a closer look at its components also reveals striking differences between countries. Consider Bangladesh, China and Uganda, three countries that have achieved considerable gains in human development since 1990, but from different starting points. All three have increased their HDI scores by about 20% since 1990. Looking at improvements in the variables behind the HDI shows the divergent paths these countries have taken to get there.

Table 1 shows improvements in life expectancy, literacy, enrolment and income in the three countries, expressed relative to their 1990 levels. China's income has increased by almost 200% over the whole period—while income gains in Bangladesh and Uganda were much lower. Bangladesh improved its life expectancy by about 10%, while Uganda's remained stagnant and China's improved by less than 10%. Bangladesh and Uganda both improved their school enrolment and literacy rates dramatically, contributing greatly to their rise in the HDI ranks, while China's rise was more modest.

These comparisons give an indication of the magnitude of different drivers of HDI progress in different countries, but they do not give a complete picture. Because of different starting points in HDI components, progress in them will have different impacts in different countries. Additionally, most of the indicators in the HDI have an upper bound of attainable values—the literacy rate cannot exceed 100%. For this reason, countries at low levels of human development are more likely to show large percentage gains.

Inequality and the HDI. By design the HDI looks at average achievements—by itself it says nothing about the distribution of human development within a country. Trying to incorporate an element of distribution in the HDI is challenging because of difficult methodological issues and a lack of data, particularly related to the health and education indicators in the HDI.

A simpler approach, explored in this year's Report, is to consider the situation of people living at the bottom of the distribution ladder. Household income and consumption surveys show staggering gaps between the poorest 20% of the population and the population average. Adjusting the HDI solely with regard to income and discounting inequalities in life expectancy and education does not capture the full scale of inequality. Even so, the results are staggering.

Consider Brazil, which ranks 63 in the global HDI ranking. The poorest 20% of the population in Brazil, even under the highly optimistic assumption that their health and education achievements reflect the global average, would rank 115—52 places lower than the average for the country (table 2). Indeed, the situation of the poorest 20% in Brazil is comparable to that in countries such as Guatemala, Honduras and Mongolia. Among other countries with the largest differences in HDI ranks for the poorest are Mexico, Chile and Argentina—highly unequal countries. But even for more nearly equal, highly developed countries such as Sweden the difference is large—there the poorest 20% would rank 25, compared with 6 for the average population.

Table 1	Improvements in HDI components for Bangladesh, China and Uganda from 1990 to 2003

Index (1990 = 100)

Country	Year	Life expectancy	Adult literacy	Combined primary, secondary and tertiary school enrolment	GDP per capita (PPP US$)
Bangladesh	2003	115	120	153	143
China	2003	106	116	129	296
Uganda	2003	102	123	193	157

Source: Human Development Report Office 2005.

Table 2	Difference between poorest 20% and national average in HDI rank for selected countries

	HDI rank		
Country	Whole population	Poorest 20%	Difference
Mexico	53	108	55
Brazil	63	115	52
Chile	36	85	49
Argentina	34	78	44
Thailand	72	108	36
Russian Federation	62	95	33
Belarus	66	98	32
China	85	115	30
United States	10	31	21
Sweden	6	25	19

adequately recognized, the perceived messages associated with the statistics presented in the Report could be misleading.

For example, relative poverty measures, such as the proportion of people with disposable income less that 50% of the adjusted national disposable income (a component of the human poverty index for selected high-income countries), are usually used to assess poverty in high-income countries. These measures are the most informative approach for point in time comparisons across these countries. But when countries experience rapid economic growth—as Ireland did during the late 1990s—relative poverty measures on their own can be misleading (box 3).

While promoting the innovative use of statistics, the Human Development Report

Office makes continuing efforts to enhance the public's understanding and to encourage proper interpretations of statistics presented in the Report. In addition to other outreach activities, the Human Development Report Office offers discussions on a wide range of measurement issues and provides extensive links to the technical information of all major international data agencies' databases through its statistics website (http://hdr.undp.org/statistics/understanding/resources.cfm).

Through policy discussions on critical, emerging human development issues, the Report often reveals, and advocates for, the need to develop innovative measures and collect new data in specific areas. As this year marks the International Year of Microfinance

---

| Box 3 | Two tales of Irish poverty |

To ensure comparability across high-income countries, most comparative databases, such as the Luxembourg Income Study (www.lisproject.org), measure poverty on a relative basis. Instead of an absolute poverty line (for example, the $1 a day international poverty line for developing countries), relative poverty measures define the poverty rate as the proportion of people with disposal income less than 50% or 60% of adjusted average national disposable income. For point in time comparisons across countries, this is the most informative approach. But when countries experience rapid economic growth—as in the case of Ireland in the late 1990s—relative poverty measures on their own can sometimes be misleading.

Based on the 50% and 60% of median income measures, the table presents two different time series of poverty estimates for Ireland—relative and anchored—for 1994–2000. A relative poverty line shifts yearly according to the annual median income of a country. An anchored poverty line maintains the initial year poverty line, adjusting it to each subsequent year only according to changes in consumer prices.

According to the relative poverty line of 60% of annual median income, the preferred measure of the European Union, poverty rose 11.3% between 1994 and 2000 in Ireland (see table). But if we set the poverty line at 60% of the 1994 median income and adjust the poverty line only by the change in consumer prices for subsequent years—the anchored poverty line approach—Irish poverty falls by 55.9% during the same period. Similar patterns are evident for the 50% of median income line—a measure favoured by most international analysts of poverty and used in the human poverty index in this Report. According to the table, a poverty rate of 11.9% in

1994 increases to 16.5% in 2000 on a relative basis, while falling by more than over three-quarters to only 3.5% using the anchored approach. The two different sets of poverty lines—relative and anchored—tell two different stories of Irish poverty trends.

It is clear that when economic conditions change rapidly, relative poverty trends do not always present a complete picture of the ways that economic change affects people's lives. The relative poverty trends suggest that not all incomes in Ireland grew at the same rate and that low incomes grew at a slower rate than higher incomes (or relative poverty would also have fallen). But even so, lower incomes grew enough to reduce the anchored poverty by almost half. In particular, social transfers rose substantially in real terms, so pensioners, for example, saw their living standards improve markedly though they still lagged behind rapidly rising incomes resulting from employment and profits. Whether this represents "pro-poor economic growth" remains debatable. But both sides of the poverty story must be recognized.

Differences between relative and anchored poverty lines for Ireland

Year	50% of median income		60% of median income	
	Relative poverty line	Anchored poverty line	Relative poverty line	Anchored poverty line
1994	11.9	11.9	20.4	20.4
1995	12.9	11.1	20.8	19.2
1996	12.3	8.5	21.8	16.6
2000	16.5	3.5	22.7	9.0
Percentage change, 1994–2000	38.7	−70.6	11.3	−55.9

Source: Nolan, Munzi and Smeeding 2005.

2005, the Report highlights the importance of access to adequate financial services by the poor to help lift their families and communities out of poverty and draws attention to the pressing need to collect better data for assessing the needs for and the impact of microfinance (box 4).

Advocating for better human development statistics

While this year's Report presents the best data currently available for measuring human development, many gaps and problems remain.

Data gaps

Gaps throughout the indicator tables demonstrate the pressing need for improvements in the availability of relevant, reliable and timely human development statistics. A stark example of data gaps is the large number of countries excluded from the HDI. The intent is to include all UN member countries, along with Hong Kong, China (SAR), and the Occupied Palestinian Territories in this Report. But because of a lack of reliable data, 16 UN member countries are excluded from the HDI and therefore from the main indicator tables (what key indicators are available for these

---

| Box 4 | **Measuring financial access** |

Economic research supports the broad view that access to deep and efficient financial sector services contributes importantly to economic growth. Poor people can particularly benefit from these services, such as loans, savings deposits, insurance and payment systems. Anecdotal evidence suggests that financial services are reaching more poor people and that, as a result, wealth increases not only for the recipients, but their communities as well. Hard data, however, on who receive what types of services and how effective these services are, and the funding sources of these services, remain scarce and at times even unhelpful: estimates of worldwide microfinance clients range from 70 million to 750 million. We need better data to understand how microfinance can reach its potential and effectively contribute to human development.

Private sector providers of microfinance need this information to channel their investments. Policy-makers and regulators, both at the national level and in bilateral and multilateral donor agencies, need to know whether and to what extent the poor have access financial services in order to measure the effectiveness of their own activities, and understand what changes, in regulation or structural reform, are needed.

The convergence of information needs between public and private interests has motivated a number of institutions to consider how best to move forward. The World Bank and the International Monetary Fund (IMF) has increased their attention to microfinance in their Financial Sector Assessment processes. The UK Department for International Development (DFID) has made progress in collecting data on access to finance in South Africa. In October 2004, the United Nations Capital Development Fund (UNCDF), the World Bank and the IMF brought together top economists and statisticians to figure out how to get better data.

West Africa shows what can be achieved in this way. Since 1993 the Central Bank of West Africa has collected detailed statistics on institutions that offer microfinance in seven West African countries. As a result, it knows that the number of institutions that provided microfinance from 1994 to 2004 increased sixfold and that the number of service points increased from 1,000 to 3,000 outlets. Furthermore, it knows that these services reach more than 12% of the economically active population of West Africa and that a 13-fold increase occurred in the value of deposits since 1994. There is also some evidence that the areas where microfinance has grown have seen particularly strong economic growth—an encouraging sign, though the impact of microfinance will clearly need to be further analyzed.

The International Year of Microcredit 2005 provides a unique opportunity to understand and address the dearth of critical information on the access of poor and low-income people to inclusive financial services, and to determine how these services can be effectively provided in the future.

Source: Fischer, Banny and Barrineau 2005.

countries are presented in table 33). Similarly, the human poverty index covers only 103 developing countries and 18 high-income OECD countries, the gender-related development index 140 countries and the gender empowerment measure 80 countries. For a significant number of countries data for the components of these indices are unreliable and out of date and in some cases need to be estimated (for the definition and methodology of the indices, see *Technical note 1*).

Data gaps in the Millennium Indicators Database (http://millenniumindicators. un.org), which is based on national statistics compiled or estimated by international data agencies, are also revealing. Despite considerable improvements in recent years, for most of the MDG indicators many countries still have no data for 1990–2003, and few have data on trends over that time (table 1). Data for some of the indicators, such as maternal mortality ratios (box 5), are particularly difficult to obtain.

Table 1	Large data gaps remain even in basic human development indicators: countries lacking data, 1990–2003

Indicator	Countries lacking trend data	Countries lacking any data
Children under weight for age	115	35
Net primary enrolment ratio	40	9
Children reaching grade 5	114	53
Youth literacy	57	29
Births attended by skilled health personnel	162	9
Female share of non-agricultural wage employment	68	15
HIV prevalence among pregnant women ages 15–24 in major urban areas	162	139
Population with sustainable access to an improved water source, rural	59	15
Population living on less than $1 a day	93	67

Note: Data refer to developing countries and countries in Central and Eastern Europe and the Commonwealth of Independent States. A country is defined as having trend data if at least two data points are available—one in 1990–96 and one in 1997–2003—and the two points are at least three years apart.
Source: Human Development Report Office, based on UN 2005f.

Inconsistencies between national and international estimates

Inconsistencies between national and international data have often been brought to light through the Report, most visibly through the HDI. Sometimes the data gap in an international data series is contested and a national estimate is claimed to be available, but more frequently the accuracy of the international estimate is questioned and a different national estimate is proposed. Such inconsistencies frequently dispute the accuracy and reliability of data presented in the Report, challenging its statistical credibility and policy impact.

Some of the differences between national and international data are inevitable. They can result from the process of international harmonization, in which national data—inconsistent with the international standards and definitions or of poor quality for other reasons—need to be adjusted. When data for a country are missing, international agencies may produce an estimate if other relevant information can be used. In some cases, the international indicator, such as GDP per capita in purchasing power parity US$, is produced mainly for international comparisons and is not directly comparable to other related national statistics.

In other cases, however, data inconsistencies may occur as a result of lack of coordination—either between national and international data agencies or among various government agencies in a national statistical system—and can be avoided. Sometimes, the most recent national statistics are not made available to the relevant international data agency in time, despite its earnest data collection efforts. Other times, when multiple sources for a given indicator exist in a country, the data submitted by a government agency are not coordinated through the central national statistical office and could be contested by the government once published in the international series. Occasionally, errors creep into the compilation of international data series.

While the primary responsibility to deal with these inconsistency issues lies with international data producers and their national and regional counterparts, all international data users should support their efforts. The Human

Box 5   Monitoring maternal mortality

Maternal mortality claims around half a million lives each year and many millions more women suffer ill health as a result of complications in pregnancy. The world is off track for the Millennium Development Goal of reducing maternal deaths by two-thirds, but it is hard to tell exactly how far off because maternal mortality ratios are notoriously difficult to measure accurately.

Nationally reported data on maternal deaths often suffer from underreporting and misclassification. Only one-third of the world's population lives in countries that maintain comprehensive statistics about human lives and deaths—vital registration—the most effective way of measuring adult (including maternal) mortality. Even in countries with good vital registration, maternal deaths, including deaths due to direct obstetric causes and to conditions aggravated by pregnancy and delivery, can be hard to identify precisely and are frequently underrecorded. Moreover, many maternal deaths in developing countries, especially those with high maternal mortality ratios, occur outside of health facilities and go completely unrecorded.

In the absence of strong vital registration systems, measuring maternal mortality—because it is relatively rare—requires large, costly household surveys or regular censuses. Even when indirect estimation techniques (such as the sisterhood method) are used in surveys (such as the Demographic and Health Surveys), the resulting estimates of maternal mortality ratios are inevitably associated with large standard errors, typically refer to an earlier period and are not suitable for assessing short-term policy impact.

In an effort to address the gaps and poor comparability of national data, the World Health Organization (WHO), the United Nations Children's Fund (UNICEF) and the United Nations Population Fund (UNFPA) have developed international estimates using a methodology that adjusts nationally reported data to account for misclassifications and underreporting, while developing model-based estimates for countries with no recent data of acceptable quality. These modelled estimates—used in this Report and in other major global monitoring reports—rely on more widely available data on fertility and coverage of skilled attendant at delivery to predict maternal mortality.

So far, three sets of international estimates have been produced separately for 1990, 1995 and 2000. Because of large ranges of uncertainty and lack of comparability due to changes in methodology, these estimates can be used only to indicate the scope of the problem and offer little insight about the trends over time.

The majority of maternal deaths—about three-quarters—are due to obstetric complications that can be successfully treated with available technology. Accordingly, process indicators—such as the proportion of births attended by skilled health personnel and coverage of emergency obstetric care—are increasingly used as proxies for assessing trends in maternal mortality and for directing public health policies and programmes to improve maternal health.

Source: Based on Abou-Zahr 2005; UN Millennium Project 2005; UNICEF, WHO and UNFPA 1997; WHO 2005.

Development Report Office has an especially important role given the Report's high profile. It has in recent years strived to be more proactive in identifying potential problems in advance, defusing potential conflicts through timely interventions with governments and international agencies and engaging in more visible public discussions about the problem and possible solutions.

In particular, the Human Development Report Office recognizes the unique role of the Report in

- Advocating for improvements in human development measurements and data through the Report, including the need for countries to adopt internationally agreed standards and definitions in basic areas of statistics and for international agencies to be more transparent and accessible with their methodologies and processes.
- Identifying potential problems and coordinating between national and international data agencies to resolve the differences.
- Improving its statistical outreach to increase the public understanding of the statistical principles and processes and to enhance the awareness of governments' own responsibilities.

| Box 6 | Dealing with data inconsistencies—the Qatar experience |

The government of Qatar noticed that certain data presented in recent *Human Development Reports* were inconsistent with official data published by Qatar, leading to disparities in a number of indices. Some of the statistics employed in the *Human Development Reports* were out of date, and others reported as unavailable did in fact exist. Human development indicator tables prepared by the Planning Council were, in some instances, at odds with those appearing in the Report.

The Planning Council of Qatar called on the advice of the Human Development Report Office, and active communication and cooperation has since been maintained, including an advisory visit by a senior member of the Human Development Report Office to Qatar in December 2004.

Since the Human Development Report relies on the statistical series published by other international data agencies, the Planning Council initiated direct contact with 22 international agencies to ensure that statistics for Qatar are accurately and comprehensively reported. This has in turn led to more active cooperation between the statistical organization of Qatar and the main statistics organizations of the United Nations.

Qatar initiated an active process of cooperation between the users and producers of statistics, aimed at a smoother and more accurate flow of information. It held a symposium in May 2004, in which representatives of the statistical organizations of a number of UN agencies took part. A strategy for more active cooperation between users and producers and more timely and accurate reporting was formulated. The strategy has since been rigorously implemented, and substantial improvements have been achieved. A follow-up symposium was held in May 2005.

Source: Aboona 2005.

| Box 7 | National strategies for the development of statistics |

Increased use of quality statistics leads to improvements in policy decisions and development outcomes. This transition to evidence-based policy-making can be achieved through implementing a statistical capacity building strategy that is fully integrated into national policy processes such as poverty reduction strategies and monitoring progress towards the Millennium Development Goals. A National Strategy for the Development of Statistics (NSDS) helps achieve this objective. An NSDS converts statistical priorities into a detailed, flexible work programme, building on the existing statistical system and ongoing improvement processes, such as the International Monetary Fund's General Data Dissemination System and the UN's Fundamental Principles for Official Statistics.

A good strategy—backed with political commitment and adequate funding—can increase the contribution of a national statistical system. It can help countries break free from a vicious circle of underfunding and underperformance. Support from the international development community, however, is crucial. Those countries most in need of better statistics are those least able to afford them. The World Bank's Trust Fund for Statistical Capacity Building is one important source of grant funding to help countries to design an NSDS. The World Bank has also launched a new programme—STATCAP—to help countries access loans and credits to support implementation of an NSDS.

The 2004 Marrakech Action Plan for Statistics (MAPS) recommends that all low-income countries prepare an NSDS by 2006 and begin to implement it by the following year in order to have high quality, locally produced data for the next major review of the Millennium Development Goals in 2010. This is an ambitious but achievable goal. Partnership in Statistics for Development in the 21st Century (PARIS21) works through advocacy, developing methodological guidelines and documentation and facilitating regional programmes with regional partner organisations. Helping countries to achieve this target is the main objective of the PARIS21 in its work programme for 2004–06. NSDS guidelines and the PARIS21 work plan can be viewed on the PARIS21 website at www.paris21.org.

Source: William 2005.

It acknowledges explicitly the role of UNDP country offices—as partners in both disseminating the Report and coordinating with governments. Through them we can improve the national capacity in managing statistical information, particularly through better communication and coordination between national and international data agencies to reduce data discrepancies.

Since last year the Human Development Report Office has taken important steps to develop better launch materials, establish a new statistical Web site and provide training to UNDP country offices and national experts. While continuing to work closely with international data agencies, the Human Development Report Office has also initiated more direct contact with national statistical offices and other government agencies. Meanwhile, many governments have increasingly recognized the implications of data inconsistencies for national policy debates and discussions and acknowledged their own role in reducing such data inconsistencies. More and more country governments, such as Qatar (box 6), are working to improve coordination with relevant international data agencies and among government agencies within the national statistical system.

Towards stronger statistical capacity

A vital part of the solution to the enormous gaps and deficiencies in statistical information is building sustainable statistical capacity in countries, an effort requiring financial and political commitment at both the national and international levels. The momentum generated by the MDG process has mobilized the entire international statistical community, and many initiatives are under way, including the development of national strategies for the development of statistics recommended by the Marrakech Action Plan for Statistics (http://unstats.un.org/unsd/statcom/doc04/marrakech.pdf) and supported by the Partnership in Statistics for Development in the 21st Century (box 7).

International statistical agencies should continue to play an active part in statistical development by improving, promoting and implementing internationally agreed standards, methods and frameworks for statistical activities, while strengthening their own statistical capacity to meet the increasing demand for better international statistics for monitoring human development.

Calculating the human development indices

The diagrams here summarize how the five human development indices used in the *Human Development Report* are constructed, highlighting both their similarities and their differences. The text on the following pages provides a detailed explanation.

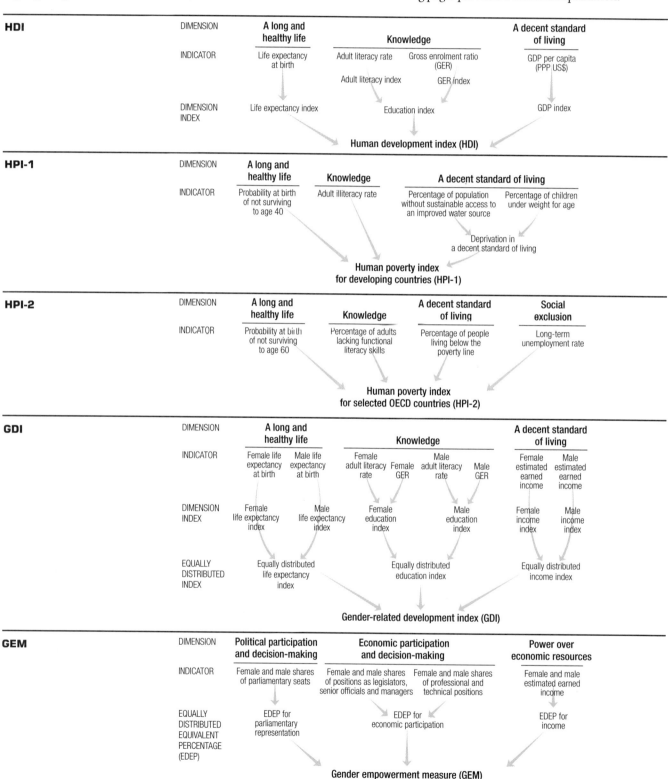

The human development index (HDI)

The HDI is a summary measure of human development. It measures the average achievements in a country in three basic dimensions of human development:

- A long and healthy life, as measured by life expectancy at birth.
- Knowledge, as measured by the adult literacy rate (with two-thirds weight) and the combined primary, secondary and tertiary gross enrolment ratio (with one-third weight).
- A decent standard of living, as measured by GDP per capita (PPP US$).

Before the HDI itself is calculated, an index needs to be created for each of these dimensions. To calculate these dimension indices —the life expectancy, education and GDP indices—minimum and maximum values (goalposts) are chosen for each underlying indicator.

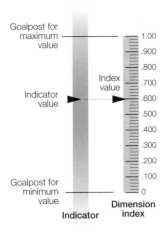

Performance in each dimension is expressed as a value between 0 and 1 by applying the following general formula:

$$\text{Dimension index} = \frac{\text{actual value} - \text{minimum value}}{\text{maximum value} - \text{minimum value}}$$

The HDI is then calculated as a simple average of the dimension indices. The box at right illustrates the calculation of the HDI for a sample country.

Goalposts for calculating the HDI

Indicator	Maximum value	Minimum value
Life expectancy at birth (years)	85	25
Adult literacy rate (%)	100	0
Combined gross enrolment ratio (%)	100	0
GDP per capita (PPP US$)	40,000	100

Calculating the HDI

This illustration of the calculation of the HDI uses data for South Africa.

1. Calculating the life expectancy index
The life expectancy index measures the relative achievement of a country in life expectancy at birth. For South Africa, with a life expectancy of 48.4 years in 2003, the life expectancy index is 0.391.

$$\text{Life expectancy index} = \frac{48.4 - 25}{85 - 25} = \mathbf{0.391}$$

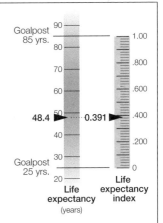

2. Calculating the education index
The education index measures a country's relative achievement in both adult literacy and combined primary, secondary and tertiary gross enrolment. First, an index for adult literacy and one for combined gross enrolment are calculated. Then these two indices are combined to create the education index, with two-thirds weight given to adult literacy and one-third weight to combined gross enrolment. For South Africa, with an adult literacy rate of 82.4% in 2003 and a combined gross enrolment ratio of 78% in the school year 2002/03, the education index is 0.809.

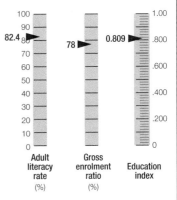

$$\text{Adult literacy index} = \frac{82.4 - 0}{100 - 0} = 0.824$$

$$\text{Gross enrolment index} = \frac{78 - 0}{100 - 0} = 0.780$$

$$\text{Education index} = 2/3 \text{ (adult literacy index)} + 1/3 \text{ (gross enrolment index)}$$
$$= 2/3 \ (0.824) + 1/3 \ (0.780) = \mathbf{0.809}$$

3. Calculating the GDP index
The GDP index is calculated using adjusted GDP per capita (PPP US$). In the HDI income serves as a surrogate for all the dimensions of human development not reflected in a long and healthy life and in knowledge. Income is adjusted because achieving a respectable level of human development does not require unlimited income. Accordingly, the logarithm of income is used. For South Africa, with a GDP per capita of $10,346 (PPP US$) in 2003, the GDP index is 0.774.

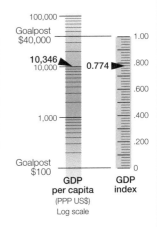

$$\text{GDP index} = \frac{\log (10,346) - \log (100)}{\log (40,000) - \log (100)} = \mathbf{0.774}$$

4. Calculating the HDI
Once the dimension indices have been calculated, determining the HDI is straightforward. It is a simple average of the three dimension indices.

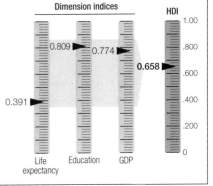

$$\text{HDI} = 1/3 \text{ (life expectancy index)} + 1/3 \text{ (education index)}$$
$$+ 1/3 \text{ (GDP index)}$$
$$= 1/3 \ (0.391) + 1/3 \ (0.809) + 1/3 \ (0.774) = \mathbf{0.658}$$

The human poverty index for developing countries (HPI-1)

While the HDI measures average achievement, the HPI-1 measures *deprivations* in the three basic dimensions of human development captured in the HDI:

- A long and healthy life—vulnerability to death at a relatively early age, as measured by the probability at birth of not surviving to age 40.
- Knowledge—exclusion from the world of reading and communications, as measured by the adult illiteracy rate.
- A decent standard of living—lack of access to overall economic provisioning, as measured by the unweighted average of two indicators, the percentage of the population without sustainable access to an improved water source and the percentage of children under weight for age.

Calculating the HPI-1 is more straightforward than calculating the HDI. The indicators used to measure the deprivations are already normalized between 0 and 100 (because they are expressed as percentages), so there is no need to create dimension indices as for the HDI.

Originally, the measure of deprivation in a decent standard of living also included an indicator of access to health services. But because reliable data on access to health services are lacking for recent years, in this year's Report deprivation in a decent standard of living is meausred by two rather than three indicators—the percentage of the population without sustainable access to an improved water source and the percentage of children under weight for age.

The human poverty index for selected OECD countries (HPI-2)

The HPI-2 measures deprivations in the same dimensions as the HPI-1 and also captures social exclusion. Thus it reflects deprivations in four dimensions:

- A long and healthy life—vulnerability to death at a relatively early age, as measured by the probability at birth of not surviving to age 60.
- Knowledge—exclusion from the world of reading and communications, as measured by the percentage of adults (aged 16–65) lacking functional literacy skills.
- A decent standard of living—as measured by the percentage of people living below the income poverty line (50% of the median adjusted household disposable income).
- Social exclusion—as measured by the rate of long-term unemployment (12 months or more).

Calculating the HPI-1

1. Measuring deprivation in a decent standard of living

An unweighted average of two indicators is used to measure deprivation in a decent standard of living.

Unweighted average = 1/2 (population without sustainable access to an improved water source)
+ 1/2 (children under weight for age)

A sample calculation: Angola

Population without sustainable access to an improved water source = 50%

Children under weight for age = 31%

Unweighted average = 1/2 (50) + 1/2 (31) = 40.5%

2. Calculating the HPI-1

The formula for calculating the HPI-1 is as follows:

$$\text{HPI-1} = [1/3 \, (P_1^{\alpha} + P_2^{\alpha} + P_3^{\alpha})]^{1/\alpha}$$

Where:

P_1 = Probability at birth of not surviving to age 40 (times 100)

P_2 = Adult illiteracy rate

P_3 = Unweighted average of population without sustainable access to an improved water source and children under weight for age

$\alpha = 3$

A sample calculation: Angola

$P_1 = 48.1\%$

$P_2 = 33.2\%$

$P_3 = 40.5\%$

$$\text{HPI-1} = [1/3 \, (48.1^3 + 33.2^3 + 40.5^3)]^{1/3} = \textbf{41.5}$$

Calculating the HPI-2

The formula for calculating the HPI-2 is as follows:

$$\text{HPI-2} = [1/4 \, (P_1^{\alpha} + P_2^{\alpha} + P_3^{\alpha} + P_4^{\alpha})]^{1/\alpha}$$

Where:

P_1 = Probability at birth of not surviving to age 60 (times 100)

P_2 = Adults lacking functional literacy skills

P_3 = Population below income poverty line (50% of median adjusted household disposable income)

P_4 = Rate of long-term unemployment (lasting 12 months or more)

$\alpha = 3$

A sample calculation: United States

$P_1 = 11.8\%$

$P_2 = 20.0\%$

$P_3 = 17.0\%$

$P_4 = 0.7\%$

$$\text{HPI-2} = [1/4 \, (11.8^3 + 20.0^3 + 17.0^3 + 0.7^3)]^{1/3} = \textbf{15.4}$$

Why $\alpha = 3$ in calculating the HPI-1 and HPI-2

The value of α has an important impact on the value of the HPI. If $\alpha = 1$, the HPI is the average of its dimensions. As α rises, greater weight is given to the dimension in which there is the most deprivation. Thus as α increases towards infinity, the HPI will tend towards the value of the dimension in which deprivation is greatest (for Angola, the example used for calculating the HPI-1, it would be 48, equal to the probability at birth of not surviving to age 40).

In this Report the value 3 is used to give additional but not overwhelming weight to areas of more acute deprivation. For a detailed analysis of the HPI's mathematical formulation, see Sudhir Anand and Amartya Sen's "Concepts of Human Development and Poverty: A Multidimensional Perspective" and the technical note in *Human Development Report 1997* (see the list of selected readings at the end of this technical note).

The gender-related development index (GDI)

While the HDI measures average achievement, the GDI adjusts the average achievement to reflect the *inequalities* between men and women in the following dimensions:

- A long and healthy life, as measured by life expectancy at birth.
- Knowledge, as measured by the adult literacy rate and the combined primary, secondary and tertiary gross enrolment ratio.
- A decent standard of living, as measured by estimated earned income (PPP US$).

The calculation of the GDI involves three steps. First, female and male indices in each dimension are calculated according to this general formula:

$$\text{Dimension index} = \frac{\text{actual value} - \text{minimum value}}{\text{maximum value} - \text{minimum value}}$$

Second, the female and male indices in each dimension are combined in a way that penalizes differences in achievement between men and women. The resulting index, referred to as the equally distributed index, is calculated according to this general formula:

$$\text{Equally distributed index} = \{[\text{female population share (female index}^{1-\epsilon})] + [\text{male population share (male index}^{1-\epsilon})]\}^{1/1-\epsilon}$$

ϵ measures the aversion to inequality. In the GDI $\epsilon = 2$. Thus the general equation becomes:

$$\text{Equally distributed index} = \{[\text{female population share (female index}^{-1})] + [\text{male population share (male index}^{-1})]\}^{-1}$$

which gives the harmonic mean of the female and male indices.

Third, the GDI is calculated by combining the three equally distributed indices in an unweighted average.

Goalposts for calculating the GDI

Indicator	Maximum value	Minimum value
Female life expectancy at birth (years)	87.5	27.5
Male life expectancy at birth (years)	82.5	22.5
Adult literacy rate (%)	100	0
Combined gross enrolment ratio (%)	100	0
Estimated earned income (PPP US$)	40,000	100

Note: The maximum and minimum values (goalposts) for life expectancy are five years higher for women to take into account their longer life expectancy.

Calculating the GDI

This illustration of the calculation of the GDI uses data for Brazil.

1. Calculating the equally distributed life expectancy index

The first step is to calculate separate indices for female and male achievements in life expectancy, using the general formula for dimension indices.

FEMALE
Life expectancy: 74.6 years

$$\text{Life expectancy index} = \frac{74.6 - 27.5}{87.5 - 27.5} = 0.785$$

MALE
Life expectancy: 66.6 years

$$\text{Life expectancy index} = \frac{66.6 - 22.5}{82.5 - 22.5} = 0.735$$

Next, the female and male indices are combined to create the equally distributed life expectancy index, using the general formula for equally distributed indices.

FEMALE
Population share: 0.507
Life expectancy index: 0.785

MALE
Population share: 0.493
Life expectancy index: 0.735

$$\text{Equally distributed life expectancy index} = \{[0.507\,(0.785^{-1})] + [0.493\,(0.735^{-1})]\}^{-1} = \textbf{0.760}$$

2. Calculating the equally distributed education index

First, indices for the adult literacy rate and the combined primary, secondary and tertiary gross enrolment ratio are calculated separately for females and males. Calculating these indices is straightforward, since the indicators used are already normalized between 0 and 100.

FEMALE
Adult literacy rate: 88.6%
Adult literacy index: 0.886
Gross enrolment ratio: 92.7%
Gross enrolment index: 0.927

MALE
Adult literacy rate: 88.3%
Adult literacy index: 0.883
Gross enrolment ratio: 88.5%
Gross enrolment index: 0.885

Second, the education index, which gives two-thirds weight to the adult literacy index and one-third weight to the gross enrolment index, is computed separately for females and males.

$$\text{Education index} = 2/3\,(\text{adult literacy index}) + 1/3\,(\text{gross enrolment index})$$

$$\text{Female education index} = 2/3\,(0.886) + 1/3\,(0.927) = 0.899$$

$$\text{Male education index} = 2/3\,(0.883) + 1/3\,(0.885) = 0.884$$

Finally, the female and male education indices are combined to create the equally distributed education index.

FEMALE
Population share: 0.507
Education index: 0.899

MALE
Population share: 0.493
Education index: 0.884

$$\text{Equally distributed education index} = \{[0.507\,(0.899^{-1})] + [0.493\,(0.884^{-1})]\}^{-1} = \textbf{0.892}$$

3. Calculating the equally distributed income index

First, female and male earned income (PPP US$) are estimated (for details on this calculation, see the addendum to this technical note). Then the income index is calculated for each gender. As for the HDI, income is adjusted by taking the logarithm of estimated earned income (PPP US$):

$$\text{Income index} = \frac{\log(\text{actual value}) - \log(\text{minimum value})}{\log(\text{maximum value}) - \log(\text{minimum value})}$$

FEMALE
Estimated earned income (PPP US$): 4,704

$$\text{Income index} = \frac{\log(4{,}704) - \log(100)}{\log(40{,}000) - \log(100)} = 0.643$$

MALE
Estimated earned income (PPP US$): 10,963

$$\text{Income index} = \frac{\log(10{,}963) - \log(100)}{\log(40{,}000) - \log(100)} = 0.784$$

Calculating the GDI continues on next page

Calculating the GDI (continued)

Second, the female and male income indices are combined to create the equally distributed income index:

FEMALE
Population share: 0.507
Income index: 0.643

MALE
Population share: 0.493
Income index: 0.784

Equally distributed income index = $\{[0.507 \, (0.643^{-1})] + [0.493 \, (0.784^{-1})]\}^{-1}$ = **0.706**

4. Calculating the GDI

Calculating the GDI is straightforward. It is simply the unweighted average of the three component indices—the equally distributed life expectancy index, the equally distributed education index and the equally distributed income index.

GDI = 1/3 (life expectancy index) + 1/3 (education index) + 1/3 (income index)
= 1/3 (0.760) + 1/3 (0.892) + 1/3 (0.706) = **0.786**

Why $\epsilon = 2$ in calculating the GDI

The value of ϵ is the size of the penalty for gender inequality. The larger the value, the more heavily a society is penalized for having inequalities.

If $\epsilon = 0$, gender inequality is not penalized (in this case the GDI would have the same value as the HDI). As ϵ increases towards infinity, more and more weight is given to the lesser achieving group.

The value 2 is used in calculating the GDI (as well as the GEM). This value places a moderate penalty on gender inequality in achievement.

For a detailed analysis of the GDI's mathematical formulation, see Sudhir Anand and Amartya Sen's "Gender Inequality in Human Development: Theories and Measurement," Kalpana Bardhan and Stephan Klasen's "UNDP's Gender-Related Indices: A Critical Review" and the technical notes in *Human Development Report 1995* and *Human Development Report 1999* (see the list of selected readings at the end of this technical note).

The gender empowerment measure (GEM)

Focusing on women's opportunities rather than their capabilities, the GEM captures gender inequality in three key areas:

- Political participation and decision-making power, as measured by women's and men's percentage shares of parliamentary seats.
- Economic participation and decision-making power, as measured by two indicators—women's and men's percentage shares of positions as legislators, senior officials and managers and women's and men's percentage shares of professional and technical positions.
- Power over economic resources, as measured by women's and men's estimated earned income (PPP US$).

For each of these three dimensions, an equally distributed equivalent percentage (EDEP) is calculated, as a population-weighted average, according to the following general formula:

$$EDEP = \{[\text{female population share (female index}^{1-\epsilon})] + [\text{male population share (male index}^{1-\epsilon})]\}^{1/1-\epsilon}$$

ϵ measures the aversion to inequality. In the GEM (as in the GDI) $\epsilon = 2$, which places a moderate penalty on inequality. The formula is thus:

$$EDEP = \{[\text{female population share (female index}^{-1})] + [\text{male population share (male index}^{-1})]\}^{-1}$$

For political and economic participation and decision-making, the EDEP is then indexed by dividing it by 50. The rationale for this indexation: in an ideal society, with equal empowerment of the sexes, the GEM variables would equal 50%—that is, women's share would equal men's share for each variable.

Where a male or female index value is zero, the EDEP according to the above formula is not defined. However, the limit of EDEP, when the index tends towards zero, is zero. Accordingly, in these cases the value of the EDEP is set to zero.

Finally, the GEM is calculated as a simple average of the three indexed EDEPs.

Calculating the GEM

This illustration of the calculation of the GEM uses data for Denmark.

1. Calculating the EDEP for parliamentary representation

The EDEP for parliamentary representation measures the relative empowerment of women in terms of their political participation. The EDEP is calculated using the female and male shares of the population and female and male percentage shares of parliamentary seats according to the general formula.

FEMALE	MALE
Population share: 0.505	Population share: 0.495
Parliamentary share: 36.9%	Parliamentary share: 63.1%

$$\text{EDEP for parliamentary representation} = \{[0.505\ (36.9^{-1})] + [0.495\ (63.1^{-1})]\}^{-1} = 46.42$$

Then this initial EDEP is indexed to an ideal value of 50%.

$$\text{Indexed EDEP for parliamentary representation} = \frac{46.42}{50} = \mathbf{0.928}$$

2. Calculating the EDEP for economic participation

Using the general formula, an EDEP is calculated for women's and men's percentage shares of positions as legislators, senior officials and managers, and another for women's and men's percentage shares of professional and technical positions. The simple average of the two measures gives the EDEP for economic participation.

FEMALE	MALE
Population share: 0.505	Population share: 0.495
Percentage share of positions as legislators, senior officials and managers: 26.2%	Percentage share of positions as legislators, senior officials and managers: 73.8%
Percentage share of professional and technical positions: 51.0%	Percentage share of professional and technical positions: 49.0%

$$\text{EDEP for positions as legislators, senior officials and managers} = \{[0.505\ (26.2^{-1})] + [0.495\ (73.8^{-1})]\}^{-1} = 38.48$$

$$\text{Indexed EDEP for positions as legislators, senior officials and managers} = \frac{38.48}{50} = 0.770$$

$$\text{EDEP for professional and technical positions} = \{[0.505\ (51.0^{-1})] + [0.495\ (49.0^{-1})]\}^{-1} = 49.99$$

$$\text{Indexed EDEP for professional and technical positions} = \frac{49.99}{50} = 1.00$$

The two indexed EDEPs are averaged to create the EDEP for economic participation:

$$\text{EDEP for economic participation} = \frac{0.770 + 1.00}{2} = \mathbf{0.885}$$

3. Calculating the EDEP for income

Earned income (PPP US$) is estimated for women and men separately and then indexed to goalposts as for the HDI and the GDI. For the GEM, however, the income index is based on unadjusted values, not the logarithm of estimated earned income. (For details on the estimation of earned income for men and women, see the addendum to this technical note.)

FEMALE	MALE
Population share: 0.505	Population share: 0.495
Estimated earned income (PPP US$): 26,587	Estimated earned income (PPP US$): 36,430
Income index = $\dfrac{26,519 - 100}{40,000 - 100} = 0.663$	Income index = $\dfrac{36,390 - 100}{40,000 - 100} = 0.910$

The female and male indices are then combined to create the equally distributed index:

$$\text{EDEP for income} = \{[0.505\ (0.663^{-1})] + [0.495\ (0.910^{-1})]\}^{-1} = \mathbf{0.766}$$

4. Calculating the GEM

Once the EDEP has been calculated for the three dimensions of the GEM, determining the GEM is straightforward. It is a simple average of the three EDEP indices.

$$GEM = \frac{0.928 + 0.885 + 0.766}{3} = \mathbf{0.859}$$

TECHNICAL NOTE 1 ADDENDUM
Female and male earned income

Despite the importance of having gender-disaggregated data on income, direct measures are unavailable. For this Report crude estimates of female and male earned income have therefore been derived.

Income can be seen in two ways: as a resource for consumption and as earnings by individuals. The use measure is difficult to disaggregate between men and women because they share resources within a family unit. By contrast, earnings are separable because different members of a family tend to have separate earned incomes.

The income measure used in the GDI and the GEM indicates a person's capacity to earn income. It is used in the GDI to capture the disparities between men and women in command over resources and in the GEM to capture women's economic independence. (For conceptual and methodological issues relating to this approach, see Sudhir Anand and Amartya Sen's "Gender Inequality in Human Development" and, in *Human Development Report 1995*, chapter 3 and technical notes 1 and 2; see the list of selected readings at the end of this technical note.)

Female and male earned income (PPP US$) are estimated using the following data:

- Ratio of the female non-agricultural wage to the male non-agricultural wage.
- Male and female shares of the economically active population.
- Total female and male population.
- GDP per capita (PPP US$).

Key
W_f / W_m = ratio of female non-agricultural wage to male non-agricultural wage
EA_f = female share of economically active population
EA_m = male share of economically active population
S_f = female share of wage bill
Y = total GDP (PPP US$)
N_f = total female population
N_m = total male population
Y_f = estimated female earned income (PPP US$)
Y_m = estimated male earned income (PPP US$)

Note
Calculations based on data in the technical note may yield results that differ from those in the indicator tables because of rounding.

Estimating female and male earned income

This illustration of the estimation of female and male earned income uses 2003 data for Switzerland.

1. Calculating total GDP (PPP US$)
Total GDP (PPP US$) is calculated by multiplying the total population by GDP per capita (PPP US$).

Total population: 7,350 (thousand)
GDP per capita (PPP US$): 30,550
Total GDP (PPP US$) = 7,350 (30,550) = 224,542,500 (thousand)

2. Calculating the female share of the wage bill
Because data on wages in rural areas and in the informal sector are rare, the Report has used non-agricultural wages and assumed that the ratio of female wages to male wages in the non-agricultural sector applies to the rest of the economy. The female share of the wage bill is calculated using the ratio of the female non-agricultural wage to the male non-agricultural wage and the female and male percentage shares of the economically active population. Where data on the wage ratio are not available, a value of 75% is used.

Ratio of female to male non-agricultural wage (W_f/W_m) = 1.324
Female percentage share of economically active population (EA_f) = 40.8%
Male percentage share of economically active population (EA_m) = 59.2%

$$\text{Female share of wage bill } (S_f) = \frac{W_f/W_m (EA_f)}{[W_f/W_m (EA_f)] + EA_m} = \frac{1.324 (40.8)}{[1.324 (40.8)] + 59.2} = \mathbf{0.477}$$

3. Calculating female and male earned income (PPP US$)
An assumption has to be made that the female share of the wage bill is equal to the female share of GDP.

Female share of wage bill (S_f) = 0.477
Total GDP (PPP US$) (Y) = 224,542,500 (thousand)
Female population (N_f) = 3,699 (thousand)

$$\text{Estimated female earned income (PPP US$) } (Y_f) = \frac{S_f (Y)}{N_f} = \frac{0.477 (224,542,500)}{3,699} = \mathbf{28,972}$$

Male population (N_m) = 3,651 (thousand)

$$\text{Estimated male earned income (PPP US$) } (Y_m) = \frac{Y - S_f (Y)}{N_m} = \frac{224,542,500 - [0.477 (224,542,500)]}{3,651} = \mathbf{32,149}$$

Selected readings

Anand, Sudhir, and Amartya Sen. 1994. "Human Development Index: Methodology and Measurement." Occasional Paper 12. United Nations Development Programme, Human Development Report Office, New York. *(HDI)*

———. 1995. "Gender Inequality in Human Development: Theories and Measurement." Occasional Paper 19. United Nations Development Programme, Human Development Report Office, New York. *(GDI, GEM)*

———. 1997. "Concepts of Human Development and Poverty: A Multi-dimensional Perspective." In United Nations Development Programme, *Human Development Report 1997 Papers: Poverty and Human Development.* New York. *(HPI-1, HPI-2)*

Bardhan, Kalpana, and Stephan Klasen. 1999. "UNDP's Gender-Related Indices: A Critical Review." *World Development* 27 (6): 985–1010. *(GDI, GEM)*

United Nations Development Programme. 1995. *Human Development Report 1995.* New York: Oxford University Press. Technical notes 1 and 2 and chapter 3. *(GDI, GEM)*

———. 1997. *Human Development Report 1997.* New York: Oxford University Press. Technical note 1 and chapter 1. *(HPI-1, HPI-2)*

———. 1999. *Human Development Report 1999.* New York: Oxford University Press. Technical note. *(HDI, GDI)*

Two sides of the poverty reduction coin— why growth and distribution matter

This year the *Human Development Report* presents new data and simulations on income, exploring the relationship between economic growth, redistribution and income poverty. Chapter 1 focuses on the international level, looking at global distribution and exploring the implications of different growth patterns for poverty reduction. The chapter draws on a global income distribution model prepared for *Human Development Report 2005* (Dikhanov 2005). The model is used to explore how different growth and distribution scenarios to 2015 might have a bearing on poverty. Trend growth projections and the $1 a day poverty line are used to determine how many fewer people would be living in poverty with a pro-poor growth pattern with the income of poor people growing at twice the average rate. Chapter 2 shifts from the global to the national level. Household expenditure surveys are used to plot income distribution patterns for three countries. Starting from the prevailing distribution, a forward-looking projection is developed to consider the impact on poverty of pro-poor growth patterns, with the income of the poor—defined as the population living below the national poverty line—rising at twice the national average.

The scenario exercises illustrate the potentially large scale benefits for poverty reduction of small changes in distribution in favour of the poor. However, the simulations used are stylized exercises. They cast some light on how the interaction of economic growth with different distribution patterns can influence prospects for poverty reduction. By definition, simulations do not help identify the specific strategies that might achieve the optimal growth distribution patterns for maximizing the speed of poverty reduction. That does not mean that the simulations in chapters 1 and 2 have no implications

for policy. As the global modeling exercise in chapter 1 demonstrates, creating conditions under which the world's poor people capture a larger share of future growth would create an enabling environment for accelerated poverty reduction. The same applies at a national level. As the pro-poor growth simulations here demonstrate, modest gains in the income share of the poor can shorten the time horizon for halving poverty. One of the central messages that emerges for policy-makers is that distribution matters both for the Millennium Development Goals and for wider poverty reduction efforts.

World income distribution

The global income distribution model used in chapter 1 provides an estimate of global income distribution for 1970–2000. These estimates are supplemented with two forward-looking scenarios for 2015. The first scenario looks at poverty in 2015 on a distribution-neutral growth projection—that is, with national income distribution held constant over time. The second scenario assumes that the income of the poor grows at twice the average rate until 2015. The scenarios are based on 1990–2002 trends in GDP growth and UN population projections for 2015. The simulations highlight the impact of different growth patterns on income inequality and income poverty. Additionally, the model looks at the dimensions of the income transfer that would be required to eliminate $1 a day poverty.

Data and methodological issues
Dikhanov (2005) is a model of world inequality accounting. It provides an approximation for global income inequality, which is narrower than a model of wealth accounting because it

does not take into account ownership of productive assets, which might be seen as a primary source of economic power and a determinant of income inequality. Nor does it take into account the notional value of non-market goods and services delivered by governments.

In effect, world inequality accounting attempts to capture income inequality among all individuals in the world. The exercise involves combining income distribution within countries and comparing incomes across countries. Global income is taken to be the sum of the reported, as well as estimated and imputed, personal consumption expenditure from national accounts data of all countries in the World Bank database. Thus national accounts data, rather than data from household surveys, are used to determine average incomes in each country. National accounts data are more suitable for comparison over time. However, such data are incomplete because they do not include the informal economy and certain categories of income. This makes it possible to scale up national accounting exercises to arrive at a global income using consistent methodology across countries. Personal consumption expenditure differs from standard GDP or GNI measurement in that it excludes some national accounting items, such as savings by firms and governments. The current exercise uses a polynomial interpolation to approximate a continuous distribution from the information provided by the underlying data.

Applying distributional information from the income and consumption surveys to average incomes yields an approximation, in national currencies, of each individual's income. For international comparisons these incomes must be converted into the same currency. Because exchange rates do not take into account price differential between countries, international comparison requires adjustments. The model converts personal consumption expenditure values in local currency into international dollars using 1999 purchasing power parities (PPPs). The PPP methodology collects information on prices through the International Comparison Program, which surveys the price for a basket of goods across more than 100 countries. An important debate has developed in recent years

over the use of PPP adjustments, specifically in relation to the $1 a day poverty line. This debate is not revisited here. Interested readers should see the list of readings at the end of this note.

Some countries lack the national accounts information needed to scale up from the national level to the global level. To obtain global totals, gap-filling procedures involving imputation were used. The techniques are detailed in notes to *World Development Indicators 2001* (World Bank 2001). Imputation procedures are applied to a relatively small group of countries, with standard national accounting providing data for over 80 percent of the global personal consumption expenditure and population.

World inequality accounting makes it possible to derive various regional subaggregates of global distribution, as well as the share of global income accounted for at each percentile level, regardless of the country in which individuals live. That is, the model creates a hypothetical world in which all people can be lined up in a single distribution, regardless of where they live. The shape and regional decomposition of the distribution is set out in chapter 1.

Simulations and results

Much heat has been generated by the debate on globalization and inequality. Polarized conclusions have been reached with regard to both trend and attribution. Studies employing different techniques and data sources have reached divergent conclusions on whether global income inequality is increasing or decreasing and on the precise role played by globalization. World inequality accounting does not resolve the global inequality debate, though it does call into question claims that globalization has been accompanied by income convergence (as claimed by some supporters of global integration) or by rapid divergence (as claimed by others). The model used in chapter 1 finds that overall inequality, as measured by the Gini coefficient, has changed little, from 67 in 1970 to 68 in 2000. This shift is probably smaller than the margin of error introduced by the data, and is thus insignificant.

As indicated earlier, the 2015 simulation compares two different growth paths for 2002–15. Both simulations use a similar growth projection. For countries with positive growth, trends for 1990–2002 are projected forward to 2015. For countries and regions with negative growth, positive future growth is assumed based on regional averages for the period 2000–06 as set out in *Global Economic Prospects 2005* (World Bank 2005).

In the first simulation the model assumes that within-country distribution stays constant—that is, increments to growth are shared to reflect the current distribution. The second assumes that the income of people below an annual income of $700 (2000 PPP US$), an amount roughly equivalent to the $1 a day poverty line, would grow at twice the rate of the population as a whole. The income growth rate of the rest of the population would be adjusted downward to keep the average income growth rate the same as in the first simulation. This pro-poor growth simulation results in 253 million fewer people living in poverty in 2015. However, much of the reduction is concentrated in East Asia and South Asia, rather than Sub-Saharan Africa, reflecting the higher average growth trends for the first two regions. The conclusion: growth and distribution matter a great deal in defining poverty reduction prospects.

National income distribution and poverty reduction

In any country the rate at which poverty declines is primarily a function of two variables: the economic growth rate and poor people's share of growth. There are complex variations within this interaction in, for example, the depth of poverty or the distance measured in income terms from the poverty line. The overall effect of growth on poverty incidence will be determined by distribution below the poverty line, as well as distribution between poor people and non-poor people. If there is a large concentration of poverty just below the line, increases in income for this group will have a large impact on poverty incidence. However, large relative increases in income for groups that are further from the poverty line produce only small reductions in the incidence of poverty. It also has to be borne in mind that any poverty threshold is, to some degree, an artificial construct that provides a partial indicator for measuring the dynamic processes associated with poverty.

Exercises and results

In chapter 2 kernel density curves are constructed for income distribution in Brazil, Kenya and Mexico. These distribution data are used in two exercises. The first considers the effect of a hypothetical transfer from top to bottom of the distribution. This is a stylized exercise, but it draws attention to a central characteristic of countries with large concentrations of poverty at one end of the distribution and wealth at the other: small transfers would substantially reduce poverty. The second exercise builds on a global income distribution simulation. It uses the national income distribution data as the basis for a simulation that examines the effect of two different growth scenarios on poverty reduction. Projecting forward trend growth rates, it simulates the impact on poverty incidence of distribution neutral growth (holding current distribution patterns constant) and pro-poor growth (in which the income of the population below the poverty line grows at twice the national rate).

Static redistribution

In a simple exercise the effect of doubling the total income share of all the people below the poverty line is considered, with an adjustment among the top 20 percent of the distribution. For practical purposes, this can be thought of as a hypothetical lump-sum transfer. Specifically, the size of the transfer received is inversely proportional to the income of the recipient. Figure 1 illustrates the impact. The black line shows the pre-redistribution pattern and the green line the post-redistribution pattern. Redistribution pushes the bottom end of the distribution up and to the right. For Kenya and, less spectacularly, Brazil and Mexico, the median poor household is taken above the poverty line. The figure shows that a doubling of poor people's income would have a large effect on the number of people in poverty and a relatively small impact on the income of the richest.

Figure 1

Doubling the income of the poor would take a small transfer from the rich

Income distribution before and after hypothetical wealth transfer

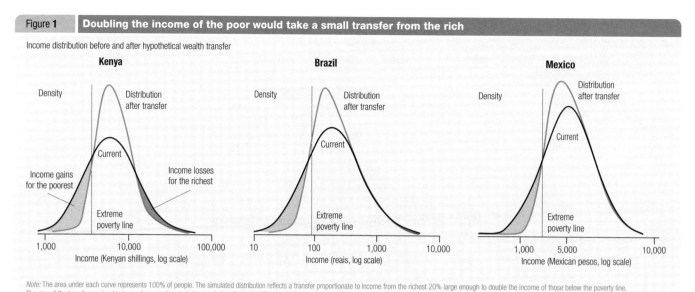

Note: The area under each curve represents 100% of people. The simulated distribution reflects a transfer proportionate to income from the richest 20% large enough to double the income of those below the poverty line. The size of the transfer received is inversely proportionate to income below the poverty line.
Source: Fuentes 2005.

Table 1 | **Pro-poor growth provides greater results**

	Kenya 1997	Brazil 2002	Mexico 2002
Doubling the income share of poor people: static transfer from the richest quintile			
Poverty rate decline	23% to 4%	22% to 7%	16% to 4%
People out of poverty (millions)	5	26	12
Transfer as share of total household income (%)	7.00	2.91	2.57
Transfer as share of richest quintile's income (%)	14.2	4.6	4.7
Year median household is out of poverty under different growth patterns			
Simulation 1 (no change in distribution)	2030	2041	2032
Simulation 2 (pro-poor growth)	2013	2022	2017

Note: The data for the national simulations are computed from household surveys that are the basis for the government's own poverty estimated and also underpin the World Bank's assessment of $1 a day poverty.
Source: Fuentes 2005.

Dynamic pro-poor growth

In a dynamic model the distribution pattern changes over time. The simulation here compares the time horizon for the median poor household crossing the poverty line under distribution-neutral growth and under the pro-poor growth scenario. Under both scenarios average per capita growth rates are assumed to follow the observed trend between 1990 and 2002—a period chosen to reflects two full economic cycles.

Table 1 summarizes the main results from both simulations. For both Brazil and Mexico the static transfer required to double income below the poverty line is equivalent to less than 5% of the income of the richest population quintile. Poverty incidence falls sharply in both countries: from 22% to 7% in Brazil and from 16% to 4% in Mexico. In Kenya less extreme disparities of wealth and a higher incidence of poverty mean that the incomes of the richest quintile would have to fall far more to finance the transfer, but the overall incidence of poverty still falls from 23% to 4%. For all three countries the pro-poor growth scenario reduces the time horizon for lifting the median household above the poverty line. For Brazil the time horizon falls by 19 years, for Mexico by 15 years and for Kenya by 17 years.

Calculations for the two scenarios are based on the following formulation. In the distribution-neutral simulation, the observed growth rate is imputed to each percentile so that:

$$Y_{it+1} = Y_{it} * e^{gi} \text{ for every percentile } i.$$

The pro-poor growth simulation assumes a growth rate for the number of poor people twice the average growth rate observed in 1990–2002, with growth rate remaining constant so that:[1]

$$Y_{jt+1} = Y_{jt} * e^{gj} \text{ for every percentile } j.$$

Percentile j is defined as those below the poverty line at the initial time t_0.

$$Y_{it+1} = Y_{it} * e^{gi} \text{ for every percentile } i.$$

Percentile i is defined as those above the poverty line at the initial time t_0.

The growth rate gj is double the observed growth rate in 1990–2002. The growth rate gi is such that the overall growth rate of the economy remains constant over time. Given that the relative weights of each percentile change every year, gi in time t is slightly higher than gi in time $t + 1$.

The data are for average per capita income of households in 100 percentiles. The welfare indicator is after-tax per capita income for the household. International poverty estimates were used for Brazil and Kenya and national computations of poverty incidence for Mexico. The simulations used the 1990–2002 per capita growth rates as reported in *Human Development Report 2004* to capture two full economic cycles for Brazil and Mexico.[2] For Kenya, since observed growth rates are negative, an optimistic yet plausible per capita growth rate of 1 percent was assumed.

Notes

1   These assumptions have two implications. First, inequality will fall every year. Second, for the overall growth rate to remain constant, the growth rate for those above the poverty line will be smaller every year, as the share of income of poor people increases.

2   Despite the presence of financial crises in both Brazil and Mexico during that period, the growth rates used are representative of long-term growth. Growth rates for 1970–2002 are lower in both countries. The difference in time horizon between growth patterns does not change significantly when using different growth rates.

Sources and selected readings

Chen, Shaohua, and Martin Ravallion. 2004. "How Have the World's Poorest Fared since the Early 1980s?" Policy Research Paper 3341. Washington, DC: World Bank.

Cornia, Giovanni Andrea, ed. 2004. *Inequality, Growth, and Poverty in an Era of Liberalization and Globalization*. Oxford: Oxford University Press.

Deaton, Angus. 2003a. "How to Monitor Poverty for the Millennium Development Goals." *Journal of Human Development* 4(3): 353–78.

———. 2003b. *Measuring Poverty in a Growing World*. NBER Working Paper: 9822. Cambridge, Mass.: National Bureau of Economic Research.

Dikhanov, Yuri. 2005. "Trends in Global Income Distribution 1970–2015." Background note for *Human Development Report 2005*. New York.

Fuentes, Ricardo. 2005. "Poverty, Pro-Poor Growth and Simulated Inequality Reduction." Background note for *Human Development Report 2005*. New York.

Kakwani, Nanak. 2004. "Poverty Measurement Matters: An Indian Story." Brasilia: United Nations Development Programme, International Poverty Centre, Brasilia.

Reddy, Sanjay G., and Thomas W. Pogge. 2003. "How Not to Count the Poor." Columbia University, New York. [http://www.columbia.edu/~sr793/count.pdf]. May 2005.

World Bank. 2001. *World Development Indicators 2001*. Washington, DC: World Bank.

———. 2005. *Global Economic Prospects 2005*. Washington, DC: World Bank.

Assessing progress towards the Millennium Development Goals

Assessing progress towards the Millennium Development Goals

This year's *Human Development Report* assesses progress towards the Millennium Development Goals (MDGs) and attempts to quantify the potential benefits of achieving the MDGs by 2015. For each country the exercise attempts to answer two distinct questions for each MDG:

● If the MDG were achieved by 2015, how many fewer people would suffer human deprivation than if progress continued along the trends of the 1990s?

● If progress continued along the trends of the 1990s, when would the MDG be achieved?

The Report makes these assessments for five MDG indicators that have reasonably reliable trend data available on a country-by-country basis (table 1).

Calculating progress towards each MDG

Progress towards each MDG is assessed by comparing average annual progress if current trends prevailed with the annual progress needed to meet the indicator, under the assumption of linear progress.

The average annual rate of progress is calculated using the general formula:

$$\alpha_0 = \frac{(x_{t_1} - x_{t_0}) / x_{t_0}}{t_1 - t_0},$$

where x_{t_1} and x_{t_0} are the values of the indicator for 1990 or the year closest to 1990 for which data are available; t_1 is the most recent year for which data are available, generally 2003; and

t_0 is 1990 or the year closest to 1990 for which data are available. For hunger and under-five mortality rates, for which the most desirable value is 0, the formula is applied without modification.

For the net primary enrolment ratio, gender equality in education (ratio of girls to boys) and share of population with access to safe water and sanitation, for which the most desirable value is 100%, progress is expressed as "shortfall reduction" according to the following formula:

$$\alpha_1 = \frac{(x_{t_1} - x_{t_0}) / (100 - x_{t_0})}{t_1 - t_0}.$$

Calculating the human cost of not meeting the MDGs

The average annual rate of progress is then used to calculate the value of the indicator on current trends in 2015:

$$x_{tMDG} = x_{t_0} + [\alpha_i(t_{MDG} - t_0)],$$

where t_{MDG} denotes 2015, the target year for achieving the MDGs and i can take the value 0 or 1 depending on the indicator.

The indicator is then multiplied by the value of its denominator, w, listed in table 1, as projected by the UN Population Division, to arrive at the total number of deprived people, p_{tMDG}, in 2015:

$$p_{tMDG} = x_{tMDG} \, w_{tMDG}.$$

The number of people deprived if the MDG is met, $\hat{p}_{tMDG}$, is also calculated for each country as the value of the indicator needed to achieve the MDG, determined by the MDG indicator (x^*), multiplied by its denominator:

$$\hat{p}_{t_{MDG}} = x^* w_{t_{MDG}} .$$

The shortfall, the difference between achieving the MDG and progress along current trends, is calculated by adding the differences between these two values for all countries not on track to achieve the MDG:

$$\text{Shortfall} = \Sigma \left(p_{t_{MDG}} - \hat{p}_{t_{MDG}} \right) \left[p_{t_{MDG}} > \hat{p}_{t_{MDG}} \right]$$

where $\left[p_{t_{MDG}} > \hat{p}_{t_{MDG}} \right]$ is equal to 1 if true and 0 if false.

Calculating the year in which MDGs are achieved on current trends

The necessary level to achieve each MDG is determined by the MDG itself. For example, the target for MDG 4 calls for reducing the under-five mortality rate by two-thirds. The level at which the MDG is achieved is thus set to the initial level multiplied by a coefficient β. For child mortality, this coefficient is set to ⅓. For hunger, it is set to ½, as determined by the MDG target. The year in which a country will achieve the MDG, $\bar{t}$, is then determined by the formula:

$$\bar{t} = t_0 + \frac{\beta x_{t_0}}{\alpha} .$$

| Table 1 | Millennium Development Goals assessed |

Target	Variable (indicator)	Source agency	Reference year t_0	Reference year t_1	Denominator used for calculating counts (w)
Goal 1. Eradicate extreme poverty and hunger					
Target 1. Halve the proportion of people whose income is less than $1 a day	People living on less than $1 a day (1993 PPP US$) (%) [a]	World Bank	1990	2000	Total population
Target 2. Halve the proportion of people who suffer from hunger	Undernourished people (%)	FAO	1990–92	1999–2001	Total population
Goal 2. Achieve universal primary education					
Target 3. Ensure that children everywhere will be able to complete a full course of primary schooling	Net primary enrolment ratio (%)	UNESCO Institute for Statistics	1990/91	2002/03	Children of primary school age
Goal 3. Promote gender equality and empower women					
Target 4. Eliminate gender disparity in all levels of education	Female net primary enrolment ratio (%)	UNESCO Institute for Statistics	1990/91	2002/03	Girls of primary school age
Goal 4. Reduce child mortality					
Target 5. Reduce by two-thirds the under-five mortality rate	Under-five mortality rate (per 1,000 live births)	UNICEF and WHO	1990	2003	Births
Goal 7. Ensure environmental sustainability					
Target 10. Halve the proportion of people without sustainable access to safe drinking water and sanitation	People with sustainable access to an improved water source (%)	UNICEF and WHO	1990	2003	Total population
	People with access to improved sanitation (%)	UNICEF and WHO	1990	2003	Total population

a. Assessment of human costs only, not timeline.

Definitions of statistical terms

Agriculture, domestic support Annual monetary value of all gross transfers from taxpayers and consumers arising from policy measures that support agriculture, minus the associated budgetary receipts, regardless of their objectives and impacts on farm production and income or on consumption of farm products.

Armed forces, total Strategic, land, naval, air, command, administrative and support forces. Includes paramilitary forces such as the gendarmerie, customs service and border guard, if these are trained in military tactics.

Arms transfers, conventional Refers to the voluntary transfer by the supplier (and thus excludes captured weapons and weapons obtained through defectors) of weapons with a military purpose destined for the armed forces, paramilitary forces or intelligence agencies of another country. These include major conventional weapons or systems in six categories: ships, aircraft, missiles, artillery, armoured vehicles and guidance and radar systems (excluded are trucks, services, ammunition, small arms, support items, components and component technology and towed or naval artillery under 100-millimetre calibre).

Births attended by skilled health personnel The percentage of deliveries attended by personnel (including doctors, nurses and midwives) trained to give the necessary care, supervision and advice to women during pregnancy, labour and the postpartum period, to conduct deliveries on their own and to care for newborns.

Birthweight, infants with low The percentage of infants with a birthweight of less than 2,500 grams.

Carbon dioxide emissions Human-originated carbon dioxide emissions stemming from the burning of fossil fuels, gas flaring and the production of cement. Emissions are calculated from data on the consumption of solid, liquid and gaseous fuels, gas flaring and the production of cement.

Cellular subscribers (also referred to as cellular mobile subscribers) Subscribers to an automatic public mobile telephone service that provides access to the public switched telephone network using cellular technology. Systems can be analogue or digital.

Children reaching grade 5 The percentage of children starting primary school who eventually attain grade 5 (grade 4 if the duration of primary school is four years). The estimates are based on the reconstructed cohort method, which uses data on enrolment and repeaters for two consecutive years.

Children with diarrhoea receiving oral rehydration and continued feeding Percentage of children (ages 0–4) with diarrhoea in the last two weeks preceding the survey who received either oral rehydration therapy (oral rehydration solutions or recommended homemade fluids) or increased fluids and continued feeding.

Consumer price index, average annual change in Reflects changes in the cost to the average consumer of acquiring a basket of goods and services that may be fixed or may change at specified intervals.

Condom use at last high-risk sex Men and women who say they used a condom the last time they had sex with a non-marital, non-cohabiting partner, of those who have had sex with such a partner in the last 12 months.

Contraceptive prevalence rate The percentage of married women (including women in union) ages 15–49 who are using, or whose partners are using, any form of contraception, whether modern or traditional.

Contributing family worker Defined according to the 1993 International Classification by Status in Employment (ICSE) as a person who works without pay in an economic enterprise operated by a related person living in the same household.

Crime, population victimized by The percentage of the population who perceive that they have been victimized by certain types of crime in the preceding year, based on responses to the International Crime Victims Survey.

Debt forgiveness, gross bilateral Forgiveness of bilateral debts of developing countries with the support of official funds of donor countries, whether owed to public or private creditors. Offsetting entries for official development assistance (ODA) principal are not subtracted. See *official development assistance (ODA) disbursed, net.*

Debt relief committed under HIPC initiative Forgiveness of loans as a component of official development assistance under the Debt Initiative for Heavily Indebted Poor Countries (HIPCs). The initiative is a mechanism for debt relief, jointly overseen by the International Monetary Fund (IMF) and the World Bank. Bilateral and multilateral creditors have provided debt relief through this framework to the 42 poorest, most heavily indebted countries since 1996.

Debt service, total The sum of principal repayments and interest actually paid in foreign currency, goods or services on long-term debt (having a maturity of more than one year), interest paid on short-term debt and repayments to the International Monetary Fund.

Earned income (PPP US$), estimated Roughly derived on the basis of the ratio of the female nonagricultural wage to the male non-agricultural wage, the female and male shares of the economically active population, total female and male population and GDP per capita (PPP US$). For details on this estimation, see *Technical note 1*.

Earned income, ratio of estimated female to male The ratio of estimated female earned income to estimated male earned income. See *earned income (PPP US$), estimated (female and male)*.

Economic activity rate, female The share of the female population ages 15 and above who supply, or are available to supply, labour for the production of goods and services.

Education expenditure, public Includes both capital expenditures (spending on construction, renovation, major repairs and purchase of heavy equipment or vehicles) and current expenditures (spending on goods and services that are consumed within the current year and would need to be renewed the following year). It covers such expenditures as staff salaries and benefits, contracted or purchased services, books and teaching materials, welfare services, furniture and equipment, minor repairs, fuel, insurance, rents, telecommunications and travel. See *education levels*.

Education index One of the three indices on which the human development index is built. It is based on the adult literacy rate and the combined gross enrolment ratio for primary, secondary and tertiary schools. For details on how the index is calculated, see *Technical note 1*.

Education levels Categorized as pre-primary, primary, secondary or tertiary in accordance with the International Standard Classification of Education (ISCED). *Pre-primary education* (ISCED level 0) is provided at such schools as kindergartens and nursery and infant schools and is intended for children not old enough to enter school at the primary level. *Primary education* (ISCED level 1) provides the basic elements of education at such establishments as primary and elementary schools. *Secondary education* (ISCED levels 2 and 3) is based on at least four years of previous instruction at the first level and provides general or specialized instruction, or both, at such institutions as middle schools, secondary schools, high schools, teacher training schools at this level and vocational or technical schools. *Tertiary education* (ISCED levels 5–7) refers to education at such institutions as universities, teachers colleges and higher level professional schools—requiring as a minimum condition of admission the successful completion of education at the second level or evidence of the attainment of an equivalent level of knowledge.

Electricity consumption per capita Refers to gross production, in per capita terms, which includes consumption by station auxiliaries and any losses in the transformers that are considered integral parts of the station. Also includes total electric energy produced by pumping installations without deduction of electric energy absorbed by pumping.

Employment by economic activity, women Female employment in industry, agriculture or services as defined according to the International Standard Industrial Classification (ISIC) system (revisions 2 and 3). *Industry* refers to mining and quarrying, manufacturing, construction and public utilities (gas, water and electricity). *Agriculture* refers to activities in agriculture, hunting, forestry and fishing. *Services* refer to wholesale and retail trade; restaurants and hotels; transport, storage and communications; finance, insurance, real estate and business services; and community, social and personal services.

Energy use, GDP per unit of The ratio of GDP (in 2000 PPP US$) to commercial energy use, measured in kilograms of oil equivalent. Provides a measure of energy efficiency by showing comparable and consistent estimates of real GDP across countries relative to physical inputs (units of energy use). See *GDP (gross domestic product)* and *PPP (purchasing power parity)*.

Enrolment ratio, gross The number of students enrolled in a level of education, regardless of age, as a percentage of the population of official school age for that level. The gross enrolment ratio can be greater than 100% as a result of grade repetition and entry at ages younger or older than the typical age at that grade level. See *education levels*.

Enrolment ratio, gross, combined for primary, secondary and tertiary schools The number of students enrolled in primary, secondary and tertiary levels of education, regardless of age, as a percentage of the population of official school age for the three levels. See *education levels* and *enrolment ratio, gross*.

Enrolment ratio, net The number of students enrolled in a level of education who are of official school age for that level, as a percentage of the population of official school age for that level. See *education levels*.

Environmental treaties, ratification of After signing a treaty, a country must ratify it, often with the approval of its legislature. Such process implies not only an expression of interest as indicated by the signature, but also the transformation of the treaty's principles and obligations into national law.

Exports, high-technology Exports of products with a high intensity of research and development. Includes high-technology products such as in aerospace, computers, pharmaceuticals, scientific instruments and electrical machinery.

Exports, manufactured Defined according to the Standard International Trade Classification to include exports of chemicals, basic manufactures, machinery and transport equipment and other miscellaneous manufactured goods.

Exports of goods and services The value of all goods and other market services provided to the rest of the world. Includes the value of merchandise, freight, insurance, transport, travel, royalties, licence fees and other services, such as communication, construction, financial, information, business, personal and government services. Excludes labour and property income and transfer payments.

Exports, primary Defined according to the Standard International Trade Classification to include exports of food, agricultural raw materials, fuels and ores and metals.

Fertility rate, total The number of children that would be born to each woman if she were to live to the end of her child-bearing years and bear children at each age in accordance with prevailing age-specific fertility rates.

Foreign direct investment, net inflows of Net inflows of investment to acquire a lasting management interest (10% or more of voting stock) in an enterprise operating in an economy other than that of the investor. It is the sum of equity capital, reinvestment of earnings, other long-term capital and short-term capital.

Fuel consumption, traditional Estimated consumption of fuel wood, charcoal, bagasse (sugar cane waste) and animal and vegetable wastes.

GDP (gross domestic product) The sum of value added by all resident producers in the economy plus any product taxes (less subsidies) not included in the valuation of output. It is calculated without making deductions for depreciation of fabricated capital assets or for depletion and degradation of natural resources. Value added is the net output of an industry after adding up all outputs and subtracting intermediate inputs.

GDP (US$) GDP converted to US dollars using the average official exchange rate reported by the International Monetary Fund. An alternative conversion factor is applied if the official exchange rate is judged to diverge by an exceptionally large margin from the rate effectively applied to transactions in foreign currencies and traded products. See *GDP (gross domestic product)*.

GDP index One of the three indices on which the human development index is built. It is based on GDP per capita (PPP US$). For details on how the index is calculated, see *Technical note 1*.

GDP per capita (PPP US$) See *GDP (gross domestic product)* and *PPP (purchasing power parity)*.

GDP per capita (US$) GDP (US$) divided by midyear population. See *GDP (US$)*.

GDP per capita annual growth rate Least squares annual growth rate, calculated from constant price GDP per capita in local currency units.

Gender empowerment measure (GEM) A composite index measuring gender inequality in three basic dimensions of empowerment—economic participation and decision-making, political participation and decision-making and power over economic resources. For details on how the index is calculated, see *Technical note 1*.

Gender-related development index (GDI) A composite index measuring average achievement in the three basic dimensions captured in the human development index—a long and healthy life, knowledge and a decent standard of living—adjusted to account for inequalities between men and women. For details on how the index is calculated, see *Technical note 1*.

Gini index Measures the extent to which the distribution of income (or consumption) among individuals or households within a country deviates from a perfectly equal distribution. A Lorenz curve plots the cumulative percentages of total income received against the cumulative number of recipients, starting with the poorest individual or household. The Gini index measures the area between the Lorenz curve and a hypothetical line of absolute equality, expressed as a percentage of the maximum area under the line. A value of 0 represents perfect equality, a value of 100 perfect inequality.

GNI (gross national income) The sum of value added by all resident producers in the economy plus any product taxes (less subsidies) not included in the valuation of output plus net receipts of primary income (compensation of employees and property income) from abroad. Value added is the net output of an industry after adding up all outputs and subtracting intermediate inputs. Data are in current US dollars converted using the *World Bank Atlas* method.

Health expenditure per capita (PPP US$) The sum of public and private expenditure (in PPP US$), divided by the population. Health expenditure includes the provision of health services (preventive and curative), family planning activities, nutrition activities and emergency aid designated for health, but excludes the provision of water and sanitation. See *health expenditure, private; health expenditure, public;* and *PPP (purchasing power parity)*.

Health expenditure, private Direct household (out of pocket) spending, private insurance, spending by nonprofit institutions serving households and direct service payments by private corporations. Together with public health expenditure, it makes up total health expenditure. See *health expenditure per capita (PPP US$)* and *health expenditure, public*.

Health expenditure, public Current and capital spending from government (central and local) budgets, external borrowings and grants (including donations from international agencies and non-governmental organizations) and social (or compulsory) health insurance funds. Together with private health expenditure, it makes up total health expenditure. See *health expenditure per capita (PPP US$)* and *health expenditure, private.*

HIPC completion point The date at which a country included in the Debt Initiative for Heavily Indebted Poor Countries (HIPCs) successfully completes the key structural reforms agreed on at the HIPC decision point, including developing and implementing a poverty reduction strategy. The country then receives the bulk of its debt relief under the HIPC Initiative without further policy conditions.

HIPC decision point The date at which a heavily indebted poor country with an established track record of good performance under adjustment programmes supported by the International Monetary Fund and the World Bank commits, under the Debt Initiative for Heavily Indebted Poor Countries (HIPCs), to undertake additional reforms and to develop and implement a poverty reduction strategy.

HIPC trust fund, bilateral pledges to the A firm obligation undertaken by an official donor to provide specified assistance to the HIPC trust fund. Bilateral commitments are recorded in the full amount of expected transfer, irrespective of the time required for the completion of disbursements.

HIV prevalence The percentage of people ages 15–49 who are infected with HIV.

HIV/AIDS prevalence, pregnant women ages 15–24 attending antenatal care in clinics in capital city Percentage of blood samples taken from women that test positive for HIV during routine sentinel surveillance at selected antenatal clinics. Data are median values of all antenatal clinics in the cities specified and are from national surveillance reports and database of census bureau.

Human development index (HDI) A composite index measuring average achievement in three basic dimensions of human development—a long and healthy life, knowledge and a decent standard of living. For details on how the index is calculated, see *Technical note 1.*

Human poverty index (HPI-1) for developing countries A composite index measuring deprivations in the three basic dimensions captured in the human development index—a long and healthy life, knowledge and a decent standard of living. For details on how the index is calculated, see *Technical note 1.*

Human poverty index (HPI-2) for selected high-income OECD countries A composite index measuring deprivations in the three basic dimensions captured in the human development index—a long and healthy life, knowledge and a decent standard of living—and also capturing social exclusion. For details on how the index is calculated, see *Technical note 1.*

Illiteracy rate, adult Calculated as 100 minus the adult literacy rate. See *literacy rate, adult.*

Immunization, one-year-olds fully immunized against measles or tuberculosis One-year-olds injected with an antigen or a serum containing specific antibodies against measles or tuberculosis.

Imports of goods and services The value of all goods and other market services received from the rest of the world. Includes the value of merchandise, freight, insurance, transport, travel, royalties, licence fees and other services, such as communication, construction, financial, information, business, personal and government services. Excludes labour and property income and transfer payments.

Income poverty line, population below The percentage of the population living below the specified poverty line:
- $1 a day—at 1985 international prices (equivalent to $1.08 at 1993 international prices), adjusted for purchasing power parity.
- $2 a day—at 1985 international prices (equivalent to $2.15 at 1993 international prices), adjusted for purchasing power parity.
- $4 a day—at 1990 international prices, adjusted for purchasing power parity.
- $11 a day (per person for a family of three)—at 1994 international prices, adjusted for purchasing power parity.
- National poverty line—the poverty line deemed appropriate for a country by its authorities. National estimates are based on population weighted subgroup estimates from household surveys.
- 50% of median income—50% of the median adjusted disposable household income. See *PPP (purchasing power parity).*

Income or consumption, shares of The shares of income or consumption accruing to subgroups of population indicated by deciles or quintiles, based on national household surveys covering various years. Consumption surveys produce results showing lower levels of inequality between poor and rich than do income surveys, as poor people generally consume a greater share of their income. Because data come from surveys covering different years and using different methodologies, comparisons between countries must be made with caution.

Infant mortality rate The probability of dying between birth and exactly one year of age, expressed per 1,000 live births.

Internally displaced people People or groups of people who have been forced or obliged to flee or to leave their homes or places of habitual residence, in particular as a result of or in order to avoid the effects of armed conflict, situations of generalized violence, violations of human rights or natural or human-made disasters, and who have not crossed an internationally recognized state border.

Internet users People with access to the worldwide network.

Labour force All those employed (including people above a specified age who, during the reference period, were in paid employment, at work, self-employed or with a job but not at work) and unemployed (including people above a specified age who, during the reference period, were without work, currently available for work and seeking work).

Legislators, senior officials and managers, female Women's share of positions defined according to the International Standard Classification of Occupations (ISCO-88) to include legislators, senior government officials, traditional chiefs and heads of villages, senior officials of special interest organizations, corporate managers, directors and chief executives, production and operations department managers and other department and general managers.

Life expectancy at birth The number of years a newborn infant would live if prevailing patterns of age-specific mortality rates at the time of birth were to stay the same throughout the child's life.

Life expectancy index One of the three indices on which the human development index is built. For details on how the index is calculated, see *Technical note 1*.

Literacy rate, adult The percentage of people ages 15 and above who can, with understanding, both read and write a short, simple statement related to their everyday life.

Literacy rate, youth The percentage of people ages 15–24 who can, with understanding, both read and write a short, simple statement related to their everyday life.

Literacy skills, functional, population lacking The share of the population ages 16–65 scoring at level 1 on the prose literacy scale of the International Adult Literacy Survey. Most tasks at this level require the reader to locate a piece of information in the text that is identical to or synonymous with the information given in the directive.

Malaria cases The total number of malaria cases reported to the World Health Organization by countries in which malaria is endemic. Many countries report only laboratory-confirmed cases, but many in Sub-Saharan Africa report clinically diagnosed cases as well.

Malaria prevention, children under age 5 The percentage of children under age 5 sleeping under insecticide-treated bednets.

Malaria treatment, children under age 5 with fever The percentage of children under age 5 who were ill with fever in the two weeks before the survey and received antimalarial drugs.

Market activities Defined according to the 1993 revised UN System of National Accounts to include employment in establishments, primary production not in establishments, services for income and other production of goods not in establishments. See *non-market activities* and *work time, total*.

Maternal mortality ratio The annual number of deaths of women from pregnancy-related causes per 100,000 live births.

Maternal mortality ratio, adjusted Maternal mortality ratio adjusted to account for well documented problems of underreporting and misclassification of maternal deaths, as well as estimates for countries with no data. See *maternal mortality ratio*.

Maternal mortality ratio, reported Maternal mortality ratio as reported by national authorities. See *maternal mortality ratio*.

Medium-variant projection Population projections by the United Nations Population Division assuming medium-fertility path, normal mortality and normal international migration. Each assumption implies projected trends in fertility, mortality and net migration levels, depending on the specific demographic characteristics and relevant policies of each country or group of countries. In addition, for the countries highly affected by the HIV/AIDS epidemic, the impact of HIV/AIDS is included in the projection. The UN Population Division also publishes low- and high-variant projections. For more information, see http://esa.un.org/unpp/assumptions.html.

Military expenditure All expenditures of the defence ministry and other ministries on recruiting and training military personnel as well as on construction and purchase of military supplies and equipment. Military assistance is included in the expenditures of the donor country.

Non-market activities Defined according to the 1993 revised UN System of National Accounts to include household maintenance (cleaning, laundry and meal preparation and cleanup), management and shopping for own household; care for children, the sick, the elderly and the disabled in own household; and community services. See *market activities* and *work time, total*.

Official aid Grants or loans that meet the same standards as for official development assistance (ODA) except that recipient countries do not qualify as recipients of ODA. These countries are identified in part II of the Development Assistance Committee (DAC) list of recipient countries, which includes more advanced countries of Central and Eastern Europe, the countries of the former Soviet Union and certain advanced developing countries and territories.

Official development assistance (ODA) disbursed, net Disbursements of loans made on concessional terms (net of repayments of principal) and grants by official agencies of the members of the Development Assistance Committee (DAC), by multilateral institutions and by non-DAC countries to promote economic development and welfare in countries and territories in part I of the DAC list of aid recipients. Includes loans with a grant element of at least 25% (calculated at a rate of discount of 10%).

Official development assistance (ODA), per capita of donor country Official development assistance granted by a specific country divided by this country's total population. See *official development assistance (ODA) disbursed, net*.

Official development assistance (ODA) to basic social services ODA directed to basic social services, which include basic education (primary education, early childhood education and basic life skills for youth and adults), basic health (including basic health care, basic health infrastructure, basic nutrition, infectious disease control, health education and health personnel development) and population policies and programmes and reproductive health (population policy and administrative management, reproductive health care, family planning, control of sexually transmitted diseases, including HIV/AIDS, and personnel development for population and reproductive health). Aid to water supply and sanitation is included only if it has a poverty focus.

Official development assistance (ODA) to least developed countries See *official development assistance (ODA) disbursed, net* and country classifications for least developed countries.

Official development assistance (ODA), untied Bilateral ODA for which the associated goods and services may be fully and freely procured in substantially all countries and that is given by one country to another.

Patents granted to residents Refers to documents issued by a government office that describe an invention and create a legal situation in which the patented invention can normally be exploited (made, used, sold, imported) only by or with the authorization of the patentee. The protection of inventions is generally limited to 20 years from the filing date of the application for the grant of a patent.

Physicians Includes graduates of a faculty or school of medicine who are working in any medical field (including teaching, research and practice).

Population growth rate, annual Refers to the average annual exponential growth rate for the period indicated. See *population, total.*

Population, total Refers to the de facto population, which includes all people actually present in a given area at a given time.

Population, urban The midyear population of areas classified as urban according to the criteria used by each country, as reported to the United Nations. See *population, total.*

PPP (purchasing power parity) A rate of exchange that accounts for price differences across countries, allowing international comparisons of real output and incomes. At the PPP US\$ rate (as used in this Report), PPP US\$1 has the same purchasing power in the domestic economy as \$1 has in the United States.

Private flows, other A category combining non-debt-creating portfolio equity investment flows (the sum of country funds, depository receipts and direct purchases of shares by foreign investors), portfolio debt flows (bond issues purchased by foreign investors) and bank and trade-related lending (commercial bank lending and other commercial credits).

Probability at birth of not surviving to a specified age Calculated as 1 minus the probability of surviving to a specified age for a given cohort. See *probability at birth of surviving to a specified age.*

Probability at birth of surviving to a specified age The probability of a newborn infant surviving to a specified age if subject to prevailing patterns of age specific mortality rates.

Professional and technical workers, female Women's share of positions defined according to the International Standard Classification of Occupations (ISCO-88) to include physical, mathematical and engineering science professionals (and associate professionals), life science and health professionals (and associate professionals), teaching professionals (and associate professionals) and other professionals and associate professionals.

Refugees People who have fled their country because of a well founded fear of persecution for reasons of their race, religion, nationality, political opinion or membership in a particular social group and who cannot or do not want to return. *Country of asylum* is the country in which a refugee has filed a claim of asylum but has not yet received a decision or is otherwise registered as an asylum seeker. *Country of origin* refers to the claimant's nationality or country of citizenship.

Research and development expenditures Current and capital expenditures (including overhead) on creative, systematic activity intended to increase the stock of knowledge. Includes fundamental and applied research and experimental development work leading to new devices, products or processes.

Researchers in R&D People trained to work in any field of science who are engaged in professional research and development (R&D) activity. Most such jobs require the completion of tertiary education.

Royalties and licence fees, receipts of Receipts by residents from non-residents for the authorized use of intangible, non-produced, non-financial assets and proprietary rights (such as patents, trademarks, copyrights, franchises and industrial processes) and for the use, through licensing agreements, of produced originals of prototypes (such as films and manuscripts). Data are based on the balance of payments.

Sanitation, improved, population with sustainable access to The percentage of the population with access to adequate excreta disposal facilities, such as a connection to a sewer or septic tank system, a pour-flush latrine, a simple pit latrine or a ventilated improved pit latrine. An excreta disposal system is considered adequate if it is private or shared (but not public) and if it can effectively prevent human, animal and insect contact with excreta.

Science, math and engineering, tertiary students in The share of tertiary students enrolled in natural sciences; engineering; mathematics and computer sciences; architecture and town planning; transport and communications; trade, craft and industrial programmes; and agriculture, forestry and fisheries. See *education levels.*

Seats in parliament held by women Refers to seats held by women in a lower or single house or an upper house or senate, where relevant.

Smoking, prevalence The percentage of men and women who smoke cigarettes.

Telephone mainlines Telephone lines connecting a customer's equipment to the public switched telephone network.

Terms of trade The ratio of the export price index to the import price index measured relative to a base year. A value of more than 100 means that the price of exports has risen relative to the price of imports.

Tuberculosis cases The total number of tuberculosis cases reported to the World Health Organization. A tuberculosis case is defined as a patient in whom tuberculosis has been bacteriologically confirmed or diagnosed by a clinician.

Tuberculosis cases cured under DOTS The percentage of estimated new infectious tuberculosis cases cured under the directly observed treatment, short course (DOTS) case detection and treatment strategy.

Tuberculosis cases detected under DOTS The percentage of estimated new infectious tuberculosis cases detected (diagnosed in a given period) under the directly observed treatment, short course (DOTS) case detection and treatment strategy.

Under-five mortality rate The probability of dying between birth and exactly five years of age, expressed per 1,000 live births.

Under height for age, children under age five Includes moderate and severe stunting, defined as more than two standard deviations below the median height for age of the reference population.

Under weight for age, children under age five Includes moderate underweight, defined as more than two standard deviations below the median weight for age of the reference population, and severe underweight, defined as more than three standard deviations below the median weight.

Undernourished population People whose food intake is chronically insufficient to meet their minimum energy requirements.

Unemployment Refers to all people above a specified age who are not in paid employment or self-employed, but are available for work and have taken specific steps to seek paid employment or self-employment.

Unemployment, long-term Unemployment lasting 12 months or longer. See *unemployment*.

Unemployment rate The unemployed divided by the labour force (those employed plus the unemployed).

Unemployment rate, youth Refers to unemployment between the ages of 15 or 16 and 24, depending on the national definition. See *unemployment*.

Wage employment in non-agricultural sector, percentage of total non-agricultural employees, female Women's share in paid non-agricultural employment. People in paid non- agricultural employment are those who during a specified reference period (for example, one week) performed some work for wage or salary in cash or in kind, as well as persons who, having already worked in their present job, were temporarily not at work during the reference period for reasons such as illness or injury, holiday or vacation, strike or lockout, educational or training leave, maternity or parental leave, reduction in economic activity, temporary disorganization or suspension of work (bad weather, mechanical or electrical breakdown, shortage of raw materials or fuels) and the like and who had a formal attachment to their job as evidenced by one or more of the following criteria: the continued receipt of a wage or salary; an assurance of return to work following the end of the contingency or an agreement as to the date of return; or a short duration of absence from the job. Non-agricultural employment refers to employment in industry or services as defined according to the International Standard Industrial Classification system (revisions 2 and 3). *Industry* refers to mining and quarrying, manufacturing, construction and public utilities (gas, water and electricity). *Services* refer to wholesale and retail trade; restaurants and hotels; transport, storage and communications; finance, insurance, real estate and business services; and community, social and personal services.

Water source, improved, population without sustainable access to Calculated as 100 minus the percentage of the population with sustainable access to an improved water source. Unimproved sources include vendors, bottled water, tanker trucks and unprotected wells and springs. See *water source, improved, population with sustainable access to*.

Water source, improved, population with sustainable access to The share of the population with reasonable access to any of the following types of water supply for drinking: household connections, public standpipes, boreholes, protected dug wells, protected springs and rainwater collection. Reasonable access is defined as the availability of at least 20 litres a person per day from a source within 1 kilometre of the user's dwelling.

Women in government at ministerial level Includes deputy prime ministers and ministers. Prime ministers were also included when they held ministerial portfolios. Vice presidents and heads of ministerial-level departments or agencies were also included when exercising a ministerial function in the government structure.

Work time, total Time spent on market and non-market activities as defined according to the 1993 revised UN System of National Accounts. See market activities and non-market activities.

Statistical references

Aten, Bettina, Alan Heston, and Robert Summers. 2001. Correspondence on data from the Penn World Table 6.0. March. Philadelphia, Penn.

———. 2002. "Penn World Tables 6.1." University of Pennsylvania, Center for International Comparisons, Philadelphia. [http://pwt. econ.upenn.edu/]. Accessed March 2005.

Aboona, Yuhanna. 2005. "Qatar's Approach towards Data Inconsistencies." Background note prepared for *Human Development Report 2005*. March. Doha.

Abou-Zahr, Carla. 2005. "Measuring Maternal Mortality." Background note prepared for *Human Development Report 2005*. April. Geneva.

CDIAC (Carbon Dioxide Information Analysis Center). 2005. Data on carbon dioxide emissions. [http://cdiac.esd.ornl.gov/trends/emis/ em_cont.htm]. Accessed April 2005.

FAO (Food and Agriculture Organization of the United Nations). 2005. *The State of Food Insecurity in the World 2004*. Rome.

Fischer, Stanley, Charles Konan Banny, and Christina Barrineau. 2005. "Measuring Financial Access." Background note prepared for *Human Development Report 2005*. April. New York.

Global IDP Project. 2005. Internally displaced people estimates. [www. idpproject.org/statistics.htm]. Accessed March 2005.

Goldshmidt-Clermont, Luisella, and Elisabetta Pagnossin Aligisakis. 1995. "Measures of Unrecorded Economic Activities in Fourteen Countries." Background paper for *Human Development Report 1995*. United Nations Development Programme, Human Development Report Office, New York.

Gwatkin, Davidson, Shea Rutstein, Kiersten Johnson, Eldaw Abdalla Suliman, Adam Wagstaff, and Agbessi Amouzou. Forthcoming. *Socioeconomic Differences in Health, Nutrition, and Population*. Second edition. Washington, D.C.: World Bank.

Harvey, Andrew S. 1995. "Market and Non-Market Productive Activity in Less Developed and Developing Countries: Lessons from Time Use." Background Paper for *Human Development Report 1995*. United Nations Development Programme, Human Development Report Office, New York.

———. 2001. "National Time Use Data on Market and Non-Market Work by Both Women and Men." Background Paper for *Human Development Report 2001*. United Nations Development Programme, Human Development Report Office, New York.

Human Development Report Office. 2005. "New Applications of the Human Development Index." Background note prepared for *Human Development Report 2005*. May. New York.

IISS (International Institute for Strategic Studies). 2004. *The Military Balance 2004–2005*. Oxford, U.K.: Oxford University Press.

ILO (International Labour Organization). 2002. *Estimates and Projections of the Economically Active Population, 1950–2010*, 4th ed., rev. 2. Database. Geneva.

———. 2003. *Key Indicators of the Labour Market*. Third edition. Geneva. [http://kilm.ilo.org/kilm/]. Accessed March 2005.

———. 2005a. *Database on International Labour Standards (ILOLEX)*. Geneva. [www.ilo.org/ilolex/english/docs/declworld.htm]. Accessed May 2005.

———. 2005b. *Laboursta Database*. Geneva. [http://laborsta.ilo.org]. Accessed March 2005.

IMF (International Monetary Fund) and IDA (International Development Association). 2004. "Heavily Indebted Poor Countries (HIPC) Initiative—Status of Implementation." August. Washington, D.C.

IPU (Inter-Parliamentary Union). 1995. *Women in Parliaments 1945–1995: A World Statistical Survey*. Geneva.

———. 2005a. Correspondence on women in government at ministerial level. March. Geneva.

———. 2005b. Correspondence on women in national parliaments. March. Geneva.

———. 2005c. Correspondence on year women received the right to vote and to stand for election and year first woman was elected or appointed to parliament. March. Geneva.

———. 2005d. *Parline Database and World Classification of Women in National Parliaments*. Geneva. [www.ipu.org]. Accessed March 2005.

ITU (International Telecommunication Union). 2005. *World Telecommunication Indicators Database*. 8th edition. [www.itu.int/ ITU-D/ict/publications/world/world.html]. Accessed March 2005.

LIS (Luxembourg Income Study). 2005. "Relative Poverty Rates for the Total Population, Children and the Elderly." Luxembourg. [www. lisproject.org/keyfigures/povertytable.htm]. Accessed March 2005.

Milanovic, Branko. 2002. Correspondence on income, inequality and poverty during the transition from planned to market economy. March. World Bank, Washington, D.C.

Nolan, Brian, Teresa Munzi, and Timothy M. Smeeding. 2005. "Two Views of Irish Poverty Trends." Background note prepared for *Human Development Report 2005*. March. Dublin.

OECD (Organisation for Economic Co-operation and Development), Development Assistance Committee. 2005a. Correspondence on agricultural support estimates. March. Paris.

———. 2005b. Correspondence on employment rates. March. Geneva.

———. 2005c. Correspondence on official development assistance disbursed. March. Paris.

———. 2005d. Correspondence on youth and long-term unemployment rates. March. Geneva.

———. 2005e. *DAC Journal: Development Cooperation 2004 Report* 6(1). Paris.

———. 2005f. *DAC Online*. Database. Paris.

OECD (Organisation for Economic Co-operation and Development) and Statistics Canada. 2000. *Literacy in the Information Age: Final Report on the International Adult Literacy Survey*. Paris.

———. 2005. *Learning a Living by Earning Skills: First Results of the Adult Literacy and Life Skills Survey*. Paris.

Ruoen, Ren, and Chen Kai. 1995. "China's GDP in U.S. Dollars Based on Purchasing Power Parity." Policy Research Working Paper 1415. World Bank, Washington, D.C.

SIPRI (Stockholm International Peace Research Institute). 2004. *SIPRI Yearbook: Armaments, Disarmaments and International Security*. Oxford, U.K.: Oxford University Press.

———. 2005a. Correspondence on military expenditure data. March. Stockholm.

———. 2005b. Correspondence on weapons transfers data. March. Stockholm.

————. 2005c. *SIPRI Arms Transfers. Database*. March. Stockholm.

Smeeding, Timothy M. 1997. "Financial Poverty in Developed Countries: The Evidence from the Luxembourg Income Study." In Sheldon H. Danziger and Robert H. Haveman, eds., *Understanding Poverty*. New York: Russell Sage Foundation; and Cambridge, Mass.: Harvard University Press.

Smeeding, Timothy M., Lee Rainwater, and Gary Burtless. 2000. "United States Poverty in a Cross-National Context." In Sheldon H. Danziger and Robert H. Haveman, eds., *Understanding Poverty*. New York: Russell Sage Foundation; and Cambridge, Mass.: Harvard University Press.

Statec. 2005. Correspondence on gross enrolment ratio for Luxembourg. May. Luxembourg.

UN (United Nations). 2002. Correspondence on time use surveys. Department of Economic and Social Affairs, Statistics Division. February. New York.

————. 2003. *World Population Prospects 1950–2050: The 2002 Revision*. Database. Department of Economic and Social Affairs, Population Division. New York.

————. 2004. *World Urbanization Prospects: The 2003 Revision*. Department of Economic and Social Affairs, Population Division. New York.

————. 2005a. *Comtrade*. Database. Department of Social and Economic Affairs, Statistics Division. New York.

————. 2005b. Correspondence on energy consumption. Department of Economic and Social Affairs, Statistics Division. March. New York.

————. 2005c. Correspondence on life expectancy at birth. Department of Economic and Social Affairs, Statistics Division. March. New York.

————. 2005d. Correspondence on traditional fuel use. Department of Economic and Social Affairs, Statistics Division. March. New York.

————. 2005e. *Database on Contraceptive Use*. Department of Economic and Social Affairs, Population Division. New York.

————. 2005f. Millennium Indicators Database. Department of Economic and Social Affairs, Statistics Division. New York. [http://millenniumindicators.un.org]. Accessed April 2005.

————. 2005g. "Multilateral Treaties Deposited with the Secretary-General." New York. [http://untreaty.un.org]. Accessed April 2005.

————. 2005h. *World Population Prospects 1950–2050: The 2004 Revision*. Database. Department of Economic and Social Affairs, Population Division. New York.

UNAIDS (Joint United Nations Programme on HIV/AIDS). 2005. Correspondence on HIV prevalence. March. Geneva.

UNDP (United Nations Development Programme). 2003. *Bosnia and Herzegovina Human Development Report 2003*. Sarajevo.

UNESCO (United National Educational, Scientific and Cultural Organization). 1997. "International Standard Classification of Education 1997." Paris. [www.uis.unesco.org/ev_en.php?ID=3813_201&ID2=DO_TOPIC]. Accessed March 2005.

UNESCO (United National Educational, Scientific and Cultural Organization) Institute for Statistics. 1999. *Statistical Yearbook*. Montreal.

————. 2003a. Correspondence on adult and youth literacy rates. March. Montreal.

————. 2003b. Correspondence on gross and net enrolment ratios and children reaching grade 5. March. Montreal.

————. 2005a. Correspondence on adult and youth literacy rates. March. Montreal.

————. 2005b. Correspondence on education expenditure. March. Montreal.

————. 2005c. Correspondence on gross and net enrolment ratios and children reaching grade 5. March. Montreal.

————. 2005d. Correspondence on students in math science and engineering. April. Montreal.

UNHCR (United Nations High Commissioner for Refugees). 2005. Correspondence on refugees by country of asylum and by country of origin. April. Geneva.

UNICEF (United Nations Children's Fund). 2004. *State of the World's Children 2005*. New York: Oxford University Press.

UNICEF (United Nations Children's Fund), WHO (World Health Organization), and UNFPA (United Nations Population Fund). 1997. *Guidelines for Monitoring the Availability and Use of Obstetric Services*. New York.

UN Millennium Project. 2005. *Who's Got the Power? Transforming Health Systems for Women and Children*. Task Force on Child Health and Maternal Health. London: Earthscan.

UNODC (United Nations Office on Drugs and Crime). 2004. Correspondence on data on crime victims. March. Vienna.

UN-OHRLLS (United Nations Office of the High Representative for the Least Developed Countries, Landlocked Developing Countries and Small Island Developing States). 2005. "List of Least Developed Countries." New York. [www.un.org/special-rep/ohrlls/ldc/list.htm]. Accessed May 2005.

WHO (World Health Organization). 2003. *Global Tuberculosis Control: WHO Report 2003*. Geneva. [www.who.int/gtb/publications/globrep/]. Accessed March 2005.

————. 2005a. Correspondence on health expenditure. March. Geneva.

————. 2005b. Correspondence on human resources for health. March. Geneva.

————. 2005c. *World Health Report 2005: Make Every Mother and Child Count*. Geneva.

William, Tony. 2005. "National Strategies for the Development of Statistics." Background note prepared for *Human Development Report 2005*. March. Paris.

WIPO (World Intellectual Property Organization). 2004. *Intellectual Property Statistics*. Publication B. Geneva.

World Bank. 2003. *World Development Indicators 2003*. CD-ROM. Washington, D.C.

————. 2005a. Correspondence on GDP per capita annual growth rates. March. Washington, D.C.

————. 2005b. Correspondence on income distribution data. April. Washington, D.C.

————. 2005c. *World Development Indicators 2005*. CD-ROM. Washington, D.C.

Classification of countries

Countries in the human development aggregates [a]

High human development (HDI 0.800 and above)

Argentina	Switzerland
Australia	Tonga
Austria	Trinidad and Tobago
Bahamas	United Arab Emirates
Bahrain	United Kingdom
Barbados	United States
Belgium	Uruguay
Brunei Darussalam	(57 countries or areas)
Bulgaria	
Canada	
Chile	
Costa Rica	
Croatia	
Cuba	
Cyprus	
Czech Republic	
Denmark	
Estonia	
Finland	
France	
Germany	
Greece	
Hong Kong, China (SAR)	
Hungary	
Iceland	
Ireland	
Israel	
Italy	
Japan	
Korea, Rep. of	
Kuwait	
Latvia	
Lithuania	
Luxembourg	
Malta	
Mexico	
Netherlands	
New Zealand	
Norway	
Panama	
Poland	
Portugal	
Qatar	
Saint Kitts and Nevis	
Seychelles	
Singapore	
Slovakia	
Slovenia	
Spain	
Sweden	

Medium human development (HDI 0.500–0.799)

Albania	Myanmar
Algeria	Namibia
Antigua and Barbuda	Nepal
Armenia	Nicaragua
Azerbaijan	Occupied Palestinian
Bangladesh	Territories
Belarus	Oman
Belize	Pakistan
Bhutan	Papua New Guinea
Bolivia	Paraguay
Bosnia and Herzegovina	Peru
Botswana	Philippines
Brazil	Romania
Cambodia	Russian Federation
Cape Verde	Saint Lucia
China	Saint Vincent and the
Colombia	Grenadines
Comoros	Samoa (Western)
Congo	São Tomé and Principe
Dominica	Saudi Arabia
Dominican Republic	Solomon Islands
Ecuador	South Africa
Egypt	Sri Lanka
El Salvador	Sudan
Equatorial Guinea	Suriname
Fiji	Syrian Arab Republic
Gabon	Tajikistan
Georgia	Thailand
Ghana	Timor-Leste
Grenada	Togo
Guatemala	Tunisia
Guyana	Turkey
Honduras	Turkmenistan
India	Uganda
Indonesia	Ukraine
Iran, Islamic Rep. of	Uzbekistan
Jamaica	Vanuatu
Jordan	Venezuela
Kazakhstan	Viet Nam
Kyrgyzstan	Zimbabwe
Lao People's Dem. Rep.	(88 countries or areas)
Lebanon	
Libyan Arab Jamahiriya	
Macedonia, TFYR	
Malaysia	
Maldives	
Mauritius	
Moldova, Rep. of	
Mongolia	
Morocco	

Low human development (HDI below 0.500)

Angola
Benin
Burkina Faso
Burundi
Cameroon
Central African Republic
Chad
Congo, Dem. Rep. of the
Côte d'Ivoire
Djibouti
Eritrea
Ethiopia
Gambia
Guinea
Guinea-Bissau
Haiti
Kenya
Lesotho
Madagascar
Malawi
Mali
Mauritania
Mozambique
Niger
Nigeria
Rwanda
Senegal
Sierra Leone
Swaziland
Tanzania, U. Rep. of
Yemen
Zambia
(32 countries or areas)

a Excludes the following UN member countries for which the human development index cannot be computed: Afghanistan, Andorra, Iraq, Kiribati, the Democratic Republic of Korea, Liberia, Liechtenstein, Marshall Islands, the Federated States of Micronesia, Monaco, Nauru, Palau, San Marino, Serbia and Montenegro, Somalia and Tuvalu.

Countries in the income aggregates [a]

High income (GNI per capita of $9,386 or more in 2003)

Andorra
Australia
Austria
Bahamas
Bahrain
Belgium
Brunei Darussalam
Canada
Cyprus
Denmark
Finland
France
Germany
Greece
Hong Kong, China (SAR)
Iceland
Ireland
Israel
Italy
Japan
Korea, Rep. of
Kuwait
Luxembourg
Malta
Monaco
Netherlands
New Zealand
Norway
Portugal
Qatar
San Marino
Singapore
Slovenia
Spain
Sweden
Switzerland
United Arab Emirates
United Kingdom
United States

(39 countries or areas)

Middle income (GNI per capita of $766–9,385 in 2003)

Albania
Algeria
Antigua and Barbuda
Argentina
Armenia
Azerbaijan
Barbados
Belarus
Belize
Bolivia
Bosnia and Herzegovina
Botswana
Brazil
Bulgaria
Cape Verde
Chile
China
Colombia
Costa Rica
Croatia
Cuba
Czech Republic
Djibouti
Dominica
Dominican Republic
Ecuador
Egypt
El Salvador
Estonia
Fiji
Gabon
Georgia
Grenada
Guatemala
Guyana
Honduras
Hungary
Indonesia
Iran, Islamic Rep. of
Iraq
Jamaica
Jordan
Kazakhstan
Kiribati
Latvia
Lebanon
Libyan Arab Jamahiriya
Lithuania
Macedonia, TFYR
Malaysia

Maldives
Marshall Islands
Mauritius
Mexico
Micronesia, Fed. Sts.
Morocco
Namibia
Northern Mariana Islands
Occupied Palestinian
  Territories
Oman
Palau
Panama
Paraguay
Peru
Philippines
Poland
Romania
Russian Federation
Saint Kitts and Nevis
Saint Lucia
Saint Vincent and the
  Grenadines
Samoa (Western)
Saudi Arabia
Serbia and Montenegro
Seychelles
Slovakia
South Africa
Sri Lanka
Suriname
Swaziland
Syrian Arab Republic
Thailand
Tonga
Trinidad and Tobago
Tunisia
Turkey
Turkmenistan
Ukraine
Uruguay
Vanuatu
Venezuela

(91 countries or areas)

Low income (GNI per capita of $765 or less in 2003)

Afghanistan
Angola
Bangladesh
Benin
Bhutan
Burkina Faso
Burundi
Cambodia
Cameroon
Central African Republic
Chad
Comoros
Congo
Congo, Dem. Rep. of the
Côte d'Ivoire
Equatorial Guinea
Eritrea
Ethiopia
Gambia
Ghana
Guinea
Guinea-Bissau
Haiti
India
Kenya
Korea, Dem. Rep.
Kyrgyzstan
Lao People's Dem. Rep.
Lesotho
Liberia
Madagascar
Malawi
Mali
Mauritania
Moldova, Rep. of
Mongolia
Mozambique
Myanmar
Nepal
Nicaragua
Niger
Nigeria
Pakistan
Papua New Guinea
Rwanda
São Tomé and Principe
Senegal
Sierra Leone
Solomon Islands
Somalia

Sudan
Tajikistan
Tanzania, U. Rep. of
Timor-Leste
Togo
Uganda
Uzbekistan
Viet Nam
Yemen
Zambia
Zimbabwe

(61 countries or areas)

a World Bank classification (effective 1 July 2004) based on gross national income (GNI) per capita. Excludes Nauru and Tuvalu because of lack of data.

Countries in the major world aggregates

Developing countries

Afghanistan	Guyana	Qatar	Cambodia
Algeria	Haiti	Rwanda	Cape Verde
Angola	Honduras	Saint Kitts and Nevis	Central African Republic
Antigua and Barbuda	Hong Kong, China (SAR)	Saint Lucia	Chad
Argentina	India	Saint Vincent and the	Comoros
Bahamas	Indonesia	Grenadines	Congo, Dem. Rep. of the
Bahrain	Iran, Islamic Rep. of	Samoa (Western)	Djibouti
Bangladesh	Iraq	São Tomé and Principe	Equatorial Guinea
Barbados	Jamaica	Saudi Arabia	Eritrea
Belize	Jordan	Senegal	Ethiopia
Benin	Kenya	Seychelles	Gambia
Bhutan	Kiribati	Sierra Leone	Guinea
Bolivia	Korea, Dem. Rep.	Singapore	Guinea-Bissau
Botswana	Korea, Rep. of	Solomon Islands	Haiti
Brazil	Kuwait	Somalia	Kiribati
Brunei Darussalam	Lao People's Dem. Rep.	South Africa	Lao People's Dem. Rep.
Burkina Faso	Lebanon	Sri Lanka	Lesotho
Burundi	Lesotho	Sudan	Liberia
Cambodia	Liberia	Suriname	Madagascar
Cameroon	Libyan Arab Jamahiriya	Swaziland	Malawi
Cape Verde	Madagascar	Syrian Arab Republic	Maldives
Central African Republic	Malawi	Tanzania, U. Rep. of	Mali
Chad	Malaysia	Thailand	Mauritania
Chile	Maldives	Timor-Leste	Mozambique
China	Mali	Togo	Myanmar
Colombia	Marshall Islands	Tonga	Nepal
Comoros	Mauritania	Trinidad and Tobago	Niger
Congo	Mauritius	Tunisia	Rwanda
Congo, Dem. Rep. of the	Mexico	Turkey	Samoa (Western)
Costa Rica	Micronesia, Fed. Sts.	Tuvalu	São Tomé and Principe
Côte d'Ivoire	Mongolia	Uganda	Senegal
Cuba	Morocco	United Arab Emirates	Sierra Leone
Cyprus	Mozambique	Uruguay	Solomon Islands
Djibouti	Myanmar	Vanuatu	Somalia
Dominica	Namibia	Venezuela	Sudan
Dominican Republic	Nauru	Viet Nam	Tanzania, U. Rep. of
Ecuador	Nepal	Yemen	Timor-Leste
Egypt	Nicaragua	Zambia	Togo
El Salvador	Niger	Zimbabwe	Tuvalu
Equatorial Guinea	Nigeria	(137 countries or areas)	Uganda
Eritrea	Occupied Palestinian		Vanuatu
Ethiopia	Territories	**Least developed**	Yemen
Fiji	Oman	**countries [a]**	Zambia
Gabon	Pakistan	Afghanistan	(50 countries or areas)
Gambia	Palau	Angola	
Ghana	Panama	Bangladesh	
Grenada	Papua New Guinea	Benin	
Guatemala	Paraguay	Bhutan	
Guinea	Peru	Burkina Faso	
Guinea-Bissau	Philippines	Burundi	

Central and Eastern Europe and the Commonwealth of Independent States (CIS)

Albania	Luxembourg
Armenia	Mexico
Azerbaijan	Netherlands
Belarus	New Zealand
Bosnia and Herzegovina	Norway
Bulgaria	Poland
Croatia	Portugal
Czech Republic	Slovakia
Estonia	Spain
Georgia	Sweden
Hungary	Switzerland
Kazakhstan	Turkey
Kyrgyzstan	United Kingdom
Latvia	United States
Lithuania	(30 countries or areas)
Macedonia, TFYR	
Moldova, Rep. of	**High-income OECD**
Poland	**countries [b]**
Romania	Australia
Russian Federation	Austria
Serbia and Montenegro	Belgium
Slovakia	Canada
Slovenia	Denmark
Tajikistan	Finland
Turkmenistan	France
Ukraine	Germany
Uzbekistan	Greece
(27 countries or areas)	Iceland
	Ireland
OECD	Italy
Australia	Japan
Austria	Korea, Rep. of
Belgium	Luxembourg
Canada	Netherlands
Czech Republic	New Zealand
Denmark	Norway
Finland	Portugal
France	Spain
Germany	Sweden
Greece	Switzerland
Hungary	United Kingdom
Iceland	United States
Ireland	(24 countries or areas)
Italy	
Japan	
Korea, Rep. of	

a United Nations classification based on UN-OHRLLS 2005.
b Excludes the Czech Republic, Hungary, Mexico, Poland, Slovakia and Turkey.

Developing countries in the regional aggregates

Arab States
Algeria
Bahrain
Djibouti
Egypt
Iraq
Jordan
Kuwait
Lebanon
Libyan Arab Jamahiriya
Morocco
Occupied Palestinian
  Territories
Oman
Qatar
Saudi Arabia
Somalia
Sudan
Syrian Arab Republic
Tunisia
United Arab Emirates
Yemen
(20 countries or areas)

East Asia and the Pacific
Brunei Darussalam
Cambodia
China
Fiji
Hong Kong, China (SAR)
Indonesia
Kiribati
Korea, Dem. Rep.
Korea, Rep. of
Lao People's Dem. Rep.
Malaysia
Marshall Islands
Micronesia, Fed. Sts.
Mongolia
Myanmar
Nauru
Palau
Papua New Guinea
Philippines
Samoa (Western)
Singapore
Solomon Islands
Thailand
Timor-Leste
Tonga
Tuvalu
Vanuatu
Viet Nam
(28 countries or areas)

South Asia
Afghanistan
Bangladesh
Bhutan
India
Iran, Islamic Rep. of
Maldives
Nepal
Pakistan
Sri Lanka
(9 countries or areas)

Latin America and the Caribbean
Antigua and Barbuda
Argentina
Bahamas
Barbados
Belize
Bolivia
Brazil
Chile
Colombia
Costa Rica
Cuba
Dominica
Dominican Republic
Ecuador
El Salvador
Grenada
Guatemala
Guyana
Haiti
Honduras
Jamaica
Mexico
Nicaragua
Panama
Paraguay
Peru
Saint Kitts and Nevis
Saint Lucia
Saint Vincent and the
  Grenadines
Suriname
Trinidad and Tobago
Uruguay
Venezuela
(33 countries or areas)

Southern Europe
Cyprus
Turkey
(2 countries or areas)

Sub-Saharan Africa
Angola
Benin
Botswana
Burkina Faso
Burundi
Cameroon
Cape Verde
Central African Republic
Chad
Comoros
Congo
Congo, Dem. Rep. of the
Côte d'Ivoire
Equatorial Guinea
Eritrea
Ethiopia
Gabon
Gambia
Ghana
Guinea
Guinea-Bissau
Kenya
Lesotho
Liberia
Madagascar
Malawi
Mali
Mauritania
Mauritius
Mozambique
Namibia
Niger
Nigeria
Rwanda
São Tomé and Principe
Senegal
Seychelles
Sierra Leone
South Africa
Swaziland
Tanzania, U. Rep. of
Togo
Uganda
Zambia
Zimbabwe
(45 countries or areas)

Index to Millennium Development Goal indicators in the indicator tables

Goals and targets from the Millennium Declaration	Indicators for measuring progress	Indicator table
Goal 1 Eradicate extreme poverty and hunger		
Target 1 Halve, between 1990 and 2015, the proportion of people whose income is less than $1 a day	1. Proportion of population below $1 (PPP) a day 2. Poverty gap ratio (incidence × depth of poverty) 3. Share of poorest quintile in national consumption	3 15
Target 2 Halve, between 1990 and 2015, the proportion of people who suffer from hunger	4. Prevalence of underweight children under five years of age 5. Proportion of population below minimum level of dietary energy consumption	3, 7 7 [a], 33 [a]
Goal 2 Achieve universal primary education		
Target 3 Ensure that, by 2015, children everywhere, boys and girls alike, will be able to complete a full course of primary schooling	6. Net enrolment ratio in primary education 7. Proportion of pupils starting grade 1 who reach grade 5 8. Literacy rate of 15- to 24-year-olds	12, 33 12 12
Goal 3 Promote gender equality and empower women		
Target 4 Eliminate gender disparity in primary and secondary education, preferably by 2005, and to all levels of education no later than 2015	9. Ratio of girls to boys in primary, secondary and tertiary education 10. Ratio of literate women to men ages 15–24 11. Share of women in wage employment in the non-agricultural sector [b] 12. Proportion of seats held by women in national parliaments	27 [c] 27 [d] 30
Goal 4 Reduce child mortality		
Target 5 Reduce by two-thirds, between 1990 and 2015, the under-five mortality rate	13. Under-five mortality rate 14. Infant mortality rate 15. Proportion of one-year-old children fully immunized against measles	10, 33 10 6
Goal 5 Improve maternal health		
Target 6. Reduce by three-quarters, between 1990 and 2015, the maternal mortality ratio	16. Maternal mortality ratio 17. Proportion of births attended by skilled health personnel	10 6
Goal 6 Combat HIV/AIDS, malaria and other diseases		
Target 7 Have halted by 2015 and begun to reverse the spread of HIV/AIDS	18. HIV prevalence among pregnant women 15–24 [e] 19. Condom use rate of the contraceptive prevalence rate 19a. Condom use at last high-risk sex 19b. Percentage of 15- to 24-year-olds with comprehensive correct knowledge of HIV/AIDS 20. Ratio of school attendance of orphans to school attendance of non-orphans ages 10–14	 9
Target 8 Have halted by 2015 and begun to reverse the incidence of malaria and other major diseases	21. Prevalence and death rates associated with malaria 22. Proportion of population in malaria-risk areas using effective malaria prevention and treatment measures 23. Prevalence and death rates associated with tuberculosis 24. Proportion of tuberculosis cases detected and cured under directly observed treatment, short course (DOTS)	9 [f] 9 [g] 9 [h] 9
Goal 7 Ensure environmental sustainability		
Target 9 Integrate the principles of sustainable development into country policies and programmes and reverse the loss of environmental resources	25. Proportion of land area covered by forest 26. Ratio of area protected to maintain biological diversity to surface area 27. Energy use (kilograms of oil equivalent) per $1 GDP (PPP) 28. Carbon dioxide emissions per capita and consumption of ozone-depleting chlorofluorocarbons (ODP tons) 29. Proportion of population using solid fuels	 22 [i] 22 [j]
Target 10 Halve by 2015 the proportion of people without sustainable access to safe drinking water and sanitation	30. Proportion of population with sustainable access to an improved water source, urban and rural 31. Proportion of population with access to improved sanitation, urban and rural	7 [k], 33 [k] 7 [l]

Index to Millennium Development Goal indicators in the indicator tables

Goals and targets from the Millennium Declaration	Indicators for measuring progress	Indicator table
Target 11 By 2020 to have achieved a significant improvement in the lives of at least 100 million slum dwellers	32. Proportion of households with access to secure tenure	

Goal 8 Develop a global partnership for development

Target 12 Develop further an open, rule-based, predictable, non-discriminatory trading and financial system. Includes a commitment to good governance, development, and poverty reduction—both nationally and internationally	*Official development assistance* 33. Net ODA, total and to least developed countries, as a percentage of OECD/DAC donors' gross national income GNI	17 [n]
	34. Proportion of total bilateral, sector-allocable ODA of OECD/DAC donors to basic social services (basic education, primary health care, nutrition, safe water and sanitation)	17
Target 13 Address the special needs of the least developed countries. Includes: tariff- and quota-free access for least-developed countries' exports; enhanced programme of debt relief for HIPCs and cancellation of official bilateral debt; and more generous ODA for countries committed to poverty reduction	35. Proportion of bilateral ODA of OECD/DAC donors that is untied 36. ODA received in landlocked countries as proportion of their gross national incomes 37. ODA received in small island developing States as proportion of their gross national incomes	17
Target 14 Address the special needs of landlocked countries and small island developing states	*Market access* 38. Proportion of total developed country imports (by value and excluding arms) from developing countries and from the least developed countries, admitted free of duties 39. Average tariffs imposed by developed countries on agricultural products and textiles and clothing from developing countries 40. Agricultural support estimate for OECD countries as a percentage of their gross domestic product	
Target 15 Deal comprehensively with the debt problems of developing countries through national and international measures in order to make debt sustainable in the long term	41. Proportion of ODA provided to help build trade capacity	18
	Debt sustainability 42. Total number of countries that have reached their HIPC decision points and number that have reached their HIPC completion points (cumulative) 43. Debt relief committed under HIPC Debt Initiative [m] 44. Debt service as a percentage of exports of goods and services	
		19
Target 16 In cooperation with developing countries, develop and implement strategies for decent and productive work for youth	45. Unemployment rate of 15- to 24-year-olds, male and female and total	21 [o]
Target 17 In cooperation with pharmaceutical companies, provide access to affordable essential drugs in developing countries	46. Proportion of population with access to affordable essential drugs on a sustainable basis	
Target 18 In cooperation with the private sector, make available the benefits of new technologies, especially information and communications	47. Telephone lines and cellular subscribers per 100 people 48a. Personal computers in use per 100 people 48b. Internet users per 100 people	13 [p] 13

a Tables 7 and 33 present this indicator as undernourished people as percent of total population.
b Table 28 includes data on female employment by economic activity.
c Table presents female (net or growth) enrolment ratio as percent of male ratio for primary, secondary and tertiary education levels separately.
d Table presents data on female youth literacy data as percent of male rate.
e Tables 9 and 33 present HIV prevalence among people ages 15–49.
f Table includes data on malaria cases per 100,000 people.
g Table includes data on children under age five with insecticide-treated bed nets, and children under age five with fever treated with anti-malarial drugs.
h Table includes data on tuberculosis cases per 100,000 people.
i Table presents this indicator as GDP per unit of energy use (2000 PPP US$ per kilogram of oil equivalent).
j Table includes data on carbon dioxide emissions per capita.
k Tables 7 and 33 include data on population with sustainable access to an improved water source for urban and rural combined.
l Table includes data on population with sustainable access to improved sanitation for urban and rural combined.
m Table 18 includes data on bilateral debt relief pledges to the HIPC trust fund, and gross bilateral debt forgiveness.
n Table includes data on official development assistance (ODA) to least developed countries as percent of total ODA.
o Table includes data on unemployment rate of 15- to 24-year-olds as total and female rate as percent of male rate for OECD countries only.
p Table presents telephone lines and cellular subscribers separately.